Learning to Program with Visual Basic

Second Edition

Patrick G. McKeown
Craig A. Piercy
University of Georgia

JOHN WILEY & SONS, INC.

To Carolyn—P.G.M.

To Estelle & Nicolas—C.A.P.

Acquisitions Editor	Beth L. Golub
Editorial Assistant	Jennifer Battista
Marketing Manager	Jessica Garcia
Senior Production Editor	Christine Cervoni
Senior Designer	Harry Nolan

This book was set by Patrick G. McKeown and printed and bound by Courier/Westford. The cover was printed by Phoenix Color, Corp.

This book is printed on acid-free paper. ∞

To order books or for customer service please call
1(800)-CALL-WILEY 225-5945.

Library of Congress Cataloging-in-Publication Data

ISBN 0-471-41862-5

Printed in the United States of America

10 9 8 7 6

PREFACE

With the introduction of Visual Basic for Windows, Microsoft took a large step toward redefining computer programming. With Visual Basic, instead of writing monolithic programs that are difficult to understand and debug, it is possible to write short sections of code that match objects on the screen. While not completely object oriented, the *object-oriented, event driven programming* approach taken by Visual Basic makes it much easier to construct large programs using the Windows interface. The newest release of Visual Basic, Visual Basic 6.0, continues in this tradition with many new features including a Web-based help system and the capability to view databases from within Visual Basic using the Data View window.

A DIFFERENT TYPE OF TEXTBOOK

After using Visual Basic in our classes for a number of years, we decided that a different type of textbook was needed: One that demonstrates the many features of the Visual Basic interface while at the same time covering the programming logic required to create information system applications regardless of the computer language used. In our classes, we have found many students who are capable of creating an interface, but have problems with the programming logic. This textbook approaches this problem by helping students learn how to program *using* Visual Basic rather than just learning how to use the Visual Basic interface.

To strike the proposed balance between interface and logic, the number of controls introduced in the first five chapters have been kept to a minimum—just enough to enable the students to write interesting programs. By minimizing the number of controls, the emphasis in the first five chapters is on students learning programming concepts that they will need to know regardless of the language they eventually use in the workplace. Three topics are the focus of these five chapters: The fundamentals of the Visual Basic interface, problem solving, and using the sequence, decision, and repetition control structures. Only after a firm foundation has been laid in the beginning chapters are more Visual Basic controls and features discussed. In the next two chapters, more advanced programming topics including arrays and user-defined general procedures are explained. In the last five chapters, topics such as passwords, menus, dialog boxes, using Visual Basic to access databases, creating graphics with Visual Basic, programmer-defined data types, direct access files, and an introduction to object-oriented programing are covered.

CHAPTER COMPONENTS

Each chapter begins with a continuing scenario of a video store start-up. This scenario poses a different, interesting business problem to be solved in each chapter. Following the scenario, are chapter sections that together provide a solution to this problem and a set of end-of-chapter projects that provide the student with opportunities to solve similar problems. Each chapter section includes four key instructional elements:

1. discussions of the solution process as it relates to the scenario or to another example
2. VB Code Boxes that provide the code to implement the solution or similar example
3. screen captures that display the result of entering and running the code
4. *It's Your Turn!* exercises at the end of each section that both test the student's knowledge of the section material and request the student to enter and run the same code.

The discussion of the solution to the problem posed by the scenario, VB Code Boxes, screen captures, and *It's Your Turn!* exercises work together to explain and demonstrate the concept being introduced, provide specific instructions to create an application, test the student's understanding of the material, and then request the reader to create the same application by implementing the Code Tables. All too often, students reading the text assume an understanding of the material without actually testing it. In this system, the instructor can easily assign the students to demonstrate their understanding of the material by completing the end-of-section exercises. Once a student has gone through the chapter and worked all of the *It's Your Turn!* exercises, they will have a working application that solves the problem posed in the scenario. In addition to the *It's Your Turn!* exercises, there are exercises at the end of each chapter that test the student's understanding of chapter material and projects that provide the students with an opportunity to create applications similar to the one covered in the text. At the end of each chapter, a running case is included that allows students to create a second project that grows with each additional chapter.

You may think it unusual that, in this day of very colorful textbooks, this textbook has no color at all. However, there is a reason for this. With the continuing rapid release of new versions of Visual Basic, it is necessary to be able to quickly revise a textbook to keep up with the new versions. We have chosen to do this by desktop publishing this book in a single color format. This in no way should detract from its usefulness in the classroom and, furthermore, enables us to offer the textbook to students at a lower price than the more elaborate books.

WHAT'S NEW IN THIS EDITION?

For prior user's of this textbook, the first thing new you will notice is that Craig Piercy has joined this effort as a co-author. Craig wrote the Vintage Videos and Joe's Tax Assistance cases for the first edition and is now a part of the team writing the textbook. You may also notice that this second edition looks a bit longer; this is due to two new chapters, more than 60 new tip boxes, and over 300 new exercises and projects. In the first case, the existing database chapter has been split into an introductory chapter and an advanced topics chapter. Introductory database topics from the previous edition are covered in Chapter 9 and a new Chapter 10 covers advanced database topics. We have also added an entirely new chapter 13 on VBScript that introduces the use of this variation of Visual Basic for electronic commerce.

The additional exercises and projects include new *It's Your Turn!* exercises, a new type of end-of-chapter exercise, and more projects to be completed. The almost 220 new *It's Your Turn!* exercises test the student's understanding of the text material in addition to the ones that have them create the application from the text. Also new to this edition are more than 60 exercises at the end of the chapter that test the student's understanding of the chapter material and 43 new projects.

SUPPORTING WEB SITE

Rather than including a disk and paper instructor's manual with the text which would increase the price of the textbook to the student, we have created a supporting Web site at

http://www.negia.net/~vbbook

for both instructors and students. The faculty section, which is password-protected, provides all of the support normally associated with a package such as this including transparencies for each chapter, a test bank, solutions to end-of-chapter exercises and projects, sample syllabi, and teaching suggestions. The student section of the

Web site includes data files needed by student and solutions to the *It's Your Turn!* exercises (instructors will also have access to this section). Students are given access to the *It's Your Turn!* solutions so they can check their work or, if they run into problems with a project, determine their error. The solutions to the *It's Your Turn!* exercises include *all* of the code from the VB Code Boxes presented in the text in a downloadable format. Both sections of the Web site have e-mail access to the authors, a bulletin board to display the occasional error that readers may discover, and new information on Visual Basic as it becomes available.

Included with the textbook is a CD-ROM that includes a working version of Visual Basic 6.0. This version of VB does not include the Help files that are available in the full version and it is not possible to create an .exe file with it. Your students can install Visual Basic on their own computer using this CD-ROM. If you or they have questions about doing this, see the accompanying Web site.

ACKNOWLEDGMENTS

Completing a text book such as this one has been made much easier by the help from a large number of people and we want to thank each of them here. Kelly Hilmer of Virginia Tech acted as a first reviewer and developed the Web site for the first edition. Estelle Piercy also read many of the chapters and provided numerous suggestions. Sarah Trammell and Jeffrey Daniels checked the *It's Your Turn!* exercises and created the solutions for them that are in the Web site. Cate Dapron and Publication Services copy edited online the textbook saving many hours of entering changes. The faculty and students of the Terry College of Business at the University of Georgia have also been very helpful in providing corrections and taking the time to discuss the project with us. At John Wiley & Sons, we want to thank my editor, Beth Lang Golub and her assistant, Jennifer Battista, the marketing manager, Jessica Garcia, and the senior production editor, Christine Cervoni, for their help with the project. And last, but far from least, we want to thank our wives, Carolyn and Estelle, for supporting us throughout this effort.

The following people reviewed at least one of the editions of the text and provided helpful comments:

Douglas B. Bock	Southern Illinois University, Edwardsville	Margaret Porciello	State University of New York, Farmingdale
Robert Foley	DeVry Institute, Decatur, GA	J.D. Robertson	Bentley College
Constanza Hagmann	Kansas State University	Ruth Sapir	SUNY Farmingdale
Bassam Hasan	Macon State College	Harrison Schofill	ITT Technical Institute, Jacksonville, FL
Donald F. Hoggan	Solano Community College	Deborah K. Smith	East Carolina University
Tim Jenkins	ITT Technical Institute, San Bernardino, CA	Stephen Solosky	Nassau Community College
Akhil Kumar	University of Colorado, Boulder	Devinder Sud	DeVry Institute, North Brunswick, NJ
David W. Letcher	The College of New Jersey	Gary Templeton	University of Alabama, Huntsville
Chuck Litecky	Mississippi State University	Marc Tower	ITT Technical Institute, Greenfield, WI
Patricia McQuaid	California Polytechnic State University, San Luis Obispo	M.A. Venkataramanan	Indiana University
Mike Mostafavi	University of Phoenix	Bruce White	Quinnipiac University
Margaret T. O'Hara	East Carolina University	Vincent C. Yen	Wright State University
Merrill Parker	Chattanooga State Technical Community College		

Patrick G. McKeown and Craig A. Piercy
Athens, GA

To the Student

Typically, the Preface to a text book is aimed at the instructor and you may not have read it. For that reason, this *To the Student* page is included to help you make the most of the instructional system that includes this textbook, an accompany CD-ROM, and the associated Web site that are designed to help you learn to program with Visual Basic. The key idea behind this system is that the only way to learn how to write computer programs in Visual Basic (or for that matter, any computer language) is to "get your hands dirty" by actually writing programs. If you use this system, we think you will easily be able to learn to program and to create fairly sophisticated computer applications in Visual Basic.

The Textbook

In the textbook, each chapter begins with the continuing saga of Vintage Videos, a start-up video store that rents only older videos. Each chapter poses a different, interesting business problem to be solved. Following the scenario, the chapter sections provide the logic and Visual Basic statements for a solution to this problem, give specific Visual Basic code to create an application, and then request you to create the same application.

If you read the text discussion of the new concepts and then use the VB Code Boxes and screen captures to complete the *It's Your Turn!* exercises, you will have a working application that solves the problem posed in the scenario. To make this work, though, you must make the effort to complete the *It's Your Turn!* exercises *on your own*. Be careful not to allow well-meaning friends or classmates to give you too much help or you will not acquire the skills needed to be a successful programmer!

The Accompanying CD-ROM

Included with this textbook is a CD-ROM that includes a working version of Visual Basic 6.0. This version of VB does not include Help files and it is not possible to create an .exe file with it. You can install Visual Basic on your own computer using this CD-ROM. If you have questions, see the associated Web site.

The Web Site

A Web site has been developed as a key part of the instructional system and you may access it at:

http://www.negia.net/~vbbook

The Web site includes sections for students and instructors. The student section includes the data files you will need to complete many of the *It's Your Turn!* and end-of-chapter exercises. It also includes the solutions to the *It's Your Turn* exercises you will need to complete the Vintage Videos application in a downloadable format. You are being given access to the *It's Your Turn!* solutions so you can check your work or, if you run into problems with a project, determine your error. The solutions to the *It's Your Turn!* exercises include *all* of the code from the VB Code Boxes presented in the text. The Web site will have e-mail access to the authors, a bulletin board to display the occasional error that you might discover, and new information on Visual Basic as it becomes available.

TABLE OF CONTENTS

6 *Working with Arrays in Visual Basic* **207**

7 *Using Functions, Subs, and Modules* **265**

1 AN INTRODUCTION TO PROGRAMMING AND VISUAL BASIC

LEARNING OBJECTIVES

After reading this chapter, you will be able to:

❖ Understand the importance of information systems in organizations.

❖ Discuss the role of computer programs and programming in information systems.

❖ List and discuss the six computer operations.

❖ Describe the difference between modern Windows-based computer languages and older procedural languages.

❖ Discuss the difference between compiled and interpreted languages.

❖ List and discuss the steps in the object-oriented, event-driven programming process.

SCENARIO: INTRODUCTION TO VINTAGE VIDEOS

The Treasure of Rio Montenegro, Ambush at Apache Pass, Starships Ahoy.... Clark chuckled to himself as he unpacked the videos from the carton. "You've got to hand it to Ed," he thought. "You won't find old titles like these at the big chain stores."

Clark Davis is an aspiring MIS student at Helene State University. Recently, he started working afternoons and weekends at his sister and brother-in-law's new video store called Vintage Videos. Ed and Yvonne Monk have established Vintage Videos to serve those video connoisseurs who prefer older, "classic" movies. Their rather broad definition of "classic" includes just about any film released before 1990. At Yvonne's urging, Ed has agreed to let Clark help out around the store to earn extra money toward his college expenses.

Carrying the new stock to the shelves, Clark heard mumbled cursing coming from the direction of the counter.

"What's the matter, Ed? More of Yvonne's cooking?" Clark quipped.

"No. Believe it or not, that's improving. Actually, it's this software. I can't seem to get it to do what I want," replied Ed. "The salesman made it sound like it was the solution to all of our problems, but it just doesn't seem to work right."

"Are you sure you know how to use it properly?"

"I think so. I've read through the manuals and even spent a few hours on the phone with the technical support. I think it just doesn't have all of the capabilities that we need."

Clark paused for a moment in thought. He sensed an opportunity here to put his recently acquired information systems knowledge to use. With some luck he might just be able to get extra credit at school and extra cash in his pocket at the same time.

He quickly suggested: "You know, Ed, I've been studying information systems at the University. Maybe, I can come up with something to help you out."

"What have you got in mind?"

"Well, I think we should evaluate Vintage Videos' IS needs and then develop a program specifically to meet those needs," Clark proposed in his best business-like voice.

"Maybe so, but wouldn't that be expensive? You know we can't afford expensive consultants or equipment," Ed replied warily.

Clark replied: "Actually, I was thinking that I could be your in-house IS consultant. I've been studying programming using Visual Basic. I think that with Visual Basic we can develop something that will work well at no great expense in extra equipment. We can discuss any extra compensation for myself after I show what can be done."

Somewhat reassured but still a little cautious, Ed answered: "I'll tell you what. Why don't we talk about what we're going to need. Then you can work up something simple just to show me what you can do. Then we can take it from there."

"That sounds reasonable," Clark said with a grin. "Why don't you buy me lunch and we can discuss it? Then I'll get to work on demonstration."

With an equal-sized grin, Ed replied: "Sure thing! How about lunch at Chez Yvonne?"

INFORMATION SYSTEMS IN BUSINESS

Many organizations are finding that in order to survive, they must be able to collect and process data efficiently and make the resulting information on their operations available to their employees. Successful organizations have found that the key to making this information available is having an effective information system that will carry out these operations. An **information system** is *the combination of technology (computers) and people that enables an organization to collect data, store them, and transform them into information.* To understand the concept of an information system fully, you need to understand the difference between data and information. **Data** are raw facts that are collected and stored by the information system. Data can be in the form of numbers, letters of the alphabet, images, sound clips, or even video clips. You are undoubtedly very familiar with many types of data, including names, dates, prices, and credit card numbers. By themselves, data are not very meaningful; however, when data are converted by the information system into **information**, the end result is meaningful. Once again, you are familiar with many forms of information, including written reports, lists, tables, and graphs. Information is what organizational employees use in their work.

To convert or process data into information electronically, software must direct the operations of the computer's operations. **Software** is composed of one or more lists of instructions called **programs**, and the process of creating these lists of instructions is termed **programming**. While computer hardware can be mass-produced on assembly lines like other consumer goods, software must be developed through the logical and creative capabilities of humans. Individuals or groups of individuals working together must develop the instructions that direct the operations of every computer in use today. The same is true whether the instructions are for the computer that controls your car's fuel system, the computer that controls the space shuttle, or the computer that prints the checks for the business at which you work.

Programming in Information Systems

While a great deal of programming work goes on at large software firms like Microsoft or Adobe Systems, much more programming is done at companies that produce non-software goods and services. While you may think that these companies could buy off-the-shelf software like word processors or spreadsheets to run their business, in most cases companies must develop their own software to meet their particular needs. In fact, it has been said that the "software needed to be competitively different is generally not available from off-the-shelf packages" and that ". . .building . . . systems for unique [competitive] capability is often the single most important activity for an . . . organization."[1] This means that no matter how good off-the-shelf software becomes, there is always going to be demand for programmers to work in businesses and not-for-profit organizations. In fact, the demand for information systems employees is accelerating and the future is very bright for persons trained in this field.

Programming is actually part of a much larger process known as **systems development.** This process involves a large scale effort to either create an entirely new information system or to update (maintain) an existing information system. In either case, systems development involves four primary steps: planning, analysis, design, and implementation. In the planning stage, it is decided what must be done to solve a problem or meet a need—create a new system, update an old one, or even, purchase a system from an outside source. Once it has been decided what must be done, the next step is to analyze the system that will be created. This may involve analyzing an existing system or analyzing the system that must be created. Once the analysis step is completed, the next step is to design the new or updated system. This design must be complete and detailed and leave nothing to chance or guesswork. Once the design is completed, the system can be implemented. It is in the implementation step that programming comes in. Programmers work with the results of the design step to create a series of computer programs that, together, will work as the needed information system. In many cases, the programmers will know little or nothing about the overall problem and must depend completely on the results of the design step. However, without the programming process, the information system will never be built or updated.

Given that programming is such an important part of building and maintaining information systems for organizations of all sizes, it is easy to see why individuals interested in working in the field of information systems must have some knowledge of computer programming. This book is written with the purpose of helping you become capable of writing computer programs that will solve business-related problems. The scenario at the beginning of the chapter involves a small business that is preparing to open its doors and is looking to create a part of its information system that will handle processing rentals of "vintage" videos. As you go through this book, this system will be expanded to handle other functions within the business.

COMPUTER OPERATIONS

Before we start our discussion of creating computer programs, it is useful to understand the six operations that all computers can carry out to process data into information. Understanding these operations will help you when you start writing programs. These operations are the same regardless of whether we are discussing multi-user mainframe computers that handle large-scale processing, such as preparing the end-of-

---

1. Martin, James, *Cybercorp: The New Business Revolution*, New York: AMACOM Books, p. 104

term grade rolls or processing the university payroll, or small personal computers that are used today by a large proportion of office workers in the United States and other developed countries. The six operations that a computer can perform are:

1. Input data
2. Store data in internal memory
3. Perform arithmetic on data
4. Compare two values and select one of two alternative actions
5. Repeat a group of actions any number of times
6. Output the results of processing

Let's now discuss each of these operations in a little more detail.

Input Data: For a computer to be able to transform data into information, it must first be able to accept input of the data that will be processed into information. Data are typically input from a keyboard or mouse, but they can also come from a barcode reader like those used at checkout terminals. Input can also come from some type of sensor or from a computer disk. For example, with a word processor, the letters of the alphabet, numbers, and punctuation symbols are the data that are processed by the computer. New documents are created by entering data from the keyboard while existing documents are loaded from your hard drive or floppy disk.

Store data in memory: Once data have been input, they are stored in internal memory. Each memory location holding a piece of data is assigned a name, which is used by the instructions to perform the processing. Since the values in a memory location can change as the process occurs, the memory locations are called **variables**. For example, when you start your word processor, the characters you enter to create a document are stored in memory.

The instructions for processing this data are also stored in memory. In the earliest days of computing, the instructions (program) were not stored in memory and had to be entered one at a time to process the data. When the *stored program* concept was developed by John von Neumann, it was a tremendous breakthrough. With a stored program, the instructions can be executed as fast as they can be retrieved from memory to convert the data into usable information.

Perform arithmetic on data: Once the data and instructions have been input and stored, arithmetic operations can be performed on the variables representing the data to process them into information. This includes addition, subtraction, multiplication, division, and raising to a power. The processing chip of the computer carries out these operations by retrieving the data from memory and then performing the processing based on instructions from the programmer.

You may ask how a word processor or computer game works if all the computer can do is perform arithmetic. The answer is that everything in a computer—numbers, letters, graphics, and so on—is represented by numbers, and all processing is handled through some type of arithmetic operation.

Compare two values and select one of two alternative actions: To do anything other than the simplest processing, a computer must be able to choose between two sets of instructions to execute. It does this by comparing the contents of two memory locations and, based on the result of that comparison, executing one of two groups of instructions. For example, when you carry out the spell-checking operation, the computer is checking each word to determine if it matches a word in the computer's dictionary. Based on the result of this comparison, the word is accepted or flagged for you to consider changing.

Repeat a group of actions any number of times: While you *could* carry out all of the above operations with a typewriter or handheld calculator, repeating actions is something the computer does better than any person or any other type of machine. Because a computer never tires or becomes bored, it can be instructed to repeat some action as many times as needed without fear of an error occurring from the constant repetition. The capability of a computer to repeat an operation is what most clearly sets it apart from all other machines.

However, if you fail to instruct the computer properly as to when to terminate the repetition, it could continue repeating the operation endlessly or until someone turns it off! Such endless or infinite loops are something all programmers must guard against. The spell-checking operation mentioned above is an example of a repeated action: The program repeatedly checks words until it comes to the end of the document.

Output the results of processing: Once the processing has been completed and the required information generated, to be of any use the information must be output. Output of processed information can take many forms: displayed on a monitor, printed on paper, stored on disk, as instructions to a machine, and so on. Output is accomplished by retrieving information from a memory location and sending it to the output device. For example, when you complete your work with a word processor, the resulting information is displayed on your monitor and you probably will also print it for distribution to others.

These six operations are depicted in Figure 1-1, where each operation is numbered.

FIGURE 1-1. Six computer operations

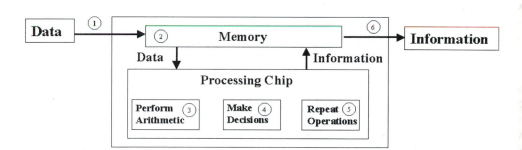

PROGRAMS AND PROGRAMMING

As mentioned above, to carry out any of the six operations just discussed, you must be able to provide instructions to the computer in the form of a program. The most important thing about programming is that it is a form of *problem solving*, and the objective is to develop the step-by-step process—the **logic**—that will solve the problem. Step-by-step logic of this type is referred to as an **algorithm**. You have worked with algorithms before; a set of directions to a party is an algorithm, as is a recipe to make spaghetti sauce or to bake a cake. Many times a program fails to work because the programmer attempts to write the program before developing the correct algorithm for solving the problem. Only after you have developed the logic of the solution can you consider actually writing the instructions for the computer.

Control Structures

While it may seem quite daunting to create the logic to solve a problem, remember that all computer programs can be created with only three types of logic or, as they are known in programming, **control structures.** The three control structures are sequence, decision, and repetition.

The **sequence control structure** includes the input, storage, arithmetic, and output computer operations discussed earlier. It is so called because all four of these operations can be performed without any need to make a decision or repeat an operation.

The **decision control structure** is the same as the decision-making computer operation discussed earlier. It enables the programmer to control the flow of operations by having the user or data determine which operation is to be performed next.

Finally, the **repetition control structure** is used to repeat one or more operations. The number of repetitions depends on the user or the data, but the programmer must include a way to terminate the repetition process.

Once you learn how to create the logic for these three control structures, you will find that writing meaningful and useful programs is a matter of combining the structures to create more complex logic.

Programming Languages

Once you have developed the logic for solving the problem, you can think about writing the actual instructions that the computer will use in implementing the logic. Computer programs must be written in one of various **programming languages.** These languages use a restricted vocabulary and a very structured syntax that the computer can understand. While a great deal of research is ongoing to create computers that can accept instructions using conversational English, currently no computers meet this criterion. So, until computers like C3-PO and R2D2, popularized in the *Star Wars* movies, are created, we are stuck with using these computer languages.

Within the computer, the data and instructions are represented in the binary number system as a series of zeros and ones. This form of representation is used because the computer's only two electrical states—on and off—correspond to 1 and 0. Using a string of transistors that act as switches, the computer can represent a number, character, or instruction as a series of on–off states. All processing is also carried out in the binary number system. For example, the computer carries out all arithmetic in binary instead of in the decimal number system that humans use.

The binary form of the instructions is called **machine language,** since this is the language that computers use to carry out their operations. An example of the machine language statements necessary to sum the digits 1 to 100 for a computer using an Intel CPU chip is shown in Figure 1-2.

FIGURE 1-2.
Machine language program

Machine Language Command	Explanation
10111000 00000000 00000000	Set Total Value to 0
10111001 00000000 01100100	Set Current Value to 100
00000001 11001000	Add Current value to Total Value
01001001	Subtract 1 from Current Value
01110101 11111011	If Current value is not 0, repeat

Programming the very first computers, which had to be done in binary, was very difficult and time-consuming. Now, we have English-like programming languages, which are referred to as **high-level languages** because they are close to the level of the programmer rather than being close to the level of the machine. Before the statements in a high-level program can be used to direct the actions of a computer, they must be translated into machine language. This process is shown in Figure 1-3, where the translator itself is a software program that can perform the process of changing high-level statements into machine-language instructions. Files on a Windows-based computer with an .exe file extension are machine-language programs that have been translated from some high-level language. They can be executed with no translation because they are already in a binary form.

FIGURE 1-3.
Language
translation process

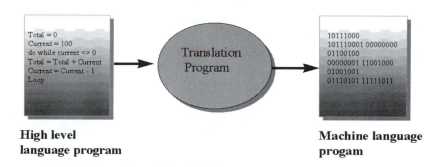

**High level
language program**

**Machine language
progam**

Depending on the type of language and the application, one of two methods is used for this translation process: **interpretation** or **compilation**. When a program is *interpreted*, the high-level language statements are converted into equivalent machine-language statements one at a time as the program is executed. The nice thing about interpreting a program is that, if the program encounters a statement with an error in it, the interpretation process stops and an error message is displayed so the user can correct it. On the other hand, executing an interpreted program is slower than executing a compiled program since each statement has to be converted to binary each time it is encountered in the program even if has been converted previously.

When a high-level language is *compiled*, the entire program is translated into machine language before an attempt is made to execute it. Compilation has an advantage over interpretation in that a compiled program will run faster than an interpreted program once all errors have been found and corrected. However, errors are more difficult to find during compilation than during interpretation. Visual Basic has an advantage over other languages in that Visual Basic projects can be interpreted during the design and testing process, but can then be compiled into an executable program when all of the errors have been removed.

*Programming in
Windows*

As you are probably aware, most personal computers today run some form of the Microsoft Windows operating system such as Windows 95, Windows 98, Windows ME, or Windows 2000/NT. The Windows operating system offers many improvements over the previous operating system for computers using Intel chips (MS-DOS). These improvements include the capability to run multiple programs at the same time, access to more memory, and a **graphical user interface (GUI)**. The basic interface for all Windows packages is the desktop, on which users work with icons that represent shortcuts to files. In addition to allowing users to "point-and-click" to access application software and utilities, all software written for Windows displays the same menu bar, with menu choices at the top of the screen, a scroll bar at the right, and the capability to expand or shrink the application's window. With Windows being the primary operating system for personal computers, learning to program in the Windows environment has become a critical skill for anybody interested in working in information systems. To program in Windows, you first need to understand a little about how Windows works.

To understand the workings of Windows, you need to understand three key concepts: windows, events, and messages. A **window** is any rectangular region on the screen with its own boundaries. All applications run in their own windows. For example, when you use your word processor, a document window displays the text you are entering and editing. When you retrieve a file, you do this from a dialog box that is a window. Similarly, when an error message is displayed, this is done in a window. Finally, the menu bar and all of the icons or buttons on the toolbar across the top or side of your screen are also windows. Figure 1-4 shows a Windows 98 screen with several types of windows displayed.

Figure 1-4.
Windows in
Windows 98

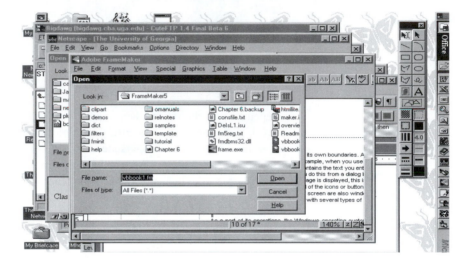

As a part of its operations, the Windows operating system is constantly monitoring all of the windows on the screen for signs of activity termed **events**. An event can be a mouse click or double-click, a keypress, or simply a change in a window caused by an entry of text in it.

When an event occurs, the corresponding window sends a **message** to the operating system, which processes the message and then broadcasts it to other windows. When they receive a message, the other windows take actions based on their own set of instructions. Programming in Windows requires that you learn how to work with windows, events, and messages. For this reason, programming in Windows is usually termed **event-driven programming,** because all actions are driven by events. While this may sound complicated, languages like Visual Basic make it easy to create Windows-based applications that work with Windows by providing you with the necessary tools.

Event-driven programming is quite different from programming under MS-DOS or on mainframe computers. In those cases, the program itself controls the actions that will take place and the order in which those actions will occur. Execution of the program starts with the first instruction and continues through the remaining instructions, making decisions as to which instructions will be executed depending on the data that are input. The main program may use smaller subprograms to handle parts of the processing. This type of programming is referred to as **procedural program-**

ming, and it works very well for such activities as processing a large number of grades at the end of the term or printing payroll checks at the end of the pay period. However, with the move toward widespread use of GUI, the trend is toward using event-driven programming.

THE VISUAL BASIC LANGUAGE

As discussed above, Visual Basic is a computer language that has been developed to help you create programs that will work with the Windows operating system. It is an event-driven language that does not follow a predefined sequence of instructions; it responds to events to execute different sets of instructions depending on which event occurs. The order in which events—such as mouse clicks, keystrokes, or even other sets of instructions—occur controls the order of events in Visual Basic and other event-driven languages. For that reason, an event-driven program can execute differently each time it is run, depending on what events occur.

In addition to being event-driven, Visual Basic has many characteristics of an **object-oriented language**; that is, it uses identifiable shapes, each of which has certain properties and can respond to a variety of events.[2] Each of the windows discussed above as a part of the Windows operating system is an object, as are a wide variety of other shapes, including command buttons, click boxes, and menus. **Properties** of objects are simply the attributes associated with the object. **Methods** are a set of predefined activities that an object can carry out. For example, the name of an object is a property and positioning the cursor on that object is a method.

An example of an object with which you are familiar might be a soccer ball. Properties of the soccer ball are its diameter, weight, color, and so on. Methods for the soccer ball include rolling and bouncing. If we apply the KICK event to the soccer ball, then, depending on its diameter and weight, it will roll and bounce a certain distance. It is important to note that the instructions for a method are already a part of Visual Basic, but the programmer must write the instructions to tell the object how to respond to an event.

Objects are combined with properties or methods by a period or dot, and objects are combined with events by an underline. Continuing the soccer ball example, we might have

Ball.Color = White

which defines the color of the ball. Similarly,

Ball.Roll

causes the ball to roll. Finally,

Ball_Kick

is the result of someone kicking the ball.

Even through Visual Basic 6 is not completely object-oriented, it has enough characteristics of object-oriented languages that we will refer to it as an **object-oriented event-driven (OOED) language**.

Working with an OOED language involves combining objects with the instructions on how each object should respond to a given event. For example, you might have a command button for which the instructions are to display a message; instructions for another button might be to exit the program or, as it is called in Visual Basic, the **project.** These instructions are referred to as the **code** for the program. The code

---

2. Visual Basic 6 is not completely object-oriented because it lacks a key characteristic (inheritance) present in true object-oriented languages like Java and C++.

for Visual Basic is written in a form of one of the oldest computer languages around—Basic, which was first used in 1960. The version of Basic used in Visual Basic has been improved in many ways, but it retains one of the key advantages of the original language: It is very easy to use and understand.

The OOED
Programming Process

Creating an application using an OOED programming language such as Visual Basic is much easier than working with a traditional programming language. Instead of having to develop the logic for the entire program as you would with a procedural language, you can divide up the program logic into small, easily handled parts by working with objects and events. For each object, you determine the events that you want the object to respond to and then develop code to have the object provide the desired response. All of the necessary messages between objects in Windows are handled by Visual Basic, thereby significantly reducing the work you must do to create an application.

The manner in which you create a Visual Basic project is also different from traditional programming. Instead of having to create an entire program before testing any part of it, with Visual Basic you can use **interactive development** to create an object, write the code for it, and test it before going onto other objects. For example, assume that you are creating a Visual Basic project that calculates the taxes on a video rental and sums the taxes and price to compute the amount due. With Visual Basic, you can create the objects and code to calculate the taxes and amount due and test them to ensure their correctness, before going on to the rest of the project.

While creating an OOED application is easier than working with a procedural language, you still need to follow a series of steps to ensure correctness and completeness of the finished product. These steps are:

1. Define problem
2. Create interface
3. Develop logic for action objects
4. Write and test code for action objects
5. Test overall project
6. Document project in writing

Let's take a brief look at each of these steps. As an example, we will use a part of the situation just mentioned, that is, creating an application to calculate the taxes and amount due on a video rental. We will return to this example and expand it in Chapter 3 when Clark Davis faces this problem with Vintage Videos.

Step One: Define
Problem

Before we can hope to develop any computer application, it is absolutely necessary to clearly define our objective, that is, the problem to be solved. Only then can we begin to develop the correct logic to solve the problem and incorporate that logic into a computer application. Ensuring that the correct problem is being solved requires careful study of why a problem exists. Maybe an organization is currently handling some repetitive process manually and wants to use a computer to automate it. Or maybe management has a complicated mathematical or financial problem that cannot be solved by hand. Or maybe a situation has occurred or will occur that cannot be handled by an existing program.

The problem identification step should include identification of the data to be *input* to the program and the desired results to be *output* from the program. Often these two items will be specified by a person or an agency other than the programmer. Much grief can be avoided if these input and output requirements are incorporated into the programmer's thinking at this early stage of program development. Unclear thinking at this stage may cause the programmer to write a program that does not correctly solve the problem at hand, or a program that correctly solves the wrong problem, or a combination of both! Therefore the programmer *must* spend as much time as is necessary to truly identify and understand the problem. In our case, the owner of Vintage Videos has found that existing computer software does not meet his particular needs and he needs a custom-developed application

Because Visual Basic is a *visual* language, a good way to understand what is required to solve the problem is to sketch the interface showing the various objects that will be part of the project. Not only does this help you understand the problem, it is also a good way for you to communicate your understanding to other people. As a part of this sketch, you should denote the input and output objects and the objects for which code is needed, the so-called **action objects.** A sketch of the proposed solution for the Vintage Videos problem is shown in Figure 1-5.

In looking at Figure 1-5, you will see one input—the price of the video—and two outputs—the taxes and the amount due. There are also two action objects—a calculation button and an exit button. If there are multiple forms, they should all be sketched with input, output, and action objects denoted as in Figure 1-5.

FIGURE 1-5. Sketch of interface for Vintage Videos

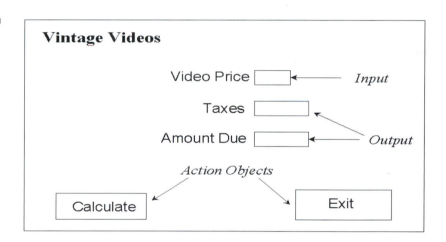

Step Two: Create Interface

Once you have defined the problem and, using a sketch of the interface, have decided on the objects that are necessary for your project, you are ready to create the interface. Creating the interface with Visual Basic is quite easy: You select objects from those available and place them on the form. This process should follow the sketch done earlier. While you have not yet been introduced to the wide variety of objects available for creating Visual Basic projects, we can work on the logic for the Vintage Videos problem with just three types of objects: buttons for action, textboxes for input and output, and labels for descriptors. The interface in Visual Basic is shown in Figure 1-6.

Step Three: Develop Logic for Action Objects

Once the problem has been clearly identified and the interface created, the next step is to develop the logic for the action objects in the interface. This is the step in the development process where you have to think about what each action object must do in

FIGURE 1-6.
Interface for
Vintage Videos

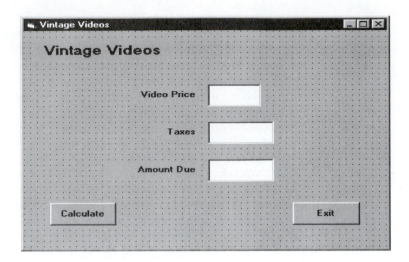

response to an event. No matter how good your interface, if you don't develop the appropriate logic for the action objects, you will have great difficulty creating a project that solves the problem defined earlier.

To help with this logical development for the action objects, there are two useful tools for designing OOED applications: IPO Tables and pseudocode. **IPO** (Input/ Processing/Output) **Tables** show the inputs to an object, the required outputs for that object, and the processing that is necessary to convert the inputs into the desired outputs. Once you have an IPO Table for an object, you can write a pseudocode procedure to complete the logic development step.

Writing **pseudocode** involves writing the code for the object in English rather than in a computer language. Once you have developed an IPO Table and the pseudocode for each object, it is a very easy step to write a **procedure** in Basic that will carry out the necessary processing.

IPO Table

Let's begin by developing the logic for the Calculate button using an IPO Table. The IPO Table for the Calculate button has as input the number of videos and the price of the videos. The processing involves the calculation necessary to compute the desired output: the amount of the sale. As mentioned earlier, in many cases the program designer will have no control over the input and output. They will be specified by somebody else—either the person for whom the application is being developed or, if you are a member of a team and are working on one part of the overall application, the overall design. Once you are given the specified input and output, your job is to determine the processing necessary to convert the inputs into desired outputs. Figure 1-7 shows the IPO table for the calculation button. IPO tables are needed for all objects that involve input, output, and processing. We won't do one for the Exit button since it simply terminates the project.

FIGURE 1-7. IPO
Table for Calculate
button

Input	Processing	Output
Video price	Taxes = 0.07 x Price	Taxes
	Amount due = Price + Taxes	Amount due

Pseudocode

Once you have developed the IPO tables for the action objects, you should then develop a pseudocode procedure for each action object. Pseudocode is useful for two reasons. First, you can write the procedure for the object in English without worrying about the special syntax and grammar of a computer language. Second, pseudocode provides a relatively direct link between the IPO Table and the computer code for the object, since you use English to write instructions that can then be converted into program instructions. Often, this conversion from pseudocode statement to computer language instruction is virtually line for line.

There are no set rules for writing pseudocode; it should be a personalized method for going from the IPO Table to the computer program. The pseudocode should be a set of clearly defined steps that enables a reader to see the next step to be taken under any possible circumstances. Also, the language and syntax should be consistent so that the programmer will be able to understand his or her own pseudocode at a later time. As an example of pseudocode, assume a program is needed to compare two values, Salary and Commission, and to output the smaller of the two. The pseudocode for this example is shown below:

```
Begin procedure
    Input Salary and Commission
    If Salary < Commission then
        Output Salary
    Else
        Output Commission
    End Decision
End procedure
```

In this pseudocode, it is easy to follow the procedure. Note that parts of it are indented to make it easier to follow the logic. The important point to remember about pseudocode is that it expresses the logic for the action object to the programmer in the same way that a computer language expresses it to the computer. In this way, pseudocode is like a personalized programming language.

Now let's write a pseudocode procedure for the Vintage Videos Calculate object. Note that the pseuocode program matches the IPO Table shown in Figure 1-7.

```
Begin procedure
    Input Video Price
    Taxes = 0.07 x Video Price
    Amount Due = Video Price + Taxes
    Output Taxes and Amount Due
End procedure
```

While we have only one object in our small example for which an IPO Table and pseudocode are needed, in most situations you will have numerous objects for which you will need to develop the logic using these tools.

Step Four: Write and Test Code for Action Objects

Once you have created the Visual Basic interface and developed the logic for the action objects using IPO Tables and pseudocode, you must write procedures in Basic for each action object. This code should provide instructions to the computer to carry out one or more of the six operations listed earlier—that is, input data, store data in internal memory, perform arithmetic on data, compare two values and select one of two alternative actions, repeat a group of actions any number of times, and output the results of processing. While creating the interface is important, writing the code is the essence of developing an application.

Since you have not yet been introduced to the rules for writing code in Basic for the various objects, we will defer a full discussion of this step until Chapter 3 and beyond. However, you should be able to see the similarity between the Visual Basic event procedure displayed in VB Code Box 1-1 and the pseudocode version shown earlier. The differences are due to the way Visual Basic handles input and output. Input is from the Text property of the first textbox, named txtVideoPrice. Output goes to the Text property of the two textboxes named txtTaxes and txtAmountDue. There are also statements that begin with the word Dim, to declare the variables, and comment statements that begin with an apostrophe (').

Once you have written the code for an action object, the second part of this step is to test that object and correct any errors; don't wait until the entire project is completed. Use the interactive capabilities of Visual Basic to test the code of each and every object as it is written. This process is referred to as **debugging**—trying to remove all of the errors or **"bugs."**

VB CODE BOX 1-1. Visual Basic computation of Taxes and Amount Due	```Private Sub cmdCalc_Click()```
	```'This object should calculate Taxes and Amount Due```
	```'given the Video Price```
	``` Dim curPrice as Currency, curTaxes as Currency```
	``` Dim curAmountDue as Currency```
	``` curPrice = txtVideoPrice.Text```
	``` curTaxes = 0.07 * curPrice```
	``` curAmountDue = curPrice + curTaxes```
	``` txtTaxes.Text = curTaxes```
	``` txtAmountDue.Text = curAmountDue```
	```End Sub```

Because Visual Basic automatically checks each line of the code of an object for syntax or vocabulary errors, the debugging process is much easier than in other languages. However, even if all the syntax and vocabulary are correct, the code for an object still may be incorrect—either in the manner in which it carries out the logic or in the logic itself. The best way to find and correct such errors is to use **test data** for which the results are known in advance. If the results for the object do not agree with the results from the hand calculations, an error exists, either in the logic or in the hand calculations. After the hand calculations have been verified, the logic must be checked. For example, if the results of the Calculate button came out different from what was expected, then we would need to look for a problem in the data or the logic.

In the case of the Calculate button, we want to determine if the code shown in VB Code Box 1-1 will actually compute and output to the textboxes the *correct* taxes and amount due for the video price entered in the first textbox. Figure 1-8 shows the result of clicking the Calculate button for a video with a price of $1.99. Note that the results, while correct, are not *exactly* what you might expect. Instead of rounded values of $.14 for the taxes and $2.13 for the amount due, the answers are the exact values of $.1393 and $2.1293. This is because we have not *formatted* the answers as dollar and cents. This will be done when we revisit this problem in Chapter 3.

While the answers for this set of test data are correct, this does not mean it will work for all test data. Testing requires that a wide variety of test data be used to assure that the code for the object works under all circumstances.

Since the Calculate button appears to work, we can now write the code for the Exit button, which consists of one instruction: End. If this command also works, then we are ready to move on to the next step in the application development process: testing the overall project.

FIGURE 1-8. Testing the Calculate button

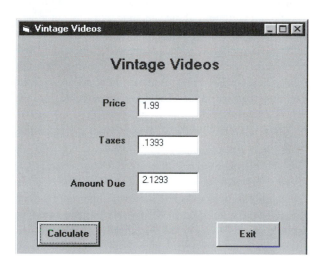

Step Five: Test Overall Project

Once you have tested the code for each action object individually, the next step is to test the overall project and correct any errors that may still exist or that may be the result of incorrect communication between objects. At this stage it is necessary to determine whether the results obtained from the project meet the objectives outlined in the Problem Definition step. If the project does not meet the final user's needs, then the developer must analyze the results and the objectives to find out where they diverge. After the analysis, the developer should trace through the program development procedure and correct the algorithm, IPO Tables, pseudocode, and final code for one or more objects to find the cause of the difference between the objectives and the final project.

Step Six: Document Your Project in Writing

An important part of writing any computer software is the documentation of the software. **Documentation** can be defined as *the written descriptions of the software that aid users and other programmers*. It includes both internal descriptions of the code instructions and external descriptions and instructions. Documentation helps users by providing instructions and suggestions on using the software. Documentation helps other programmers who may need to make changes or correct the programs.

Internal documentation usually includes *comments* within the program that are intermingled with the program statements to explain the purpose and logic of the program elements. In VB Code Box 1-1, the statements beginning with an apostrophe (') are examples of internal documentation. This type of documentation is essential to the maintenance of software, especially by someone other than the original programmer. By being able to read the original programmer's purpose for a part of a program or a program statement, a different programmer can make any needed corrections or revisions. Without internal documentation, it can be extremely difficult for anyone to understand the purpose of parts of the program. And, if a programmer is unclear about what's going on in the program, making needed changes will be very difficult. In this text, because we will be explaining the code in detail, we do not include the level of internal documentation that *should* be found in the projects you create both here and in your work.

Written documentation includes books, manuals, and pamphlets that give instructions on using the software and also discuss the objectives and logic of the software. The documentation should include a user's guide and programmer documentation. The *user's guide* provides complete instructions on accessing the software, entering data, interpreting output, and understanding error messages. The *programmer documentation* should include various descriptive documents that allow for maintenance of the software. These may include pseudocode of sections of the program, a listing of the program, and a description of required input values and the resulting output.

Final Comments on the Programming Process

Creating applications in an OOED language like Visual Basic is easy and fun. However, there is one caveat to this statement: You still must be able to develop the logic for the action objects and write the code to make them respond appropriately to events. In this text, we will spend the first five chapters concentrating on two things: showing you how to create a fairly simple interface and discussing the key elements involved in writing code. While creating the interface can be very interesting, you should not lose sight of the overall goal, which is to produce applications that respond to events in an appropriate manner. The only way to make this happen is to be able to write code that works!

SUMMARY

In this chapter, you have been introduced to the process of developing applications for information systems in organizations. While off-the-shelf software is of great use to individuals and organizations, in many cases organizations are finding that they must develop their own software to be competitive in today's world. This chapter also covered the six operations that all computers can carry out:

1. Input data
2. Store data in internal memory
3. Perform arithmetic on data
4. Compare two values and select one of two alternative actions
5. Repeat a group of actions any number of times
6. Output the results of processing

You also learned about the difference between high-level languages and machine language and about the requirement that high-level languages be translated into machine language before the computer can use them. The difference between Windows-based, event-driven, object-oriented (OOED) computer languages and older procedural languages was discussed, as was the concept of objects in programming. Each object has certain properties and methods that respond to a restricted set of events. Next, we discussed the steps in the OOED programming process, which are as follows:

1. Define problem
2. Create interface
3. Develop logic for action objects

4. Write and test code for action objects

5. Test overall project

6. Document project in writing

IPO Tables and pseudocode were discussed as tools to help in the all-important second step: developing the logic for objects. No matter how good the design or the interface, without the correct logic and the corresponding correct computer code, the objects will not be able to respond appropriately to events.

KEY TERMS

action objects
algorithm
bugs
code
compilation
control structures
data
debugging
decision control structure
documentation
event-driven programming
events
graphical user interface (GUI)
high-level language

information
information system
interactive development
interpretation
IPO (Input/Processing/Output)
   Tables
logic
machine language
message
methods
object-oriented event-driven
   (OOED) language
object-oriented language
procedural programming

procedure
programming
programming languages
programs
project
properties
pseudocode
repetition control structure
sequence control structure
software
systems development
test data
variables
window

EXERCISES

1. Every month you collect your loose change in a jar on your dresser. At the end of the month, you sort and roll the coins and deposit them in your savings account. Describe what you would do using steps that follow the three basic control structures: sequence, decision and repetition. By following your steps, you should be able to handle one year worth of coins.

2. Develop a list of properties and methods for each of the following common objects below.

    a. a pet cat

    b. an automobile

    c. a video tape

    d. a document created using word processing software

    e. a list of customers and their contact information

3. For the following scenarios, describe the inputs, outputs and processing steps using an IPO table.

    a. You are balancing your checkbook. You have a stack of items that need to be added to the checkbook record including: deposit slips, ATM withdrawal receipts, and copies of checks used. You need to add the items and keep a running total of the balance for each item.

b. You are planning your schedule for the next school term. Assume that you will successfully complete your current courses.

c. You have a personal web page on which you post a news page about your band/sports team/debate club/etc. You wish to automate the creation of your news page.

4. An algorithm is a step-by-step logical procedure for accomplishing a task or solving a problem. Write an algorithm that lists the steps that you would take for the following tasks or problems.

a. You are going from your home to your first class of the day.

b. You are searching on the Internet for a course research topic.

c. You are attempting to beat a friend while playing a simple game (tic-tac-toe, hangman, etc.).

5. Write a brief problem description for the programs that correspond to the following sets of IPO and pseudocode. What control structures are used in the logic for each set?

a.

Input	Processes	Output
exchange rate amount in dollars	read exchange rate get amount in dollars calculate amount in foreign currency display amount in for- eign currency	amount in for- eign currency

```
Begin Procedure
    Read exchange rate
    Get amount in US dollars
    Amount in foreign currency = exchange rate * amount in US dollars
    Display amount in foreign currency
End Procedure
```

b.

Input	Processes	Output
tax rate item 1 price item 2 price item 3 price : item k price	read tax rate get prices for all items purchased calculate subtotal calculate sales tax calculate total price print subtotal, sales tax and total price	subtotal sales tax total price

```
Begin Procedure
        Read tax rate
        Repeat
                Get item price
        Until all item prices obtained
        Calculate subtotal = sum of all prices
        Calculate sales tax = subtotal * tax rate
        Calculate total price = subtotal + sales tax
        Print subtotal, sales tax and total price
End Procedure
```

c.

Input	Processes	Output
grade average 1	get each grade average	letter grade 1
grade average 2	determine letter grade	letter grade 2
grade average 3		letter grade 3
:		:
grade average k		letter grade k

```
Begin Procedure
        Repeat
                Get next grade average
                If grade average >= 90
                        next letter grade = A
                ElseIf grade average >= 80
                        next letter grade = B
                ElseIf grade average >= 70
                        next letter grade = C
                ElseIf grade average >= 60
                        next letter grade = D
                Else
                        next letter grade = F
                End If
                Write next letter grade
        Until all grades are assigned
End Procedure
```

PROJECTS

1. Assume that a student takes three quizzes and the score for each quiz is input. The output should be the average score on the three quizzes. Sketch the interface for this problem if textboxes will be used for input and output and a Compute button will calculate the average score. Also, create an IPO Table and pseudocode for the Compute button.

2. Chris Patrick works for the Shrub and Turf Lawn Care Company. He is paid a 10 percent commission on the value of lawn care contracts that he sells. Assume that the input includes the number of sales and the price charged for such contracts (assume it is the same for all contracts.) Output should include the total value of the sales and Chris's commission on the sales. Sketch the interface for this problem if textboxes are

used for input and output. Assume that two buttons are used: one for computing total value of the sales and one for computing Chris's commission. For each button, develop an IPO Table and the pseudocode procedure.

3. Acme, Inc., leases automobiles for its salespeople and wishes to create an application that will determine the gas mileage for each type of automobile. Input should include the make of the automobile, the beginning odometer reading, the ending odometer reading, and the gallons of gasoline consumed. Output should include the miles per gallon for the car being tested. Sketch the interface for this problem if textboxes are used for input and output. Assume that a Calculate button is used for computing the gas mileage. Develop an IPO Table and the pseudocode procedure for this Calculate button. [Note: Gas mileage = (Ending odometer reading – Beginning odometer reading)/ Gallons used.]

4. Smith and Jones, Inc., wishes to determine the breakeven production volume for a new product. Breakeven volume is defined as the number of units that must be produced and sold for the total cost of production to equal the total revenue. The formula used to calculate the breakeven point is (Fixed cost of production)/(Selling price per unit – Variable cost per unit). The company also wants to know the Total revenue and Total cost values at the breakeven point where:

Total revenue = Selling price x Number produced

Total cost = Fixed cost + (Variable cost x Number produced)

Input for this problem includes the Fixed cost of production, the Unit price, and the Unit cost for the new product. Output should include the Breakeven volume as well as the Total cost and Total revenue at the breakeven point. Sketch the interface for this problem if textboxes are used for input and output. Assume that one button is used for calculation of Breakeven volume and Total revenue/Total cost at the Breakeven volume. Develop an IPO Table and the pseudocode procedure for this button.

5. Cover-Your-Wall, Inc., specializes in selling wallpaper to "do-it-yourselfers." The company would like a computer program to determine the number of rolls needed to cover a room. This calculation depends on the area to be covered. This value is computed for a rectangular room with an eight-foot ceiling using the following formula:

Room area = (2 x length x 8) + (2 x width x 8) – (window area) – (door area)

Then the number of rolls needed is found by:

number of rolls = (room area)/(roll area)

Design a project that will enable customers to enter data about their room and the type of wallpaper they are using and determine the number of rolls needed. Assume that input includes length and width of the room in feet, window area and door area for the room in square feet, and the roll area in square feet for the type of wallpaper being considered. Output should include the room area and the number of rolls needed to cover the room. Sketch the interface for this problem if textboxes are used for input and output. Assume that one button is for computing the room area and another for computing the number of rolls needed. Develop IPO Tables and the pseudocode procedures for these buttons.

6. The loan officers of LowHomeLoans.com wish to provide a simple tool for computing the maximum loan payment that a borrower can expect to afford. They want to incorporate two "rules of thumb:"

1) The maximum monthly payment should not exceed 28% of the borrowers gross monthly income and
2) The maximum monthly payment should not exceed 36% of the borrowers gross monthly income minus monthly debt payments.

Here the monthly payment will include principle, interest, taxes and insurance. Assume that input includes the gross monthly income and the monthly debt payments. Output should include the maximum monthly payment based on gross income alone and maximum monthly payment based on gross income minus monthly debt. Sketch the interface for this problem using only textboxes, labels and command buttons. Develop an IPO table and the pseudocode procedures for these buttons.

7. Gregor Samsa was having difficulties getting up this morning. He had spent much of the night thinking about a project at the medium-sized exterminating company that he owns and operates. He has been losing money lately due to problems with the company's billing system and he feels that it should be upgraded or replaced. After looking around, he has found several alternative systems that might work for him. One criteria that he will use to choose between the alternative systems will be the net present value (NPV). As he attempts to roll out of bed, Gregor decides to have one of his IS people build him a simple NPV calculator. The NPV for a project may be calculated using:

$$NPV = -I_0 + (F_1/(1+k)) + (F_2/(1+k)^2) + ... + (F_n/(1+k)^n) + (S_n/(1+k)^n)$$

Here, I_0 represents the initial investment; F_i represents the net cash flow in period i; S_n represents the salvage value of the project at the end of it's useful life (period n); k represents the minimum required annual rate of return; and n represents the lifetime of the project in years. Develop the IPO, sketch the interface, and write pseudocode for the action objects in your interface. You may assume that the useful life will be a maximum of 10 years. What changes would you need to make if this assumption is relaxed, that is, the program should work for any amount of years?

PROJECT: JOE'S TAX ASSISTANCE

"No! I'm sorry, Mrs. Twipple. You can't claim your cats as dependents."

"But I look after them all the time. I feed them, clean up after them, take them for walks,..."

"That's just not the way the tax laws work. Anyway, I think I have enough information to complete your return. Why don't you come back next week at the same time and I'll have something worked up for you." Joe gave a sigh of relief as Mrs. Twipple headed for the door.

Joe Jackson retired over a year ago after 30 years as an auditor for a government agency. Since retirement Joe had plenty of time for hobbies, visiting with his granddaughter Zooey, and volunteering for various programs. Most recently, he had been spending one day a week with the Internal Revenue Service's Volunteer Income Tax Assistance (VITA) program, in which volunteers like Joe offer free tax assistance to people in the community, many of whom do not have the means or the education to complete their own returns.

To stretch his legs, Joe walked out into the hallway and over to the water fountain. The day was nearing an end, but he noticed at least three parties still in line for tax assistance. "It shouldn't take so long to help all these people," Joe mused. "There has got to be a way to speed up the process." He decided to put off thinking about this for the moment and asked the next couple to step into the office.

Later, on the drive home, Joe began to think of ways to improve his efficiency. The main problem, he thought, was how to handle all of the information obtained from each VITA client. At times, the amount of paper generated was enormous.

Finally a possible solution occurred to Joe: "Maybe Zooey can help me come up with something."

His granddaughter, no doubt with some financial assistance from her parents, had presented Joe with a laptop at Christmas. "It's time you joined the information age, Grandpa, and I'm going to help you do it," she had explained. Since that time, she had shown Joe how to use various software programs, how to get "on-line" and "surf," and even a thing or two about programming.

Joe came to a decision: "Yep, tomorrow I'll explain to Zooey what I want to do and we can get to work programming. Maybe we can use that Visual Basic thing-a-ma-bob that she was talking about."

Questions

1. Think about the information needs that Joe would come across in his work with tax returns.

2. Would Visual Basic be a useful tool in helping Joe handle these needs?

3. Develop an opening screen for Joe's VITA program.

2   USING VISUAL BASIC TO CREATE A FIRST PROJECT

LEARNING OBJECTIVES

After reading this chapter, you will be able to:

❖ Point out the elements of the Visual Basic development environment, including the title bar, menu bar, toolbar, initial form window, Toolbox, Project Explorer window, Properties window, and Form Layout window.

❖ Discuss the use of the form in creating a Visual Basic project.

❖ Understand controls and their properties.

❖ Use the label, command button, and image controls from the Toolbox to create an interface on the form.

❖ Use a message box for output from the project.

❖ Use the Code window to write the event procedure for a command button.

❖ List the different types of files that make up a Visual Basic project and be able to save a project to disk.

❖ Use the various Visual Basic help facilities to answer questions or solve problems encountered when creating a project.

SCENARIO: OPENING SCREEN FOR VINTAGE VIDEOS

Clark leaned back from the kitchen table and rubbed his stomach. "Not bad, Sis. Did you find a new flavor of Hamburger Helper?"

"Very funny, little brother. You know that beggars can't be 'choosers' when it comes to a free lunch," Yvonne responded.

"Didn't you know? This is a business lunch," said Clark.

"That's right," Ed interjected in corroboration. "Clark's going to use some of his high-priced education to write a Visual Basic program for us down at the store."

"That sounds interesting, but what's wrong with the software that you bought a couple of weeks ago?" Yvonne inquired.

"Well, I'm not very happy with it. Clark says that with Visual Basic he can write a program that will do exactly what we want. From what he tells me it sounds like a good idea. Anyway, I'm willing to give it a chance," declared Ed.

"Okay, but why do you want to use Visual Basic? I mean, what makes you think it would be better than another language, for instance?" Yvonne inquired further.

"You've used Windows before, haven't you? Visual Basic is specifically designed to write programs for use with Windows." Clark explained professorially. "One of the hardest parts of writing traditional programs is designing and writing the interface between the user and the program. Visual Basic takes care of most of that for you. With it you can design the window and add things like menus and buttons very easily."

"You mean like the buttons I click with the mouse on Ed's video Blackjack game?" asked Yvonne.

"Exactly. The major part of the programming involves writing what the program will do when objects like the button are clicked or selected. Visual Basic handles all the stuff like knowing when the button is clicked or when a menu is requested," Clark continued.

Concluding her interrogation, Yvonne asked, "When can you show us something?"

"I've got to work on a school project in the computer lab at school this afternoon. I thought I could work up an opening screen with a button or two just to show you what I'm talking about. Then we can talk contract," replied Clark. "Oh, and Ed, you and Yvonne need to think about what you want the program to do."

Ed responded: "Well, right off the bat, I'd like to see it display our name and a catchy slogan in large type. Something like 'Vintage Videos: Oldies but Goodies!' I'd also like to have some type of picture representing the fact that we rent videos. And... maybe a button to click to display a welcome message for our employees... when we start needing them!"

"Great. Then I'll get to school and think about this opening screen. Maybe after this project, we can work on a program to catalog Yvonne's Hamburger Helper recipes," Clark added as he ducked out the door.

Comments on Scenario

As noted in the scenario, Visual Basic does make it much easier to create the interface between the user and the program. This chapter will introduce you to creating program interfaces. In the process, we will show you how to create an opening screen for Vintage Videos that will include three elements:

1. The name Vintage Videos and the store's slogan in a large typeface
2. A picture representing the fact that they rent videos
3. A button that can be clicked to display a welcome message.

By the end of this chapter, you should be able to replicate these operations in other situations.

GETTING STARTED WITH VISUAL BASIC

To start Visual Basic in Windows, you can either double-click the Visual Basic icon on the desktop or select the Visual Basic menu item from the Programs list on the Start Menu. Either way, the first thing you will see when you start Visual Basic is a dialog box like that shown in Figure 2-1. This dialog box has a variety of icons from which you can choose, and three tabs—New, Existing, and Recent. The Existing and Recent tabs are used to open existing Visual Basic projects. Except for the Standard EXE icon, which is highlighted, you should ignore the remainder of the icons and simply click on Open to start a new Visual Basic project. (If the check box at the bottom left of the dialog box has been checked, this box will not appear and you will automatically start a new project.)

When you start a new Visual Basic project, the Visual Basic **Integrated Development Environment (IDE)** is displayed as shown in Figure 2-2, and you are in Visual

FIGURE 2-1.
Opening dialog
box for Visual
Basic

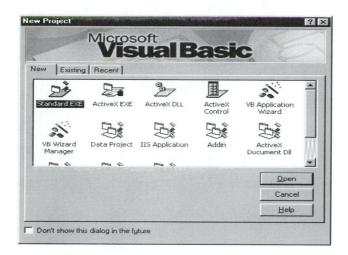

Basic's **Program Design mode**. (There are two other modes, Run and Break, which we will discuss later.) Key elements of the Integrated Development Environment are pointed out in this figure.

The key elements of the Visual Basic IDE are the project title bar, the menu bar, the toolbar, the Toolbox, the form, the Project Explorer window, the Properties window, and the Form Layout Window. The first three of these elements should be familiar to you from other Windows software. The title bar shows the name of the project—initially Project1. It also shows that you are in the design mode. The menu bar has a variety of menu options, beginning with File and ending with Help, that makes it possible to carry out the operations necessary to create a Visual Basic project. As we go through the creation of Visual Basic projects, we will discuss the various menu options. The toolbar contains icons that replicate the most commonly used menu options. In Visual Basic, as in many Windows applications, there is more than one toolbar available to you; the standard toolbar is what is displayed initially. You can also customize the toolbars by adding or deleting icons.

You should be aware that the Visual Basic IDE shown in Figure 2-2 is the default **multiple document interface (MDI) environment**. This is denoted by the **Project Window** having a white background. In the MDI environment, it is possible to make a Form window part of the larger Project window, like in Excel or Word. With the MDI Interface, you can also resize both the project window and the Form window within it by using the mouse to drag the corner or side of the window in any direction.

It is also possible in Visual Basic 6 to use the older **single document interface (SDI)** that was the default for earlier versions of Visual Basic, and the default can be changed to SDI. If the background screen shows through, then your system has been changed to SDI. The difference between the MDI interface and the SDI interface will not be important to us.

You will notice that there are black squares on the bottom, right-hand side, and corners of the form—these are its **sizing handles** which can be used to change the size of the form with the mouse. As the size is changed, a series of values at the far right end of the toolbar will change indicating the form's size in **twips.** There are 1440 twips per inch *when printed*. The initial size of the form is 4800 x 3600.

FIGURE 2-2. Visual Basic Development Environment

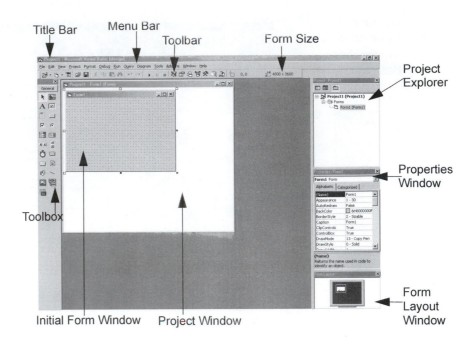

The Form Window

In the middle of the Visual Basic development environment is the **Form window**. This object is key to the creation of any Visual Basic project since other objects are placed on it during the design process. The Form window is shown in Figure 2-3. Note that it also has a title bar, which contains the name of the form (initially Form1). There are also the typical Windows minimize, maximize, and exit controls. More important, the Form window has a grid of dots to help you position objects. When an object is placed on the form, it will automatically "snap" to the nearest dot. Objects can thus be lined up on a row or column of dots to provide a pleasing appearance.

FIGURE 2-3. Form window

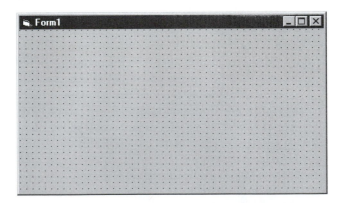

The Toolbox

The **Toolbox** holds the objects that are placed on the form to create the Visual Basic project. These objects are commonly referred to as **controls**, since they control the response of the project to events such as mouse clicks. Such controls include the three we used in our example in Chapter 1—the command button, the label, and the text

Figure 2-4. Default Toolbox

box. The default Toolbox is shown in Figure 2-4 and Table 2-1 shows the icon for each control, its name, and its action. You should recognize many of them from using other applications.

TABLE 2-1: Default Toolbox Controls

Icon	Name	Action
	pointer	Selects another control; moves controls around screen
	picture box	Displays an image; responds to events
	label	Displays text (read only; no input)
	text box	Displays and inputs text
	frame	Acts as container for other controls
	command button	Responds to events
	check box	Responds to being checked
	option button	Responds to being on or off
	combo box	Acts as drop-down list box
	list box	Displays list of text items
	vertical and horizontal scroll bars	Responds to scrolling by determining a value
	timer	Determines time between events
	drive list box	Displays a list of disk drives
	directory list box	Displays a list of directories
	file list box	Displays a list of files
	shape	Used to draw shapes
	line	Used to draw lines
	image	Displays an image on screen
	data	Provides a link to a database
	OLE	Used for OLE (Object Linking and Embedding) operations

In addition to the controls shown in Figure 2-4 and listed in Table 2-1, there are many **custom controls** that can be added to your Toolbox. Some of these controls are available with Visual Basic, but you must add them to the default Toolbox; they can be added individually or as a group.

*Project Explorer
Window*

On the right side of the Visual Basic development environment are three windows. The top window is the **Project Explorer window;** like the Windows Explorer that is a part of Windows, the Project Explorer enables you to view the code that causes an object to respond to events, to view an object, or to view the folders that are part of a Visual Basic project. In Figure 2-5, the Project Explorer window shows the current project (Project1) with one form (Form1). If there are multiple forms or other objects in the project, they will also be shown here. We will demonstrate the use of this window as we create projects with multiple objects.

FIGURE 2-5.
Project Explorer
window

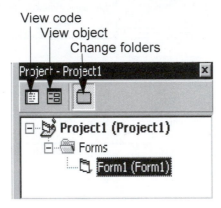

Properties Window

Beneath the Project Explorer window in Figure 2-2 is the **Properties window** for the Visual Basic object that is currently highlighted. Since there is only one object—the form—the properties for it are currently shown in the Properties window with the default caption—Form1—for this form being highlighted. When other objects are added to the form their properties can also be displayed in the Properties window. However, it is important to note that the properties for only one object can appear in the Properties window and that to view the properties for another object, you must click that object. We will discuss the use of the Properties window in more detail when we create our first project later in this chapter.

Form Layout Window

The final window on the right side of the screen is the **Form Layout window.** This window displays a picture of a computer screen with the current form name (Form1) in it. You can use the mouse to move the form around, thereby controlling where the project will be displayed when you run your project.

You can resize all three of these windows—the Project Explorer window, the Properties window, and the Form Layout window—by dragging a corner, the top, or bottom, and you can even remove them from the screen by clicking the termination x-symbol in the upper right-hand corner of the window. The toolbar icons or the View command from the menu bar can then be used to display them again.

Mini-Summary 2-1: Getting started with Visual Basic

1. The Visual Basic development environment is a typical Windows-based application with title bar and menu bar. It also has a Toolbox and toolbar.

2. The Project window contains the form that is used to create Visual Basic applications.

3. The Properties window is used to modify object properties and the Project Explorer shows the files that are a part of the project. The Form Layout window shows the location of the form when the project is executed.

It's Your Turn!

1. What are the three basic modes of Visual Basic?

2. List and describe the key elements of the Visual Basic development environment.

3. Which of the toolbox controls would be most appropriate for each of the following?

    a. Add a permanent indicator on the form.

    b. Provide a list of items for the user to select.

    c. Provide a space for users to enter input.

    d. Allow a user to mark one or more from several options.

    e. Provide a means for the user to begin an action.

4. In order to get a feel for sizes in Visual Basic, perform the following conversions:

    a. 7200 twips = _____ inches

    b. _____ twips = 3 inches

    c. 6840 twips = _____ inches

    d. _____ twips = 0.5 inches

5. What is the difference between SDI and MDI?

6. From Windows, access Visual Basic by double-clicking the Visual Basic icon or by using the Programs option from the Start menu. Did the Visual Basic opening dialog box appear? If so, what did you do to access the Visual Basic development environment?

7. If your system is *not* set to MDI, check with your instructor on how to use the Tools menu option to set it to the MDI option.

8. Click on the maximize icon in the upper left-hand corner of the Project (white) window to fill the space. Do *not* maximize the form window; instead use the form's sizing handles to change its size to about 6915 x 3825 twips.

9. Point out the various parts of the opening screen for Visual Basic. Where is the Toolbox? Do you have the same default Toolbox as shown in Figure 2-4? If not, what additional controls have been added?

10. Close the Properties window by clicking on the close button in its top right corner. See if you can make it reappear by choosing the appropriate option from the View menu. What is the hot-key for viewing the Properties window? Control Properties?

CONTROL PROPERTIES

As we said earlier, all objects have properties that define them. Visual Basic properties include the object's name, its caption, whether it is visible, its size, and so on. To learn about properties in Visual Basic, we will use the object that is a part of every project: the form.

When Visual Basic is started, it automatically loads a form on the screen. This is the initial form, and for the next few chapters it is the only form we will consider. Since this is the only object on the screen, the Properties window automatically displays the properties for the form, as shown in Figure 2-6. Note that the current name of the form—Form1—is displayed at the top of the Properties window after the word "Properties." The name of the form is also displayed in the Object box along with the type of object—in this case, form. If there were other objects on the form, clicking the down arrow on the Object box would display a drop-down list box of these objects, and clicking on one of these other objects would display its properties.

FIGURE 2-6.
Properties window for form

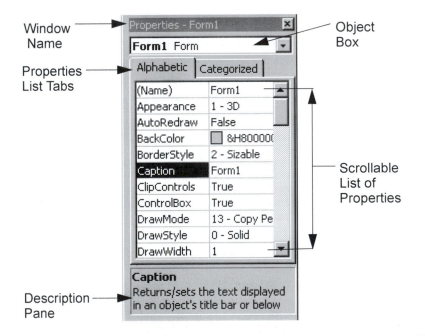

TIP: If the Properties window is not visible on the screen, press the F4 function key to make it visible.

The Properties List tabs enable you to view the list of properties in one of two ways: alphabetically or categorically. Since the default method of listing the properties is to put them in alphabetical order, that is what is shown here. Note, however, that the Name property is shown first even though alphabetically it would not come first. If you were to select the Categorized tab, the properties would be grouped by categories, such as Appearance, Behavior, and Position. For example, the background and foreground colors and the font for the object's caption would be included under Appearance.

Finally, the Description Pane at the bottom of the screen provides a brief description of the property that is currently highlighted in the Properties window—in this case, the Caption property.

For the current form, we want to change only two properties: the Name and the Caption. The Name property is used to refer to the object in the Visual Basic code that defines the way the object responds to an event, and the Caption property is the text that the object displays to the user. While they could be the same, in practice they seldom are. You can use almost any text for the object Caption property, since its purpose is to identify the control to the user. However, we need to pay close attention to the Name property.

The Name Property

An object's Name property must start with a letter and can be a maximum of 40 characters long. It can include numbers and underline (_) characters, but it cannot include punctuation or spaces. For the name of the form, we should use something that reminds us of the purpose of the project; in this case, it is being done for Vintage Videos, so we could name it simply "Vintage." However, the name should also indicate the type of object being referred to—in this case, a form. For purposes of naming objects, Microsoft has developed a list of prefixes that correspond to types of objects. For example, *frm* is for a form, *cmd* for a command button, and *lbl* for a label. As we take up each object, we will use the appropriate prefix. In addition, a complete list of the Microsoft Visual Basic object prefixes can be found on the VB Web help site.

If we take both objectives into account—that is, a name that reminds us of the purpose of the object and a prefix that matches the type of object—a good name for this form is *frmVintage*. While Visual Basic is not sensitive to the case you use in naming objects, the prefix is usually shown in lowercase letters and the mnemonic part of the name begins with a capital letter.

Changing an Object's Properties

All objects have a set of default properties that are automatically displayed in the Properties window. To change an object's property, you must first give the object the **focus** by clicking on it. Then use the Properties window's scroll bar to find the property you wish to change. In the case of the Name property, if the properties are in alphabetical order, it is already at the top of the list. Next, click in any column for the property you wish to change to highlight it and type a new value, automatically replacing the old value. Finally, press **ENTER**. For example, to change the Name property, highlight it and type the new name: **frmVintage** to replace the default name. (Note: The new name, frmVintage, is not actually in boldface in the Properties window, but we will use this method to distinguish text you should input from normal text.)

When the Name property of the form is changed, the new name is displayed at the top of the Properties window, in the Object box, and in the right column of the Name property row. If the Forms folder is open in the Project Explorer window, the new name is also displayed there. It is also displayed on the form in the Form Layout window.

The Caption property of the form will be displayed in the title bar of the form, so we want a caption that will be in line with the purpose of the project. In this case, the name of the video store would be an appropriate caption. To create a new caption for the form, simply highlight the current one in the Properties window (Form1) and change it to **Vintage Videos.** Notice that the new caption now appears in the title bar of the form.

> **TIP:** To quickly jump to a property, hold down the Ctrl and Shift keys together along with the first letter of the property. For example, simultaneously pressing Ctrl, Shift, and the letter c will highlight the Caption property.

Mini-Summary 2-2: Changing the Properties of a Visual Basic Object

1. To change a property of a control, first select the control by clicking on it. If the Properties window is not visible, you may display it by pressing F4.

2. Move the cursor to the Properties window and select the property to be changed (scroll if necessary to view the property).

3. Enter the new setting for the selected item and press **ENTER** to accept the change.

It's Your Turn!

1. Click anywhere in the initial form to ensure that it has the focus. If the Properties window is not visible, press **F4** to make it visible. If it is not already in alphabetical order, click on the "Alphabetical" tab.

2. Highlight the Name property in the Properties window and change it to **frmVintage**. Note the effect on the Properties window. Does the form itself change in any discernible way?

3. Note all of the locations on the screen where the new name for the form is displayed.

4. Highlight the Caption property and change it to **Vintage Videos**. How does the form change?

5. Highlight the **Enabled** property. What does this property do according to its description in the lower section of the properties window?

6. Which properties primarily affect the form's appearance?

7. Experiment with changing the **Backcolor** property by highlighting it and clicking the down arrow. Next, click the **Palette** tab and select a color. To return to the original grey color, click the System tab and select Active Border.

ADDING A CONTROL TO THE FORM

Now that you have seen how to access Visual Basic and have become familiar with the opening screen and the Properties window, we are ready to work with controls in the Toolbox to begin creating a project. However, we first need to recall the six-step process for doing this, presented in Chapter 1:

    1. Define problem

    2. Create interface

    3. Develop logic for action objects

4. Write and test code for action objects

5. Test overall project

6. Document project in writing.

Defining the Problem

In our case, the problem was defined in the Vintage Videos scenario at the beginning of the chapter. The owner of Vintage Videos wants an opening screen that will display the store's name along with some type of picture representing videos. He also wants to be able to click a button and display an opening message. Based on this description, we can sketch the interface for this problem. Such a sketch is shown in Figure 2-7.

In Figure 2-7, note that we have three types of controls on the sketch of the opening screen for Vintage Videos: one control that displays the name of the video store and its slogan, a second control that displays a picture of video camera, and a third control that is a button with the caption "Click Me First!" In an actual situation, before we start to create the interface in Visual Basic, we would need to have the client approve this sketch. If the owner of Vintage Videos likes this proposed interface, we can go ahead to the second step, which is to create the interface.

FIGURE 2-7.
Sketch of interface for Vintage Videos opening screen

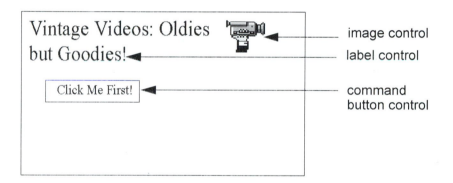

Create the Interface

To create an interface for the Visual Basic project that matches the sketch shown in Figure 2-7, we need to access Visual Basic and display the development environment shown earlier as Figure 2-2. Next, we need to decide what controls to use. In this case, we need to use a **label** control to display the store name and slogan, an **image** control to display the picture of a video camera, and a **command button** control that will be clicked to display a welcoming message. When you move the mouse pointer over any control in the Toolbox, a **ToolTip** is displayed showing the type of control. The label, image, and command button controls are shown in Figure 2-8.

FIGURE 2-8. Controls for opening screen

There are two ways to select a control and place it on the blank form. You can click it once to *draw* it any size anywhere on the form, or you can double-click it to automatically position the default size in the center of the form. In the first case, if you position the cursor over the control, click it once, and move the pointer back to the form, the cursor becomes a crosshair. If you click the left mouse button and *hold* it down, you can "draw" the outline of the control by dragging the crosshairs up, down, left, right, or diagonally. When you are "drawing" the control using the mouse, a set of numbers will appear at the bottom right-hand corner of the control outline and at the right end of the toolbar giving the size of the control in twips.

 label control

 image control

 command button control

┌───┐
│ **TIP:** The distance between dots on the grid is 120 twips. │
└───┘

Once you release the mouse button, the label area will be bounded by its sizing handles, with which you can change the size of the label. You will also notice that there are no grid dots in the control area and that there is a default caption in the upper left-hand corner of the label. If you click anywhere within the control area, and hold the mouse button down, you can drag the control to any other location on the form.

In the second case, if you double-click a control, it automatically appears in the center of your screen with its sizing handles. As with the form object, you can resize the control with these sizing handles. You can also move it anywhere on the screen. While the choice whether to draw the control or double-click it on the screen is usually one of personal preference, there are times when you must draw the control. We will point out these situations when they come up. Figure 2-9 shows the result of drawing the label on the form in preparation for creating the store name and slogan. Note that the default caption is "Label1," which is also the default name for this label..

> **TIP:** If you have a label control already located in the center of the screen, it is best to draw any additional controls. Otherwise, you may have trouble distinguishing between the existing label control and the new controls.

FIGURE 2-9. Label control drawn in form

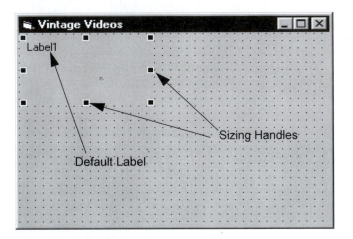

Once the label control is on the form, the next step is to change its name and caption. As with the form, you use the Properties window to change these properties of the label. To do this, first check the Object box in the Properties window to make sure the focus is on the label; if it does not show *Label1*, click the label control to highlight it. Next, click the name row of the Properties window and change it to **lblVintage**. Notice that we have used the lbl prefix for this object name since it is a label, and that the rest of the name is the same as that of the form. This will not cause any confusion since one name begins with frm and the other with lbl. When you change the name for the label, notice that the caption does not change. Typically, the only time the name and caption of a control are the same is before you change either of them.

To change the caption for the lblVintage label, use the same approach as you did for the form: Highlight the Caption property and change it—in this case to **Vintage Videos: Oldies but Goodies!** Note that while you are entering the new caption, it is being changed in the label at the same time. Notice also that while the caption in the label changes to the new setting, the text is not large enough to act as an eye-catching heading for the form. To increase the size of the label caption, we need to change the label **Font** property.

dialog
box icon

When you select the Font property for a control, an icon with three dots is displayed. This indicates that clicking on this icon will display a dialog box in which we can make changes to the font of the corresponding label. This dialog box is shown in Figure 2-10 with list boxes that enable you to change the font type (currently MS Sans Serif), the font style (currently Regular), and the font size (currently 8 points). Since we want the label caption to stand out, we need to change the font style to Bold and the font size to 14 points. Clicking **Ok** executes these changes. Finally, since the label caption text will "wrap" within the defined label size, we need to use the sizing handles to change the size of the label to display it on two lines like the sketch. The results of these operations are shown in Figure 2-11.

FIGURE 2-10. The Font dialog box

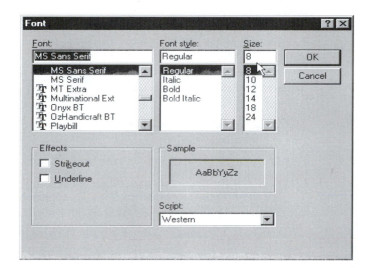

FIGURE 2-11. Completed label control

Mini-Summary 2-3: Adding a Control to a Form

1. Select the control you want to add to the form in the Toolbox.

2. Either click the control once to draw it on the form, or double-click the control to position it in the center of the form.

3. If you clicked the control once, use the crosshair to "draw" it on the form by holding the left mouse button down.

4. In either case, drag the control to the desired position and use the sizing handles to adjust it to the desired size.

5. Change the properties for the control as discussed earlier.

It's Your Turn!

1. Add a label control to your form by drawing it in the upper left-hand corner of the form.

2. Add a second label to your form by double-clicking the label icon in the Toolbox. Move this second label around the screen with your mouse. Resize it to be approximately one-half the width of the form.

3. If the second label does not have the focus, click on it once. Now press the **Delete** key to delete the second label.

4. Click the first label (the one you drew in the upper left-hand corner of the form) and change its Name property to *lblVintage*.

5. Change the Caption property of this label to **Vintage Videos: Oldies but Goodies!**. Change the Font property of this label to have a font style of Bold and a size of 14 points. (Leave the font type as is.) Use the handles on the label to resize it as necessary to make the result appear like that shown in Figure 2-11.

ADDING MORE CONTROLS TO THE FORM

We are now ready to add the image control to the right of the label and to add the command button control beneath it. The process of doing this is the same as for the label control added earlier: Either click the control in the Toolbox once and draw the label on the form, or double-click the control to place the label in the center of the form and then position it as desired.

Adding the Image Control

To add the image control to the form, single-click it and draw it to the right of the existing label control. Change the Name property to **imgVintageLogo** and use the sizing handles to enlarge it so its height and width are the same as the height of the label control. The image control does not have a Caption property, but it does have a **Picture** property you can use to insert a graphic image. To do this, select the Picture property and click the dialog box icon to display a list of folders in the Visual Basic folder. Go *up* one level and select the *Common* folder from which you should select the *Graphics* folder. From this folder, select the *Icons* folder and then the *Misc* folder. (From previous use, a folder may appear automatically when you click on the dialog box icon.) This will display a variety of icons from which to choose. Find the camera icon (*Camera.ico*) and select it to be inserted into the image control.

> **TIP:** Graphics, such as camera.ico, are available on the CD that comes with your text. To include them on your computer when installing Visual Basic, you must choose the *Custom Installation* and ensure that graphic files are selected by clicking the appropriate check box.

When you insert the Camera.ico file into the image control, it does not automatically expand to fill the current size of the control; in fact, the image control *shrinks* to fit the size of the icon. Even if you resize the image control, the picture within it does not change. To enlarge the image control and the icon simultaneously, you must change the **Stretch** property of the image control to True from its default value of False. To do this, first expand the size of the control using the sizing handles. Next, select the Stretch property from the Properties window and click on the down arrow. This will display a drop-down list box with values of True and False in it. Select **True** and the picture within the image control will expand to fit the size of the control. The top portion of the resulting screen will look like that shown in Figure 2-12 .

True/False Selection

> **TIP:** To force a label to automatically fit its contents, change the Autosize property to True.

FIGURE 2-12.
Result of adding image control

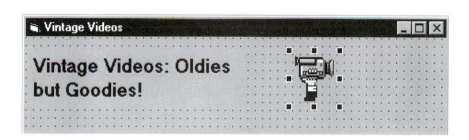

Adding a Command Button Control

Now that you have added the two controls to the Vintage Videos form that are primarily for appearance purposes, you are ready to add the command button control that, when clicked, will display a message. To add the command button control, double-click the corresponding icon in the Toolbox to display it in the center of the form, and then move it to immediately beneath the label control. Change the Name property of the command button control to **cmdMessage** and replace the default Caption property with the message **Click me first!**. As you did with the label control, change the Font property so that the Caption is displayed in 12-point boldface type. If the message wraps down to a second line on the command button, use the sizing handles to lengthen the button so the caption is displayed on a single line. The result of these actions will be a screen like that displayed in Figure 2-13.

FIGURE 2-13.
Result of adding
command button
control

> **TIP:** Often you will use several similar control objects as part of your interface, for example several labels that have the same font typeface and size. You may be able to save some time by creating the first of these control objects then copying and pasting it as necessary. However, when asked if you would like to create a control array, answer NO until these are discussed in a later chapter.

It's Your Turn!

1. Draw an image control to the right of the existing label control so that its height and width are approximately the same as the height of the label control. Use the form grid to help you make this adjustment. Change the Name property for the image control to **imgVintageLogo**.

2. What properties of the image control may be used to set it to an exact size? Do the command button and label controls also have these properties?

3. Insert the \Graphics\Icons\Misc\Camera.ico file as the Picture property for the image control and change its Stretch property to **True.** The resulting image should be like that shown in Figure 2-13.

4. Add a command button to the form with a Name property of **cmdMessage** and a caption of **Click me first!**. Change the Font property to have the caption displayed in 12-point boldface type. The result should appear like that shown in Figure 2-13.

ADDING CODE TO THE PROJECT

Now that you have a completed the interface, the next steps in the application development process are to develop the logic for the action objects in the project and to write and test the code for them. There is only one action object—the command button—in the Vintage Videos project, and the logic is very simple: Display the "Welcome to Vintage Videos" message when the command button is clicked. The only input is the mouse-click event and the only output is the message. There is no processing to speak of.

*Write and Test Code
for Action Objects*

Once you have created the logic for the action objects, the next step is to write and test the code for each of the action objects. There is only one action object in the Vintage Videos project: the command button. The code for this object must display a welcome message when it is clicked.

To do this, we need a very useful Visual Basic operation: the **message box**. When the project is executed and the command button is clicked, a message box with a message placed there by the project developer will appear on the screen. This message box will remain on the screen until the user clicks the Ok button. To display a message box when the command button is clicked, we need to add code for the command button click event. To do this, double-click the command button on the form to display the **Code window** as shown in Figure 2-14.

FIGURE 2-14. Code
window for
command button

Object List Box   Events/Procedures List Box

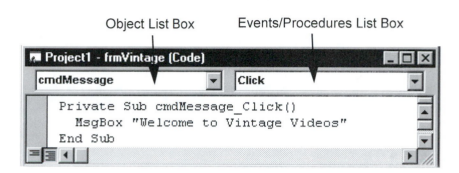

The Code window is the place in the Visual Basic development environment where we enter the code that will cause the various objects to respond as we want them to. This code is called an **event procedure** because it defines how the object will respond to an event. Note that it shows the name of this control—cmdMessage—in the **Object list box** in the top left of the window and the current event—Click—in the **Events/Procedures list box** in the top right side of the Code window. The Code window for the other objects in this project—the form, label, and image controls—can be accessed by clicking the down arrow on the Object list box. Similarly, if we wanted to add code for other events for the command button, say the double-click event, we could reach the appropriate Code window for those events by clicking the down arrow on the Events/Procedures list box.

When you access the Code window, the first and last lines of the event procedure are already displayed with a blank line between them. The last word of the first line—Click( )—tells us that this is the code procedure for the Click event for the cmdMessage command button. This is the default procedure for the command button control. However, as we shall see later, you do not have to use the default event for a control.

To display a dialog box with a message in it when the cmdMessage control is clicked, you should move the cursor to the blank line and add a single line of code to this procedure:

```
MsgBox "Welcome to Vintage Videos"
```

as shown in Figure 2-14. Note that for better readability you should indent the instruction by pressing the Tab key. Visual Basic will check lines of code that you enter and alert you to obvious vocabulary and syntax errors. However, it cannot catch all errors, especially errors that are based on invalid logic.

View Object

To return to the form object, click on the View Object button in the Project Explorer window. To return to the Code window, you can double-click the control for

View Code

Run

Stop

which you wish to add code or click the View Code button in the Project Explorer window.

Once you have entered the single instruction in the command button Code window and returned to the form object, you are ready to test your project by executing it. You can do this in a number of ways, but we suggest you use the VCR-type Run button on the toolbar. When you click this button, the grid dots on the form will disappear and you will be in **Run Time**. You can now click the command button to determine if you have entered the code correctly. If you have, the message box shown in Figure 2-15 will appear. Note that there are no grid dots on the form, because the grid disappears when the project is executed. Note also that the title bar of the message box has a caption of "Project1." This is the current (default) name of the project. Any message boxes displayed in the project use the project name as their default title. In a later chapter, you will learn how to control the title bar caption for a message box. If you click Ok on this window, it will disappear. To terminate the execution of the project, click the VCR-type Stop button on the toolbar.

FIGURE 2-15.
Message window
displayed

If you have not entered the code correctly, you may receive an error message and the Code window will be displayed with the probable error highlighted. You should correct the error and click the Run button again. Some errors will not generate an error message; instead they will result in the project not carrying out the desired results. These errors are usually the result of an error in the underlying logic, so you will need to go back and check the IPO Tables and pseudocode to find the error. Once you have found it, you must transfer the correction in logic to the code for the control and start the error-checking process again.

> **TIP:** You can execute a project by selecting the Start option from the Run submenu (denoted as **Run|Start**) or by pressing the F5 function key. You can stop the execution of a project by selecting **Run|End.**

Test Overall Project and Document It

Normally, after you have coded and tested each individual action object, you are ready to test the overall project and document it. However, in this very simple first project these steps are unnecessary. In later projects, we will discuss the process of carrying out these steps.

Mini-Summary 2-4: Writing and Testing an Event Procedure

1. To add code for a control, double-click it to display the Code window with the first and last lines of the procedure already entered.

2. Enter the code for the control between the existing first and last lines of the procedure.

3. Click the View Object button on the Project Explorer window to display the form.

4. Click the Run button on the toolbar to execute the project.

5. Test the functionality of the control; if an error occurs, correct it in the Code window.

6. Terminate the execution of the control by clicking the Stop button on the toolbar.

It's Your Turn!

Completing these questions will enable you to create the Visual Basic project discussed in the text.

1. Double-click the cmdMessage command button and add the single instruction after the first line in the Code window as shown in Figure 2-14:

```
Msgbox "Welcome to Vintage Videos"
```

(If there is already an *Option Explicit* statement in the code window, simply type this line of code after it. We will explain this in the next chapter.)

2. Notice that when you clicked the cmdMessage command button some Visual Basic code was automatically generated. What is the significance of this automatically generated code? How do the automatically generated statements indicate their corresponding action object and event?

3. Click the View Object button in the Project Explorer window to display the form. Click the Run button and then click the cmdMessage command button. Your form should look like Figure 2-15.

4. Click the Ok button on the message box and then click the Stop button.

5. Click the View Code button, change the term "Msgbox" in the message box statement to "Msbbox" and run the project again. What happens? Correct your error and run it again to make sure you did not add other errors.

6. Terminate the execution of your project and display the form again.

WORKING WITH FILES IN VISUAL BASIC

Now that you have a little experience working with Visual Basic, we will take a closer look at the menu bar and toolbar to work with files in Visual Basic The menu bar contains options that correspond to submenus that contain all of the commands needed for working with the development environment. The toolbar contains icons corresponding to the more commonly used menu commands. As in other Windows applications, you access an option from the menu bar by clicking on the option or by pressing the Alt key and, while holding it down, pressing the underlined letter. For example, you can access the File option by clicking on the word File in the menu bar or by pressing the Alt+F key combination. Once you have a submenu, you can select commands or submenus from it in a similar manner. Figure 2-16 shows the top half of the File menu. An icon beside a submenu option indicates that this option is also available on a toolbar.

FIGURE 2-16.
A portion of the
File submenu

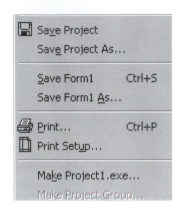

The Standard Toolbar Clicking an icon on the toolbar is a shortcut way of carrying out the most popular commands. In addition, the location and size in twips of the current object are shown at the right end of the toolbar. ToolTips are available to help remind you of the purpose of each of the toolbar icons. For example, Figure 2-17 shows the result of positioning the pointer over the Save Project icon. The icons for the Standard toolbar and their names, corresponding menu options, and use are shown in Table 2-2. .

> **TIP:** The location values on the toolbar can be handy in making sure that objects on the form are exactly lined up horizontally or vertically. Simply watch these values as you add objects to the form.

FIGURE 2-17.
ToolTip in Toolbar

In addition to the Standard or default toolbar, there are three toolbars that contain icons for specialized operations. For example, the Debug toolbar contains icons representing all of the operations you will need to find errors in your projects. You may display one or more of these specialized toolbars by selecting them from the **View|Toolbar** menu option.

Files in Visual Basic When you have completed a project or when you have to stop work before finishing, you need to save your work to disk so you can retrieve it later for more work. In addition, you should save your work frequently, especially before attempting to execute your application. To save a project, you first need to understand the files that are a part

TABLE 2-2: Toolbar Icons and corresponding menu selections

Icon	Name	Menu Option	Action
	Add Standard EXE	File | Add Project	Add a standard.EXE project as a part of this project group (.vbg file)
	New Form	Project | Add Form	Add a new form to the current project
	Menu Editor	Tools | Menu Editor	Start the Menu Editor (creates menus—to be covered in Chapter 8)
	Open Project	File | Open Project	Open an existing project
	Save Project	File | Save Project	Save current project file and all related files under same names
	Cut	Edit | Cut	Used in code editor to cut a section of code
	Copy	Edit | Copy	Used in code editor to copy a section of code
	Paste	Edit | Paste	Used in code editor to paste a section of code
	Find	Edit | Find	Used in code editor to find a character or string of characters
	Undo	Edit | Undo	Used in code editor to "undo" most previous action
	Redo	Edit | Redo	Used in code editor to "redo" a previously undone action
	Run	Run | Start	Execute the current project
	Break	Run | Break	Pause execution of project to look for errors
	Stop	Run | Stop	Stop execution of project
	Project Explorer	View | Project Explorer	Display Project Explorer window
	Properties Window	View | Properties Window	Display Properties window
	Form Layout Window	View | Form Layout Window	Display Form Layout window
	Object Browser	View | Object Browser	Display information about available objects
	Toolbox	View | Toolbox	Display Toolbox
	Data View Window	View | Data View Window	Display a window in which certain types of databases can be viewed and manipulated directly
	Visual Component Manager	View | Visual Component Manager	This tool enables you to publish, find, and reuse components

of it. First, recall that a **file** is *a group of data, instructions, or information to which a name can be applied.* In Visual Basic, each project has one **project file** with a .vbp extension and at least one **form file** with an .frm extension. If the project has multiple forms, then there will be an .frm file for each form in the project. In addition to the .frm files, if any forms have image or picture controls then there will also be a **binary form file** with an .frx file for each such form. Projects can also include **module files,** which are composed solely of code and have a .bas extension. Such modules are often written to be shared by multiple forms.

> **TIP:** Since the files that make up a Visual Basic project are related, it is easier to keep up with them if they are all stored in a folder specifically created for that project.

Finally, a type of file created by Visual Basic is the **Workspace file**, with a .vbw extension. This file keeps track of the windows that were left open when you exited Visual Basic so the next time you can start where you left off. You should not worry about .vbw files, because Visual Basic will create them as needed. Figure 2-18 provides an overview of the Visual Basic file structure.

FIGURE 2-18.
Visual Basic file structure

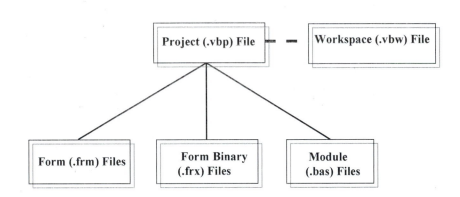

Saving Visual Basic Files

Save File

New Folder

To save a *new* Visual Basic project and any related forms, click the Save icon on the toolbar or select **File | Save** from the menu bar. When you do this, a Save File As dialog box will be displayed for your system's default drive and folder (usually the location of the Visual Basic program), with the form name you assigned earlier being shown as the current filename for the first form. For example, *frmVintage.frm* will be the default name for the current form. Before saving any files, you should switch to your data disk and create a new folder in which to save them. This is also done from the Save As... dialog box by clicking the New Folder icon, entering an appropriate name for the folder, and pressing **ENTER**. In our case, an appropriate folder name would be **Chapter2**.

> **Warning!** If you use *long* file names, Windows often limits the space in the root folder of a floppy disk to less than the 1.44 Mbytes available on the disk. For this reason, we **strongly** suggest you place each chapter's files in a different folder.

Once a new folder is created, you should switch to it in order to save your form file. Since there is no reason to include the *frm* prefix in the file name, it should be saved under a new name, say, **Vintage2.frm.** To save it, double-click the existing name to highlight it, enter the new form filename, and press **ENTER**. Note: do *not* include the file extension in the file name. Visual Basic will automatically add the appropriate extension. Even if you do include the extension, Visual Basic will treat it as part of the file name and include *another* extension. If there were additional forms or modules, their filenames will also be shown here for you to accept or change. Figure 2-19 shows the File Save As... dialog box after creating a new Chapter2 folder and saving the form file as Vintage2.frm.

FIGURE 2-19. File dialog box

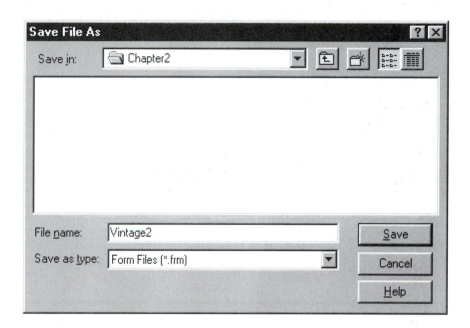

After the form file has been saved, Visual Basic will display *project1.vbp* as the current filename of the overall project in a Save File As... dialog box. As with the default form name, you will also want to change this name to something more appropriate, say, **Vintage.vbp**. It is not necessary for you to change the filename for binary form (.frx) or workspace (.vbw) files, since Visual Basic automatically gives them the same name as the corresponding form (.frm) or project (.vbp) file.

Once you have changed the default filenames, clicking on the Save icon will automatically save them again without displaying the file dialog boxes. Only if you select **File | Save Project as...** or **File | Save** *filename.frm* **as...** will the file dialog box be displayed.

A word of warning: When you save a project file and its associated form and module files, the project file will always look for files with the names you assigned at that time. If you change the names of the form or module files without resaving them as a part of the project, the project file will not be able to find them and will not be able to execute properly.

When you have completed your work on a project, you can exit Visual Basic by selecting the Exit option from the File submenu (**File | Exit**).

> **TIP:** DO NOT change the names of the form or module files without resaving the project file; otherwise the project will not recognize your new filenames.

Retrieving a Saved Project

Retrieving a previously saved project from disk is very easy. When you first access Visual Basic, you can retrieve a project by clicking either the Recent tab or the Existing tab on the Opening Dialog box. Clicking on the Recent tab displays a list of projects that have been opened recently, while clicking on the Existing tab will display an open file dialog box for the default drive and directory with project files listed. In either case, you can click on a project filename and retrieve it into the Visual Basic development environment, where you can modify and/or execute the project. You do not have to worry about retrieving form, binary form, or module files; retrieving the project file automatically retrieves any files related to the project.

Open Project

If you are already in the development environment, then you can click on the Open Project icon on the Toolbox or use the **File | Open Project** menu option to open an existing project from a open file dialog box.

Starting a New Project

Instead of retrieving an existing project, you will often want to start a new project. Because Visual Basic has the capability to work with a group of projects, it is important that you go about starting a new project in the appropriate way. Otherwise, Visual Basic will add the new project to an existing project in a **Project Group**, which has a .vbg extension. To start a new project that is *not* a part of a Project Group, you *must* use the **File | New Project** menu option instead of using the first icon on the toolbar, which you might think does the same thing. This is not the case; clicking the first icon on the toolbar creates a Project Group composed of the existing project and the new project. If this occurs, simply use the **File | New Project** option to start the new project *without saving* the Project Group file.

Mini-Summary 2-5: Working with Files in Visual Basic

1. There are 21 operations that can be executed from the toolbar. All of these operations correspond to commands available from the menu bar.

2. The types of files that make up a Visual Basic project include form files (.frm), the project file (.vbp), binary form files (.frx), module files (.bas), and the workspace file (.vbw).

3. You can save a project through the toolbar Save File icon or through the File | Save menu option. Similarly, you can open a saved project through the Open Project toolbar icon or the File | Open menu option.

4. To start a new project, select **File | New Project**.

It's Your Turn!

1. Describe the meaning of each of the following Visual Basic file extensions:

    a. .vbp

    b. .frm

    c. .vbw

    d. .frx

    e. .bas

Completing the remaining questions will enable you to create the Visual Basic project discussed in the text.

2. Use the Save icon on the toolbar or select the **File | Save** menu option to save the project and form files. In the File Save As dialog box, change to the a:\ drive and click the New Folder icon to create a new folder named **Chapter2** on your data disk and press **ENTER**.

3. For a form filename, enter **Vintage2.frm** and press **ENTER**. (Do not add an frm extension!)

4. For a project filename, enter **Vintage2.vbp** and press **ENTER**. (Do not add a vbp extension!)

5. Select **Programs | Windows Explorer** from the Windows Start menu and check to make sure the .vbp and .frm files have been saved on your data disk in the appropriate folder.

6. Use the **File | Exit** menu option to exit the Visual Basic development environment. Now start Visual Basic again and retrieve the Vintage2.vbp file from the a:\ drive using either the Recent tab or the Existing tab on the Visual Basic dialog box. Use the Run icon to execute the project. Terminate it by clicking the Stop icon.

7. Use the **File | New Project** menu option to start a new project. Now exit Visual Basic without saving the project.

USING VISUAL BASIC HELP

Visual Basic is a very powerful development platform that offers many more capabilities than can be discussed in an introductory programming text such as this. Fortunately, Visual Basic also offers developers a powerful Help system that offers help on virtually any possible question. In fact, there are four types of help available to you in Visual Basic: the Help menu option, context-sensitive help, Web-based help, and Auto help. You should note that the first two types of help will only work if the Microsoft Developer's Network (MSDN) help system has been installed on your system. If you are using the Visual Basic disk that comes with this book or the MSDN help system has not been installed on your system, then you will need to use the Web-based help for answers to specific questions.

Regardless of whether you are using the MSDN help system or Web-based help, the same Web interface is used. This means that help is displayed in the same format as Web pages, and navigation among the pages is handled via the familiar Back, Forward, Stop, Home, and Print icons on the browser toolbar. Another new feature about Visual Basic 6 Help is that it is combined with Help for the other computer languages that are a part of Microsoft's Visual Studio 6—that is, Visual Basic, Visual C++, Visual FoxPro, Visual InterDev, Visual J++, and Visual VouchSafe. However, this should not cause any problems for you in seeking aid from Visual Basic Help whether you are using the MSDN system or the Web.

Using Web-based help

Because many of you will be using the Web-based help system rather than the MSDN help system, we will concentrate on showing you how to use this system. If, on the other hand, you do have the MSDN system, because of the consistent look and feel between the two systems, selecting **Help** from the Visual Basic menu bar will result in very similar screens to those that we are showing here. To access the Web-based help, open Internet Explorer, Netscape, or another Web browser and enter as the URL:

> http://msdn.microsoft.com/library/default.asp

This will display the opening MSDN Library page for the Web-based help display as shown in Figure 2-20.

FIGURE 2-20.
MSDN Library
initial page

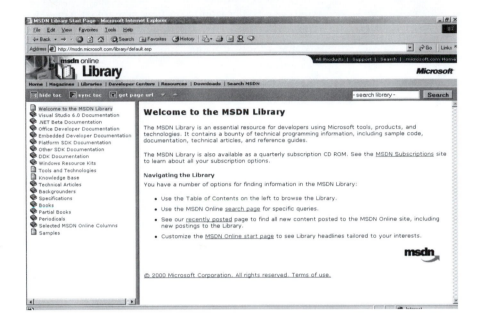

Notice the Web interface with a list of items (the Table of Contents—TOC) on the left, a corresponding Web page on the right, and three icons at the top of the screen: *Hide TOC, Sync TOC,* and *Get URL.* Clicking the first of these results in the list of items on the left being hidden. Clicking on the Sync TOC icon will display the Table of Contents on the left. Finally, clicking the third icon will result in the URL of the current help page being displayed. The MSDN item is initially highlighted on the left side and a graphic displaying a Welcome page is displayed on the right. To view help on Visual Basic (or any other topic), you must "drill down" by clicking on a book icon. In our case, this requires clicking once to "open" the *MSDN Library Visual Studio 6.0* book and then on *Visual Basic Documentation* book icon, and finally, on the book icon for the *Visual Basic Start Page.* When this process is completed, the page shown is displayed along with a new set of links on the left side of the page.

You will probably be most interested in the link to the *Programmer's Guide* within the page which contains such items as *Visual Basic Basics* and *What you can do with Visual Basic* or the links to *Getting Started* and *Reference* on the left of the page. Note that on the left side of the screen, you can see the result of "drilling down" with the MSDN and Visual Basic documentation books being shown as "open."

If the *Reference* link on the left is clicked, you can then drill down to find information on a particular item. For example, to find help on command buttons, you would click on *Language Reference, Objects,* and the letter *C.* This will display a list of objects whose names begin with the letter "C". Finally, clicking on *CommandButton* results in the help screen shown in Figure 2-22 being displayed.

FIGURE 2-21. Visual Basic Start Page

FIGURE 2-22. Visual Basic Help screen for *commandbutton control*

Regardless of whether you are using the MSDN help system or the Web-based systems, Visual Basic Help is based on the same **hypertext** principles as the World Wide Web: Clicking on an underlined word for which a pointed finger is displayed provides more information on that topic. Many Visual Basic Help screens will provide information on related topics, examples, and, for objects, information on properties, methods, and events that relate to those objects. For example, if you clicked on *Properties* in the screen shown in Figure 2-22, a list of all the properties for the commandbutton control will be displayed from which you can select one to view more information.

If you are using the MSDN help system, you can also reach the same type of Help screen by selecting the Index or Search options from the Help menu. The difference between using Index and using Search is that, with the Search option, MSDN searches *every word* in the entire Visual Studio Help system for an occurrence of the term you have entered rather than indexing just important terms as is done with the Index tab. For example, if you enter "box" in the Index system, you will find six references, but if you enter the same word in the Search system, you will find over 500 different references to "box," each with multiple Help topics in which the word occurs. For this reason, you should be very specific about the term for which you are searching.

Context sensitive help[1] and Auto Help

If the MSDN help system is installed on the computer on which you are working, context sensitive help is also available to you. With **context sensitive help,** positioning the pointer on a control on a form or word in the Code window and pressing the F1 function key will result in Visual Basic trying to provide context sensitive help on the item to which you are pointing. While it is not always perfect in matching the help provided to your needs, it does a very good job on most things. For example, if you position the pointer on the command button in the Vintage Video application and press **F1**, the same help screen shown earlier in Figure 2-22 will be displayed. Similarly, if you position the cursor on the MsgBox instruction in the Code window and press **F1**, a help screen on using this instruction will be displayed. In many situations, Context Sensitive help can be the fastest way to obtain information on a control, code instruction, or other feature of Visual Basic.

In addition to the type of help where you are actively looking for information, Visual Basic can automatically provide you several types of information as you work. In the process of entering code, you may have already noticed the little boxes that pop up with information about the statement you are entering. These boxes are a part of Microsoft's effort to have Visual Basic "think ahead" and provide you with information you need to complete the statement. There are three kinds of **Auto Help**: Auto List Members, Auto Quick Info, and Auto Data Tips. The Auto List Members help displays a box of items that can be used to complete a statement. Auto Quick Info displays the syntax necessary to complete the statement at the current cursor location. Auto Data Tips displays the value of the variable over which the cursor is placed. (Note: This type of help works even if you do not have the MSDN help system installed.)

For example, if you enter the first part of a MsgBox statement, say, *MsgBox,* the Auto Quick Info help will pop up with the syntax for completing the Message Box statement as shown in Figure 2-23. This means it is not necessary for you to remember the syntax for each and every statement.

Figure 2-23. Use of Auto Help

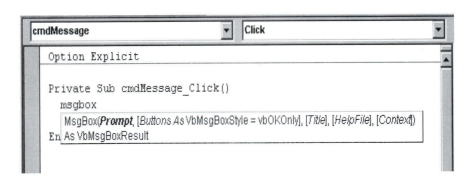

Mini-Summary 2-6: Visual Basic Help

1. If the MSDN help system is installed, there are three types of help available to you: the Help menu option, Context Sensitive help, and Auto Help. If the MSDN system is *not* installed, you can access help over the Web.

2. Using the Web-based help, you must "drill down" to the information you need through a series of lists of items.

3. If you are using the MSDN help system, you can also use the Index and Search Help Menu options to search for the help you need.

4. Also, if you are using the MSDN help system, you can obtain context sensitive help. With context sensitive help, you can locate the cursor on a control on the form or word in the Code window and press F1 to obtain help on that control or code statement.

5. If you are typing a statement, Auto Help will try to "think ahead" and provide information on completing that statement. Auto Help is available even if you do not have the MSDN help system.

It's Your Turn

1. Switch to a Web browser and enter the URL:

  http://msdn.microsoft.com/library/default.asp

Click on the book icon beside MSDN Visual Studio Library 6.0 to open this book. Then click the book icon beside Visual Basic Documentation to open this book. Now click on the **Visual Basic Start Page** to display the page shown in Figure 2-21. Click on any topic on this page and then click the **Back** button to return to the Visual Basic Start Page.

2. Click **Reference** book icon, then the **Language Reference** icon, and the **Objects** icon. Finally, click the letter **I** and select **Image Control** to display information on the Image Control. Click on **Properties** to display information on the Properties for the Image Control. Select **Picture** to display information on the Picture property. Click the **Back** button *twice* to return to the Help page about the Image Control.

If you have the MSDN Visual Basic help system, complete the following exercises:

3. Select Help from the menu bar, select the Index option from the Help menu, and enter **Image Control** into the input box. Select the Visual Basic reference for the Image Control to display information on the Image Control. Click on **Properties** to display information on the Properties for the Image Control. Select **Picture** to display information on the Picture property. Click the **Back** button to return to the Help page about the Image Control.

4. Click the Search option Help screen and enter **Image Control** into the input box. How many matches did you find? Select **File | Exit** to exit the Help System.

5. Position the pointer on the Image control in the Vintage Video application and click it to give it the focus. Now press **F1**. You should see the same information on this control as was displayed in Exercise 3.

6. Display the code window for the Vintage Video application. Position the pointer at the end of the first lines of the cmdMessage_Click() event procedure and press **ENTER** to open up a blank line. Type **MsgBox** and press the **SPACEBAR** once. You should

now see the same Auto Info help as was shown in Figure 2-23. Press **ESC** to exit the Auto Info help and then select **File | Exit** to exit Visual Basic without saving the revised Vintage Videos application.

7. If MSDN help is installed, use it to find the answers to the following:

    a. What is the Rnd function?

    b. Can the Refresh method for a command button be used on an MDI form?

    c. How much memory is used by a Single data type variable?

    d. Which arguments are required for the Inputbox function?

    e. What does ADO stand for?

8. Repeat the previous question using Web-based help if MSDN help is not installed.

SUMMARY

In this chapter, we have concentrated on providing a guided tour through the Visual Basic development environment. Understanding this environment is essential to being able to create information system applications in Visual Basic. The development environment includes the menu bar, toolbar, Toolbox, Form window, Project Explorer window, Properties window, and Form Layout window. The menu bar provides access to all of the commands needed to create applications, and the toolbar has icons corresponding to the more popular commands. The Toolbox has icons corresponding to various controls that can be dragged on the Form window to create an interface. The Project Explorer window shows the files that make up the project, and the Properties window displays the properties of the controls on the Form. The Form Layout window displays the appearance of the project when it is completed.

Creating an interface involves selecting a control from the Toolbox and drawing it on the form or double-clicking the control to display it in the center of the form. In this chapter, we used the label, command button, and image controls to create an interface. Once a control is positioned on the form, the next step is to select a property in the Properties window and change it. In this chapter, we changed properties for three controls and for the form.

Once the interface has been created, the next step is to write the code for the action objects on the form. This is done by double-clicking a control and entering the instructions for it in the Code window to respond to a specific event.

We then looked at the toolbar and discussed the 20 operations that can be executed from it. We noted that these operations correspond to commands available from the menu bar. We also discuss the various types of files that make up a Visual Basic project including the form file (.frm), project file (.vbp), binary form file (.frx), module file (.bas), and workspace file (.vbw). You can save a project through the toolbar Save File icon or through the File | Save menu option. Similarly, you can open a saved project through the Open Project toolbar icon or the File | Open menu option.

We also discussed the Visual Basic Help System. If the MSDN help system is installed, there are three types of help available to you: the Help menu option, Context Sensitive help, and Auto Help. If the MSDN system is *not* installed, you can access help over the Web. Using the Web-based help, you must "drill down" to the information you need through a series of lists of items. If you are using the MSDN help system, you can also use the Index and Search Help Menu options to search for the help you need.

Also, if you are using the MSDN help system, you can obtain context sensitive help. With context sensitive help, you can locate the cursor on a control on the form or word in the Code window and press F1 to obtain help on that control or code statement. If you are typing a statement, Auto Help will try to "think ahead" and provide information on completing that statement. It is available even if you do not have the MSDN help system.

NEW VISUAL BASIC ELEMENTS

Controls/Objects	Properties	Methods	Events
Form object	Name Caption		
label control	Name Caption Font		
command button control	Name Caption Font		Click
image control	Name Picture		

NEW PROGRAMMING STATEMENTS

MsgBox "message"

KEY TERMS

Auto Help
binary form file
Code window
context sensitive help
controls
custom controls
default event
event procedure
Events/Procedures list box
file
focus
form file

Form Layout window
Form window
hypertext
integrated development environment (IDE)
message box
module file
multiple document interface (MDI) Environment
Object list box
Program Design mode
Project Explorer window

project file
Project Group
Properties window
run time
Single Document Interface (SDI) Environment
sizing handles
toolbar
ToolTip
Toolbox
twips
workspace file

EXERCISES

1. Describe two techniques for adding controls to a form at design time.

2. Suppose that you want a form that is exactly 5 inches wide by 4 inches high. What form properties would you set? What values would you set them?

3. Suppose that you will be using four command buttons on your form. You would like for all four command buttons to be the same size. In addition, you would like to line them up vertically along their right edge with equal spacing between them. Which command button properties would you set? Provide an example of how you would set these property values.

4. Compare the properties of the form, command button, label, and image controls. What properties do they have in common? What properties are different?

5. When will the following code be executed? Describe what occurs when it is executed.

```
Private Sub imgActiveImage_Click()
    MsgBox "Hi kids. Welcome to my program."
End Sub
```

6. Using Visual Basic, create a simple project that includes a form, a command button, and a message that appears when the button is clicked. Test and save your project and exit Visual Basic. Using any file utility, such as Windows Explorer, change the file name of the .frm file. Re-enter Visual Basic and re-load your project. What happens when the project attempts to load? What occurs when you try to run the project? What error did the instructions lead you to make? Why does this error occur? Can you determine how to correct the problem?

PROJECTS

1. Use the **File | New Project** menu option to create a Visual Basic interface that will correspond to the sketch shown in Figure 2-24. Give appropriate names to your controls. Assume that when you click the CommandButton control, a message is displayed that reads, "Professor Beige's Grading Program." The question mark symbol can be found at \graphics\icons\misc\question.ico in the Visual Basic directory. Use 16-point Arial font for the label. Use the Form Layout window to position the form so it will appear in the center of the screen when you execute the project. Test your project and correct any problems. Save the form as **Ex2-1.frm** and the project as **Ex2-1.vbp**. Place them in a folder named **Ex2-1** in the Chapter2 folder on your data disk. Use the Windows Explorer tool to determine what other files were created when you created the project files.

FIGURE 2-24.
Sketch of interface for Exercise 1

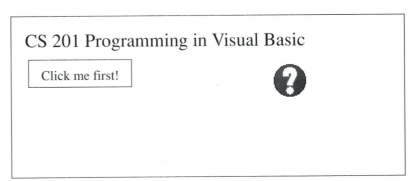

2. Use the **File | New Project** menu option to create a Visual Basic interface that will implement the sketch shown in Figure 2-25. Give appropriate names to your controls. Assume that when you click the CommandButton control, a message is displayed that

reads, "When completed, this button will start the program." The world symbol can be found at \graphics\icons\elements\world.ico. Use 18-point Times New Roman font for the label. Use the Form Layout window to position the form in the top right corner of the screen. Test your project and correct any problems. Save the form as **Ex2-2.frm** and the project as **Ex2-2.vbp**. Place them in a folder named **Ex2-2** in the Chapter2 folder on your data disk.

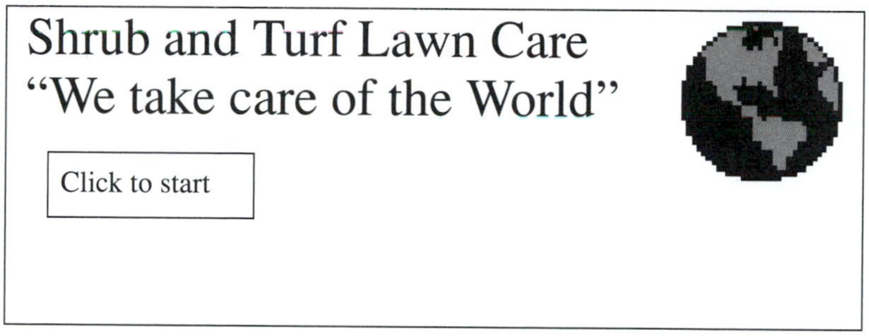

FIGURE 2-25.
Sketch of interface for Exercise 2

Shrub and Turf Lawn Care
"We take care of the World"

Click to start

3. Create a Visual Basic interface that will implement the sketch shown in Figure 2-26. Give appropriate names to your controls. Assume that when you click the command button control, a message is displayed that reads, "When completed, this program will compute gas mileages." The cars symbol can be found at \graphics\icons\industry\cars.ico. Use 18-point Arial Black font for the label. Use the Line control with its Border Style property set to "dashed" to create the dashed line beneath the label. Change the Backcolor property of the form to yellow using the Palette tab. (Yellow is in the third row, fourth from the left.) Also, change the Backcolor property on the label to the same color. Use the Form Layout window to position the form so it will be in the top left corner of the screen when you execute the project. Test your project and correct any problems. Save the form as **Ex2-3.frm** and the project as **Ex2-3.vbp**. Place them in a folder named **Ex2-3** in the Chapter2 folder on your data disk.

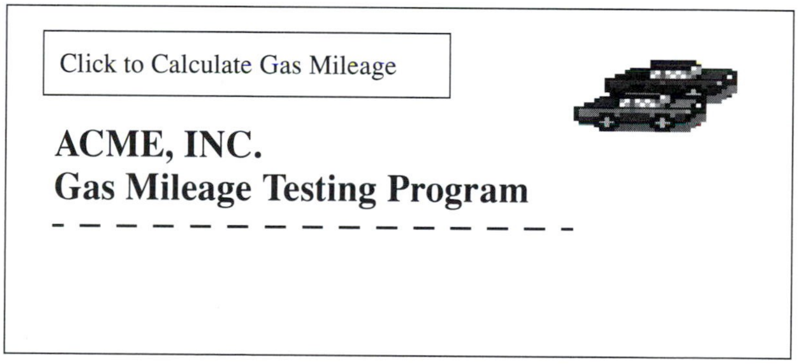

FIGURE 2-26.
Sketch of interface for Exercise 3

Click to Calculate Gas Mileage

ACME, INC.
Gas Mileage Testing Program
- - - - - - - - - - - - - -

4. Smith and Jones, Inc., needs you to create a Visual Basic interface that will implement the sketch shown in Figure 2-27. Give your controls appropriate names. Assume that when you click the top CommandButton control, a message is displayed that reads, "When completed, this button will calculate breakeven volume and revenue/costs." The graph symbol can be found at \graphics\icons\office\graph01.ico. Use 18-point

Impact font for the label. Use the Line control with its Border Style property set to "solid" to create the line beneath the label. Change the Backcolor property of the form to white using the Palette tab (white is in the first row, first column). Also, change the Backcolor property on the label to the same color. Save the form as **Ex2-4.frm** and the project as **Ex2-4.vbp**. Place them in a folder named **Ex2-4** in the Chapter2 folder on your data disk.

FIGURE 2-27.
Sketch of interface for Exercise 4

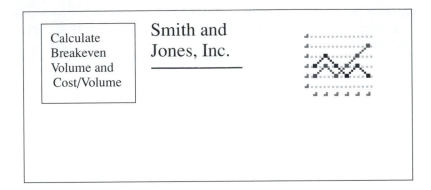

5. Cover-Your-Walls, Inc., has requested your services to create an interface for a Visual Basic program that will compute room area and number of rolls of wallpaper needed. A sketch is shown in Figure 2-28. Assume that when you click the command button control, a message is displayed that reads, "When completed, this button will calculate room area and number of rolls required." The house symbol can be found at \graphics \icons\misc\house.ico. Use 16-point Desdemona font for the label. Change the Backcolor property of the form to white using the Palette tab (white is in the first row, first column). Also, change the Backcolor property on the label to the same color. Save the form as **Ex2-5.frm** and the project as **Ex2-5.vbp**. Place them in a folder named **Ex2-5** in the Chapter2 folder on your data disk.

FIGURE 2-28.
Sketch of interface for Exercise 5

6. Anyone who has watched television late at night has noticed (among other strange programming) various pitches for "get-rich-quick" schemes. Some of these make the outrageous claim that they can help you double your money in a very short time. A simple "rule of thumb" that can be used to estimate the number of years required to double your money is known as the "rule of 72." Using the rule of 72 the approximate number

of years to double an investment is equal to 72 divided by the annual percentage returned (for a savings account this would be the interest rate). This rule assumes that the interest is compounded annually and is not taxed. Design a Visual Basic program to be used in applying the rule of 72 using an IPO, pseudocode, and a sketch of the interface. Make sure that your interface is intuitive and visually pleasing from a user's perspective. Begin implementing your program by creating a partial interface in Visual Basic using the controls that you know. Feel free to experiment with other controls on your form. Save the form as **Ex2-6.frm** and the project as **Ex2-6.vbp**. Place them in a folder named **Ex2-6** in the Chapter2 folder on your data disk.

7. Professional and hard-core amateur athletes often use a heart monitor to check their heart rate during training. The monitor will indicate whether or not the heart rate is within an acceptable range of values. For those of us who are somewhat less than professional in our training, there is a pair of simple formulas that can be used to determine this range called the target heart rate zone. We can then monitor our heart rate during aerobic exercise and try to maintain it within this zone. The lower limit of the zone may be estimated as 60% of the difference between 220 and your age. The upper limit of the zone may be estimated as 75% of the difference between 220 and your age. Design a Visual Basic program to determine your target heart rate zone. Use an IPO, pseudocode, and a sketch of the interface. Make sure that your interface is intuitive and visually pleasing from a user's perspective. Begin implementing your program by creating a partial interface in Visual Basic using the controls that you know. Feel free to experiment with other controls on your form. Save the form as **Ex2-7.frm** and the project as **Ex2-7.vbp**. Place them in a folder named **Ex2-7** in the Chapter2 folder on your data disk.

8. Have you ever wondered which size pizza actually provides the most pizza for your pizza buying dollar? Round pizzas are often identified by their diameter. The size of the pizza in square inches may be computed using the formula for the area of a circle (area $= \pi * \text{diameter}^2 / 4$). The price of the pizza per square inch may then be calculated by dividing the total price by the pizza's area. Design a Visual Basic program to be used in determining the area of a pizza in square inches and the price per square inch. Use an IPO, pseudocode, and a sketch of the interface. Make sure that your interface is intuitive and visually pleasing from a user's perspective. Begin implementing your program by creating a partial interface in Visual Basic using the controls that you know. Feel free to experiment with other controls on your form. Save the form as **Ex2-8.frm** and the project as **Ex2-8.vbp**. Place them in a folder named **Ex2-8** in the Chapter2 folder on your data disk.

PROJECT: JOE'S TAX ASSISTANCE (CONT.)

It was Saturday and Zooey was scheduled to come to Joe's house to give him a lesson on the laptop. Joe was getting excited about developing his tax assistance program, and he could hardly wait to tell her about it. He had even risen early and written down some of his thoughts.

Joe was sitting in the den looking over his notes when Zooey came walking in, followed by her mother Janet (Joe's daughter), and his wife Angela.

"Hi, Grandpa," said Zooey as she gave him a hug. "I can stay for a while. Mom's taking Granny to the mall and she'll pick me up afterwards."

"The way they shop we might have all night to work. Maybe you should put your things in the guest room," Joe replied and promptly received a playful slap on the shoulder from Angela.

"Be good, dear," she said. "Janet and I won't spend all of your money . . . if you're nice."

Janet added, "And with summer vacation starting in a month or two, I might bring Zooey over and take Mom shopping more often."

Joe knew when he was outnumbered; nevertheless he remained defiant: "Zooey can come over whenever she likes, but I don't know about the shopping. Maybe we can sell the program we're going to develop in order to support the shopping habit."

With a smile the two ladies departed, while Joe and Zooey got down to business.

"I brought a couple of Visual Basic books we used in school like you asked, Grandpa. What's up?" Zooey inquired.

Joe had already explained to Zooey over the phone that he wanted to create a program that would be a useful tool with his VITA work. He showed her the standard 1040 form, and they began to discuss how the program might be designed. Of course, Joe realized that there might be some trial and error involved, especially since he was a novice programmer, but Zooey assured him that, according to her computer instructor, writing a program is often an "iterative" process.

Zooey considered the form. "You know, Grandpa," she said, "there are objects in Visual Basic that look a lot like the parts of the 1040 form. For instance, the little boxes that you fill in are just like text boxes in Visual Basic. Also, there are things like option and check boxes that would be good for some of these items. In fact, did you know that the pages you create in Visual Basic are called 'forms' too?"

"You don't say?" Joe responded. "So you think that we can come up with something for the tax form?"

"Most definitely!" Zooey exclaimed. "Let me show you a few of the things Visual Basic can do, like forms and command buttons. Then we can start figuring out how to use them with the tax form."

Having already set up the computer, the two began to concentrate on the screen as Zooey demonstrated a few things. Joe's mind began to race at the possibilities as he watched her demonstration.

Questions

1. Obtain and examine an IRS 1040 tax form. Develop a strategy for breaking it into manageable parts for the Visual Basic program.

2. Design an opening screen for Joe's VITA program. This screen will serve as the main form of the program. Use labels and command buttons. The screen should include a command button corresponding to each separate section of the tax form following the strategy you develop in question 1. For each of these buttons, write code for displaying a message box when the button is clicked. Each message box should display a short message describing the future action of the button. In addition, include a command button to end the program. Be sure to name each object, edit the captions, and adjust sizes and positions appropriately.

3. Run and test your program.

3 VARIABLES, ASSIGNMENT STATEMENTS, AND ARITHMETIC

LEARNING
OBJECTIVES

After reading this chapter, you will able to:

❖ Declare and use different types of variables in your project.

❖ Use text boxes for event-driven input and output.

❖ Use a four-step process to write code for event procedures.

❖ Write Visual Basic instructions to carry out arithmetic operations.

❖ Describe the hierarchy of operations for arithmetic.

❖ Understand how to store the result of arithmetic operations in variables using assignment statements.

❖ Use comments to explain the purpose of program statements.

❖ Discuss using Visual Basic functions to carry out commonly used operations.

❖ Use command buttons to clear text boxes, print a form with the PrintForm method, and exit the project.

❖ Describe the types of errors that commonly occur in a Visual Basic project and their causes.

SCENARIO:
CALCULATING
AMOUNT DUE AT
VINTAGE
VIDEOS

The next morning, Ed and Yvonne were busy shelving videos and preparing for their approaching "Grand Opening" when Clark arrived at Vintage Videos.

"Fire up the computer, guys! Your chief programmer has arrived for the demonstration!"

"'Morning, Clark. The computer's on. Go ahead and get set up while we finish shelving these Stooges flicks," Ed said in greeting.

Yvonne peered at Clark slyly and said: "Hey, Ed, doesn't Clark kind of remind you of Moe? He's the smart stooge."

Ed chuckled. "I almost want to agree, but wouldn't that make us Larry and Curly?"

"Okay, you stooges, it's all set. Come and take a look," Clark "Moe" Davis commanded.

Clark started the program as Yvonne and Ed did their best stooge walks to the counter.

"Notice it looks just like most Windows programs," Clark began. "Keep in mind that it's just a simple demo right now."

"Cute picture, but what does the program do?" Yvonne asked.

"First, it does the normal things that any Windows program does." Clark demonstrated: "See, you can minimize the window by clicking here, and maximize it by clicking here. You can also drag it around with the mouse. These kinds of things are built into any Visual Basic program. The work is in adding items to the form like the picture and the button and then writing code that tells the program to perform a task when a particular item is selected. Here, Ed, you try it."

Ed took the mouse and clicked on the "Click Me" button. The message box saying "Welcome to Vintage Videos" appeared.

Clark explained further: "I added all the items that you see in the main window and wrote the program that makes the box appear when you click the button. I'm thinking about having the message appear each time you open the program."

"It looks pretty good, but it doesn't do much. Are you sure that we can get a program that will satisfy our needs?" Ed inquired carefully. "Also, how do you get out of the program?"

"That's why you need to tell me what you WANT it to do. I made the demo just to give you an idea of what we can do in Visual Basic. I hope it will give you some ideas for what we can put into the program. As far as exiting the program, I can easily add a button that will let you quit the program," Clark responded persuasively.

"I'd like to have something that we can use when a customer rents a video. I want to be able to enter the name of the customer, the name of the video, and the price of the video, then let the computer determine the amount due by computing the sales tax and adding it to the price. I also want to be able to print the results and clear them so another transaction can be added," Joe said. "Can you do something like that?"

"Sure. That shouldn't be too difficult. I'm sure you'll want to add something else later, but that's a good place to start. I'll get going this afternoon."

"My little stooge Moe can do it for sure!" Yvonne said as she rolled her eyes and bopped Clark playfully on the head.

The Prototyping Development Process

As we said in Chapter 1, application development is an important part of developing an information system. In the Vintage Videos scenario, we are witnessing a type of systems development called **prototyping**. In prototyping, the client and the developer work together to rapidly create a working prototype of the information system. In this case, the programmer, Clark, has created a prototype in the form of an opening screen, which he demonstrates to the client, Ed. Based on the prototype, the client learns about the capabilities of the development tool, Visual Basic, and makes suggestions as to ways to improve the prototype. In this case, Ed has requested that the prototype include a way of entering the customer name, video name, and video price and a way for the prototype application to compute the sales tax and amount due. He also wants to be able to print the form, clear text boxes, and exit the project.

On the basis of these client suggestions and requests, a new version of the prototype will be developed and demonstrated to the client. This iterative process will continue until a working application is developed that meets the client's needs. This prototyping process of application development will be the basis for the continuing discussion of the Vintage Videos case.

WORKING WITH VARIABLES

Recall from Chapter 1 that a computer can carry out six basic operations:

1. Input data
2. Store data in internal memory
3. Perform arithmetic on data
4. Compare two values and select one of two alternative actions
5. Repeat a group of actions any number of times
6. Output the results of processing.

In Chapter 2, we created a Visual Basic project that carried out only two of these operations by responding to input in the form of a mouse click to output a message. In this chapter, we are going to expand that project to handle input in the form of the name of the customer, the name of the video being rented, and the rental price. The project must then use arithmetic operations on data to compute the sales tax on the video and add this amount to the rental price to compute the amount due. The project must output the sales tax and amount due that are calculated and respond to a mouse click to print the form, clear text boxes, and terminate execution of the project.

To do this, we will need to carry out Steps 1–3 and 6; that is, we need to store both data and instructions in the computer's memory, perform arithmetic on the data, and output the results of the processing. In this chapter we will not need to compare two values or repeat a group of actions.

Variables

To be able to carry out any type of arithmetic operation, you need to understand the manner in which data are stored in the computer's internal memory. Internal memory can be thought of as a very large number of boxes called **memory cells** arranged in a manner similar to post office boxes. In each memory cell, one and only one data item can be stored at a time. To store a new value in the memory cell, you must destroy the old value. However, you can retrieve and use a value from a memory cell without destroying it.

Because memory cells can have different values stored in them, they are commonly referred to as **variables**. The location of the memory cell remains the same, but different values may reside there at different times during the execution of the program. For example, a memory cell (variable) called Number may begin with a value of 10, have this changed to 0, and then to –20.

Changing the value of a variable involves destroying the contents of the memory cell and resupplying the cell with a new value. So, in a computer program when we speak of a variable or a variable name, these terms refer to a memory cell in the computer's memory. The *value of a variable* in a program is the *current value* in the memory cell with the same name.

Naming Variables

Because data are stored in variables, in order to perform a desired operation, both you and the computer must be able to refer to a variable. To identify variables, you must assign names to them. Once this is done and a variable name is used in the program, there is no uncertainty as to which variable is being referenced. For example, if you have given a variable a name of Number and it has a value of 10 stored in it, then you can change the value stored in Number by using the appropriate instructions and referring to Number. Note that the name of the memory cell and its contents are *not* the same. If a variable is named B, this does *not* mean it has the symbol "B" stored in it.

Variables are named in Visual Basic through a combination of the letters A through Z, the digits 0 through 9, and the underscore (_). Variable names are not allowed to contain any other *special* characters, and they must *always* start with a letter. Visual Basic recognizes up to 255 characters in a name, but you will probably never want to create a variable name this long! Visual Basic is *case-insensitive*, that is, case is not considered in variable names. For example, a variable named *NUMBER* is the same as a variable named *Number* or *number*. However, it is often useful to use upper- and lowercase letters in variable names, especially when words are combined to create a variable name. Doing this helps you understand the purpose of the variable. For example, *InterestRate* is easier to understand than *interestrate*. You should avoid using all capitals for variable names, since they can make the name difficult to understand.

A naming convention is also considered standard when using variables. The standard convention is to prefix the variable name with a three-letter indicator related to the variable data type. Variable data types will be discussed shortly. For example, a variable representing a tax amount that is declared as a currency data type may be named curTaxes following this convention. This convention will be followed throughout the text.

In addition to these rules about variable names, another rule is that a variable name may not be one of the restricted **keywords** in Visual Basic. These are words that Visual Basic uses as a part of its language. For example, you could not use the keyword Print as a variable name. However, it is valid to imbed a keyword in a variable name. For this reason, it would be valid to use PrintThis as a variable name. Visual Basic is very helpful in alerting you to keywords and errors in variable names. Keywords are displayed in blue and errors in red. For example, if you tried to use Print as a variable name, Visual Basic would display an error message and show the word Print in red. If this happens, change the variable name and try again.

A common practice is to choose a name that in some way helps the programmer to remember the quantity being represented by the variable. Such devices that aid the programmer's memory are termed **mnemonic variable names**. The use of mnemonic variable names is considered good programming practice. With an upper limit of 255 characters in Visual Basic, this is usually easy to do. The only problem with using long variable names is that they can be cumbersome to work with in the programming process. For that reason, it is a good idea to make sure the variable name represents the quantity but does not become too long. Table 3-1 shows quantities and a typical name for the variable corresponding to each of those quantities.

TABLE 3-1: Example variable names

Item	Variable Name
Video rental price	curVideoPrice
Amount due	curAmountDue
Taxes due	curTaxes
Interest on home mortgage	curMortageInterest
Year-to-date earnings	curYTDEarnings
Employee's last name	strEmpLastName

Data Types

Different types of data can be stored in a computer's internal memory. Visual Basic supports 14 standard data types as well as user-defined data types. The data types you will use most often for your work include String, Single, Double, Integer, Long Integer, Currency, Date, and Boolean (true or false).

The **String data type**, prefixed *str*, is used to store any string of ASCII symbols or characters that is enclosed in quotation marks. For example, a String variable might hold "120 Hilltop Rd." All of the remaining data types listed above are considered **numeric data types,** because they store numeric data and can be used in arithmetic processing. It is important to remember that Numeric variables are very different from the numbers stored as String variables. Numerical variables can be used in arithmetic operations—addition, subtraction, multiplication, and so on. String variables, on the other hand, *should not* be used in such operations. The primary purpose of String variables is to provide for the input, output, and manipulation of sets or *strings* of characters.

Integers and **Long Integers** are designed to be used only with whole numbers, and they cannot have any fractional portion. **Single** and **Double** precision numbers can contain a decimal point and are used for calculations that require fractional values. These are referred to as **floating point operations**, since the position of the decimal point is not fixed. If you need to work with currency or other values in which you need up to four decimal places of accuracy, then you would use the **Currency** data type. Since the decimal point does not *float* in this data type, this is a **fixed point operation.** You might not think of the **Date** or **Boolean** data types as being Numeric, but both can be used in arithmetic processing. For example, if you subtract 100 from May 14, 2001, the answer is Feb. 3, 2001. Similarly, the Boolean type corresponds to values of 0 (false) or –1 (true), so if a value is multiplied by a Boolean variable, depending on the value of the Boolean variable, its sign may be changed.

Good programming practice calls for the type of variable to be shown as a prefix to the variable name just like prefixes are used as a part control names. For example, we used *cur* as a prefix for a variable that will hold currency data. We will use these prefixes whenever we declare variables. Table 3-2 displays the characteristics of each Numeric data type along with the standard three letter prefix for each data type and other pertinent information about the data type.

In Table 3-2, the *Range* refers to the values that can be represented by this type of constant. A value involving an E followed by a number means that value raised to that power of 10. For example, 2.5E2 is the same as 2.5×10^2. *Precision* in the table refers to how accurately this type of constant can store numbers. For example, Integers and Long Integers cannot store numbers with fractions, so they are accurate to only the whole number part of a value. Similarly, a Single variable can be accurate to only the first seven digits that are stored in it. So, 23,561.1903 is accurate to only the first seven digits, or 23,561.19, with the last two decimal places being lost.

Finally, the *Number of Bytes* refers to the amount of internal memory required to store this constant, where one byte equals eight bits. In general, the greater the range and precision, the greater the number of bytes required to store the data type.

In addition to the String and Numeric data types, Visual Basic offers the **Variant** data type. A Variant data type can take on any of the other data types as needed. This generally occurs in the coding process when you fail to declare the type of variable you are using and Visual Basic has to "guess" at the data type by using a Variant type variable. In general, it is not a good idea to have Visual Basic do this, so you should always

TABLE 3-2: Characteristics of numeric data types

Numeric Data Type	Prefix	Range	Precision	Number of Bytes
Single	sng	1.4E-45 to 3.4E38 and −3.4E38 to −1.4E-45	Seven significant digits	4
Double	dbl	4.9E-324 to 1.8E308 and −1.8E308 to −4.9E-324	Fifteen significant digits	8
Currency	cur	−922,337,203,685,477.5808 to 922,337,203,685,477.5807	Four places to right of decimal	8
Integer	int	−32,768 to 32,767	Whole numbers	2
Long	lng	−2,147,483,648 to 2,147,483,647	Whole numbers	4
Date	dtm	January 1, 100, to December 31, 9999	Not applicable	8
Boolean	bln	True or False	Not applicable	2

"declare" the data type for each variable you use in your project. We will discuss this process in more detail next.

Using the coding convention prefixes for objects and variables can provide several advantages including:

❖ Your code follows a standard that allows anyone who reads the code to immediately determine the data type of the variable;

❖ Words that are normally reserved as Visual Basic keywords may be used as part of an object or variable name, for example strPrint;

❖ You can name different objects with practically the same name. For example, imagine that you have a form with a label and a text box used to enter a user's age. If prefixes are used, you may name your text box txtAge, the corresponding label lblAge, and even an integer variable that may receive the value of the text box as intAge.

Declaring Variables   Good programming form requires that you always inform Visual Basic of the data type you wish to be used with a given variable. This operation, termed *declaring variables*, is usually the first code instruction that is entered into an event procedure for a control. While variables can be declared in a number of ways, the most common declaration form uses the Dim keyword in combination with the variable name and the data type; that is,

Dim *variable name* **as** *data type*

where you supply both the variable name and the data type (use the data types given in Table 3-2 or, for a String variable, use the keyword String.)

For example, to declare a variable called curMyIncome as currency, the statement would be:

```
Dim curMyIncome as Currency
```

Similarly, to declare a variable called strHerName as a String type, the statement would be:

```
Dim strHerName as String
```

You may combine multiple declarations on one line by separating them by commas, *so long as each declaration has both a variable name and a data type.* For example, to combine the two previous declarations on one line, you would enter:

```
Dim curMyIncome as Currency, strHerName as String
```

Failure to have a data type for a variable in the Dim statement will result in that variable being declared as a Variant type variable. For example, the declaration:

```
Dim curMySalary, curYourSalary as Currency
```

will result in curMySalary being declared to be a Variant type variable and curYourSalary to be a Currency type variable.

> **TIP:** However you declare a variable in terms of upper- and lower-case letters, Visual Basic will always change the case of the variable in later references to fit the declaration. This can be useful for a quick check on the variables that you are using.

Using the Option Explicit Statement

Throughout this book, we will always declare variables since it is our belief that the programmer should always be in control. Failure to declare variables leaves it up to Visual Basic to use the Variant type, which can lead to problems when Visual Basic makes the wrong decision as to how a variable should be used. To ensure that you always declare variables, you should modify Visual Basic to automatically insert the **Option Explicit** statement in every project. This statement requires that all variables be declared and generates an error message if any are not. While you could add this statement yourself in every project you create, it is much easier to have Visual Basic do it for you. To have Visual Basic add the Option Explicit statement, do the following:

1. If you have not done so already, start Visual Basic.

2. From the menu bar, select **Tools | Options | Editor.**

3. From the Options dialog box, click the check box to the left of **Require Variable Declaration** to turn it *on*. (If it is already checked, do nothing!) The Options dialog box with the appropriate check box pointed out is shown in Figure 3-1.

4. Click **Ok** to return to the form window of Visual Basic. Until you uncheck the check box, you must declare all variables for any new forms added to the current project or for all forms on any new projects. NOTE: adding the Option Explicit statement will not change the current project; only future projects are affected.

Mini-Summary 3-1: Variables and data types

1. Variables correspond to memory locations in the computer in which data and results are stored. They are assigned names by the programmer and used in the program.

2. A variety of data types can be stored in the memory locations; all are referred to by their variable names.

3. It is a good idea to declare variables as to the type of data on which they correspond. Variables are declared with the Dim statement.

4. The Option Explicit statement forces all variables to be declared in a program. It is possible to automatically include this statement in every program.

FIGURE 3-1.
Requiring
declaration of
variables

Variable
Declaration
Check Box

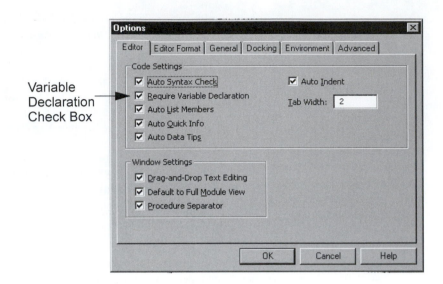

It's Your Turn!

1. Give the most appropriate data type for each of the following values:

     a. 23
     b. 7.56
     c. True
     d. $100.87
     e. 9534
     f. 10089.34512

2. Create a variable name for each of the following quantities and give the appropriate data type:

     a. Time until arrival
     b. Take-home pay
     c. Discount rate
     d. Shipping rate per pound
     e. Failure rate per 1000
     f. Pass or fail?

3. Write instructions to declare the variables for which you created names in the previous exercise.

4. For each of the following short scenarios, list the variables that you would need to solve the problem. In your list include the variable name, its data type, and the declaration statement that you would use.

     a. W. Loman makes a living as a traveling salesman. In order to properly maintain his vehicle, Mr. Loman faithfully records the odometer reading (total miles a car has traveled) and the gallons of gas purchased. He then uses these values to calculate the miles per gallon for his vehicle since the last fill-up.

     b. Joe "Bull" Cigar occasionally checks the prices of the shares of stock that he owns in the financial pages of his local newspaper. When he checks, he records the date, the closing price of the stock, and the number of shares traded. Bull would like to be able to save this information in a file on his computer. In addition, he would like to be able to calculate the percent change in stock price since his initial investment.

c. Tiger "Golden Bear" Shark is new to the professional golf circuit. He would like a simple program for his palm device in which he can keep a record of his performance by hole on the various courses that he plays. He will need to enter the name of the course, the date, the hole number, the hole par, his score on the hole, and comments about the hole. In addition, he would like the program to calculate his total score for a round and how far over/under par.

5. Choose **Tools|Options|Editor** from the menu. If the **Require Variable Declaration** option is not checked, do so now. Click **Ok** to return to the main screen.

6. Access Visual Basic, select **Existing,** change to the **Chapter2** folder on the a:\ drive and double-click **Vintage2.vbp** to retrieve the project you created in Chapter 2.

7. If the Code window is not displayed, click the View Code button in the Project Explorer window. If **Option Explicit** is declared at the top of the screen, do nothing; otherwise, click the down arrow for the Object list box to display the (General) object and the (Declarations) section; then enter **Option Explicit.**

8. Use the **File|Save as...** option to create a new folder with a name of **Chapter3**. Then save the form as **Vintage3.frm** and the project as **Vintage3.vbp** in the Chapter3 folder on your data disk.

EVENT-DRIVEN INPUT

Now that you understand the use of variables to represent the contents of a memory cell, the next question is: How do we get data into these variables? This is accomplished through some type of input. By **input** we mean using the keyboard, mouse, or other means to enter data into a variable. There must *always* be some form of input for processing of data into information to take place. In procedural languages, there are some types of input or read statements that enter data directly into a variable. However, for input to occur in event-driven languages like Visual Basic, where the user typically enters data into a control on the screen, an event must transfer the data from the control to a variable. This is important to note: While you can enter data into a control, if the appropriate event does not take place, then the data will never be used in the program. (This is not to say that we will never input data directly into variables; it does mean that transferring data from a control to a variable is more in keeping with the event-driven nature of Visual Basic).

text box The control commonly used for event-driven input is the **text box**, into which data can be easily entered. Once data have been entered into a text box, you can use an event like clicking a command button to transfer the data to a variable, which can then be used in some type of computation. The text box can also be used to display processed information. The property of the text box that enables it to be used for input and output is its **Text property**. The Text property is *always* equal to whatever is displayed in the **Edit field** of the text box, that is, the area in the text box in which you may enter, edit, or display text. To enter text in the text box, you simply click the mouse pointer inside the blank area to change it to a vertical line and type the text. You may edit existing text by placing the pointer in the text box at the desired location and using the word processing editing keys to change the text.

> **TIP:** To improve the appearance of the labels by right-justifying them, you can change the Alignment property for the label from Left to Right.

To add a text box to a form, you select it from the Toolbox, place it on the form, and change its name and other properties, just like you did with the label, image, and command button controls in Chapter 2. The text box is the control in the Toolbox with the letters **ab** in it. The Name property of the text box should be changed to begin with a prefix of *txt*. The text box does not have a Caption property, but it does have the Text property that is displayed in the text box. The default value for the Text property is *text* combined with a number, say, *text1*. This default property is usually deleted as a part of the design process. Figure 3-2 shows a form with a text box centered in the upper half. Note that we have also added a label which describes this text box as *First Number* and that the text box is empty because we deleted the default value for the Text property of the text box. The name of the text box is *txtFirstNum* and the name of the label is *lblFirstNum*.

text box
icon

> **TIP:** You can easily delete the Text property for a highlighted text box by double-clicking it in the Properties window and pressing **Del**. If you then highlight another text box, the focus will still be on the Text property, enabling easy deletion of it.

FIGURE 3-2. Text box added to form

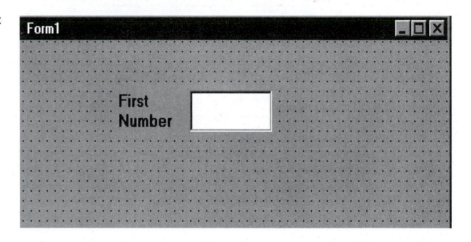

Creating a Simple Calculator

As an example of using a text box for input (and output), let's add two more text boxes and accompanying labels to the form shown in Figure 3-2. Let's also add two command buttons and a line to create a very simple calculator that sums the contents of the top two (input) text boxes and displays the result in the third (output) text box. The Sum command button transfers the contents of the two input text boxes to variables, carries out the addition, and transfers the results to the output text box. The Clear command button clears the text boxes and places the cursor back in the top text box. The line control acts as a separator between the input and output text boxes. The resulting form is shown in Figure 3-3 and the Name and Caption properties (where appropriate) are shown in Table 3-3. In all cases, the Font properties for the captions have been set to 10 points with Bold style.

FIGURE 3-3. Simple calculator

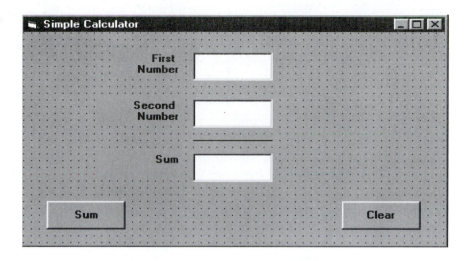

TABLE 3-3: Controls for Calculator

Control	Name	Caption
form	frmSimple	Simple Calculator
text box	txtFirstNum	not applicable
text box	txtSecondNum	not applicable
text box	txtSum	not applicable
label	lblFirstNum	First Number (right-justified)
label	lblSecondNum	Second Number (right-justified)
label	lblSum	Sum (right justified)
command button	cmdSum	Sum
command button	cmdClear	Clear
line	linSeparator	none

Using Assignment Statements to Input Data

To transfer the contents of the text boxes to variables, you must use an assignment statement. An **assignment statement** gives a variable a value by setting it equal either to an existing quantity or to a value that is computed by the program. In the case of transferring the contents of a text box to a variable, the variable is set equal to the Text property of the text box. The general form of an assignment statement is:

Control property or *variable = value, variable, expression,* or *property*

Note that the Control property or variable being assigned a value appears on the left side of the equals sign, with a value, variable, expression, or Control property appearing on the right. This is an important rule that must always be followed in the assignment statement. For example, an assignment statement might be:

curAmountDue = curPrice + curTaxes

where curAmountDue is a variable to which the sum of the curPrice and curTaxes is being assigned.

We will discuss other applications of assignment statements in more detail later in this chapter, but for now we are interested in assigning the Text property of the text boxes to variables, summing those variables, and transferring the sum to a third text box. Since all of this is accomplished by the cmdSum command button, we need to double-click this control to open its Code window and declare three variables—intFirst, intSecond, and intSum—that will be used in the actual summation. Next, we need to use assignment statements to transfer the Text property of the text boxes to the variables intFirst and intSecond. These statements are shown in VB Code Box 3-1.

VB Code Box 3-1. Code to input two numbers	```Private Sub cmdSum_Click Dim intFirst as Integer, intSecond as Integer Dim intSum as Integer intFirst = txtFirstNum.Text intSecond = txtSecondNum.Text End Sub```

All controls, including the text boxes in VB Code Box 3-1, have a **default property** which does not have to be included with the control name in an assignment statement. For example, the Text property is the default property for the text box. Similarly, the Caption property is the default property for the label control. This means that the assignment statements in VB Code Box 3-1 could have been written as:

```
intFirst = txtFirstNum
intSecond = txtSecondNum
```

However, for ease of understanding in this text, we will always include the property with the object.

> **TIP:** In most places in your project, if you have the help system installed, you can position the pointer on a control, property, function, or other entity and press **F1** to display context-sensitive help about it.

Using Functions

In looking at the assignment statements in VB Code Box 3-1, notice that intFirst and intSecond are Integer variables, but the Text property of any text box is a character string. This means that we have Numeric variables being set equal to String quantities—something that should be avoided since it requires Visual Basic to decide how to handle the mismatch of types. While Visual Basic *usually* handles this appropriately by converting the quantity on the right to the variable type on the left, it is not wise to leave this conversion up to Visual Basic. Instead, we need to use a built-in Visual Basic function to carry out the conversion. A **function** is an operation that takes one or more arguments and returns a single value. A common form of a function is:

variable = functionname(arg1, arg2, ...)

where arg1, arg2, and so on are the arguments of the function and the value is returned through the function name in an assignment or other statement. You might want to think of any function as a *black box* into which arguments are fed and from which a single value is returned, as shown in Figure 3-4. We do not need to know how it works to use it; we only need to know the name of the function, the appropriate form of the arguments and the type of value to be returned.

Not all functions require arguments. For example, the Date function returns the system date on your computer with no arguments. Regardless of whether a function does or does not require arguments, all are used in a similar manner.

FIGURE 3-4.
Function as black
box

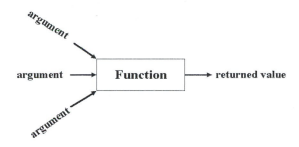

In our case, we will use the **Val()** function to convert the Text property from a string to a number, which is then assigned to a Numeric variable. For example, instead of

```
intFirst = txtFirstNum.Text
```
the appropriate statement is
```
intFirst = Val(txtFirstNum.Text)
```
The revised code for the cmdSum command button using the Val function is shown in VB Code Box 3-2:

VB CODE BOX 3-2. Code to use Val() function in inputting numbers	```Private Sub cmdSum_Click() Dim intFirst as Integer, intSecond as Integer Dim intSum as Integer intFirst = Val(txtFirstNum.Text) intSecond = Val(txtSecondNum.Text) End Sub```

You might ask, why not use the text boxes directly for this computation? The answer to this question involves the nature of the Text property of a text box: It is a String, and as such it must be converted into a Numeric variable before being used in any type of calculation. If you try to use the Text property in a calculation, in some cases it will be converted into a Variant data type while in others it will remain as a String. In either case, the results can end up surprising and *wrong!*

*Computing and
Displaying the Sum*

Now that we have the contents of the two text boxes transferred to variables, the next step is to sum these two variables and display the result in the output text box. Once again, we use assignment statements to carry out these operations. In the first case, we use the summation sign (+) to sum the variables intFirst and intSecond, with the result being assigned to the variable Sum. This assignment statement will appear as:
```
intSum = intFirst + intSecond
```
In the second case, it might appear that we simply assign the value of the variable intSum to the Text property of the text box txtSum. However, we have the reverse of the problem we had before; we are now assigning the value of an Integer variable to a text box that is a String. To make sure that this conversion is handled correctly, we need to use the **Str()** function, which converts the Numeric argument into a character string. In this case, the assignment statement is:
```
txtSum.Text = Str(intSum)
```
If we add these two statements to the Code window for the cmdSum command button, we arrive at the code shown in VB Code Box 3-3. This is *all* the code you need to use our Simple Calculator. If you enter an Integer value in the top text box and a second Integer value in the second text box, and click the cmdSum command button,

the sum of the two values will be displayed in the bottom text box. For example, if we enter 20 and 30 and click the command button, the sum, 50, will be displayed.

VB CODE BOX 3-3. Code for cmdSum command button	``` Private Sub cmdSum_Click() Dim intFirst as Integer, intSecond as Integer Dim intSum as Integer intFirst = Val(txtFirstNum.Text) intSecond = Val(txtSecondNum.Text) intSum = intFirst + intSecond txtSum.Text = Str(intSum) End Sub ```

Properties and Methods

Note that the Text property for the txtSum text box is shown appended to the text box name with a period. This **dot notation** is the way that properties are set at run time. The general form for setting a property at run time is:

> ***object.property = value***

The same notation is used to invoke a method for a control. Recall that methods define the actions that a control can carry out. The general form for using a method at run time is:

> ***object.method***

For example, a method that is associated with a text box is the **SetFocus** method. This method shifts the cursor to the text box whenever it is invoked. If we wanted to put the cursor in the txtFirstNum text box, the statement would be:

```
txtFirstNum.SetFocus
```

We will use this method later in the Calculator example.

In comparing the use of properties and methods, you should note one crucial difference: *A control **property** can be used in an assignment statement, but a control **method** can never be used in an assignment statement.* So, if you ever see a control followed by a period and name in an assignment statement, the name must refer to a property. Conversely, if you see a control followed by a period and name by itself, then the name must refer to a method.

> **TIP:** Note that when you type the name of an object in your code, a context-sensitive pop-up menu appears just after typing the period. This menu provides a listing of all properties and methods available for the object that you typed.

Clearing Text Boxes

After we use this calculator for one set of numbers, to use it again we need to clear the text boxes and set the focus back to the first text box. To do this, we need to add code to the cmdClear command button that sets the Text property of each text box to an empty string ("") and uses the SetFocus method to position the cursor in the txtFirstNum text box. The code for this command button is shown in VB Code Box 3-4.

VB CODE BOX 3-4. Code for cmdClear command button	``` Private Sub cmdClear_Click() txtFirstNum.Text = "" txtSecondNum.Text = "" txtSum.Text = "" txtFirst.Setfocus 'Set focus back to first text box End Sub ```

> **TIP:** The null string ("") does *not* contain any spaces between the pair of quotation marks.

If 20 and 30 are entered in the top two text boxes of the Calculator project and Sum is clicked, the result is shown in Figure 3-5. If the Clear button is then clicked, all three text boxes will be cleared and the focus will be set back to the top text box.

FIGURE 3-5.
Running the simple calculator

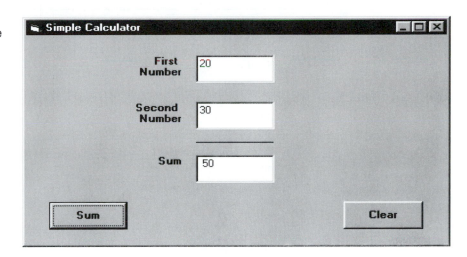

Four-Step Coding Process

Virtually all coding for Visual Basic projects follows this form: Input data, process it, and output the results. To write this code, you should use a four-step coding process to carry out these operations. The four steps are as follows:

1. Decide what variables and constants will be needed and declare them.

2. Input data from text boxes or other input controls (to be discussed later).

3. Process data into information using arithmetic or string operations and store in variables.

4. Output values of variables to text boxes or other output controls.

For the Simple Calculator, three variables (intFirst, intSecond, and intSum) are needed, so they should be declared. Next, the values for the intFirst and intSecond variables are input from text boxes. Third, these two variables are processed by summing them. Finally, the result of this processing is output to another text box. Obviously, all of these operations come *after* the logic for the problem has been developed using IPO Tables and pseudocode.

Mini-Summary 3-2: Event-driven input

1. Input in a Visual Basic program is often event-driven. A value is entered into a text box and then transferred to a variable with an event such as clicking a command button.

2. An assignment statement is used to transfer the contents of the text box to a variable and to make arithmetic calculations with the variables.

3. The Val() function is used to convert the string contents of the text box to a numeric variable. The Str() function converts numeric variables into strings for storage in text boxes.

4. Control properties can be used in assignment statements, but control methods cannot.

Mini-Summary 3-2: Event-driven input (Continued)

5. Text boxes may be cleared by setting equal to a null or empty string. The SetFocus method positions the cursor in a text box.

6. A four-step coding process should be used to write programs in Visual Basic.

It's Your Turn!

1. Assume the following variable declarations have been made:

Dim intN As Integer
Dim sngPi As Single
Dim sngAlpha As Single

Determine which of the following are valid Visual Basic assignment statements. If they are not valid explain why they are not.

a. sngPi = 3.141592
b. intN +1 = intN
c. sngAlpha = 1
d. sngAlpha = sngAlpha
e. 3 = intN
f. intN = intN + 1
g. intN = "Five"

2. For each of the following, what is the value displayed in txtAnswer after the code completes execution?

```
a.    Private Sub cmdCalculate_Click()
          Dim intFirst As Integer
          Dim intSecond As Integer
          Dim intAnswer As Integer
          intFirst = 5
          intSecond = 3
          intAnswer = intFirst + intSecond
          txtAnswer.Text = intAnswer
      End Sub

b.    Private Sub cmdCalculate_Click()
          txtR.Text = Str(0.07)
          txtS.Text = Str(4.5)
          txtAnswer.Text= Str(Val(txtR.Text) + Val(txtS.Text))
      End Sub

c.    Private Sub cmdCalculate_Click()
          Dim intA As Integer
          Dim intB As Integer
          Dim intAnswer As Integer
          intAnswer = intA + intB
          txtAnswer.Text = ""
      End Sub
```

3. Explain what is wrong with the following statement:

```
txtName.Setfocus = On
```

Completing the remaining questions will enable you to create the Visual Basic project discussed in the text.

4. Start Visual Basic and open a new standard EXE form. Change the Caption property of the form to **Simple Calculator** and change the Name property of the form to **frmSimple**.

5. Add three text boxes, three corresponding labels, and the line control as shown in Figure 3-3. (You will need to *draw* the line control to position it correctly.) Change the font for the labels to **10 point bold**.

6. Add command buttons in the lower lefthand and righthand areas of the form. Use the names and captions (where appropriate) shown in Table 3-3 for the controls on this form.

7. Open the Code window for the **cmdSum** command button and enter the code shown in VB Code Box 3-3.

8. Open the Code window for the **cmdClear** command button and enter the code shown in VB Code Box 3-4. Change the font for both command buttons to be **10 point bold**.

9. Close the Code window and click the **VCR Run** button. Enter **20** in the top text box and **30** in the second text box. Click the **Sum** command button. Your result should look like Figure 3-5. Now click the **Clear** command button to clear all text boxes and set the focus back to the top text box. Test your project with a few other combinations of Integers, both positive and negative. When these are completed, click the **VCR Stop** button.

10. Create a new folder called **Simple** in the Chapter3 folder on your data disk. Save the project with a form filename of **simple.frm** and a project name of **simple.vbp** in this new folder.

11. Experiment with the use of the Text property by adding a new command button with a Caption of **Test** and a Name of **cmdTest**. The Code window for this command button should have only one line:

txtSum.Text = txtFirstNum.Text + txtSecondNum.Text

12. Run the project again with values of **20** and **30**. Click the **Test** command button. What happens? Note that the two numbers have been concatenated rather than being summed. Exit Visual Basic without saving the revised version of this project.

USING ASSIGNMENT STATEMENTS FOR CALCULATIONS

Now that you have seen and used assignment statements to transfer input and output to and from text boxes and to carry out a simple calculation, you are ready to consider more complex uses of assignment statements. However, in all cases, the same idea as before applies; that is, you always have the variable or control property on the left side of the equal sign and a value, variable, expression, or Control property on the right side. While the term *expression* in our discussion of assignment statements is a common one in algebra, it needs to be defined for programming: An **expression** is *a combination of two or more variables and/or constants with operators*. We already saw one example of an expression when we summed the two variables in the Simple Calculator, that is, intFirst + intSecond. In this discussion, we will cover numerous other situations involving expressions.

To understand our definition of an expression, we need to understand two new terms in it: constants and operators. A **constant** is a quantity that does not change. Numbers are constants, as are strings enclosed in quotation marks. For example, 73 and –0.453 are numeric constants and "Visual Basic" is a string constant. Constants are used frequently in expressions when the same value applies to all situations. For example, the circumference of a circle is always 3.14157 times the diameter of the circle (where 3.14157 represents Pi). In this case, 3.14157 is a constant in the expression.

Operators are symbols used for carrying out processing. The plus sign we used in the Simple Calculator example is an operator. There are four types of operators: arithmetic, concatenation, comparison, and logical. Arithmetic operators are used to carry out arithmetic calculations. Concatenation operators are used to combine String variables and constants. Comparison operators are used to compare variables and constants. Finally, logical operators are used for logical operations. For the time being, we will concentrate on the arithmetic operators shown in Table 3-4.

You should already be familiar with all of these operations, with the possible exception of integer division and the use of the Modulus operator. Integer division is differentiated from standard division in that with integer division both the divisor and the dividend are rounded to integers and the quotient is truncated to an integer. For example, if A = 7.111 and B = 1.95, then A\B will result in 7.111 being rounded to 7, B being rounded to 2, and the quotient of 7 divided by 2 will be truncated to 3. As a result, 7.111\1.95 yields an integer value of 3.

The Modulus operation finds the integer remainder that results from integer division of the two operands. For example, if we use the same two values of A and B as above, A MOD B will yield a value of 1 (7.111\1.95 = 7\2 = 3 with remainder of 1)

We can construct arithmetic expressions by combining variables, constants, and arithmetic operators. Examples of valid arithmetic expressions in assignment statements are shown in Table 3-5.

TABLE 3-4: Arithmetic Operators

Operator	Function	Example	Result
( )	Grouping	(A+B)	Groups summation operation
^	Exponentiation	Radius^2	Squares Radius
–	Negation	–Amount	Changes sign of Amount
*	Multiplication	3*Price	Multiplies Price by 3
/	Division	PayRaise/Months	Divides PayRaise by Months
\	Integer Division	Number\3	Performs integer division of Number by 3
Mod	Modulus	15 Mod 2	Remainder from dividing 15 by 2
+	Addition	Price + Taxes	Sums Price and Taxes
–	Subtraction	Salary – Deductions	Subtracts Deductions from Salary

All of the examples in Table 3-5 should be clear, with the possible exception of the examples involving the variable intCounter. In these two examples, we first *initialize*

TABLE 3-5: Examples of Valid Expressions in Assignment Statements

Expression	Result
curTakeHome = curSalary – curTaxes – curDeductions	TakeHome value is equal to Salary minus Taxes and Deductions.
curInterest = curPrincipal * sngInterestRate	Interest value is equal to Principal times Interest Rate.
sngArea = 3.14157*sngRadius^2	Value of Pi is multiplied by Radius squared to compute area of a circle.
curUnitCost = curTotalCost/intUnits	Unit Cost is equal to Total Cost divided by number of Units.
intRoundUp = intBig\intLittle + intBig Mod intLittle	The remainder of integer division of Big by Little (Big Mod Little) is added to the result of integer division of Big by Little to compute the Roundup value.
intCounter = 0	The variable Counter is set equal to zero.
intCounter = intCounter + 1	The variable Counter is set equal to *old* value of Counter plus 1.

the variable to zero and then increment it by one. These two instructions provide two key concepts to remember. First, you should never assume that the value of any variable is automatically zero or anything else. It may retain a value from a previous use, so any variable that will appear later should always be initialized on the *right* side of an assignment statement.

Second, whenever the same variable appears on both sides of an assignment statement, the value of a variable on the *right* side of the equals sign is the *current value* of that variable and the value of the variable on the *left* side of the equals sign is the *new value* of the variable. Having two different values of the same variable in the same assignment statement does not confuse the computer, because it makes any needed calculations on the right side of the equals sign using current values. It then takes the resulting value and places it in the variable on the left side of the equals sign. This way there is no confusion between old and new values of the same variable.

At this point, we need to consider a major syntax error that can occur when in the use of an assignment statement: An expression can never appear on the left side of the equals sign. For example, an *invalid* assignment statement is:

```
X + Y = Z + Q
```

Note that the expression consisting of two variables and an operator on the left of the equals sign violates the rule about expressions on the left side of the equals sign.

The Hierarchy of Operations

An important question may come to mind when you're using arithmetic operators: In what order will the operators be used? For example, consider the following expression in an assignment statement:

```
Cost = F + V*D + S*D^2
```

Note that there are two summations, two multiplications, and an exponentiation operation. The order in which these operations are carried out will determine the value of the expression, which in turn will be assigned to the variable, Cost, on the left side of the equals sign. However, there is no ambiguity about the order of arithmetic operations in this or any expression on the right side of an assignment statement, because the hierarchy of operations will control the order in which the operations are performed. For Visual Basic, the **Hierarchy of Operations** is:

1. Parentheses
2. Raising to a power
3. Change of sign (negation)
4. Multiplication or division
5. Integer division
6. Modulus
7. Addition or subtraction

Note that the arithmetic operators were listed in Table 3-4 in the same order as the hierarchy of operations. In case of a tie, work from left to right.

Returning to our example, since there are no parentheses in the expression F + V*D + S*D^2, according to the hierarchy of operations the arithmetic operations will carried out in the following order:

1. D will be raised to the second power.
2. V will then be multiplied by D, and S will be multiplied by D-squared.
3. F and the two products found in Operation 2 will be summed.

If F = 100, V = 200, D = 30, and S = 2, this expression will be evaluated as follows:

1. D^2 = 900
2. V*D = 6,000 and S*D^2 = 1,800
3. F + V*D + S*D^2 = 100 + 6000 + 1,800 = 7,900

and the variable Cost will be equal to 7,900.

You should be aware that parentheses can have a dramatic effect on the result of evaluating an expression. For example, consider the same expression as before but with parentheses around F + V; that is, the assignment statement is now:

Cost = (F + V)*D + S*D^2

In this case, F and V will be summed before being multiplied by D, yielding a result that is very different from the one we got before. Using the same values as before, we now have:

1. F + V = 300
2. D^2 = 900
3. (F + V)*D = 9,000 and S*D^2 = 1,800
4. 9,000 + 1,800 = 10,800

and Cost equals 10,800 instead of 7,900.

String Operators

For String variables and constants, the only valid operation is that of combining two strings into one. This operation, which is performed using the plus sign (+) or the ampersand (&), has the effect of adding the second String variable or constant to the end of the first. For example, if we have the assignment statement strBigDay = "May" + " Day" (or "May" & " Day"), the result is that strBigDay is now equal to "May Day." None of the other operators has any meaning for operations with strings.

> **TIP:** While both the ampersand (&) and plus (+) symbols do the same thing when combining strings, they work differently when used with numeric values. This may cause some confusion if you wish to concatenate two numeric values. It may be best to use the ampersand (&) only for concatenation.

Symbolic Constants

In creating an application in Visual Basic or any other language, you never work entirely with variables only. Often you are working with constants in expressions or by themselves. While it is possible to use the actual Numeric constant or String constant (enclosed in quotation marks), if a quantity is not going to change in your project it is advisable to give this quantity a name and data type just like you do for variables. For example, if you are working with an interest rate that is going to remain the same throughout your program at say, 0.07, you might want to give this value a name of sng-IntRate, define it as a Single data type, and use it, rather than the actual value, in your processing. If you decide at a later time that you want to change the interest rate from its current value, you simply change it at the point in your project where you have named it. The same rules and conventions apply to names for constants as apply to names for variables. Named constants are often referred to as **symbolic constants** since you are using a symbolic name for the actual value or string.

Assigning a name to a constant is usually done at the beginning of an event procedure—even before you declare variables. The form of the constant definition statement is:

Const *constant name* as *variable type* = *value or expression*

where you supply both the constant name and value portions of the statement. For example, to create a symbolic constant called IntRate with a value of 0.07, the statement would be:

```
Const sngIntRate as Single = 0.07
```

and if you also wanted to define a constant for the number of years in the investment as being 12, the statement would be:

```
Const intNumYears as Integer = 12
```

As with declaring variables, it is possible to define more than one symbolic constant on a line by separating them with commas. For example, the two constant definitions shown above could be combined as:

```
Const sngIntRate as Single = 0.07,intNumYears as Integer = 12
```

Mini-Summary 3-3: Using assignment statements for calculations

1. Assignment statements are used for calculations by setting variables equal to expressions where an expression is a combination of variables, constants, and operators.

2. Arithmetic operators include grouping, exponentiation, negation, multiplication, division, integer division, modulus, addition, and subtraction. The Hierarchy of Operations controls the order in which these operations are carried out.

3. String operators include the plus sign and ampersand for concatenation.

4. Symbolic constants can be defined at the beginning of the program to store values that will not change during the program.

It's Your Turn!

1. Write appropriate assignment statements for the following situations:

   a. The total cost for the sale of multiple items is the unit price times the number of units sold.

   b. The net sales price after applying a discount is equal to the gross sales price times (1 − discount rate). For example, if the gross price is $500 and the discount rate is 0.15, the net price is equal to 500 x (1 − 0.15).

   c. The value of an amount of money some number of years in the future is equal to the amount of money times (1 + rate of return) raised to the number-of-years power. For example, if the amount of money is $1,000, the rate of return is 0.12, and the number of years is 5, the future value is equal to 1000 x $(1+.12)^5$.

   d. The depreciated value of a piece of machinery using straight line depreciation is equal to the original value minus the depreciation, where the depreciation is equal to the original value divided by the life of the machinery times the number of years since it was put into service.

   e. The amount due for a sale is equal to the sales price times (1 + tax rate).

2. Evaluate the following expressions to determine the value assigned to the variable on the left of the equals sign.

   a.   Y = 3^2*4–1*2+3
   b.   X = 3^(2*4)–1*(2+3)
   c.   sngAverage = ((70 + 80)/2 + 65)/2
   d.   strState = "New York"
        strCity = strState & " City"

3. Declare constants for the following values:

   a. Pi (3.14157)
   b. The exchange rate between British Pounds and U.S. Dollars (1.62)
   c. The number of feet in a mile (5,280)

4. Given that sngTwo = 2.0, sngThree = 3.0, sngFour = 4.0, intNum = 8, and intMix = 5 and that the appropriate variable declarations have been made, find the value assigned to the given variable for each of the following.

```
a. sngW = (sngTwo + sngThree) ^ sngThree
b. sngX = (sngThree + sngTwo / sngFour) ^ 2
c. sngY = intNum / intMix + 5.1
d. intZ = intNum / intMix + 5.1
```

5. Write variable declaration statements and assignment statements for the following that calculates the given expression and assigns the results to the specified value.

   a. Rate times Time to DIST

   b. Square root of (A^2+B^2) to C

   c. 1/(1/R1 + 1/R2 + 1/R3) to Resist

   d. P times $(1+R)^N$ to Value

   e. Area of triangle (one-half base times height) of base B and height H to Area

APPLICATION TO SCENARIO

So far you have learned about text boxes, assignment statements, and expressions. We are now ready to apply them to the Vintage Videos scenario using the six-step development process presented in Chapter 1; that is, define problem, create interface, develop logic for action objects, write and test code for action objects, test overall project, and document project in writing.

Define Problem

Recall that the video shop owner wants to extend the project created in Chapter 2 to input the renter's name, the video rented, and the price for the video and then use this information to calculate the taxes due on the rental price and add these taxes to the rental price to compute the amount due. He also wants to have a way of printing the result of the computations, clearing the text boxes, and exiting the project. To ensure that we understand his request, we need to sketch the interface. In this case, this involves adding additional features to the sketch created in Chapter 2 (Figure 2-8). The resulting sketch is shown in Figure 3-6.

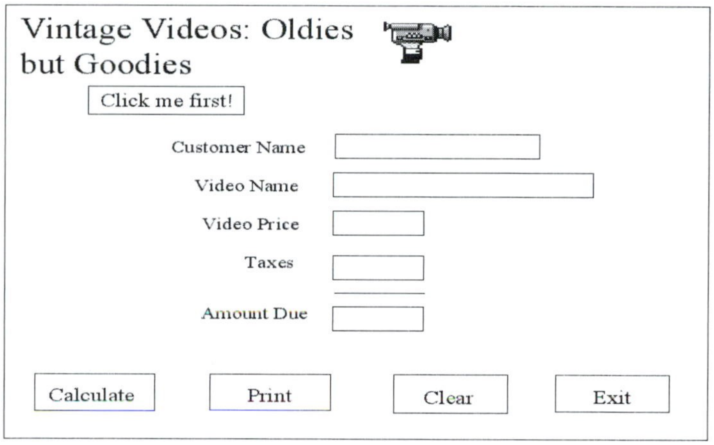

FIGURE 3-6.
Revised Vintage Videos sketch

Create Interface

Note that, in the sketch in Figure 3-6, that five text boxes for input and output and five corresponding labels have been added to the form along with a line control to separate the amount due text box from the others. Four additional command buttons—to calculate the taxes and amount due, to print the form contents, to clear the text boxes, and to exit the project—are required in addition to the existing command button that displays a welcoming message. No other controls are required for this project.

If you retrieve the Vintage3.vbp project from the Chapter3 folder, you can add the required controls from the Toolbox and modify their properties to create an interface that matches the sketch. The resulting form is shown in Figure 3-7, with the pertinent properties for the new controls shown in Table 3-6. Note that the Font property is set at 8 points with Bold style for the new labels and at 10 points with Bold style for the new command buttons.

Develop Logic for Action Objects

On the revised Vintage Videos form, there are four new action objects: the Calculate, Print, Clear, and Exit command buttons. Of these, the Calculate command button is the only one that involves input, processing, and output. As such, it is the only object for which we need to develop the logic using an IPO Table and pseudocode. The Clear

FIGURE 3-7.
Expanded interface
for Vintage Videos

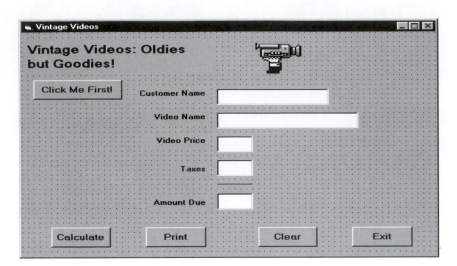

TABLE 3-6: New Controls for Vintage Videos Application

Control	Name	Caption
text box	txtCustName	not applicable
text box	txtVideoName	not applicable
text box	txtVideoPrice	not applicable
text box	txtTaxes	not applicable
text box	txtAmountDue	not applicable
label	lblCustName	Customer Name
label	lblVideoName	Video Name
label	lblVideoPrice	Video Price
label	lblTaxes	Taxes
label	lblAmountDue	Amount Due
line	linSeparator	none
command button	cmdCalc	Calculate
command button	cmdPrint	Print
command button	cmdClear	Clear
command button	cmdExit	Exit

> **TIP:** The order in which you add text boxes to the form controls the order that the cursor will follow when the **Tab** key is pressed. If the order is incorrect, you can change it in the Properties window with the **TabIndex** property of the text box. Make the TabIndex property for the first text box = 0, the second = 1, and so on.

button clears the text boxes and sets the focus back to the Customer Name text box. The Print and Exit buttons involve only single instructions to print and exit the application.

Input to the cmdCalc command button includes the customer name, video name, and video price. Processing includes computing the tax on the video price and adding it to the video price to determine the total amount due. Output should include the tax and the total amount due. The IPO Table for the Calculation command button is shown in Figure 3-8.

FIGURE 3-8. IPO Table for Calculate button

Input	Processing	Output
customer name video name video price	taxes = price times tax rate amount due = price + taxes due	taxes amount

The pseudocode for the Calculate command button shown below converts the IPO into structured English. Note that there is no mention of text boxes in the input and output statements in the pseudocode, because the pseudocode is intended to present the logic of the operation with no concern for the details.

```
Begin Procedure Calculate
    Input customer name
    Input video name
    Input video price
    Taxes = video price times tax rate
    Amount due = video price + taxes
    Output taxes
    Output amount due
End procedure
```

Write and Test Code   As noted earlier, there are four new action objects for which we need to write code: the click events for the Calculation, Clear, Print, and Exit command buttons. The code for the Calculation command button should follow the pseudocode, except that it uses text boxes for input and output. If we apply the four-step process for writing code to this problem, the resulting code is as shown in VB Code Box 3-5.

VB CODE BOX 3-5. Code for Calculate button

```
Private Sub cmdCalc_Click()
    Const sngTaxRate as Single = 0.07 'Use local tax rate
    Dim curPrice As Currency, curAmountDue As Currency
    Dim curTaxes As Currency
    curPrice = CCur(txtVideoPrice.Text)
    curTaxes = curPrice * sngTaxRate
    curAmountDue = curPrice + curTaxes
    txtTaxes.Text = Str(curTaxes)
    txtAmountdue.Text = Str(curAmountDue)
End Sub
```

Note in the code that a symbolic constant, sngTaxRate, is declared to be equal to the local sales tax rate (0.07). If the sales tax rate changes or the application is used in another jurisdiction, we can easily change the sales tax rate by changing this statement. Since the tax rate does not normally change from use to use, we declare it as a constant rather than inputting it for each use. Note also that the variables are declared as Currency rather than Single, since the values stored in them will be in dollars and cents. Also, the CCur function is used to convert between the String data type and the Currency date type, and the Str() function is used in the other direction. Some of the more commonly used conversion functions are shown in Table 3-7.

TABLE 3-7: Commonly Used Conversion Functions

Conversion Function	Purpose
CBool	Converts argument to Boolean data type
CCur	Converts argument to Currency data type
CDate	Converts argument to Date data type
CInt	Converts argument to Integer data type
CSng	Converts argument to Single data type
CDbl	Converts argument to Double data type

> **TIP:** While the Val( ) function is useful in converting user inputted strings to numbers, it may be best to avoid it in favor of the functions shown in Table 3-7 since they provide specific conversions.

Note that in VB Code Box 3-5 we have also added a **comment** to the statement defining the tax rate by beginning it with apostrophes. Comments are a form of **internal documentation** that is used to explain part of a program. Comments can be on a line by themselves or added to the end of another statement as was done here. Comments are displayed in green on the screen to distinguish them from executable code. Any text begun with an apostrophe or the keyword *Rem* is ignored by the computer and is there for explanation purposes only. You should include comments in your code wherever it will help explain the purpose of the program or a specific statement. As we noted in Chapter 1, since we explain all code in the text, we will add comments here only to explain code that might otherwise be misunderstood. Your instructor may want you to add more comments, and, almost certainly, if you do any coding in your professional life, comments will be *required*.

Figure 3-9 shows an example of running the project with sample data (Customer Name = *George Burdell*, Video Name = *Spartacus*, and Video Price = *2.99*) and clicking the Calculate command button. The resulting Taxes value is 0.2093 and the Amount Due is 2.1993.

Formatting Output   Note that the values output in the Taxes and Amount Due text boxes are shown not as dollars and cents but with four decimal places. To control the form of the numeric items or dates in output, we need to use the **Format(*expression, format*)** function. In this function, *expression* is any valid expression that is to be formatted and *format* is a

FIGURE 3-9. Vintage
Videos application

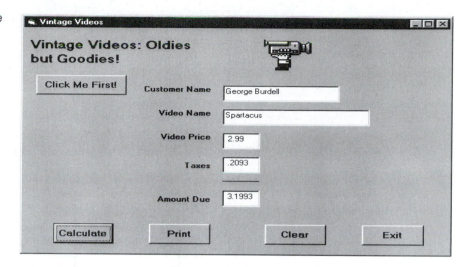

valid **format expression**. The more commonly used Numeric format expressions are shown in Table 3-8, where each format expression is enclosed in quotation marks in the Format function. For example, to format a number as currency with two decimal places, the format expression would be "currency"; to format it as percent, the expression would be "percent."

> **TIP:** If you do not include the format expression, the Format( ) function will return the same result as the Str( ) function.

TABLE 3-8: Numeric Format Expressions

Format Expression	Result
Currency	Display number with dollar sign, thousands separator, and two digits to the right of the decimal point.
Fixed	Display number with at least one digit to the left and two digits to the right of the decimal point.
Standard	Display number with thousands separator and at least one digit to the left and two digits to the right of the decimal point.
Percent	Display number multiplied by 100 with a percent sign (%) on the right and two digits to the right of the decimal point.
Scientific	Use standard scientific notation.

In the Vintage Videos project, we will format the txtTaxes text box as currency by replacing the statement involving the Str( ) function with a statement using the Format( ) function, as shown below:

```
txtTaxes = Format(curTaxes, "currency")
```

Similarly, to format the txtAmountDue text box as currency, the statement would be:

```
txtAmountDue = Format(curAmountDue, "currency")
```

It is also possible to format the values in the input text boxes using the Format function by including the same text box on the left side of the assignment statement and on the right side in the Format function. For example, to format the contents of the txtVideoPrice as currency, the statement might be:

```
txtVideoPrice.Text = Format(txtVideoPrice.Text,"currency")
```

If we replace the two statements in the cmdCalc command button Code window that use the Str( ) function with statements that use the Format( ) function and we then add a statement that formats the txtVideoPrice text box, the final code for this object will appear as shown in VB Code Box 3-6. If we run the revised project with the same sample data as before, the new result will be as shown in Figure 3-10. Note that all monetary values are now shown as currency.

VB CODE BOX 3-6. Code to compute and display taxes and amount due	``` Private Sub cmdCalc_Click() Const sngTaxRate as Single = 0.07 'Use local tax rate Dim curPrice As Currency, curAmountDue As Currency Dim curTaxes As Currency curPrice = CCur(txtVideoPrice.Text) curTaxes = curPrice * sngTaxRate 'Compute taxes curAmountDue = curPrice + curTaxes 'Compute amount due txtTaxes.Text = Format(curTaxes, "Currency") txtAmountDue.Text = Format(curAmountDue, "Currency") txtVideoPrice.Text = Format(curPrice, "Currency") End Sub ```

FIGURE 3-10. Result of running revised project

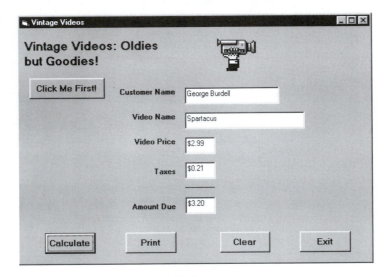

Mini-Summary 3-4: Developing the Vintage Videos Application

1. The Vintage Videos application can be developed using the six-step process discussed in Chapter 1. The code is written using the four-step process discussed earlier in this chapter.

2. IPO Tables and pseudocode are useful for developing the logic of the code.

3. In addition to the Val function, there are a number of other conversion functions that convert string data to a specific numeric data type.

4. To control the form of output, the Format function should be used with a variety of format expressions.

It's Your Turn!

1. Describe what appears in the txtAnswer textbox after each of the following is executed. If you are not sure, create a form and write the code in Visual Basic to find out.

```
a. Private Sub cmdCalculate_Click()
     Dim sngValue As Single
     sngValue = 56.789
     txtAnswer.Text = Format(sngValue, "currency")
   End Sub
```

```
b. Private Sub cmdCalculate_Click()
     Dim sngValue As Single
     sngValue = 456.7891
     txtAnswer.Text = Format(sngValue, "fixed")
   End Sub
```

```
c. Private Sub cmdCalculate_Click()
     Dim sngValue As Single
     sngValue = 65.432
     txtAnswer.Text = Format(sngValue, "standard")
   End Sub
```

```
d. Private Sub cmdCalculate_Click()
     Dim sngValue As Single
     sngValue = 1.543
     txtAnswer.Text = Format(sngValue, "percent")
   End Sub
```

```
e. Private Sub cmdCalculate_Click()
     Dim sngValue As Single
     sngValue = 0.00235
     txtAnswer.Text = Format(sngValue, "scientific")
   End Sub
```

2. Describe what appears in the txtAnswer textbox after each of the following is executed. If you are not sure, create a form and write the code in Visual Basic to find out.

```
a. Private Sub cmdCalculate_Click()
     Dim sngValue As Single
     sngValue = 0
     txtAnswer.Text = CBool(sngValue)
   End Sub
```

```
b. Private Sub cmdCalculate_Click()
     Dim sngValue As Single
     sngValue = 3.6
     txtAnswer.Text = CInt(sngValue)
   End Sub
```

```
c. Private Sub cmdCalculate_Click()
     Dim sngValue As Single
     sngValue = 36038
     txtAnswer.Text = CDate(sngValue)
   End Sub
```

Completing the remaining questions will enable you to create the Visual Basic project discussed in the text.

3. Retrieve the **Vintage3.vbp** project from your data disk and add the five text boxes, five labels, four command buttons, and one line control as shown in Figure 3-6.

4. Change the Name properties for all of the new controls to match those shown in Table 3-6. Delete the Text property for the text boxes and add the appropriate captions to the label and command button controls. Your resulting form should look like that shown in Figure 3-7.

5. Add the code shown in VB Code Box 3-5 to the Code window for the Click event for the cmdCalc command button. Add the End statement to the Code window for the Click event for the cmdExit command button.

6. Run the project and test the **Calculate** command button with the following sample data:

```
Customer Name: George Burdell
Video Name: Spartacus
Video Price: 2.99
```

The result should be the same as shown in Figure 3-9.

7. Change the data and test the Calculate button again. If the results are correct, terminate the project and go to the next exercise. If there is an error in the results, terminate the project and modify the code to correct the error.

8. Change the statements that use the Str( ) function to assign the output to the txtTaxes and txtAmountDue text boxes to use the Format( ) function with the Currency format expression. Also, Format the txtVideoPrice text box. Your code should be the same as that shown in VB Code Box 3-6. Run your project again with the same data as in Exercise 4. Your result should look like Figure 3-10.

9. Use the **Save** icon to save the form and project under the same names as before.

PRINTING THE FORM, CLEARING ENTRIES, AND EXITING

In addition to computing the taxes and amount due on a video rental, Ed, the video store owner, asked Clark to make it possible for users to print the results, clear the previous entries in preparation for the next customer, and exit the project.

Printing the results is very easy; it requires only one instruction: **PrintForm**. PrintForm is a method just like SetFocus is a method. The PrintForm method is an activity of a form that prints an exact image of the form using the Windows printer. The complete form of the PrintForm statement is:

formname.**PrintForm**

If no form name is given, the current form is printed.

If the PrintForm instruction is included in the code for the cmdPrint command button and the button is clicked for a transaction, the result will look exactly like the on-screen form, with a white background but without the title bar.

Clearing Entries

In preparation for the next customer, the owner of Vintage Videos wants to be able to clear the existing entries and to set the focus to the customer name text box. This means that the Text property of the text boxes must be set to an empty string, as was done with the Simple Calculator example, and the SetFocus method used with the txt-

CustName text box. The complete code for the cmdClear button is shown in VB Code Box 3-7. When the cmdClear is clicked, all text boxes are blanked out and the focus set to txtCustName.

Exiting the Project   The code for the Exit button is very simple; it consists of one word: **End**. This will cause the project to terminate, just as if you had clicked the VCR Stop button .

VB CODE BOX 3-7. Code to clear entries	`Private Sub cmdClear_Click()`
	`    txtCustName.Text = ""`
	`    txtVideoName.Text = ""`
	`    txtVideoPrice.Text = ""`
	`    txtTaxes.Text = ""`
	`    txtAmountDue.Text = ""`
	`    txtCustName.SetFocus`
	`End Sub`

Mini-Summary 3-5: Printing the form, clearing entries, and exiting

1. The contents of the form can be printed using the PrintForm command.

2. The application can be exited with the End command.

It's Your Turn!

1. Open the **Vintage3.vbp** project. Open the Code window for the Print command button and add the **PrintForm** instruction.

2. Open the Code window for the Clear command button and add the code shown in VB Code Box 3-7.

3. Run the project again with the previous customer and video. If you are connected to a printer, print the form. In any case, clear the entries and enter a customer name of **Sam Cassell**, a video name of ***Sands of Iwo Jima***, and a price of **$1.99**. Print the form and then clear the form. Add new data of your choosing and click Calculate again.

4. Exit the project and save the form and project under the same name.

MORE ON USING FUNCTIONS   You have already used four built-in functions—Val( ), Str( ), CCur( ), and Format( )—in creating the Simple Calculator and the Vintage Videos application, so you have some knowledge of their use. In addition to these four, there are many other built-in functions that serve a variety of useful purposes. There are built-in functions for converting data types, working with dates and time, performing financial operations, working with strings, and carrying out different mathematical operations. Examples of commonly used built-in functions are shown in Table 3-9. Check the online Help for others. You will probably recognize many of them from working with spreadsheet software.

As an example of using one of the financial functions, we will create an application that will determine the monthly payment necessary to repay a loan. In looking at Table 3-9, you can see that we will need to use the Pmt( ) function for this purpose. The Pmt function has the following form: **Pmt(*rate, nper, pv*),** where ***rate*** = the periodic interest rate as a decimal fraction, ***nper*** = the number of months over which the loan is to be repaid, and ***pv*** = the *negative* of the loan amount. For example, if you borrowed $10,000 at a 12% annual interest rate for five years, the appropriate form of the function would be: Pmt(.01, 60, –10000), where we have changed the 12% annual rate to a

TABLE 3-9: Visual Basic Functions

Function	Type	Purpose
Abs	Mathematical	Returns absolute value of a number
Sqr	Mathematical	Returns square root of a positive number
FV	Financial	Returns future value of an annuity
PV	Financial	Returns present value of an annuity
IRR	Financial	Returns internal rate of return
Pmt	Financial	Returns periodic payment to pay off a loan
UCase/LCase	String	Converts a string to all upper/lower case
Len	String	Returns length of string
Date	Date/Time	Returns date on computer system clock
Datevalue	Date/Time	Returns date for string argument

1% (0.01) monthly rate and have converted the number of years to 60 months. It is important that the interest rate and the number of months match.

> **TIP:** Always be sure to understand completely how a function should be used, what parameters are required or optional and what it returns before using it in your code. Functions with similar names do not necessarily operate in the same way.

Creating the Interface   To create the interface to compute the monthly payment required to repay a loan, we need to add the three input text boxes for the amount of the loan, the duration of the loan in months, and the interest rate as a percentage. We will also need an output text box for the monthly payment and two command buttons, one to compute the monthly payment and one to exit the project. We will assign names to the text boxes that correspond to the data to be displayed there, that is, *txtAmount, txtMonths, txtRate,* and *txtPayment.* The labels will be given similar names. At the top of the form there should be a large label named *lblHeading,* which should have a Font property of 14-point Bold. The txtPayment text box should have the same font property. The two command buttons should be named *cmdCompute* and *cmdExit,* with Bold Font properties for their captions. The resulting form is shown in Figure 3-11.

Note that we have added a label with a percentage symbol after the txtRate text box. Doing this will allow us to enter the interest rate as a whole number without for-

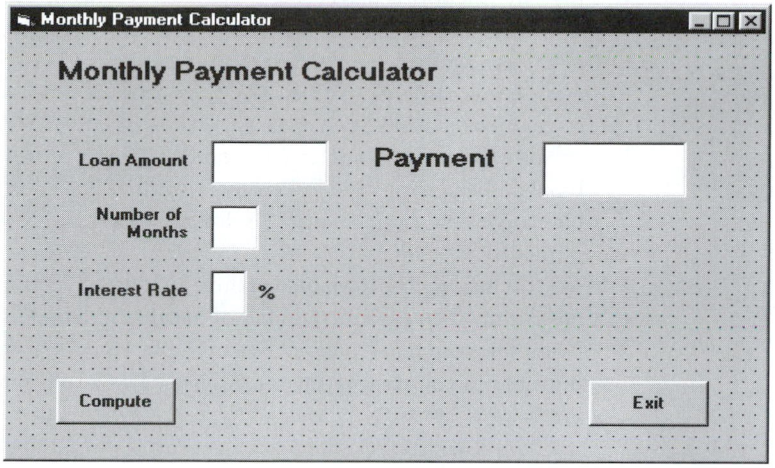

FIGURE 3-11.
Interface for
Payment Calculator

matting it. We do this because formatting a number as a percent precludes using it later in calculations.

*Computing the
Monthly Payment*

For this project, we need to develop the logic for only one action object—*cmdCompute.* For this control, the input includes the loan amount, number of months, and interest rate. The processing involves using the Pmt function to generate the required monthly payment, which is then output. Since this is so straightforward, we will dispense with the IPO Table and pseudocode for this situation.

For the cmdCompute command button, the code to compute the monthly payment is very simple: Transfer the contents of the three text boxes to variables, use the variables in the Pmt( ) function to determine a payment value, transfer the result of the payment value to the txtPayment text box, and format all text boxes appropriately. For the interest rate, we need to convert the contents of the txtRate textbox to a Single data type variable and divide it by 100 to convert it to a decimal fraction. We then have to divide the result by 12 to convert it into a *monthly* interest rate. With the CSng() conversion function, this can be done in one statement (where Rate is the variable):

```
sngRate = (CSng(txtRate.Text)/100)/12
```

The code for the cmdCompute command button is shown in VB Code Box 3-8.

VB CODE BOX 3-8. Code to compute monthly payment	```Private Sub cmdCompute_Click()```

```
Private Sub cmdCompute_Click()
    Dim curAmount As Currency, intMonths As Integer
    Dim sngRate As Single
    Dim curPayment As Currency
    curAmount = CCur(txtAmount.Text)
    intMonths = CInt(txtMonths.Text)
    sngRate = (CSng(txtRate.Text) / 100) / 12
    curPayment = Pmt(sngRate, intMonths, -curAmount)
    txtPayment.Text = Format(curPayment, "Currency")
    txtAmount.Text = Format(curAmount, "Currency")
End Sub
```

Several things are of note in VB Code Box 3-8. First, as in the Vintage Videos application, we declare the curAmount and curPayment variables to be Currency instead of Single. intMonths is declared to be Integer and sngRate to be Single since they are not dollars and cents. Second, we use the CCur( ), CInt( ), and CSng( ) conversion functions instead of the Val( ) function. Finally, we have formatted the contents of the txtAmount and txtPayment text boxes as Currency. However, we have not formatted the contents of the txtRate text box since we want it to remain as an *annual* interest rate instead of being displayed as a monthly interest rate. As mentioned earlier, because of the way the Percent Numeric format expression works, if the txtRate text box had been formatted as Percent *before* the calculation, it would *not* have been possible to convert the formatted result back to a numeric value and use it in the calculation.

To test the cmdCompute command button, we will run the project and enter values for the loan amount, number of months, and interest rate, and then click the cmd-Compute command button. For example, for a loan of $3,000 for 36 months at 8 percent, the monthly payment is $256.03. The result of using this data is shown in Figure 3-12.

FIGURE 3-12.
Monthly Payment
Calculator

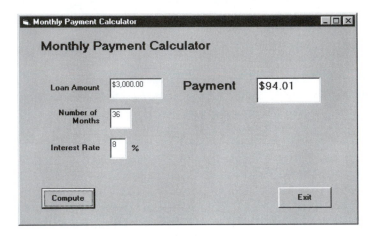

Mini-Summary 3-6: More on using functions

1. In addition to the conversion functions (CInt, CStr, and so on), there are many other functions.

2. These include scientific, mathematical, financial, string, and date/time functions.

3. The Pmt function is useful for computing the monthly payment on a loan amount.

It's Your Turn!

1. Describe what is displayed in the text box after the following assignment statements are executed.

```
a. txtAnswer.Text = Abs(-3)

b. txtAnswer.Text = Sqr(25)

c. txtAnswer.Text = UCase("VB is fun")

d. txtAnswer.Text = Len("VB is fun")

e. txtAnswer.Text = Sqr(Len("four"))
```

Completing the remaining questions will enable you to create the Visual Basic project discussed in the text.

2. Use **File | New Project** to start a new project. For this project, add the controls shown in Figure 3-11 with the names and properties shown in Table 3-10.

TABLE 3-10: Information for Exercise 1

Control	Name	Caption	Font/Other
Form	frmMonthPay	Monthly Payment Calculator	
Label	lblHeading	Monthly Payment Calculator	14-point Bold
Label	lblLoanAmt	Loan Amount	Bold
Label	lblNumMonths	Number of Months	Bold
Label	lblIntRate	Interest Rate	Bold
Label	lblPercentSign	%	Bold
Label	lblPayment	Payment	14-point Bold
Text Box	txtAmount	N/A	
Text Box	txtMonths	N/A	
Text Box	txtRate	N/A	
Text Box	txtPayment	N/A	14-point Bold
Command Button	cmdCompute	Compute	Bold
Command Button	cmdExit	Exit	Bold

3. Open the Code window for the cmdCompute command button and add the code shown in VB Code Box 3-8. Also, add the code for the cmdExit command button.

4. Test your project for a loan amount of **$3,000** for **36** months at **8**% interest rate. The results should look like that shown in Figure 3-12. Test it also for a loan amount of **$10,000** for **60** months at **7.3**%. If your project runs correctly, save the form in a folder called **MonthPay** as **MonthPay.frm** and the project as **MonthPay.vbp** within the **Chapter3** folder on your data disk. If there are errors, correct them and then save it.

ERRORS IN VISUAL BASIC

In creating the three projects discussed in this chapter, you may have encountered an error message from Visual Basic, or, worse than that, you received no message but your project failed to run correctly. Ideally, in either of those cases, you were able to find your error by comparing your work to the descriptions in the text. Unfortunately, when you begin creating projects with no explicit instructions to follow, you are likely to run into a variety of errors, or as they are commonly known in the programming community, **bugs**. (There is an apocryphal story about the source of this term, which we won't bore you with here!)

Finding errors is a very important part of program development that often takes as long as all the other steps combined, even when special testing software is used to detect errors. Writing bug-free software is inherently difficult, because the logic supporting the program is inflexible. In most engineering projects, a margin of error is built into the design specifications, so a bridge, for example, usually will not collapse if an element is defective or fails. With computer software, on the other hand, *each* program instruction must be absolutely correct. Otherwise, the whole program may fail. This is a significant problem given the ever-increasing complexity of modern programs. For example, between 1983 and 1992, the average size of a typical application software package increased tenfold, from 100,000 lines of computer code to 1 million lines.

Other errors that can occur during execution include the incorrect use of data or the inadvertent request by the user that the computer perform a meaningless operation, for example, dividing by zero. The code for an object will execute until it encounters an error; then it will stop, display a message telling why it has abnormally terminated the program execution, and highlight the line of code that may be causing the error. If possible, test data that can test all portions of the code should be chosen. If this is not done, errors in any untested section of the project will not be discovered. If an error *is* detected, then the programmer must trace through both the logic of the code and the actual language statements to find it. If a logic error goes *undetected*, the results can be catastrophic.

In general, there are three types of errors that you may encounter in creating Visual Basic projects: syntax errors, run time errors, and logic errors. **Syntax errors** are usually caused by incorrect grammar, vocabulary, or usage. Using a keyword for a variable name, using a keyword incorrectly, and entering an assignment statement with an expression on the left of the equals sign are all examples of syntax errors. Fortunately, Visual Basic will catch almost all syntax errors when they are entered. For example, if you tried to use the Dim keyword twice in the same declaration statement, Visual Basic would immediately alert you to this error when you attempted to press **ENTER** at the end of the line, as shown in Figure 3-13. You would receive a similar error message if you tried to use a variable name beginning with a number or a variable name with a period embedded in it. Occasionally, Visual Basic will not catch your syntax error until you attempt to run the program, but the result is the same: You must correct the syntax before proceeding. The best way to avoid these errors is to adhere to the rules regarding variable names, use of keywords, and appropriate use of assignment statements and operators in expressions.

FIGURE 3-13.
Incorrect use of keyword

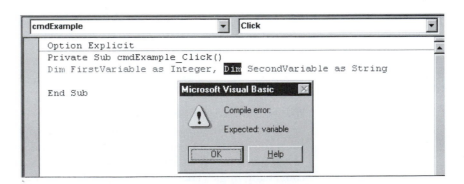

Run time errors occur when the program is running, and they are almost always associated with an error in programmer logic or input data. For example, if you have a project that requires a division operation and either the data or the logic requires a division by zero, a run time error will occur. When this occurs, Visual Basic will terminate the execution of the project and display the Code window with the line in which the error most likely occurred highlighted. At this point, you can correct the error if it involves a problem with the program statement, click the Run icon, and continue running the program. If the error is one of input (long experience has shown that a large percentage of all errors are errors of input), then you must terminate execution of the project and enter correct data. Even with Visual Basic's help, run time errors are more difficult to find and correct than syntax errors. For this reason, programmers will often include "error trapping" and input validation statements in the project to avoid run time errors. For example, a statement will be included that will test a divisor to determine if it is not equal to zero before it gets used in an expression.

> **TIP:** When error messages appear while you are testing your program, don't simply press End and ignore them. The message will provide valuable clues as to a problem in your code and possibly how to fix it. Selecting Debug will show the line in which your coding error first causes a problem.

Logic errors are errors that result from incorrect program design, and they usually are not caught until the program has been tested extensively or is already in use. The much-discussed Year 2000 bug is a good example of a logic error. This error was caused by the failure of designers of today's programs to consider the fact that the year 2000 would eventually arrive. Instead, the designers assumed that all date arithmetic could be handled by using just the last two digits of any year. For example, to determine the year a loan would mature, simply add the number of years for the term of the loan to the last two digits of the current year. When it is now 1998 and the term of the loan is, say, five years, you end up with a maturity of 03 causing confusion for the computer about whether this refers to 1903 or 2003. While using only the last two years of the date saved a great deal of disk space at a time when disk space was scarce, it is now causing a great deal of grief for those programmers who are charged with correcting the logic error.

Debugging Projects
Debugging is the art and science of finding run time and logic errors in computer programs. We don't include syntax errors in this search, because Visual Basic will find almost all of them for you. In debugging a project, you should start by testing each object as it is created, giving special attention to the input statements. Be sure to use test data that will check all possible options in an object; this will catch many of the errors. To help in this process, Visual Basic provides a group of debugging tools, which we will discuss in later chapters. Finally, when all else fails, ask someone else to look at your code. Many times fresh eyes can find errors that have evaded you for hours!

SUMMARY
In this chapter, we have discussed ways of carrying out two more of the six computer operations discussed in previous chapters: storing data in internal memory and carrying out arithmetic operations on that data. We also discussed ways of inputting that data and outputting the result of the processing. In terms of storing data in internal

---

Mini-Summary 3-7: Errors in Visual Basic

1. There are three major types of errors in Visual Basic: syntax errors, run time errors, and logic errors. Programming errors are commonly referred to as *bugs*.

2. Syntax errors are usually found immediately by Visual Basic. Run time errors are also often caught by Visual Basic when the program is running. However, logic errors are not found by Visual Basic and must be found by the programmer.

3. The process of finding and removing errors is referred to as *debugging*.

---

memory, we discussed the use of variables to represent data that are stored in internal memory and ways of declaring the data type for each variable. The importance of declaring variables was emphasized.

Event-driven input using text boxes and assignment statements was discussed next. In this type of input, the user enters data in a text box and then uses an event to transfer the data to a variable, which is then used in the processing step. The Str( ) and Val( ) functions were introduced as means of translating between the data type of the variables and the String format of the text boxes. For all functions, there can be multiple arguments but only one value returned.

Assignment statements for performing calculations were discussed, as was the use of arithmetic and string operators. The hierarchy of operations that controls the order in which arithmetic operations are carried out was also discussed. Symbolic constants were introduced as a method of using a name to represent a constant in a program.

In addition to the Val( ) and Str( ) functions, there are a variety of other conversion functions that can be used to convert string data to specific data types. Output can be formatted through the use of the Format( ) function. For formatting numbers there are a number of commonly used format expressions, including Currency, Fixed, Standard, Percent, and Scientific.

The PrintForm method can be used to print an image of the form. It is possible to clear text boxes by setting their Text property to an empty value (" ") and the text box SetFocus method can be used to position the cursor in a text box. The project can be exited through the use of the End command.

In addition to the conversion functions and the Format function, other functions enable us to carry out complex operations easily in such areas as converting data types, working with dates and time, finance, and mathematics. The Pmt function is a useful function for computing the monthly payment necessary to repay a loan amount.

The various types of errors that can occur in the development of a Visual Basic program—syntax errors, run time errors, and logic errors—were also discussed in this chapter. The process of finding and removing errors is referred to as debugging.

NEW VISUAL BASIC ELEMENTS

Controls/Objects	Properties	Methods	Events
text box control	Name Text	SetFocus	
form object		PrintForm	

NEW PROGRAMMING STATEMENTS

Statement to declare a variable
Dim variable name as type

Statement to force all variables to be declared
Option Explicit

Statement to assign a value to a constant
Const constant name as type = value

Assignment Statement
Control property or variable = value, variable, expression, or control property

Statement to use a function
Variable = functionname(arg1, arg2, ...)

Statement to end execution of a project
End

KEY TERMS

assignment statement	format expression	run time errors
bugs	function	string data type
comments	internal documentation	symbolic constant
constant	logic errors	syntax errors
debugging	memory cells	text box
default property	mnemonic variable names	Text property
Edit Field	numeric data type	variables
fixed point operations	operator	variant data type
floating point operations	prototyping	

EXERCISES

1. Write a single Visual Basic statement to accomplish each of the following:

   a. Declare the variable blnStatus as Boolean.

   b. Assign "Nicolas" to the variable strFirstName.

   c. Assign the value 0.85 to the txtPercent text box to appear in Percent format.

   d. Set the focus to the txtScore text box.

   e. Increment the variable intCounter by 1.

2. What happens when each of the following is executed? Why?

```
a. Private Sub cmdCalculate_Click()
     Dim strAddress As String
     strAddress = "543 Elm Street"
     txtAnswer.Text = Val(strAddress)
   End Sub
```

```
b. Private Sub cmdCalculate_Click()
     Dim strAddress As String
     strAddress = "543 Elm Street"
     txtAnswer.Text = CInt(strAddress)
   End Sub
```

3. What happens when the following code is executed? Why does this occur? How can it be corrected?

```
Private Sub cmdCalculate_Click()
  Dim intNumber As Integer
  intNumber = 42000
End Sub
```

4. Use the Visual Basic Help facility or the MSDN on-line library to answer the following questions.

   a. What can cause a Type Mismatch error?

   b. What is the data type of the value returned by the Msgbox function?

   c. What does the Left function do? What are the arguments required?

   d. What is the value and data type of the vbOKOnly constant?

   e. What methods are available for the command button?

5. When are two variables that have been assigned the same value not equal? Create an interface with one text box and one command button. Write the following code for the command button.

```
Private Sub cmdCalculate_Click()
  Dim sngA As Single
  Dim dblB As Double
  sngA = 8.05006
  dblB = 8.05006
  txtAnswer.Text = sngA - dblB
End Sub
```

What is the result in the text box after executing the code? What would it be if the values stored in memory for each variable are equal? Why do you think the result comes out this way? What does this imply for your calculations?

PROJECTS

1. Review your design for Exercise 1 in Chapter 1 and then retrieve **Ex2-1.vbp** from your data disk. Add five text boxes and corresponding labels and modify the properties for the text boxes and labels as needed. The first text box should allow the user to input the student's name, and the next three text boxes are for input of the three quiz scores. The last text box is to display the average of the three quiz scores. Add a line control above this text box.

   Use a command button to sum the three test scores and compute and display the average of the three scores (use the Fixed Numeric format for the average.) Add command buttons to print the form, to clear the text boxes and set the focus back to the student name text box, and to exit the project. Test your project with a student name of **Chris Patrick** and test scores of **71**, **79**, and **85**. Save the resulting project as **Ex3-1.frm** and **Ex3-1.vbp** in the Chapter3 folder on your data disk.

2. Review your design for Exercise 2 in Chapter 1 and then retrieve **Ex2-2.vbp** from your data disk. Add four text boxes and corresponding labels and modify the properties for the text boxes and labels as needed. The first text box should allow the user to input the customer's name. The next two text boxes should allow the user to input the square footage for a lawn and the cost per square foot for a given type of treatment. The fourth text box should display the cost of the treatment, which is equal to the square footage times the cost per square foot. Add a line control above this text box.

Use a command button to compute and display the treatment cost. Format the cost per square foot and treatment cost as dollars and cents. Add command buttons to print the form, to clear the text boxes and set the focus back to the square footage text box, and to exit the project. Test your project with a customer name of **Caroline Myers** with square footage of **3250** square feet and a treatment cost of **$.002** per square foot. Save the resulting project as **Ex3-2.frm** and **Ex3-2.vbp** in the Chapter3 folder on your data disk.

3.   Review your design for Exercise 3 in Chapter 1 and then retrieve **Ex2-3.vbp** from your data disk. Add four text boxes and corresponding labels and modify the properties for the text boxes and labels as needed. The first text box should allow the user to input the make of the car being tested. The second and third text boxes should allow the user to input the miles driven and the gallons of gas used. The fourth text box should display the miles per gallon, which is equal to the miles driven divided by the gallons used. Add a line control about this text box.

Use a command button to compute and display the miles per gallon (use the Fixed Numeric format). Add command buttons to print the form, to clear the text boxes and set the focus back to the automobile name text box, and to exit the project. Another command button should provide for the user to exit the project. Test your project with a **Toyonda** make of car that was driven **225** miles on **7.3** gallons of gas. Save the resulting project as **Ex3-3.frm and Ex3-3.vbp** in the Chapter3 folder on your data disk.

4.   Review your design for Exercise 4 in Chapter 1 and then retrieve **Ex2-4.vbp** from your data disk. Add five text boxes and corresponding labels and modify the properties for the text boxes and labels as needed. The first text box should allow the user to input the fixed cost of production, while the next two text boxes are for input of the unit cost and unit price values. The fourth text box should display the breakeven volume, which is equal to Fixed cost/(Unit price − Unit cost). The fifth text box should display the Breakeven revenue (Cost), which is equal to Breakeven volume times Unit price. Replace the message in the command button with the code necessary to make these calculations and display the results. Format the Breakeven volume using the Standard Numeric format. Format all other text boxes to be dollars and cents. Add command buttons to print the form, to clear the text boxes and set the focus back to the fixed cost text box, and to exit the project. Test your project with a Unit price of **$25**, Unit cost of **$15**, and Fixed cost of **$1,000**. Save the resulting project as **Ex3-4.frm** and **Ex3-4.vbp** in the Chapter3 folder on your data disk.

5.   Review your design for Exercise 5 in Chapter 1 and then retrieve **Ex2-5.vbp** from your data disk. Add seven text boxes and corresponding labels, and modify the properties for the text boxes and labels as needed. The first text box should allow the user to input the customer's name. The next four text boxes should allow the user to input the length of the room, the width of the room, the window area, and the door area. The sixth text box should display the room area and the seventh text box should display the number of rolls needed. Add a line control above this text box.

Replace the message in the command button with the calculations to compute the room area and number rolls of wallpaper needed. **Note:** Because the number of rolls calculated must be an integer, you should use Integer division to calculate the number of rolls and *then* add one (+1) to the result to account for the fractional remainder of a roll. Use the Fixed Numeric format to format all text boxes *except* the number of rolls.

Add command buttons to print the form, to clear the text boxes and set the focus back to the customer name text box, and to exit the project. Test your project for a **20' x 15'** room with **2** doors, each of which is **21** square feet, and **4** windows, each of which is **12** square feet. Assume that each roll of wallpaper will cover **45** square feet. Save the resulting project as **Ex3-5.frm** and **Ex3-5.vbp** in the Chapter3 folder on your data disk.

6.   Modify the Simple Calculator example to replace the single command button with four command buttons: one for addition, one for subtraction, one for multiplication, and one for division (assume you are dividing the contents of the top text box by the contents of the second text box). Use the arithmetic operators (+, –, *, or /) as the Caption property for each command button. Also, add a command button to exit the project. Try your calculator for various values in the two text boxes. Specifically, try to divide by zero and see what happens. Save your project as **Ex3-6.frm** and **Ex3-6.vbp** in the Chapter3 folder on your data disk.

7.   Modify the Monthly Payment Calculator to calculate the future value of a series of fixed value payments into an annuity for some number of months at a fixed interest rate. (Hint: The FV( ) function works *exactly* like the Pmt( ) function except that the fixed payment replaces the loan amount in the function and the future value is returned instead of the payment required.) You will need to modify the command button code and the labels. Test your annuity calculator with a fixed payment of **$100** per month for **10** years (120 months) at a **12** percent annual interest rate (1% monthly). Save your project as **Ex3-7.frm** and **Ex3-7.vbp** in the Chapter3 folder on your data disk.

8.   The library at Yeehaw Technical Institute needs an application that will compute the overdue fines for books as they are returned. As a first version of this application, assume that the borrower's name, the days overdue, and the fine per day (which differs depending on whether the borrower is a faculty member, a grad student, or an undergraduate) are entered in text boxes and that the Total fine due (Days overdue x Daily fine) is output by clicking a command button. Create an interface using text boxes, labels, and command buttons. Develop an IPO Table and pseudocode for this problem and then create a project that will carry out the logic using Visual Basic. It should have Calculate, Clear, Print, and Exit buttons. Try out your project with the following data:

> Borrower's name: **Jody Silver**
> Days overdue: **10**
> Daily fine: $**.25**

Save your project as **Ex3-8.frm** and **Ex3-8.vbp** in the Chapter3 folder on your data disk.

9.   Bob's Bike Factory produces custom-made bikes in four basic models. The price of the basic model plus the price of accessories determine the total price. Some distributors get special discounts, which are subtracted from the price before sales taxes are added. Develop an IPO Table and pseudocode for this project, a sketch of the form, and a Visual Basic project that has a form with a title and a logo for Bob's Bike Factory (e.g., a bike icon—use graphics/icons/industry/bicycle.ico) plus Calculate, Clear, Print, and Exit buttons. The final project should have the following features:

> 1.   The price of the model, the discount rate, and the number of bikes are input via text boxes. The tax rate is set in the code.

2. The discount (if any), taxes due, and total amount due are computed by a Calculate button and are output to text boxes with appropriate labels.

Try out your project with the following data:

Bikes ordered: **10 Model Red Racers**

Price: **$1499.99** each

Tax rate: **7**%

Discount: **15**%

Save your project as **Ex3-9.frm** and **Ex3-9.vbp** in the Chapter3 folder on your data disk.

10. Reckoning that they might amuse themselves on their PDAs while waiting in the snow and rain for dangerous weather phenomena, the meteorologists at The Weather Channel need a simple program to allow them to convert temperatures from Fahrenheit to Celsius. The interface would be composed of two textboxes and a command button. They would simply type the Fahrenheit temperature (F) into the first textbox, click the button and the corresponding Celsius temperature (C) would appear in the second textbox. The conversion relationship between the two is: $C = 5/9*(F-32)$. Design and create a Visual Basic program for this application. Try out your project with a Fahrenheit temperature of 32 degrees which should result in a Celsius temperature of 0 degrees. Save your project as **Ex3-10.frm** and **Ex3-10.vbp** in the Chapter3 folder on your data disk.

11. A currency trader would like a simple program to calculate the equivalent value of various foreign currencies for a given amount in US$. Assume that a VB program would utilize two textboxes to input the amount in US$ and the exchange rate. Also, an appropriately labeled textbox is used to display the equivalent amount of the foreign currency. The amount of foreign currency is calculated by simply multiplying the amount in US$ by the exchange rate. Assume that the calculation is performed when a command button is clicked. Design and create a Visual Basic program for this application. Try your project to convert US dollars to UK pounds with an exchange rate of 0.69. Check your newspaper for examples of other exchange rates to use in testing your project. Save your project as **Ex3-11.frm** and **Ex3-11.vbp** in the Chapter3 folder on your data disk.

12. Financial ratios are often used as a measure of a company's performance. They are important as indicators of the company's health that may be used in management and investment decisions. Several commonly used financial ratios are:

a. The Current Ratio is used to predict the capability of a company to pay its current liabilities. The Current Ratio is calculated by dividing Current Assets divided by Current Liabilities.

b. The Quick Ratio provides more liquid test for paying Current Liabilities. The quick ratio is equal to (Current Assets - Inventory) / Current Liabilities.

c. The Receivables Turnover Ratio represents the average time for a firm to convert receivables to cash. This ratio is equal to Net Sales divided by Accounts Receivable.

d. The Average Collection Period indicates the average number of days to turn over accounts receivable. The Average Collection Period is equal to 365 divided by the Receivables Turnover Ratio.

e. The extent that a firm depends on loans versus the resources from stakeholders and other owners is measured by the Debt to Equity Ratio. Debt to Equity is equal to the Total Liabilities divided by Owner's Equity.

f. Return on Investment (ROI) represents the capability of a company to earn profits for its owners. ROI = Net Income / Owner's Equity.

Design and create a Visual Basic program for calculating these ratios. Save your project as **Ex3-12.frm** and **Ex3-12.vbp** in the Chapter3 folder on your data disk.

13. On what day and date will Easter fall this year? How about the next? What about in the year 2053? Since the Easter holiday always falls on a Sunday you could narrow it down, but how could you pinpoint it exactly. The actual date of Easter each year is determined by the Catholic church. In A.D. 325, church leaders decided that Easter should fall on the first Sunday after the first full moon occurring on, or after the spring equinox (the day in March on which day and night have equal length and which marks the beginning of Spring). This sounds difficult enough, but any calculations must also take into account the fact that our calendar is not perfect and must be corrected every so often. Fortunately, an algorithm has been developed that will allow us to calculate the exact date of Easter for any given year.

a. Choose a year and call it X.

b. Divide X by 19 to get a quotient (which is ignored) and a remainder A.

c. Divide X by 100 to get a quotient B and a remainder C.

d. Divide B by 4 to get a quotient D and a remainder E.

e. Divide 8B+13 by 25 to get a quotient G and a remainder (which we ignore).

f. Divide 19A+B-D-G+15 by 30 to get a quotient which we ignore and a remainder H.

g. Divide A+11H by 319 to get a quotient M and a remainder (which is ignored).

h. Divide C by 4 to get a quotient J and a remainder K.

i. Divide 2E+2J-K-H+M+32 by 7 to get a quotient (which is ignored) and a remainder L.

j. Divide H-M+L+90 by 25 to get quotient N and a remainder (which is ignored).

k. Divide H-M+L+N+19 by 32 to get a quotient (which we ignore) and a remainder P.

l. Easter Sunday will be the Pth day of the Nth month.

Design and create a Visual Basic program for calculating the date of Easter for any year entered by the user. For the year 2001, Easter fell on April 15th (this gave everyone in the US an extra day to do their taxes). Save your project as **Ex3-13.frm** and **Ex3-13.vbp** in the Chapter3 folder on your data disk.

PROJECT: JOE'S TAX ASSISTANCE (CONT.)

After a long afternoon of programming, Joe sat back and looked at his watch. "Wow, it's 6:00 already. Where did the time go?"

"That's another thing about computers. They seem to always make the clocks run faster," Zooey asserted. "What do you think so far, Grandpa?"

As he clicked the buttons on the main form, his eyes lit up. "It's looking good, my girl. I can't get over how the messages appear when I click here—and to know that we made it do that."

"Don't get too excited yet. The program will be able to do more impressive things than that," she responded. "Let me show you a few more things before Mom and Granny get back."

"OK. You know, I nearly forgot about the ladies. They ought to be back soon."

"In this program, you're going to have to perform some calculations. For that you'll need to use variables, arithmetic operators, and some functions," Zooey explained. She then began telling Joe about the different types of variables. Another hour went by as she went as far as explaining various functions.

"You know, Zooey, my head is about to bust," Joe sighed. "You've really taught me a lot today."

"I think what we need to do now is start working on some of the other forms for the program."

Joe picked up the 1040 and looked it over. "Some of these look kind of complicated, but there are a couple parts that I think we can do with what you've shown me so far. For instance, the Income part looks like it could be done with text boxes for entering the information and then a calculation at the end to add them up."

"Now you're cooking, Grandpa. I think the Adjusted Gross Income section can be done like that, too," she added.

Before they could get started again, Angela and Janet walked into the den with an armload of packages apiece.

"Well, did you buy out the stores?" Joe asked with cautious humor as he rose to greet them with a hug.

"Not quite. We might have to go back for another trip later," Janet threatened. "Are you ready to send Zooey home with me?"

"So soon? Maybe you could go shopping some more. We're getting a lot done." Joe cried.

"Well, haven't we changed our tune," teased Angela.

"That's okay, Grandpa. I've had enough for today. Besides, you know enough to continue with the next part by yourself," Zooey encouraged. "Just watch the clock this time."

Questions

1. Design a section on the form for the Income portion of the 1040 form. Use text boxes and labels for the user to enter the appropriate information such as the VITA client's name, Social Security number, and income. Include buttons for clearing the text boxes and calculating the total income. Write code for the Clear button which will cause all of the text boxes to appear empty when clicked. Include code for the Calculate button which calculates the total income, stores it as a variable and displays the value in the Total Income text box.

2. Design a section on the form for the Adjusted Gross Income portion of the 1040 form. Use text boxes and labels for the user to enter the appropriate information. Include buttons for clearing the text boxes, calculating the total income, and for returning to the main form. Add code to the Clear button which will cause the Adjusted Gross Income text boxes to appear empty along with the Income text boxes. Include code for the Calculate button which calculates the total adjusted gross income deductions and the adjusted gross income, stores them as variables and displays them as values.

3. Run and test your program.

4 THE SELECTION PROCESS IN VISUAL BASIC

LEARNING OBJECTIVES

After reading this chapter, you should be able to:

- Understand the importance of the selection process in programming.
- Describe the various types of decisions that can be made in a computer program.
- Discuss the statement forms used in Visual Basic to make decisions.
- Understand the various comparison operators used in implementing decisions in Visual Basic.
- Use the If-Then-Else, If-Then-ElseIf, and Case decision structures.
- Use the list box control to select from a list of alternatives.
- Work with complex comparison structures and nested decisions to handle more sophisticated selection processes.
- Use the scroll bar to input integer values.
- Use the Form_Load event to execute a procedure when a form is loaded.
- Work with the debugging toolbar to find program errors.

SCENARIO: USING DECISIONS AT VINTAGE VIDEOS

Clark was concentrating on the mail he was carrying as he walked through the door of Vintage Videos and ran into John Wayne. The momentary surprise wore off when he realized that it was only a life-size cardboard display. Nevertheless, he breathed a sigh of relief that he wouldn't have to do a quick draw.

"Howdy, Pardner," said Ed as he emerged from the back room with an armload of movie posters.

"Hi, Ed. I picked up the mail and brought along the next version of our program to show you," Clark replied. "This place is beginning to look great. You're almost ready to open."

"Yeah, we're almost there. Yvonne's out getting a few last-minute supplies. Let me see what you have for us."

Clark started the program and clicked the "Click me first" button to display the "Welcome to Vintage Videos" message. After he clicked "OK," he and Ed examined the main form.

Clark explained the program: "Here you can enter the customer's name and then the name of the video. Then you can type the price of the video here. After that, you simply press the Calculate button and the taxes and total automatically appear in these boxes."

Ed tried the program several times. "Not bad, but can we have the welcome message displayed automatically?"

"Sure. But more important, what do you think of the main window of the program? Any changes that you want there?" Clark asked.

"Right now, I can think of a couple of things," Ed answered. "First, we need to force our cashiers to input the renter's name and the video name before continuing."

"No problem," Clarke replied. "What else?"

"Well, you know that our price structure is pretty much fixed. We plan on charging $2.99 for the more-difficult-to-obtain "classic" movies, $1.99 for regular videos, and $0.99 if the video is for kids. Can you make the program figure the prices based on the type of movie?"

"I think so. Is that all?"

"That's all I can think of at the moment," replied Ed.

"Okay, I'll get to work on that. I have some free time this afternoon before my next class."

Ed smiled and with a passable impression of the Duke said, "Well, pilgrim, that's a mighty fine program you've got goin'. Keep up the good work and you'll go far. That's a promise you can bank on in Denver."

Discussion of Scenario

After reviewing the prototype information system application for Vintage Videos, the owner has made several requests of the developer which we will discuss in this chapter. Several of these enhancements involve having the project make decisions about whether the customer name and video name have been entered before continuing with processing the price data. A decision must also be made about the price depending on the type of video: classic, regular, or kids. In addition, the owner wants the welcome message to pop up automatically when the program starts. All of these features will be added to the prototype application in this chapter.

FIGURE 4-1. List of video types

As with the previous versions of the prototype, the development process should start with a sketch of the new interface that will be shown to the client to ensure that there is mutual understanding between the developer and the client about what is needed. In this case, since the interface is changing very little, the sketch will be the same as before, except for the addition of a list of available video types (shown in Figure 4-1) from which the user can select. This list of video types will be placed in the upper right-hand corner of the form. In addition, the "Click Me First!" button will be deleted.

THE SELECTION PROCESS

In Chapter 1, we listed the six operations a computer can carry out: input data, store data in internal memory, perform arithmetic on the data, compare two values and select one of two alternative actions, repeat a group of actions any number of times, and output the result of processing. In Chapters 2 and 3, we considered using all of the operations in Visual Basic *except* for making decisions and repeating a group of actions. In this chapter, we will discuss in detail how to compare two values and then select an action based on the outcome of the comparison; repeating a group of actions will be discussed in the next chapter.

The process of selection is important to the capability of a computer program to carry out useful processing. If a computer could not select between alternatives, its use would be restricted to only those activities for which the order of processing never deviates. As you know, this would be a very unreasonable situation. In our daily lives, we are constantly making decisions to select among alternatives whether it is something as simple as what to have for lunch or as complex as choosing a career. The same is true for computer programs; to be truly useful, they must be able to select between alternative courses of action. For example, if you were writing a program to compute the weekly payroll for a company, there would be a number of decisions to be made: Is the employee salaried or hourly? Is he or she full- or part-time? Did the employee work any overtime hours this week? Does the employee participate in a tax deferral system? And so on. Each decision would have some impact on either the employee's gross salary or net (take home) salary, and the program must process the data that are input to make these decisions.

Another way of thinking about the selection process is that it affects the flow of control within the program. That is, the selection that is made determines the next statement or set of statements to be executed. In procedural programs, this was virtually the only way a program could be controlled once it was started. However, in event-driven programs, we know that the user has much more control over the flow of control, since nothing happens until either the user or the program causes an event to occur. This does not take away from the importance of the selection process; it just makes it a part of an event procedure.

Anatomy of a Decision

Every decision in a computer program must compare two values to determine which of two alternative statements or sets of statements will be executed. One alternative will be executed if the comparison is true and another alternative will be executed if the comparison is false. In each case, the alternatives to be executed are valid Visual Basic statements. The two values to be compared can be variables, constants, expressions, control properties, or any combination of these three. The only restriction is that both values being compared must be of the same broad data type, that is, Numeric or String.

For the salary example discussed above, consider the overtime decision. In this decision, the number of hours worked is compared to 40. If the comparison is true, that is, more than 40 hours were worked, then the employee should be paid at the regular rate for the first 40 hours and should receive overtime pay at the rate of time and a half for hours worked over 40. If the comparison is false—that is, 40 hours or fewer are worked—then the employee should be paid at the regular pay rate for all hours worked. In this case, the values being compared are Single data type variables and constants, and they are being compared for an inequality.

Types of Decisions

In computer programming, there are two basic decision structures: two alternatives and many alternatives. In the above payroll example, the decision as to whether or not the employee worked more than 40 hours is an example of a decision with two alternatives—more than 40 hours worked or 40 hours or fewer worked. On the other hand, a decision involving shipping costs for a letter or parcel is an example of a multiple-alternative decision structure, because the alternatives include standard ground shipment, two-day shipment, and overnight delivery. In a multiple-alternative decision, it is assumed that the alternatives are mutually exclusive and include all possible situations. This may mean that one of the alternatives is "everything else." In either case—two-alternative or multiple-alternative—the true/false test is still used and an alternative is executed or not executed.

In the two-alternative decision structure, the **If-Then-Else decision structure** should be used. In this decision structure, there is a single condition that is true or false. If the condition is true, then the true alternative is implemented; if the condition is false, the false alternative is implemented. The general form of the If-Then-Else decision structure in pseudocode is shown below:

```
If condition is true then
        implement true alternative
Else
        implement false alternative
End decision.
```

where the term *else* means the condition being tested was not true. Note that the true and false alternatives have been indented. This is for ease of understanding only; it has no effect on the decision structure.

In no case are both alternatives implemented; if the true alternative is implemented, the decision structure is exited. If the false alternative is implemented, the true alternative is skipped.

For the payroll example, the pseudocode version of decision structure is:

```
If employee works more than 40 hours then
        employee pay = regular pay + overtime pay
Else
        employee pay = regular pay
End decision.
```

For the multiple-alternative situation, the general form in pseudocode for three possible alternatives is:

```
Select one:
        Condition 1 is true: implement alternative 1
        Condition 2 is true: implement alternative 2
        Condition 3 is true: implement alternative 3
End Selection.
```

In this situation, the first condition is tested to determine if it is true; if it is, the first alternative is implemented, no other conditions are tested, and the decision structure is terminated. If the first condition is false, the second condition is tested in the same manner and so on until one condition is found to be true. If none of the conditions is true, the decision structure is terminated with no action being taken.

For example, the pseudocode version of the shipping example is:

```
Select Shipping Mode
        Standard ground: cost = standard ground cost
        Two-day shipment: cost = two day cost
        Overnight: cost = overnight shipment cost
End Selection.
```

There can be many variations and combinations of these two decision structures. For example, there may be no false alternative for the two-alternative decision structure, or a two-alternative decision structure may be "nested" inside the multiple-alternative decision structure as one of the alternatives. The tests of whether a customer name or video name has been entered in the Vintage Videos application are both examples of a two-alternative decision with no false alternative. We will explore some of these variations as we go through the use of decisions in Visual Basic.

THE TWO-ALTERNATIVE DECISION STRUCTURE

Implementing the two-alternative and multiple-alternative decision structures in Visual Basic involves learning the correct syntax for the decision statements and the appropriate form for the conditions that are tested to determine if they are true or false. Failure to carry out either of these correctly will result in either a syntax error or a logic error. Since both the statement syntax and the condition forms are different for the two decision structures, we will discuss them in separate sections. However, in both cases the idea is the same: We must determine if a condition is true or false and take appropriate action for each situation.

Recall that the two-alternative decision structure occurs when there is a single condition that must be tested to determine if it is true or false. In Visual Basic the **If-Then-Else** statement for this decision structure is:

> **If** *condition is true* **then**
> > *statements for true alternative*
>
> **Else**
> > *statements for false alternative*
>
> **End if**

Notice that the form of the Visual Basic two-alternative decision structure is virtually identical to that of the pseudocode version, with the exception that *end if* is used to terminate the decision structure. The results of true and false conditions on the two-alternative decision are shown in Figure 4-2.

FIGURE 4-2. The two-alternative decision

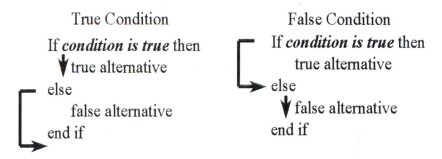

The If-Then Condition

The main thing you need to understand to use this decision structure is the form of the *condition* part of the statement. In Visual Basic, the decision condition has the form:

> **test expression1** *comparison operator* **test expression2**

where

> **test expression** = variable, constant, or expression

and

> **comparison operator** = one of six comparison operators in Table 4-1.

In this decision structure, the objective is to compare *test expression1* on the left to *test expression2* on the right to determine if the relationship defined by the comparison operator is true. The condition must evaluate to true or false; there is nothing in between.

Using the six comparison operators defined in Table 4-1, we can compare any two variables, constants, expressions, or control properties. The only requirement is that the data type for the two expressions being compared be the same; that is, compare

TABLE 4-1: Comparison Operators

Name	Operator Symbol	Example	Meaning
Equal to	=	strEmpCode = "S"	Is employee code equal to "S"?
Greater than	>	intHours > 40	Are hours worked greater than 40?
Greater than or equal to	>=	curRevenue >= curCosts	Is Revenue greater than or equal to Costs?
Less than	<	curThisYear < curLastYear	Is this year's revenue less than last year's revenue?
Less than or equal to	<=	curMySalary <= curYourSalary	Is MySalary less than or equal to YourSalary?
Not equal to	<>	intNumber <> 0	Is Number not equal to zero?

strings to strings and numbers to numbers. Trying to compare a string to a number will result in invalid results. For example, we can compare an alphanumeric Pay Code to the character constant "S" to determine if they are the same. Or we can compare the variable Hours to the constant 40 to determine if Hours worked is greater than or equal to 40. However, trying to compare Pay Code to the Integer constant 40 would not result in valid results..

> **TIP:** Since Boolean variables are either true or false, it is possible to write a condition that consists only of the Boolean variable name.

Let's see how we would apply the two-alternative decision structure to the payroll example. To do that, we will create a small project that will compute wages for hourly employees. The project will have four text boxes: one for the employee name, one for the number of hours worked, one for the hourly wage rate, and one for the resulting wage for this employee. If employees work more than 40 hours, then they should be paid at their regular pay rate for the first 40 hours and at their overtime rate for each hour over 40. If employees work 40 hours or fewer, they should be paid at their regular rate for all hours worked. For example, assume that an employee is paid $10 per hour. If the employee works 35 hours, he will be paid 35*$10 = $350. However, if the employee works 48 hours, he will be paid $10 per hour for the first 40 hours and time and a half for all hours over 40. In this case, the amount paid will be equal to 40*$10 + 1.5*(48 − 40)*$10, or $400 for regular time + $120 for overtime = $520 for the 48 hours of work. The decision structure in pseudocode for this situation is shown below:

```
If Hours > 40 then
        Pay = 40 * PayRate + 1.5 * (Hours - 40) * PayRate
Else
        Pay = Hours * PayRate
End Decision
```

The interface for this example is shown in Figure 4-3, with the four text boxes and corresponding labels and two command buttons—one to compute the pay due the employee and one to exit the application. The text boxes are named *txtName*, *txtPayRate*, *txtHours*, and *txtPay*, and the corresponding labels are given similar names.

FIGURE 4-3.
Interface for payroll computation

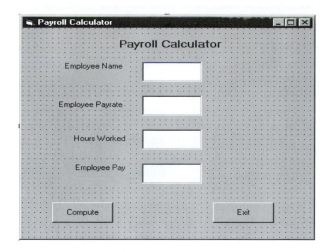

The code for the command button to compute the employee's pay (*cmdCompute*) is shown in VB Code Box 4-1. Note that we format the rate and pay as currency *after* computation. The Exit command button (*cmdExit*) has the standard End statement.

VB CODE BOX 4-1. Code to compute payroll	```Private Sub cmdCompute_Click()```

```
Private Sub cmdCompute_Click()
  Dim curPayRate As Currency, sngHours As Single
  Dim curPay As Currency
  curPayRate = CCur(txtPayRate.Text)
  sngHours = CSng(TxtHours.Text)
  If sngHours >= 40 Then 'Compare hours work to 40
    curPay = curPayRate * 40 + 1.5 * curPayRate * (sngHours - 40)
  Else
    curPay = curPayRate * sngHours
  End If
  txtPay.Text = Format(curPay, "currency")
  txtPayRate.Text = Format(txtPayRate.Text, "currency")
End Sub
```

To test this application, use the data we used earlier, that is, curPayRate = *$10* and sngHours = *35* or *48*, for an employee named *Ben Sibley*. In the first case, the resulting curPay should be $350, and in the second case, the resulting curPay should be $520, as seen in Figure 4-4 after the Compute button has been clicked. You should also test it with some other data for which you know the resulting pay.

Mini-Summary 4-1: If-Then-Else Statements

1. Decisions are an important element of any computer program, because they affect the flow control of a program.

2. There are two types of decision structures: those with two alternatives and those with many alternatives.

3. Two-alternative decisions are handled by the If-Then-Else structure.

Mini-Summary 4-1: If-Then-Else Statements (Continued)

4. The two-alternative decision structure uses a comparison condition to determine if a comparison is true or false. The result of this comparison determines which statements are executed.

5. Comparison operators include equal to, greater than, greater than or equal to, less than, less than or equal to, and not equal to.

FIGURE 4-4.
Running the payroll calculator

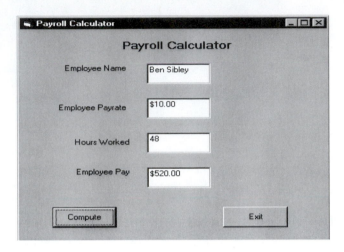

It's Your Turn!

1. Assuming that intL and intM are integer variables with intL = 9 and intM = –3, and that sngX = –4.25, sngY = 0, and sngZ = 43.5 are Single variables, find the values (True or False) of the following logical expressions:

    a. intL <= intM

    b. -2*intL <= 8

    c. sngX^2 < Sqr(intZ)

    d. CInt(sngZ) = (5*intL-3*.5)

    e. sngY <> 0

2. Write logical expressions to express the following conditions:

    a. X is greater than 5

    b. R is negative

    c. A is not equal to B

    d. M is not negative

    e. Half of Z is greater than or equal to twice Y

3. Write two-alternative decision structures for the following situations (in each case, unless directed to otherwise, do not worry about input and output; just work with the appropriate variables, which we will assume have already been declared).

a. If taxable income is greater than $30,000, then taxes are $4,500 plus 28% of the taxable income over $30,000. If taxable income is less than or equal to $30,000, taxes are 15% of taxable income.

b. If the amount to be withdrawn from an ATM is less than the existing balance, subtract the amount from the balance to compute the new balance. Otherwise, use a message box to display an "Insufficient Funds" message.

c. At the Jones Company, if a salesperson generates $10,000 or less in revenue for a month, she is paid a commission of 10% of the revenue she generates. If she generates more than $10,000 in revenue, she is paid $100 plus a commission of 12% of the revenue.

4. Complete the following exercises to create the Payroll Calculator.

a. Start Visual Basic and choose a new Standard EXE form. Create an interface like that in Figure 4-3. Give the form a name of **frmPayroll** and a caption of **Payroll Calculator**. For the text boxes and labels, use the names and captions shown in Table 4-2. Add two command buttons with names of **cmdCompute** and **cmdExit** with captions of **Compute** and **Exit**, respectively.

TABLE 4-2: Text Boxes and Labels for Payroll Application

Text Box Name	Label Name	Caption
txtName	lblName	Employee Name
txtPayRate	lblPayRate	Employee Payrate
txtHours	lblHours	Hours Worked
txtPay	lblPay	Employee Pay
	lblHeading	Payroll Calculator

b. Open the Code window for the Click event for the cmdCompute command button and add the code shown in VB Code Box 4-1. Also add the **End** instruction to the cmdExit command button code.

c. Run your project and enter the following data: Name = **Ben Sibley**, Pay rate = **$10**, and Hours worked = **35**.

d. Change the hours worked to **48** and compare your results to those shown in Figure 4-4. Test your project further by changing the pay rate to **$11.50** and the hours worked to both **38** and **47**. Compare the answer against your hand calculations.

e. Create a new folder on your data disk with a name of **Chapter4**. Create a subfolder called **Payroll**. Save your form as **Payroll.frm** and your project as **Payroll.vbp** in this folder.

APPLICATION TO SCENARIO

For the Vintage Videos scenario, we need to determine if the customer and video names have been entered in the appropriate text boxes. This involves determining if either text box is empty—that is, if there is a null string in the text box. To determine this, we need to use a two-alternative decision structure with no false alternative. The form of this decision structure is this:

> **If** *condition is true* **Then**
> 　　*true alternative is implemented*
> **End If**

Note that, in this decision structure, if the condition is true, then the true alternative is executed; otherwise, nothing happens and the decision structure is terminated.

For the scenario, if either text box is empty, then the project needs to request that a name be entered. One way to do this would be to use a Msgbox to alert the user to the missing entry. However, the user could ignore this message and still not enter a name in the text box. Another way—one that *forces* the user to respond—is the Input-Box function. The **InputBox()** function has the form:

> *variable or control property* = **Inputbox(***prompt)*

where the prompt is a message enclosed in quotation marks requesting the user to input a certain data item. When the project encounters this function, a box is displayed on the screen with the prompt for data. For the scenario, the appropriate use of the InputBox function would be:

```
txtCustName.Text = Inputbox("Please input the member name.")
```

Note that we have set the Text property of the Customer Name text box equal to the InputBox, so that whatever the user enters in the InputBox will automatically go into the customer name text box. The resulting InputBox is shown in Figure 4-5 with a customer name entered. When the user presses **ENTER,** the name will be transferred to the Text property of the txtCustName text box. If the user presses the **Cancel** button, a zero-length string ("") is returned.

This If-Then-Else decision structure is an example of an important feature that should appear in all applications: **validation**. In validation, the project developer tries to validate user input *before* it can cause problems for the project. In this case, the validation mechanism checks if a name has been entered and, if one has not, requests one. In so doing, it avoids later problems. Any project you create should include some validation to avoid problems later on.

FIGURE 4-5. Use of InputBox

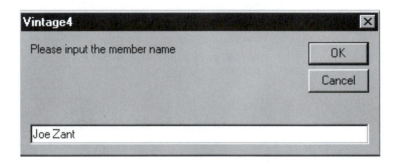

It is important to remember that the InputBox function cannot be used by itself like a Msgbox; a variable or control property must be set equal to the InputBox function to receive the user's input. Another important feature of the InputBox function is that it *always* returns a string. This means that if you are entering a number that will be transferred to a Numeric data type variable, you must use the appropriate conversion function, such as Val( ), to convert the string returned by the InputBox function to a number. For example, if you are using an InputBox function to enter a quiz score, the appropriate statement would be:

```
intQuizScore = CInt(InputBox("Please enter a quiz score"))
```

where QuizScore is a Integer data type variable. Note that two right-hand parentheses are needed at the end of the statement to match the two left-hand parentheses earlier in the statement. We don't have to worry about this in the current example, because the Text property of the text boxes is also a string.

> **TIP:** The number of right-hand parentheses in *any* expression **must** match the number of left-hand parentheses.

To test the Customer Name and Video Name text boxes to determine whether something has been entered in them, the code shown in VB Code Box 4-2 would need to be added to the existing code for the Click event of the cmdCalc button in the Vintage Videos project (saved earlier as Vintage3.vbp.) This new code would be entered immediately after the existing declaration statements and before the computation of taxes and amount due.

VB CODE BOX 4-2. Additional code to validate input	```
	If txtCustName.Text = "" Then 'Check for customer name
	    txtCustName.Text = InputBox("Enter name and try again.")
	    Exit Sub 'No customer name entered
	End If
	If txtVideoName.Text = "" Then 'Check for video name
	    txtVideoName.Text = InputBox("Enter video name and try again.")
	    Exit Sub 'No video name entered
	End If
	``

Note in VB Code Box 4-2 that we have checked if a customer name and a video name have been entered in the text boxes by comparing the Text property to a zero-length string (""). If the comparison is found to be true, then the InputBox function requests the user to enter the appropriate name and click Calculate again. The cmd-Calc event procedure is then exited via the *Exit Sub* instruction. This precludes the program from continuing until both customer name and video name have been input.

If there is anything (including spaces) in either text box, then the comparison is false and the corresponding If-Then decision structure is exited with nothing happening. If you run the Vintage Videos project with this additional code and fail to enter either a customer name or a video name, then you will be requested to do so when you click the cmdCalc command button.

> **TIP:** An empty string is different from one that has blank spaces. If there are spaces in the empty string representation, the comparison will fail.

Mini-Summary 4-2: Validation of Input

1. It is possible to have only a true alternative in the two-alternative decision structure.

2. Validation of input is an important part of any computer program.

3. An InputBox can be used to input data directly to a variable or control property.

It's Your Turn!

1. Assume that as part of a program you wish to obtain the user's age in years. You design the interface so that the user will enter their name in a text box. When a button is clicked, the age will be stored to a variable. You then want to make sure that the value entered for the age is a positive number. If the value entered is not positive, you will ask for and obtain the correct value from the user, store the correct value in the variable and display it in the textbox. Write Visual Basic code that will carry this out.

Completing the remaining questions will enable you to create the Visual Basic project discussed in the text.

2. Retrieve the **Vintage3.vbp** project from the Chapter3 folder on your data disk. Add the code shown in VB Code Box 4-2 to the Click event for the cmdCalc command button immediately after the existing declaration statements. Test the resulting project by first failing to enter the customer name and clicking the cmdCalc command button. Test it again by failing to enter the video name. In both cases, use a video price of **$1.99**.

3. Save the current form as **Vintage4.frm** and the project as **Vintage4.vbp** in the Chapter4 folder on your data disk.

THE MULTIPLE-ALTERNATIVE DECISION STRUCTURE

When there are more than two alternatives to choose from, the If-Then-Else decision structure is inappropriate. Instead, Visual Basic provides two ways to handle the multiple alternatives: If-Then-ElseIf and Select Case decision structures. They work equally well, and you can choose which you want to use (or your instructor may tell you which one he or she favors). In either case, a condition is tested to determine if a given alternative should be executed. If the condition is found to be false, this corresponding alternative will not be executed. If all conditions are found to be false, then none of the alternatives will be executed. As an example involving multiple alternatives, we will use a situation very familiar to all readers: deciding on a letter grade based on a quiz average. (Later, we will apply the multiple-alternative case to the Vintage Videos scenario.) In this case, the multiple alternatives are usually the grades A, B, C, D, and F and the condition being tested is whether the quiz average is above a certain level. For our purpose, we will assume that the instructor is using the 90-80-70-60 scale for assigning grades. The pseudocode for this decision is shown below (where Integer averages are being used):

```
If average is 90 or higher then grade is A
     Else if average is 80 or higher then grade is B
     Else if average is 70 or higher then grade is C
     Else if average is 60 or higher then grade is D
     Else grade is F
End decision
```

Note in the pseudocode that we start with the highest grade and move down through the possible breakpoints for grades. Had we started at the lowest grade and tested if the average was 60 or higher, then everybody meeting this criterion, including those with much higher grades, would receive a grade of D and the decision structure would be terminated. For this reason, it is important that the conditions are ordered in the appropriate manner to provide the desired results.

Using the If-Then-ElseIf Decision Structure

For the multiple-alternative situation, the **If-Then-ElseIf** decision structure is a natural extension of the If-Then-Else structure, where there can be multiple ElseIf statements after the original If statement. Each ElseIf statement tests a comparison condition like the one used to test the original If statement and has one or more instructions to execute if it is true. As with the If-Then-Else decision structure, the original If statement is tested first. If it is true, then none of the ElseIf statements is tested. If the original If comparison condition is false, then the first ElseIf comparison condition is tested. If it is found to be true, the corresponding set of instructions is executed and the decision structure is terminated. If the first ElseIf condition is false, each subsequent ElseIf statement is tested in order until one is found to be true or until the general-purpose Else statement is encountered. In this situation, the Else is executed when the original If statement and *all* ElseIf statements are false.

The general form of the If-Then-ElseIf decision structure is shown below for three alternatives and for an alternative when all conditions prove to be false.

> **If** *condition1 true* **then**
> > **first set of statements**
> **ElseIf** *condition2 true* **then**
> > **second set of statements**
> **ElseIf** *condition3 true* **then**
> > **third set of statements**
> **Else**
> > **last set of statements**
> **End if**

In this decision structure, there can be as many ElseIf statements as necessary as long as each one is mutually exclusive of all other ElseIf statements. In other words, overlapping conditions are not allowed. If all test conditions prove to be false, the statements after the Else keyword are executed. Note: The Else statement is not necessary; if it is deleted and all test conditions prove to be false, the decision structure is exited with no statements being executed. Figure 4-6 shows the flow of control in this decision structure when *condition3* is the true condition.

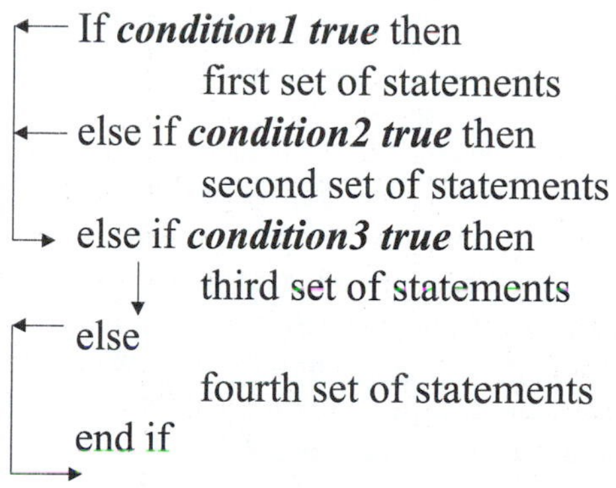

FIGURE 4-6. Flow of control for multiple-alternative decisions

```
If condition1 true then
        first set of statements
else if condition2 true then
        second set of statements
else if condition3 true then
        third set of statements
else
        fourth set of statements
end if
```

Determining a Letter Grade

To implement the grade assignment logic, let's create a small project in which we can enter the name and quiz average for a student and determine the corresponding letter grade. The interface for this project is shown in Figure 4-7, where the form has four labels, three text boxes, and two command buttons. The form is named *frmLetterGrade* and the heading label is named *lblHeading*. The text boxes are named *txtName*, *txtAverage*, and *txtLetter* and the labels are given corresponding names. The two command buttons, named *cmdLetter* and *cmdExit*, determine the letter grade and exit the project, respectively.

FIGURE 4-7.
Interface for letter grade determination project

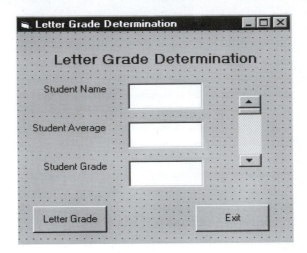

To input the average value, we will use a new control: the **scroll bar**. The scroll bar allows you to use an analog device to input values. There are vertical and horizontal scroll bars that, respectively, begin with *vsb* and *hsb* prefixes. In this case, we will use the vertical scroll bar with a name of *vsbAverage*. The key property of the scroll bar is the **Value** property, which is an Integer. The Value property responds to the **Change** event as the scroll bar is moved. The limits on the Value property can be set through the **Max** and **Min** properties. It is also possible to control the amount the value changes when the scroll bar arrows are clicked through the **SmallChange** property. The amount of change that occurs when the interior of the scroll bar is clicked is set through the **LargeChange** property.

For example, to use the scroll bar for a student's average, the Max property would be set to 100 and the Min property set to 0. The Largechange property might be set to 10 to allow for larger changes in the average and the SmallChange property set to 1 for unit changes. This will result in an Integer average value between 0 and 100. No matter what the SmallChange and LargeChange properties are, the user can always "drag" the scroll bar to any value between the Max setting and the Min setting.

The first event procedure we need to write is to transfer the result of moving the scroll bar to the corresponding text box. As mentioned earlier, this is accomplished in the default scroll bar Change event procedure. We need to assign the Value property of the scroll bar to the Text property of the txtAverage text box. The code for this event procedure is shown in VB Code Box 4-3.

The only other code for this project goes in the Click event procedures for the cmdLetter and cmdExit command buttons. The If-Then-ElseIf decision structure is

| VB CODE BOX 4-3. Change event code for scroll bar | ```Private Sub VsbAverage_Change()
    txtAverage.Text = Str(vsbAverage.Value)
End Sub``` |
|---|---|

implemented in the cmdLetter command button to determine and display the appropriate letter grade for this person. This code is shown in VB Code Box 4-4.

| VB CODE BOX 4-4. Code for letter grade determination | ```Private Sub cmdLetter_Click()
    Dim intAverage as Integer, strLetterGrade as String
    intAverage = CInt(txtAverage.Text)
    If intAverage >= 90 then 'Check quiz average
        strLetterGrade = "A"
    ElseIf intAverage >= 80 then
        strLetterGrade = "B"
    ElseIf intAverage >= 70 then
        strLetterGrade = "C"
    ElseIf intAverage >= 60 then
        strLetterGrade = "D"
    Else
        strLetterGrade = "F"
    End If
    txtLetter.Text = strLetterGrade
End Sub``` |
|---|---|

Note that no conversion is required to assign the strLetterGrade variable to the Text property of txtLetter, since both are String data types. If the project is run for a sample student, the results are as shown in Figure 4-8.

FIGURE 4-8. Letter Grade project

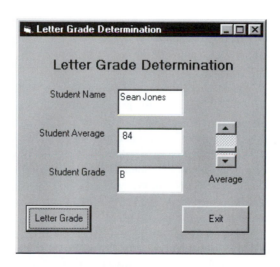

Using the Select Case Decision Structure

The second decision structure for handling multiple alternatives is the **Select Case** decision structure in which there can be as many Case statements as necessary as long as each one is mutually exclusive of all others. In other words, overlapping conditions are not allowed. If all test conditions prove to be false, the statements after the Case Else keywords are executed. Note: The Case Else statement is not necessary; if it is deleted and all test conditions prove to be false, the decision structure is exited with no statements being executed. The form of the Select Case decision structure for three alternatives and an Else alternative is shown below:

> **Select Case** *expression*
> **Case** *condition1 is true*
>   *First set of statements*
> **Case** *condition2 is true*
>   *Second set of statements*
> **Case** *condition3 is true*
>   *Third set of statements*
> **Case Else**
>   *Last set of statements*
> **End Select.**

The test condition in the Select Case decision structure is different from those in the If-Then-ElseIf decision structure. It can take on one of three forms: A single value or expression, a range of values, or a comparison condition like those used in the If-Then-Else and If-Then-ElseIf decision structures. These three forms are shown in Table 4-3.

TABLE 4-3: Select Case Comparison Conditions

Test Condition	Condition format	Example	Condition is true if:
Value or Expression	One or multiple values or strings separated by commas	Case 91, 92, 93,	Average = 91, 92, or 93
Range of Values	A range of values defined by high and low values separated by keyword To	Case 90 To 100	Average is between 90 and 100 inclusive
Comparison Condition	A comparison condition preceded by the keyword *Is*	Case Is > 89	Average is greater than 89

In each case, the test conditions refer to a student average, and each must follow the keyword Case. It is also possible to create very complex decision structures by combining all three test condition forms in the same Case statement. In these three forms of the Select Case test condition, it should be obvious that the first form is useful in looking for individual values or letters of the alphabet and the second form is useful in checking to determine if the test expression falls in a range of values. If you use the *To* keyword to define a range, the first value must be less than the second or an error will occur. Finally, the last form is useful for working with comparison expressions of the form discussed earlier.

> **TIP:** When a value may cause more than one condition to be true, only the first True condition will be evaluated and its corresponding action executed.

To apply the Select Case decision structure to the letter grade example, we need to rewrite the cmdLetter event procedure to replace the If-Then-ElseIf decision structure with Select Case. Since we are searching for values that are greater than or equal to some cutoff value, the third Select Case test expression form appears to be the best fit.

However, it would also be easy to use the second test expression form. The revised code for the cmdLetter command button is shown in VB Code Box 4-5.

| **VB CODE BOX 4-5.** Code for letter grade determination using Select Case | ```
Private Sub cmdLetter_Click()
   Dim intAverage as Integer, strLetterGrade as String
   intAverage = CInt(txtAverage.Text)
   Select Case intAverage
      Case Is >= 90
         strLetterGrade = "A"
      Case Is >= 80
         strLetterGrade = "B"
      Case Is >= 70
         strLetterGrade = "C"
      Case Is >= 60
         strLetterGrade = "D"
      Case Else
         strLetterGrade = "F"
   End Select
   txtLetter.Text = strLetterGrade
End Sub
``` |

If the If-Then-ElseIf decision structure is replaced with the Select Case decision structure shown in VB Code Box 4-5 and the project is executed with the same test data as before, the same letter grade should result.

While we have used numeric values for the Select Case decision structure, the same approach will work with character strings. In that case, the alphabetical ordering must be used to define a range. For example, it would be possible to use Case "A" to "Z" but not Case "M" to "A," because "A" comes before "Z" and "M" in the alphabetical ordering.

Mini-Summary 4-3: If-Then-ElseIf and Select Case Decision Structures

1. Multiple alternatives can be handled with either the If-Then-ElseIf or the Select Case decision structures.

2. The If-Then-ElseIf decision structure is an extension of the If-Then-Else decision structure in which multiple logical conditions can be tested in the ElseIf statements.

3. Scroll bars can be used to input values through movement up and down or right and left.

4. The Select Case decision structure uses three different types of conditions to test whether an alternative should be implemented: a list of values, a range of values using the To keyword, and a comparison condition using the Is keyword.

5. Either alternative decision structure can be used in almost all situations.

It's Your Turn!

1. Write Select Case conditions to test for each of the following:
   a. An age value is either 10, 20, or 30.
   b. A salary is between $50,000 and $100,000.
```

c. A gender is either "m" or "f".

d. A textbox called txtName is not empty.

e. A weight is below 150 pounds.

2. For each of the following, determine the result that is displayed in txtResult.

a. If sngX = 0.5? If sngX = -1.8? If sngX = 53.9?

```
Private Sub cmdCalculate_Click()
    Dim sngX As Single
    If (sngX <= 0) Then
        txtResult.Text = -sngX
    ElseIf (sngX < 1) Then
        txtResult.Text = sngX ^ 2
    Else
        txtResult.Text = 1
    End If
End Sub
```

b. If strResponse = "g"? If strResponse = "H"? If strResponse = "Y"?

```
Private Sub cmdCalculate_Click()
    Dim strResponse As String
    Select Case strResponse
    Case "g", "G"
        txtResult.Text = "50% discount"
    Case "h", "H"
        txtResult.Text = "30% discount"
    Case "i", "I"
        txtResult.Text = "10% discount"
    Case Else
        txtResult.Text = "No discount"
    End Select
End Sub
```

c. If intZ = -4? If intZ = 2? If intZ = 4? If intZ = 1? If intZ = 0? If intZ = 8?

```
Private Sub cmdCalculate_Click()
    Dim intZ As Integer
    Select Case intZ
    Case 1, 2, 3
        txtResult.Text = 5
    Case 2 To 5
        txtResult.Text = 5 / intZ
    Case Is >= 0
        txtResult.Text = 5 * intZ
    Case Else
        txtResult.Text = 0
    End Select
End Sub
```

3. Write If-Then-ElseIf and Select Case statements for the following situations:

a. Assume that the property tax on a home on South Beach is based on the market value of the home: 10% for homes over $200,000, 8% for homes over $100,000, and 6% for homes $100,000 or less. Write statements to determine the appropriate tax if the market value is known.

b. Assume that the FAST Parcel Service charges according to the distance a package is shipped: $1.00 per pound for over 1,000 miles; $.75 per pound for over 750 miles, and $.50 per pound for 750 miles or less. Write statements to determine the shipping charge if weight and distance shipped are known.

Completing the remaining questions will enable you to create the Visual Basic project discussed in the text.

4. To create the Letter Grade project, complete the following exercises:

a. Start Visual Basic (or select File | New Project) and open a Standard EXE form with a name of **frmLetterGrd** and a caption of **Letter Grade Determination**. Create the interface shown in Figure 4-7 using the text box and label names and properties shown in Table 4-4. Also, add two command buttons with names of **cmdLetter** and **cmdExit** and captions of **Letter Grade** and **Exit,** respectively. Finally, add a vertical scroll bar named **vsbAverage** with the lblScrollBar label beneath it.

TABLE 4-4: Text Boxes and Labels for Letter Grade Determination Project

Text Box Name	Label Name	Label Caption
txtName	lblName	Student Name
txtAverage	lblAverage	Student Average
txtLetter	lblLetter	Student Grade
	lblHeading	Letter Grade Determination
	lblScrollBar	Average

b. Define the properties for the vsbAverage scroll bar to be Max: **100**, Min: **0**, LargeChange: **10**, and SmallChange: **1**.

c. Add the code shown in VB Code Box 4-3 to the Change event procedure for the vsbAverage scroll bar. Add the code shown in VB Code Box 4-4 to the Click event procedure for the cmdLetter command button. Add the **End** instruction to the Click event procedure for the cmdExit command button.

d. Run your project for **Sean Jones** with an average of **82**. Try it on **Alice West** with an average of **58**. Try a few other names and averages to ensure the project is running as expected. After you have corrected any errors, save the form as **LetterGrd.frm** and the project as **LetterGrd.vbp** in the Chapter4 folder on your data disk.

e. Reverse the vsbAverage Max and Min properties to be **0** and **100** and test the revised project. Note the difference in the way the scroll bar now works. Save the form and project with the same names as before.

f. Revise the code in the Click event procedure for the cmdLetter command button to use the Select Case decision structure shown in VB Code Box 4-5. Test your project with the same data as before. After you have corrected any errors, save the form as **LetterCase.frm** and the project as **LetterCase.vbp** in the Chapter4 folder on your data disk.

APPLICATION TO SCENARIO

In the Vintage Videos scenario, the owner of the store has asked Clark to add features that will make it possible to enter the type of video and to automatically compute a price. While we could use an InputBox to input the type of video, there is an easier way to do this that does not require the user to type anything. As mentioned in Chapter 3 on programming errors, a large percentage of all run time errors can be traced to errors on input. It is all too easy for a user to misspell a word or to reverse the capitalization. Even if a single letter is being entered, there can still be problems with capitalization. For this reason it is always wise, if at all possible, to avoid having the user key in data, especially where the data concerns text.

Fortunately, Visual Basic provides a variety of controls that enable projects to be created that do not require the user to key in large amounts of data. You have already seen one of these controls earlier in this chapter—the scroll bar. Recall that the scroll bar allows the user to input numeric data by moving the scroll bar either vertically or horizontally. Other controls that are useful for displaying textual or numeric data in a list format are the list box and the combo box. With a **list box**, a list of data are displayed at all times. With the **combo box**, it is possible to display the data in a drop-down list box of the type you have probably used with the Windows operating system. While both controls can be used for input and output, in this chapter a list box will be used to input the video type instead of having the user enter it. In the next chapter, we will use a combo box as well.

The List Box Control

The list box is much like an extended text box in that it displays multiple text entries in a list. If the size of the list box as defined by the user is insufficient to display all items in the list, a scroll bar is automatically added that enables the user to scroll up or down to see the remaining list items. Just as for the text box, the default property for the list box control is the Text property. However, in this case the Text property refers to the item in the list that the user has highlighted by clicking on it.

list box

The list box icon in the Toolbox looks like a list with a scroll bar on the right-hand side. It is added to the form just like any other control. When a list box is placed on the form, the default name (*List* plus a number; for example, *List1*) is displayed. When you change the name, the new name will be displayed in the list box until list items are added. The three-letter prefix for list box names is *lst*. For example, if you wanted a list box to display the video types, an appropriate name would be *lstTypes*.

> **TIP:** You can change the look of the list box from a simple listing to a list with checkboxes by setting the Style property. The checkboxes can be useful if you want to allow for multiple items to be selected at the same time.

In addition to the number of text items displayed, one key way that the list box differs from the text box is in how data or information is placed in it. With the text box, we usually set the Text property to a null string at design time and then change it with an assignment statement at run time. With the list box, while you cannot modify the Text property at run time, you can create the list of items either at design time or at run time. If you are creating a list of items that will be the same every time you run the project and that is fairly short, you will probably want to create it at design time. On the other hand, if the contents of the list box will change from use to use, then you will *have* to add the items to the list in run time through a list of program instructions. Similarly, if the list of items to be added to the list box is long, then you will probably want to add them at run time by reading from a file (discussed in the next chapter.)

Since for Vintage Videos we have a short list of items that will be the same for every execution of the application, we will add the items to the list box at design time through the **List** property of the list box. When you click on the List property in the Properties browser and then click on the down arrow, a drop-down list box is displayed into which you can enter items to go on the list. To move to the next line after adding an item, press the **Ctrl-ENTER** key combination. (If you accidentally press **ENTER** and are exited from the drop-down list, you can always repeat the process to add items to the end of the list.) NOTE: You can only add items to the *end* of the drop-down list, so plan your list carefully before starting to add items to it. (You can also delete items from the drop-down list with the Delete and Backspace keys.)

> **TIP:** If necessary, you can increase the width of the List property drop-down list box by using the mouse to widen the Property browser.

Figure 4-9 shows the new list box added to the Vintage Videos form, with items being added to the List property in the Properties browser. Note that the name of the list box has been changed to lstTypes and it is displayed in the list box. Note also that we have entered two items, "Kids" and "Regular," pressing **Ctrl-ENTER** after each one. Since we have not pressed **ENTER** yet, they do not yet appear in the list box. When the third Item, "Classic," is input and **ENTER** is pressed, the List property items will replace the Name property in the list box.

FIGURE 4-9. List box and use of List property

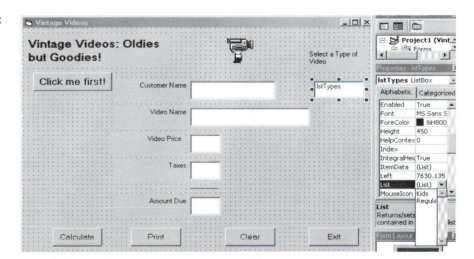

Note that when you add items to a list box as was done in Figure 4-9, a binary form file with an *frx* extension is created. This file must accompany the frm and vbp files in order for the list box to display the added items.

Adding Code

Once all three video types have been entered in the lstTypes list box, the next step is to add code to respond to the Click event for the list box. We also need to modify the code in the cmdCalc command button to ensure that the user has selected a type of video by clicking on it to highlight a type in the list box. Earlier we said that when an item is highlighted, the list box Text property is automatically set equal to that item. For example, if *Regular* is highlighted in the lstTypes list box, then the Text property for the list box is set equal to *Regular*.

To add the code for the Click event for the lstTypes list box, we need to double-click it to display the Code window for the Click event. While either of the two multiple-alternative decision structures could be used in this situation, the Select Case decision structure is more appropriate because of the efficient manner in which it selects a single code or word from among several possibilities and executes the corresponding statements. The code for the pricing decision is shown in VB Code Box 4-6. ,

| **VB CODE BOX 4-6.** Code for lstTypes click event | ```
Private Sub lstTypes_Click()
    Dim strVideoType As String, curPrice As Currency
    strVideoType = lstTypes.Text
    Select Case strVideoType 'Check type selected
        Case "Kids"
            curPrice = 0.99
        Case "Regular"
            curPrice = 1.99
        Case "Classic"
            curPrice = 2.99
    End Select
    txtVideoPrice.Text = Format(curPrice, "currency")
End Sub
``` |
|---|---|

Note in VB Code Box 4-6 that the VideoType String variable has been set equal to the (default) Text property of lstTypes. We then check to see which of the three possibilities—"Kids," "Regular," or "Classic"—the VideoType variable matches and set the price accordingly. This price is then formatted as Currency and transferred to the txtVideoPrice text box.

> **TIP:** When comparing strings, everything, even the case, must match exactly.

If this section of code is entered in the lstTypes list box Click event Code window, we are almost finished. However, what if the user fails to select a video type from the list box? In this case, the Text property for lstTypes does not equal any of the three video types and the price in txtVideoPrice text box will not change. To check for this, we need to insert a validation statement in the code for the cmdCalc command button. Like the previous validation statements, it will be a single-alternative If-Then-Else statement that checks for an empty string for the Text property of the lstTypes list box. In this case, if an empty string is found, a message box alerts the user to this condition and instructs the user to make a selection from the list box and to press the cmdCalc
```

command button again. Until the user selects a video type from the list box, he or she will not be able to calculate any values for this video. The new validation code is shown in VB Code Box 4-7 (where the VideoTypes variable has been declared as a String). This code should be inserted immediately before the price assignment in the cmdCalc event procedure.

| **VB CODE BOX 4-7.** Additional code for cmdCalc | ```strVideoType = lstTypes.Text
If strVideoType = "" Then 'Check for video type
  MsgBox "Select a video type and try again."
  Exit Sub 'No video type selected
End If``` |
|---|---|

It is also necessary to clear the list box at the same time that the text boxes are cleared. The statement to do this is:

```
lstTypes.Text = ""
```

and it should be added to the cmdClear_Click event procedure. The complete code for the cmdCalc command button is shown in VB Code Box 4-8.

| **VB CODE BOX 4-8.** Complete code for cmdCalc_Click event procedure | ```Private Sub cmdCalc_Click()
    Const sngTaxRate As Single = 0.07 'Use local tax rate
    Dim curPrice As Currency, curAmountDue As Currency
    Dim curTaxes As Currency, strVideoType As String
    If txtCustName.Text = "" Then 'Check for customer name
        txtCustName.Text = InputBox("Enter name and try again.")
        Exit Sub 'No customer name entered
    End If
    If txtVideoName.Text - "" Then 'Check for video name
        txtVideoName.Text = InputBox("Enter video name and try again.")
        Exit Sub 'No video name entered
    End If
    strVideoType = lstTypes.Text
    If strVideoType = "" Then 'Check for video type
      MsgBox "Select a video type and try again."
      Exit Sub 'No video type selected
    End If
    curPrice = CCur(txtVideoPrice.Text)
    curTaxes = curPrice * sngTaxRate 'Compute curTaxes
    curAmountDue = curPrice + curTaxes 'Compute amount due
    txtTaxes.Text = Format(curTaxes, "currency")
    txtAmountDue.Text = Format(curAmountDue, "currency")
    txtVideoPrice.Text = Format(curPrice, "currency")
End Sub``` |
|---|---|

Figure 4-10 shows the project being executed where the customer's name is Shelli Keagle and she is renting *Bambi*, which is classified as a "Kids" type video.

Mini-Summary 4-4: Using List Boxes

1. A list box can be used to display multiple lines of text, each of which can be selected by clicking on it.

2. The default property of the list box is the Text property, which is equal to the selected item.

3. The list box Click event can be used to check which value has been selected.

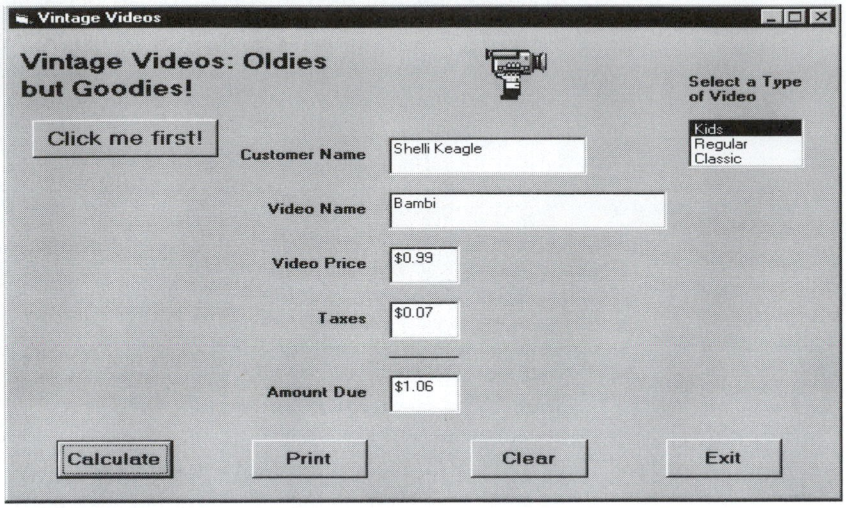

FIGURE 4-10.
Execution of project
with list box

It's Your Turn!

1. Update the Vintage Videos project by completing the following exercises:

   a. Open **Vintage4.vbp**. Add a list box control named **lstTypes** in the upper right-hand section of the form and a label to describe it. Change the List property for lstTypes to include the entries **Kids**, **Regular**, and **Classic**. Remember to press **Ctrl-ENTER** after each entry except the last; at that point, press **ENTER**. The list box should look like Figure 4-9.

   b. Add the code shown in VB Code Box 4-6 for the lstTypes Click event. Run your project and test this code to ensure that the correct price is being shown in the price text box. Remember, the String constants in the Select Case statements must be *exactly* the same as the items in the lstTypes list box or the decision structure will not work correctly.

   c. Modify the code for the cmdCalc command button to insert the code shown in VB Code Box 4-7. Your final code should appear like that shown in VB Code Box 4-8.

   d. Add a statement to the cmdClear_Click event procedure to clear the lstTypes list box.

   e. Test your modified project with a customer name of **Shelli Kagle,** a video name of *Bambi*, and a video type of **Kids**. Your result should appear like that shown in Figure 4-10. Also, try it for another type of video.

   f. Save your project and form under the same names as before.

2. Modify the Payroll project by completing the following exercises:

   a. Open **Payroll.vbp** and add a list box control named **lstPayRate**. Change the List property to include 4 payrates: **$5.25**, **$8.50**, **$10.00**, and **$12.50**.

   b. Add code for the lstPayRate Click event to input the payrate value from this list box to the txtPayRate text box.

    c. Test this project with all four payrates and the number of hours worked both below and above 40 hours. Once you are sure everything is correct, save it under the same name.

MORE COMPLEX DECISIONS

So far, we addressed only fairly simple decision structures in that only one condition was being considered. However, it is possible to encounter situations with more complex decision conditions. For example, in the Payroll Computation project, we may need to consider both salaried and hourly workers. Since salaried workers are typically not paid for overtime hours, we would need to pay them for 40 hours regardless of how many hours they actually worked. To do this, we would first need to check if a worker is salaried or hourly; if she is hourly, we would then need to make a decision as to how much she would be paid by checking the number of hours worked. If she is salaried, she is paid for 40 hours. This is an example of a decision as an alternative for another decision, a so-called **nested decision**.

Another situation that you might encounter would be one in which the alternative selected depends on more than one condition. This situation is referred to as a **compound condition**, since we combine multiple conditions. For example, in the Letter Grade Determination project, assume the professor considers both the quiz average and the number of absences in assigning a letter grade. A student must have an average of at least 90 *and* have no more than 3 absences to make an A grade, 80 and have no more than 5 absences to make a B, 70 and have no more than 7 absences to make a C, and so on.

We will discuss both nested decisions and compound conditions in this section.

Nested Decisions

Whenever a decision structure is one of the alternatives of a decision, this is referred to as a nested decision, since one decision is said to be *nested* in another decision. For example, in the payroll situation mentioned above with salaried and hourly employees, it must be decided if an employee's pay status is hourly *before* the decision about overtime versus regular time can be made. If the employee is not hourly, then no such decision needs to be made.

In working with nested decisions, the key point to remember is that any nested decisions must be completely carried out within a true or false alternative; it is not possible to have a nested decision completed outside of the alternative in which it appears. For the payroll example, the overtime decision must be completely handled within the true alternative of the hourly/salaried decision. This is shown in pseudocode form in the pseudocode shown below:

```
If PayStatus = Hourly Then
    If Hours > 40 then
        Pay = 40 * PayRate + 1.5 * (Hours - 40) * PayRate
    Else
        Pay = Hours * PayRate
    End Decision
Else
    Pay = 40 * PayRate
End Decision
```

Note in the pseudocode for the nested payroll decision that the PayStatus is checked first; if it is found to be Hourly, then, and only then, is the number of hours checked to make the overtime decision. If the PayStatus is *not* Hourly, then the employee is paid for 40 hours regardless of the number of hours she actually worked. It is in nested decisions such as this that indenting is of great use, because it clearly shows the level of each decision. In this case, the overtime decision is indented one level and its alternative is indented to a second level. This clearly shows these statements are alternatives for this decision and not for the pay status decision. On the other hand, the false alternative for the pay status decision is indented only one level to show its relationship to that decision structure. We will use the same type of indentation in the Visual Basic code.

In Visual Basic, let's add a list box named lstPayType to the payroll form with two items: *Hourly* and *Salaried*. Now we select one item from the list box and use it to determine the employee's pay. In this case, the code to compute a value for the variable curPay is shown in VB Code Box 4-9 (where strPayType has been previously declared as a String type variable.)

VB CODE BOX 4-9. Visual Basic code for nested payroll decision	```
	strPayType = lstPayType.Text
	If strPayType = "Hourly" Then 'Check pay status
	    If sngHours > 40 then 'Pay status is hourly
	        curPay = curPayRate * 40 + 1.5 * curPayRate * _
	        (sngHours - 40)
	    Else
	        curPay = curPayRate * sngHours
	    End if
	Else 'Pay status is salaried
	    curPay = curPayRate * 40
	End if
	``

Note that the statement to assign a value to curPay is sufficiently long that it is continued on the second line using the underline continuation character (_). There *must* be a space before the continuation character. You *cannot* continue a string constant contained in quotation marks. You must terminate the string constant and concatenate it with the remainder of the string after the continuation. For example, to continue a long string constant, you would do the following:

```
Msgbox("This is an extremely long string " & _
"constant that must be continued to the next line")
```

Compound Conditions

When a decision depends on a condition that involves two or more expressions, we have a compound condition. The modified grading condition mentioned earlier is an example of just such a condition, in which a student must achieve an average of at least 90 *and* have no more than three absences in order to earn a grade of A. In this case, the *and* is referred to as a **logical operator** since it operates on the logic of the true/false condition.

There are six logical operators, four of which are shown in Table 4-5. (We have not shown the other two—Imp and Eqv—because they are seldom used except in very specialized situations.) In addition to the name of the logical operator, Table 4-5 also contains a short description of each logical operator and an example using the operator (it is assumed that X = 20, Y = 10, and Z = 50).

It is important to note that each condition in a compound condition must be independent of the other conditions so it can be evaluated on its own. This means you could *not* have a statement of the form:

```
If X > 15 and < 25
```
because the second half of the statement cannot be evaluated independent of the first half.

TABLE 4-5: Logical Operators

Operator	Description	Example
And	Both conditions must be true for entire condition to be true	X > 15 *And* Z < 100 is true because both conditions are true
Or	One or both conditions must be true for entire condition to be true	X > 15 *Or* Y > 20 is true because one condition (X>15) is true
Not	Reverses a condition	*Not* (Y>5) is false because Y >5 is true
Xor	One and only one condition is true	X > Y *Xor* Y > Z is true because first condition is true and second is false

To rewrite our Letter Grade example to include the number of absences in the requirement for a grade, we need to use the And operator. We will assume that a second scroll bar named *vsbAbsences* is being used to input the number of absences and that the appropriate code has been added to its Change event to transfer the number of absences to a text box called txtAbsences. With these additions, the revised code for the cmdLetter command button for the Letter Grade example is shown in VB Code Box 4-10.

VB CODE BOX 4-10. Revised code for grade decision	```Private Sub cmdLetter_Click()```

```
Private Sub cmdLetter_Click()
    Dim intAverage as Integer, strLetterGrade as String
    Dim intAbsences as Integer
    intAverage = CInt(txtAverage.Text)
    intAbsences = CInt(txtAbsences.Text)
    If intAverage >= 90 and intAbsences <= 3 then
        strLetterGrade = "A"
    ElseIf intAverage >= 80 and intAbsences <= 5 then
        strLetterGrade = "B"
    ElseIf intAverage >= 70 and intAbsences <= 7 Then
        strLetterGrade = "C"
    ElseIf intAverage >= 60 and intAbsences <= 9 then
        strLetterGrade = "D"
    Else
        strLetterGrade = "F"
    End if
    txtLetter.text = strLetterGrade
End sub
```

Mini-Summary 4-5: Complex Decisions

1. Complex decisions can be implemented as nested decisions or compound conditions.

2. Nested decisions involve a decision being one of the alternatives of another decision.

Mini-Summary 4-5: Complex Decisions (Continued)

3. Compound conditions combine conditions using one of the logical operators: And, Or, Not, and Xor.

4. Each condition in a compound decision must be able to be evaluated by itself.

It's Your Turn!

1. For each of the following, write a compound condition or nested decision that will allow the appropriate alternative to be selected:

   a. When the value of an integer variable intAge is between 20 and 65, output the result "Employment Age", otherwise do nothing.

   b. When a Single variable sngTemp is less than 32, output the result "Very Cold"; when sngTemp is from 32 to less than 50, output the result "Cold"; when sngTemp is from 50 to less than 65, output the result "Cool"; when sngTemp is from 65 to less than 80, output the result "Warm"; otherwise output the result "Hot."

   c. When a marital status code, strMarStatCode, is "m" or "M", output the result "Married"; when the code is "s" or "S", output the result "Single"; otherwise give a message about an incorrect code and exit the subroutine.

   d. When a Single variable, sngSales, is less than $50, the value of the Single variable sngCommission is $0; when sngSales is between $50 and $500, inclusive, the value of sngCommission is 10% of sngSales; when sngSales is greater than $500, the value of sngCommission is $50 plus 8% of sngSales above $500.

2. For the following, determine the value that is displayed in the txtResult text box:

   a. When txtX.Text = 5 and txtY.Text = 3? When txtX.Text = -5 and txtY.Text = 3? When txtX.Text = 5 and txtY.Text = -3? When txtX.Text = -5 and txtY.Text = -3?

```
Private Sub cmdGo_Click()
    Dim intX As Integer
    Dim intY As Integer
    intX = CInt(txtX.Text)
    intY = CInt(txtY.Text)
    If intX > 0 And intY > 0 Then
        txtResult.Text = intX * intY
    ElseIf intX < 0 And intY < 0 Then
        txtResult.Text = -intX * intY
    ElseIf intX > 0 And intY < 0 Then
        txtResult.Text = intX * intY
    ElseIf intX < 0 And intY > 0 Then
        txtResult.Text = -intX * intY
    End If
End Sub
```

   b. When txtX.Text = 5 and txtY.Text = 3? When txtX.Text = -5 and txtY.Text = 3? When txtX.Text = 5 and txtY.Text = -3? When txtX.Text = -5 and txtY.Text = -3?

```
Private Sub cmdGo_Click()
    Dim intX As Integer
    Dim intY As Integer
    intX = CInt(txtX.Text)
    intY = CInt(txtY.Text)
    If (intX > 0 And intY > 0) Or (intX > 0 And _
      intY < 0) Then
        txtResult.Text = intX * intY
    End If
    If (intX < 0 And intY < 0) Or (intX < 0 And _
      intY > 0) Then
        txtResult.Text = -intX * intY
    End If
End Sub
```

c. When txtX.Text = 5 and txtY.Text = 3? When txtX.Text = -5 and txtY.Text = 3? When txtX.Text = 5 and txtY.Text = -3? When txtX.Text = -5 and txtY.Text = -3?

```
Private Sub cmdGo_Click()
    Dim intX As Integer
    Dim intY As Integer
    intX = CInt(txtX.Text)
    intY = CInt(txtY.Text)
    If intX > 0 Then
        If intY > 0 Then
            txtResult.Text = intX * intY
        Else
            txtResult.Text = -intX * intY
        End If
    Else
        If intY > 0 Then
            txtResult.Text = -intX * intY
        Else
            txtResult.Text = intX * intY
        End If
    End If
End Sub
```

3. For each of the following compound conditions, write two conditions that are its opposite—that is—conditions that will be True when the original is False, and vice versa. Write one of your conditions using the Not operator and one without.

    a. `intW > 10 And intW < 20`

    b. intK = 5 Or intJ <=5

    c. (intM < 0 or intN < 0) And intP < 0

    d. Not ((intA > 0 Or intB >0) Or Not (intA > 0 Or intB >0))

4. Nick's mom is making videos of Nick's favorite television shows while he is on duty with the National Guard in Bosnia. She wants to create a program that, when a day and time are entered, will remind her which show to record and what channel it is on. Write a selection structure that will implement the following table:

5. The local hobby shop is starting a club for collectors of wooden railway system products. For each $10 purchase, a club member will receive a point. After 5 points have been accumulated, the member will receive a 3% discount on each subsequent

TABLE 4-6: Nick's show schedule

Day	Time	Show and Channel
Monday	11:00 a.m.	Bob the Builder, Nickelodeon
Monday	12:00 noon	Clifford, PBS
Wednesday	9:00 a.m.	Rolie Polie Olie, Disney
Wednesday	1:00 p.m.	Rolie Polie Olie, Disney
Friday	11:00 a.m.	Bob the Builder, Nickelodeon

purchase. After 10 points have been accumulated, the member will receive a 5% discount on each subsequent purchase. After 20 points have been accumulated, the member will receive a 7.5% discount on each subsequent purchase. Finally, a club member who accumulates 50 points will receive a 10% discount on each purchase. Write a selection structure that will determine the discounted price of an item based on the actual price and the number of points accumulated. Additional points should be added based on the discount price.

Completing the remaining questions will enable you to create the Visual Basic project discussed in the text.

6. Modify the Payroll project by completing the following exercises:

a. Open the **Payroll.vbp** project and add a list box control named **lstPayType** and a label to describe the list box. Use the List property to add two items to the list box: **Hourly** and **Salaried**. Declare a variable **PayType** as string.

b. Modify the code for the cmdCompute command button control so the payroll decision matches that shown in VB Code Box 4-9.

c. Test your new payroll project by selecting **Hourly** for both **35** and **45** hours worked at a payrate of **$10.00** per hour. Do the same again except select **Salaried** as the PayType. You should get different answers for the two pay types for 45 hours.

d. Save the payroll form and project with the same names as before.

7. Modify the Letter Grade project by completing the following exercises:

a. Open the **LetterGrd.vbp** project and, immediately below the txtAverage text box, add a new text box control named **txtAbsences** with an appropriate label. Also, add a second scroll bar control named **vsbAbsences** with a Min property of **10** (if they have more than 9 absences it won't change their grade) and a Max property of **0**. Set both the LargeChange and SmallChange properties to **1**. Finally, add appropriate labels for the new scroll bar.

b. Add the necessary code to the Change event procedure for the vsbAbsences control to transfer its Value property to the txtAbsences text box. Modify the code for the cmdLetter command button control to match that shown in VB Code Box 4-10.

c. Test your revised grading project with various values for the average and the number of absences. In particular, test the effect of the number of absences on the letter grade. For example, what letter grade is assigned a student with an average of 95 and 5 absences? 2 absences?

d. Save the letter grade assignment form and project with the same names as before.

8. Look at the form of the Select Case decision structure. Is there any reason why we could not use nested decisions in it? How about using compound conditions in a Select Case decision structure?

USING THE FORM_LOAD EVENT

The last change the owner of Vintage Videos has requested is that the welcome message appear automatically when the project begins, rather than only when the user remembers to click the "Click me first!" command button. To cause any code to be executed when the project is initiated, you must use the Load event for the form (commonly referred to as the Form_Load event). As the name implies, the **Form_Load event** occurs when the form is loaded. This event is triggered for the main form when you first start the project and is triggered for any other form when it is loaded into memory. To enter code for the Form_Load event, you simply double-click anywhere on the form to open the Form_Load event procedure Code window. Just as the Click event is the default event for command buttons, the Load event is the default event for the form.

Our objective for opening the Form_Load event is to enter the same code that now exists for the Click event for the cmdMessage command button. Actually, we want to *move* the code from the cmdMessage command button to the Form_Load event and then delete the button altogether. While we could simply retype the code in the Form_Load event procedure, we can also use the editing capabilities of the Code window to expedite the process. When you open the Code window for the Form_Load event, you can display the code for the cmdMessage Click event procedure (if it is not displayed already) by using the vertical scroll bar. When the code for this event procedure is visible, use the mouse to highlight it, the Cut icon on the toolbar to *cut* it (shortcut keys: **Ctrl-x**), and the Paste icon to *paste* it (shortcut keys: **Ctrl-v**) in the Form_Load event Code window. [If you want to copy only a section of code, you would use the Copy icon (shortcut keys: **Ctrl-c**) instead of the Cut icon.] Figure 4-11 shows the line of code for the cmdMessage Click event procedure highlighted and ready to be moved to the Form_Load event procedure.

Cut

Paste

Copy

FIGURE 4-11. Moving code from one event procedure to another

```
Private Sub cmdExit_Click()
    End
End Sub
Private Sub cmdMessage_Click()
    MsgBox "Welcome to Vintage Videos"
End Sub
Private Sub cmdPrint_Click()
    PrintForm
End Sub
Private Sub Form_Load()

End Sub
```

Once you have moved the code from the cmdMessage Click event procedure to the Form_Load event procedure, it will be executed every time the form is loaded when the project is started. Since we don't need the cmdMessage command button any more, we need to delete it. To do this, display the form and click on the button to highlight it. You can then delete it by pressing the **Delete** key or by using the **Edit | Delete** option. You should delete the beginning and ending lines of code in the Code window for the now non-existing cmdMessage command button to keep the Code window from being filled with extraneous lines of code.

It's Your Turn!

1. Modify the Vintage Videos project by completing the following exercises:

   a. Open the project **Vintage4.vbp** and then open the Form_Load event Code window. Move the welcoming message from the cmdMessage command button event procedure to the Form Load event procedure.

   b. Delete the cmdMessage command button and delete the corresponding event procedure code.

   c. Test the Form_Load event by starting the project several times. If it works, save the form and project under the same name as before.

A FIRST LOOK AT VISUAL BASIC'S DEBUGGING TOOLS

View Toolbars submenu

As we noted in the last chapter, Visual Basic has a wide array of debugging tools. To help you with your projects as they become more complex and have a greater chance of including errors, we will introduce these debugging tools in this chapter. In later chapters, we will extend this discussion to other tools.

A primary aid to debugging is the Debug toolbar, which you can display by selecting Toolbars from the View menu item. In the **View | Toolbars** submenu, you will see the various toolbars that are available with Visual Basic: Debug, Edit, Form Editor, and Standard. There is also an option to customize a toolbar but we will not discuss that here. To view the Debug toolbar, click the check box at the left of the Debug option. The resulting toolbar is shown in Figure 4-12 with the various icons labeled. While you will not understand all of these now, their purpose will become clear to you in later chapters. Some of these options are also on the Standard toolbar.

> **TIP:** If you prefer the keyboard to using the mouse, there are several hot keys that can be used for the debugging features. These include: F8—Step Into; F5—Run, Shift-F8—Step Over, and F9—Toggle Breakpoint.

FIGURE 4-12.
Debug toolbar

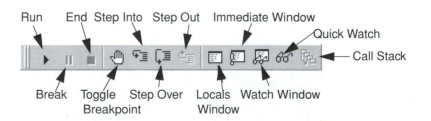

*Using the Break
Command and the
Immediate Window*

In looking at the Debug toolbar, notice the two vertical lines (second option from left; also on Standard toolbar). If you click on these while a project is running, they will *break* the project execution and put you into **break mode**. Since you can click the Run icon again to restart the project, the break mode does not end the project; it just *pauses* it. Once you enter the break mode, you can then access other debugging options. One of these is the **Immediate window,** which is the small window with the *Immediate* caption that "pops up" when you run your project. When you click on the break option, the project Code window and the Immediate window are displayed. When the Immediate window is on the screen, you can use it to display the current status of variables with the **Print** *variables* statement.

For example, assume that in the Vintage Videos project, you made a mistake in the lstTypes Click event procedure: Instead of *Classic,* you used *Classics* (with an *s)* in the Case statement. Then, when you ran the project and clicked on the *Classic* option, a price of $0.00 was displayed, as shown in Figure 4-13, because there was no match for *Classics* in the Case statement.

FIGURE 4-13. Error in Vintage Videos input

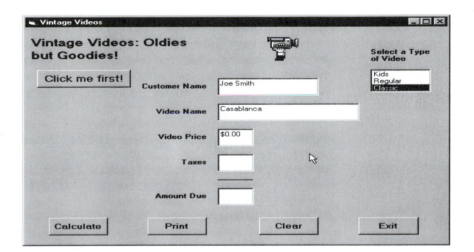

To find the cause of this error, you need to click the break icon on either the Standard toolbar or the Debug toolbar. When you do this, the Immediate window is displayed on top of the project Code window. If you then click in the Immediate window and enter

```
Print lstTypes.Text
```

the current value for the Text property of the lstTypes list box will be displayed in the Immediate window, as shown in Figure 4-14.

> **TIP:** You may use the question mark as a shortcut for the Print command.

Note that the value of the Text property for lstTypes is seen to be *Classic,* while the Select Case statement in the Code window uses *Classics.* After seeing this, you can change the Select Case statement to match the value of lstTypes and click on the Run icon to restart the project with the correct code. If you click again on the *Classic* item in the lstTypes list box, the correct price is displayed in the Video Price text box.

FIGURE **4-14.** Use of Immediate window to display variable

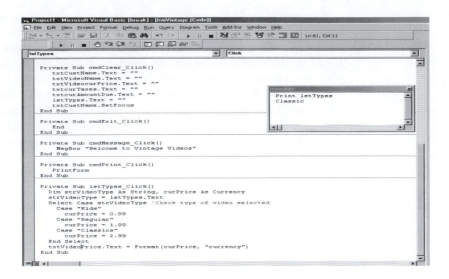

When you encounter an error message in Visual Basic, the project is automatically switched to the break mode so you can use the Immediate window to print values to look for the cause of the error.

> **TIP:** It is often advisable to use a control property in the Immediate window, since variable values are lost when you leave an event procedure.

It's Your Turn!

1. If it is not already open, open **Vintage4.vbp** and modify the Click event procedure for the lstTypes control to change the **Case "Classic"** statement to **Case "Classics"** and run the project. Enter the data shown in Figure 4-13 and click on **Classic**. When a value of $0.00 is displayed, click on the break icon, type **Print lstTypes** in the Immediate window, and press **ENTER**. Your result should look like Figure 4-14.

2. Modify the Case statement back to **"Classic"** and click on the Run icon. Click on the Classic option again and you should see $2.99.

SUMMARY

In this chapter, you have been introduced to the selection process of programming, which involves comparing two values and, on the basis of that comparison, selecting one of two or more alternatives to execute. The selection process is very important in programming, because it allows the program to make decisions based on the data. Without the selection process, all programs would simply execute the code straight through, with no deviation from a set procedure.

The types of selection processes that we discussed involved two alternatives and many alternatives. In the two-alternative decision type, there is one comparison condition and two alternatives: one for the true comparison condition and one for the false condition. Only one of the two alternatives can be executed, and then the decision structure is terminated. This decision type is implemented in Visual Basic through the If-Then-Else decision structure. It is also possible to have a one-alternative decision type by including only a true alternative. In this case, if the comparison condition is false, no alternative is implemented and the decision structure is terminated. This one-alternative case is implemented in Visual Basic through the If-Then decision structure.

For the many-alternative decision type, there are multiple conditions with an alternative for each condition. The conditions are tested, and when a true condition is encountered the corresponding alternative is selected. There may also be an alternative that is implemented if *all* conditions are found to be false. In any case, when a condition is found to be true and an alternative is executed, no other conditions are tested and the decision structure is terminated. The multiple-alternative decision type is implemented in Visual Basic through the If-Then-ElseIf and Select Case decision structures.

The scroll bar and list box controls were also discussed in this chapter. The scroll bar is an analog control that returns an integer value depending on the movement of the slider bar. The Change event is the default event for both vertical and horizontal scroll bars.

The list box, which can be used as a means of displaying several alternatives, was also discussed. In a list box, you can select an alternative by clicking on it. The Click event for this control was used in combination with the Select Case decision structure to select a type of video and display its price in the corresponding text box.

Two types of more complex decisions were also discussed: nested decisions and compound conditions. With nested decisions, at least one alternative of a decision structure is itself a decision structure. Only if this alternative is executed will the nested decision be implemented. An important feature of nested decisions is that decisions cannot overlap; the inner decision must be completed totally within the alternative in which it is found. With complex conditions, one or more of the logical operators (And, Or, Not, and Xor) are used to combine two or more conditions to make a decision. It is important to remember that each condition in a compound condition must be able to be evaluated by itself.

Finally, we discussed the use of the Form_Load event as a way of executing instructions every time the project is started. You were then introduced to the Debug toolbar and the various operations available from it. The use of the break icon and the Immediate window were also covered in this chapter. A complete list of the Vintage Videos code from this chapter is shown in VB Code Box 4-11.

NEW VISUAL BASIC ELEMENTS

Controls/Objects	Properties	Methods	Events
scroll bar control	Name Value Max/Min/Largechange/SmallChange		Change
list box control	Name Text List		Click
Form object			Load
Immediate Window		Print	

| VB CODE BOX 4-11. Complete code for Vintage Videos project | ```
Option Explicit
Private Sub cmdCalc_Click()
    Const sngTaxRate As Single = 0.07 'Use local tax rate
    Dim curPrice As Currency, curAmountDue As Currency
    Dim curTaxes As Currency, strVideoType As String
    If txtCustName.Text = "" Then 'Check for name
       txtCustName.Text = InputBox("Enter name and try again.")
       Exit Sub 'No customer name entered
    End If
    If txtVideoName.Text = "" Then 'Check for video name
    txtVideoName.Text = InputBox("Enter video name and try again.")
       Exit Sub 'No video name entered
    End If
    strVideoType = lstTypes.Text
    If strVideoType = "" Then 'Check for video type
      MsgBox "Select a video type and try again."
       Exit Sub 'No video type selected
    End If
    curPrice = CCur(txtVideoPrice.Text)
    curTaxes = curPrice * sngTaxRate 'Compute Taxes
    curAmountDue = curPrice + curTaxes 'Compute amount due
    txtTaxes.Text = Format(curTaxes, "currency")
    txtAmountDue.Text = Format(curAmountDue, "currency")
    txtVideoPrice.Text = Format(curPrice, "currency")
End Sub
Private Sub cmdClear_Click()
    txtCustName.Text = ""
    txtVideoName.Text = ""
    txtVideoPrice.Text = ""
    txtTaxes.Text = ""
    txtAmountDue.Text = ""
    lstTypes.Text = ""
    txtCustName.SetFocus
End Sub
Private Sub cmdExit_Click()
    End
End Sub
Private Sub Form_Load()
    MsgBox "Welcome to Vintage Videos"
End Sub
Private Sub cmdPrint_Click()
    PrintForm
End Sub
``` |
|---|---|

NEW PROGRAMMING STATEMENTS

Statements for two-alternative decision
If *condition is true* **then**
   statements for true alternative
Else
   statements for false alternative
End if
```

NEW PROGRAMMING STATEMENTS (CONTINUED)

Statements for one-alternative decision
If *condition is true* **then**
  statements for true alternative
End if

Statement to use InputBox *variable or control property* = **InputBox**(*"prompt"*)

Statements for multiple-alternative decision using If-Then-Elseif form
If *condition1 is true* **then**
  first set of statements
Elseif *condition2 is true* **then**
  second set of statements
ElseIf *condition3 true* **then**
  third set of statements
Else
  last set of statements
End if

Statements for multiple-alternative decision using Select Case form
Select Case *expression*
Case *condition1*
  First set of statements
Case *condition2*
  Second set of statements
Case Else
  Last set of statements
End Select

KEY TERMS

Break mode	If-Then-Else decision	nested decision
Combo Box	If-Then-ElseIf decision	Select Case decision
compound condition	Immediate window	scroll bar
Form_Load event	list box	validation
If-Then decision	logical operator	

EXERCISES

1. Based on what you have read and your practice with Visual Basic, answer the following questions.

   a. What are the various types of decisions in a computer program?

   b. What statement forms are available in Visual Basic to make decisions? When should each be used?

   c. What are comparison operators? List those that are available in Visual Basic.

   d. What are logical operators? List those that are available in Visual Basic.

   e. Describe the new controls that were presented in this chapter.

2. What will be shown in the txtResult textbox after each of the following is executed?

a.

```
Private Sub cmdGo_Click()
    Dim strResponse As String
    strResponse = "Hiya!"
    If strResponse <> "" Then
        txtResult.Text = "Not Empty"
        Exit Sub
    End If
    txtResult.Text = "Empty"
End Sub
```

b.
```
Private Sub cmdGo_Click()
    If txtResult.BackColor = vbRed Then
        txtResult.BackColor = vbGreen
        txtResult.Text = "Green"
    Else
        txtResult.BackColor = vbRed
        txtResult.Text = "Red"
    End If
End Sub
```

c.
```
Private Sub cmdGo_Click()
    Dim intDist As Integer
    Dim sngCost As Single
    intDist = 23 * 5
    If intDist <= 100 Then
        sngCost = 5
    ElseIf intDist > 100 And intDist <= 500 Then
        sngCost = 8
    ElseIf intDist > 500 And intDist < 1000 Then
        sngCost = 20
    Else
        sngCost = 12
    End If
    txtResult.Text = sngCost
End Sub
```

d.
```
Private Sub cmdGo_Click()
    Dim strGender As String
    Dim strMarStatus As String
    Dim strCode As String
    strGender = "F"
    strMarStatus = "m"
    If strGender = "m" Or strGender = "M" Then
        If strMarStatus = "s" Or strMarStatus = "S" Then
            strCode = "AA"
        Else
            strCode = "AB"
        End If
    End If
    If strGender = "f" Or strGender = "F" Then
        If strMarStatus = "s" Or strMarStatus = "S" Then
            strCode = "BA"
        Else
```

```
                strCode = "BB"
            End If
        End If
    txtResult.Text = strCode
End Sub
```

3. Write Select Case blocks for the following scenarios:

a. In the Spring, a certain city classifies a pollen index of less than 10 as "pleasant," 11 to 20 as "slightly unpleasant," 21 to 30 as "unpleasant," and over 30 as "stay inside." Write a Select Case block which uses a variable intPollenIndex to generate the appropriate message.

b. The local library checks out more than just books these days. With the different types of media available for checkout, a more complex mode of determining overdue charges is required. Write a Select Case block that will determine the amount of a fine based on the item and the number of days overdue. The late fees for each item are listed in Table 4-7.

TABLE 4-7: Library late fees

Item	Fine per day
General books	Each day, $0.10
New books	First 10 days, $0.10 Over 10 days, $0.20
Video tape	First 3 days, $0.25 4 to 6 days, $0.50 Over 6 days, $1.00
Audio tape	First week, $0.20 Over 7 days, $0.40

c. Tropical storms are classified as hurricanes based on their wind speeds and storm surges. Generally, a minimum hurricane has sustained winds of at least 74 miles per hour (mph). A storm that is a hurricane can be classified into 5 categories based on the Saffir/Simpson classification scale: Category 1—sustained winds of 74 to 95 mph; Category 2—sustained winds of 96 to 110 mph; Category 3—sustained winds of 111 to 130 mph; Category 4—sustained winds of 131 to 155 mph; Category 5—sustained winds above 155 mph. Write a Select Case block that will determine the hurricane category based on the wind speed in mph.

d. If you have eaten at a Chinese restaurant, you may have noticed placemats depicting the Chinese zodiac. Each year in the Chinese calendar is associated with a particular animal. The 12-year cycle is rat, ox, tiger, rabbit, dragon, snake, horse, ram, monkey, rooster, dog, and boar. The year 1900 is a year of the rat, 1901 is a year of the ox, and so on, with 1912 being another year of the rat. If you know when someone was born, you can calculate the difference between their year of birth and 1900 and use this to determine in which year of the Chinese zodiac the person was born. Write a Select Case block that will determine the Chinese year based on the difference between a year of birth and 1900.

4. For each of the following, explain what is wrong with the code. What error messages would you see, if any? What can you do to fix it?

```
a. Private Sub cmdGo_Click()
     Dim intX As Integer
     intX = 5
     If intX = txtInput.Text Then
       txtResult.Text = "They are the same"
     End If
   End Sub
```

```
b. Private Sub cmdGo_Click()
     Dim intX As Integer
     intX = CInt(txtX.Text)
     intY = CInt(txtY.Text)
     If intX > 0 And (intY < 0 And intX < 0) Then
       txtResult.Text = "Hurray, it's True!"
     End If
   End Sub
```

5. Use the Visual Basic Help facility or the MSDN on-line library to answer the following questions.

a. What can the LCase and UCase functions be used for?

b. What is the value of the Listbox ListIndex property if no item is selected? If the first item in the listbox is selected?

c. What is the difference between a Form's Load and Activate events?

d. What is the difference between the Debug menu commands Step Into and Step Over?

PROJECTS

1. From the Chapter3 folder on your data disk, open the project **EX3-1.vbp** and add validation statements to the code for the command button that sums and averages the three quiz scores. These validation statements should check that the user has entered a student name and three quiz scores. If the name or a quiz score is missing, use an **InputBox** to request an entry from the user. Test your revised project with a student name of **Ashley Hyatt** and quiz scores of **75, 90,** and **80.** However, do not enter the name or the last quiz score until requested to do so by the project. Save your revised project as **Ex4-1.frm** and **Ex4-1.vbp** in the Chapter4 folder on your data disk.

2. From the Chapter3 folder on your data disk, open the project **EX3-2.vbp** and add validation statements to the code for the command button that computes the treatment cost. These statements should check that the user has entered a customer name and the number of square feet. If the name or square footage has been omitted, an **InputBox** should request this information. Also, assume that there are two types of treatment: **Pre-emergence** at **$0.004** per square foot and **Fertilizer** at **$0.001** per square foot. Add a list box with the two types of treatments, from which the user can select one. Based on the user's selection, the project should compute the treatment cost. Test your revised project with a customer name of **Todd Allman**, a square footage of **4,000,** and **Pre-emergence** treatment. However, do not enter the name until requested to do so by the project. Save your revised project as **Ex4-2.frm** and **Ex4-2.vbp** in the Chapter4 folder on your data disk.

3. From the Chapter3 folder on your data disk, open the project **EX3-3.vbp** and add a validation statement to the code for the command button that computes the miles per gallon to ensure that the miles driven is not zero. If it is zero or has not been entered, display an error message and terminate the computation of the miles per gallon. Test your project with an **Altissan** make of car that used **10.5** gallons of gas. Do not enter the miles driven until after you have first clicked the command button. At that time, enter **285** miles and click it again. Save your revised project as **Ex4-3.frm** and **Ex4-3.vbp** in the Chapter4 folder on your data disk.

4. From the Chapter3 folder on your data disk, open the project **EX3-4.vbp** and assume that the company makes only two products: Widgets and DoHickeys. The unit price and unit cost for each of these items is shown in Table 4-8 and the fixed cost of production is the same for both products. A list box should display the names of the products. The user should select the item for which the breakeven cost is being computed. Based on this selection, the unit price and cost information shown below should be used to compute the breakeven amount. Test your project to compute the breakeven cost for both products if the fixed cost is **$1,000**. Test it again if the fixed cost is **$5,000**. Save your revised project as **Ex4-4.frm** and **Ex4-4.vbp** in the Chapter4 folder on your data disk.

TABLE **4-8**: Unit price and costs

Product	Unit Price	Unit Cost
Widgets	$25	$15
DoHickeys	$35	$30

5. From the Chapter3 folder on your data disk, open the project **EX3-5.vbp** and assume that the wallpaper company sells two types of wallpaper: Standard, which has 50 square feet per roll at a cost of $15 per roll, and Premium, with 37.5 square feet per roll at a cost of $25 per roll. A list box should display the two types of wallpaper from which the user can choose. Add the capability to clear the list box selection to the existing Clear button. Test your project to compute the number of rolls needed and cost to wallpaper the room for both products if the room is **12.5** feet by **20** feet with a door area of **42** square feet and a window area of **36** square feet. Save your revised project as **Ex4-5.frm** and **Ex4-5.vbp** in the Chapter4 folder on your data disk.

6. Open the project **EX3-1.vbp** (or **EX4-1.vbp** if you completed it) and add a text box to display the letter grade earned by the student. Also add a corresponding label to describe the contents of the text box. Add the necessary code to the command button that computes the average score to assign the student a letter grade based on Table 4-9. Also, add a welcoming message that is displayed when you start the project. Test the resulting project for the data shown in Project 1. Also text your project for a variety of other quiz scores. Save your revised project as **Ex4-6.frm** and **Ex4-6.vbp** in the Chapter4 folder on your data disk.

7. Open the project **EX3-2.vbp** (or **EX4-2.vbp** if you completed it) and add (or modify) a list box with types of treatments and a descriptive label. Assume that users will input the square footage directly into the text box or from a scroll bar. They will then choose a type of treatment from the list box and determine a price per square foot based

TABLE 4-9: Grading scale

Average	Letter Grade
93 and above	A
at least 85 but less than 93	B
at least 77 but less than 85	C
less than 77	F

on Table 4-10. Also, add a welcoming message that is displayed when you start the project and add the capability to clear the list box selection to the existing Clear button. Test your revised project with a customer name of **Todd Allman**, a square footage of **4,000**, and **Premium Grass Fertilizer** treatment. Test it for the other treatments. Save your revised project as **Ex4-7.frm** and **Ex4-7.vbp** in the Chapter4 folder on your data disk.

TABLE 4-10: Product data

Treatment	Price per Square Foot
Pre-emergence	.004
Broadleaf Weed	.002
Regular Fertilizer	.001
Premium Grass Fertilizer	.005

8. Modify the project you completed in Project 6 to consider the number of quizzes taken. To receive a grade of A, in addition to the quiz score requirement, the student must have taken all 3 quizzes; for a B, they must have taken at least 2 quizzes, and for a C, they must have taken at least 1 quiz. (If no quizzes are taken, the grade is an F.) Test your project for the same data as for Exercise 1 (where 3 quizzes were taken). Also test it on a student with a quiz scores of **92** and **96** for **2** quizzes. Save your revised project as **Ex4-8.frm** and **Ex4-8.vbp** in the Chapter4 folder on your data disk.

9. Revise the project you created for Project 4 in this chapter to use a list box to handle four products. The four projects and their unit costs and unit prices are shown in Table 4-11. Also, add a welcoming message that is displayed when you start the project. Finally, add the capability to clear the list box selection in preparation for the next product. Test your project to compute the breakeven cost for all products if the fixed cost is $1,000. Test it again if the fixed cost is $5,000. Save your revised project as **Ex4-9.frm** and **Ex4-9.vbp** in the Chapter4 folder on your data disk.

TABLE 4-11: Product data

Product	Unit Price	Unit Cost
Widgets	$25	$15
DoHickeys	$35	$30

TABLE 4-11: Product data (Continued)

Product	Unit Price	Unit Cost
Whatzits	$9.50	$4.50
ThingaMabobs	$12.25	$9.75

10. Revise the project you created for Project 5 in this chapter to use a list box to handle five types of wallpaper. The five types of wallpaper and the square feet per roll are shown in Table 4-12. Also, add a welcoming message that is displayed when you start the project. Finally, add the capability to clear the list box selection in preparation for the next type of wallpaper to the existing Clear button. Test your project to compute the number of rolls needed for each type of wallpaper for the data given in Project 5. Save the revised project as **Ex4-10.frm** and **Ex4-10.vbp** in the Chapter4 folder on your data disk.

TABLE 4-12: Wallpaper data

Wallpaper Type	Square footage per roll	Cost per roll
Standard	50	$15
Premium	37.5	$25
Jumbo	60	$20
Double	75	$45
Triple	112.5	$65

11. John Galt, who recently moved to California, has been reeling over his gas bill. He can't believe the recent amounts due, so he decides to build a Visual Basic program to double-check the gas company's calculations. John finds out the following after a call to his gas company. Each month the meter is read. The meter presents a four-digit number representing cubic meters of gas. The difference between the current month's reading and the previous month's reading is then used to calculate the amount owed. Note that, since only four digits are available on the meter, the current reading may be less than the previous reading. For example, the previous reading may be 9780, and the current one may be 0408. Your code should take this into account. The company charges for gas based on the rates shown in Table 4-13. Design and create a Visual Basic program for calculating John's gas bill. Save the project as **Ex4-11.frm** and **Ex4-11.vbp** in the Chapter4 folder on your data disk.

TABLE 4-13: Gas rate chart

Gas Used	Rate
First 80 cubic meters	$10.00 minimum cost
Next 120 cubic meters	$0.10 per cubic meter
Next 200 cubic meters	$0.05 per cubic meter
Above 400 cubic meters	$0.025 per cubic meter

12.   Howard Roark, a prominent architect, has recently turned his attention to ensuring that his buildings conform to the Uniform Federal Accessibility Standards (UFAS). The purpose of these standards is to make sure that public areas, such as lobbies and corridors, are accessible for all users, including those in wheelchairs. A couple of the standards concern the dimensions that are required for a turn around an obstruction in a corridor. If the obstacle is 48 inches or more wide, then the aisle width must be at least 36 inches and the turn width of the corridor must be at least 36 inches. If the obstacle is less than 48 inches, then the aisle width must be at least 42 inches and the turn width of the corridor must be at least 48 inches. Design a Visual Basic program that will determine whether or not a design specification for a turn meets the UFAS requirements. Howard should be able to enter the widths of the obstacle, the aisle, and the turn. Then a message should appear notifying him whether or not the design is within specifications. Save the project as **Ex4-12.frm** and **Ex4-12.vbp** in the Chapter4 folder on your data disk.

13.   Mr. Roark's architecture firm is interested in energy conservation in the houses that they build. Howard knows that sunlight through a window during the day can contribute significantly to a rise in the average daily indoor temperature of a room. The Average Indoor Temperature in a well-insulated room may be calculated as:
(Heat Gain Factor * Window Area)/(Heat Loss Factor * Room Area) + Average Outdoor Temperature.

The area of the window is calculated using its width in feet times its height in feet. Similarly, the area of the room in square feet is calculated using its width in feet times its length in feet. The heat gain and loss factors depend on whether or not the window is single or double paned according to Table 4-14. Design and create a Visual Basic program that computes the average daily temperature in a well-insulated room. What is the average daily indoor temperature in a 20-by-25-foot room with a single-paned 5-by-5-foot window and an average outdoor temperature of 35.4 degrees? Save the project as **Ex4-13.frm** and **Ex4-13.vbp** in the Chapter4 folder on your data disk.

TABLE 4-14: Window heat factors

Window Type	Heat Gain Factor (HGF)	Heat Loss Factor (HLF)
Single-paned	1540	13
Double-paned	1416	9.7

14.   After placing an ad for a job position on an online Job Search Service, Estelle's Placement Service needs to process just over 100 electronically submitted forms from applicants. In order to expedite the handling of these forms and possibly others in the future, Estelle hires a young Visual Basic programmer to develop a program that will allow her to enter information from the form. Then, after clicking a button, she will receive a score and status for the applicant. The score will be calculated based on how well the applicant's information conforms with various requirements for the position. A rule will be incorporated into the program for each requirement that will determine the number of points to be awarded the applicant for that requirement. After all rules have been evaluated, a total score will have been calculated. If the total score is less than 10, then the applicant will be deemed "unacceptable" for the position. If the score is between 10 and 20, then the applicant is "possible" for the position. A score above 20 will mean that the applicant is "desirable." Points will be awarded based on the rules

incorporated in Table 4-15. Design and create a Visual Basic program that will determine an applicant's score and status. Save the project as **Ex4-14.frm** and **Ex4-14.vbp** in the Chapter4 folder on your data disk.

TABLE 4-15: Resume evaluation rules

Criteria	Criteria Values	Scores
Education level	College (4 yr)	5
	College (2 yr)	3
	High school	1
Education field	Industrial engineering	5
	Business	3
	Other	1
Experience (years)	More than 5	5
	3 to 5	3
	Less than 3	1
Experience (field)	Manufacturing	5
	Other	2
Computer literate?	Yes	5
	No	0

PROJECT: JOE'S TAX ASSISTANCE (CONT.)

After a day of shopping, it was Angela's habit to pamper herself by taking a long bath, retiring to bed with a good mystery, and reading herself to sleep. Alas, tonight was to be a different story. Just as she nodded off from Agatha Christie's *Murder at the Vicarage*, Joe burst in with his laptop.

"Honey, are you asleep?" he inquired.

"Wha . . . ," said Angela.

"Let me show you my program," Joe interrupted as he beamed proudly.

Angela had seen Joe like this before, and she knew that if she wanted to get to sleep anytime soon she had better give in.

"Oh goody, dear, I've been waiting up to see it! Please show it to me," she acquiesced.

The sarcasm was lost on Joe as he positioned the laptop on the bed next to Angela.

"See, here is the form. Notice that it has parts that are very much like some of the sections on the 1040 tax form. Here's one where you can put in all of the person's income. Look! When I type something here a message shows up reminding me to fill out Schedule F and..."

"Hey, slow down, buddy. You're going too fast for me." Angela declared. "Let me try a few buttons."

"Okay, click there and see what happens," Joe said as he turned the mouse over to Angela. "Notice how the total income has been calculated."

"I'm impressed, Joe. You created all this yourself?"

"Well, Zooey helped with the main form and she taught me what to do for the other parts."

"I guess this proves that you can teach an old dog new tricks. If you keep this up, you'll have the whole Tax Code made into a program by next tax season," Angela teased. "Are you coming to bed soon?"

"I'm not ready for bed yet. I've been reading about how to get the program to make decisions using something called If-Then statements. I want to give that a try first," he replied.

"You mean like, IF you leave me alone, THEN I can go to sleep?"

"Yeah, something like that. Only you can take it even further and add an alternative using If-Then-Else statements," said Joe.

"I think it's the ELSE part that you should worry about."

Joe gave her a quick kiss and said, "I get the message. Good night, dear."

As Joe gathered his things and left the room, Angela retrieved her book from the floor where it had fallen. Perhaps a few more chapters with Miss Marple would calm her down again.

Questions

1. Add a section to the form for determining whether or not the client will get a tax refund with the following specifications. Include one text box and an accompanying label for a refund. Include one text box and an accompanying label for an amount owed. Add the button: Calculate Refund. Add code to the Clear button to clear the new text boxes and reset variables. For the Calculate Refund button, write code which will make a decision on whether the client will receive a refund or will have to pay. If the client receives a refund, the amount should appear in the refund text box. If the client owes taxes, the amount should appear in the amount owed text box.

2. Run and test your program.

3. Practice using the debugging tools. Add the Immediate window to print a control value, say, a list box.

5 THE REPETITION PROCESS IN VISUAL BASIC

LEARNING OBJECTIVES

After reading this chapter, you will be able to:

❖ Understand the importance of the repetition process in programming.

❖ Describe the various types of loops that can be carried out in an OOED computer language.

❖ Discuss the statement forms used in Visual Basic to handle repetition, and understand the use of pre- and post-test loops.

❖ Use the event-driven, For-Next, While-loop, and Until-loop repetition structures in creating projects.

❖ Understand the concepts of variable scope and static variables.

❖ Use the combo box control to select from a list of alternatives.

❖ Understand the use of files to permanently store data and information.

❖ Work with nested loops.

❖ Create an executable version of a Visual Basic project.

❖ Use debugging tools in Visual Basic to find and correct errors.

SCENARIO: MULTIPLE VIDEOS AT VINTAGE VIDEOS

Clark was just putting some finishing touches on the latest edition of the Vintage Videos program when Yvonne walked in with a box of supplies.

"Can you give me a hand, Clark?" she asked.

"Sure, Sis. What have you got?" he replied.

"Just a few more decorations for tomorrow's grand opening... and our costumes," Yvonne replied.

"All right. Were you able to get me the cowboy costume like I asked?" Clark inquired.

"No, but I think that you'll look cute in the one I found," she responded. Then, quickly changing the subject, she asked, "How is the program coming?"

Clark was a little suspicious but decided to answer Yvonne's question before pressing further. He explained: "The program is coming along. I've just added an automatic calculation capability to it. All you have to do is to select a video type—Kids, Regular, or Classic—and the program automatically determines the price."

He demonstrated how to use the list box to select a video type and how the program checks to ensure that all appropriate information has been entered when the Calculate button is clicked. He selected a kids video, and the proper price appeared in the text box.

"So the computer can make choices?" Yvonne asked.

"Yes, depending on how it's written, different things can happen depending on the current conditions. That's not all. You can also get it to repeat commands if you want. This can save lots of time typing because you don't have to type the same commands over and over. Also, sometimes you're not sure how often certain commands should be repeated so you can let the program decide. You can get the program to repeat commands like this by writing structures called loops."

"Are you going to use loops in the program?"

"In fact, the next thing I'm going to add will use loops. Ed wants to be able to enter more than one video per customer and then calculate the total. I'm also going to add a window so the full list of videos is included in a receipt that can be printed, instead of printing the entire form. He also wants to start checking if the customer is a member, and, if not, to add their name to our membership list. And while I'm at it, he wants the capability to remove members from the list. And . . . Oh! He also wanted me to make the program capable of running on computers which don't have Visual Basic installed in preparation for the day when we have multiple check out stations."

"Great," Yvonne replied. "I was thinking, though, that since we are opening tomorrow and the program is not finished, shouldn't we have something else set up to record transactions."

"Ed and I have that covered. We plan to keep notes in this notebook on each transaction in addition to using the program. It's a common practice when trying out a new program."

"I see. That way you'll have a backup of all of the information," she said.

"That's right, and we can also use the notes to see what else we might need in the program." Clark hesitated a moment and then asked, "So what costume did you get me?"

"Since they didn't have what we originally talked about, I thought we could all dress in costumes that were related somehow. So I looked through what they had and found three from the same old movie," Yvonne explained.

"I'm afraid to ask, but what movie was it?"

"*Peter Pan*! I'm going to be Tinkerbell, Ed will be Captain Hook, and you can be Peter Pan. Don't worry, you'll look good in tights," she said.

Clark groaned a little at the thought and hoped that none of his friends would drop by.

Comments on Scenario

After reviewing the prototype information completed in Chapter 4, the owners of Vintage Videos are requesting that another type of functionality be added. Instead of assuming that each customer will only rent one video, the project needs to be capable of allowing a customer to rent multiple videos, each of which will be listed on a receipt that can be printed. While the project you completed in Chapter 4 worked well for one video per customer, this is an unrealistic assumption and we need to revise that application to handle multiple videos for each customer. The revised project will also determine whether a customer is a member of Vintage Videos. If the customer is not a member, then he or she will be enrolled as a member for future reference. To add this increased functionality, we need to be able to repeat actions in Visual Basic or, as Clark mentions in the scenario, to use loops. In addition, Clark has been requested to create a version of the application that will run on computers that do not have Visual Basic installed—a so-called **executable** (.exe) version.

As with all project designs, we need to begin by designing the interface, which is an extension of the existing Vintage Videos interface, to include the features requested by Ed, the store owner. A sketch of the revised interface is shown in Figure 5-1, with the new elements pointed out.

FIGURE 5-1.
Revised Vintage Videos interface

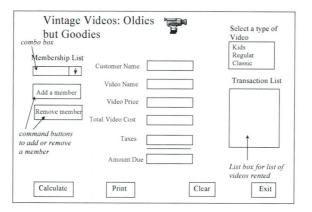

Note that we have added a sixth text box that will display the total cost of the videos this customer rents. In addition, we have added a drop-down list (combo) box that will display the names of all Vintage Video's members. We have also included command buttons to add a customer name to this list in the text box or to delete a name from the list. A list box has been added that will display a list of videos rented, and the Calculate button will handle the process of summing the prices, computing the taxes on the sum, and adding the taxes to the sum to compute the amount due. This will be done for each video that is rented.

To help you understand how this interface will operate, here is a list of steps that will be followed in renting videos:

1. Check the combo box to see if the customer is a member. If they are, add their name to the customer name text box.

2. If the customer is already a member, go to the next step; if not, add the name to the membership list by clicking the *Add a member* button.

3. If the customer is a member, but his or her name needs to be removed from the membership list; do this by clicking the *Remove Member* button.

4. Enter the name of the video in the *Video Name* text box and click the video type to display the price.

5. Click the *Calculate* button to:
    a. add the price of this video to the previous total video cost;
    b. compute taxes, add them to the total video cost, and display the total in the *Amount Due* text box;
    c. add the name and price of the video to the *Transaction List* list box.

6. When all videos have been added to the list, click the *Print* button to add the total cost of videos, the taxes on the videos, and the amount due to the *Transaction List* list box and print the contents of this list box.

7. Click the *Clear* button to clear all information from the list boxes in preparation for the next customer.

8. Click the *Exit* button to save the revised list of members and to exit the application.

Note that in this revised project all of the command buttons at the bottom of the form have been modified and additional controls need to be added to the form. This will require modifying your existing single-video Vintage Videos project to add the new controls to the form and to revise the code for existing controls. We will do this after we discuss loops in general.

INTRODUCTION TO LOOPS

In the first four chapters of this book, we have discussed five of the six operations that computers can carry out. In this chapter, we will discuss the sixth and final computer operation: Repeat a group of actions any number of times. This operation is the one that really makes the computer a useful tool, because a computer can repeat an operation as many times as needed without making mistakes due to boredom or tiredness like a human being might. Whether it be processing thousands of payroll checks, simulating millions of years of geological development, or searching for a name in a list, computers can repeat an operation over and over again with great ease.

You should be familiar with repetition, because you have had to repeat operations in many situations. For example, when you balance your checkbook, you must repeatedly determine if a check has cleared and, if not, subtract that check's amount from the balance shown on your bank statement. You must also do this for each deposit during the last month and, if it is not shown on your statement, add the amount of the deposit to your bank balance. In both cases, there is an action to be repeated—commonly referred to as the *body of the loop*—and some condition that indicates the end of the repetition process—a *termination condition*. If the loop does not have a body, then nothing happens in the repetition process. If the loop does not have a valid termination condition, then the loop will continue until stopped by the user either aborting the loop or turning the computer off. This last situation is often referred to as an **endless** or **infinite loop** and is something you should guard against in your programming.

Types of Loops

Loops can be classified into three types: event-driven, determinate, and indeterminate. The latter two types of loops occur in both OOED and procedural languages, but the first type is restricted to an OOED language. An **event-driven loop** is one in which the repetition is driven by an event occurring—say, by a command button being clicked. A **determinate loop** is one for which you *know* in advance how many repetitions will occur, and an **indeterminate loop** is one where you *do not know* how many repetitions will occur.

An event-driven loop with which you should be familiar occurs at the grocery checkout counter. In this case, the event that activates the repetition is the checkout clerk passing a grocery item over the laser beam to determine its price. This loop is terminated by the clerk ceasing the checkout operation, printing a receipt, and clearing the register for the next customer.

An example of a determinate loop would be a loop that computes the outstanding balance for a loan for each month of the repayment period. Recall that we used the

Pmt( ) function to find the monthly payment on a loan in Chapter 3. With a determinate loop, we can compute and display the balance after each payment. In this case, the number of months determines the number of repetitions.

On the other hand, an example of an indeterminate loop is one that computes the balance for each month *until* the balance is less than some predefined amount. In this case, we do not know in advance how many repetitions it will take for the balance to reach the desired amount.

It should be noted that an event-driven loop is actually a form of indeterminate loop since the number of events usually is not known in advance. If we compare it to the traditional indeterminate loop, we see that it uses events to control the number of repetitions, while the traditional form of the indeterminate loop uses either input data or values generated by the program to control the number of repetitions. In a sense, the traditional indeterminate loop is *data-driven*.

We will discuss each of these types of loops using the same simple examples before proceeding to the Vintage Videos scenario.

Repetition Example

To help you understand the repetition process, we will use a simple example to demonstrate various loop structures. This example will involve entering, counting, and summing Integer values. We will also add them to a list box. In this situation, the repetition involves repeatedly entering a number, increasing a counter by one, and adding the number to the current sum to arrive at a new sum. It also involves adding the value to a list box so there will be a record of the values entered. When the loop is terminated, the number of integers and their sum should be displayed in text boxes.

The summing process involves inputting a value and adding it to the current sum. The counting process involves adding one to a counter for each value that is input and summed. The only difference between summing and counting is that counting always adds one to a counter while summing adds some value to an existing sum.

In the process of working with this example, you should become comfortable with working with loops. We will then turn our attention back to the Vintage Videos scenario to develop the application for it.

Initializing Variables

Anytime you sum or count values, it is important that the variables be *initialized* to zero before the repetition process and that the summing and counting processes occur for each value that is input. While all variables are initialized to zero when they are declared, it is also important to initialize summing and counting variables if the project will be run for different sets of values; otherwise, the initial values for the variables will be whatever they were after the previous execution of the loop.

> **TIP:** Initializing variables can be even more important when variables have a higher level scope (discussed in next section).

It's Your Turn!

1. Give an example, other than the one given in the text, of a process in your daily life where repetition is important.

2. List the types of loops that are possible in Visual Basic. Which one is not possible in a procedural language? Why?

3. Which type of loop would work best for each of the following everyday scenarios: determinate, indeterminate, or event-driven?

    a. Keeping score for a 10-frame game of bowling.

    b. Recording the results of a set of baseball pitches until the batter is out.

    c. Adding up the prices for each item on an order form.

    d. Increasing an auction bid as long as the bid amount is less than a predefined maximum.

4. Why is it important that your loops have a stopping mechanism?

EVENT-DRIVEN LOOPS

With procedural programming, it was necessary to write code to create a loop, but in OOED programming we can actually create a loop just by repeating an event, say, clicking a button. We will start our discussion of summing and counting integers by using an event-driven loop that uses a command button to repeat the summation process. The form for this example is shown in Figure 5-2. Notice that it has an input text box, a text box for the sum, a text box for the number of values, and a list box to display the values that were entered. There are also three command buttons: one for calculating the current sum and counter value, one to clear the text boxes, and one to exit the project.

FIGURE 5-2. Form for event-driven loop

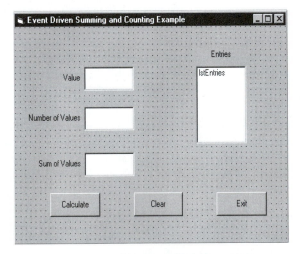

The first command button, which we will name *cmdCalc*, adds the contents of the first text box (*txtTheValue*) to the sum of all previous values and displays the sum in the last text box (*txtSum*). It also adds one to the previous number of entries and displays this value in the second text box (*txtNumValues*). This command button also adds the value to the list box (*lstEntries*) and, finally, clears the existing value in *txtTheValue*.

The second command button (*cmdClear*) clears all values from the text boxes, clears the list box, and sets the variables that sum and count the values back to zero. The final command button (*cmdExit*) exits the project.

Variable Scope

Note that, in this project, we have a new situation: The variables that sum and count the number of input values appear in two event procedures—cmdCalc and cmdClear. If we simply declare them as usual in each event procedure, the processing in one event procedure will have *no* effect on the processing in the other event procedure. This is due to a concept in Visual Basic known as **variable scope**, which does not allow one procedure to "know" about variables declared in another procedure. Variables declared in an event procedure are referred to as **local variables**, and they are protected from *contaminating* each other. However, if the variables are declared at the *form level* rather than at the *procedure level*, then all event procedures that are a part of this form will "know" about them. This concept is shown in Figure 5-3 for a single form where both procedures "know" about the form-level variables. If there are multiple forms that need to know about a variable, then this needs to be declared at the *project level* using a Basic module. This will be discussed in more detail in Chapter 7 when we discuss multiple forms.

FIGURE 5-3.
Concept of variable scope

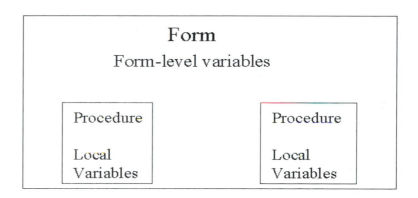

TIP: If the same variable is declared at both the form level and the procedure level, the procedure-level declaration will override the form-level declaration. You should **avoid** double-declaring of variables!

In the case of the sum and counting variables that appear in both the cmdCalc and cmdClear event procedures, we need to declare them at the form level in the Declarations procedure of the General object. To declare variables at the form level, simply click on the Code icon in the Project Explorer window to display the Code window. If you have not yet entered code for any of the objects for a project, you will automatically see the Declarations procedure of the General object. You will note that the Option Explicit instruction is already there since we set up our environment to have this instruction appear automatically for all projects. The result of declaring the variables at the form level is shown in Figure 5-4. Like all declarations, whether at the procedure level, the form level, or the project level, this declaration also automatically initializes the declared variables to zero.

If you have already entered code for at least one event procedure, then you will need to click on the Object drop-down list box at the top of the Code window to display a list of objects and select the **General** object. Finally, select the **Declarations**

Code icon

FIGURE 5-4.
Form-level variable
declaration

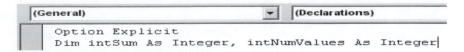

procedure from the Procedure drop-down list box next to the Object drop-down list box and enter the declarations. If you need to view your declarations, you should select General from the Object drop-down list box.

While we know that variables declared at any level are automatically initialized to zero, it is still good practice to initialize them in the program. For the intSum and int-NumValues variables, we will do this in the Form_Load event procedure as shown in VB Code Box 5-1.

VB CODE BOX 5-1. Code for the Form_Load event procedure	```Private Sub Form_Load intSum = 0 intNumValues = 0 End```

Static Variables

In addition to declaring variables to be form-level variables so they will be known to all procedures in the form, you can also declare a local variable to be *Static*. A **Static variable** is one that retains its value between executions of an event procedure. Normally, a local variable will be reset to zero between events, but when it is declared Static, the variable retains its value until the project is terminated. The form of the Static declaration statement is:

Static *variable* **as** *type,* *variable* **as** *type, etc.*

For example, if we had declared the intSum and intNumValues variables as Static variables instead of as form-level variables, they would have retained their values between clicks of the Calculate button. However, we would not have been able to set them to zero at the end of the event-driven loop. For the event-driven loop, the Clear button was used to reset the values. In this case, they would have retained their values until the project was terminated or the Clear button was clicked.

It is also possible to make *all* variables in an event procedure static by replacing the Private keyword in the sub name statement with the Static keyword. The general form of this is:

Static Sub *control name_event name()*

Code for the Calculate Button

The pseudocode for the Calculate command button to input, sum, count, and add the entries to a list box is shown below:

```
Sum and count procedure
    Input Value
    Add Value to Sum
    Increment Number of values by 1
    Display Sum and Number of values
    Add value to list box
End procedure
```

Note that there is no reference to *repeating* the loop or to a loop termination condition, because all repetition will be controlled by the user clicking the Calculate button. We also do not need to explicitly initialize the summing and counting variables to zero, because this is done in the Form_Load procedure and when they are declared at the form level.

The complete Visual Basic code for the Calculate button is shown in VB Code Box 5-2. In looking at this code, you will notice that, after the summation and counting statements, there are two additional statements that clear the txtNumValues text box and put the cursor back into it. To carry out this latter action, the SetFocus method is appended to the name of the text box. When you click the Calculate button, the txtNumValues text box will be cleared and the cursor will be placed there by the SetFocus method for the next value to be entered. You should also notice that while the intTheValue variable is declared in this event procedure, the intSum and intNumValues variables are not, since they were declared at the form level.

VB CODE BOX 5-2. Code for Calculate button	```
	Private Sub cmdCalc_Click()
	    Dim intTheValue As Integer
	    intTheValue = CInt(txtTheValue.text)
	    intSum = intSum + intTheValue
	    intNumValues = intNumValues + 1
	    txtSum.Text = Str(intSum)
	    txtNumValues.Text = Str(intNumValues)
	    lstEntries.AddItem str(TheValue) 'Add value to list box
	    txtTheValue.Text = ""
	    txtTheValue.SetFocus 'Set focus back to txtTheValue
	End Sub
	``

We have used another new method in this procedure: The **AddItem** method. This method is used to add items to a list box at run time, instead of at design time as we did in Chapter 4. The AddItem method is used with list and combo boxes to add String data to the list. Like all methods, it is appended to the object with a period followed by the item to be added. Note that since a list box is made up of strings, we convert the Integer variable intTheValue to a string before adding it to the list box

The code for the Clear button shown in VB Code Box 5-3 is very simple; it clears all text boxes and the list box, sets the variables intSum and intNumValues to zero, and sets the focus back to the txtTheValue text box in preparation for the next use. Clearing the list box requires us to use a third new method: the **Clear** method, which applies to list and combo boxes. As with the other methods, you simply append it with a period to the object to be cleared.

VB CODE BOX 5-3. Code for Clear button	```
	Private Sub cmdClear_Click()
	    txtTheValue.Text = ""
	    txtSum.Text = ""
	    txtNumValues.Text = ""
	    intSum = 0
	    intNumValues = 0
	    lstEntries.Clear 'Clear list box
	    txtTheValue.SetFocus 'Set focus back to txtTheValue
	End sub
	``

Executing an Event-Driven Loop

To run the event-driven loop project, you simply enter an integer in the txtTheValue text box and click the Calculate button to add this integer to the current sum and to add one to the number-of-values variable. The sum will appear in the txtSum text box and the number of entries (including this one) will appear in the txtNumValues text box. Also, when you click the Calculate button, the txtTheValue text box will be cleared and the cursor will be placed back there.

To make the use of this project even easier, the TabIndex property of some controls can be set at design time. You can do this in such a way that when the project begins the cursor is automatically located in the txtTheValue text box, and when you press the **TAB** key after entering a number, the focus jumps to the Calculate button. When the focus is on the Calculate button, a dotted line is displayed around the caption and you can simply press the **ENTER** key on the keyboard instead of having to click the button with the mouse. To have this occur, at design time set the TabIndex property to zero for the txtTheValue text box and to one for the cmdCalc button. If you run your project for values of 123, 456, 789, –135, and 246, the result will appear as shown in Figure 5-5. The complete code for this project is shown in VB Code Box 5-4. .

Button with focus [Calculate]

FIGURE 5-5. Execution of summing and counting example

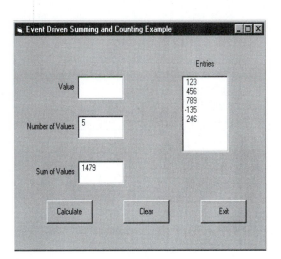

Mini-Summary 5-1: Event-Driven Loops

1. Event-driven loops are a special type of loop that is possible with OOED languages. Repetition is controled by the user repeating an event.

2. An event-driven loop is repeated by an event, such as a mouse click occurring.

3. Variable scope determines the level at which a variable is known—procedure level, form level, or project level.

4. The SetFocus method is used to position the cursor in a text box.

5. The AddItem method is used to add items to a list box or a combo box at run time.

6. The Clear method is used to clear the contents of a list box or a combo box.

| VB CODE BOX 5-4. Complete code for event driven input loop | ```
Option Explicit
Dim intSum As Integer, intNumValues As Integer
Private Sub Form_Load
   intSum = 0
   intNumValues = 0
End
Private Sub cmdCalc_Click()
   Dim intTheValue As Integer
   intTheValue = CInt(txtTheValue.Text)
   intSum = intSum + intTheValue
   intNumValues = intNumValues + 1
   txtSum.Text = Str(intSum)
   txtNumValues.Text = Str(intNumValues)
   lstEntries.AddItem Str(intTheValue) 'Add value to list box
   txtTheValue.Text = ""
   txtTheValue.SetFocus 'Set focus back to txtTheValue
End Sub
Private Sub cmdClear_Click()
   txtTheValue.Text = ""
   txtSum.Text = ""
   txtNumValues.Text = ""
   intSum = 0
   intNumValues = 0
   lstEntries.Clear 'Clear list box
   txtTheValue.SetFocus 'Set focus back to txtTheValue
End Sub
Private Sub cmdExit_Click()
   End
End Sub
``` |

It's Your Turn!

1. To create a project to input, count, and sum a series of values, complete the following exercises:

   a. Create a form like that shown in Figure 5-2 using the control names, labels, and captions (where necessary) discussed in the text. Name the form **frmEvent-Driven** and give it the caption shown in Figure 5-2.

   b. Add the code shown in Figure 5-4 and VB Code Box 5-1 to declare the **intSum** and **intNumValues** variables as *form-level* as Integer variables and to initialize them to zero.

   c. Add the code for the Calculate and Clear buttons as shown in VB Code Box 5-2 and VB Code Box 5-3. Also, add the **End** statement to the Exit button. Finally, set the **TabIndex** property for txtTheValue to be **0** and for cmdCalc to be **1**.

2. Run your project with the data shown in the text, that is, **123, 456, 789, −135**, and **246**. Your result should appear like that shown in Figure 5-5. Can you see why we call this an *event-driven loop*? Clear the text boxes and test your project with the following values: **101, 73, −451, 23**, and **−202**.
```

3. Create a folder named **Chapter5** on your data disk using the **File | Save As** option. Save your form as **EvntDrvn.frm** and your project as **EvntDrvn.vbp** in the Chapter5 folder.

4. Go into your Code window to the cmdCalc event procedure code and add the following declaration:

Static intSum as Integer, intNumValues as Integer

5. Now run your project again with the two sets of data used previously. What happens when you click the Clear button after the first data set? What happens when you begin to enter the second set of data? Were the intSum and intNumValues variables reset to zero? Why or why not? Exit your project, but do *not* save this revised project. Run it again with a new data set. Are the variables reset to zero this time? Exit your project again but do *not* save this revised project.

DETERMINATE LOOPS

As mentioned above, the second loop type is the *determinate loop*, for which you *know* the number of repetitions in advance. While you could create an event-driven loop like the one discussed previously and repeatedly click a button until the number of repetitions has occurred, this can quickly become tedious. Instead, we will use a type of loop that is available in Visual Basic to handle this situation.

For-Next Loops

When the number of repetitions is known in advance, the **For-Next loop** is appropriate. The form of this loop is as follows:

    For *variable = start value* **to** *end value* **Step** *change value*
        statements that compose body of loop
    Next *variable*

where   *variable* = the counter variable in the loop

        start value = the beginning value of the counter variable

        end value = the ending value of the counter variable

        change value = the amount the counter variable changes each time through the loop

and   **Next** *variable* = the end of the For loop

If there is no ambiguity about which For-Next loop is being terminated, the *variable* part of the Next statement is optional. However, if it appears, it *must* match the variable name in the For statement. Also, if the Step part of the statement is omitted, the change value is assumed to be one.

Figure 5-6 points out these parts of the For-Next loop for a simple example where the objective is to sum the first ten integers (1–10). It is also assumed that all variables have been previously declared and the summation variable, intSum, has been initialized to zero.

FIGURE 5-6. Parts of a For-Next loop

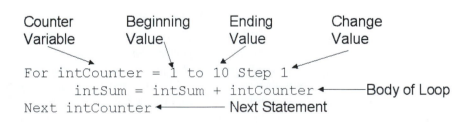

```
Counter          Beginning        Ending           Change
Variable         Value            Value            Value


For intCounter = 1 to 10 Step 1
      intSum = intSum + intCounter  ————Body of Loop
Next intCounter ————— Next Statement
```

In a For-Next loop, the Next statement adds the change value to the current value of the counter variable on each repetition. This new value is compared to the ending value to determine whether or not the loop should be terminated. The loop is terminated when the counter variable is greater than the end value. If the loop is *not* terminated, the Next statement transfers control back to the For statement after the body of the loop has been executed. If the loop is terminated, control is transferred to the statement in the program that immediately follows the Next statement. Notice in Figure 5-6 that the body of the loop is indented. Just as in decision structures, indenting the body of a loop is a good way to make it clear what the loop is repeating.

Note that the Step part of the statement was equal to one in our first example of the For-Next loop. Since the change value was one, it was not required but was shown for demonstration purposes. On the other hand, if we wished to count backward from 10 to 1, we would need to use a change value of –1 and begin and end values of 10 and 1, respectively. The For statement in this case is:

```
For intCounter = 10 to 1 Step -1
```

The *Step –1* part of this For statement is necessary to have the loop count backward. Otherwise, the loop will *not* be executed at all. For example, if we changed the For statement to leave out the Step –1, that is,

```
For intCounter = 10 to 1
```

then there would be NO output. The loop would terminate immediately since the beginning value, 10, is greater than the ending value, 1, and the Step value is positive. In this case the loop would not repeat at all.

> **TIP:** Although it is allowed by Visual Basic, it can be dangerous to modify the loop counter variable within the loop. This should usually be avoided.

Application to Summing and Counting Example

To apply the For-Next loop to the summing and counting example discussed previously, we will use the Calculate button to input and sum the values, assuming that we know in advance the number of values that will be entered. We must also use an Input-Box to input the values to be summed. This is because the For-Next loop, once initiated by a command button or other event, will *not* pause to allow you to enter a new value in the txtNumValues text box. If you tried to use a text box for input with a For-Next loop, the value you input before initiating the loop would be summed as many times as the loop repeats and no other values would be entered.

With the For-Next loop in this example, the only input outside of the loop is the number of values from the txtNumValues text box. The For-Next loop will handle the input and summing of the values; there is no need to count because the For-Next loop also handles this task. It was not necessary to declare any form-level variables in this event procedure, because all of the inputs and calculations are being done in one event procedure—cmdCalc.

To modify the event-driven loop project, delete the txtTheValue text box and add a button named *cmdPrint* with a caption of *Print*. This button will be used later in the application. At the code level, delete the form-level declaration of intSum and intNumValues, since they are declared at the procedure level, and replace the existing code in the cmdCalc with the code in VB Code Box 5-5.

In looking at the code, we see that after the summation variable is initialized, a validation If-Then decision structure is used to check if the user has entered a value in the txtNumValues text box. If not, a MsgBox warns the user that the text box is empty

VB CODE BOX 5-5. Code for cmdCalc event procedure	

```
Private Sub cmdCalc_Click()
    Dim intTheValue as Integer, intSum as Integer
    Dim intNumValues as Integer, intCounter as Integer
    intSum = 0
    If txtNumValues.Text = "" then 'Number not entered
        Msgbox "Please enter number of values to be summed"
        Exit Sub 'Do not go into loop
    End If
    intNumValues = CInt(txtNumValues.Text)
    For intCounter = 1 to intNumValues
        intTheValue = CInt(InputBox("Enter next value"))
        intSum = intSum + intTheValue
        lstEntries.AddItem Str(intTheValue)
    Next
    txtSum.Text = Str(intSum)
    lstEntries.AddItem "Sum is " & str(intSum)
End Sub
```

and the sub is exited. This keeps the For-Next loop from trying to run a zero number of times.

If the txtNumValues.Text value is not zero, then the intNumValues variable is set equal to it and the For-Next loop takes over. It runs from 1 to intNumValues, inputting each value with an InputBox, adding it to the sum, and adding it to the list box. The last two lines move the sum to a text box and to the list box. Note that a label ("Sum is ") is concatenated using an ampersand with the String version of the sum variable (Str(intSum)). This alerts the user to the fact that this value is the sum.

The cmdClear event procedure for the For-Next loop example is shown in VB Code Box 5-6. The code for it is very similar to that for the event-driven example, except that no variables are reset to zero and the focus is set to the txtNumValues text box rather than to the now non-existent txtTheValue text box. When this project is run for the same data as before—that is, five values, which are 123, 456, 789, –135, and 246—the result is as shown in Figure 5-7.

VB CODE BOX 5-6. Code for cmdClear event procedure	

```
Private Sub cmdClear_Click()
    txtNumValues.text = ""
    txtSum.Text = ""
    lstEntries.Clear 'Clear list box
    txtNumValues.SetFocus 'Set focus to txtNumValues
End Sub
```

Printing the Contents of a List Box

For-Next loops are not always used to input data; actually they are more often used for working with lists of items. One such use of a For-Next loop is to print the contents of a list or a combo box. In Chapter 6 we will discuss a variety of other situations where For-Next loops are used to work with lists.

To print the contents of a list box, first we must know how many items are in the list box. Second, we must have a way of identifying each item in the list box. Finally, we must have a way of sending the items in the list box to the printer.

To determine the number of items in a list box, you can use the **ListCount** property of the list box. This property keeps up with how many items have been added to a list box. For example, in Figure 5-7, the value of lstEntries.ListCount would be 6 since there are six items in the list box (five values and the sum).

FIGURE 5-7. Result of running project with For-Next loop

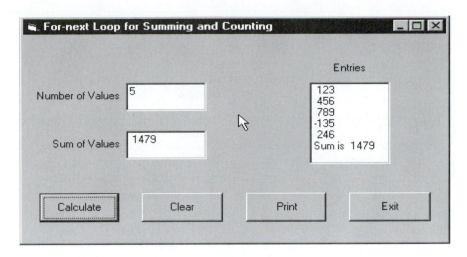

To identify the items in a list box, we can use the run-time **List( )** property of the list box. We used the design-time version of the List property to add items to the list box, but the run-time version of the List( ) property specifies an item in the list box. The first item is always numbered as zero and goes up to the number of items in the list box (ListCount) *minus 1*. Because ListCount is equal to the number of items in the list box and List( ) starts at zero, the List( ) property of the last item is ListCount − 1. This means that the first item is identified as List(0), the second item as List(1), and so on to the last item, which is identified as List(ListCount −1). In the example in Figure 5-7, lstEntries.List(0) is 123, lstEntries.List(1) is 456, lstEntries.List(2) is 789, and so on down to lstEntries.List(5), which is "Sum is 1479."

Now that you know how many items there are in any list box (ListCount) and how to identify items in the list box with the run-time List( ) property, the only thing we do not yet know is how to communicate with the printer. This is handled with the **Printer** object and the **Print** method with a statement of the form:

> **Printer.Print** *item to be printed*

For the list box, the item to be printed is one of the items in the list box. Since these items are identified by the List( ) property of the list box, we can use a For-Next loop to print all items in the lstEntries list box in the example with the following three statements (assuming intCounter has been declared as an Integer variable):

```
For intCounter = 0 to lstEntries.ListCount - 1
    Printer.Print lstEntries.List(intCounter)
Next
```

In this For-Next loop, the intCounter variable goes from 0 to lstEntries.ListCount − 1 and the lstEntries.List(intCounter) property is equal to each item in the list box. As a result, all items are printed. To cause the printer to actually print the list, you must include the Printer.EndDoc statement after the Next statement. If the code shown in VB Code Box 5-7 is added to the cmdPrint event procedure, then clicking the Print button will print the six items displayed in the list box.

> **TIP:** The Print statement by itself (no object used) will result in the output being printed in the upper left-hand corner of the form.

VB CODE BOX 5-7. Code to print contents of lstEntries	```Private Sub cmdPrint_click() Dim intCounter as Integer For intCounter = 0 to lstEntries.ListCount - 1 Printer.Print lstEntries.List(intCounter) Next Printer.EndDoc End Sub```

Printing to the Immediate Window

You may not have a printer connected to your computer or your instructor may not want you to use the computer laboratory printer to print the contents of the list box. If either of these circumstances is the case, then you should replace the Printer object in VB Code Box 5-7 with the **Debug** object. This will cause your output to be displayed in the same **Immediate window** as was discussed in Chapter 4 for debugging purposes. It can also be used in place of the Printer object to test a project without wasting large amounts of paper or if no printer is available. When you use the Debug object instead of the Printer object, whatever would have printed on paper is now printed to the Immediate window. Since you are not using the Printer object, you should also remove, or "comment out," the last statement in the code, Printer.End-Doc.

> **TIP:** If your Immediate window is not visible when you run your project, you can make it visible with the **View|Immediate window** menu selection.

Figure 5-8 shows the Immediate window that results from using the Debug.Print command. Note that you may have to scroll the Immediate window to see all of your output. Also, since the Immediate window retains the results of previous runs, you should delete the contents after each run by returning to design mode, highlighting the contents, and pressing the delete key (**DEL**). Note: You *cannot* delete the contents of the Immediate window while the project is running! The complete code for the For-Next input loop is shown in VB Code Box 5-8.

> **TIP:** If the project screen disappears from sight when you display the Immediate window, you will find it as an icon on the Windows task bar at the bottom of the screen and can redisplay it by clicking the icon.

FIGURE 5-8. Use of Immediate window for printed output

```
Immediate
123
456
789
-135
246
Sum is   1479
```

Mini-Summary 5-2: For-Next Loops

1. If the number of loops is known in advance, then you can use a For-Next loop. For-Next loops have a For statement, statements in the body of the loop, and a Next statement.

2. A For statement has a numeric counter variable, a beginning value, an ending value, and an optional Step value. The Step value must be negative to count down.

3. For-Next loops are often used to work with lists such as list or combo boxes. With list or combo boxes, the ListCount property indicates the number of elements in the list and the Run Time List( ) property is used to designate which element is being printed.

4. It is possible to print to either the Printer or Debug objects with the Print method. Output to the Debug object appears in the Immediate window.

| **VB CODE BOX 5-8.** Complete code for For-Next input loop | ```
Private Sub cmdCalc_Click()
   Dim intTheValue as Integer, intSum as Integer
   Dim intNumValues as Integer, intCounter as Integer
   intSum = 0
   If txtNumValues.Text = "" then 'Number not entered
      Msgbox "Please enter number of values to be summed"
      Exit Sub 'Do not go into loop
   End if
   intNumValues = CInt(txtNumValues.Text)
   For intCounter = 1 to intNumValues
      intTheValue = CInt(InputBox("Enter next value"))
      intSum = intSum + intTheValue
      lstEntries.AddItem Str(intTheValue)
   Next
   txtSum.Text = Str(intSum)
   lstEntries.AddItem "Sum is " & Str(intSum)
End Sub
Private Sub cmdClear_Click()
   txtNumValues.Text = ""
   txtSum.Text = ""
   lstEntries.Clear 'Clear list box
   txtNumValues.SetFocus 'Set focus to txtNumValues
End Sub
Private Sub cmdPrint_click()
   Dim intCounter as Integer
   For intCounter = 0 to lstEntries.ListCount - 1
      Printer.Print lstEntries.List(intCounter)
   Next
   Printer.EndDoc
End Sub
Private Sub cmdExit_click()
   End
End Sub
``` |
```

It's Your Turn!

1. For each of the For-Next... loops shown on the next page, what values will be displayed in the text boxes, txtRes1 and txtRes2, after the loop has been completely executed?

a.
```
Private Sub cmdGo_Click()
    Dim intCounter As Integer
    Dim intSum As Integer
    For intCounter = 1 To 10
        intSum = intSum + intCounter
    Next intCounter
    txtRes1.Text = intCounter
    txtRes2.Text = intSum
End Sub
```

b.
```
Private Sub cmdGo_Click()
    Dim intCounter As Integer
    Dim intSum As Integer
    For intCounter = 2 To 8 Step 2
        intSum = intSum + intCounter
    Next intCounter
    txtRes1.Text = intCounter
    txtRes2.Text = intSum
End Sub
```

c.
```
Private Sub cmdGo_Click()
    Dim intCounter As Integer
    Dim intSum As Integer
    For intCounter = 20 To 10 Step -2
        intSum = intSum + intCounter
    Next intCounter
    txtRes1.Text = intCounter
    txtRes2.Text = intSum
End Sub
```

d.
```
Private Sub cmdGo_Click()
    Dim intCounter As Integer
    Dim intSum As Integer
    For intCounter = 3 To 20 Step 5
        intSum = intSum + intCounter
    Next intCounter
    txtRes1.Text = intCounter
    txtRes2.Text = intSum
End Sub
```

2. For each of the following For-Next . . . loops, what error has been made? How should it be corrected?

a.
```
For intCounter = 5 To 1
    intSum = intSum + intCounter
Next intCounter
```

b.
```
For intCounter = 2 To 6 Step 2
    intSum = intSum + intCounter
Next intSum
```

```
c.    ' sum the numbers from 1 to 10
      For intCounter = 1 To 10
          intCounter = intCounter + intCounter
      Next intCounter
```

To revise the project that inputs, counts, and sums values to use a determinate loop, complete the following exercises.

3. If it is not already open, open **EvntDrvn.vbp** and delete the text box used to enter values (txtTheValue) and the corresponding label. Add a command button with a name of **cmdPrint** and a caption of **Print**. Change the name of the form to be **frm-ForNext** and the caption for the form to match that shown in Figure 5-7.

4. Delete the code for the cmdCalc and cmdClear buttons and the form-level declarations in the General Declarations area. Add the code in VB Code Box 5-5 to the cmd-Calc event procedure and the code in VB Code Box 5-6 to the cmdClear event procedure.

5. Test your project with the data given in the text—five values: **123, 456, 789, −135,** and **246**.

6. Test your project with the following data—six values: **−34, 107, −301, 202, 782,** and **15**.

7. Modify the code in VB Code Box 5-7 to print the contents of the list box to the Debug object (Immediate window) with the Print button. (Change **Printer** to **Debug** and delete the **Printer.EndDoc** statement.) Run your project again with the same data as in Exercise 3 above and click the Print button to print to the Immediate window. Exit the project, delete the contents of the Immediate window, and run your project again with the same data as in Exercise 4 above and print to the Immediate window.

8. If you have a printer connected to your computer and your instructor tells you to do so, modify the code in the **Print** button to print to a printer. Be sure to add back the **Printer.EndDoc** statement.

9. Save your project as **ForNext.frm** and **ForNext.vbp** in the Chapter5 folder.

INDETERMINATE LOOPS

The third classification of loops is the indeterminate loop, for which the number of repetitions is not known in advance. While the number of repetitions for an event-driven loop can be known or not known in advance, in this section we will consider loops that are data-driven, either by values generated in the code or by input. In all cases, the loops will be executed within a single control rather than in multiple controls.

There are four types of indeterminate loops in Visual Basic:

1. Looping *until* some condition is true with the termination condition *before* the body of the loop.

2. Looping *while* some condition is true with the termination condition *before* the body of the loop.

3. Looping *until* some condition is true with the termination condition *after* the body of the loop.

4. Looping *while* some condition is true with the termination condition *after* the body of the loop.

*Classifying
Indeterminate Loops*

The four types of indeterminate loops listed above can be classified in two ways: as pre-test or post-test loops or as While or Until loops. The first two types of loop are referred to as **pre-test loops** because the termination condition comes *before* the body of the loop, and the second two types of loop are referred to as **post-test loops** because the termination condition comes *after* the body of the loop. The choice of a pre-test loop or a post-test loop depends on whether or not the loop should always execute at least one repetition. Because the termination condition comes after the body of the loop, a post-test loop will always repeat at least once. A pre-test loop, on the other hand, may not repeat at all, because the termination decision before the body of the loop may keep the loop from executing.

The first and third types of loop listed above are also referred to as **Until loops**, and the second and fourth types of loop are referred to as **While loops**. The difference between the two types is that in an Until loop, the loop continues *until* a termination condition *becomes true*, but in a While loop, the loop continues *while* a termination condition *is true*. In general, either type of loop can be used for any situation so long as the termination condition is set up correctly.

The form of the pre-test loops is:

Do Until (or While) *condition*
   body of loop
Loop

and the form of the post-test loops is:

Do
   body of loop
Loop Until (or While) *condition*

The *condition* part of these statements is the same as the comparison conditions used in the If-Then-Else statement. In a pre-test Do While loop, if the condition being tested is true, then control is transferred to the body of the loop for another repetition of the loop. If the condition is false, control is transferred out of the loop and to the statement immediately following the Loop statement.

> **TIP:** The statements within an indeterminate loop must eventually cause the termination condition to be satisfied; otherwise an infinite loop results.

On the other hand, in a pre-test Do Until loop, if the condition being tested is false, then control is transferred to the body of the loop for another repetition of the loop. If the condition is true, control is transferred out of the loop and to the statement immediately following the Loop statement. Figure 5-9 shows the Do While and Do Until processes for a pre-test loop.

In a post-test loop, the body of the loop is executed and then the *condition* is tested. If the condition being tested in the Loop While statement is true, control is transferred back to the Do statement at the top of the loop and then to the body of the loop for another repetition of the loop. If the condition is false, control is transferred out of the loop and to the statement immediately following the Loop While statement.

> **TIP:** If the program appears to be doing nothing when you run it and does not respond to mouse clicks or key presses, you probably have an infinite loop in progress. You should terminate it by pressing the Ctrl+Break key combination.

FIGURE 5-9. Pre-test
indeterminate loop

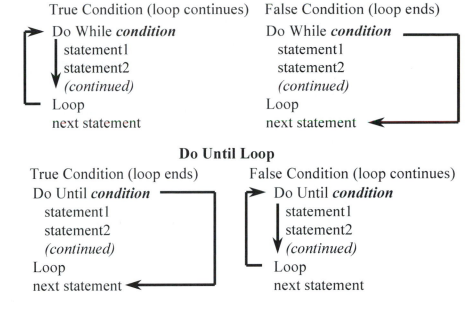

For the post-test Until loop, if the condition being tested in the Loop Until statement is false, control is transferred back to the Do statement at the top of the loop and then to the body of the loop for another repetition of the loop. If the condition is true, control is transferred out of the loop and to the statement immediately following the Loop Until statement.

As an illustration of indeterminate loops, consider the case of initializing a variable to 10 and repeatedly subtracting 2 from it *while* the variable is greater than zero. When the variable becomes less than or equal to zero, the loop terminates and control passes to the statement immediately following the Loop statement. The statements to do this for a pre-test While loop are shown in VB Code Box 5-9 (note that the body of the loop is indented; this helps a reader understand what is being repeated):

VB CODE BOX 5-9. Using While loop to count backwards	```intValue = 10```
	 ```Do While intValue > 0```
	 ``` MsgBox "Value = " & str(intValue)```
	 ``` intValue = intValue - 2```
	 ```Loop```

If a project is created with a single command button and these statements are entered in the Code window for that control, the values 10 8 6 4 2 will be displayed in a series of message boxes. The values that are displayed are all positive, since the loop is terminated by the Do While statement when Value becomes less than or equal to zero.

Note that the Do While statement in this example can be replaced with an equivalent Do Until statement that will continue to subtract 2 from the variable *Until* the variable is less than or equal to zero; that is,

```
Do Until Value <= 0
```

This same loop can also be created as a post-test While loop with the following statements:

```
intValue = 10
Do
    MsgBox "Value = " & Str(intValue)
    intValue = intValue - 2
Loop While intValue > 0
```

An equivalent Loop Until statement would be:

```
Loop Until intValue <= 0
```

Processing an Unknown Number of Values from a File

One way to input, sum, count, and display values when the number of values is unknown is to use an event-driven loop like the one discussed earlier. In that case, the user entered values in a text box and clicked a button to process each value. Essentially, the user entered an unknown number of values, using the command button event to continue the process *while* values remained to be summed (or *until* no more values remained).

We could also input and process an unknown number of values using a pre-test Do While loop or Until loop, with input coming from an InputBox like that used for the For-Next loop. However, with the event-driven loop capability of languages like Visual Basic, this is unnecessary. This does not mean that indeterminate loops will never be used for keyboard input; it just means we will not use them in this text for this type of input. Instead, we will use them to input values from a data file.

A **data file** is a *collection of data stored on magnetic or optical secondary storage in the form of records*. A **record** is a *collection of one or more data items that are treated as a unit*. Files are identified by the computer's operating system with **filenames** assigned by the user. Files are important to processing data into information because they provide a permanent method of storing large amounts of data that can be input whenever needed for processing into information. There are three types of data files in widespread use: Sequential access files, direct access files, and database files. **Sequential access files** are files from which the data records must be input in the same order that they were placed on the file. **Direct access files** are files that can be input in any order. While **database files** are widely used for data storage, they must be accessed with a database management system and cannot be input directly into a Visual Basic project. In this chapter, we will discuss reading from and writing to sequential access files. Direct access files will be discussed in Chapter 11 and database files will be discussed in Chapter 9.

Sequential access files replicate the action of entering data from a keyboard, since you enter data from a keyboard one after the other just like they would be read from a sequential access file. The number of records on a sequential access file is often unknown, but there is an invisible binary marker at the end of the file called the **EOF** (end of file) **marker**. While this precludes the use of a For-Next loop for inputting data from a sequential file, it does not affect the use of a Do While loop or a Do Until loop, because these loops can input data until the EOF marker is encountered (or while it has not been encountered).

TIP: As your program code gets longer, splitting the screen enables you to look at widely separated parts of the code. Do this by dragging the small separator just above the right scroll bar of the code window into position. To remove the split, simply double-click it.

Data Input from Sequential Access Files

To input data from a sequential access file, such a file must first exist. The easiest way to create a sequential access file is to use a text editor like WordPad or NotePad. When you type data into a text editor and then save it as a *text file* (not a *Word* file), an EOF marker is automatically placed at the end of the file. Figure 5-10 shows a sequential access file being created in NotePad where each record consists of a single Integer value. (We recommend using NotePad instead of WordPad to create data files, because NotePad automatically saves them as text files. WordPad automatically saves files as MS Word files, which will not work as data files.)

FIGURE 5-10.
Creating a sequential file in Notepad

Once you have a sequential access file, you must first *open* it in the project before data can be input from it. This is accomplished with an Open statement of the form:

Open "*filename*" for Input as #*n*

where *filename* must include the drive and folder where the file is located and *n* is a number between 1 and 511. This is the number that Visual Basic will use to refer to the file. For example, from a floppy data disk in drive a:, opening a file named "Sum-Data.txt" as number 10 would require the following statement:

```
Open "a:\SumData.txt" for Input as #10.
```

The Open statement must be executed before any data can input from or output to a sequential file. At some point before the project is terminated, the file should be closed with the Close statement:

Close #*n*.

For example, to close the same file opened earlier, the statement would be:

```
Close #10.
```

To input data from a sequential file once it has been opened, you use the Input #*n* statement:

Input #*n*, *list of variables*

where *n* must match the number assigned earlier to the file and *list of variables* is a list of variable names for which data will be entered. There must be a one-to-one match between the list of variables and the data on the file, in terms of both data type and number of items being input. For example, to input data into a variable called intTheValue from the sequential access file opened earlier as #10, the statement would be:

```
Input #10, intTheValue
```

As an example of using a Do Until loop to sum and count values that are input from a sequential file, we will use the same form as we did for the For-Next loop. However, the code will be decidedly different; instead of inputting the number of values to be input, we will count them as they are input from the sequential access file and display this number in the text box. The cmdCalc event procedure to accomplish this is shown in VB Code Box 5-10.

| VB CODE BOX 5-10. Code for cmdCalc event procedure | ```
Private Sub cmdCalc_Click()
    Dim intTheValue As Integer, intSum As Integer
    Dim intNumValues As Integer
    Open "a:\SumData.txt" For Input As #10 'Open data file
    intSum = 0
    intNumValues = 0
    'Input, sum, and count data items and add to list box
    Do Until EOF(10) 'Input to end of file
      Input #10, intTheValue
      intSum = intSum + intTheValue
      intNumValues = intNumValues + 1
      lstEntries.AddItem Str(intTheValue)
    Loop
    txtNumValues.text = Str(intNumValues)
    txtSum.Text = Str(intSum)
    lstEntries.AddItem "Sum is " & Str(intSum)
    Close #10
End Sub
``` |
|---|---|

The code necessary to clear the form is almost the same as that for the For-Next example. The only difference is that there is no need to set the focus to the txtNum-Values text box, because all input comes from the sequential file. The code for the cmdClear event procedure is shown in VB Code Box 5-11. Note that we do not need to change the code for the Print button, because it used the ListCount property of the list box to determine the number of items in the list box and does not depend on the Calculate button or the Clear button for any information.

> **TIP:** If errors occur when reading a file, they may be caused by the file instead of your code. Check for such things in the file as: an extra line at the end of the file, string values that are not enclosed in quotes, and missing delimiters (for example, a missing comma).

If this project is executed with the sequential data file called a:\SumData that was shown in Figure 5-10, the results are as shown in Figure 5-11 and the code for an indeterminate input loop is shown in VB Code Box 5-12 .

Mini-Summary 5-3: While and Until Loops

1. Do While and Do Until loops can be used when the number of repetitions is not known in advance and the termination of such loops depends on a comparison condition.

2. Do While and Do Until loops can be pre-test or post-test loops, depending on where the decision condition is located relative to the body of the loop.

3. Sequential access files can be used to work with data that must be processed in the same order that it was input. Values are input from a sequential access file with the Input #n statement.

5. A sequential access file must be opened and assigned a number between 1 and 511. The file is referred to by this number in the code. The file must also be closed.
```

VB Code Box 5-11. Code for cmdClear event procedure	```Private Sub cmdClear_Click()```

```
Private Sub cmdClear_Click()
   txtNumValues.Text = ""
   txtSum.Text = ""
   lstEntries.Clear
End Sub
```

Figure 5-11. Results of using Until loop to input, sum, and count values

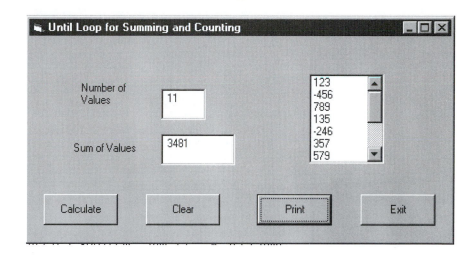

It's Your Turn!

1. For each of the following loops, what values will be displayed in the text boxes, txtRes1 and txtRes2, after the loop has been completely executed?

```
a. Private Sub cmdGo_Click()
      Dim intCounter As Integer
      intCounter = 0
      txtRes2.Text = 0
      Do While intCounter < 5
         txtRes2.Text = txtRes2.Text + intCounter
         intCounter = intCounter + 1
      Loop
      txtRes1.Text = intCounter
   End Sub

b. Private Sub cmdGo_Click()
      Dim intCounter As Integer
      intCounter = 0
      txtRes2.Text = 0
      Do While intCounter <= 5
         txtRes2.Text = txtRes2.Text + intCounter
         intCounter = intCounter + 1
      Loop
      txtRes1.Text = intCounter
   End Sub
```

| **VB CODE BOX 5-12.** Complete code for indeterminate input loop | ```
Private Sub cmdCalc_Click()
   Dim intTheValue As Integer, intSum As Integer
   Dim intNumValues As Integer
   Open "a:\SumData.txt" For Input As #10 'Open data file
   intSum = 0
   intNumValues = 0
   'Input, sum, and count data items and add to list box
   Do Until EOF(10) 'Input to end of file
     Input #10, intTheValue
     intSum = intSum + intTheValue
     intNumValues = intNumValues + 1
     lstEntries.AddItem str(intTheValue)
   Loop
   txtNumValues.Text = Str(intNumValues)
   txtSum.Text = Str(intSum)
   lstEntries.AddItem "Sum is " & Str(intSum)
   Close #10
End Sub
Private Sub cmdPrint_Click()
   Dim intCounter as Integer
   For intCounter = 0 to lstEntries.ListCount - 1
      Printer.Print lstEntries.List(intCounter)
   Next
   Printer.EndDoc
End Sub
Private Sub cmdPrint_Click()
   Dim intCounter as Integer
   For intCounter = 0 to lstEntries.ListCount - 1
      Printer.Print lstEntries.List(intCounter)
   Next
   Printer.EndDoc
End Sub
Private Sub cmdExit_Click()
   End
End Sub
``` |

```
c. Private Sub cmdGo_Click()
      Dim intCounter As Integer
      intCounter = 0
      txtRes2.Text = 0
      Do
         txtRes2.Text = txtRes2.Text + intCounter
         intCounter = intCounter + 1
      Loop Until intCounter = 5
      txtRes1.Text = intCounter
   End Sub

d. Private Sub cmdGo_Click()
      Dim intCounter As Integer
      intCounter = 0
      txtRes2.Text = 0
      Do
         txtRes2.Text = txtRes2.Text + intCounter
         intCounter = intCounter + 1
```
```

```
        Loop While intCounter <= 5
        txtRes1.Text = intCounter
    End Sub
```

2. For each of the following loops, make corrections so that they will work as the comments indicate.

```
a.  Private Sub cmdGo_Click()
    ' add numbers from 1 to 10
        Dim intCounter As Integer
        intCounter = 0
        txtRes2.Text = 0
        Do
            intCounter = intCounter + 1
            txtRes2.Text = txtRes2.Text + intCounter
        Loop While intCounter <= 10
    End Sub
```

```
b.  Private Sub cmdGo_Click()
    ' calculate 5 factorial
        Dim intCounter As Integer
        intCounter = 5
        txtRes2.Text = 0
        Do
            intCounter = intCounter - 1
            txtRes2.Text = txtRes2.Text * intCounter
        Loop Until intCounter = 0
    End Sub
```

```
c.  Private Sub cmdGo_Click()
    ' add even numbers between 0 and 10
        Dim intCounter As Integer
        intCounter = 0
        txtRes2.Text = 1
        Do While intCounter = 10
            txtRes2.Text = txtRes2.Text + intCounter
            intCounter = intCounter + 2
        Loop
    End Sub
```

3. For each of the following loops, convert the While condition to an equivalent Until condition or vice versa.

```
a.  intCounter = 0
    Do While Not (intCounter = 10)
        intCounter = intCounter + 1
    Loop
```

```
b.  intCounter = 5
    blnFlag = True
    Do
        intCounter = intCounter - 1
        If intCounter = 3 Then blnFlag = False
    Loop Until Not blnFlag And intCounter = 0
```

```
c.  intCounter = 10
    Do Until intCounter = 0
        intCounter = intCounter - 1
    Loop
```

```
d.  Do Until EOF(1)
        Input #1, strName, intAge
        lstDisplay.AddItem strName & "   " & intAge
    Loop
```

4. Assume that you have a sequential file with an unknown number of records. Each line in the file contains the following information in this order: first name, second name, age, gender, and marital status. Design and write code that will read this file and display each line in a list box.

5. To create a project that will input values from a file and count and sum them, complete the following exercises:

   a. Open NotePad from the Windows Accessories folder and enter the data shown in Figure 5-10. Be sure not to add extra blank lines at the end of the file, as this will lead to an incorrect value for the number of values in the data file. Save this file to the root folder of your data disk as **a:\SumData.txt**.

   b. Open **ForNext.vbp** and change the name of the form to be **frmUntilLoop** and change the caption to match that shown in Figure 5-11.

   c. Modify the code for the cmdCalc event procedure to match that shown in VB Code Box 5-10. Also, change the code for the cmdClear event procedure to match that shown in VB Code Box 5-11.

   d. Run your project and click the **Calculate** button. The result should appear like that shown in Figure 5-11.

   e. Save your form and project as **UntilLoop.frm** and **UntilLoop.vbp** in the Chapter5 folder on your data disk.

6. It is very easy to make your program more flexible by inputting the name of the file using an InputBox. To do this, modify the code for the cmdCalc event procedure to declare **strTheFileName** as a String variable and to add the following line of code before the Open statement:

```
strTheFileName = InputBox("Input filename for data file")
```

Also, modify the Open statement to replace "a:\SumData.txt" (including the quotation marks) with **strTheFileName** (with no quotation marks) as shown below:

```
Open strTheFileName for Input as #10
```

This will allow you to input the filename for the data file.

7. Run your revised project and input **a:\SumData.txt** as the filename of the data file. Use NotePad to create another text data file similar to SumData.txt with a different name. Run your project with new data file.

8. Save your project as **InputName.frm** and **InputName.vbp** in the Chapter5 folder.

APPLICATION TO SCENARIO

Now that you have a good understanding of the repetition process in Visual Basic, we are ready to apply this understanding to the multiple-video Vintage Videos application. You should have already created a portion of the form in earlier chapters. However, we need to add new controls to it. These include a combo box to list member names, a command button to add customer names to the list of names, a command button to delete members from the combo box, a list box to display videos as they are processed, a text box to display the total cost of the videos, and labels for the combo and list boxes. With the exception of the combo box, you should already know how to add all of the new controls and set their properties. We will assume that an empty list box with a name of *lstVideos*, command buttons named *cmdAdd* and *cmdDelete*, a text box named *txtTotalCost*, and appropriate labels have also been added to the form as shown earlier in Figure 5-1.

Combo Boxes

A **combo box** is a combination of a text box and a list box. It has a text box portion that is displayed at all times and a drop-down list of items that can be displayed by clicking on the down arrow. One property of note for the combo box is the **Style** property, which can be set at design time to Drop Down combo (the default), Simple Combo, or Drop Down list. With the default Drop Down combo style, you can use the drop-down list to select an item or you can type a value into the text box. In either case, the Text property is set equal to the selected item or typed value. With the Simple combo style, the list portion of the combo box is always displayed like a list box, but the top-most item is still a text box. Finally, with the Drop Down list style, there is no text box portion and you must select from the drop-down list. We will use the default style for this application.

combo box

To add a member-names combo box, select the combo box icon from the toolbox. It looks much like the list box icon with the addition of a drop-down arrow on the top. The prefix for the combo box name is *cbo*, so we will give it a name of *cboMembers*. As in a text box, the Text property is initially set to the name of the combo box and should be deleted. Finally, since this combo box will have a list of members that will change from day to day, we will add them at run time instead of at design time. The final version of the revised form is shown in Figure 5-12.

. Form for multi-video application

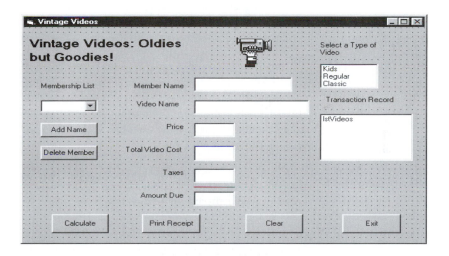

Required Operations

As noted at the beginning of the chapter, there are a variety of new operations that must be included in the multi-video application. They are summarized here in the order in which they must occur when the application runs:

1. Member names are added to the combo box from a data file when the project is started.
2. The combo box is manually searched for a customer name; if the name is found, it is clicked to add it to the customer name text box.

3. If the name is not in the combo box, the Add button is clicked to add the customer name to the combo box.

4. A video name is entered, and a video type is selected from the list box. The Calculate button is clicked to calculate the total price, taxes, and amount due and to add the video name and price to a transaction list box. This is done for each video that is rented.

5. The Print button is clicked to add total video price, taxes, and amount due to the list box and print the contents of this list box as a receipt.

6. The Clear button is clicked to clear the text box and list box entries in preparation for the next customer.

7. If a name is found in the combo box and needs to be deleted, the Remove button is clicked to execute this operation.

8. The Exit button is clicked to save the membership list to the same data file for the next day's use and to exit the project.

Let's discuss how we will handle each of these requirements.

Adding a list of members to a combo box

To create the combo box of member names, we need to input names from a sequential file and add them to the cboMembers combo box. Since the number of members may change each day, it will be unknown and we will need to use a Do Until EOF() loop to input the names from the file. The pseudocode for this operation is shown below:

```
Open file
Repeat Until end of file encountered
    Input Name
    Transfer name to combo box
end of loop
Close file
```

Since the combo box must be filled before any other events can occur, we need to write the code for it in the Form_Load event procedure. To do this, we simply double-click on the form to display the Form_Load Code window. The code that needs to be entered follows the logic of the pseudocode and is shown in VB Code Box 5-13, where the file that stores the member names is named *members.txt* and is on a floppy disk in the a: drive.

VB CODE BOX 5-13. Visual Basic code for the Form Load event	```Private Sub Form_Load() Dim strName As String lstVideos.AddItem "Welcome to Vintage Videos" Open "a:\members.txt" For Input As #1 Do Until EOF(1) 'Input names and add to combo box Input #1, strName cboMembers.AddItem strName Loop Close #1 End Sub```

To make the search for a customer's name easier, we will assume that the customer's full name is listed in last-name-first fashion with the last and first names separated by a comma. Since Visual Basic takes a comma as the delimiter between variable items, we must do something to make sure Visual Basic gets the entire name and not just the last name. One way to do this would be to input two String variables—say, strLastName and strFirstName—and then concatenate them when they are added to the cboMembers combo box. However, since we are going to save this combo box back to the file, this would require "unconcatenating" the names before writing them to file, something we would like to avoid.

Another way to handle the two names is to enclose the entire name in quotation marks to force Visual Basic to interpret it as one string rather than two. For example, instead of entering:

```
Watson, Betsy
```

as a name in the file, the employee must enter it as:

```
"Watson, Betsy"
```

so the first name is not interpreted as another string. Since this matches our need to write the names back to the file, we will use this approach.

Another helpful feature of combo and list boxes is that they can be **sorted**, that is, arranged in alphabetical or numerical order. Since we are listing names with the last name first, if the **Sorted** property of the combo box is set to true, then the names will appear in alphabetical order according to last name.

You should be aware that the Click event is *not* the default event for the combo box; instead, the **Change** event is. For this reason, we will need to switch to the Click event if we want to use it.

Transferring name from combo box to customer name text box

To check if the customer is a member, the clerk can manually search the cboMembers combo box. If the customer's name is in the list, it can be quickly transferred to the customer name text box using the combo box Click event (not the default Change event). The only statement in the event procedure will be the one that sets the Text property of the txtCustName text box equal to the Text event of the cboMembers combo box. This statement is:

```
txtCustName.Text = cboMembers.Text
```

Adding customer name to combo box

If the customer's name is not found in the cboMembers combo box, then we want to add it to the list by entering it the txtCustName text box in last name first form and clicking on the *Add a member* command button. This will add the name in the text box to the combo box with the following statement:

```
cboMembers.Additem txtCustName.Text
```

When the name is added to the list, since the Sorted property of the combo box is turned on, the name is automatically added in the appropriate alphabetical order.

As with any type of input, we need to validate that a name is actually in the txtCustName text box before we try to add it to the combo box.

Processing multiple videos

After the customer name has been checked, the project must be able to process multiple videos using the Calculate button. This is an event-driven loop of the type used earlier to sum and count multiple values. As in the single video project, the name of the video must be entered in the txtVideoName text box and the price must be determined by selecting the video type from the lstTypes list box. The Calculate button will not continue if the customer name, video name, or video price is missing.

Once the necessary information has been entered, the cmdCalc event procedure adds the rental price to the sum of the prices to find the total price, calculates the taxes for this total price, and finds the amount due by adding the taxes to the total price. To do this, the TotalCost variable is declared at the form level as a Currency data type variable to retain its value between calculations and to make it available to other event procedures. It will be initialized to zero in the Form_Load event. The cmdCalc event procedure will also add the name and price of the video to the lstVideos list box as well as clearing the video name and video price text boxes and the text property of the lstTypes list box. Finally, the focus is set back to the video name text box.

The statement to add the video name and price to the lstVideos list box uses concatenation to combine the video name, two spaces, and the previously formatted contents of the txtVideoPrice text box before adding the combined string to the list box. The statements to do this are:

```
lstVideos.AddItem strVideoName & "  " & txtVideoPrice.Text
```

The revised portion of the cmdCalc event procedure that sums the prices of the multiple videos, formats the text boxes, adds the video names to the list box, clears the text boxes, and sets the focus to the video name text box in preparation for the next video is shown in VB Code Box 5-14 (some statements are not changed).

VB CODE BOX 5-14. Revised code for end of cmdCalc event procedure	`curPrice = CCur(txtVideoPrice)`
	`curTotalCost = curTotalCost + curPrice 'Add price to total cost`
	`curTaxes = curTotalCost * curTaxRate 'Compute taxes`
	`curAmountDue = curTotalCost + curTaxes 'Compute amount due`
	`txtTotalCost.Text = Format(curTotalCost, "currency")`
	`txtTaxes.Text = Format(curTaxes, "currency")`
	`txtAmountDue.Text = Format(curAmountDue, "currency")`
	`txtVideoPrice.Text = Format(curPrice, "currency")`
	`lstVideos.AddItem txtVideoName.Text & " " txtVideoPrice.Text`
	`lstTypes.Text = ""`
	`txtVideoName.Text = ""`
	`txtVideoPrice.Text = ""`
	`txtVideoName.SetFocus 'Set Focus to video name text box`
	`End Sub`

Printing the lstVideos list box and clearing entries

Printing the lstVideos list box is accomplished with a For-Next loop like that used earlier to print the list of values. However, before printing the list box, we need to add the total video cost, the taxes on this amount, the total amount due, and a message of the form "Thanks for your business!" to the list box after the existing entries. The code for this is shown in VB Code Box 5-15.

VB CODE BOX 5-15. Code for cmdPrint event procedure	`Private Sub cmdPrint_Click()`
	`    Dim intNumber As Integer, intCounter As Integer`
	`    lstVideos.AddItem "Total video price " + _`
	`        txtTotalCost.Text`
	`    lstVideos.AddItem "Taxes  " + txtTaxes.Text`
	`    lstVideos.AddItem "Total price =  " + _`
	`        txtAmountDue.Text`
	`    lstVideos.AddItem "Thanks for your business!"`
	`    intNumber = lstVideos.ListCount`
	`    For intCounter = 0 To intNumber - 1`
	`      Debug.Print lstVideos.List(intCounter)`
	`    Next`
	`End Sub`

Note that we have used the Debug object instead of the Printer object. To actually send this to the printer, you would change this line of the code to use the Printer object and add the Printer.EndDoc statement at the end of the procedure.

To clear the entries, we simply need to set all text boxes to a null string (" "), set the curTotalCost variable to zero, and clear the lstVideos list box with the statements:

```
curTotalcost = 0
lstVideos.Clear
```

Removing names from the membership list

While the ability to delete individuals from the membership list is not needed just as Vintage Videos is opening its doors for business, it will be necessary as the membership list grows. To remove an item from a combo box or list box, use the RemoveItem method. This method is the reverse of the AddItem method with one exception: Instead of giving the string to be added, you must provide the number of the item to be removed through the **ListIndex** property of the list box or combo box. This property is equal to the number of the item currently selected in the list box or combo box. For example, cboMembers.ListIndex is equal to the number of the currently selected item in the cboMembers combo box.

To be able to click the Remove Member command button to remove the currently selected item in the cboMembers combo box, the only statement needed is:

```
cboMembers.RemoveItem cboMembers.ListIndex
```

However, if the combo box is empty or no item has been selected, attempting to remove a member will result in an error message. For that reason, we need to check the value of cboMembers.ListIndex to ensure that it is greater than -1 (if the combo box is empty or no name has been selected, the ListIndex property is equal to -1). The resulting code for the cmdDelete_Click event procedure is shown in VB Code Box 5-16.

VB CODE BOX 5-16. Code to delete name from list	```Private Sub cmdDelete_Click() If cboMembers.ListIndex > -1 Then cboMembers.RemoveItem cboMembers.ListIndex Else MsgBox "No name selected or list is empty" End If End Sub```

Saving membership list to file and exiting project

The membership list may change during the day as customers are added to it. We need to be able to save it to disk so that the revised membership list will be used the next time this project is run. Just as we can input data from a file, we can also save data and information to a file. As with inputting data from a file, the file must first be opened. However, the Open statement is different, with *Output* replacing *Input*. The general form of the Open statement for output is:

Open "*filename*" for Output as #*n*

For example, to output to the file **a:\members.txt**, the statement is:

```
Open "a:\members.txt" for Output as #10
```

Once a file has been opened for output, to store the revised membership list to the file, we need to use the Write statement of the following form:

Write #*n, variable list.*

This statement will insert commas between items and quotation marks around strings as they are written to the file. This will allow the file to be input later using the *Input #n* statement, which requires that values be separated by commas.

To output the entire list of names in cboMembers to a file, we will use a For-Next loop to repeat the Write statement for each name on the list. The code to do this is shown in VB Code Box 5-17 and includes the End statement to exit the project.

VB CODE BOX 5-17. Code for cmdExit event procedure	```Private Sub cmdExit_Click()```

```
Private Sub cmdExit_Click()
  Dim intNumMembers As Integer, strMemberName As String
  Dim intCounter As Integer
  Open "a:\members.txt" For Output As #10
  intNumMembers = cboMembers.ListCount
  For intCounter = 0 To intNumMembers - 1
    strMemberName = cboMembers.List(intCounter)
    Write #10, strMemberName
  Next
  Close #10
  End
End Sub
```

Running the Project   After the code for all of the event procedures has been input, we are ready to run the project for a customer named Ben Dyer who is renting three movies—*Bambi* (Kids), *Spartacus* (Classic), and *Stripes* (Regular). Figure 5-13 shows the form after the data for *Bambi* and *Spartacus* have been entered. Figure 5-14 shows the Immediate window after the Print button has been clicked. The complete code for the Vintage Videos project up to this point is shown in VB Code Box 5-18.

FIGURE 5-13.
Running multiple-video project with sample data

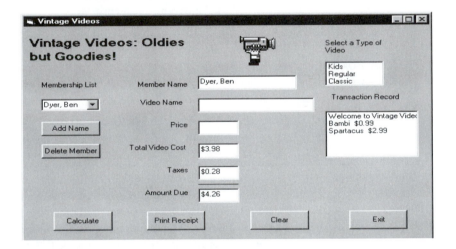

FIGURE 5-14.
Output to Immediate Window

VB CODE BOX 5-18. Complete code for Vintage Videos	

```vb
Option Explicit
Dim TotalCost As Currency
Private Sub cboMembers_Click()
    txtCustName.Text = cboMembers.Text
End Sub
Private Sub cmdAdd_Click()
   If txtCustName.Text <> "" Then
        cboMembers.AddItem txtCustName.Text
   End If
End Sub
Private Sub Form_Load()
   Dim strName As String
   lstVideos.AddItem "Welcome to Vintage Videos"
   Open "a:\members.txt" For Input As #1
   Do Until EOF(1) 'Input names and add to combo box
     Input #1, strName
     cboMembers.AddItem strName
   Loop
   Close #1
End Sub
Private Sub cmdCalc_Click()
   Const sngTaxRate As Single = 0.07 'Use local tax rate
   Dim curPrice As Currency, curAmountDue As Currency
   Dim curTaxes As Currency, strVideoType As String
   If txtCustName.Text = "" Then 'Check for name
      txtCustName.Text = InputBox("Enter name and try again.")
      Exit Sub 'No customer name entered
   End If
   If txtVideoName.Text = "" Then 'Check for video name
     txtVideoName.Text = InputBox("Enter video name and _
        try again.")
     Exit Sub 'No video name entered
   End If
   strVideoType = lstTypes.Text
   If strVideoType = "" Then 'Check for video type
     MsgBox "Select a video type and try again."
     Exit Sub 'No video type selected
   End If
   curPrice = CCur(txtVideoPrice)
   curTotalCost = curTotalCost + curPrice 'Add price to total
   curTaxes = curTotalCost * curTaxRate 'Compute taxes
   curAmountDue = curTotalCost + curTaxes 'Compute amount due
   txtTotalCost.Text = Format(curTotalCost, "currency")
   txtTaxes.Text = Format(curTaxes, "currency")
   txtAmountDue.Text = Format(curAmountDue, "currency")
   txtVideoPrice.Text = Format(curPrice, "currency")
   lstVideos.AddItem txtVideoName.Text & " " & txtVideoPrice.Text
   lstTypes.Text = ""
   txtVideoName.Text = ""
   txtVideoPrice.Text = ""
   txtVideoName.SetFocus 'Set Focus to video name text box
End Sub
```

VB CODE BOX 5-18. Complete code for Vintage videos (cont.)	

```vb
Private Sub cmdClear_Click()
   txtCustName.Text = ""
   txtVideoName.Text = ""
   txtVideoPrice.Text = ""
   txtTaxes.Text = ""
   txtAmountDue.Text = ""
   lstTypes.Text = ""
   txtCustName.SetFocus
   txtTotalCost.Text = ""
   curTotalCost = 0
   lstVideos.Clear
End Sub
Private Sub cmdDelete_Click()
   If cboMembers.ListIndex > -1 Then
      cboMembers.RemoveItem cboMembers.ListIndex
    Else
      MsgBox "No name selected or list is empty"
    End If
End Sub
Private Sub cmdPrint_Click()
  Dim intNumber As Integer, intCounter As Integer
  lstVideos.AddItem "Total video price " + txtTotalCost.Text
  lstVideos.AddItem "Taxes  " + txtTaxes.Text
  lstVideos.AddItem "Total price =  " + txtAmountDue.Text
  lstVideos.AddItem "Thanks for your business!"
  intNumber = lstVideos.ListCount
  For intCounter = 0 To intNumber - 1
    Debug.Print lstVideos.List(intCounter)
  Next
End Sub
Private Sub cmdExit_Click()
  Dim intNumMembers As Integer, strMemberName As String
  Dim intCounter As Integer
  Open "a:\members.txt" For Output As #10
  intNumMembers = cboMembers.ListCount
  For intCounter = 0 To intNumMembers - 1
    strMemberName = cboMembers.List(intCounter)
    Write #10, strMemberName
  Next
  Close #10
End Sub
Private Sub lstTypes_Click()
  Dim strVideoType As String, curPrice As Currency
  strVideoType = lstTypes.Text
  Select Case strVideoType 'Check type of video selected
    Case "Kids"
      curPrice = 0.99
    Case "Regular"
      curPrice = 1.99
    Case "Classic"
      curPrice = 2.99
  End Select
  txtVideoPrice.Text = Format(curPrice, "currency")
End Sub
```

It's Your Turn!

1. Open NotePad and create a *text* file called **a:\members.txt** with the following names entered one to a line in last-name-first order with the entire name enclosed in quotation marks: **Ben Dyer, Lonnie Stams, Alice Goodly, Betsy Watson, Suzy Arons, Ann Carroll, Jimmy Triesch, Ashley Hyatt, Chris Patrick, Sam Jones, Carolyn Myers, Pat George, Margo Kidd, Ben Sibley,** and **Joe Smith.** For example, the first name would be entered as "Dyer, Ben". Also, do not add an extra line to the end of the file.

2. Modify the Vintage Videos project by completing the following exercises.

    a. Open the **Vintage4.vbp** project and add the controls shown in Table 5-1 in the locations shown in Figure 5-12. Change the control names and, where appropriate, add a caption. Also, change the label beside the customer name text box to have a caption of **Member Name** and the caption for the label beside the video price text box to be **Price.**

TABLE 5-1: Controls Added to Vintage Videos Form

Control	Name	Caption
command button	cmdAdd	Add Name
command button	cmdDelete	Delete Member
combo box	cboMembers	
label (above combo box)	lblMembers	Membership List
text box	txtTotalCost	
label (beside text box)	lblTotalCost	Total Cost
list box	lstVideos	
label (above list box)	lblTranVideos	Transaction Record

    b. Change the Sorted property for **cboMembers** to **True** and clear its Text property.

    c. Open the Form_Load event and delete the existing code there. Enter the code shown in VB Code Box 5-13 to input the names from the **a:\members.txt** file to the combo box. Run your project and test this event procedure. If you click on the down arrow, you should see the first few names.

    d. Exit the project, double-click the *cboMembers* combo box, and use the Procedure drop-down list box to switch to the **Click** event instead of the Change event. Next, enter this line of code into the Click event procedure:
```
txtCustName.Text = cboMembers.Text
```

    e. Double-click the cmdAdd command button and enter these three lines of code into the Click event procedure:
```
If txtCustName.Text <> "" then
  cboMembers.AddItem txtCustName.Text
End If
```

f. Double-click the cmdDelete command button and enter the code shown in VB Code Box 5-16 to remove members from the combo box.

g. Run your project and look for **Adams, Bill** in the combo box. Since he is not in the member list, add his name to the customer name text box and click the *Add Name* button to add him to the list.

h. Check the combo box for **George, Patrick**. You should find that this person is a member. Click the *Delete Member* button to remove him from the list. Go back to the combo box and verify that **Adams, Bill** has been added to the list and that **George, Patrick** has been removed.

3. Exit the project and declare the variable cur**TotalCost** as a form-level Currency data type variable. Next, double-click the Calculate button to modify the existing event procedure so that the lines *starting* with **Price = CCur(txtVideoPrice.Text)** match the code shown in VB Code Box 5-14.

4. Run the project and verify that **Ben Dyer** is a member and use the Calculate button repeatedly to add these three videos: *Bambi* **(Kids)**, *Spartacus* **(Classic)**, and *Stripes* **(Regular)**. The sum of video prices should be $5.97, the taxes should be $0.42, and the amount due should be $6.39.

5. Exit the project, double-click the Print button, and erase the existing code. Replace it with the code shown in VB Code Box 5-15. Double-click the Clear button and add the following lines to its event procedure:

```
txtTotalCost.Text = ""
curTotalCost = 0
lstVideos.Clear
```

6. Run your project with the same customer name and videos shown above and click the Print button. The Immediate window should appear like that shown in Figure 5-14.

7. Exit the project, double-click the Exit button, and add the code shown in VB Code Box 5-17 (you do not need to re-enter the **End** statement). Run your project and determine that a customer named **Andy, Brown** is not a member. Add his name to the membership list. Assume Andy rents one video: *How the West Was Won* **(Regular)**. Exit your project and then run it again to ensure that Andy's name was added to the end of the membership file and is displayed in the combo box.

8. Save the form as **Vintage5.frm** and the project as **Vintage5.vbp** in the Chapter5 folder on your data disk. An **.frx** file should be saved along with the files since you have both a graphic and a list box.

NESTED LOOPS

Just as decision structures can be nested, loops also can be nested. In the case of nested loops, there is an outer loop and an inner loop. As with decision structures, the inner loop *must* be completely contained within the outer loop. Nested loops are used whenever it is necessary to repeat an inner loop all of the way through for each repetition of the outer loop. An analogy may be drawn between nested loops and the way an automobile's odometer works. Recall that the tenths wheel on the odometer must make one complete revolution before the miles wheel advances one mile. In this analogy, the tenths wheel is the inner loop and the miles wheel is the outer loop.

While there can be any combination of nested For-Next, While, and Until loops, to combine any of these loops with an event-driven loop requires that the event-driven loop be the outer loop. In this brief discussion of nested loops, we take a look at nested For-Next loops. In future chapters, there will be situations where other combinations of loops are required.

Nested For-Next loops have a For-Next loop within a For-Next loop. When this combination is used, the inner For-Next loop will go through all its values for each value of the outer For-Next loop. There are three key programming rules to remember about using nested For-Next loops:

1. Always use different counter variables for the outer and inner For-Next loops.
2. Always have the Next statement for the inner For-Next loop *before* the Next statement for the outer For-Next loop.
3. Always include the counter variable in the Next statements to distinguish between the loops.

As an example of nested For-Next loops, consider the situation where the outer loop counts from 1 to 5 and the inner loop counts from 10 to 100 by 10s. The values of the inner and outer counter variables are summed as the bodies of the loops. This code is shown in VB Code Box 5-19.

| **VB CODE BOX 5-19.** Nested For-Next loops | ```
Dim intInside as Integer, intOutside as Integer
Dim intInnerSum as Integer, intOuterSum as Integer
intInnerSum = 0
intOuterSum = 0
For intOutside = 1 to 5 'Start outer loop
   For intInside = 10 to 100 Step 10 'Start inner loop
      intInnerSum = intInnerSum + intInside
      'Find Inner Sum
   Next intInside 'End inner loop
   intOuterSum = intOuterSum + intOutside 'Fin Outer sum
Next intOutside 'End Outer loop
MsgBox("Inner sum = " & str(intInnerSum))
MsgBox("Outer sum = " & str(intOuterSum))
``` |
| --- | --- |

If the code in VB Code Box 5-19 is executed, the result will be an outer sum of 15 and an inner sum of 2,750. Note that the inner loop results in a sum of 550, but the inner loop is repeated five times, resulting in the larger value.

CREATING AN EXECUTABLE FILE

The last change requested by the owners of Vintage Videos is for Clark to create a version of the information system that will run on computers that do not have Visual Basic installed. This can be done by creating an **executable (.exe) file** that can be executed on any computer on which it is installed.

Creating an executable file is very easy with Visual Basic; you simply select the **File|Make** *filename***.exe** option, where *filename* is the name of the project vbp file. When you select this option, Visual Basic automatically compiles (rather than interprets) the code for the action objects into a binary file—the *.exe* (executable) file. You are given a option to change the name of the .exe file, or you can leave it the same as the *.vbp* file (the default filename). It will be saved in the same folder as the .vbp file.

In the process of compiling the project into an .exe file, you may find errors that you did not find during your previous testing. If this occurs, then you should correct the error and start the compilation process over again.

When the .exe file has successfully been created, you can execute it by double-clicking on it in Windows Explorer. Alternatively, you can create a shortcut to it on the
```

Windows
Shortcut

desktop and then execute the project by double-clicking the shortcut. You can create a shortcut on the desktop by completing these three steps:

1. Display the file in Windows Explorer.

2. *Right*-click the file name and select *Create Shortcut.* This will create a file called ShortCut to Vintage5 (assuming that Vintage5 is the name you selected for the exe file).

3. Click the shortcut file and drag it to the desktop icon in Explorer (at the top of the left-hand column). This will create on the desktop an icon of the same name, which can be double-clicked to execute the Vintage Videos application.

It's Your Turn!

1. For each of the following nested loops, what values will be displayed in the text boxes, txtRes1 and txtRes2, after the loop has been completely executed?

```
a. Private Sub cmdGo_Click()
      Dim intLoop1 As Integer
      Dim intLoop2 As Integer
      txtRes1.Text = 0
      txtRes2.Text = 0
      For intLoop1 = 1 To 3
         For intLoop2 = 1 To 3
            txtRes1.Text = txtRes1.Text + intLoop1
            txtRes2.Text = txtRes2.Text + 1
         Next intLoop2
      Next intLoop1
   End Sub

b. Private Sub cmdGo_Click()
      Dim intLoop1 As Integer
      Dim intLoop2 As Integer
      txtRes1.Text = 0
      txtRes2.Text = 0
      For intLoop1 = 1 To 2
         For intLoop2 = 3 To 1 Step -1
            txtRes1.Text = txtRes1.Text + intLoop1
            txtRes2.Text = txtRes2.Text + 1
         Next intLoop2
      Next intLoop1
   End Sub

c. Private Sub cmdGo_Click()
      Dim intLoop1 As Integer, intLoop2 As Integer
      txtRes1.Text = 0
      txtRes2.Text = 0
      For intLoop1 = 1 To 3
         For intLoop2 = intLoop1 To 4
            txtRes1.Text = txtRes1.Text + intLoop1
            txtRes2.Text = txtRes2.Text + 1
         Next intLoop2
      Next intLoop1
   End Sub
```

```
d. Private Sub cmdGo_Click()
     Dim intLoop1 As Integer
     Dim intLoop2 As Integer
     txtRes1.Text = 0
     txtRes2.Text = 0
     intLoop1 = 4
     Do While intLoop1 > 0
        intLoop2 = 0
        Do
           txtRes1.Text = txtRes1.Text + intLoop2
           txtRes2.Text = txtRes2.Text + 1
           intLoop1 = intLoop1 - 1
           intLoop2 = intLoop2 + 1
        Loop Until intLoop2 = 3
     Loop
   End Sub
```

2. Compile your **Vintage5.vbp** file into an .exe file with the same name in the Chapter5 folder.

3. Go into Windows Explorer, find the **Vintage5.exe** file, and double-click it to execute the project.

4. Exit the project and then follow the three steps given in the text to create a shortcut to the .exe file on the desktop.

5. Go to the desktop by minimizing all windows and double-click the shortcut icon to run the project. Exit the project.

DEBUGGING LOOPS

It can easily be said that projects that involve loops are an order of magnitude more difficult to debug than projects without loops. Because these projects involve repetition, there are multiple values to check for correctness. Input using loops can easily run into errors, especially when files are involved. There are also problems with infinite loops when the termination condition is incorrectly stated. To find and correct errors in projects with loops, Visual Basic has provided a variety of tools. We will consider some of these tools in this chapter and others in subsequent chapters. The tools we consider in this chapter are printing with the Debug object to the Immediate window, the Watch window, and the Locals window combined with a program breakpoint.

Using the Debug Object

One easy way to find out what's happening inside a loop is to use the Debug object to print values for each repetition of the loop. These values will be printed to the Immediate window. If you are not displaying input values in a list box, then this is an excellent way of checking the input. Remember: Input errors cause a large proportion of the errors you will encounter, and this is even more true when loops are used to input data from files.

For example, in the project we created earlier to use an Until loop to input values from a file and sum and count those values (*UntilLoop.vbp*), assume that the sum of those values is equal to zero. To find the error, you could insert the following statement in the event procedure for the Calculation button immediately before the end of the loop:

```
Debug.Print intTheValue, intSum, intNumValues
```

If your error is that you used the multiplication sign (*) instead of the addition sign (+), the result of using the Debug object is shown in Figure 5-15. Note that the input values appear to be correct; but the Sum value remains at zero throughout the loop, indicating that the error is somewhere in the calculation. Note that the Immediate window can be resized as necessary to allow you to view more of the output.

FIGURE 5-15. Use of Immediate window to display values in loop

Immediate		
123	0	1
−456	0	2
789	0	3
135	0	4
−246	0	5
357	0	6
579	0	7
680	0	8

Using the Watch and Locals Windows

Immediate window

Locals window

Watch window

Quick Watch

On the Debug toolbar there are three icons for windows that you can use to help find errors in your programs. These are the Immediate window, the Locals window, and the Watch window. You have already used the Immediate window, both to print a value when needed and as the destination for the Debug.Print instruction. The other windows also provide very useful information about what's going on in your project.

The Locals window can be used to display the values of all variables that are *local* to an event procedure. For example, in the cmdCalc event procedure in the project discussed earlier, if the intSum value is incorrect, we might want to look at the value of variables local to the cmdCalc event procedure.

Finally, the last window on the Debug toolbar is the Watch window. This window allows us to *watch* the values for a specific variable or expression as the project is executed. The easiest way to set a watch is to locate the cursor on a variable or an expression in a procedure and click the Quick Watch icon on the Debug toolbar. This will display a window like the one shown in Figure 5-16, from which you can select *Add* to add this variable or expression to the list of variables or expressions to be watched.

FIGURE 5-16. Adding a Watch on a variable

However, because a loop will execute so quickly that you cannot watch the values as they fly by in the Locals window or the Watch window, you need to either use the Step commands or set a **breakpoint** to stop execution of the project. In this chapter, we will show you how to use the latter strategy, and in later chapters we will cover the Step commands.

To set a breakpoint in a project and put it into *break mode* at a particular point in the project, position the cursor on the line at which you would like the project to pause

Toggle
Breakpoint

and click the Toggle Breakpoint icon on the Debug toolbar. If you do this, the line of code is highlighted in red. When this line of code is encountered in the project, the execution pauses until you click the Run icon again. This will enable you to look at information in either the Locals window or the Watch window.

For example, if we set a breakpoint on the last line of code in the loop in the cmd-Calc event procedure in UntilLoop.vbp; add watches on the intSum, intNumValues, and intTheValue variables; and turn on viewing both the Watch and Locals windows, the result will be as shown in Figure 5-17.

Note that execution has stopped on a breakpoint as indicated by the highlighted line and, as indicated by the status line at the top of the screen, the project is now in **break mode**. Note, too, that all variable values for this event procedure up to *but not including* the breakpoint line of code are shown in the Locals window, which is displayed above the Code window. Also, the values of the Watch variables are shown in the Watch window in the lower portion of the screen.

> **TIP:** Anytime the project is in break mode, you can position the cursor over any variable and the value will be displayed in a box. This is pointed out in Figure 5-17 for the intSum variable.

By repeatedly clicking the Run icon, we can watch the variables in both windows to see how they change for each repetition of the loop. Since the value of intSum never changes from zero, we know that the problem must be in the statement that calculates this value. The breakpoint can be toggled off by clicking the appropriate icon again. The Watch and Locals windows can be closed by clicking the close button in each window.

FIGURE 5-17.
Debugging
windows

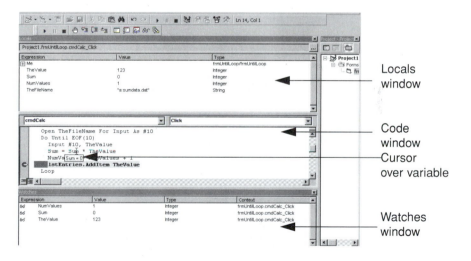

Breakpoints are also useful for debugging infinite loops. If you encounter a situation where a project with a loop appears to do *nothing* when you run it, you probably have an infinite loop. When this occurs, you should press the **CTRL+BREAK** key combination to stop the endless loop. You should add a breakpoint and some watches on the variables to determine why the loop is not encountering a termination condition.

It's Your Turn!

1. Open **UntilLoop.vbp** and change the line that calculates the sum to be:

```
intSum = intSum * intTheValue
```

2. Run the project and note the value that is displayed for the sum of the values. It should be zero. Now, add this statement before the end of the loop:

```
Debug.Print intTheValue, intSum, intNumValues
```

and run your project again. Your output should look like that shown in Figure 5-15. If the Immediate window is not visible, click the appropriate icon on the Debug toolbar to display it.

3. Use the Quick Watch icon to add a watch on the three variables in the cmdCalc event procedure (intTheValue, intSum, and intNumValues). Display the Watch and Locals windows by clicking the appropriate icons on the Debug toolbar, and run the project again.

4. You were not able to learn anything about the bug in the last exercise because you did not set a breakpoint within the loop. Position the cursor on the last line before the Loop instruction and turn on the breakpoint by clicking the appropriate icon on the Debug toolbar. Run your project again and repeatedly click the Run icon to view different values in the Locals and Watch windows as the loop progresses.

5. Terminate execution of the project, turn the breakpoint off, and close the Watch and Locals windows. Do *not* save the project.

SUMMARY

In this chapter, we have discussed the use of loops in Visual Basic projects. Without loops, computer programs would be of little use, since loops are what enable users to repeat an action as many times as desired or needed. All loops have a body that is repeated and a termination condition that causes the loop to stop. Without a correct termination condition, the loop could continue endlessly, resulting in an infinite loop.

There are three types of loops in an OOED language like Visual Basic: event-driven loops, determinate loops, and indeterminate loops. Event-driven loops, which are possible only in an OOED language, are repeated by the user repeatedly performing an event such as a mouse click.

Determinate loops are loops for which the number of repetitions is known in advance. In Visual Basic, determinate loops are implemented with the For-Next loop. In a For-Next loop, the For statement includes a counter variable; the beginning and ending values for the counter; and the Step value, which is the amount by which the counter variable is increased each time through the loop. You can count up or down with a For-Next loop depending on the parameters in the For statement.

Indeterminate loops are those for which the number of repetitions is *not* known in advance. In Visual Basic, data-driven indeterminate loops are implemented by the While loop and the Until loop. In both types of loop, the termination condition uses a condition like that used in If-Then-Else decision structures. Both types of loops can be either pre-test loops, in which the termination condition occurs *before* the body of the loop, or post-test loops, in which the termination condition occurs *after* the body of the loop.

When an unknown number of values is input, a sequential file is a good way to store and input the values, using either an Until or While loop. Files must be opened before data can be input from them or output to them.

Combo boxes, which are a combination of a text box and a list box, were also introduced in this chapter. For-Next loops can also be used to print the contents of a list box or combo box or to write them to a file.

Nested loops consist of one loop inside of another. The inner loop must complete all repetitions before the outer loop can complete a single repetition.

Executable (.exe) files can be created in Visual Basic by compiling a project using the File|Make command. The executable file can then be run on any Windows computer regardless of whether or not it has Visual Basic loaded on it.

Debugging of loops can be handled by using the Debug object to print values to the Immediate window. Loops can also be debugged by setting a breakpoint in the loop and setting a Watch on one or more variables. The values of the variables will appear in the Watch window. We can also turn on the Locals window and view the values for all local variables when a breakpoint occurs.

NEW VISUAL BASIC ELEMENTS

Controls/Objects	Properties	Methods	Events
combo box control	ListIndex Name Text Sorted Style	AddItem RemoveItem	Change Click
Debug object		Print	
Printer object		Print EndDoc	
list box control	ListCount List( ) ListIndex Sorted	AddItem RemoveItem Clear	

NEW PROGRAMMING STATEMENTS

Statement to define a variable as being Static **Static** variable as type
Statements for For-Next loop **For** variable = start value **to** end value **Step** change value   statements to compose body of loop **Next** variable
Statements for While or Until pre-test loop **Do While** (or **Until**) condition   body of loop **Loop**

NEW PROGRAMMING STATEMENTS (CONTINUED)

Statements for Until or While post-test loop **Do**   body of loop **Loop Until** (or **While**) condition
Statement to open a sequential access file for Input **Open** "filename" **for Input as** #n
Statement to close a sequential access file **Close** #n
Statement to input a list of values from a sequential access file **Do Until EOF(n)**   **Input #n**, variable **Loop**
Statement to open a sequential access file for Output **Open** "filename" **for Output as** #n
Statement to output a known number of list items to a file **For intCounter = 0 to intNumItems - 1**   **Write #n**, variable **Loop**

KEY TERMS

break mode	event-driven loop	post-test loop
breakpoint	executable file	pre-test loop
data-driven loop	filename	record
data file	general object	sequential access file
database file	indeterminate loop	static variable
determinate loop	infinite loop	Until loop
direct access file	local variable	variable scope
endless loop	nested loop	While loop
EOF Marker		

EXERCISES

1. Write Visual Basic program segments to:

   a. Print the first 50 positive numbers.

   b. Print the value of intX and decrease intX by 0.5 as long as intX is positive.

   c. Obtain a list of names using a loop and input box until the Cancel button is clicked.

   d. Print the square roots of the first 25 positive integers.

   e. Calculate and display the squares of consecutive positive integers until the difference between a square and the preceding one is greater than 50.

2. Any looping structure may be written in several ways. For each of the following, convert the given looping structure into the requested looping structure that will achieve the same results. Additional variables and selection statements may be required.

a. Convert the following to use a Do While loop.

```
Private Sub cmdGo_Click()
    Dim intLoop As Integer
    Dim intResult As Integer
    intResult = 0
    For intLoop = 10 To 0 Step -1
        intResult = intResult + intLoop
    Next intLoop
    txtResult.Text = intResult
End Sub
```

b. Convert the following to use a For-Next loop.

```
Private Sub cmdGo_Click()
    Dim intLoop As Integer
    Dim intResult As Integer
    intResult = 0
    intLoop = 0
    Do Until intLoop = 10
        intResult = intResult + intLoop
        intLoop = intLoop + 2
    Loop
    txtResult.Text = intResult
End Sub
```

c. Convert the following to use a For-Next loop. intMax will be a nonnegative number that is entered into a text box by the user. Your new code should work the same as the original no matter what nonnegative value has been entered.

```
Private Sub cmdGo_Click()
    Dim intLoop As Integer, intMax As Integer
    Dim intResult As Integer
    intResult = 0
    intLoop = 0
    intMax = txtMax.text
    Do
        intResult = intResult + intLoop
        intLoop = intLoop + 1
    Loop Until intLoop = intMax
    txtResult.Text = intResult
End Sub
```

3. Write Visual Basic code segments for each of the following:

a. A sequential data file called dogs.txt contains a listing of dogs and their stats. Each line contains the dog's name, weight, and age, respectively. Code is needed to read this file as input to a Visual Basic program.

b. Code is needed to write a listing of television programs to a sequential data file called TV.txt. On each line of the file a program's name, day of week, time of day, and length in minutes should be written.

c. Code is needed that will allow a new program to be added to the file of part b. Each new program should be added to the end of the file without losing the current data in the file.

4. For each of the following, explain what is wrong with the code. What error messages would you see, if any? What can you do to fix it?

a. This code should add the numbers from 1 to 10.

```
Private Sub cmdGo_Click()
   Dim intLoop As Integer
   intLoop = 0
   txtResult.Text = 0
   Do
      txtResult.Text = txtResult.Text + intLoop
   Loop Until intLoop = 10
End Sub
```

b. This code should find the product of the numbers from 1 to 10.

```
Private Sub cmdGo_Click()
   Dim intLoop As Integer
   Dim intResult As Integer
   intResult = 1
   For intLoop = 1 To 10
      intResult = intResult * intLoop
   Next intLoop
   txtResult.Text = intResult
End Sub
```

c. The following code should write the contents of a list box to a file called Emp-Data.dat on the a: drive when the Save button is clicked. Then, when the Load button is clicked, the listbox should be loaded from the file. Each line of the list box currently holds information about an employee, including name, age, gender, and salary. For example, the first line might be: Joe Smith 30 m 50000.

```
Private Sub cmdSave_Click()
   Dim intLoop As Integer
   Open "a:Empdata.dat" For Output As #1
   For intLoop = 0 To lstDisplay.ListCount
      Write #1, lstDisplay.List(intLoop)
   Next intLoop
   Close #1
End Sub

Private Sub cmdLoad_Click()
   Dim intLoop As Integer, strName As String
   Dim intAge As Integer, strgender As String
   Dim intsalary As Integer
   lstDisplay.Clear
   Open "a:Empdata.dat" For Input As #1
   Do While Not EOF(1)
      Input #1, strName, intAge, strgender, intsalary
      lstDisplay.AddItem strName & " " & intAge & " " & _
        strgender & " " & intsalary
   Loop
   Close #1
End Sub
```

5. Use the Visual Basic Help facility or the MSDN on-line library to answer the following questions.

a. What Visual Basic statement may be used to exit a Do loop prematurely?

b. What is the difference between the debug commands Step Into and Step Over?

c. How can you write a For-Next loop that will print all available screen fonts?

d. What built-in Visual Basic function will return an integer that represents the next file number available for use by the Open statement?

PROJECTS

1.   Create a project that will enable an instructor to input a student's name and quiz scores. The name should be posted to a list box before any quiz scores are input. There should be a command button that will input the quiz scores and sum, count, and post the quiz scores to a list box as they are entered. Based on these quiz scores, a second command button should compute the student's quiz average and assign a letter grade using the typical 90-80-70-60 cut-off values. The average grade and quiz score should also be posted to the list box. Be careful—if a student takes zero quizzes, he or she automatically receives a letter grade of F. You should be able to print the information in the list box and clear all information in preparation for the next student. Test your project with the student names and quiz scores in Table 5-2. Save your project as **Ex5-1.frm** and **Ex5-1.vbp** in the Chapter5 folder on your data disk.

TABLE 5-2: Student Data

Name Quizzes>>	1	2	3	4	5	6	7	8
Ashley Patrick	73	82	69	77	81	73		
Ben Oakes	88	83	92	79	85			
Nancy Wilson	88	91	89	93	87	90	89	93

2.   Open project **Ex4-2.vbp** (**Ex4-7.vbp** if you completed it) and modify it to count the customers and to keep a running total of the sales for each day. An existing command button should enable the user to input the name and use the price and square footage to compute the amount of the sale. Customer names and the amount of the sale should be posted to a list box. The total sales for the day and the number of customers served should also be added to the list box by clicking a new command button. It should also be possible to print the list box and to clear all entries in preparation for the next business day. Test your project with the data in Table 5-3 and then save it as **Ex5-2.frm** and **Ex5-2.vbp** in the Chapter5 folder on your data disk.

TABLE 5-3: Customer Data

Name	Square Footage	Treatment
John Jarret	3,000	Pre-emergence
Beth Anderson	5,500	Broadleaf weeds
Kelly Smith	6,500	Regular Fertilizer
Sally Jones	3,500	Regular Fertilizer
Andy Silverman	5,000	Premium Fertilizer

3.   Open project **Ex4-3.vbp** and modify it to count the number of automobiles tested and to keep a running sum of the average gas mileage computed for each vehicle. An existing command button should enable the user to input the type of automobile, the miles driven, and the gallons of gas used. It should then compute and display the miles

per gallon. Automobile types and their gas mileage should be posted to a list box. Another command button should compute the average miles per gallon for *all* vehicles tested, and this value should also be posted to the list box along with the total number of vehicles tested. It should be possible to print the contents of the list box and to clear all entries. Test your project with the data in Table 5-4 and then save it as **Ex5-3.frm** and **Ex5-3.vbp** in the Chapter5 folder on your data disk. (Hint: be careful of zero cars!)

TABLE 5-4: Automobile Data

Type of Automobile	Miles Driven	Gallons of Gas Used
Atlissan	270	10.5
Lexiadillac	400	20.5
Meruick	425	22.3
Toyonda	300	9.8
Chrysillis	350	20.0

4. Modify the project you created for Exercise 1 in this chapter to allow the instructor to input the number of quizzes taken by a student from a scroll bar and then input the individual quiz scores using a For-Next loop and InputBox. Your output for the project should be the same as that for Exercise 1. Use the data given in Table 5-2 to test this project. Save your project as **Ex5-4.frm** and **Ex5-4.vbp** in the Chapter5 folder on your data disk. Warning: watch out for zero quizzes being entered!

5. Modify the project you created for Exercise 2 in this chapter to allow the user to input the number of customers from a scroll bar and then input the name, treatment type, and square footage for each customer using a For-Next loop and InputBoxes. Your output for the project should be the same as that for Exercise 2. Use the data given in Table 5-3 to test this project. Save your project as **Ex5-5.frm** and **Ex5-5.vbp** in the Chapter5 folder on your data disk.

6. Modify the project you created for Exercise 3 in this chapter to allow the user to input the number of automobiles tested from a scroll bar and then input the automobile type, miles driven, and gallons of gas used for each automobile type using a For-Next loop and InputBoxes. Your output for the project should be the same as that for Exercise 3. Use the data given in Table 5-4 to test this project. Save your project as **Ex5-6.frm** and **Ex5-6.vbp** in the Chapter5 folder on your data disk. Also, create an executable file for this project and save it with the same name as the project file.

7. Modify the project you created for Exercise 1 in this chapter to allow the instructor to input the quiz scores for the first student (Ashley Patrick) from a sequential access file. Your output for the project should be the same as that for Exercise 1. Use the data given in the first row of Table 5-2 to create this file and give it name of *Ashley_Patrick.txt* (where an underline is used to connect the first and last names) and save it to the root folder of your data disk. Test your project to ensure you get the same results as you did for Ashley in Exercise 1. Save your project as **Ex5-7.frm** and **Ex5-7.vbp** in the Chapter5 folder on your data disk. Also, create an executable file for this project and save it with the same name as the project file.

8. Modify the project you created for Exercise 7 in this chapter to allow the instructor to input the quiz scores for the students from a series of sequential access files, that is, there is a separate sequential file for each student with his and her name as the name of the file like was done in Exercise 7. Your output for the project should be the same as that for Exercise 1. Use the data given in Table 5-2 to create the remaining files needed to test this project on your data disk. Hint: You will need to input the filename for each student's data file before you open it and input data from it. Save your project as **Ex5-8.frm** and **Ex5-8.vbp** in the Chapter5 folder on your data disk. Also, create an executable file for this project and save it with the same name as the project file.

9. Modify the project you created for Exercise 2 in this chapter to input a list of customers to a combo box from a file called *a:\customer.txt*. Then compare a customer's name to the names in the combo box to determine if this is a new customer. If the customer is new, alert the user and add the customer's name to the combo box and the customer name text box. Add statements to the cmdExit event procedure as needed to save the contents of the combo box to the file for use the next day. Your output for the project should be the same as that for Exercise 2. Use the data given in Table 5-3 to create the data file, and then test this project with those same names and data. Also test it with a name of **Lance Motowick** and **3,600** square feet of **Premium Fertilizer**. Save your project as **Ex5-9.frm** and **Ex5-9.vbp** in the Chapter5 folder on your data disk. Also, create an executable file for this project and save it with the same name as the project file.

10. Create a VB project to automatically input an unknown number of golfer names and golf scores from a file called *a:golfer.txt*. Create this file using the data shown in Table 5-5. Hint: To input a name and a value from a file, the Input statement should be of the form:

```
Input #n, variable1, variable2
```

and the data should be entered in the file with a name and the score on the same line, separated by a comma.

These names and scores should be loaded into a list box and the number of golfers and average of all scores computed and displayed text boxes with appropriate labels. There should also be a second list box of all golfers with a score less than 90. You should also add an Exit button. Hint: To see how to add a name and score to a list box, review how the video name and price were added to a list box. Save your project as **Ex5-10.frm** and **Ex5-10.vbp** in the Chapter5 folder on your data disk.

TABLE 5-5: Golfer Data

Golfer	Score
Fred Smith	93
Larry Vinings	101
Hugh Smith	88
Al Nimmi	79
Archie Card	83
Ben Brown	98

11. Create a project that will allow the user to select a personal computer from among the five listed in Table 5-6.

TABLE 5-6: Computer Data

Type of PC	Price
Basic	$595
Standard	$795
Standard Plus	$995
Special	$1,195
Special Plus	$1,395

These computer types should be input into a list box from which the user can select the one that is being sold. Depending on which computer type is selected, the project should display the product's name in a text box and the price in a second text box. The user should be able to select the number of items sold using a scrollbar (minimum = 1 and maximum = 10). Based on the price and number sold, the application should display the Sale Amount in a text box and add the computer type and number sold to a "Computers Sold" list box. This project should be able to handle multiple customers, keep a running total of sales, and count the number of each type computer sold. At the end of the day, a summary of number of each type sold and total sales volume should be added to the list box. It should be possible to print the contents of the list box and exit the project with command buttons. Save your project as **Ex5-11.frm** and **Ex5-11.vbp** in the Chapter5 folder on your data disk.

12. The Net Present Value (NPV) of a project may be calculated using the formula:

$$NPV = -I_0 + F_1/(1+k) + F_2/(1+k)^2 + \cdots + F_n/(1+k)^n + S/(1+k)^n$$

where I_0 is the initial investment, k is the minimum required rate of return, n is the lifetime of the project, F_i is the cash flow in period i, and S is the salvage value for the project after period n. Create a Visual Basic project that will calculate and display the NPV for any project. This means that your code must accommodate any number of periods in a project's lifetime. A project with an initial investment of $5000, a minimum rate of return of 6%, a seven-year lifetime with the cash flow for each year equal to $1000, and no salvage value, will have an NPV of $582.30. Save your project as **Ex5-12.frm** and **Ex5-12.vbp** in the Chapter5 folder on your data disk.

13. Depreciation of assets is a real-world accounting problem that requires computer assistance to do it in the volume that large corporations require. Depreciation is the allocation of the cost of an asset over a period of time for accounting and tax purposes. There are several methods available for making these allocations. Each method takes the original value of the asset (Depreciation Basis), the number of years over which the asset is to be used (Useful Life), and a calculation rule to determine the amount to depreciate each year. The Book Value is the current value of the asset after depreciation has been subtracted each year. For example, if the asset cost $10,000 and the depreciation in the first year is $2,000, then the book value after the first year is $8,000 (equal to $10,000 minus $2,000). The book value for a given year is calculated by simply subtracting the depreciation from the previous year's book value. The original book value is

equal to the Depreciation Basis:

Book Value = Book Value – Depreciation.

Three classic methods of depreciation are:

Straight-Line depreciation: Straight-line depreciation is the simplest method and uses the basis of an asset and the useful life of the asset to assign equal depreciation to each period, or:

Depreciation = Depreciation Basis / Useful Life.

Sum-of-the-years'-digits: The sum-of-the-years'-digits method computes a different fractional depreciation for each year. The denominator of each fraction is the sum of the digits from 1 to N, where N is the useful life of the asset. The denominator is the same each year. The numerator is $N–Y+1$, where Y is the period number. The formula for this is:

Depreciation = Depreciation Basis * (Useful Life – Year + 1) / Sum of digits in Useful Life

Double declining balance: The double declining balance uses a fixed percentage of the prior year book value to calculate depreciation. The percentage rate is $2/N$, where N is the useful life of the asset. The formula may be written:

Depreciation = Book Value for previous year * 2 / Useful Life Loan Amortization

Create a Visual Basic project that will allow a user to select a depreciation method from a list box, and enter the depreciation basis, useful life, and lifetime of the asset in years into text boxes. When a button is clicked, the year, amount depreciated, and book value will be displayed in a listbox for each year of the asset's life. The results for a $10,000 asset depreciated over 8 years for each method are shown in Table 5-7. Save your project as **Ex5-13.frm** and **Ex5-13.vbp** in the Chapter5 folder on your data disk.

TABLE 5-7: Depreciation Data

Straight-Line			Sum of Years' Digits			Double Declining Balance		
Yr.	Dep.	B.V.	Yr.	Dep.	B.V.	Yr.	Dep.	B.V.
1	$1250	$8750	1	$2222.22	$7777.78	1	$2500	$7500
2	$1250	$7500	2	$1944.44	$5833.34	2	$1875	$5625
3	$1250	$6250	3	$1666.67	$4166.67	3	$1406.25	$4218.75
4	$1250	$5000	4	$1388.89	$2777.78	4	$1054.69	$3164.06
5	$1250	$3750	5	$1111.11	$1666.67	5	$791.02	$2373.05
6	$1250	$2500	6	$833.33	$833.34	6	$593.26	$1779.78
7	$1250	$1250	7	$555.56	$277.78	7	$444.95	$1334.83
8	$1250	$0	8	$277.78	$0.0	8	$333.71	$1001.12

14. If a loan with a beginning balance of X dollars, which carries a monthly interest rate of k percent, is to be paid off in n months, the monthly payment M may be calculated using:

$$M = X*k*(1+k)^n/((1+k)^n-1)).$$

During this time period, some of each monthly payment is used to repay that month's accrued interest, and the rest is used to reduce the balance owed. The amount of accrued interest I for any month is:

I = Current Balance * k

Write a Visual Basic program to display an amortization table that displays the payment number, the amount of the monthly payment, the interest for that month, the amount of the payment applied to the principle, and the new balance. Use your program to produce an amortization table for a $120,000 loan to be repaid in 20 years at 7% APR. Note: Assume 12 months per year. Save your project as **Ex5-14.frm** and **Ex5-14.vbp** in the Chapter5 folder on your data disk.

15. Have you ever purchased a lottery ticket? If so, what were the odds of winning? Most of the state lotteries these days are conducted by choosing r numbered balls from a set of n numbered balls. A mathematical formula can be used to calculate the number of different ways that you can select r items from a collection of n items when order is not important may be written as:

Number of Combinations = n * (n–1)/2 * (n-1)/3 * ⋯* (n–r–1)/r

Suppose that you are playing a lottery in which 5 balls are chosen from a collection containing 20 distinct balls. The number of ways in which 5 balls may be selected from this collection is 15,504. You can compute this using the preceding formula with n = 20 and r = 5. This result indicates that the odds of winning this lottery with a single ticket are 1 in 15,504.

Create a Visual Basic program for calculating the odds of winning a lottery for any values of n and r. Your code should validate that the inputted values of n and r satisfy the relationship of $r < n$.

How could you change your code for a lottery in which the first p balls are selected from one collection of n balls, and the next q balls are selected from a second set of m balls?–Save your project as **Ex5-15.frm** and **Ex5-15.vbp** in the Chapter5 folder on your data disk.

16. If you save $100 per year at 5% interest compounded yearly, how much money will you have in 5 years? What about 10 years? What if you save at 6% interest instead? It is often beneficial to prepare a table that can be used to help compare possible scenarios such as these. An example of such a table for equal investments of $100 at the beginning of each year is shown in Table 5-8. The balance at the end of any year using an interest rate k may be calculated using:

End of Year Balance = (1 + k) * Beginning of Year Balance

For a five year term, one could start with a balance of $100, calculate the end of year balance, add $100 for the next year's investment, then use this new balance as the beginning of year balance for year 2. This process may then be repeated until the balance at the end of year 5 is obtained. (The values in the table reflect the balance before the next year's investment is made.)

Write a Visual Basic program that will create a table like that in Table 5-8 for any amount of yearly investment provided by the user. What would be the balance after investing $500 for 20 years at 7% interest? Save your project as **Ex5-16.frm** and **Ex5-16.vbp** in the Chapter5 folder on your data disk.

TABLE 5-8: Compound Interest Table

Yearly investment = $100							
	5 Years	10 Years	15 Years	20 Years	25 Years	30 Years	35 Years
5%	$581	$1322	$2268	$3474	$5015	$6981	$9491
6%	$597	$1396	$2466	$3897	$5813	$8377	$11808
7%	$614	$1477	$2687	$4385	$6766	$10105	$14787
8%	$634	$1565	$2933	$4944	$7898	$12239	$18616
9%	$653	$1657	$3201	$5578	$9234	$14860	$23516
10%	$671	$1752	$3494	$6297	$10814	$18086	$29799

PROJECT: JOE'S TAX ASSISTANCE (CONT.)

The next Friday night, Joe was watching Zooey playing on the varsity softball team. After the game, she was going to spend the weekend with her grandparents. It was a close game, but Zooey's team came out on top, 5 to 4.

Joe was waiting by the car after the game when Zooey walked up.

"Hi, Grandpa! How'd you like the game?" she greeted.

"You played a good game. That was a nice catch over by the left field line, by the way." Joe said as they climbed in the car and headed for home.

"I'm surprised you were paying attention. The way Granny talks, you've been thinking of nothing but our program all week."

Joe appeared thoughtful as he said, "I've been wrapping up a few people's returns and haven't had much time to work on it. I did get a chance to read about looping structures, though. In fact, I was thinking that the softball game has a lot of loops in it."

"C'mon, Grandpa, what are you talking about?" Zooey quizzed.

"Just think about it for a moment. The whole game is kind of like a FOR . . . NEXT . . . loop. If you had a variable representing the number of an inning and the play that happens during the inning representing the body of the loop, you could imagine that the game is a loop written as FOR inning = 1 to 7 . . . NEXT inning. Of course, I'm assuming that the game doesn't go into extra innings."

Zooey was starting to understand, and she prodded him a little: "Is that all? I can think of a couple more actions in the game that could be modeled as a loop. Did you read about nesting loops?"

"Oh, yes, you mean having one loop inside of another. Let me think . . . " Joe said.

"Beeep, time's up. What about each team's at-bat? You could think of it as a conditional DO loop—for example, DO. . . UNTIL outs = 3," Zooey explained.

"Okay, smarty pants, I've got another one for you. An individual player's at bat, and the process of pitching the ball occurs over and over until something happens: Either the ball is hit or the player is struck out or walked. Another conditional DO loop."

"You've got the idea, Grandpa. Basically, loops can be used whenever something needs to be repeated," said Zooey, encouragingly. "Do you have any ideas about using loops in our program?"

"Yes, there are a few places where they could be useful. When a person has a dependent the name and social security number will need to be entered. If they have more than one, this will need to be repeated for each dependent. Also, if a person wishes to itemize deductions instead of taking the standard deduction each one would need to be entered along with the amount. This could be entered using a repeating process using InputBoxes.

They pulled into the driveway and Zooey could tell that Joe was ready to get to work on the program.

"Let me say hello to Granny and take a shower before we get started tonight, Grandpa. Remember, we've got all weekend."

"You're right, Zooey. I can hold my horses a little longer," Joe said. "Then we can put a loop in for the exemptions section."

Questions

1. Add a section to the form for entering the client's exemptions. Leave some space for check boxes that can be added in a later chapter. Include one text box and an accompanying label for displaying the number of exemptions claimed. Place a list box for displaying the list of dependent names, Social Security numbers, and relationship to taxpayer. The list box should be large enough to display a reasonable number of dependents (up to 5) and wide enough to display the dependent's name. Add a button with the caption "Add Dependent". For the Add Dependent button, write code which will display a series of InputBoxes with the first requesting the first and last name of the dependent, the second requesting the dependent's social security number, and a third InputBox requesting the relationship of the dependent to the taxpayer. The process of adding dependents should continue as long as the user clicks the Add Dependent command button. A variable used for counting the number of dependents should also be calculated as each one is added and the final result displayed in the appropriate text box. It should also be possible to click a Print command button to print the contents of the dependents list box and to clear the list box and number of dependent text box. Include appropriate looping structures and selection statements in your code.

2. Run and test your program. Use the debugging tools whenever possible.

6 WORKING WITH ARRAYS IN VISUAL BASIC

LEARNING OBJECTIVES

After reading this chapter, you will be able to:

❖ Understand the use of control, list, and table arrays in Visual Basic projects.

❖ Use control arrays to work with groups of controls using a single name.

❖ Work with check boxes and option buttons.

❖ Describe the difference between arrays and combo boxes, list boxes, and similar controls.

❖ Declare the maximum index value for a list array and understand the errors that occur when declared upper limits on index values are exceeded.

❖ Input data into an array from the keyboard or a file using loops.

❖ Manipulate array data to find the sum and average of array values, the largest or smallest value in an array, or a particular value.

❖ Work with multiple arrays to match values in one array to those in another.

❖ Output the result of array processing to a control, the printer, or the Immediate window.

❖ Declare, input, process, and output two-dimensional arrays.

❖ Use Step operations to step though an array operation to find and correct an error.

SCENARIO: WORKING WITH LISTS AT VINTAGE VIDEOS

Resplendent in his Peter Pan costume, Clark stood and surveyed the store. Balloons and posters adorned the walls and counters. After only a couple of hours, the grand opening of Vintage Videos was shaping up to be a success. Several customers had already come to check out the new store, watch classic movie snippets on the monitors around the store, and sample the free popcorn. Ed had even signed up a few new members.

As Clark straightened a few boxes on the shelves, he noticed that Ed was having some problems with the computer.

"Clark, can you give me a hand here?" Ed called. "I mean that literally, because I can't seem to operate the mouse right with this hook on."

"Aye, aye, Cap'n," Clark replied as he walked to the counter. "How has the program been working today in action with real customers?"

"It's great so far! I like the way we can get the final receipt totaled," exclaimed Ed. "It's also very easy to enter new customers. I prefer using the program to just writing them down in the books."

"Isn't technology grand," said Clark. "I'm sure we'll find some more problems to fix as we use the program. So far, though, is there anything else that you think you can use?"

"As a matter of fact, there is. Several customers have asked me and Yvonne for a particular video. We've been so busy getting ready and we've put so many boxes on the shelves that we can't remember where everything is yet. Or even if we have the particular video."

Clark nodded and said, 'I think I see where you're going with this. You want to be able to look up videos on the computer."

"That's right. I want to be able to type a video name and then let the computer tell me whether or not we have it." Ed went on: "It would also be nice to know where a video is if we do have it."

"I think I can do something like that, but I'll need some help," Clark responded. "I can add another form to the program where you can enter the name of a video to look up. We are going to need a list of the videos and their locations so I can store it in the computer. Can you or Yvonne make one up?"

"That sounds good. I'll ask Yvonne to start making a list. Maybe as Tinkerbell she can use a little pixie dust to speed up the job."

Clark chuckled as he began to think of the design for the new form.

At that moment a customer approached with two videos. Ed asked for the customer's name and typed it into the Add Member Name text box. He then entered the title, chose the type, and pressed the Calculate button for each video in turn. After both of the videos were entered, Ed clicked on Print Receipt and the final total was calculated. Ed handed the receipt and the videos to the man and wished him a nice day.

Ed then turned to Clark and said, "You know, it would be nice to click a button rather than highlighting the correct type of video and then clicking it. Can you make that change too?"

"That should be an easy change. But I still don't think it will solve your problems using the mouse with that hook!"

Comments on Vintage Videos Scenario

In the Vintage Videos application, the owners have asked Clark to replace the list box of types of videos with *option buttons,* with one button for each type of video. With an option button, only one button at a time can be clicked. They have also asked him to extend the existing application to enable a clerk to answer a customer's query regarding whether the store carries a particular video and, if so, its price and location in the store. Answering this query will require that the clerk enter the video name or part of a name and have the application search the list of videos and respond with all videos by that name or portion of a name.

For example, if the customer is looking for a video with the word *Starfighter* in its name, then the application should respond with all videos in the store with this word in their name. This list might include *Starfighters Away* and *The Last Starfighter.* The clerk would then tell the user that both videos are $1.99 and are located in the Sci-Fi (science fiction) section of the store.

Using Lists and Tables

In Chapters 4 and 5 we discussed the use of list and combo boxes for displaying and working with lists of names and other types of information. The capability to display lists of data and information is one of Visual Basic's strengths, because so much of the information you work with in business applications—client names, prices, part numbers, and so on—is in the form of lists. Working with lists can include arranging them in a desired order, finding a particular item in the list, and working with values on two or more lists. In addition to working with lists of data and information, Visual Basic can handle groups of controls such as option buttons.

Visual Basic's abilities extend in yet another area: tables of information. While working with tables may be new to you, it involves many of the same operations as working with lists. In this chapter we will discuss working with both lists and tables.

USING CONTROL ARRAYS

check box

option button

In Visual Basic, a group of controls that work together is referred to as a **control array**. Creating a control array is very easy; you simply add two or more controls with the same name and Visual Basic will automatically create a control array by that name. Each control in the array is distinguished by a number called an **index**. The controls in a control array are assigned index values, starting with zero for the first control added to the form, one for the second control added, and so on.

Two new controls that are commonly used in control arrays are check boxes and options buttons. The **check box** is a small square control that can be "checked" by clicking it. It is commonly used when the user is making multiple selections from a list. **Option buttons** are small round controls that can also be selected by clicking. However, where multiple check boxes can be selected, only one option button in a group can be selected. Option buttons are often referred to as **radio buttons**, since they are like the buttons you use to select stations on your radio—only one can be clicked at a time.

To demonstrate the use of check boxes and option buttons, we will place two check boxes and three option buttons on a blank form and display a message box to indicate which check box or option button has been selected. Check boxes are added to the form in the same way as other controls. To create a control array of check boxes, first you should give all the boxes the same name (the *chk* prefix is used for check boxes). When the second check box (or other control) is added with the same name, you will be queried as to whether you want to create a control array. You should answer *yes* to this query. The query is shown in Figure 6-1 when the second check box with a name of *chkSelect* is added to the demonstration form. Once this is done, the controls will be treated as a control array with each individual control having a separate index value. Note: The order in which you add the controls is critical, because the index value for a control depends on the order in which that control was added to the form. You can check the index value for a control in a control array in the Properties window for the control.

FIGURE 6-1. Query about creating a control array

While a control array of check boxes is added directly to the form, option buttons (which are named with a *opt* prefix) are commonly grouped in a container. While the

frame

form itself can be used as the container, this allows only one group per form and restricts the use of option buttons. Instead, a special container control is commonly used to group the option buttons. This control is the **frame control**, which you should add before adding any option buttons (the *fra* prefix is used to name frame controls).

TIP: A frame can hold other controls because it is a container object. Other container objects include the form and picture box controls.

Once the frame has been added, you can add the option buttons by drawing (*not* double-clicking) them into the frame and giving them all the same name. For example, to add three option buttons in a frame to the demonstration form, you would first add a frame named *fraDemo* and then draw three option buttons in it, all with the same name: *optDemo*. If a caption is added to each check box and option button, the resulting form will appear as shown in Figure 6-2, where the check boxes and option buttons are pointed out. If you widen the Properties Explorer window, you will see that the first check box is named chkSelect(0), the second check box is named chkSelect(1), and so on. Similarly, the first option button is named optDemo(0); the second button is named optDemo(1), and so on. Also, if you select the frame and move it, you will notice that the option buttons will move with it. The frame control also allows you to have multiple sets of option buttons on a form by grouping each set separately from the others.

FIGURE 6-2. Form demonstrating control arrays

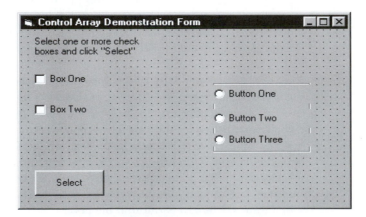

TIP: Another way to add an option button to a frame is to double-click the toolbox option button icon to add the option button to the form and then use **Edit|Cut** and **Edit|Paste** to transfer it to the frame.

Coding the Check Box Control Array

The code for the check boxes is handled differently from the code for the option buttons. Since the user can select multiple check boxes, we need to wait until the cmdSelect button is clicked to execute any code. On the other hand, since only one of the option buttons can be clicked, we can execute the code when one of the buttons is selected. For the check boxes, we will assume that the user can select the first check box or the second check box, the first and second boxes together, or no check boxes at all. In each case, the **Value** property of the appropriate check box is checked to determine if it is True or False. If it is True, then the corresponding check box has been selected. The code for cmdSelect, to determine which check box or combination of check boxes has been selected, is shown in VB Code Box 6-1.

| **VB CODE BOX 6-1.** Code for check box control array | ```
Private Sub cmdSelect_Click()
    If chkSelect(0).Value And Not chkSelect(1).Value Then
        MsgBox "Box One selected"
    ElseIf Not chkSelect(0).Value And chkSelect(1).Value Then
        MsgBox "Box Two selected"
    ElseIf chkSelect(0).Value And chkSelect(1).Value Then
        MsgBox "Boxes One and Two selected"
    Else
        MsgBox "No boxes selected"
    End If
End Sub
``` |
|---|---|

Note that the same name—chkSelect—is used for each element in the check box control array, with the each of various check boxes being differentiated by its index, that is, chkSelect(0), chkSelect(1), and so on. Also note that the Value property must come *after* the index. The Value property is not actually compared to True since it is automatically either True or False; it is only necessary to check if its current property is True. To check if it is False requires the use of the Not operator to convert a False property to True. In this case, if the first check box is selected but not the second one, then the first condition is True; if the second check box is selected but not the first one, the second condition is True. If only the third check box is selected, then the third condition is True. If the first *and* second check boxes are selected, the third condition is True. If no check boxes are selected, then the Else condition is True.

> **TIP:** The complete name of a control that is part of a control array always includes the index values.

Coding the Option Button Control Array

To add code for the option buttons, simply double-click any of the buttons to open the Code window for the optTypes control array. You will know you are working with a control array by the different opening line of the event procedure, as shown below:

```
Private Sub optDemo_Click(Index As Integer)
```

where the name of the control array of option buttons is *optDemo*.

This is different from previous sub statements, because the index value is being *passed* to the event procedure; this means that the index of the option button that was clicked is now known to the event procedure. If you click the first button, the index value in the event procedure is 0, if you click the second button, the value is 1, and so on. You can use this index value in a Select Case statement to determine which button was clicked. The code for the option buttons is shown in VB Code Box 6-2.

Application to Vintage Videos Scenario

In the Vintage Videos scenario, the objective is to replace the lstTypes list box with option buttons where only one option can be clicked. To do this, we add the *fraTypes* frame first and then draw the three option buttons in it, all with the same name: *optTypes*. If a caption identifying each button is added, the resulting form will appear as shown in Figure 6-3, where the option buttons are pointed out. If you widen the Properties Explorer window, you will see that for the Kids button the name is optTypes(0); for the Regular button it is optTypes(1); and for the Classic button it is optTypes(2).
```

| **VB Code Box 6-2.** Code for option buttons | ```
Private Sub optDemo_Click(Index As Integer)
    Select Case Index
    Case 0
        MsgBox "Button One selected"
    Case 1
        MsgBox "Button Two selected"
    Case 2
        MsgBox "Button Three selected"
    End Select
End Sub
``` |

Figure 6-3. Vintage form with option buttons

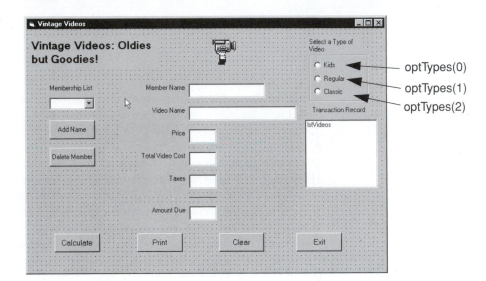

Clearing check boxes or option buttons requires that their Value property be set to *False*. This will result in none of the check boxes or option buttons being selected after the clearing operation.

The code to select a video price using the optTypes option buttons is similar to that used for the optDemo option buttons and is shown in VB Code Box 6-3. The code to clear the optTypes option buttons in preparation for entering the next video shown in Code Table 6-4 needs to be added to the cmdCalc_Click( ) event procedure. Note that a For-Next loop is used to set the option button Value property to False for all three option buttons.

Mini-Summary 6-1: Control Arrays

1. A control array is a group of the same type control that is assigned a single name. Check boxes and option buttons are often grouped into a control array. The Value property is set to true when a check box or option button is selected.

2. The individual controls are identified by the control array name and an index value which is determined by the order that they are added to the form. Option buttons are usually grouped using the frame control

3. The Select Case decision structure can be useful in working with a control array.

4. Check boxes and option buttons can be cleared by setting their Value property to False.
```

VB CODE BOX 6-3. Code to select prices using option buttons	```Private Sub OptTypes_Click(Index As Integer) Dim curPrice As Currency Select Case Index Case 0 curPrice = 0.99 Case 1 curPrice = 1.99 Case 2 curPrice = 2.99 End Select txtVideoPrice.Text = Format(curPrice, "currency") End Sub```

VB CODE BOX 6-4. Code to clear Opt-Types option buttons	```For intCounter = 0 to 2 OptTypes(intCounter).Value = False Next```

It's Your Turn!

1. Why do we use a control array rather than a group of individual controls?

2. In a control array, how is each individual control identified?

3. What decision structure works well with control arrays? Why?

4. Why are option buttons and check boxes often used as control arrays?

5. A form contains three text boxes and a control array called cmdOperation consisting of 4 command buttons. Describe how the following code will work when one of the buttons of the control array is clicked.

```
Private Sub cmdOperation_Click(Index As Integer)
  Select Case Index
  Case 0
     txtResult.Text = Val(txtFNum.Text) + Val(txtSNum.Text)
  Case 1
     txtResult.Text = Val(txtFNum.Text) - Val(txtSNum.Text)
  Case 2
     txtResult.Text = Val(txtFNum.Text) * Val(txtSNum.Text)
  Case 3
     txtResult.Text = Val(txtFNum.Text) / Val(txtSNum.Text)
  End Select
End Sub
```

To create the check box and option button example, complete the following:

6. Use **File | New Project** to create a new standard EXE Visual Basic project. Name the form **frmDemo** and give a caption of **Control Array Demonstration Form**.

7. Add a check box control array composed of two check boxes. Give it a name of **chkSelect**. Add a label above with a caption of **Select one or more check boxes and click "Select"**.

8. Add a command button named **cmdSelect**. Add the code shown in VB Code Box 6-1 to the cmdSelect command button. Test it by selecting various combinations of check boxes.

9. Add a frame, delete its caption, and give it a name of **fraDemo**. *Draw* a three option buttons in this frame to create a control array named **optDemo**.

10. Add the code shown in VB Code Box 6-2 to the optDemo control array Click event. Test your code by clicking each of the buttons.

11. Add a command button named **cmdClear** with a caption of **Clear.** Add code *like* that shown in VB Code Box 6-4 to clear both the check boxes and option buttons.

12. Use the **File | Save** dialog box to create a new folder named **Chapter6** and save the current project as **ControlDemo.frm** and **ControlDemo.vbp**.

To create the revised Vintage Videos application, complete the following exercises *after* opening the **Vintage5.vbp** project from the Chapter5 folder:

13. Select and delete the lstTypes list box and delete the code for the corresponding event procedure. Also, remove **all** references to the lstTypes list box in the code for the Calculate and Clear buttons. In place of the lstTypes list box, add a frame called **fraTypes**. Delete the caption for this frame.

14. Draw three option buttons, all named **optTypes**, in the frame to create the control array. Give the option buttons captions of **Kids**, **Regular**, and **Classic**. Widen the Properties Explorer window to see the names given to the buttons in the control array.

15. Double-click any of the option buttons in the control array and add the code shown in VB Code Box 6-3.

16. Add the code shown in VB Code Box 6-4 to the cmdCalc_Click( ) event procedure to clear the optTypes option buttons in preparation for the next video. Note: you will need to declare the counter variable (IntCounter) as an Integer at the beginning of the event procedure.

17. Test your project to be sure that the option buttons display the correct prices in the txtVideoPrice text box. Save the form as **Vintage6.frm** and the project as **Vintage6.vbp** in the **Chapter6** folder.

WORKING WITH LISTS AS ARRAYS

While it is possible in Visual Basic to display and work with lists using controls like combo and list boxes, there comes a time when there are simply too many items to depend on visual tools. Instead, you need to store the data or information in memory as a list or table or, as it is termed, an **array**. Arrays provide a way of working with long lists in memory in the same way as working with shorter lists using Visual Basic list and combo box controls. We can input items into the list, initialize them to some value, process them to find their sum and average, find the largest or smallest item in a list, look up an item in a list, or rearrange a list in alphabetical or numerical order. One difference between lists stored as arrays and lists stored as controls is that list and combo boxes respond to control properties like *Sorted*, but arrays do not respond to any control properties. Another difference is that while Visual Basic controls like combo boxes and list boxes store only text in the form of character strings, arrays can be declared to hold any type of data you wish. However, it is important to note that an array can store *only* one type of data. For example, an array can store String data or Currency data, but not both. Finally, there is no array operation that corresponds to the ListCount property, so the number of elements in the array must be input or calculated whenever the array is to be processed. There is no way to look this value up as you can with a list box.

Arrays hold multiple values or strings the same way combo and list boxes do—by giving each value or string a number or numbers that define its position in the list or table. In a combo box or list box, the position of an item is determined by the List( ) property, but in a list array the position is determined by the index or **subscript** of the array element. As an example of this, consider a list box called lstPrices and an array called curPrices, as shown in Figure 6-4.

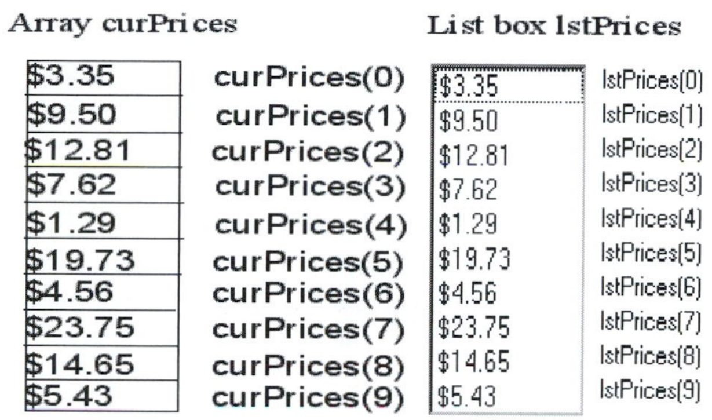

FIGURE 6-4.
Comparing arrays and list boxes

In this example, the list box holds a series of character strings, but the curPrices array holds a series of Currency type values. The strings in the list box are designated as lstPrices.List(0), lstPrices.List(1), lstPrices.List(2), and so on, while the Currency values in the array are designated as curPrices(0), curPrices(1), curPrices(2) and so on, where the numbers in parentheses after the variable names are the index values. That is, the index for the first curPrices value is 0, the second is 1, and so on. When you want to refer to an element of an array, you *must* always give the index value for that element. (Note: The elements in both the list and the array have been formatted as currency to display the dollar sign.)

> **TIP:** Visual Basic will generate a "Subscript out of Range" error if you try to refer to an array element that does not exist.

For example, the necessary code to sum the first ten values in the curPrices array and display the results in a text box is shown in VB Code Box 6-5:

VB CODE BOX 6-5.
Code to sum prices in array

```
curSumPrice = 0
For intCounter = 0 to 9
    curSumPrice = curSumPrice + curPrices(intCounter)
Next intCounter
txtPrice.text = Format(curSumPrice, "currency")
```

In summary, each item in an array is identified by two things:

1. The name of the array

2. The position of the item in the array (its index), which must be an Integer constant, variable, or expression.

Array Operations

To work with an array, you must first declare it. You declare an array the same way you would any other type of variable—at the procedure, form, or project level, depending on how many forms and objects must be able to *see* and use the array.

Once the array is declared, you must either input or create the items in the array just as you would with a combo or list box. Even if you do not see the values in an array, they are there. Once the data are in the array, you can manipulate the various array elements to carry out a wide variety of operations, including those described earlier (that is, initializing, summing, averaging, finding maximum or minimum values, and finding a specific element).

Once you have completed the array manipulation or processing, you must have a way to output the results of the manipulations. In Visual Basic, combo boxes and list boxes are a very convenient way to display the result of list array manipulation.

Declaring an Array

You must declare any array you use so that Visual Basic knows that it is a list of variables and not a single-value variable. While declaring single-valued variables is a good practice to use in programming, you *must* declare an array for it to be used in the project. Arrays in Visual Basic can be declared as fixed-size arrays or dynamic-size arrays. A **fixed-size array** has a specific amount of memory set aside for it, while a **dynamic array** has no fixed amount of memory set aside for it but the memory needed is defined in each module or procedure that uses it with the *ReDim* statement. For the purpose of our discussion in this chapter, we will restrict ourselves to fixed-size arrays.

If an array is declared in an event procedure, then only that procedure will know about the array, and, unless the array is declared with the *Static* keyword, its values will be reset to zero each time the event procedure is terminated. If the array is declared at the form level, then all procedures on that form will be aware of the array and will be able to use it in computations. The array values will not be reset to zero *unless* you leave that form. Finally, as will be discussed in Chapter 7, an array can be declared globally in a Basic module so that all forms and procedures can use it.

The general form of an array declaration statement for a list array is:

Dim *ArrayName(max index value)* as *variable type*

This declaration statement defines the upper limit on the index for the array, with the lower limit being set to zero by default. Attempting to go outside of these upper and lower limits will result in an error.

For example, if the curPrices array discussed earlier has an upper limit on the index of 9, then the declaration would be:

```
Dim curPrices(9) as Currency
```

Note that this allows a total of 10 prices to be stored, with the index starting at zero.

> **TIP:** You can change the default lower limit from zero to one by adding the statement: **Option Base 1** before any array declarations in the Declarations procedure of the General object.

When you declare the upper limit on the index value, you are putting an absolute restriction on the value of the index. If you try to use an index above the declared upper limit, an error will result. For example, if you declare curPrices with a maximum index value of 9 and try to use it in a For-Next loop that runs from 1 to 12, then a "Subscript out of range" error message will result, as shown in Figure 6-5.

FIGURE 6-5. Error due to exceeding declared upper limit on index

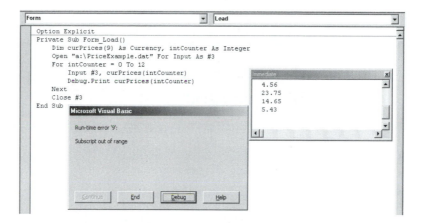

This error means that you have attempted to reference an index value higher than the declared upper limit. If this occurs, you have the option of ending execution or viewing the code by clicking on *Debug.* If you select Debug, you can then change the code and try to continue running the project (usually, in this situation, changing the upper limit value will require you to restart the execution of the project).

Up to now, we have assumed the lower limit was 0, but you can define both the upper and lower limits on the index values with the *To* keyword. The form of this type of declaration for a one-dimensional array is:

Dim *ArrayName(lower limit* To *upper limit)* as *variable type*

For example, to declare an array called strEmpName to be of the String data type and to have a lower limit of 100 on the index values and an upper limit of 200, the statement would be:

```
Dim strEmpName(100 to 200) as String
```

If you declare an array to have a lower limit other than zero, then the index values *must* fall within the range you define. For the above declaration, if you try to refer to strEmpName(99), you will receive the same "Subscript out of range" error that you did when you exceeded the upper index limit. In making this type of declaration, you must have an upper limit that is larger than the lower limit; otherwise, you will encounter a compile error stating that "Range has no values."

TIP: When you specify the lower bound of an array, you may set the bounds to any integer values including negative values. Just remember that the bounds are inclusive and the lower bound must be less than the upper bound.

Mini-Summary 6-2: Arrays

1. Arrays are lists or tables of data that have a single name. Individual array elements are identified by the array name and one or more subscripts or index values.

2. To be used in Visual Basic, an array must be declared; arrays can be fixed-size or dynamic-size.

Mini-Summary 6-2: Arrays (Continued)

3. The default lower limit on an array index is zero, but this can be changed to a different lower limit in the array declaration.

4. It is not possible to exceed the upper limit or to go below the lower limit on the array index values.

It's Your Turn!

1. List the similarities and differences between a list box and a one-dimensional array.

2. By what two things is every array element defined?

3. How many array elements are in each array declared by the following dimension statements?

   a. Dim intNum(10) As Integer
   b. Dim lngCount(0 to 5) as Long
   c. Dim curSalary(1 to 100) As Integer
   d. Dim sngTemp(-260 to 120) As Integer

4. Write the statements to declare the following arrays:

   a. A list of names with a maximum index of 50
   b. A list of prices with a maximum index of 100
   c. A list of the number of quizzes taken by students where there are 100 students in the class
   d. A list of values for which the index values will run from 25 to 50

INPUTTING VALUES TO AN ARRAY

Once you have declared an array, values can either be input or assigned to it. In this section, we will discuss inputting values to an array; in the next section, we will consider assigning values to an array. An important rule about input to an array is that inputting data to an array must always be done one element at a time. It is not possible to input an entire array in one operation.

Inputting a value into a single element of an array is just like inputting a value to a single-value variable, except that you *must* include the index for the array element. For example, to use an Input Box to input a value to curPrices(3), which was declared earlier as an array of Currency, the statement is:

```
curPrices(3) = Ccur(InputBox("Please input a price"))
```

While single-value input like this is possible, most of the time you will want to input multiple values into an array using a loop. This can be an event-driven loop, a For-Next loop, or a While or Until loop, depending on the circumstances. For example, in the project shown in Figure 6-5, the array values were input from a file using a For-Next loop

Event-Driven Array Input

If input is to be from the keyboard and you do not know the number of values to be input, an event-driven loop is most appropriate. This will work very much like the loop in Chapter 5 that input, summed, and counted an unknown number of values, except that the array values will be input to an array instead of being added to a list box. Also, since they are being input to an array and stored in memory, the values need not be summed immediately. The index for the array will correspond to the value of the counting variable for each value that is input. To demonstrate this type of array input, assume that a list of prices is to be stored in an array called curPrices, as shown earlier in Figure 6-4, and that a form similar to that used to input and sum values in Chapter 5 will be used to input and display the array of curPrices, as shown in Figure 6-6.

FIGURE 6-6. Form for working with curPrices array

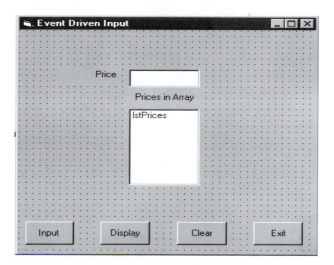

This form has a text box for inputting prices and a list box for displaying the array *after* it is completely input. There are also Input, Display, Clear, and Exit buttons. The Input button does just that; it inputs the prices from the textbox into the array after they are entered from the keyboard. The Display button transfers the array values into the list box, and the button clears the list box using *lstPrices.Clear.* The exit button exits the project. The curPrices array and the intNumPrices variable are declared at the form level, since they must be known to more than one event procedure (Input and Display). The curPrices array is declared to be a Currency data type with a maximum index of 25. The code for declaring the array and variable and for the Input and Display buttons is shown in Figure 6-7.

FIGURE 6-7. Code window for event-driven array input

```
Option Explicit
Dim curPrices(25) As Currency, intNumPrices As Integer
Private Sub cmdClear_Click()
  lstPrices.Clear
End Sub
Private Sub cmdDisplay_Click()
  Dim intCounter As Integer
  For intCounter = 0 To intNumPrices - 1
    lstPrices.AddItem Format(curPrices(intCounter), "currency")
    Debug.Print curPrices(intCounter)
  Next intCounter
End Sub
Private Sub cmdExit_Click()
  End
End Sub
Private Sub cmdInput_Click()
  curPrices(intNumPrices) = CCur(txtPrice.Text)
  intNumPrices = intNumPrices + 1
  txtPrice.Text = ""
  txtPrice.SetFocus
End Sub
```

In the cmdInput event procedure, the contents of the txtPrice text box are assigned to the curPrices array with an index of intNumPrices. The variable intNum-Prices is then incremented, the text box is cleared, and the focus is set back to it. Because its initial value is zero from the declaration at the form level, intNumPrices is incremented *after* the name is assigned to the array.

In the cmdDisplay event procedure, a For-Next loop is used to display the contents of the curPrices array by adding them to a list box. Note that the For-Next loop starts at zero and runs to *intNumPrices – 1* and not intNumPrices. This is true because intNumPrices counts the absolute number of elements in the array but the array index starts at zero. This makes intNumPrices one more than the index value of the last array element. In fact, this will be true in general for all For-Next loops that involve the int-NumPrices value. Finally, as shown in Figure 6-7, the cmdClear button clears the list box and the cmdExit button exits the project.

If you run this project and add the prices listed earlier to the text box one at a time, you can see the current contents of the array by clicking on cmdDisplay. Note that clearing the list box *does not* clear the array, and you can add a few prices, check the status of the array, clear it, and then add more prices to the array. Figure 6-8 shows this project after five prices have been added.

The remaining prices can be added and displayed in the same manner. It is *very important* to note that once the array elements have been entered, they will remain in memory until the project is exited.

FIGURE 6-8. Result of inputting and displaying a partial list of prices

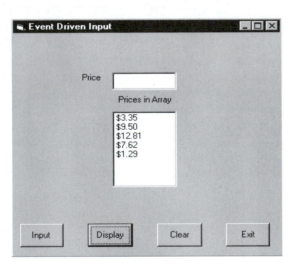

Array Input Using For-Next Loops

If the number of values in the array is known, then you can use a For-Next loop to input the values into the array from the keyboard or from a file. For this to be done, it must be assumed that the number of array elements will be input first, followed by the array values themselves. If keyboard input is to be used, then the For-Next loop to input data using an inputbox is shown in VB Code Box 6-6. This replaces the code that input the same array using an event-driven loop (Prices( )).

Array Input from Files

Typically, arrays are sufficiently large that keyboard input becomes very tedious. For that reason, a more realistic situation is one in which an unknown number of array values are input from a sequential access file, as was done in Chapter 5. Also, if the data

VB CODE BOX 6-6. Code for array input from keyboard using a For-Next loop	```
	Private Sub Input_click()
	    Dim intCounter
	    intNumPrices = CInt(InputBox("How many prices?"))
	    For intCounter = 0 to intNumPrices - 1
	        curPrices(Counter) = cCur(InputBox("Input next price"))
	    Next
	End sub
	``

are in a file, knowing the number of data values to be input is unnecessary as long as there is an EOF marker at the end of the file. For these reasons, we will concentrate on file input for an unknown number of elements using an Until or While loop.

To input an unknown number of array elements from a sequential access file opened as #*n*, the general form of the Do Until input loop is:

> ***intCounter = 0***
>
> **Do Until EOF(*n*)**
>
> > **Input #*n*, *ArrayName(intCounter)***
> >
> > ***intCounter = intCounter + 1***
>
> **Loop**

Note in this general form that the data values are input directly from the file into the array element defined by *ArrayName(intCounter)*, where the variable intCounter has been defined as an Integer variable. There is no need to input the data value to a variable and then add this variable to a combo box or list box.

> **TIP:** If you set the default lower limit to 1 with the Option Base 1 instruction, then you need to insert the statement *intCounter = 1* before the Until input loop. In addition, all For-Next loops will run from 1 to the value of intCounter (not intCounter − 1).

As an illustration of using a Do Until loop to input data from a sequential access file, recall the example in which we created an array of prices using event-driven input. In that example, input was from a text box and the array was displayed in a list box. Using a Do Until loop in the Form_Load event procedure to input an array will be similar, except that there will be no input text box or input button and the code to input the file is shown in VB Code Box 6-7.

VB CODE BOX 6-7. Code to input array elements from a file	```
	Private Sub Form_Load()
	    intNumPrices = 0
	    Open "A:\Prices.txt" For Input As #5
	    Do Until EOF(5)
	        Input #5, curPrices(intNumPrices)
	        intNumPrices = intNumPrices + 1
	    Loop
	    Close #5
	End Sub
	``

All other event procedures remain the same since they depend on the array that is created in the Form_Load event procedure. No matter how the array is created, the Display, Clear, and Exit buttons still work the same way. If this revised project is run with a data file called "a:\Prices.txt" that is created with the same prices as shown in Figure 6-4, the result of clicking the Display button will be as shown in Figure 6-9.

FIGURE **6-9.** Result of displaying array of prices

Mini-Summary 6-3: Array Input

1. Arrays must be input one value at a time. They can be input as single elements or using any of the three types of loops discussed earlier.

2. Event-driven loops and For-Next loops are good for keyboard input; While and Until loops are good for input from a file.

3. In any case, each array element must be input using its subscript value.

It's Your Turn!

1. When using event-driven input to populate an array, why must the counter variable be declared at the form level? What would have happened if we had declared it in the event procedure as a Static variable?

2. Why does the For-Next loop for displaying the contents of an array run to the number of elements in the array *minus* one?

3. Explain why clearing a list box displaying the contents of an array does not clear the array itself?

4. Why is file input often the best way to input data to an array?

5. What kind of loop is used to input data from a file? Why is a For-Next loop *not* appropriate for file input?

6. Describe the result of executing each of the following Visual Basic code segments:

```
a. Private Sub cmdGo_Click()
     Dim intCounter As Integer
     Dim intNum(4) As Integer
     Dim strName(4) As String
     For intCounter = 0 To 4
       intNum(intCounter) = intCounter + 1
       strName(intCounter) = InputBox("Name, please:")
       lstDisplay.AddItem intNum(intCounter) & ".  " _
```

```
                      & strName(intCounter)
            Next intCounter
         End Sub
 b.  Private Sub cmdGo_Click()
         Dim intCounter As Integer
         Dim intNum(20) As Integer
         Dim strName(20) As String
         Dim strResponse As String
         intCounter = 0
         Do
           strResponse = InputBox("Name, please:")
           If strResponse <> "" Then
             intCounter = intCounter + 1
             intNum(intCounter) = intCounter
             strName(intCounter) = strResponse
             lstDisplay.AddItem intNum(intCounter) & ".   " _
                 & strName(intCounter)
           End If
         Loop Until strResponse = ""
         End Sub
```

7. To create a form that will use event-driven input to populate an array, complete the following exercises:

    a. Create the form shown in Figure 6-6, using the control properties shown in Table 6-1. Name the form **frmEvntDrvnInput** and give it the caption shown in the figure.

TABLE 6-1: Control Properties for Event Driven Input Form

Control Name	Caption	Control Name	Caption
txtPrice		lblPrice	Price
lstPrices		lblPriceList	Prices in Array
cmdInput	Input	cmdClear	Clear
cmdDisplay	Display	cmdExit	Exit

    b. Add the code shown in Figure 6-7 to the General declarations area for the form and to the Click event procedures for the Input and Display command buttons.

    c. Run the project with the data shown in Figure 6-4. Add five prices, click the display button, clear the list box, add the remaining five prices, and click the display button again. You should see all ten prices. Save the form as **Evnt-DrvnInp.frm** and the project as **EvntDrvnInp.vbp** in the Chapter6 folder.

8. To revise this project to use input from a file, complete the following exercises:

    a. Modify the form for the event-driven input project by deleting the txtPrice text box and corresponding label, the Input command button, and the cmdInput_Click( ) event procedure. The other command buttons need to arranged as shown in Figure 6-9. The form should be named **frmUntilInput** with a caption of **Until Loop Array Input.**

    b. Add the code shown in VB Code Box 6-7 to the Form_Load event procedure.

    c. Use NotePad to create a text file in the root folder of your floppy disk called **Prices.txt**, with the prices shown in Figure 6-4. Run your revised project and click the Display button after the disk activity on the a: drive has stopped. It should look like Figure 6-9.

    d. Save your revised project as **UntilInput.frm** and **UntilInput.vbp**.

9. Modify the array limits on the curPrices array to have a maximum index of 5. Run your project again. What happens? Do NOT save the project.

10. Change the index limits for this project to be *10 To 15* and run it again. What happens? Return the limits to the original values.

PROCESSING WITH ARRAYS

Inputting data into an array is only the first step in using it. There are a large number of processing activities that can be handled best by arrays, including initializing array elements to some value, summing and averaging the values in an array, finding the largest or smallest value in a list, working with multiple lists, finding a particular value in a list, and sorting a list into a desired order. In this chapter, we will cover the first five of these operations; the last operation, sorting a list, will be covered in Chapter 7. It is important to note that, in all cases, the For-Next loop is the best way to process arrays, since the For-Next Loop counter matches the index values of the array.

Initializing Array Elements

It is quite often necessary to initialize all values of the array to zero or some other value. This requires a For-Next loop to refer to each value of the array. For example, if a list array of Integer values called intScores has a declared upper limit of 100, then to initialize all values in this array to some value other than zero, say, −1, the statements would be:

```
For intCounter = 0 to 100
  intScores(intCounter) = -1
Next
```

As you have probably already noticed, processing arrays often requires the use of a For-Next loop. In fact, working with arrays is a very important use for For-Next loops. The Integer counter variable in a For-Next loop matches up very well with the Integer index values of the array elements. If you want to go through the elements of a list array, then you need only use a For-Next loop with starting and ending values that match the declared lower and upper limits of the array index values. If the actual number of array elements is less than the declared number (a common occurrence), the index value of the last used array value can be used in the For-Next loop instead of the declared upper limit. For example, even though the Scores array presented earlier had all of its elements initialized to −1, if the last index of an element that actually is used is only 25, then the For-Next loop to process the array would be:

```
For intCounter = 0 to 25
```

Finally, just as it is not necessary to go up to the upper limit on an index value, it also is not necessary to start at the lower limit. In many situations, it is more appropriate (or easier to understand) to start at 1 rather than at 0. That is, even though an array has been declared to have a zeroth element, if it is more natural to start with the element with an index of one, there is no problem with doing this.

*Summing and
Averaging Values*

Once you have an array of values, it is very easy to sum and average them using For-Next loops to add each array element to the sum and then divide the sum by the number of elements. To implement this procedure in Visual Basic, we will use the same file of 10 prices as before (*a:\Prices.txt*); we will modify the project used to input an unknown number of values (*UntilInput.*vbp) and add a command button to find and display the sum and average (*cmdAverage*) in text boxes (*txtSum* and *txtAverage*) with corresponding labels. The code for the cmdAverage_Click( ) event procedure is shown in VB Code Box 6-8. The result of running this project and clicking the *Display* and *Sum and Average* buttons is shown in Figure 6-10.

| **VB CODE BOX 6-8.** Code to compute the sum and average of array elements | ```Private Sub CmdSumAverage_Click()
  Dim curSum as Currency, intCounter as Integer
  Dim curAverage as Currency
  curSum = 0
  For intCounter = 0 to intNumPrices - 1
    curSum = curSum + curPrices(intCounter)
  Next
  If intNumPrices >0 then
    curAverage = curSum/intNumPrices
  Else
    MsgBox "No values to average!"
    Exit Sub
  End If
  txtSum.Text = Format(curSum, "currency")
  txtAverage.Text = Format(curAverage, "currency")
End``` |
|---|---|

Note in VB Code Box 6-8 that the For-Next loop to compute the sum runs from zero to intNumPrices – 1, for the same reason that it did in the cmdDisplay_Click( ) event procedure. On the other hand, the average is computed by dividing the sum by intNumPrices since this value is the actual absolute number of elements in the array. Note that we check to ensure that intNumPrices is *not* zero before we try to divide by it. Attempting to divide by zero is very common error that is often caused by input errors resulting in no values being input. We will assume that this project is saved as SumAverage.frm and SumAverage.vbp.

FIGURE 6-10. Form to compute the sum and average of array values

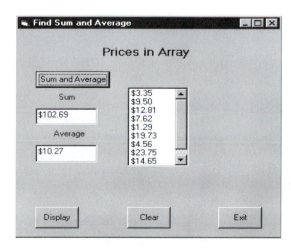

Finding the Largest (Smallest) Value in a List

A common operation in working with lists is finding the largest or smallest value in the list. By *value*, we mean a numeric value or a character string. For numeric values, it is obvious what larger and smaller mean, but what about for character strings? For character strings, the alphabetical ordering holds; that is, the letter A is *smaller* than the letter B because it comes first in the alphabetical ordering. Similarly, lower-case letters come *after* upper-case letters, and digits come before the alphabetic characters. The order of characters is known as the **collating sequence** and it includes all 256 characters that Visual Basic recognizes. You can see the complete collating sequence by entering and running the code shown in VB Code Box 6-9 in the Form_Load event for a new project.

| **VB CODE BOX 6-9.** Displaying the collating sequence | ```
Private Sub Form_Load()
  Dim intCounter As Integer
  For intCounter = 0 To 255
    Debug.Print Chr(intCounter);
  Next
End Sub
``` |
|---|---|

This code uses the **Chr()** function to convert the Integer values of the For-Next counter variable into the corresponding characters. To reverse this operation and find the position of a particular character in the collating sequence, you would use the Asc() function with the character as the argument of the function. For example, if we entered:

```
Debug.Print Asc("A")
```

the number 65 would be printed in the Immediate window.

To find the largest value in an array, each item in the list must be compared to the currently known largest value. If an item in the list is larger than the currently known largest value, the item in the list becomes the largest known value. This comparison process continues until all items in the list have been compared to the currently known largest value, at which time the comparisons end and the largest value is known. The pseudocode for this logic is shown below (to find the smallest value, simply reverse the direction of the inequality from greater than to less than):

> Begin procedure to find largest value
> Set largest value to first item in list
> Repeat beginning with second item to last item
>   If item in list > largest value then
>   Largest value = item in list
>   End decision
> End repeat
> Display largest value
> End procedure

Note that the largest value is initialized to the first item in the list and then compared to every item in the list, starting with the second item. The largest value must be compared to something, and the first item in the list is a convenient value to be used.

To see how this works, assume you have the same list of 10 prices as shown in Figure 6-4 and you want to find the largest value. If we walk through the pseudocode shown above for these prices, the results are as follows:
```

Set Largest = curPrices(0) = \$3.35
Set intCounter = 1
Is curPrices(1) = \$9.50 > \$3.35? Yes, so Largest = curPrices(1) = \$9.50
Is curPrices(2) = \$12.81 > \$9.50? Yes, so Largest = curPrices(2) = \$12.81
Is curPrices(3) = \$7.62 > \$12.81? No, so no change
Is curPrices(4) = \$1.29 > \$12.81? No, so no change
Is curPrices(5) = \$19.73 > \$12.81? Yes, so Largest = curPrices(5) = \$19.73
Is curPrices(6) = \$4.56 > \$19.73? No, so no change
Is curPrices(7) = \$23.75 > \$19.73? Yes, so Largest = curPrices(7) = \$23.75
Is curPrices(8) = \$14.65 > \$23.75? No, so no change
Is curPrices(9) = \$5.43 > \$23.75? No, so no change
End of array, so Largest = \$23.75

To implement this procedure in Visual Basic, we will use the same file of 10 prices as before (*a:\Prices.txt*) and extend the form used earlier to input, sum, and average an unknown number of values (*SumAverage.vbp*). A command button to find the largest value (*cmdFindMax*) and a text box (*txtMaxPrice*) to display the largest value in the array with a corresponding label should be added. The code for the cmdFindMax_Click( ) event procedure is shown in VB Code Box 6-10, and the result of clicking the *Display* and *Find Max* buttons is shown in Figure 6-11.

| **VB CODE BOX 6-10.** Code to find the maximum price in the curPrices array | ```Private Sub cmdFindMax_Click()
  Dim intCounter As Integer, curLargest As Currency
  curLargest = curPrices(0)
  For intCounter = 1 To intNumPrices - 1
    If curPrices(intCounter) > curLargest Then
      curLargest = curPrices(Counter)
    End If
  Next
  txtMaxPrice.Text = Format(curLargest, "currency")
End Sub``` |
| --- | --- |

FIGURE 6-11. Form to find maximum value

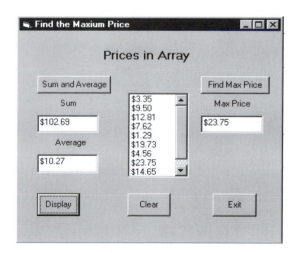

Mini-Summary 6-4: Processing with Arrays

1. Typical array operations include initializing all array elements to sum value, summing and averaging the array values and finding the largest or smallest value in the array.

2. For-Next loops are very useful for working with arrays since the counter variable often matches the index of the array.

3. Summing and averaging involves adding each value of the array to a summation variable while at the same time counting the number of elements.

4. Finding the largest or smallest value involves multiple comparisons of array elements to the current largest (smallest) value until all elements have been checked.

It's Your Turn!

1. Why do we say that, in many cases, the For-Next loop is the best way to process an array?

2. Why would it be necessary to initialize an entire array to some value?

3. What is the collating sequence and what does it have to do with decisions?

4. What operations do the Chr( ) and Asc( ) functions carry out?

5. Assume that the following declarations have been made:

```
Dim intArray1(4) As Integer
Dim intArray2(4) As Integer
```

Also assume that the intArray2 initially contains the following values:

0	1	2	3	4
10	13	7	24	2

Describe the contents of the arrays after each of the following Visual Basic code segments have been executed.

```
a. Private Sub cmdGo_Click()
     Dim intI As Integer
     For intI = 0 To 4
       intArray1(intI) = 1
     Next intI
   End Sub

b. Private Sub cmdGo_Click()
     Dim intI As Integer
     Dim intTemp As Integer
     intTemp = intArray2(0)
     For intI = 0 To 3
       intArray2(intI) = intArray2(intI + 1)
     Next intI
     intArray2(4) = intTemp
   End Sub
```

```
c. Private Sub cmdGo_Click()
     Dim intI As Integer
     Dim intTemp As Integer
     For intI = 0 To 4
       intArray1(intI) = intArray2(intI) + 10
     Next intI
   End Sub
d. Private Sub cmdGo_Click()
     Dim intI As Integer
     Dim intTemp As Integer
     For intI = 0 To 4
       If (intArray2(intI) Mod 2) > 0 Then
         intArray1(intI) = intArray2(intI)
       Else
         intArray1(intI) = intArray2(intI) + 1
       End If
     Next intI
   End Sub
```

6. To modify the UntilInput.vbp project to find the sum and average price in the list, complete the following exercises:

   a. Add the **cmdSumAverage** command button with a caption of **Sum and Average**. Also add the **txtSum** and **txtAverage** text boxes with corresponding labels. Change the name of the form to be **frmSumAverage** and give it a caption of **Find Sum and Average**. The resulting form should look like Figure 6-10.

   b. Add the code shown in VB Code Box 6-8 to the **cmdSumAverage _Click( )** event procedure.

   c. Run the project and click the Sum and Average button. You should see a sum of $102.69 and an average of $10.27.

   d. Save the form as **SumAverage.frm** and the project as **SumAverage.vbp** in the Chapter6 folder on your data disk.

7. To modify the current project to find the maximum price in the list, complete the following exercises:

   a. Add the **cmdFindMax** command button with a caption of **Find Max Price**. Also add the **txtMaxPrice** text box, with a corresponding label. Change the name of the form to be **frmFindMax** and give it a caption of **Find Maximum Price**. The resulting form should look like Figure 6-11.

   b. Add the code shown in VB Code Box 6-10 to the **cmdFindMax_Click( )** event procedure.

   c. Run the project and click the Find Max Price button. You should see a maximum price of $23.75.

   d. Save the form as **MaxPrice.frm** and the project as **MaxPrice.vbp** in the Chapter6 folder on your data disk.

8. Modify the project to find the *minimum price* in the data file. Change the name and caption of the form to match its new purpose. Run your project with the same a:\Prices.txt data file as before. What is the minimum price in the list?

9. Save this form as **MinPrice.frm** and this project as **MinPrice.vbp** in the Chapter6 folder on your data disk.

10. To display the Visual Basic collating sequence, open a new Standard EXE file and enter the code shown in VB Code Box 6-9 in the Form_Load event procedure. Run the project and, if the Immediate window is not already displayed, use **View | Immediate window** to display it. Note that the first characters are not printable. What character precedes the letter *a*? The letter *A*? Save the form as **Collating.frm** and the project as **Collating.vbp** in the Chapter6 folder on your data disk.

FINDING ITEMS AND WORKING WITH MULTIPLE LISTS

As mentioned earlier, in addition to finding the largest or smallest value in a list, typical processing operations on lists include finding a particular item in a list and working with multiple lists. In this section we will take up these two operations, and then in the next section we will apply them to the Vintage Videos scenario. To discuss these two operations, we will assume that instead of the prices being just a random list, each price in the list is associated with a part identifier as shown in Table 6-2.

TABLE 6-2: Part Identifiers and Prices

Part Identifier	Price	Part Identifier	Price
V23-5W	$3.35	V24-5V	$19.73
X37-3K	$9.50	X44-8T	$4.56
Q55-8S	$12.81	Q49-3K	$23.75
R12-7T	$7.62	V24-2T	$14.65
T17-6Y	$1.29	R13-8W	$5.43

For example, the part with identifier V23-5W has a price of $3.35, while the part with identifier X37-3K has a price of $9.50. Since the part identifier is a character string and the price is a Currency data type, they must be stored in separate arrays. This will also allow us to find the item with largest or smallest price easily by searching the price array or to find a particular item in the list by searching the identifier array.

Project Objectives

The objective of this project will be twofold:

1. Find the part with the maximum price and display the part identifier and price; and

2. Find the part with a specified identifier and display the part identifier and price; if the part is not on the list, display a message.

To work with two arrays to achieve these objectives, we need to modify the form used to find the maximum price. Specifically, we need to expand the width of the list box used to display the prices so that both the identifier and the price can be displayed on one line in the list box. We also need to widen the text box that was used to display price to now display the part identifier and the price for the highest priced item in the list. Since we also want to search the list for a particular identifier, we need to add another command button (*cmdFind*) to execute the search and add a text box (*txtFound*) to display the identifier and price for the item once it is found. Finally, the labels need to be modified to describe the revised or new text boxes, and the name of the list box needs to be changed to *lstParts*. The final form should look like Figure 6-12.

Inputting Values into Two Arrays

To input the part identifiers and prices from a file, we need to declare a second array, *strPartID*, at the form level as a String data type. The Input statement in the Do Until input loop that is in the Form_Load event procedure needs to be modified slightly as shown below:

```
Input #5, strPartID(intNumPrices), curPrices(intNumPrices)
```

The first two lines of data on the file would appear as follows, where the data items are separated by commas:

```
V23-5W, 3.35
X37-3K, 9.50
```

When the Input statement reads these data items, strPartID(0) will be equal to V23-5W and curPrices(0) will be equal to 3.35. Similarly, strPartID(1) = X37-3K and curPrices(1) = 9.50. Note that for a given part, the index values for the strPartID and curPrices array elements are the same. This means that the array index acts as a *link* between the two arrays and if you find a price, you can find the corresponding part ID through the index value and vice versa.

To display the two items on the same line in the list box, we need to modify the statement in the cmdDisplay event procedure that adds items to the lstParts list box to concatenate the part identifier with the formatted part price. The statement to do this is:

```
lstParts.AddItem strPartId(intCounter) + "   " _
& Format(curPrices(intCounter), "currency")
```

If data on a:\Prices.txt are modified to include the part identifier for each part, as shown in Table 6-1, and the input and lstParts.AddItem statements in the Form_Load event procedure are modified as shown above, running the program and clicking the *Display* button will result in the form shown in Figure 6-12.

FIGURE 6-12. Part identifier and price displayed in list box

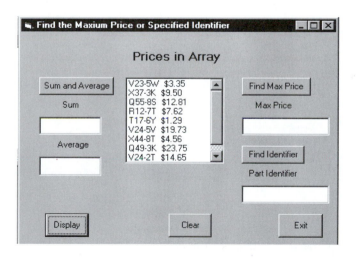

Finding a Specified Part Identifier

To search for a part identifier in the parts list to find its price, we need to use a For-Next loop to compare the part identifier to every part identifier in the parts list. Before the loop, the user enters the part identifier that is to be found in an InputBox. In addition, a **flag** variable is set to False. Within the loop, if a match is found between the part identifier that was input and a part identifier on the parts list, an If-Then decision sets the flag to True and saves the index of the part identifier. If no match is found, the flag variable remains False.

After the loop, the status of the flag variable is checked; if it is True, then the part identifier is on the parts list and you can use the array index of the part identifier array to find it. If the flag is False, the part identifier is not on the parts list. The pseudocode for this operation is shown below:

```
Begin procedure to find part identifier
Input part identifier
Set Flag to False
Repeat for each part in parts list
        If part identifier = identifier on parts list then
                Flag = True
                Save index of part identifier on parts list
        End decision
End repeat
If Flag = True
        Use saved index to display part identifier and price
Else
        Display message that part not on parts list
End decision
End procedure
```

The flag variable in the Visual Basic version of the above pseudocode will be a Boolean variable that is initially set to False and then set to True if a match is found in the loop. After the loop, the status of the flag variable is checked; if it is True, the part identifier and price are displayed in a text box. If the flag variable is False, a message is displayed that the part is not on the parts list. Another variable is intPriceIndex, which is set to the array index of the part identifier that is a match. This variable is then used to display the part identifier and price after the loop. The code for the cmdFind button is shown in VB Code Box 6-11.

VB CODE BOX 6-11. Code to search for part identifier in parts array	

```
Private Sub cmdFind_Click()
    Dim intCounter As Integer, intResults As Integer
    Dim strFindPartID as String, blnFound As Boolean
    Dim intPriceIndex as Integer
    strFindPartID = InputBox("Input identifier to find")
    blnFound = False
    For intCounter = 0 To intNumPrices - 1
        If UCase(strFindPartID) = UCase(strPartId(intCounter))Then
            blnFound = True
            intPriceIndex = intCounter
            Exit For
        End If
    Next
    If blnFound Then
        txtFound.Text = strPartId(intPriceIndex) & "   " & _
        Format(curPrices(intPriceIndex), "currency")
    Else
        MsgBox "Part not found", vbExclamation, _
        "Price Search"
    End If
End Sub
```

Several things are of note in this code. First, if the part identifier is found, the For-Next loop is exited with the *Exit For* instruction. This has the same effect as if the loop had ended normally. This saves processing time by not looking for the part identifier after it has already been found. Second, to check the status of the Boolean variable blnFound, you do *not* need to actually compare it to True; Boolean variables are already True or False, so no comparison is necessary. Finally, we have added second and third parameters to the MsgBox, and it is now being used as a function to assign a value to the variable Results. The new parameters are a Visual Basic constant that displays an exclamation sign—VBExclamation— and a title, "Price Search."

More on the Message Box

Up to this point, we have used the MsgBox as a statement to display a message in a dialog box. However, it is possible to include other parameters with the MsgBox to display a designated title as well as icons and buttons. The form of the message box with additional parameters is:

MsgBox *message, buttons, title*

where *buttons* is one or more internal Visual Basic constants, such as vbExclamation or vbYesNoCancel, that display one or more buttons and/or an icon. Similarly, *title* is a title string for the dialog box. For example, using the MsgBox function in VB Code Box 6-11 will result in the dialog box shown in Figure 6-13.

FIGURE 6-13
Message Box with exclamation mark

> **TIP:** It is possible to use the plus sign (+) to combine two or more of the Visual Basic constants to display icons and buttons.

In addition to adding a title, icons, and buttons to the MsgBox, it is also possible to treat it as a *function* and use it to learn which of the buttons the user clicked. As with any function, the parameters must be enclosed in parentheses and the MsgBox function must appear in an expression as shown below:

intVariable = **MsgBox**(*message, buttons, title*)

The value of *intVariable* can be checked to determine which button on the dialog box the user clicked.

For example, assume you used the following instruction in a project:

```
intResults = MsgBox("Write over old file?", vbYesNoCancel)
```

In this case, the user would be presented with a dialog box with the prompt and three buttons—Yes, No, and Cancel—one of which must be clicked. It would then be possible to use an If-Then-ElseIf or Select Case decision structure to check the status of the Integer variable *intResults* to determine which button the user clicked: Yes to write over the old file, No to not write over the old file, or Cancel to cancel the entire operation. If the user clicks the *Yes* button to overwrite old file, the intResults variable will be equal to 6; if the user clicks *No* to not overwrite the old file, the intResults variable will be equal to 7; and if the user clicks *Cancel* to cancel the entire operation, then intResults will be equal to 2. However, you do not have to remember these values, since they can be replaced with the Visual Basic constants vbYes, vbNo, and vbCancel. The code to check if the user clicked the Yes button would be:

```
If intResults = vbYes then
```

Figure 6-3 shows the most commonly used internal Visual Basic constants, along with commonly used buttons and the values they return.

If the code in VB Code Box 6-11 is entered in the cmdFind_Click( ) event procedure, this button is ready to test. To do this, run the project, click the Find Identifiers

TABLE 6-3: Visual Basic Internal Constants and Values Returned from the MsgBox Function

Button Constant	Description	Value Returned	Visual Basic Constant	Description
vbOKOnly	Display **OK** button only	1	vbOk	**OK** button clicked
vbOKCancel	Display **OK** and **Cancel** buttons	2	vbCancel	**Cancel** button clicked
vbYesNoCancel	Display **Yes**, **No**, and **Cancel** buttons	3	vbAbort	**Abort** button clicked
vbYesNo	Display **Yes** and **No** buttons	4	vbRetry	**Retry** button clicked
vbCritical	Display **Stop sign**	5	vbIgnore	**Ignore** any buttons
vbQuestion	Display a **question mark**	6	vbYes	**Yes** button clicked
vbExclamation	Display an **Exclamation mark**	7	vbNo	**No** button clicked
vbInformation	Display **Information Message** icon			

> **TIP:** There are many internal Visual Basic constants; go to the *Language Reference* section of the Web Help system and look in the *MsgBox Function* section to see them.

button, and enter (for example) **V24-5V**. If this is done, the following will be displayed in the txtMaxPrice text box:

```
V24-5V    $19.73
```

However, if you enter **Z93-Q1**, a message like that shown in Figure 6-13 will be displayed, since this part identifier is not on the parts list.

Finding the Part Identifier with the Highest Price

To find and display the part identifier and price corresponding to the part with the highest price, it is only necessary to modify the cmdFindMax_Click( ) event procedure to save the array index for the maximum price, as was done when a matching part identifier is found. This requires adding a statement that stores the index of the current largest price to the loop that searches for the maximum price. This statement will store the array index at the same time that the value of the largest price is saved. We will also need to include a statement that adds the part identifier and price to the txtMaxPrice text box. The revised cmdFindMax_Click( ) event procedure is shown in VB Code Box 6-12.

If the project is run and the Find Max Price button is clicked, the part identifier and price for the highest priced part will appear as shown below:

```
Q49-3K    $23.75.
```

This has been a fairly big project, so to help you with the code, we have shown all of the code for the MaxPrice.vbp project in one place in VB Code Box 6-13.

| **VB Code Box 6-12.** Code to save index for part with highest price | ```
Private Sub cmdFindMax_Click()
  Dim intCounter As Integer, curLargest As Currency
  Dim intMaxIndex as Integer
  curLargest = curPrices(0)
  For intCounter = 1 To intNumPrices - 1
    If curPrices(intCounter) > curLargest Then
      curLargest = curPrices(intCounter)
      intMaxIndex = intCounter
    End If
  Next
  txtMaxPrice.Text = strPartId(intMaxIndex) & "   " & _
  Format(curPrices(intMaxIndex), "currency")
End Sub
``` |
|---|---|

| **VB Code Box 6-13.** Complete code for PartsList project | ```
Option Explicit
Dim curPrices(25) As Currency, intNumPrices As Integer
Dim strPartID(25) As String
Private Sub cmdClear_Click()
  lstParts.Clear
  txtSum.Text = ""
  txtAverage.Text = ""
  txtMaxPrice.Text = ""
  txtFound.Text = ""
End Sub
Private Sub cmdDisplay_Click()
  Dim intCounter As Integer
  For intCounter = 0 To intNumPrices - 1
    lstParts.AddItem strPartID(intCounter) + " " _
    + Format(curPrices(intCounter), "currency")
    Debug.Print curPrices(intCounter)
  Next
End Sub
Private Sub cmdFind_Click()
  Dim intCounter As Integer, intResults As Integer
  Dim strFindPartID As String, blnFound As Boolean
  Dim intPriceIndex As Integer
  strFindPartID = InputBox("Input part identifier to find")
  blnFound = False
  For intCounter = 0 To intNumPrices - 1
    If UCase(strFindPartID) = _
        UCase(strPartID(intCounter)) Then
      blnFound = True
      intPriceIndex = intCounter
      Exit For
    End If
  Next
  If Found Then
    txtFound.Text = strPartID(intPriceIndex) & " " & _
    Format(curPrices(intPriceIndex), "currency")
  Else
    MsgBox "Part not found", vbExclamation, "Price Search"
  End If
End Sub
``` |
|---|---|

| VB CODE BOX 6-13. Complete code for PartsList project (cont.) | ```vb
Private Sub cmdExit_Click()
  End
End Sub
Private Sub cmdFindMax_Click()
  Dim intCounter As Integer, curLargest As Currency
  Dim intMaxIndex As Integer
  curLargest = curPrices(0)
  For intCounter = 1 To intNumPrices - 1
    If curPrices(intCounter) > curLargest Then
      curLargest = curPrices(intCounter)
      intMaxIndex = intCounter
    End If
  Next
  txtMaxPrice.Text = strPartID(intMaxIndex) & " " & _
  Format(curPrices(intMaxIndex), "currency")
End Sub
Private Sub cmdSumAverage_Click()
  Dim curSum As Currency, intCounter As Integer
  Dim curAverage As Currency
  curSum = 0
  For intCounter = 0 To intNumPrices - 1
    curSum = curSum + curPrices(intCounter)
  Next
  If intNumPrices = 0 then
    curAverage = curSum / intNumPrices
  Else
    MsgBox "No values to average!"
    Exit Sub
  End If
  txtSum.Text = Format(curSum, "currency")
  txtAverage.Text = Format(curAverage, "currency")
End Sub
Private Sub Form_Load()
  intNumPrices = 0
  Open "a:\Parts.txt" For Input As #5
  Do Until EOF(5)
    Input #5, strPartID(intNumPrices), _
      curPrices(intNumPrices)
    intNumPrices = intNumPrices + 1
  Loop
  Close #5
End Sub
``` |

Mini-Summary 6-5: Finding Array Elements and Working with Multiple Lists

1. It is possible to work with multiple list arrays by matching the index values for the arrays.

2. Finding a specific array value involves comparing each array element to the desired value. A flag is often used to indicate whether a match has been found.

3. The MsgBox can be used with multiple parameters to display a title and icons and/or buttons. By treating the MsgBox as a function, it is possible to determine which button the user clicked.
```

It's Your Turn!

1. Assume that the following declarations have been made:

```
Dim strArray1(4) As String
Dim curArray2(4) As Currency
```

Also assume that the arrays initially contain the following values:
strArray1

0	1	2	3	4
Thomas	Henry	Percy	Gordon	Skarlooey

curArray2

0	1	2	3	4
10.99	12.65	11.55	12.65	9.69

Describe the contents of the txtAnswer text box after the following Visual Basic code segments have been executed:

```
Private Sub cmdGo_Click()
  Dim strSearch As String
  Dim intI As Integer
  Dim blnFound As Boolean
  Dim intPos As Integer
  strSearch = InputBox("Enter name:")
  blnFound = False
  For intI = 0 To 4
    If UCase(strArray1(intI)) = UCase(strSearch) Then
      blnFound = True
      intPos = intI
      Exit For
    End If
  Next intI
  If blnFound Then
    txtAnswer.Text = strArray1(intPos) & _
    " costs " & curArray2(intPos)
  Else
    txtAnswer.Text = "Item not found"
  End If
End Sub
```

2. Use NotePad to modify the **Prices.txt** file to add the part identifiers shown in Table 6-2 (with a comma after each one) before each price (no need to add the price again). Save the text file as **Parts.txt**.

3. To modify the **MaxPrice.vbp** project to search for part identifiers, complete the following exercises:

    a. Modify the **MaxPrice.frm** form by widening the existing list and text boxes to be able to display both the part identifier and the price; rename the list box as **lstParts**. Give the form a name of **frmPartsList** and give it the caption shown in **Figure 6-12**.

b. To the right of the list box, add a new command button and a new text box named **cmdFind** and **txtFound**, respectively. The text box should be wide enough to display a part identifier and price. In addition, modify existing labels and captions and add new labels and captions so your form looks like that shown in Figure 6-12.

c. Add the following to the General declarations section:
```
Dim strPartID(25) as string
```

d. Modify the Form_Load event procedure to input the part identifier and price in the Do Until loop. This will require changing the Open statement to appear as shown below:
```
Open "a:\Parts.txt" for Input as #5
```
and modifying the Input statement as follows:
```
Input #5,strPartID(intNumPrices),curPrices(intNumPrices)
```

e. Modify the cmdDisplay_Click( ) event procedure so the statement that adds the part identifier and price to the list box appears as shown below:
```
lstParts.AddItem strPartID(intCounter) + "   " _
& Format(Prices(intCounter), "currency")
```

f. Run the project and click the display button. All ten part identifiers and prices should now be in the list box. You may have to scroll down to see all of them.

g. Add the code shown in VB Code Box 6-11 to the cmdFind_Click( ) event procedure. Run the project, click the Find Identifier button, and enter **T17-6Y**. What price is displayed? Click the button again and enter **R73-0S**. Is this part identifier in the list?

h. Modify the cmdFindMax_Click( ) event procedure so that it is like that shown in VB Code Box 6-12. Run your project and click this button. You should find that the part identifier for the highest priced part is Q49-3K.

i. Modify the cmdClear_click( ) event procedure to reflect changing the name of the list box to *lstParts*.

j. Save the revised form as **PartsList.frm** and the project as **PartsList.vbp** in the Chapter6 folder on your data disk.

4. Modify the MsgBox used in the cmdFind_Click( ) procedure so that it displays Yes, No, and Cancel buttons. Add instructions that will display another MsgBox indicating which button was clicked when a part identifier is not found. Test your project with a part identifier that is not in the parts list. Modify this further to also include a stop sign icon. Do *not* save this version of your project.

APPLICATION TO SCENARIO

Now that you have some understanding of arrays, we can turn our attention to the Vintage Videos scenario. Recall that the video store owners are responding to inquiries from their customers about whether they carry certain videos, and, if they do, their rental price and where they are located in the store. While Ed and Yvonne know about virtually every video in the store, their employees do not. To respond to these inquiries, they have asked Clark to come up with a way for store clerks to search for a video by name and, if it is found, display the price and the location in the store.

In responding to this request for an additional feature for the video information system he has been creating, Clark quickly realized that there is no room on the current form for the controls that would be needed to enter a video name, search for and display the names of videos that are like the one entered, and then display the price of the video the customer was interested in and its location in the store. About the best he can do on the current form is add a button that requests the name of the video to be found and transfers control to a second form where the actual information is displayed.

Working with Multiple Forms

In the first five chapters of this book, we have restricted our attention to projects that involve only a single form. However, Visual Basic gives you the capability to easily create and manage projects that involve multiple forms. You can create projects in which new forms are displayed when the user requests additional functionality as in the scenario or projects in which new forms automatically "pop up" as needed to respond to a user or program request.

Add form

To add a second form to an existing project, use the **Project|Add Form** menu selection or click on the Add Form icon on the toolbar. In either case, the Add Form dialog box will be displayed unless it has been discontinued by a previous user. (You can discontinue displaying this dialog box by clicking the check box in the bottom left-hand corner.) This dialog box contains a wide variety of types of forms that you can add to your project and modify to fit your needs. You can also choose to add existing forms to this project. However, for the time being we will restrict ourselves to adding a new blank form by clicking the Open button.

FIGURE 6-14 Project Explorer window

When a new form is added to a project, the existing form is replaced by a blank form and the new form's name (initially *Form1*) is added to the Project Explorer window above the original form (*frmVintage*), as shown in Figure 6-14. To view the original form again, simply double-click its name in the Project Explorer window. Do the same to return to the new form. The new form should be named with a *frm* prefix and saved with a *frm* extension as a part of the overall project. In our case, the new form will be named *frmVideos* and will be saved as *Videos.frm* as a part of the Vintage.vbp project.

Once you add a new form to the project, you may add controls and code to it as you did with the original form. This form also has its own Form_Load event, which occurs when it is loaded and displayed. The control names for the second and successive forms can be the same as for the main form, since they are attached to a different form. In fact, the complete name of any control is:

formname.controlname

but you do not need to include the *formname* portion of the name unless a control on another form is being referred to.

The question is, then, How do you load and display a second form? The answer is, with a single instruction in an event procedure in the original form:

formname.Show

where *formname* is the name of the form to be displayed and Show is the method that handles this operation. If the form is not already loaded into memory, the Show method loads it too.

To hide the second form and display the original form again, the command is:

formname.Hide

which hides the form named *formname*, but does not unload it from memory.

For example, to display the video form, the command would be:

```
frmVideos.Show
```

and it would be included as an instruction in a new command button, *cmdFindVideo*, on the main form, frmVintage. This button should have a caption of *Find Video* and should be placed beneath the Add Name command button.

If this new button is added to the main form, it will allow the clerk to switch to the video form to answer a customer's question regarding whether the store carries a particular video and, if it does, how much the rental on it is and where it is located in the store. There should be a button on this new form to hide it so the main form is once again displayed. The resulting main form is shown in Figure 6-15.

FIGURE 6-15.
Revised frmVintage to access second form

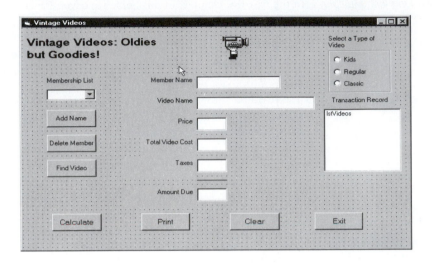

The Videos Form

Now that a new form has been added to the project and a button to display it has been added to the main form, we are ready to design and program this form. There should be a way for the clerk to type in a name or part of a name and have all videos that match the entry displayed in a list box, or, if no matching entries are found, then a message to that effect should be displayed. From the list of matching entries, the clerk can ask which one the customer is looking for and then display the name, price, and location of that video. For example, if a customer is looking for a video that has the word *ghost* in the title but is not sure of anything beyond that, the clerk can enter this word and display three videos with *ghost* in the title: *The Ghost and Mrs. Muir, Ghost,* and *Ghostbusters.* If the customer decides that the movie he is interested in is *The Ghost and Mrs. Muir,* then the clerk can click on this movie and find that it rents for $1.99 and is in the Drama section of the store. The design for a form to handle this operation is shown in Figure 6-16.

FIGURE 6-16.
Design for Videos form

This form does not need to be as large as the main form since it contains only a text box (*txtSearch*), a list box (*lstVideos*), two command buttons (*cmdSearch* and *cmd-Back*), and various labels. The name or partial name of the video to be searched for is entered in txtSearch, and then cmdFind is clicked. A list of videos matching the entry is listed in lstVideos, and if one is clicked, the list is replaced with more information about that particular video.

This form will require code in the cmdFind button to search for videos matching the entry in txtSearch and code for the Click event of lstVideos to find the video matching the one selected from the list. Entering this code on the second form is just like entering it for the main form—you simply double-click the control and enter the code in the Code window.

Since it is necessary to store information on the video name, video price, and video location, three arrays are needed. Because these arrays will be used in two different event procedures, the arrays and the number of elements in the arrays must be declared at the form level. The video name array and video location array will be String data types while the video price array will be a currency data type array. Declaring form-level variables for the frmVideo form is the same as doing it for any other form—you declare them in the Declarations procedure of the General event for the form. The declarations for this form are shown in Figure 6-17. (Note: To add the declarations, go to the Option Explicit statement, press **ENTER**, and add them.)

FIGURE 6-17.
Declaring arrays for videos form

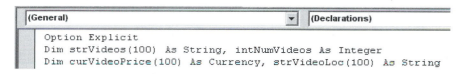

```
(General)                                          ▼  (Declarations)

    Option Explicit
    Dim strVideos(100) As String, intNumVideos As Integer
    Dim curVideoPrice(100) As Currency, strVideoLoc(100) As String
```

Note that we have declared the arrays to hold a maximum of 101 video names, prices, and locations. Obviously, as Vintage Videos continues to add new "old" videos, there will quickly be more than 101 in stock and the array declarations will need to be enlarged. While the entire problem of array size is easily handled using *dynamic arrays*, their use can become confusing. So, for this chapter's purposes, we will use fixed-size arrays.

Once the arrays have been declared at the form level, the next step is to write the code to input the list of videos when the form is loaded in the Form_Load event procedure. This code is very similar to that used earlier to input the part identifiers and prices from a file. If the file name is *Videos.txt* and it is stored on a floppy disk in the a: drive, the code to input names, prices, and locations into the *strVideos, curVideoPrice*, and *strVideoLoc* arrays is shown in VB Code Box 6-14.

Mini-Summary 6-6: Using Multiple Forms

1. It is possible to have multiple forms in a project. The Hide and Show methods are useful for switching between these forms.

2. A new form can be added using the **Project|New Form** menu option or the New Form icon on the toolbar.

3. If a control on one form is referred to on another form, the form name must be included as a part of the control reference.

| **VB CODE BOX 6-14.** Code for frmVideos Form_Load event procedure | ```
Private Sub Form_Load()
  Open "a:\videos.txt" For Input As #2
  Do Until EOF(2)
    Input#2,strVideos(intNumVideos),_
    curVideoPrice(intNumVideos),strVideoLoc(intNumVideos)
    intNumVideos = intNumVideos + 1
  Loop
  Close #2
End Sub
``` |

It's Your Turn!

1. To modify the Vintage Videos project to use a second form, complete the following exercises:

   a. Open the **Vintage6.vbp** project and add the **cmdFindVideo** command button to the form below the Delete Member command button. Use **Find Video** as the caption. The resulting form should look like Figure 6-15.

   b. Double-click cmdFindVideo and add the instruction

      frmVideos.Show

      to the Click event procedure.

   c. Use the **Project|Add Form** menu selection or the **Add Form** icon to add a new form to the **Vintage6.vbp** project. Name it **frmVideos** and give it a caption of **Video List**. Add the controls shown in Table 6-4. The result should look like Figure 6-16.

TABLE 6-4: Controls for frmVideos Form

Control Name	Caption	Control Name	Caption
txtSearch		lstVideos	
lblSearch	Enter Video Name	lblVideos	Find a Video
cmdSearch	Search	cmdBack	Back

   d. Resize the form to be as small as possible while keeping the text box large enough to enter a search string and keeping the list box wide enough to display video names, prices, and locations.

   e. Add the declarations shown in Figure 6-17 to the Declarations procedure of the General object for the frmVideos form.

   f. Add the code shown in VB Code Box 6-14 to the Form_Load event procedure to input the video names, prices, and locations.

2. Use NotePad to create a file called **Videos.txt** with the videos shown in Table 6-5 plus 20 or so other pre-1990 videos of your choosing. Be sure and include the video name and location in quotation marks. For example, the first entry should be:

   "Ghost", 1.99, "Drama"

(You may also download this data file from the Chapter 6 section of the text web site).
```

TABLE 6-5: Videos for Videos.txt data file

Video Name	Video Price	Video Location
Ghost	1.99	Drama
Ghostbusters	1.99	Comedy
Sons of Katie Elder	1.99	Western
Bambi	0.99	Kids
Star Wars (original)	2.99	Sci-Fi
The Ghost and Mrs. Muir	1.99	Drama

3. Add the instruction

```
debug.Print strVideos(intNumVideos), _
curVideoPrice(intNumVideos), strVideoLoc(intnumVideos)
```

to the Form_Load event procedure after the Input statement and run your project. Click the **Find Video** button on the main form to display the Video List form. All of the video information should appear in the Immediate window.

4. When your project works correctly, remove the Debug.Print instruction and save the form as **Videos.frm**. Save the main form without changing its name and save the project as **Vintage6.vbp** in the Chapter6 folder on your data disk.

SEARCHING FOR VIDEOS

The logic to search for the video name or partial name is very much like that used earlier to search for a part identifier, with one exception: Since we are searching for a partial name, we need to use a String function that will determine if a word or sequence of characters is a **substring** of a longer string sequence. This is the **InStr( )** function. The form of this function is:

InStr(*string to search, search string*)

where *string to search* is the character string that is being searched for an occurrence of the second parameter *search string*. If the search string is found as a substring of the string to search, InStr( ) returns the position at which it begins. If no match is found, InStr( ) returns zero. Thus, to determine if a match was found, all that is necessary is to determine if InStr( ) returned a nonzero value.

For example, InStr("Ghostbusters", "Ghost") returns a nonzero value of 1, since Ghost is a substring of Ghostbusters that begins at the first character. Similarly, InStr("Ghostbusters", "bust") also returns a nonzero value. However, since InStr( ) does a *case-sensitive* comparison, InStr("Ghostbusters", "Bust") returns zero since "Bust" is not in "Ghostbusters." One way to avoid this problem is to use the **UCase()** function to convert all strings to upper case before doing any comparisons. If this is done, InStr(UCase("Ghostbusters"), UCase("Bust")) returns a nonzero value, since "BUST" is a substring of "GHOSTBUSTERS."

If the user enters a partial title, like *ghost*, then multiple titles may be returned. Each title should be added to the list box—unless there are too many, in which case a message should be displayed requesting a more specific search word. For example, to search for all videos with "the" in their title would result in far too many videos being listed to be of any help. The code for the cmdSearch_Click( ) event procedure to search for videos matching the search string is shown in VB Code Box 6-15.

| **VB CODE BOX 6-15.** Code to search for video name | ```
Private Sub cmdSearch_Click()
  Dim strVideoName As String, intCounter As Integer, _
  intNumMatches As Integer
  strVideoName = txtSearch.Text
  lstVideos.Clear
  lstVideos.AddItem "Video Name"
  For intCounter = 0 To intNumVideos - 1
    If InStr(UCase(strVideos(intCounter)), _
    UCase(strVideoName)) > 0 Then
      intNumMatches = intNumMatches + 1
      lstVideos.AddItem strVideos(intCounter)
    End If
  Next
  If intNumMatches = 0 Then
    MsgBox ("No matching videos found! Try again.")
  ElseIf intNumMatches <= 5 Then
    lstVideos.AddItem Str(intNumMatches) & " videos found"
  Else
    lstVideos.Clear
    MsgBox ("Too many matching videos!")
  End If
End Sub
``` |
|---|---|

Note in VB Code Box 6-15 that a For-Next loop is used to compare the character string entered in txtSearch to each video name entered earlier. If the character string is found to be a substring of the video name, the video name is added to the list box and the number of matches counter is incremented. After the For-Next loop, the number of matches is checked to determine if no matches were found or if too many (> 5) matches were found. If too many were found, the list box is cleared when the Ok button on the message box is clicked.

If one to five videos that matched the search string were found, the user can then click on any one of them in the list box to display price and location. The code is similar to that shown in VB Code Box 6-15, except that since an exact match is desired here, the InStr( ) function is *not* used. The code for the lstVideo_Click( ) event is shown in VB Code Box 6-16.

| **VB CODE BOX 6-16.** Code to search for exact match of video name | ```
Private Sub lstVideos_Click()
  Dim strVideoName As String, intCounter As Integer
  strVideoName = lstVideos.Text
  lstVideos.Clear
  For intCounter = 0 To intNumVideos - 1
    If strVideoName = strVideos(intCounter) Then
      lstVideos.AddItem strVideoName & "  " & _
      Format(curVideoPrice(intCounter), "currency") & _
      "  " & strVideoLoc(intCounter)
      Exit For
    End If
  Next
End Sub
``` |
|---|---|

In this code, lstVideos is cleared, and once the match is found, the name, price, and location are displayed in the list box. Figure 6-18 shows the frmVideos form after the string *ghost* is searched for and after *The Ghost and Mrs. Muir* is clicked.

FIGURE 6-18.
frmVideos after search and after selecting a video

 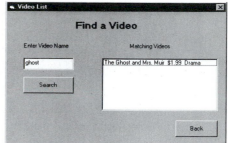

The only thing left to do in this project is to add an instruction to the cmdBack button to clear the information on the Videos form and hide it. This code is shown in VB Code Box 6-17 and the complete code for the new Videos form operations is shown in VB Code Box 6-18.

| **VB CODE BOX 6-17.** cmdBack_Click event procedure | ```
Private Sub cmdBack_Click()
    txtSearch.Text = ""
    lstVideos.Clear
    frmVideos.Hide
End Sub
``` |
|---|---|

It's Your Turn!

To complete the frmVideos form, complete the following exercises.

1. Add the code shown in VB Code Box 6-15 to the cmdSearch_Click( ) event procedure.

2. Add the code shown in VB Code Box 6-16 to the lstVideos_Click( ) event procedure.

3. Add the code shown in VB Code Box 6-17 to the cmdBack_Click( ) event procedure.

4. Run your project, switch to the frmVideos form, and enter **ghost** in the txtSearch text box. Click the **Search** button to display the videos shown on the left side of Figure 6-18. Click on **The Ghost and Mrs. Muir** selection in the list box to display the information on this video shown on the right side of Figure 6-18. Click on **Back** to return to the main form. Save the two forms and the overall project using the same names as before.
```

| **VB CODE BOX 6-18.** Complete code for Videos form | ```vb
Option Explicit
Dim strVideos(100) As String, intNumVideos As Integer
Dim curVideoPrice(100) As Currency, strVideoLoc(100) As String
Private Sub cmdBack_Click()
  txtSearch.Text = ""
  lstVideos.Clear
  frmVideos.Hide
End Sub
Private Sub cmdSearch_Click()
 Dim strVideoName As String, intCounter As Integer, _
 intNumMatches As Integer
 strVideoName = txtSearch.Text
 lstVideos.Clear
 lstVideos.AddItem "Video Name"
  For intCounter = 0 To intNumVideos - 1
    If InStr(UCase(strVideos(Counter)),_
    UCase(strVideoName)) > 0 Then
      intNumMatches = intNumMatches + 1
      lstVideos.AddItem strVideos(intCounter)
    End If
  Next
  If intNumMatches = 0 Then
    MsgBox ("No matching videos found! Try again.")
  ElseIf intNumMatches <= 5 Then
    lstVideos.AddItem Str(intNumMatches) + " videos found"
  Else
    lstVideos.Clear
    MsgBox ("Too many matching videos")
  End If
End Sub
Private Sub Form_Load()
  Open "a:\videos.txt" For Input As #2
  Do Until EOF(2)
    Input #2, strVideos(intNumVideos), _
    curVideoPrice(intNumVideos), strVideoLoc(intNumVideos)
    intNumVideos = intNumVideos + 1
  Loop
  Close #2
End Sub
Private Sub lstVideos_Click()
  Dim strVideoName As String, intCounter As Integer
  strVideoName = lstVideos.Text
  lstVideos.Clear
  For intCounter = 0 To intNumVideos - 1
    If strVideoName = strVideos(intCounter) Then
      lstVideos.AddItem strVideoName & " " & _
      Format(curVideoPrice(intCounter), "currency") & _
      " " & strVideoLoc(intCounter)
      Exit For
    End If
  Next
End Sub
``` |
```

WORKING WITH TWO-DIMENSIONAL ARRAYS

Now that we have worked with one-dimensional arrays of lists of items, we will consider situations where a two-dimensional array or table is needed. There are many situations in business where tables are used, including tables of intercity shipping charges, income tax tables, and tables of unemployment statistics by month and city, and many more.

Two-dimensional arrays share many characteristics with one-dimensional arrays, so much of this discussion will be an extension of the earlier part of this chapter. The first thing to note is that these tables require two index values or subscripts for the array, with the first index giving the row position and the second subscript giving the column position.

Declaring Two-Dimensional Arrays

To declare a two-dimensional array (a table), you must provide the maximum row and column index values. The general form for declaring a table array is:

Dim *ArrayName(max row index, max column index)* as *var type*

For example, if the maximum row index is 10 and the maximum column index is 20 for an array that will hold Single data type values, the declaration statement is:

```
Dim sngNumberTable(10, 20) as Single
```

Like lists, table arrays start both the row and column index values at zero; therefore, in the example, sngNumberTable will hold 11 rows and 21 columns for a total of 11 x 21 = 231 elements.

To illustrate, assume we have a table of revenues for products and regions (in millions of dollars) for a computer company, as shown in Table 6-6.

TABLE 6-6: Product Revenues by Region (in millions of dollars)

Product	NorthEast	SouthEast	MidWest	West
PCs	53.5	62.1	27.1	41.5
Storage	24.7	23.5	27.3	20.3
Memory	15.1	11.3	17.9	20.7

If we wanted to store this information in a two-dimensional array, we would first declare the maximum row index in the first position, and then the maximum column index in the second position. For our example this would be:

```
Dim curRevenue(2,3) as Currency
```

As in list arrays, the index values for the first row and first column are zero.

In the table above, the revenue for PCs in the NorthEast region is in the element curRevenue(0,0), because PCs is the first row and NorthEast is the first column. Likewise, the element curRevenue(2,3) gives the Revenue for Memory in the West region. Each element of the table is uniquely defined by its row and column position.

Input for Two-Dimensional Arrays

All of the methods for handling input with lists also work for tables. The most commonly used method of input for tables is a nested For-Next loop, where the outer loop is used to input the rows of an array and the inner loop is used to input the columns. This means that all of the elements of the first row are input first, followed by all the elements of the second row.

For example, in the Product Revenues table above, the statements necessary to read the revenue data from a file on an item-by-item basis for each row in the

Form_Load event procedure are shown in VB Code Box 6-19. This assumes that revenue.txt has only one value per line.

| **VB CODE BOX 6-19.** Form_Load event procedure to input data for two dimensional array | ```Private Sub Form_Load()
  Dim intProduct As Integer, intRegion As Integer
  Dim curRevenue(10,10) as Currency
  Open "a:\revenue.txt" For Input As #10
  For intProduct = 0 To 2
    For intRegion = 0 To 3
      Input #10, curRevenue(intProduct,intRegion)
    Next intRegion
  Next intProduct
End Sub``` |
|---|---|

The Input #10 statement will read all of the first row, then all of the second row, then all of the third row, as shown in Table 6-7:

TABLE 6-7: Revenue Data

Read first	53.5	62.1	27.1	41.5
Read second	24.7	23.5	27.3	20.3
Read third	15.1	11.3	17.9	20.7

If we reverse the row and column counters in the For-Next loop, then the order of input would read all of the first column, then all the second column, and so on through all four columns.

Processing Tables

As in one-dimensional arrays, data manipulation on two-dimensional arrays is performed on an element-by-element basis. While these operations were performed with a single For-Next loop for list arrays, tables often require nested For-Next loops, especially if all values in the array are involved in the operation.

For example, suppose we want to know the total revenues by product and by region. To make these calculations, we need to use nested For-Next loops to cover all elements. Assume that we have a form with three command buttons—one for product totals, one for regional totals, and one to exit the project—and a list box for output.

To find the product totals, we need to sum across the rows and add the sum to the list box with an appropriate message. To find the regional totals, we need to sum down columns, adding the sums to the list box. The Code window for this form is shown in VB Code Box 6-20, and the form after the product totals button has been clicked is shown in Figure 6-19 .

Mini-Summary 6-7: Two-Dimensional Arrays

1. In Visual Basic, tables are processed as two-dimensional arrays, with the first index referring to the row and the second referring to the column of the table.

2. Nested For-Next loops are usually the best way to input and process two-dimensional arrays.

VB CODE BOX 6-20.
Working with 2-dimensional arrays
	``
	Option Explicit
	Dim curRevenue(2, 3) As Currency
	Private Sub cmdProducts_Click()
	    Dim curProductSum As Currency, intProduct As Integer
	    Dim intRegion As Integer
	    lstSums.Clear
	    lstSums.AddItem "Totals by Product"
	    For intProduct = 0 To 2
	        curProductSum = 0
	        For intRegion = 0 To 3
	            curProductSum = curProductSum + _
	            curRevenue(intProduct, intRegion)
	        Next intRegion
	        lstSums.AddItem Str(intProduct) & " " & _
	        Format(curProductSum, "currency")
	    Next intProduct
	End Sub
	Private Sub cmdRegion_Click()
	    Dim curRegionSum As Currency, intProduct As Integer
	    Dim intRegion As Integer
	    lstSums.Clear
	    lstSums.AddItem "Totals by Region"
	    For intRegion = 0 To 3
	        curRegionSum = 0
	        For intProduct = 0 To 2
	            curRegionSum = curRegionSum + _
	            curRevenue(intProduct, intRegion)
	        Next intProduct
	        lstSums.AddItem Str(intRegion) & " " & _
	        Format(curRegionSum, "currency")
	    Next intRegion
	End Sub
	``

FIGURE 6-19.
Results of finding sums by product

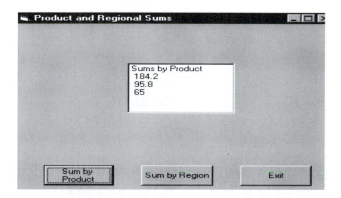

It's Your Turn!

1. How many array elements are in each array declared by the following dimension statements?

   a. Dim intNum(4, 4) As Integer

   b. Dim strID(0 to 3, 0 to 5) as String

   c. Dim sngData(-2 to 2, -5 to 10) as Single

2. Declare two-dimensional arrays as follows:

   a. Salaries in five departments for the four quarters of the year.

   b. Sales for 10 companies for each of the 12 months of the year.

   c. Unemployment statistics for each of the 50 states for the last 10 years.

3. Create a data file named **a:\Revenue.txt** for the data shown in Table 6-3. Enter the numeric data (not the headers) one per line for the first row, then the second row, and, lastly, the third row.

4. Create the form shown in Figure 6-19 and input the code shown in VB Code Box 6-19 to input the revenue data into a two-dimensional array. Next, enter the code shown in VB Code Box 6-20 for the two command buttons. Run this project to compute and display the product and region totals.

5. Add a button to compute and display the grand total of the sales and add the code to exit the project. Save the project as **Revenue.frm** and **Revenue.vbp** in the Chapter6 folder on your data disk.

USING THE STEP COMMANDS FOR DEBUGGING

In Chapter 5, we discussed the use of watches, breakpoints, and windows to debug your projects. In addition to these tools, Visual Basic allows you to *step* through your code one line or one event procedure at a time. When combined with the Immediate, Locals, and Watch windows, this capability allows you to view the changes that occur in variables as each line of code is executed. You can also step around event procedures that contain long loops or code that you believe to be correct. You can also step out of a procedure if you do not want to continue to watch it one line at a time. The three Step commands are available from the Debug submenu or from the Debug toolbar. The Debug toolbar icons are shown in Figure 6-20.

FIGURE 6-20. Step commands on Debug toolbar

If you click the Step Into icon in break mode or if you click it instead of the Run icon to run the program, you can then *step through* the code by repeatedly clicking this icon or pressing the shortcut key **F8**. If you turn on the Locals window or set a watch on one or more variables, you can watch their values as you step through the code.

For example, assume that instead of using the greater-than sign (>) in the search for videos that match the search string in the Vintage Videos project, you inadvertently entered the greater-than-or-equal-to sign (>=) in the line of code, as shown below:

```
If InStr(UCase(strVideos(intCounter)),UCase(strVidName)) > = 0 Then
```

When the project is executed with this line of code, no matter what you enter as the search string, you always receive the message *Too many matching videos!* To find this error, you can combine the Step commands with the Watch and Local windows. The first thing to do is to go into the Code window and position the cursor over each of the variables being compared and click the Quick Watch icon on the Debug toolbar to add these variables to the Watch window, which will then be displayed on the screen. You should also click the Locals window icon to display the Locals window on the screen.

> **TIP:** When debugging, it is often helpful to set a break at a point past code that has already been tested and then step into the code from that point.

With these two windows displayed along with the Code window, you are ready to start stepping through the program. If you click the Step Into icon, the first line of the Form_Load event procedure for the main form is displayed with yellow highlighting. However, since you are not interested in this event procedure, you will want to click the Step Out icon to avoid watching it. The main form will be displayed and you can choose to click the Find a Video button. This will display the Form_Load event procedure for the frmVideos form. Since you are not interested in this either, you will want to click the Step Out icon.

Finally, you are ready to search for a video by entering it into the text box and clicking the Search button to display the cmdSearch_Click( ) event procedure. By repeatedly clicking the Step Into icon (or the **F8** key), you can watch the values for the Local variables and the Watch variables as the procedure executes. You may notice that there is a plus sign in the Watch window beside the Videos variable name; this indicates that this variable is an array, and clicking the plus sign will display the items in the array. Figure 6-21 shows the screen after several iterations of the search loop. Note that in the Locals window the intCounter and intNumMatches variables are equal, meaning that *every video name* matches the search string and indicating a problem with the search criteria in the If-Then statement.

> **Tip**: When stepping through a project, you still need to carry out all of the operations of the project by, say, clicking on command buttons or entering data. If the form becomes minimized, you can display it by clicking the corresponding icon on the Windows task bar.

It's Your Turn!

1. Modify the **Vintage6.vbp** project so that the If-Then statement in the cmdSearch_Click( ) event procedure in the frmVideo form uses a greater-than-or-equal-to sign (>=) instead of a greater-than sign (>).

2. Set watches on the strVideoName and strVideos variables in this procedure and turn on the Locals window.

3. Click the Step Into icon to start the execution of the project. Use the Step Out icon to avoid watching the Form_Load event procedures for either form. Go as directly as possible to the cmdSearch_Click( ) event and step through it watching both the Locals and Watches windows. Click the plus sign beside the Videos variable name to see all of the items in this array.

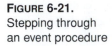

FIGURE 6-21.
Stepping through
an event procedure

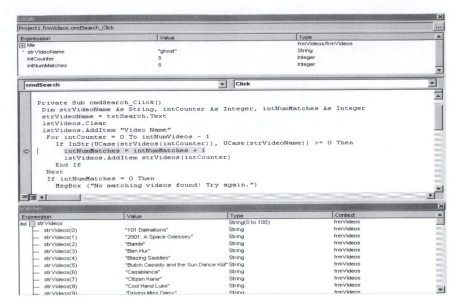

4. Stop the execution and correct the error you introduced earlier. Once again, step though the project to see how the search procedure should work. Stop the execution of the project but do not save it.

SUMMARY

In this chapter, we have studied control arrays, list arrays, and table arrays. A *control array* is a group of Visual Basic controls all of which have the same name. A *list array* is a list of values or strings that are referred to as a single entity. A *table array* is an array with both rows and columns.

In a control array, the individual controls are distinguished by a number called an index, with the first control having an index of zero, the second an index of one, and so on. The order in which controls are added to the form determines their index value. Using a control array makes it easy to refer to all of the elements in a single event procedure through their index values. A control array can be used to create a group of check boxes or option buttons, the difference being that only one option button can be selected but multiple check boxes can be selected. A frame control is used to group the option buttons, and a Select Case decision structure is used to determine which option button is clicked. The frame control can also be used to create multiple groups of controls.

In a list array, the array name is declared, along with the maximum value for the index or subscript that is used to distinguish between the array elements. As in control arrays and the List( ) property of a list box, the index for a list array starts at zero. Unlike a list box, however, a list array must have the value of the index known or computed in the code. To input the elements of an array, if the number of elements is known, a For-Next loop can be used, with the counter variable matching the array index values. If the number of elements is not known, an Until or While loop is the best way to input the array from a file, but the index value must be computed as the values are input.

Many operations can be accomplished using an array, including initializing them to some value, summing and averaging values in a list, finding the maximum or minimum value in a list, finding a particular value in a list, and working with multiple lists. For-Next loops are the most common way to process arrays. Finding the sum and averages uses a For-Next loop to add each array value to a sum. Finding the maximum or minimum value (or string) in a list involves using a For-Next loop to compare each value in the list to the current maximum or minimum value and, if the current value is larger or smaller, replacing the maximum or minimum value with the current value.

Finding a particular value or string in a list involves using a For-Next loop to search for matches between the search value or string and each value in the list. Flag variables are used to indicate that a match has been found and to indicate the index of the value in the list that matches the search string.

Multiple lists can be handled by matching the index values in each list to corresponding elements of the array. If a maximum or minimum value or a search string is found in one list, the corresponding elements in the other lists are found by the matching index.

Two-dimensional or table arrays allow you to work with tables in the same way that list arrays are used to work with lists. Working with two-dimensional arrays usually involves using nested For-Next loops for input and manipulation.

Adding forms to a project was also discussed in this chapter. The additional forms enable you to place groups of operations on individual forms rather than crowding them onto a single form. The commands necessary to view or hide the additional forms were also discussed.

Arrays can be debugged using the Step commands on the Debug menu or toolbox. These commands enable you to step through the code in an event procedure, watching the values of variables as each instruction is executed. You can also use these commands to step out of a procedure or to step over procedures rather than going through them.

NEW VISUAL BASIC ELEMENTS

Control/Object	Properties	Methods	Events
check box control	Name Value		
option button control	Name		Click
frame control	Name		
Form object		Hide/Show	

NEW PROGRAMMING STATEMENTS

Statement to declare the size of an array **Dim** ArrayName(max index value) as variable type
Statement to declare the size of an array, specifying minimum and maximum index limits **Dim** ArrayName(min index vale to max index value) as variable type
Statement to display a message box with buttons/icons and a title **MsgBox** message, buttons, title
Statement to input an array from a sequential access file intCounter = 0 **Do Until EOF(n)**   **Input #n**, ArrayName(intCounter) **Loop**
Statement to determine which button on the message box is clicked variable = **MsgBox(**message, buttons, title)
Statement to determine if search string is a larger string variable = **InStr(**string to search, search string)
Statement to declare a two-dimensional array **Dim** ArrayName(max row index, max column index) as variable type

KEY TERMS

array

collating sequence

control array

dynamic-size array

fixed-size array

flag

index

radio button

subscript

EXERCISES

1. Declare an array for each of the following scenarios:

   a. A hobby shop sells a popular wooden railway system that includes 150 different items. The proprietor needs an array to store an alphanumeric product ID for each different item.

   b. A survey has questions with responses ranging from –3 (strongly disagree) to 3 (strongly agree). The survey analyst needs an array to store a count of each possible response.

   c. A department store chain has six stores, and each store has the same 10 departments. The chain would like to store the weekly sales of all departments in one array.

2. Write a Visual Basic code segment for each of the following scenarios:

   a. Myleig Hiers, a regional furniture chain, is going out of business and needs to closeout its inventory. It decides to begin by offering 20% off for all furniture models. Prices for each of its 1200 furniture models are stored in a one-dimensional array called curFurnPrices(). Write a Visual Basic program segment that will calculate values for a new array called curDiscFurnPrices() that will hold the new discount price for each model.

b. Lens Makers creates custom eyewear quickly and at a reasonable price. Its inventory includes 220 frame styles. Information about the frames is stored in three different arrays: strProductID( ), strFrameStyle( ), and curPrice( ). Write a Visual Basic program segment that will allow the user to enter a product ID and then display the corresponding frame style and price.

c. The Big Chips Cookie Company records the number of cases of cookies produced each day over a four-week period. These values are stored in an array, intCases(3, 4), which includes the number of cases for each day (five per week) of the week. Write a code segment that would request a week number and a day from the user and then display the corresponding number of cases produced.

3. Describe the output displayed in txtResult after each of the following code segments is executed.

a.
```
Private Sub cmdGo_Click()
    Dim strLetters(10) As String, intJ As Integer
    Dim strTemp As String, intPos As Integer
    strTemp = strLetters(0)
    intPos = 0
    For intJ = 1 To 10
      If strLetters(intJ) < strTemp Then
        strTemp = strLetters(intJ)
        intPos = intJ
      End If
    Next intJ
    txtResult.Text = strTemp & " in pos. " & intPos
End Sub
```

b.
```
Private Sub cmdGo_Click()
    Dim intArr1(4) As Integer, intArr2(4) As Integer
    Dim intI As Integer, intJ As Integer
    txtResult.Text = 0
    For intJ = 0 To 4
      txtResult.Text = txtResult.Text + _
        intArr1(intJ) * intArr2(intJ)
    Next intJ
End Sub
```

c.
```
Private Sub cmdGo_Click()
    Dim intArr1(1 To 3, 1 To 3) As Integer
    Dim intArr2(1 To 3, 1 To 3) As Integer
    Dim intI As Integer, intJ As Integer
    Dim intTemp As Integer
    txtResult.Text = 0
    For intJ = 1 To 3
      For intI = 1 To 3
        If intArr1(intI, intJ) > intArr2(intI, intJ) Then
          strTemp = strTemp + intArr1(intI, intJ)
        Else
          strTemp = strTemp + intArr2(intI, intJ)
        End If
      Next intI
    Next intJ
    txtResult.Text = strTemp
End Sub
```

4. For each of the following, explain what is wrong with the code. What error messages would you see, if any? What can you do to fix it?

a. The following code should initialize each item in the array to zero:

```
Private Sub cmdGo_Click()
    Dim intArray(4) As Integer
    Dim intI As Integer
    For intI = 1 To 5
        intArray(intI) = 0
    Next intI
End Sub
```

b. The following code segment should load intArray2 with the values of intArray1:

```
Private Sub cmdGo_Click()
    Dim intArray1(4) As Integer
    Dim intArray2(4) As Integer
    Dim intI As Integer
    For intI = 0 To 4
        intI(intArray1) = intI(intArray2)
    Next intI
End Sub
```

c. The following code segment should load intArray2 with the values of intArray1 times 10:

```
Private Sub cmdGo_Click()
    Dim intArray1(4, 4) As Integer
    Dim intArray2(4, 4) As Integer
    Dim intI As Integer
    Dim intJ As Integer
    For intI = 0 To 4
      For intJ = 0 To 4
        intArray1(intI, intJ) = intArray2(intJ, intI * 10)
      Next intJ
    Next intI
End Sub
```

5. Use the Visual Basic Help facility or the MSDN on-line library to answer the following questions.

a. What effect does declaring a variable as Static have on the variable?
b. When do the following events occur with a form object: Load, Unload, Activate, Deactivate, GotFocus, LostFocus?
c. What is a dynamic array?
d. What is the difference between passing variables ByRef and ByVal?

PROJECTS

1. Assume that a list of student names and quiz averages are stored in a sequential file called **a:\Students.txt**. Create a project to input this data and store it in two arrays. The project should also determine the appropriate letter grade on a 90-80-70-60 scale and add it to a corresponding array. Add a button to display the name, quiz average, and letter grade in a list box. Add another command button that will display the name, quiz average, and letter grade in text boxes for the students with the highest and lowest quiz scores. Add another button to find the average of the quiz averages. Create a file called **Student.txt** with the data in Table 6-8. Save your project as **Ex6-1.frm** and **Ex6-1.vbp**. in the Chapter6 folder on your data disk.

TABLE 6-8: Student Quiz Averages

Student	Quiz Average
Booker, Alice	77
Bounds, Nancy	83
Carter, Jay	92
Ertel, Dean	63
Spafford, Phil	55
Boatright, Ann	66
Patrick, Chris	88
Burgell, George	93

2.   Assume that a list of customer names and sales amounts are stored in a sequential file called **a:\CustSales.txt**. Create a project to input this data and store it in two arrays. Add a button to display the customer name and sales amount in a list box. Add command buttons that will display the name and sales amounts in text boxes for the customers with the highest and lowest sales and the average sales. Create a test file from the data shown in Table 6-9. Save your project as **Ex6-2.frm** and **Ex6-2.vbp** in the Chapter6 folder on your data disk.

TABLE 6-9: Sales for Customers

Customer Name	Sales
Calfos, Dennis	$3,456
Batson, Rick	$5,120
Jones, Mary	$7,490
Hitchcock, April	$5,435
Abernathy, Ann	$9,710
Smith, Jeff	$8,604

3.   Create a project to input an unknown number of golfer names and golf scores from a file called **a:\golfer.txt**. These names and scores should be stored in two arrays. The project should also determine the appropriate designation for the golfer according to Table 6-10.

TABLE 6-10: Golfer Categories

Score	Designation
70 or less	Professional
71–79	Club Champ
80–89	Good
90–99	Fair
100 and above	Duffer

Add a button to display the golfer name, score, and designation in a list box. Add another command button that will display the name and scores in text boxes for the golfers with the highest and lowest scores. Use the data shown in Table 6-11 to test your project. Save your project as **Ex6-3.frm** and **Ex6-3.vbp** in the Chapter6 folder on your data disk.

TABLE 6-11: Golf Scores

Golfer	Score
Fred Smith	93
Larry Vinings	101
Hugh Smith	88
Al Nimmi	79
Archie Card	83
Ben Brown	98

4. Create a project that will find the Zip code for a city name that the user inputs. Assume that the name and Zip code for each city are input from a sequential file into two arrays. The user inputs a city for which she wants the Zip code and presses a command button to display it in another text box. Use the city names and Zip codes shown in Table 6-12 in a file called **ZipCodes.txt** to test your project. Save your project as **Ex6-4.frm** and **Ex6-4.vbp** in the Chapter6 folder on your data disk.

TABLE 6-12: Zip Codes

City	Zip Code
Bishop	30621
Athens	30601
Bogart	30622
Comer	30629
Hull	30646
Watkinsville	30677

5. Write a program to input a list of age ranges and associated insurance premiums into two arrays. Add a command button to display the age ranges and premiums. Then add text boxes to input a person's name and age and a command button to display the corresponding insurance premium in a third text box. For example, if the data in Table 6-13 were input and a person had an age of 39, his premium would be $95. Save your project as **Ex6-5.frm** and **Ex6-5.vbp** in the Chapter6 folder on your data disk.

6. Modify the project you created for Exercise 1 to add a second form to which the user can switch by clicking a button on the main form. When loaded, the second form inputs the same file as the main form does. On the second form, the user should be able to input a student name in a text box and click a button to display the student's name and average score in text boxes. Also, the user should be able to click an option button

TABLE 6-13: Insurance Categories

Age	Premium
20 or younger	$50
between 21 and 30	$65
between 31 and 40	$95
between 41 and 50	$135
between 51 and 60	$195
61 or older	$250

to select a value and have a list box display the names of all students with a score above that value. The option buttons should correspond to the 90-80-70-60 scale. Save the second form as **Ex6-6Two.frm** and save the project as **Ex6-6.vbp** in the Chapter6 folder on your data disk. (Don't change the name of the main form.)

7. Modify the project you created for Exercise 2 to add a second form to which the user can switch by clicking a button on the main form. When loaded, the second form inputs the same file as the main form. On the second form, the user should be able to input a customer's name in a text box and click a button to display the customer sales in another text box. Also, the user should be able to click an option button to select a value and have a list box display the names of all salespeople selling less than this value. The option buttons should correspond to sales of $8,000, $6,000, $4,000, and $2,000. Save the second form as **Ex6-7Two.frm** and save the project as **Ex6-7.vbp** in the Chapter6 folder on your data disk. (Don't change the name of the main form.)

8. Modify the project you created for Exercise 3 to add a second form to which the user can switch by clicking a button on the main form. When loaded, the second form inputs the same file as the main form. On the second form, the user should be able to input a golfer name in a text box and click a button to display the golfer's name and score in text boxes. Also, the user should be able to click an option button to select a score and have a list box display the names of all golfers with a score above that score. The option buttons should correspond to 70, 80, 90, and 100. Save the second form as **Ex6-8Two.frm** and save the project as **Ex6-8.vbp** in the Chapter6 folder on your data disk. (Don't change the name of the main form.)

9. Create a project to declare a two-dimensional array that contains the total employee salaries for three departments for each of the first six months of the year. Input the data in Table 6-14 using the Form_Load event procedure. Add buttons and a list box to the form. The buttons should compute and display the average monthly salaries for each department and the total salaries for each month. Save your project as **Ex6-9.frm** and **Ex6-9.vbp** in the Chapter6 folder on your data disk.

TABLE 6-14: Payroll Data by Month

Dept.	Jan.	Feb.	Mar.	April	May	June
Personnel	$24,500	22.800	23,100	25,600	24,900	24,100

TABLE 6-14: Payroll Data by Month (Continued)

Dept.	Jan.	Feb.	Mar.	April	May	June
Engineering	$33.800	33,900	33,100	32,500	34,900	35,200
Sales	$28,300	27,900	26,500	29,500	30,100	29,300

10. Mega-Home Warehouse sells, among other things, lawn mowers. Past experience has indicated that the selling season is only six months long, lasting from April 1 through September 30. The sales division has forecast the sales for next year as shown in Table 6-15.

TABLE 6-15: Lawn Mower Demand Each Month

Month	Demand
April	40
May	20
June	30
July	40
August	30
September	20

All lawn mowers are purchased from an outside source at a cost of $80.00 per lawn mower. However, the supplier will sell them only in lots of 10, 20, 30, 40, or 50; monthly orders for fewer than 10 mowers or more than 50 are not accepted. Discounts based on the size of the lot ordered are shown in Table 6-16.

TABLE 6-16: Discounts

Lot Size	Discount (%)
10	5
20	5
30	10
40	20
50	25

For each order placed, the store is charged a fixed cost of $200 to cover shipping costs, insurance, and so on, regardless of the number ordered (except no charge for a month if no order is placed). Assume that the orders are placed at the first of the month and are received immediately. The store also incurs carrying charges of $12.50 for each mower that remains in stock at the end of any month.

Write a Visual Basic program to calculate the total seasonal cost, the price that must be charged per mower in order for Mega-Home Warehouse to break even, and the price that must be charged to realize a profit of 30%. Try your program with various ordering policies (different combinations of orders per month) and determine which is best. Save your project as **Ex6-10.frm** and **Ex6-10.vbp** in the Chapter6 folder on your data disk.

11. Suppose that in a certain city in the South, the pollen count is measured at two-hour intervals, beginning at midnight. These measurements are recorded for a one-week period and stored in file. The first line of the files contains the pollen count for day 1, the second line for day 2, and so on. An example file is shown in Table 6-17.

TABLE 6-17: Pollen Count File

32	33	31	35	37	42	44	45	47	45	41	39
33	32	31	36	42	51	47	50	55	50	46	39
38	35	36	37	37	41	42	42	40	39	37	36
32	33	35	37	42	44	46	47	49	51	47	43
39	40	42	45	47	47	48	49	51	53	52	50
38	39	39	42	43	43	45	46	47	48	47	44
37	39	40	40	41	44	46	46	47	47	46	45

Write a Visual Basic program to produce and display a weekly report of the pollen count. The report should consist of a table showing the pollen count for each day and time. In the margins of the table, display the average pollen count for each day and the average pollen count for each sampling time. Save your project as **Ex6-11.frm** and **Ex6-11.vbp** in the Chapter6 folder on your data disk.

12. With a computer simulation, a computer program is developed that will behave in a manner similar to a real-life process. Then the program may be used to study how the process might behave under various conditions without the risks that might be associated with developing the real system. In order to more closely model reality, computer simulations usually incorporate variables whose value is determined at random based on specified distributions while the simulation is running. Because the values of these random variables may be different each time the simulation is executed, many experiments are conducted with the model, and statistics are accumulated.

To get a feel for computer simulation, create a simple Visual Basic program to simulate the rolling of a single six-sided die. A single roll of a die is easily simulated using the Rnd function in the following formula:

intDie = Int((6 * Rnd) + 1) .

The Rnd function will return a random value between 0 and 1. The rest of the formula serves to scale the values to between 1 and 6 and then truncate them to only integer values.

Your Visual Basic program should allow the user to enter a number of rolls of a die to throw. Then, when a button is clicked, that number of die rolls will be simulated. Each time a specific number appears on the die, 2 for instance, a count should be incremented in order to keep up with the total number of times each value appears during the rolls. After the rolls have been completed, a histogram illustrating the number of times a die value has appeared should be displayed. For example, after a simulation of 500 rolls, your histogram may look like:

```
Histogram of Dice Rolls
* = 5 Rolls
1 - ************** 77
2 - ***************** 93
3 - ****************** 96
4 - ************** 80
5 - ************** 81
6 - ************ 73
```

Save your project as **Ex6-12.frm** and **Ex6-12.vbp** in the Chapter6 folder on your data disk.

13. An employee data file for the Books Detective Agency includes a record for each employee that includes the employee's name, department, age, salary, and year of employment. For example:

"Elvis Cole", "Domestic", 34, 45000, 95

"Sharon McCone", "Corporate", 27, 60000, 98

"Kinsey Milhone", "Domestic", 23, 10000, 1

"Joe Pike", "Security", 32, 78001, 96

Mr. M. Books, the owner of the agency, wishes to have a computer program that will allow him to manage and query this file. The program should include buttons that allow Mr. Books to load the file into a list box and several arrays, add or remove records from the list, and save changes to the file. As the data file is read, compute and display the total and average age and the total and average salary. These values should be updated whenever modifications are made to the list.

In addition, set up queries, as code in a single query command button. Queries should allow Mr. Books to search the results based on department, age, salary, and year of employment. Use text boxes and list boxes to allow the user to provide query parameters. For example, you might use a text box for the user to enter age and a list box listing the options >, <, >=, <=, <>, =. If the user enters the age 30 for the age parameter and selects <, then the query results would display only those records with an age less than 30. Similar strategies may be used for the other items to query. Your code must be able to display records that satisfy all query parameters that are selected. Finally, include a Clear Query button to reset the query parameters and clear the result list box. Save your project as **Ex6-13.frm** and **Ex6-13.vbp** in the Chapter6 folder on your data disk.

PROJECT: JOE'S TAX ASSISTANCE (CONT.)

The next morning Joe was sitting by the pool reading the newspaper while Zooey was swimming some laps. Angela emerged carrying a tray of cold drinks.

"It's about time you two relaxed a little bit," Angela said. "You seem to be working on Joe's program every free minute."

"Thanks for the lemonade, dear," Joe replied. "We deserve a break. We got quite a bit done last night. Didn't we, Zooey?"

"That's right, Granny. Grandpa is really learning how to program. He should come out of retirement for a new career."

Noticing the smug look on Joe's face, Angela laughed and said, "As busy as he is in retirement, a job would probably be like a vacation."

Joe sighed. "You're right," he said. "I've got a lot going on, but this programming is kind of fun. We keep adding items to it and I keep learning how to do more. Zooey and I worked something called loops into the program yesterday. I'm not sure what she's going to teach me today."

"I was thinking of a couple things. First, our form is getting kind of crowded with everything on the same page. I think that we can break it up into multiple forms," Zooey explained.

"Hmm....," Joe thought, "I think I see what you mean. Maybe have a separate form for each of the sections of the 1040 tax form. That would make the program more organized."

"I agree. It shouldn't be too hard either. We can cut and paste the code and controls to new forms and then add buttons for loading the new forms and returning to the main form," Zooey responded. "I also thought that we could look at arrays today," she added.

"Arrays . . . that sounds interesting. What are they?" Joe inquired.

"They're another kind of variable," responded Zooey. "Actually, they're more like a whole group of related variables, each with a similar name."

"You mean like a family," said Angela. "Maybe the Jackson array."

"Could be. The name of the array is used as part of the name for all the variables in it, and each individual variable of the array is referred to by a number representing its position in the group. So Grandpa might be Jackson(0), and Granny, you would be Jackson(1). Since I'm part of your family, I could be stored as Jackson(2)."

"How is that different from a regular variable? Why not just store each of us under a different variable name, like JOE, ANGELA, and ZOOEY?" Joe asked.

"The advantage of using an array is that we can use another variable to specify the position that we want to refer to in the array. This makes an array very useful when using loops. We can change the position variables each time a loop is incremented."

"I see. Jackson(k) could refer to any one of us depending what k is," Angela piped in.

"That's right, Granny. Maybe you should start programming with us," Zooey said with a grin.

"No, thanks. But I do see how you can get caught up in it," replied Angela. "I'll leave the programming to you 'pros.' If you need any help, though, I'll be out here by the pool."

Questions

1. For each section of the main form created so far, design and create a corresponding new form. Each new form should include the same controls and code as its corresponding section. They should each contain a clear button for clearing the data. In addition, include a button on each form that will close the form and return to the main form. On the main form, add buttons for loading each of the new forms.

2. Alter your code for the Exemptions form to include an array. The array will be used to store the values entered for each dependent. The array should be declared as a string and have two index variables. Dimension the array so that it is large enough to store a reasonable maximum number of dependents. The code should store the entries of the dialog box in the array until all dependents are entered. Then use a loop to load the list box from the values in the array.

3. Run and test your program.

7   USING FUNCTIONS, SUBS, AND MODULES

LEARNING OBJECTIVES

After reading this chapter, you will be able to

❖ Understand the importance of general procedures and modules in programming with Visual Basic.

❖ Describe the difference between event procedures and general procedures.

❖ Create general procedures by using the menu system and by entering them directly.

❖ Understand the difference between the two types of general procedures: sub procedures (subs) and functions.

❖ Describe the relationship between arguments and parameters in general procedures.

❖ Write functions to return single values and sub procedures to process multiple values.

❖ Create sub procedures to search, sort, and print arrays.

❖ Use the Code module to declare variables globally or create global general procedures.

❖ Understand the difference between passing by value and passing by reference in sub procedures.

SCENARIO: LISTS AT VINTAGE VIDEOS (CONT.)

Yvonne stretched and sighed as Ed locked the door. "What a long day that was," she exclaimed.

"But satisfying, wasn't it, Tinkerbell?" replied Ed with a smile. Opening day had been a success at Vintage Videos, albeit a tough one for all concerned.

He came over and gave her a congratulatory hug and kiss. "Imagine, the first day of our new video store is over," said Ed. "Where's Clark? It's time to break out the bubbly and celebrate."

"The last time that I saw him, he had gone into the back room with the laptop. I guess he's either doing some homework or working on our store program," answered Yvonne. "I'll fetch him," she added.

She disappeared into the back and presently reappeared with Clark in tow. Clark's hair was tousled, his Peter Pan tights were wrinkled, and he looked a little bleary-eyed.

"Here he is. I found him asleep with his head on the keyboard," Yvonne said.

With a sheepish grin, Clark explained: "When it started to slow down a little, I took my laptop and went back to work on the video program. I guess the long day got to me. Anyway, I was able to add a video search capability to the program before nodding off. You want to see it?"

"Okay," said Ed. "Then we'll head to our place, get out of these costumes, and celebrate. You know that all work and no play will make Clark a dull 'lost' boy."

Clark copied the new program onto the store PC and started it for Ed and Yvonne. He then allowed Yvonne to take control of the mouse as he directed her through the new parts of the program. She and Ed successfully searched for a few videos that Clark suggested and they were suitably impressed.

"I entered a few videos into an array and then wrote the program to search through the array," Clark explained. "We still need to get a complete list of all the videos and their locations . . ."

Yvonne interrupted. "I've been working on that and I almost have it completed. Of course, we'll have to set up a system to add new videos that come in to the list."

"That's right," Ed jumped in. "I've also got another problem with the program that's come up today. On a positive note, we signed up over 60 new members, but this makes the member list on the program a little cumbersome, especially as it gets even bigger. I can see where it will be hard to scroll through the list looking for a member's name."

"Why don't I add a search procedure for members, too?" Clark offered. "I think we should store some more information about members. We might run into a few people with the same name—you know, two John Smiths or Mary Johnsons. If we add some more information, we can keep them separated more easily."

Yvonne eagerly rejoined the conversation with, "Why don't we store the phone number along with the name? The two John Smiths probably won't live together, and if customers are late returning videos we can call them if we want to. Would it also be possible to print a list of members or videos in alphabetical order if needed?"

Ed added, "I've also been thinking about late fees. While we don't have any right now, they will certainly become a factor the longer we are in operation. We need to add existing late fees to customers' bills when they rent new videos."

Clark thought for a moment and said, "Yes, I can think of a couple of ways to do it. I think I'll try something first with arrays, but if we store any other information on customers, we'll probably have to do something with a database. I feel better after my nap, so I can start it right away."

"Hold it, big fellow," Yvonne cried. "You've done enough for one day and it will keep until tomorrow. Right now it's party time."

After turning out the lights and locking up, the three headed out together to celebrate the successful grand opening of Vintage Videos.

Comments on Vintage Videos Scenario

In Chapter 6, we discussed using arrays to store and process information. In the Vintage Videos scenario, several extensions to the existing prototype information system are required, including:

1. A way of adding videos to the system as they come into the store.

2. A better system for managing the membership list to check if a customer is a member, add new members, and delete old ones.

3. The capability to add late fees to a customer's bill.

4. A system to print an alphabetical list of members or videos as needed.

It has also been suggested that customer phone numbers be made a part of each customer's record so that customers with similar names can be differentiated. Meeting these requests from the store owners is going to require Clark to make even greater use of arrays. The names, phone numbers, and late fees will also be stored in arrays that can be searched for names in a manner similar to that used for searching for videos.

To respond to the request for an alphabetical printing of the membership list or list of videos, both lists will have to be sorted. While it is possible to sort a list in a list box or combo box using the *Sorted* property, this only works to sort on the first item on each line. If you want to sort the list based on another part of the line, you will need to use arrays that are sorted by the code rather than by the Sorted property of the list-box. Doing this is going to require us to use a complete new type of procedure--the *general procedure*. However, before tackling the application of new material to Vintage Videos, we will discuss it in general using smaller examples.

USING GENERAL PROCEDURES

Through the first six chapters of this text, we have concentrated on the fundamentals of programming using assignment statements, decision structures, loops, and arrays. In this chapter, we will consider more complex programs that carry out a variety of activities using multiple forms. Creating projects for more complex situations requires that we use the Julius Caesar approach to programming: Divide and conquer! By this we mean that instead of trying to think about the entire project all at one time, we should divide it up into pieces that are more easily programmed. You have already been doing this with the Visual Basic event procedures that you have been writing for each control on your forms. Each event procedure carries out a piece of the project, thus dividing it up into small pieces. For example, when you write an event procedure for the Click event of a command button, you are taking care of that part of the overall project without having to worry about other controls and events. This is one of the reasons Visual Basic has become such a popular programming language.

While event procedures are extremely useful in creating projects, they are associated with a particular event, and unless you remove the word *Private* that precedes an event procedure, it is not available to other forms. There are many situations where you want to write code that is *not* associated with a particular event or that will be available to multiple forms or both. To do this, we need to use **general** (rather than *event*) **procedures**.

A general procedure tells the project how to carry out a specific task that is not associated with an event. General procedures must be defined in the General object of the form and then *invoked* elsewhere on the form. Invoking a general procedure involves referring to it in another general or event procedure. For example, if you wrote a general procedure called FindMax to find the maximum value in a list, you would have to refer to FindMax in the code whenever you wanted it to find the maximum value. Compare this to an event procedure, which reacts to some event caused by the user or by the system. For example, in Chapter 6, a button had to be clicked to activate the Click event procedure to find the maximum value in a list.

There are two types of general procedures that the user can write and include in the project: sub procedures (also called *subroutines*) and function procedures. Figure 7-1 shows the relationship between event procedures and the two types of general procedures.

General procedures are *general* because they are not associated with any specific event or control and can be invoked by any part of the project. They are a form of

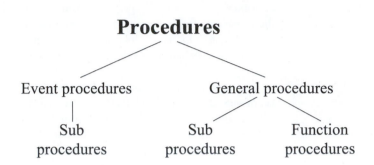

Figure 7-1.
Relationship
between general
and event
procedures

reusable code since they can be invoked repeatedly throughout the project or saved and installed in other projects where a specific task is required. Rather than writing the same code over again in each location, you could create a general procedure that is invoked every time you want to do this. For example, the general procedure FindMax mentioned earlier could be used to find the maximum value in a list in several different places in a project. It could also be saved and used in other projects where finding the maximum value in a list is needed.

Another reason for using a general procedure is to reduce the complexity of event procedures. Instead of placing all of the input, output, and logic in an event procedure, it is possible to place some or all of the logic in one or more general procedures and have just the input and output statements in the event procedure. This is another way of dividing up the work that can enable you to separately test and debug parts of an event procedure.

Types of General Procedures

As mentioned above, there are two types of general procedures: functions and sub procedures. A **sub procedure** (hereafter referred to simply as a **sub**) is similar to an event procedure in that it is a unit of code that performs a specific task within a program but *returns* no value. Like event procedures, general sub procedures begin with the word *Sub* plus a name and end with *End Sub*. Subs can have arguments passed to them the values of which can be changed in the sub and passed back to the calling procedure. For example, a sub to sort a list of names will have the list and the number of names in the list passed to it, and those names will be rearranged in the sub and passed back.

On the other hand, a **function procedure** (or more simply, a **function**) is similar to the built-in functions that we have been using since Chapter 3 in that arguments are passed to it and are processed to compute a single value that is returned through its name. The FindMax general procedure discussed earlier should be written as a function, since a single value—the maximum value in the list—is returned. Figure 7-2 shows the primary purposes of a sub and a function.

Note that two of the arguments passed to the sub are modified by it and one is not. It is possible for none, some, or all of the arguments to be modified by the sub. On the other hand, while it is possible to modify the arguments of a function, this is not its primary purpose so none are modified here.

Whether to use a function or a sub depends on whether a single value is to be returned. If it is, then a function should be used; otherwise, a sub should be used. While there are both built-in functions and subs, in this chapter we will be discussing

FIGURE 7-2.
Primary purposes
of sub and function
procedures

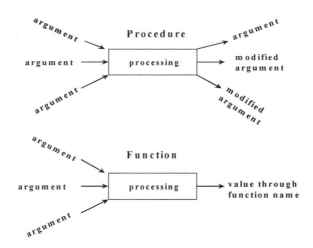

programmer-defined general procedures, that is, subs and functions that are created by the person developing the project.

Mini-Summary 7-1: General Procedures

1. General procedures are units of code that are not associated with a specific event and that can be used anywhere on a form or in the project as needed.

2. There are two types of general procedures: function procedures and sub procedures.

3. Function procedures return a value through their names, while subs do not return a value. However, subs are very useful for modifying the arguments passed to them.

It's Your Turn!

1. List the differences between an event procedure and a general procedure.

2. Give some reasons for using general procedures in a Visual Basic project.

3. Why would you use a general procedure even if the operation occurs only once in the project?

4. List the primary purposes of functions and subs. Also, list the main differences between them.

5. Why is the name important in a function but not in a sub procedure?

6. For each of the following situations, tell whether you should use a function or a sub and why.

    a. Determine the number of occurrences of the letter *A* in a list of strings.

    b. Input a list of strings and create a new list of all the strings that begin with the letter *A*.

    c. Input a list of integers and find their sum.

d. Input a list of integers and place them in order from largest to smallest.

WORKING WITH GENERAL PROCEDURES

In either type of general procedure—that is, function or sub—you must first decide where the procedure will be used (invoked). Once you have made this decision, then you can design and write the general procedure to accomplish the desired purpose. Deciding where the general procedure will be invoked is a part of the overall design of the project. If an operation will be repeated in a project or if the logic in an event procedure is complicated, then a general procedure can be of great help in reducing both the amount of code to be written and the complexity of the programming. For example, both the membership list and the video list need to be searched, so a sub may be useful for handling this operation on both forms. Similarly, both lists need to be sorted, so this may also be a place for a sub.

Designing a general procedure is much like designing an event procedure: You must decide what you want it to do, what the input and desired output are, and what logic is required to convert the input into the desired output. Input for a general procedure is usually through the arguments that pass values to it, but it is possible to use other forms of input. Similarly, output for a function is usually through its name, and output from a sub is usually through the arguments. However, in both cases it is possible to use other forms of output. Pseudocode is very important for developing the logic of a function or sub, and we will demonstrate its use here.

Invoking a Function or Sub

You invoke a function that you have written just like you invoke a Visual Basic built-in function—by placing it on the left side of an assignment statement or by including it in any statement that would use a variable, say, a Debug.Print statement. In any case, you invoke the function by referring to the function name with the arguments in parentheses (where *arg1, arg2, ..., argn* are the arguments passed to the function):

variable = functionName(arg1, arg2, ..., argn)

For example, if you have created a function called intFindMax that will find the maximum value between two Integer variables named intOne and intTwo and you want to display the maximum value in a text box (txtMaxValue), the statement to invoke this function would be:

```
txtMaxValue = Str(intFindMax(intOne, intTwo))
```

Note that we have used a data type prefix for the function. This is typically done because functions return a value of a specific type, and using the data type prefix tells us what type value will be returned.

On the other hand, you invoke a sub by referring to its name and arguments in a separate line of code, with the arguments listed after the name separated by commas. The arguments are *not* enclosed in parentheses as they are with functions. The general form of a sub reference is shown below:

subName arg1, arg2, ..., argn

For example, assume you have created a sub called Reverse to reverse the values in two Currency data type variables, curFirst and curSecond. After this sub is invoked, the variable curFirst is now equal to the old value of curSecond and curSecond is equal to the old value of curFirst. Invoking Reverse would be done as follows:

```
Reverse curFirst, curSecond
```

When a function or sub is created, it is a part of the *General* object of the form in which it is being created. If the general procedure is a *Public* procedure, it will be avail-

> **TIP:** You can also invoke a procedure by using the **Call** statement plus its name and enclosing any parameters in parenthesis. For example, to invoke the cmdExit event procedure, you would enter the command **Call cmdExit_Click**. To invoke the Reverse sub you would enter **Call Reverse(curFirst, curSecond)**.

able to any other forms or general procedures in the project. However, to invoke a sub or function declared on another form, you must include the name of the form as a part of the name of the sub or function. For example, to invoke the Reverse sub mentioned earlier from Form2 when it was created on Form1, the command is:

```
Form1.Reverse First, Second
```

Creating Subs and Functions

To create subs or functions, use the **Tools|Add Procedure** menu option to add a general procedure. This menu option will display a dialog box like that shown in Figure 7-3 in which you can enter the name of the function or sub, select the type, and indicate whether it will be a private or a public function. In most cases, you will simply want to fill in a name and select Function or Sub to display the first and last lines of the function or sub.

FIGURE 7-3. Dialog box for adding a procedure

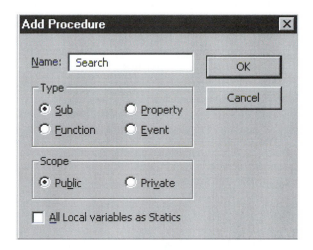

To add a function or sub without using the Tools|Add Procedure menu selection, go to the end of any event or general procedure in the Code window and press **ENTER** to open up a line. Then enter the word **Function** or **Sub** plus the procedure name and press **ENTER** to create the same two lines as before.

Once you have created the first and last lines of the function, you must include the list of parameters that will be used in the general procedure between the parentheses in the first line (the **Sub** or **Function definition statement**). **Parameters** are name and type specifiers that are separated by commas and must include the data type in the same way as Declaration statements do.

The Function Definition Statement

The Function definition statement includes the name of the function followed by the list of parameters with type specifiers. Also, since the name of the function returns a value, the name *must* be declared as a data type. The general form of the Function definition statement is:

Function *FuncName(parameter1* **as** *type, parameter2* **as** *type, ...)* **as** *type*

For example, the Function definition statement for the intFindMax function mentioned earlier would be:

```
Function intFindMax(intNum1 as Integer, intNum2 as Integer) as Integer
```

It is important to note that the parameter types and the type of the function don't have to be the same. It would be entirely possible for the intFindMax function to return a String or other type of variable if its purpose was changed.

An important rule for creating functions is that, since the value of the function is returned through the function name, *the function name should be assigned a value in the function*. This means that the function name *should* appear on the left side of an assignment statement or a value for it should be input. Failure to assign a value to the function name will result in the function not returning a value. For the FindMax example, this name is assigned a value in an If-Then-Else decision structure:

```
If intNum1 > intNum2 then
    intFindMax = intNum1
Else
    intFindMax = intNum2
End if
```

The Sub Definition Statement

The general form of the Sub definition statement is similar to that of the Function definition statement, with the keyword *Sub* instead of *Function*:

Sub *SubName (parameter1* as *type, parameter2* as *type, ...)*

Note that there is no data type definition for a sub since it returns no value through the name. In fact, the name of a sub has no meaning other than to link the Sub definition statement to the statement invoking the sub. Since no value is returned through the sub name, it is *incorrect* to define a data type for the sub.

For example, the Sub Procedure definition statement for the sub named Reverse mentioned earlier that reverses two values would be:

```
Sub Reverse(curFirst as Currency, curSecond as Currency)
```

where curFirst and curSecond are the parameters for this sub.

Matching Parameters and Arguments

The parameters in Function and Sub definition statements must match the arguments that appear in the statement invoking the function or sub, both in number and in data type. That is, the number of parameters should match the number of arguments. Similarly, the data type of a parameter should match the data type for the corresponding argument. This is required because the parameters and arguments are the linkages between the definition statement and the statement invoking the function or sub. (While it is possible to have optional arguments, we won't consider that situation in this text. Also, if a parameter is defined as a Variant data type, the corresponding argument can be of any data type. However, since we are avoiding the Variant data type in this text, we won't consider this situation here.)

For example, if there are three parameters in a Sub definition statement, with the first two being Integer data types and the last one being a String data type, then there must be three arguments in the statement invoking the sub, with the first two being integers and the third one being a string. Figure 7-4 shows the relationship between the Sub definition statement and the statement invoking the sub. In this figure, the name of the sub (*SubName*) must be the same in the statement invoking the sub and in the Sub definition statement. Also, the number of arguments matches the number of parameters and their types match. That is, the first two arguments (*arg1* and *arg2*) must be Integer data types and the last argument (*arg3*) must a String data type.

FIGURE 7-4.
Relationship between Sub definition statement and statement invoking the sub

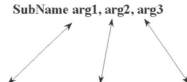

Statement invoking sub procedure

SubName arg1, arg2, arg3

Sub SubName(Parm1 as Integer, Parm2 as Integer, Parm3 as String)

Sub procedure definition statement

This type of argument–parameter matching holds for functions as well. This is shown in Figure 7-5 for a function that has two Integer parameters and one String parameter and returns a Single data type value.

FIGURE 7-5.
Relationship between Function definition statement and statement invoking the function

Statement invoking function procedure

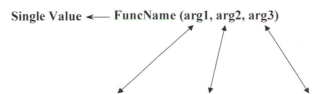

Single Value ◄—— FuncName (arg1, arg2, arg3)

Function FuncName(Parm1 as Integer, Parm2 as Integer, Parm3 as String) as Single

You have undoubtedly noticed in our examples that the variable names used as parameters in the functions and subs are not the same as the names used in the argument list. The reason for this is: The parameter names are variables in the sub that share the same memory location as the corresponding arguments in the statement invoking the function or sub. This means that the same general procedure can be used with different arguments as long as the arguments match the parameters. For example, you could use the Reverse( ) sub shown above to reverse another pair of Currency values by calling it with a different set of arguments, as shown below:

```
Reverse curMySalary, curYourSalary
```

> **TIP:** You can define some parameters as optional by placing the **Optional** keyword in front of the corresponding parameter. If it is used, all parameters listed after the first **Optional** keyword must be optional, too.

Array Arguments

Special attention must be given to arguments and parameters in functions and subs that are arrays. In both the argument list and the parameter list, fixed-size arrays are referenced by the name of the array followed by open and closed parentheses. For example, to invoke a sub to sort an array of String data type elements called Customers( ) with the number of elements in the array equal to intNumCustomers, the statement would be:

```
Sort intNumCustomers, strCustomers()
```

and the Sub definition statement would be:

```
Sub Sort(intNumber as Integer, strList() as String)
```

where the parentheses after the Customers argument and List parameter indicate that they are arrays and have been declared previously.

Notice also that we have used a generic variable name as the parameter in the Sub definition statement since it can be used to work with multiple lists.

Mini-Summary 7-2: Working with Functions and Subs

1. Both functions and subs must be invoked by an event procedure or a general procedure, and they must be defined in the General object of the form or Code module.

2. Functions and subs can be created by using the menu or by entering either word plus a name anywhere in the Code window.

3. When a function or sub is defined, there must be a one-to-one correspondence between the arguments in the calling event or general procedure and the parameters in the function or sub.

It's Your Turn!

1. What Visual Basic menu option can be used to add a general procedure?

2. How can you refer to another event procedure from within an event or general procedure?

3. When referring to a sub with arguments, how is it different to the reference to functions with arguments (there are at least two differences.)

4. How are sub and functions different in the way in which they return values?

5. Write a statement to invoke each of the following general procedures:

    a. Public Function sngConvert(intFeet as Integer)
    b. Public Function strBldMsg(strWords( ) As String, intNum As Integer)
    c. Public Sub Random(intSeed As Integer, sngRNum As Single)
    d. Public Sub Merge(intArr1( ) As Integer, intArr2( ) As Integer)

6. For each call statement below, write a corresponding general procedure definition statement. The variable prefixes indicate the appropriate data type.

    a. blnAge = blnAgeValidate(strAge)
    b. intCount = intCntChar(strPhrase, strChar)
    c. LongAverage lngArr( ), intNum
    d. Call MatInv(intArr( ), intSize, intArrInv( ))

7. Using the function intFindMax discussed in the text, write the statement to invoke it in a Debug.Print statement.

8. Using the sub Reverse discussed in the text, write the statement to invoke it with two Integer variables, intHigh and intLow.

9. Rewrite the statement to invoke a function named *intFindMaxList* in a Debug.Print statement if an array of integers called **intNumbers()** and the number of integers called **intHowMany** are passed to the function. Write the Function definition statement for intFindMaxList.

USING FUNCTIONS: AN EXAMPLE

For a general procedure to be used, it must be created and then invoked in an event procedure or another Sub or Function general procedure. In this section, we will discuss creating and using functions. Subs will be discussed in a later section.

Using programmer-defined functions is just like using built-in functions in that they usually appear in an assignment or other statement where the value of the function can be utilized. A programmer-defined function is useful when the project involves a specific operation that returns a single value. If the operation is going to be executed multiple times, reusing the function reduces the amount of code that must be written. Even if the operation is executed only once in a project, a function is often still very useful in dividing up the input, output, and logic between the event procedure and the function.

The Function definition statement is like that shown earlier, and includes the name with a data type prefix, the parameter list, and the data type of the function. The data type of the function must match the data type used in the invoking statement. This means that if the function is defined as a Single data type, it cannot be used in an operation requiring a String data type.

> **TIP:** You can call a function without using its return value just by calling it as if it were a sub procedure rather than a function.

For example, if you wanted to be able to compute the taxes due on some level of income for some number of exemptions, a function would be appropriate since a single value—the taxes due—is returned. To see this, assume a form is created in which the user can input his or her income in a text box and input the number of exemptions using a scroll bar. Clicking the Compute button inputs the user's gross income and number of exemptions and invokes a function called *curComputeTaxes* to compute the taxes due for this income and number of exemptions. The Taxes Due value is displayed in a text box. A form for this purpose is shown in Figure 7-6, and the code for the scroll bar Change event and the command button Compute event procedure that invokes the curComputeTaxes function is shown in VB Code Box 7-1.

Creating the Function

In this example, we will create the function by using the Add Procedure menu option and then entering the appropriate code. Keep in mind that the function name should be assigned a value in the function by having it appear on the left side of an assignment statement or by having the user input a value for it.

The logic for this example is embodied in the tax rates and brackets shown in Table 7-1 for single taxpayers for the 2000 tax year. Taxable income is found by subtracting $2,800 for each exemption plus the Standard Deduction ($4,400). For example, if your gross income is $60,000 with one exemption, your taxable income will be $60,000 − $2,800 − $4,400 = $52,800 and your taxes will be $3,937.50 + 0.28 * ($52,800 − $26,250) = $11,371.50.

The curComputeTaxes Function definition that embodies this logic is shown in VB Code Box 7-2. Note that the function type is defined as Currency data type since it

FIGURE 7-6. Form to compute income taxes using a function

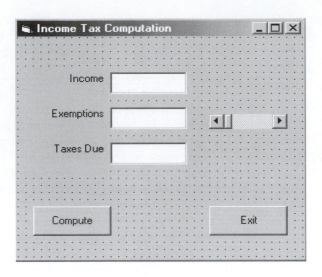

VB CODE BOX 7-1. Event procedure for Compute button	

```
Private Sub hsbExemptions_Change()
    txtExemptions.Text = Str(hsbExemptions.Value)
End Sub
Private Sub cmdCompute_Click()
  Dim intNumExemptions As Integer, curIncome As Currency
  intNumExemptions = CInt(txtExemptions.Text)
  curIncome = CCur(txtIncome.Text)
  txtTaxes.Text = Format(curComputeTaxes(intNumExemptions, _
  curIncome), "currency")
End Sub
```

TABLE 7-1: Tax Rates and Brackets

Taxable Income	Taxes Due
$0–$26,250	15% of taxable income
$26,250–$63,550	$3937.50 plus 28% of taxable income over $26,250
$63,550–$132,600	$14,385.50 plus 31% of taxable income over $63,550
$132,600–$288,350	$41,170.50 plus 36% of taxable income over $132,600
$288,350 and over	$86,854.50 plus 39.6% of taxable income over $288,350

returns a monetary value. Note also that a Case statement is used to compute the taxes due, and the name of the function, curComputeTaxes, is set equal to the expression that computes the taxes. The parameter *intNumExm* matches the *intNumExemptions* argument in the event procedure and *curGrossIncome* matches the *curIncome* argument. If you execute the project with an income of $60,000 with one exemption, an income tax of $11,371.50 will be displayed.

To create this function, you should either use the **Tools | Add Procedure** menu option or insert a blank line after any *End sub* statement and enter **Function curComputeTaxes** and press **ENTER**. You should then modify the first line to include the parameters and to define the type of the function. The code for the body of the function is shown in VB Code Box 7-2. Combining this code with that shown earlier in VB Code Box 7-1 provides all of the code necessary to run this project.

> **TIP:** To see a list of the functions and subs in a form or Code module, select the **General** object and click on the **Procedures** drop-down box.

| VB CODE BOX 7-2. Function to compute income taxes | ```
Public Function curComputeTaxes(intNumExm As Integer, _
curGrossIncome As Currency) as Currency
  Dim curTaxIncome As Currency
  curTaxIncome = curGrossIncome - 4400 - intNumExm * 2800
  Select Case curTaxIncome
  Case Is <= 26250
    curComputeTaxes = 0.15 * curTaxIncome
  Case Is <= 63550
    curComputeTaxes = 3937.50 + 0.28 * (curTaxIncome - 26250)
  Case Is <= 132600
    curComputeTaxes = 14385.50 + 0.31 * (curTaxIncome - 63550)
  Case Is < 288350
    curComputeTaxes = 41170.50 + 0.36 * (curTaxIncome - 132600)
  Case Else
    curComputeTaxes = 86854.50 + 0.396 * (curTaxIncome - 288350)
  End Select
End Function
``` |
|---|---|

Mini-Summary 7-3: Using Functions

1. A common use of a function is to create a single value that is assigned to a variable or is output.

2. A function may or may not have arguments passed to it.

3. The name of the function must be assigned a value in the function.

It's Your Turn!

1. Why do we have to write functions if there are so many built-in functions already?

2. Why is a function the appropriate general procedure to use to compute income tax?

3. Write a function to do each of the following:

   a. Find and return the maximum of three integer values.

   b. Return the sum of all values between any two integer values.

   c. Return a value of true if an entered number is positive and false if the value is negative.

   d. Given an array of integer values, find and return the value closest in absolute value to the average.
```

To create a project to determine the taxes due for a given income and number of exemptions, complete the following exercises.

4. Use the **File|New Project** to open a blank form which you should name **frmIncomeTax**. Give it a caption of **Income Tax Computation** and add a scrollbar named **hsbExemptions** to input the number of exemptions (Max property = 1, Min property = 10, LargeChange = 1, SmallChange = 1, and Value = 1). The resulting form should appear as shown in Figure 7-6

5. Write the code for the Change event of the scrollbar to transfer its Value property to the corresponding text box. Enter the code shown in VB Code Box 7-1 for the **Change** event of the scrollbar to transfer its Value property to the corresponding text box. This code box also includes the code for the **cmdCompute _Click()** event procedure to compute the income taxes for the income and number of exemptions entered on the form using the curComputeTaxes function. You should enter it also.

6. Use the **Tools|Add Procedure** to add a function named **curComputeTaxes** to the Code window. Modify the Function definition line and add the parameter list. Add the code shown in VB Code Box 7-2 to this function.

7. Run your project and test it with an income of **$60,000** and **1** exemption. The income tax should be $11,371.50. Create a new folder on your data disk named **Chapter7** and save the form as **IncomeTax.frm** and the project as **IncomeTax.vbp** in this new folder.

USING SUBS: SORTING EXAMPLE

As mentioned earlier, programmer-defined subs are useful when the arguments will be modified by the general procedure and no value will be returned through the general procedure name. If the processing is executed multiple times, reusing the sub will reduce the amount of code that must be written. Even if the processing is carried out only once in a project, a sub is often still very useful in reducing the complexity of the programming. The Sub definition statement is like that shown earlier and includes the name of the sub and the parameter list with type specifications.

For example, assume you wanted to use a sub to sort the lists of part identifiers and prices discussed in Chapter 6 in order of the prices. To do this, we will use the PartList.vbp project and Parts.txt file created in that chapter to find the maximum price in the list or to search for a specific parts identifier. Figure 7-7 shows the form for that project after a command button is added to sort the list according to price. Recall that there are two arrays associated with this project—strPartID( ) and curPrices( )—and the number of items in both arrays is equal to intNumPrices.

You may ask, Why not just use the Sorted property of the lstPrices list box to sort this list? That would work if the parts were to be sorted according to their identifier, since it appears first in the list box. However, to sort them according to the price, which appears second in the list box, we need to write a sub to rearrange the arrays themselves. This also has the advantage of rearranging the actual arrays, which is not done when the list box is sorted.

Since the curPrices( ) and strPartID( ) arrays were declared at the form level, they are known to all event procedures on the form. That means we can pass them to a Sort sub from within the cmdSort_Click event procedure as shown in VB Code Box 7-3.

FIGURE 7-7.
Modified parts list
form

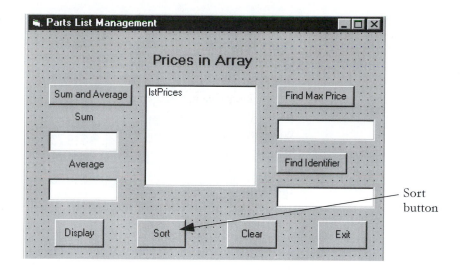

VB CODE BOX 7-3.	```cmdSort_Click()```
Event procedure for	``` Sort curPrices(), strPartID(), intNumPrices```
Sort button	```End sub```

Sorting Arrays

Sorting an array is a commonly used operation in processing data into information. This operation is similar to finding the maximum (or minimum) value in an array or finding an element in the array, because it involves pairwise comparisons. However, it goes further in also requiring repositioning of array elements. To help you understand the sorting process, we will use the list of ten prices (curPrices( )) from the Parts List project discussed in Chapter 6. This array is shown in Figure 7-8.

Figure 7-8. curPrices Array

Prices(0)	$3.35
Prices(1)	$9.50
Prices(2)	$12.81
Prices(3)	$7.62
Prices(4)	$1.29
Prices(5)	$19.73
Prices(6)	$4.56
Prices(7)	$23.75
Prices(8)	$14.65
Prices(9)	$5.43

There are a variety of algorithms for sorting lists, but we will use sort procedure that, while not very fast, is easy to understand. Called the **Bubble Sort**, in this sorting process a For-Next loop is used to compare each array element to the next one and if they are out of order, reverse them. For example, if the Prices( ) array is being ordered from smallest to largest, the Prices(0) element is compared to Prices(1). Since Prices(0) < Prices(1), no changes are made. Next, Prices(1) is compared to Prices(2), and once again, no changes are made. Next, Prices(2) is compared to Prices(3), and since Prices(2) > Prices(3), they are reversed. The result of this reversal is shown in the *left-most* set of prices in Figure 7-9 along with the remaining comparisons and reversals for the array.

Note in Figure 7-9 that, including the reversal of curPrices(2) and curPrices(3) which is not shown, there are five reversals of array elements due to a price being higher than the next price in the list. Note also that after this loop the largest value is at the bottom, but the array is not completely sorted. Even though this sorting algorithm is called the *Bubble Sort* because the lowest values *bubble* their way to the top of the list, in actuality, the largest values *sink* to their relative positions at the bottom of the list on each pass through the loop.

To completely sort the array, the comparison–reversal loop must be repeated as many times as necessary to sort the array. How do we know when the array is sorted? Note that if no reversals are made in the comparison–reversal loop, then the array is sorted. This indicates that we need a loop to repeat the comparison–reversal loop *until* no reversals are made. This is a situation where we use nested loops, with the outer

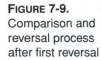

FIGURE 7-9.
Comparison and
reversal process
after first reversal

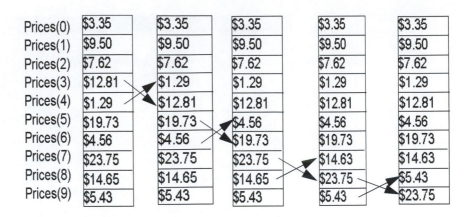

loop being a Do Until loop and the inner loop being a For-Next loop. The pseudocode for this process is shown below:

```
Begin Sort procedure
    Repeat until no reversals made
        Repeat for each pair of values
            If value > next value then
                Reverse values
            End decision
        End repeat
    End repeat
End Procedure.
```

Implementing this pseudocode in Visual Basic requires that we address several programming issues:

1. How do we handle the For-Next loop and decisions to carry out the pairwise comparisons on array elements?

2. How do we reverse two array elements?

3. How do we handle the nested DoUntil and For-Next loops so that the array is repeatedly searched until no reversals have been made?

> **TIP:** You can use Exit Sub or Exit Function to cause Visual Basic to immediately terminate the current procedure. However, they should be used sparingly.

Carrying Out Pairwise Array Comparisons

To carry out the pairwise comparisons for the curPrices( ) array with index values that run from 0 to intNumPrices − 1, the For-Next loop runs from the first array element to the next to last, with each element being compared to the one that follows it. Note that the loop stops at the next to last array element because there is no *next* element after the last one. If the last element of the array has index intNumValues − 1, the index for the next to last array element will be intNumPrices − 2. This means that the first statement of the For-Next loop will be:

```
For intCounter = 0 to intNumPrices - 2
```

Using the intCounter variable for the curPrices( ) array, the current value is cur-Prices(intCounter) and the *next* value will be curPrices(intCounter + 1). This means that the pairwise comparisons are of the form:

```
If curPrices(intCounter) > curPrices(intCounter + 1) then
```

If the comparison is found to be True and the two array elements are out of order, then they should be reversed. The form of the For-Next loop and comparisons is as shown in VB Code Box 7-4 (where it is assumed that a sub will be used to reverse the two array elements):

VB **C**ODE **B**OX 7-4. Code to reverse two price elements	```For intCounter = 0 to intNumPrices - 2 If curPrices(intCounter) > curPrices(intCounter + 1) then Reverse curPrices(intCounter), curPrices(intCounter + 1) End if Next```

Using a sub to reverse the array elements is an example of reducing the complexity of code. Even though we do not yet know the logic that will go into the sub, we can write the statement to invoke it and handle creating the sub later.

Reversing Array Elements

The key to the sorting process is being able to reverse two array elements when they are found to be out of order. Reversing two array elements is not as simple as just setting one element equal to the other. That is, these two statements will **not** reverse two string array elements:

```
strList(intCounter) = strList(intCounter + 1)
strList(intCounter + 1) = strList(intCounter)
```

In fact, all these two statements will accomplish is setting the two array elements to the *same* value, the original value of strList(intCounter + 1). For this reason, we need to use a *temporary* variable to carry out the reversal—as shown in Figure 7-10 for cur-Prices(3) and curPrices(4), which are initially out of order.

FIGURE **7-10.** Use of temporary variable to reverse two values

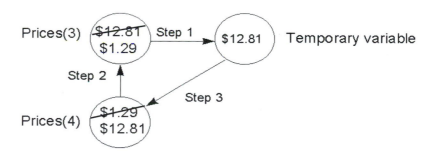

In Step 1 of the reversal process, the temporary variable is set equal to cur-Prices(3). In Step 2, curPrices(3) is set equal to curPrices(4). Finally, in Step 3 cur-Prices(4) is set equal to the temporary variable. In the process, the value of curPrices(3) is changed to $1.29 and the value of curPrices(4) is changed to $12.81. In each case, the *old* value for the array element is replaced by the *new* value, as shown by the values being struck out. This process can be generalized by replacing curPrices(3) and cur-Prices(4) with curPrices(intCounter) and curPrices(intCounter + 1).

The Reverse sub to handle reversing two elements in the For-Next loop is shown in VB Code Box 7-5. It is not necessary to use arrays in the sub, because two specific array elements—curPrices(intCounter) and curPrices(intCounter + 1)—are passed to the array. They match the curFirst and curSecond parameters in the Sub definition statement. The temporary variable, curTemp, is declared as a Currency data type local variable.

VB Code Box 7-5. Sub to reverse two values	```Public Sub Reverse(curFirst as Currency, curSecond as _```
	 ```Currency)```
	 ``` Dim curTemp as Currency```
	 ``` curTemp = curFirst```
	 ``` curFirst = curSecond```
	 ``` curSecond = curTemp```
	 ```End sub```

Repeating the For-Next Loop until the Array Is Sorted

The last issue to be dealt with in the sorting process is using nested loops with a Do Until outer loop that repeats a For-Next inner loop until the array is sorted. We already know that the array will be sorted when there are no reversals in the For-Next loop, so we can use this fact to terminate the Do Until outer loop. One way to do this is to use a Boolean variable called blnNoReversal that is set to False *before* the Do Until loop and then reset to True within the Do Until before the start of the For-Next loop. Within the For-Next loop, if any reversals occur, then blnNoReversal is set to False. If blnNoReversal is still True after the For-Next loop, this means there were no reversals, the Do Until loop can be terminated, and the array is sorted. The assignment of blnNoReversal to False before the Do Until loop ensures that the Do Until loop will complete at least one repetition.

The pseudocode for this process is shown below, and the Visual Basic code for the complete Sort sub that will go in the Code module is shown in VB Code Box 7-6.

```
Begin Sort procedure
    Repeat until no reversals made
        If value > next value then
            Reverse values
        End decision
    End repeat
End procedure
```

Note that parameters called curtList1( ), strList2( ), and intNumList are defined to match the arguments in the statement that invokes the sub. Also, since the curPrices( ) array is being used to sort both the curPrices( ) and strPartID( ) arrays, whatever is done to the curPrices( ) array should also be done to the strPartID( ) array. This requires a second sub called ReverseStr to reverse the String data type strPartID( ) array, since the Reverse sub was created to reverse Currency data type elements. The ReverseStr sub will look *exactly* like the Reverse sub for Currency type data variables except that the curFirst, curSecond, and curTemp variables will be String data type instead of Currency type.

When the cmdSort command button and the associated code is added to the PartList.frm form from Chapter 6 and the Sort, Reverse, and ReverseStr subs are added to the General object of the PartsList.vbp project, the project can be executed.

VB CODE BOX 7-6.
Code for sub to sort
an array
	``
	Public Sub Sort(curList1() As Currency, _
	strList2() As String, intNumList As Integer)
	  Dim blnNoReversal As Boolean, intCounter As Integer
	  blnNoReversal = False
	  Do Until blnNoReversal
	    blnNoReversal = True
	    For intCounter = 0 To intNumList - 2
	      If curList1(intCounter) > curList1(intCounter + 1) Then
	        Reverse curList1(intCounter),curList1(intCounter + 1)
	        ReverseStr strList2(intCounter),strList2(intCounter+1)
	        blnNoReversal = False
	      End If
	    Next
	  Loop
	End Sub
	``

If this is done, the form shown in Figure 7-11 will result from clicking on the Sort and Display buttons in that order.

FIGURE 7-11.
Displaying part identifiers and prices

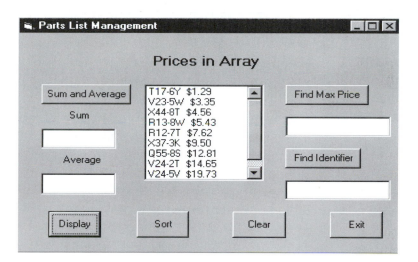

Note that the parts are displayed in increasing order of price starting with the part that has ID number T17-6Y with a price of $1.29. All of this code *except* for the Sort sub which is shown above is shown again in VB Code Box 7-7.

Mini-Summary 7-4: Using Subs: Sorting Example

1. A sub is often used for manipulating the arguments passed to it.

2. A sub can invoke another sub; for example, a sub to sort an array can invoke a sub to reverse two array elements.

3. Sorting an array requires that nested loops be used to repeat the comparison–reversal process until the array is sorted.

| VB CODE BOX 7-7. New code for PartsList.vbp project | ```
Public Sub cmdSort_Click()
    Sort curPrices(), strPartID(), intNumPrices
End Sub
Public Sub Reverse(curFirst as Currency, curSecond as _
Currency)
    Dim curTemp as Currency
    curTemp = curFirst
    curFirst = curSecond
    curSecond = curTemp
End Sub
Public Sub Reversestr(strFirst as String, strSecond _
as String)
    Dim strTemp as string
    strTemp = strFirst
    strFirst = strSecond
    strSecond = strTemp
End Sub
``` |
|---|---|

It's Your Turn!

1. What is accomplished by the following sub procedures? What variables and data types should be passed to them when they are invoked? Describe what is passed back as the result.

```
a. Public Sub ASub(intArr() As Integer, intTop As _
      Integer, intX As Integer, intY As Integer)
      Dim intN As Integer
      intX = intArr(0)
      intY = intArr(0)
      For intN = 1 To 4
        If intArr(intN) < intX Then
          intX = intArr(intN)
        End If
        If intArr(intN) > intY Then
          intY = intArr(intN)
        End If
      Next intN
    End Sub

b. Public Sub BSub(intArr1() As Integer, intArr2() _
      As Integer, intSize as Integer, intArr3() As Integer)
      Dim intN As Integer
      For intN = 0 To (intSize * 2) Step 2
        intArr3(intN) = intArr1(intN / 2)
      Next intN
      For intN = 1 To (intSize * 2 + 1) Step 2
        intArr3(intN) = intArr2((intN - 1) / 2)
      Next intN
    End Sub
```
```

```
c. Public Sub CSub(strOne As String, strTwo _
       As String, strThree as String, blnStatus as Boolean)
   If strOne < strTwo Then
      strThree = strOne & strTwo
      blnStatus = True
   Else
      strThree = ""
      blnStatus = False
   End If
End Sub
```

2. Write sub procedures to do each of the following:

    a. Write a sub procedure that returns the name of a month and the number of days in the month based on an integer passed to it (1 = Jan., 2 = Feb., etc.)

    b. Write a sub procedure that calculates the new monthly balance of a checking account after passing to it: a beginning balance; an array of deposits and the number of deposits for the month; and an array of withdrawals and the number of withdrawals for the month. Assume that there are service charges of $5 per month, $0.05 for each withdrawal, and $0.02 for each deposit.

    c. Write a sub procedure that will print a table stored in a two-dimensional array that is passed to it. Assume that the number of rows and the number of columns will also be passed to the sub.

To continue the PartsList project from Chapter 6, complete the following exercises.

3. Open the **PartsList.vbp** project from the Chapter 6 folder, add a command button to sort the arrays (*cmdSort*), and give it a caption of **Sort** as shown in Figure 7-7.

4. Open the Code window for cmdSort and add the single line of code:

```
Sort curPrices(), strPartID(), intNumPrices
```
to sort the curPrices( ) and strPartID( ) arrays.

5. Use the **Tools | Add Procedure** menu option to create the first and last lines of the **Reverse** sub. Enter the code shown in VB Code Box 7-5 for this sub. Do the same to create the first and last lines of **ReverseStr** sub and copy the code from the Reverse sub into it. Change all declarations from the Currency data type to the String data type.

6. Start another sub by entering the words **sub Sort** and enter the code shown in VB Code Box 7-6. Run your project and sort the arrays with the Sort button. Display the resulting arrays in the list box.

7. Modify the cmdSumAverage event procedure to use a function called **curSum** that sums the prices for the parts and a function called **curAverage** that uses the result of the Sum function to compute the average price for the parts.

8. Save the project as **PartList7.frm** and **PartList7.vbp** in the Chapter 7 folder.

9. How would you change the Sort sub to create a sub named **PartSort** that will sort on the basis of the strPartID( ) array rather than on the curPrices( ) array?

APPLICATION TO VINTAGE VIDEOS

Now that you have a good understanding of general procedures, we can turn our attention to using them for an enlarged Vintage Videos project. In considering the new requirements, it is obvious that more forms and controls will be needed to handle the additional functionality. For example, instead of the store clerks manually scanning the combo box of member names, a form like that used to search for videos can be used. This requires us to think about the overall design of the project. A design that matches the needs expressed by the video store owners is shown in Figure 7-12.

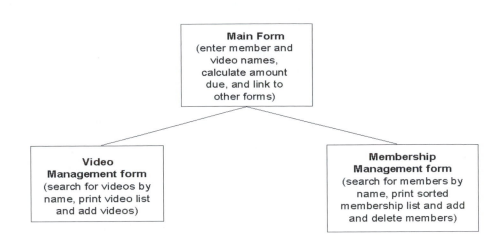

Note that in Figure 7-12 there are now two secondary forms instead of just one. The secondary form on the right is for managing the membership list and the secondary form on the left is for managing the list of videos. In both cases, the forms provide the capability to search for items on the list and display matching items in a list box, add items to the list, and print the list in alphabetical order.

The new membership management form (*frmMembers*) is shown in Figure 7-13, with a list box to display the names (*lstMembers*), a text box to enter the search string (*txtSearch*), and a button to initiate the search (*cmdSearch*). In addition, there are buttons to add names to the list (*cmdAdd*), delete names from the list (*cmdDelete*), to print the list of names (*cmdPrint*), and to return to the main form (*cmdBack*). If one of the member names in the list box is clicked, then that person's name and late fees are transferred to the main form.

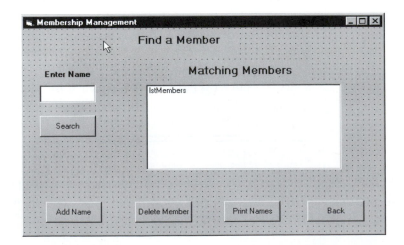

With the new form and added functionality for existing forms, project management becomes an essential feature of application development. Project management involves developing forms with a consistent *look and feel,* so the user can easily understand from previous experience how to use them. There must also be a straightforward navigation pattern between the forms to avoid the user becoming lost. For example, for the expanded Vintage Videos project, the two secondary forms should have a similar interface and should be designed so that clicking on a *Back* button will always take the user back to the main form. Project management also requires that the developer be consistent in naming forms and controls and declaring variables; otherwise, debugging the project will quickly become a nightmare.

> **TIP:** You can copy a command button from one form to another by selecting it and using the **Edit|Copy** and **Edit|Paste** menu commands.

Modifying the frmVideos form

In addition to adding a new form, we also need to modify the frmVideos form to add videos and to print a list of sorted videos. The resulting form will look as shown in Figure 7-14.

FIGURE 7-14.
Modified frmVideos form

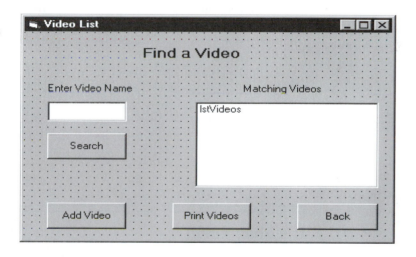

Modifying the Main Form

Since late fees should be included in the amount-due calculation, the main form needs to be modified to include a new text box (*txtLateFees*) that will display them. They must also be included in the calculation of amount due and added to the list box that is printed as a receipt. In addition, there is no longer a need for a combo box with member names, and the Add Name and Delete Member buttons need to be replaced with a single *Check Name (cmdCheckName)* button. This command button should transfer control to the membership management form added earlier and set the focus on the text box used to search for a customer's name using the following commands:

```
frmMembers.Show
frmMembers.txtSearch.SetFocus
```

The revised main form is shown in Figure 7-15, with the changes pointed out.

To include the late fees in the amount due calculation in the cmdCalc_Click( ) event procedure requires that we first validate that there is value in the txtLateFees text box before making this calculation. If the late fees text box is empty, this means the

FIGURE 7-15.
Revised main form

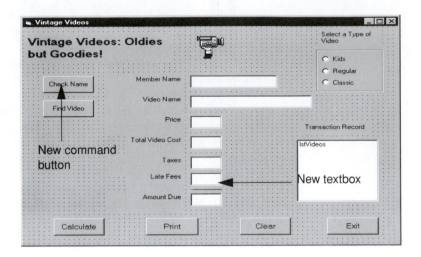

clerk has not checked if the customer is a member since doing so would result in either a late fee ($0 or some value) for an existing member or a zero value for a new member. If the text box is empty, a message should be displayed instructing the user to click the Check Members button and the procedure exited. If the late fees text box is *not* empty, we can proceed with the calculation of amount due. This requires a new variable, *curLateFees*, to be declared as Currency. This variable is then set equal to txtLate-Fees.Text and added to the total cost and taxes to determine the amount due. The contents of the LateFees text box should also be added to the transactions list box in the cmdPrint event procedure with an appropriate descriptor before the amount due is added to the list box. The new code to validate the contents of the late fees text box and, if it is not empty, use it in the calculation of amount due is shown in VB Code Box 7-8 along with the new code to display the late fees in the transaction list box. Note that existing code is clearly pointed out in this code box and does *not* need to be added.

It's Your Turn!

1. What is meant by the term *look and feel* when it refers to computer applications?

2. What is a shortcut way to move a command button from one form to another?

To revise the Vintage Videos project to manage the membership list, complete the following exercises.

3. Start Visual Basic, open the **Vintage6.vbp** project, and add a new form named **frmMembers** with a list box (**lstMembers**), a text box (**txtSearch**), five command buttons (**cmdSearch, cmdAdd, cmdDelete, cmdPrint,** and **cmdBack**), and corresponding captions and labels as shown in Figure 7-13. Code the **cmdBack** button to display frmVintage. Save this form as **Members7.frm** in it the Chapter7 folder on your data disk.

| VB CODE BOX 7-8. New code for cmd-Calc and cmdPrint event procedures on frmVintage | ```
Private Sub cmdCalc_Click   (Existing code)
Const sngTaxRate as Single = 0.07   (Existing code)
Dim curLateFees as Currency

Existing code goes here

curTaxes = curTotalCost * sngTaxRate (Existing code)
If txtLateFees.Text = "" then
   MsgBox "Click Check Members button and try again", _
   vbCritical, "Membership status not checked"
   Exit Sub 'User did not click Check Members button
End If
curLateFees = CCur(txtLateFees.Text)
curAmountDue = curTotalCost + curTaxes + curLateFees
txtLateFees.Text = Format(LateFees, "currency")
txtTotalCost.Text = Format(TotalCost, "currency") (Existing code)

Existing code goes here

End Sub (Existing code)
Private Sub cmdPrint_Click

Existing code goes here

lstVideos.AddItem "Taxes " + txtTaxes.text (Existing code)
lstVideos.AddItem "Late Fees " + txtLateFees.text

Existing code goes here

End Sub (Existing code)
``` |
|---|---|

4. Modify the existing **frmVideos** form to add buttons to print the list of videos (**cmdPrint**) and to add videos (**cmdAdd**). The resulting form should look like Figure 7-14. Why is there no problem with using the same names for controls on both forms? Save this form again with the modifications as **Videos7.frm** to the Chapter7 folder on your data disk.

5. Modify the main form by adding the **txtLateFees** text box beneath the *txtTaxes* text box with an associated label. Delete the *Member List* label, the *cboMembers* combo box, the *cmdAdd* command button, the *cmdDelete* command button, and any associated event procedures. Also, delete the code in the Form_Load event procedure and cmdExit event procedures that pertains to cboMembers.

6. Add a new command button (**cmdCheck**) with a caption of **Check Name** with these two lines of code:

```
frmMembers.Show
frmMembers.txtSearch.SetFocus
```
The result should look like Figure 7-15.

7. Modify the cmdCalc_Click( ) event procedure to declare a new variable, **curLateFees**, as Currency and add the new code shown in VB Code Box 7-8 immediately after the calculation of taxes.
```

8. Modify the cmdPrint_Click( ) event procedure to add **txtLateFees** to the LstVideos list box with an appropriate descriptor before adding the Amount Due value as also shown in VB Code Box 7-8.

9. Save the main form as **Vintage7.frm** and the project as **Vintage7.vbp** in the Chapter7 folder on your data disk.

GLOBAL DECLARATIONS AND THE CODE MODULE

In Figure 7-12, we designed a revised version of the Vintage Videos project that involves three forms: a main form and two secondary forms that manage the membership and video lists by searching for member or video names, adding members or videos, and sorting and printing the respective lists. Because at least two forms must *know* about each list, we need to use a different type of declaration for the lists—global declarations in which all forms and general procedures are aware of the declared variable. Similarly, if we want all forms to know about a general procedure, the easiest way to make this possible is create a global general procedure.

In a **global declaration**, the scope of global variables, as compared to form-level variables or procedure-level variables, includes all parts of the project. Recall that the scope of a form-level variable is the current form and the scope of a procedure-level variable is the current procedure. Global declarations are carried out in the Code module portion of the project. The **Code module** is a section of pure code that is known to all forms in a project. It contains only declarations and general procedures, no controls or event procedures. Figure 7-16 shows the concept of scope for global, form-level, and procedure-level variables. In each case, the elements below a variable declaration *know* about those variables but not in the other direction. That is, procedures know about the form-level variables and the forms and procedures all know about the global variables, but the Code module does not know about the variables at the form level or procedure level. This is a way of protecting variables from inadvertent contamination.

FIGURE 7-16.
Scope of global variables

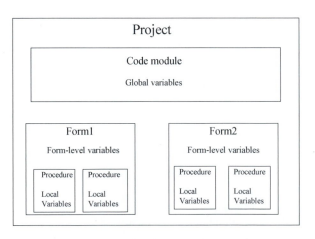

We add a Code module to the project by using the **Project|Add Module** menu selection, and it has a *.bas* extension. When this menu option is selected, unless a prior user has discontinued it, a dialog box will be displayed from which you can select a new or existing module. (If the dialog box is not displayed, a new module named Module1.bas will automatically be added.) The only indication that a module has been added is the addition of the module name to the Project Explorer window beneath any existing forms and the appearance of a blank Code window with **[Module1(Code)]** in the title bar. For example, if a module is added to the Vintage7.vbp project, the Project Explorer window will appear as shown in Figure 7-17. As with any other object, you can rename the Code module in the Properties window. You should also save it when you save the project or exit Visual Basic.

FIGURE 7-17 Addition of module

The actual declaration of global variables occurs in the *Declarations* procedure of the *General object* of the Code module. Initially, this is the only object and procedure in the Code module, so it is the one that is automatically displayed when you add the Code module or select it from the Project Explorer window. Declaring a variable globally is just like declaring it at the form level or control level, except that the keyword *Public* is used instead of the keyword *Dim* in the declaration. The general form for globally declaring variables is:

Public *varName1* as *type*, *varName2* as *type*, ...

For example, if you wanted to declare an Integer data type variable *intNumMembers* so that it would be known to all forms and procedures in a project, the appropriate statement in a Code module would be:

```
Public intNumMembers as Integer
```

While declaring variables globally is necessary for multiple forms to know about them, declaring a variable globally means that any changes to that variable in a procedure will change it everywhere in the project. This means that you must be careful when you change a global variable, because the change may have far-reaching effects.

Once global variables are declared globally in the Code module, it is not necessary or even useful to declare them again in a general or event procedure. In fact, if a global variable is declared again in any type of procedure, then all values will be zeroed out when this procedure is executed and it will not know about the contents of the global variables. For this reason, once a variable is declared globally, declaring the same variable again in a procedure is a *bad* idea.

> **TIP:** You cannot declare an array using the Public keyword in a **form** module. Attempting to do so will generate a compiler error.

Global Variables vs. Passing Variables

You may ask, Why pass variables to a general procedure rather than just declaring everything as global variables? There are two reasons for passing variables instead of using global variables. First, if we used global variables instead of passing variables, there would be the possibility of inadvertently changing a global variable within a procedure. Second, using global variables instead of passing variables would mean that subs or functions could not be used in multiple locations in the project. If functions and subs used a specific global variable rather than a local variable corresponding to the argument variable, it would work only with that specific global variable.

In general, global variables are useful for making multiple controls aware of a variable, but care should be taken when they are used within functions and subs. If the value of a global variable is changed within a function or sub, then it is changed everywhere—even if that was not intended! You can avoid this potential problem by copying the global argument variable to a local parameter variable to protect it from contamination and to allow a function or sub to be used in multiple situations.

*Global General
Procedures*

Just as variables declared globally in the Code module are known to all forms in the project, general procedures created in the Code module are also known to all forms. While a function or sub created in a form with a *Public* keyword is known to other forms, invoking it is more difficult because you must include the form name as a part of the function or sub name. It is easier and more straightforward to create the function or sub in the Code module so it can be invoked with just its name.

Just as creating functions and subs in a form is done in the *General* object, creating a function or sub in the Code module is also done in the *General* object, either by using the **Tools | Add Procedure** menu option or by creating an empty line in the Code module and typing the *Function* or *Sub* keyword plus the procedure name. We will demonstrate this shortly in the Vintage Videos project.

*Application to Vintage
Videos*

Since at least two forms in the Vintage Videos scenario need to know about each list, we need to globally declare the arrays needed to process the membership and video lists. For the membership list, we want the number of members and the lists of member names, phone numbers, and late fees to be known to all parts of the project. In this case, after a Code module has been added to the project, the Declaration statements area is shown in VB Code Box 7-9.

VB CODE BOX 7-9. Global declarations for Vintage Videos project	`Public strMembers(100) as String, curLateFees(100) as Currency`
	`Public strPhoneNumbers(100) as String, intNumMembers as Integer`
	`Public strVideos(100) as String, curVideoPrice(100) as Currency`
	`Public strVideoLoc(100) as String, intNumVideos as Integer`

With these declarations, the main and secondary forms will know about the name, phone number, and late fees for the member. They will also be aware of the name, location, and price for each video. Since these variables are declared globally, the declaration of the three video arrays at the form level in frmVideos needs to be deleted.

*Inputting the
Membership and
Video Lists*

Since the arrays for the membership and video lists are now declared globally, we can input both in the Form_Load event procedure for the main form. This will allow us to avoid reloading the videos list every time we go to the frmVideos form to search for a video. The easiest way to make this change is to move the code from the frmVideos Form_Load event procedure to the frmVintage Form_Load event procedure. The existing frmVintage Form_Load event procedure also needs to be modified to input the member's phone number and late fees, if any, in addition to the member's name. The revised frmVintage Form_Load event procedure code is shown in VB Code Box 7-10.

Mini-Summary 7-5: Global Declarations and the Code Module

1. Global variables are declared in a Code module and are known everywhere in the project.

2. Any change to a global variable is reflected everywhere in the project.

3. Global general procedures are declared in a Code module which is saved with a *.bas* extension.

| **VB CODE BOX 7-10.** Revised Form_Load event procedure for frmVintage | ```
Private Sub Form_Load()
  lstVideos.AddItem "Welcome to Vintage Videos"
  Open "a:\members7.txt" For Input As #1
  Do Until EOF(1)
   Input #1, strMembers(intNumMembers), _
   strPhoneNumbers(intNumMembers), curLateFees(intNumMembers)
   intNumMembers = intNumMembers + 1
  Loop
  Close #1
  Open "a:\videos.txt" For Input As #2
  Do Until EOF(2)
    Input #2, strVideos(intNumVideos), _
    curVideoPrice(intNumVideos), strVideoLoc(intNumVideos)
    intNumVideos = intNumVideos + 1
  Loop
  Close #2
End Sub
``` |

It's Your Turn!

1. Why should you be careful about declaring variables as global level variables?

2. Under what circumstances would it be appropriate to declare a variable as a global variable rather than passing it between procedures?

3. Use NotePad to modify the existing **Members.txt** text file to add phone numbers and late fees amounts to existing names as shown in Table 7-2 or you may download the modified file from the Chapter 7 section of the text Web site.

TABLE 7-2: Data for Members.txt File

Name	Phone Number	Late Fees
Stams, Lonnie	555-1294	$2.12
Goodly, Alice	555-4244	$3.18
Watson, Betsy	555-8590	$0
Arons, Suzy	555-3587	$16.00
Carroll, Ann	555-3700	$4.26
Triesch, Jimmy	555-9021	$10.65
Hyatt, Ashley	555-5355	$0
Patrick, Chris	555-9238	$3.20
Jones, Sam	555-8100	$4.24
Myers, Carolyn	555-9475	$0
Dyer, Ben	555-4505	$9.60
Kidd, Margo	555-1203	$5.30
Sibley, Ben	555-1032	$0
Smith, Joe	555-0023	$0
Adams, Bill	555-8163	$3.20
Brown, Andy	555-7096	$19.20

4. While still in NotePad, add the name shown below to the list and then save the file as **Members7.txt**. in the root folder of your data disk.

Smith, Joe	555-1234	$12.80
```

To modify the Vintage Videos project to use a code module, complete the following exercises (save all files to the **Chapter7** folder on your data disk):

5. Clear all existing code *except* the **End** command from the cmdExit event procedure as it is no longer correct.

6. Use the **Project|Add Module** menu option to add a Code module to the Vintage7.vbp project. Use the Project Explorer to rename this module as **modVintage7**.

7. Add the four lines of global declarations shown in VB Code Box 7-9 to the modVintage7 module. Save this module as **Vintage7.bas**. Remove the form-level declarations in frmVideos.

8. Modify the existing **frmVintage** Form_Load event procedure to input the arrays for the membership list; that is, input strMembers( ), strPhoneNumbers( ), and curLateFees( ) from the **Members7.txt**. data file.

9. Move the code from the frmVideos Form_Load event procedure to the frmVintage Form_Load event procedure. The resulting frmVintage Form_Load event procedure should appear like that shown in VB Code Box 7-10.

10. Temporarily add For-Next loops at the end of the frmVintage Form_Load event procedure to print the contents of the membership and video list arrays to the Immediate window.

11. Test the revised version of the project to ensure that all the membership and video information is being correctly input to the arrays and output to the Immediate window. Delete the For-Next loops used to test the project, and save all project files under their current names.

SEARCHING FOR MEMBER AND VIDEO NAMES

In the Vintage Videos scenario in Chapter 6, we included an event procedure to search for a partial name of a video in the list of videos and display the videos in a list box. In this chapter, we want to carry out the same operation to search for a partial name in the list of members. Since we are carrying out the same operation on two different lists, this is a situation where a sub may be useful to reuse the same code.

Since both the membership and video lists use two String arrays and one Currency array, we can use the same sub to search through both of them. If there had been a different number or different types of arrays, we would have had to use two different subs that use similar logic. In either case, using subs for the search process will reduce the complexity of the programming process.

The common Search sub will be invoked in the cmdSearch_Click( ) event procedures on the frmVideos or frmMembers form. In this case, the logic used for the Search sub will be similar to that used for the cmdSearch_Click( ) event procedure in frmVideos, which we discussed in Chapter 6. Because the results of the search will be added to list boxes on different forms, we need to pass a variable to the sub that designates the list box to which the matching entries should be added. The pseudocode for this process is shown on the next page.

Note in the pseudocode that when a match is found, the counter for the number of matches is incremented and then, depending on which list is being processed, the appropriate matching elements are added to a list box. The actual Visual Basic code to implement this Search sub is shown in VB Code Box 7-11.

Begin search procedure
    Repeat for each item in list
        If SearchString is substring of list item then
            Increment Number of matches Counter
            If Membership list then
                Add Name, Phone Number and Late Fee to member list box
            Else
                Add Video Name to video list box
            End decision
        End decision
    End repeat
End procedure

VB CODE BOX 7-11. Code for Search sub	```Public Sub Search(strSearch As String, strList1() As _``` ...

```
Public Sub Search(strSearch As String, strList1() As _
String, strList2() As String, curList3() As Currency, _
intNumItems As Integer, strWhich As String)
  Dim intNumMatches As Integer, strFound As String
' Procedure searches for strSearch in List1(). If matches are
' found, 1 or 3 array values are added to appropriate list box
  Dim intCounter As Integer
  intNumMatches = 0
  For intCounter = 0 To intNumItems - 1
    If InStr(UCase(strList1(intCounter)),UCase(strSearch)) > 0 Then
      intNumMatches = intNumMatches + 1
      If strWhich = "Members" Then
        frmMembers.lstMembers.AddItem strList1(intCounter) _
          & "   " & strList2(intCounter) & "   " & _
          Format(curList3(intCounter), "currency")
      Else
        frmVideos.lstVideos.AddItem strList1(intCounter)
      End If
    End If
  Next
  If intNumMatches = 0 Then
    MsgBox ("No matching entries found! Try again.")
  ElseIf intNumMatches > 5 Then
    MsgBox ("Too many matching entries!")
    frmMembers.lstMembers.Clear
    frmVideos.lstVideos.Clear
  End If
End Sub
```

> **TIP:** Internal comments should be used wherever they help a reader understand the code.

Note in the Search sub that there are six parameters: *strSearch, strList1( ), strList2( ), curList3( ), intNumItems,* and *strWhich.* The first parameter is the partial member video name or member name being searched for, and the next three parameters are the three lists associated with the membership list or the video list. intNumItems is the number of elements in the lists and strWhich is a string that designates the form and list box to which the array elements are added. Note also that there are two lines of comments that provide information on what this sub does and how it does it. Since this sub will be used in different situations, its purpose is not evident from its location, so comments are useful in explaining its purpose.

In the sub itself, whenever a match is found between the Search string (*strSearch*) and an item in the list of names (*strList1( )*) using the InStr( ) function, the parameter *strWhich* is checked to determine the list box to which the information from the arrays should be added. Note that the *complete name* of each list box is used—that is, the form name combined with the list box name. For example, if the membership list is being searched and the strWhich variable is equal to *Members*, then elements from all three lists are added to the frmMembers.lstMembers list box.

If no matches are found or if too many matches are found, a message box is displayed. In the latter case, all of the entries will be displayed initially, but will be cleared from the list box when the user clicks Ok on the message box.

As mentioned above, the invoking procedures for the Search sub are the cmdSearch_Click( ) event procedures in the frmVideos and frmMembers forms. For the frmMember form, the invoking cmdSearch_Click( ) event procedure is shown in VB Code Box 7-12.

VB Code Box 7-12. frmVintage code to invoke the Search sub for members	<pre>Private Sub cmdSearch_Click()
	    Dim strFindName As String
	    lstMembers.Clear
	    strFindName = txtSearch.Text
	    Search strFindName, strMembers(), strPhoneNumbers(), _
	    curLateFees(), intNumMembers, "Members"
	End Sub</pre>

Note that the event procedure is very simple since all of the important logic is in the Search procedure. The frmVideos version of this cmdSearch_Click( ) event procedure will be the same as this one, except that the strFindName variable is set equal to txtVideos.Text and the last five arguments are replaced with strVideos( ), strVideoLoc( ), curVideoPrice( ), intNumVideos, and "Videos".

If the project is run and the Check Name command button on the main form is clicked, the new frmMembers form will be displayed. On this form, a partial name, say, *smi*, can be entered to search for anybody with a last name beginning with *smi, SMI,* or *Smi*, and the Search command button can be clicked. The results are as shown in Figure 7-18, where two persons named *Smith, Joe* are listed along with their phone numbers and late fees.

The lstMembers Click Event

Once a list of names has been displayed in the list box on the frmMembers form, the next step is for the user to click on the correct name and display it on the main form along with the late fees associated with this person. If the customer's name is not found, the user can click on the Add Name button to add this person's name and phone number to the membership arrays (since the person is a new member, he or she will not have any late fees). We will consider the lstMembers_Click( ) event procedure first and then consider the cmdAdd_Click and cmdDelete_Click event procedures.

In Chapter 6, we discussed the lstVideos_Click( ) event procedure that finds the video matching the name selected by the user by searching the video name array for an exact match. Unfortunately, we cannot use the same approach for the membership list, because the member names may be exactly the same. However, since each line in the list box is one long character string, we can use character string functions to extract the information from the list box and transfer it to the main form.

FIGURE 7-18.
Result of Search
sub

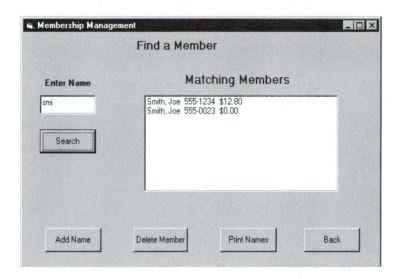

To extract the name and late fees from a list box, we first need to look at the structure of the information in the list box. Each line of the list box is composed of the member's name, phone number, and late fees separated by two spaces as shown below (where **b** indicates a space, x represents a character, and n represents a digit):

`xxxxxx,bxxxxxbbnnn-nnnnbb$nn.nn`

For example, one of the names shown in Figure 7-18 is:

`Smith, Joe  555-1234  $12.80`

There are numerous character string functions available in Visual Basic to help us extract the name and late fees amount. You have already used some of these functions, including Str( ), UCase( ), Format( ), Asc( ), Chr( ), and InStr( ). Other useful character string functions are shown in Table 7-3.

In our case, since the member name is at the left end of the list box character string, we only need to determine where it ends and then use the Left( ) function to extract it. Similarly, since the late fees amount is at the right end of the character string, we need to determine its length with the **Len()** function and then use the Right( ) function to extract it. To find where the name ends, we can use the InStr( ) function to search for two blanks and then back up one position. Similarly, to find where the late fees amount begins, we can use InStr( ) to find the location of the dollar sign, use its position to determine the length of the late fees string, and then extract it. Once extracted, both strings should be transferred to the appropriate text boxes in frmVintage.

For example, if strExample = "Smith, Joe 555-1234 $16.80" with two spaces after the name, then to find the two spaces, we would use InStr(strExample, "   ") which equals = 11. Similarly, Left(strExample, 10) = "Smith, Joe". Also, since Len(strExample) = 28 and InStr(strExample, "$") = 23, the length of the late fees string is equal to 28 − 23 = 5, and we can extract the late fees string via Right(strExample, 5) = "$16.80". The code for the lstMembers_Click( ) event procedure is shown in VB Code Box 7-13.

TABLE 7-3: String Functions

Function Name	Operation	Example
Len(*string*)	Returns number of characters in *string*	Len("Smith, Joe") = 10
InStr(*string*,*substring*)	Returns location of *substring* in *string*	InStr("Smith, Joe", ",") = 6
Left(*string*, N) or Right(*string*, N)	Returns the leftmost or rightmost N characters in *string*	Left("Smith, Joe", 3) = "Smi" Right("Smith, Joe", 3) = "Joe"
Mid(*String*, P, N)	Returns N characters from *string* starting at P^{th} character	Mid("Smith, Joe, 3, 2) = "it"
LTrim(*string*) or RTrim(*string*)	Trims blank characters from left (right) end of *string*	LTrim(" Smith, Joe") = "Smith, Joe"

| **VB CODE BOX 7-13.** Code for lstMembers_Click event procedure | ```
Private Sub lstMembers_Click()
  Dim strMemberInfo As String, intNumChar As Integer
  Dim intTwoBlankPos As Integer, strMemberName As String
  Dim intDollarSignPos As Integer, strLateFeeAmount As String
  strMemberInfo = lstMembers.text
  intNumChar = Len(strMemberInfo)'Find length of lstMembers
  intTwoBlankPos = InStr(strMemberInfo, "  ") 'Find two blanks
  strMemberName = Left(strMemberInfo, intTwoBlankPos - 1)
'Name is at left side of lstMembers
  intDollarSignPos = InStr(strMemberInfo,"$") 'Find $ sign
  intNumChar = intNumChar - intDollarSignPos 'Find $$ length
  strLateFeeAmount = Right(strMemberInfo, intNumChar)
'Late fee amount is at right end of lstMembers
  frmVintage.txtCustName.Text = strMemberName
  frmVintage.txtLateFees.Text = strLateFeeAmount
'Move name and late fees to frmVintage
  lstMembers.Clear
  frmMembers.Hide
  frmVintage.txtVideoName.SetFocus
End Sub
``` |

Mini-Summary 7-6: String Functions

1. String functions can be used to search for parts of a string or to extract a substring from within a longer string.

2. Useful string functions include UCase, InStr, Len, Right, Left, and Mid.

It's Your Turn!

1. Using the Instr( ) function, create a user-programmed function that, when passed a string and a character, will count the number of times that the character occurs in the string.

2. Describe the purpose and operation of the function at the top of the next page.
```

```
Public Function strAFun(strWord as String) As String
  Dim intN As Integer
  intN = Len(strWord)
  strAFun = ""
  Do
    strAFun = strAFun & Right(strWord, 1)
    strWord = Left(strWord, Len(strWord) - 1)
  Loop Until Len(strWord) = 0
End Function
```

To modify the Vintage Videos application to search for member names or videos, complete the following exercises.

3. Use the Project Explorer to open the **modVintage7** Code module and use the **Tools|Add Procedure** menu option to create the first and last lines of the **Search** sub. Add the code shown in VB Code Box 7-11.

4. Open the **cmdSearch_Click( )** event procedure on the frmMembers form and add the code shown in VB Code Box 7-12.

5. Open the **lstMembers_Click( )** event procedure and add the code shown in VB Code Box 7-13.

6. Open the cmdSearch_Click( ) event procedure on the frmVideos form, delete all but the first three lines of code, and add the following instruction to invoke the Search sub:

```
Search strVideoName, strVideos(), strVideoLoc(), _
  curVideoPrice(), intNumVideos, "Videos"
```

7. Save the project under the same name.

ADDING TO, DELETING FROM, AND PRINTING LISTS

The owners of the Vintage Videos store have requested that they be able to add members and videos to the respective lists as well as to delete members. Adding members or videos is fairly straightforward, but deleting a member requires more effort.

A straightforward way to add members or videos to the lists is to use the Input-Box function to request information on the new member or video. In the case of a new member, we can assume that after the member name and phone number are entered and added to the membership arrays, the new member name is added to the txtCustName text box on frmVintage. Then, the focus is set back to the Video Name text box on the main form, ready to input the name of the first video to be rented. In addition, the late fees is set equal to zero and copied to the txtLateFees text box on frmVintage. Finally, the current form is hidden. The code for the frmMembers.cmdAdd_Click( ) event procedure is shown in VB Code Box 7-14.

On the other hand, the staff of the video store may need to enter multiple videos, so we need an event-driven input loop controlled by the Add Videos button on the Videos form. That is, by repeatedly clicking on this button, we can enter multiple videos. The code for the cmdAdd_Click( ) event procedure on the frmVideos forms is shown in VB Code Box 7-15.

VB CODE BOX 7-14. Code to add members to the membership list on frmMembers	```Private Sub cmdAdd_Click() strMembers(intNumMembers) = InputBox("Enter new name:") frmVintage.txtCustName.Text = strMembers(intNumMembers) strPhoneNumbers(intNumMembers) = InputBox("Enter phone number:") LateFees(intNumMembers) = 0 frmVintage.txtLateFees.Text = 0 intNumMembers = intNumMembers + 1 frmVintage.txtVideoName.SetFocus frmMembers.Hide End Sub```

VB CODE BOX 7-15. Code to add videos to the video list on frmVideos	```Private Sub cmdAdd_Click() Videos(intNumVideos) = InputBox("Enter new video:") VideoLoc(intNumVideos) = InputBox("Enter video location:") VideoPrice(intNumVideos) = CCur(InputBox("Enter video price:")) intNumVideos = intNumVideos + 1 End Sub```

Deleting a member

In the previous version of the Vintage Video application, we were able to delete members from the combo box by using the combo box RemoveItem command. However, now that the membership list is stored in arrays, there is no corresponding command to carry out this activity. For that reason, we must write a procedure to delete members information from the arrays just as we did to sort an array.

While you may think that deleting an element of an array is nothing more than simply setting the element to be deleted to zero or a blank, this is not the case. Setting the element to a zero or blank does not delete it from the array; it just changes the contents of the array element. To delete an array element in a one-dimensional array, it is necessary to move each element *below* it up one position to replace the contents of the array element and then subtract one from the number of elements in the array. Moving the array elements up has the effect of writing over the element to be deleted with the element below it and then repeating the process until the end of the array is reached. In the process, only the element to be deleted is lost. For the curPrices array, if curPrices(5) is to be deleted, this process is shown in Figure 7-19. Note that after the deletion, there is no curPrices(9) value since the number of elements in the array has been reduced by one.

The pseudocode for the logic behind this process is shown below where the index of the element to be deleted is assumed to be known and is equal to a variable called *DeletedIndex*. By Setting each array element equal to the array element that comes after it, we *write over* the element to be deleted..

```
Begin deletion procedure
     Repeat for each element starting with DeletedIndex
          ArrayElement(Index) = ArrayElement(Index + 1)
     End repeat
End procedure.
```

To delete a member from the strMembers array, we must first find the person to be deleted using their phone number which is assumed to be unique. Next, we would delete their name, phone number, and late fees from the appropriate arrays. We can write the first process as a function since it is to return a single value—the array index

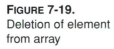

FIGURE 7-19.
Deletion of element
from array

of the person to be deleted. The second process should be written as a procedure which deletes the array elements corresponding to this index. The intFindDelete function to find the array index of the person with the matching phone number is shown in VB Code Box 7-16.

VB CODE BOX 7-16. Function to find array index	```Public Function intFindDelete() As Integer Dim intCounter As Integer, strFindPhoneNum As String intFindDelete = -1 strFindPhoneNum = InputBox("Input phone number to be deleted") For intCounter = 0 To intNumMembers - 1 If strPhoneNumbers(intCounter) = strFindPhoneNum Then intFindDelete = intCounter Exit For End If Next End Function```

Note that the function name is initially set equal to -1 in the intFindDelete function. If no matching phone number is found that is matches that input by the user, it will stay at this value which will be checked in the Delete sub procedure. The Delete sub procedure is shown in VB Code Box 7-17.

In looking at the Delete sub procedure, note that the value of the index is first checked to see if it is not negative; if it is, then no matching phone number was found and the deletion process is aborted. If the index is not negative, then the user is queried if they are sure they want to delete the record for this phone number. If they do, then a For-Next loop going from the index to be delete to the next to last record (Numbers - 2) is used to move the array elements up for the strMembers, strPhoneNumbers, and curLateFees arrays (which were declared globally), and the number of elements in the array (intNumMembers) is reduced by one. If the user decides not to delete the record for this phone number, the process is terminated.

A common way to go about this deletion process would be to find the phone number of the member to be deleted using the Search command button and then to use the Delete command button to actually delete the record. If this is done, you should be aware that the name will *not* be deleted from the list box since there is no direct connection between the arrays and the search list box. However, if you were to click the Search button again, the record would not be displayed.

| **VB CODE BOX 7-17.** Sub to delete array element | ```
Public Sub Delete(intFoundIndex As Integer)
   Dim intCounter As Integer, strOkToDelete As String
   If intFoundIndex >= 0 Then
     strOkToDelete = InputBox("Ok to delete record for " _
     & strPhoneNumbers(intFoundIndex) & " Y or N ?")
   Else
     MsgBox "No one with that phone number!", _
     vbExclamation
     Exit Sub
   End If
   If UCase(strOkToDelete) = "Y" Then
     For intCounter = intFoundIndex To intNumMembers - 2
       strMembers(intCounter) = strMembers(intCounter + 1)
       strPhoneNumbers(intCounter) = strPhoneNumbers(intCounter + 1)
       curLateFees(intCounter) = curLateFees(intCounter + 1)
     Next
     intNumMembers = intNumMembers - 1
   Else
     MsgBox "Record not deleted", vbInformation
   End If
End Sub
``` |

To implement the delete procedure, a single line needs to be added to the cmdDelete_Click( ) event procedure:

```
Delete(intFindDelete)
```

Now when the Delete command button is clicked, the user will be requested to enter a phone number. If this is a valid phone number, they will then be queried as to whether they want to delete this record as seen in Figure 7-20 for the member with phone number of 555-0023. If they answer in the affirmative, the member's record is deleted from the arrays.

FIGURE 7-20.
Message box to check for deletion of record

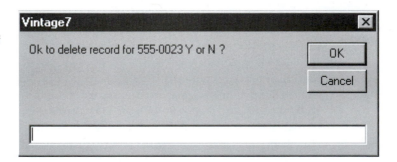

Sorting and Printing a List

To print either list in alphabetical order, we need to sort the corresponding arrays and print them. Since these arrays are not shown in a list or combo box, we need to sort them. Because both the membership and video lists use three similar arrays, we can use a single Sort sub (*Sort*) like that discussed earlier. We can also use a single sub to print the resulting sorted lists (*PrintInfo*). The frmMembers.cmdPrint_Click( ) event procedure that invokes the Sort and PrintInfo subs to sort and print the membership information is shown in VB Code Box 7-18. If we use the same Reverse( ) and Revers-
```

eStr( ) subs as were written for the earlier Sort example, the sub to sort the membership and video lists in order of member names or video names is shown in VB Code Box 7-19.

| **VB Code Box 7-18.** cmdPrint event procedure to print sorted membership list | ```
Private Sub cmdPrint_Click()
  Sort strMembers(), strPhoneNumbers(), curLateFees(), _
    intNumMembers
  PrintInfo strMembers(), strPhoneNumbers(), curLateFees(), _
    intNumMembers
End Sub
``` |
|---|---|

| **VB Code Box 7-19.** Code for Sort sub | ```
Public Sub Sort(strList1() As String, strList2() As String, _
curList3() As Currency, intNum As Integer)
 Dim blnNotSwitched As Boolean, intCounter As Integer
 Dim intNextToLast As Integer
 blnNotSwitched = False
 intNextToLast = intNum - 2
 Do Until blnNotSwitched
    blnNotSwitched = True
    For intCounter = 0 To intNextToLast
      If strList1(intCounter) > strList1(intCounter + 1) Then
        ReverseStr strList1(intCounter), strList1(intCounter + 1)
        ReverseStr strList2(intCounter), strList2(intCounter + 1)
        Reverse curList3(intCounter), curList3(intCounter + 1)
        blnNotSwitched = False
      End If
    Next
  Loop
End Sub
``` |
|---|---|

Note we are using the *full name* to refer to the cmdPrint event procedure, because there is also a cmdPrint event procedure in the frmVideos form. The frmVideos.cmdPrint_Click( ) event procedure to sort and print the video information event procedure will be the same as the frmMembers.cmdPrint_Click( ) event procedure, except for the arguments in each statement invoking the Sort and PrintInfo subs.

The PrintInfo( ) sub to print the sorted lists to the Immediate window using the Debug object is shown in VB Code Box 7-20. Note that we have used the semi-colon delimiter and the **Tab(n)** function. This combination allows us to control the column (n) in which each value is printed. If the membership list is printed, the result is as shown in Figure 7-21.

| **VB Code Box 7-20.** Code for Print sub | ```
Public Sub PrintInfo(strList1() As String, strList2() As _
String, curList3() As Currency, intNumItems As Integer)
  Dim intCounter As Integer
  For intCounter = 0 To intNumItems - 1
    Debug.Print strList1(intCounter);Tab(20); _
    strList2(intCounter); Tab(30); _
    Format(curList3(intCounter),"currency")
  Next
End Sub
``` |
|---|---|
```

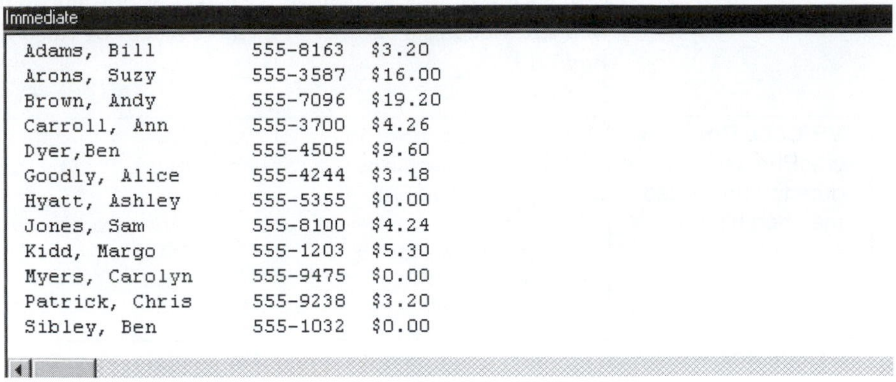

FIGURE 7-21.
Results of printing
the membership list

```
Immediate
  Adams, Bill        555-8163    $3.20
  Arons, Suzy        555-3587    $16.00
  Brown, Andy        555-7096    $19.20
  Carroll, Ann       555-3700    $4.26
  Dyer,Ben           555-4505    $9.60
  Goodly, Alice      555-4244    $3.18
  Hyatt, Ashley      555-5355    $0.00
  Jones, Sam         555-8100    $4.24
  Kidd, Margo        555-1203    $5.30
  Myers, Carolyn     555-9475    $0.00
  Patrick, Chris     555-9238    $3.20
  Sibley, Ben        555-1032    $0.00
```

Modifying the cmdClear and cmdExit Event Procedures

The final modifications we need to make to the Vintage Videos project are to change the cmdClear_Click and cmdExit_Click event procedures. In the first case, we need to add a line to zero out the late fees before starting a new customer. In the second case, we need to save both the membership list and the video list to files using the Write #*n* instruction. We were saving the members' names from the combo box to file, but now that all information is stored in arrays, this event procedure needs to be modified as shown in VB Code Box 7-21.

VB CODE BOX 7-21.
frmVintage code to
exit the project

```
Private Sub cmdExit_Click()
  Dim intCounter As Integer
  Open "a:\members7.txt" For Output As #10
  For intCounter = 0 To intNumMembers - 1
    Write #10, strMembers(intCounter), _
      strPhoneNumbers(intCounter), curLateFees(intCounter)
  Next
  Open "a:videos.txt" For Output As #3
  For intCounter = 0 To intNumVideos - 1
    Write #3, strVideos(intCounter), _
      curVideoPrice(intCounter), strVideoLoc(intCounter)
  Next
  Close #3
  Close #10
  End
End Sub
```

Summary of changes to Vintage Videos Project

We have made a large number of changes and additions to the Vintage Videos project in this chapter—so many that a summary table of the new and modified general and event procedures may be helpful to you. Instead of displaying all of the code for this project, which would take at least four pages, we will use two tables to show you where the code in the various VB Code Boxes should appear, that is, in the code module (modVintage7), the main Vintage Videos form (frmVintage), the membership information form (frmMembers), or the video information form (frmVideos). Table 7-4 lists each VB Code Box in order and indicates what is new about the procedure, its location, and its status, that is, is it new to this chapter or a modification of previous code. On the other hand, Table 7-5 shows the four elements of the Vintage.vbp project, that is, the code module, frmVintage, frmMembers, and frmVideos and lists the VB Code Boxes that contain code that is new or modified in this chapter for that element. If an event procedure is not shown in either table, it is not changed from previous chapters and remains in the Vintage Videos (Vintage.vbp) unchanged. You should consider these two tables to be a *roadmap* to the changes and modifications that have taken place int his chapter. .

TABLE 7-4: Location of Code in VB Code Boxes

VB Code Box	General or event procedure	Location	Status
7-8	cmdCalc_Click	frmVintage	Modified
7-9	Global variable declarations	modVintage7	New
7-10	frmVintage Form_Load event procedure	frmVintage	Modified
7-11	Public Sub Search procedure	modVintage7	New
7-12	cmdSearch_Click event procedure	frmMembers	New
7-13	lstMembers_Click event procedured	frmMembers	New
7-14	cmdAdd_Click event procedure	frmMembers	New
7-15	cmdAdd_Click event procedure	frmVideos	New
7-16	Public Function intFindDelete procedure	modVintage7	New
7-17	Public Sub Delete procedure	modVintage7	New
7-18	cmdPrint_Click event procedure	frmMembers	New
7-19	Public Sub Sort procedure	modVintage7	New
7-20	Public Sub PrintInfo procedure	modVintage7	New
7-21	cmdExit_Click	frmVintage	Modified

TABLE 7-5: Location of New or Modified Code in Vintage.vbp

modVintage7	frmVintage	frmMembers	frmVideos
VB Code Box 7-9	VB Code Box 7-8	VB Code Box 7-12	VB Code Box 7-15
VB Code Box 7-11	VB Code Box 7-10	VB Code Box 7-13	
VB Code Box 7-16	VB Code Box 7-21	VB Code Box 7-14	
VB Code Box 7-17		VB Code Box 7-18	
VB Code Box 7-19			
VB Code Box 7-20			

Mini-Summary 7-7 Adding to, Deleting From, and Printing Lists

1. Adding to an array is simply a matter of increasing the number of elements in the array and copying the new value into the last position in the array.

2. Deleting from an array requires that all elements *below* the element to be deleted be copied up one position and the number of elements decreased by one.

Mini-Summary 7-7 Adding to, Deleting From, and Printing Lists (Continued)

3. The same sort sub can be used to sort different sets of arrays as long as they are the same data types.

4. The semicolon and Tab characters can be used to print arrays in exact positions either on the printer or to the Debug object.

It's Your Turn!

To modify the Vintage Videos application to add a new member or video name, delete an existing member, or print member names or videos, complete the following exercises.

1. Add the code shown in VB Code Box 7-14 to the frmMembers.cmdAdd_Click( ) event procedure. Add the code shown in VB Code Box 7-15 to the frmVideos.cmdAdd_Click( ) event procedure.

2. Add the code shown in VB Code Box 7-18 to the frmMembers.cmdPrint_-Click( ) event procedure. Modify this code to invoke the same subs with the arguments **strVideos( )**, **strVideoLoc( )**, **curVideoPrice( )**, and **intNumVideos,** instead of the membership list arguments. Add this code to the frmVideos.cmdPrint_Click( ) event procedure.

3. Open the Code module and enter the code shown in VB Code Box 7-19 to create the Sort sub. Also, add the code shown in VB Code Box 7-5 to create the Reverse sub. Modify this code by changing the Currency declarations to be String data type declarations to create the ReverseStr sub.

4. Add the code shown in VB Code Box 7-20 to the Code module to print the two lists.

5. Add a single line to the frmVintage.cmdClear_Click( ) event procedure to clear the txtLateFees text box.

6. Replace the existing code in the frmVintage.cmdExit_Click event procedure with the code shown in VB Code Box 7-21. Run your project and test the additional code by adding a new member named **Joe Smith** with the phone number **555-1122**. (Remember to add the name in last-name-first form.) Also, add the videos shown in Table 7-6 to the list of videos.

TABLE 7-6: New Videos

Name	Location	Price
Easy Rider	Drama	$1.99
A Fistful of Dollars	Western	$1.99
Sleeping Beauty	Kids	$.99

7. Test the project by failing to check a customer name. You should be forced to check a customer name before any calculations can be made.

To search for and delete a member using their phone number, complete the following exercises:

8. Open the code module and create the Integer-valued function named **intFindDelete** shown in VB Code Box 7-16.

9. Also in the code module, add the sub procedure **Delete** shown in VB Code Box 7-17. For the cmdDelete_Click( ) event procedure add the single line of code:

```
Delete(intFindDelete)
```

10. Test your delete procedure by searching for all members with a last name beginning with *Smi*. You should find three names. Now delete the member with telephone number of *555-0023*. Search again and you should now see only two names.

To complete the project, carry out the following exercises:

11. Test the Print buttons on both forms. Both lists should be printed in alphabetical order by the name.

12. Finally, use the Exit button to exit the project. Now, run it again and click both print buttons. The member and videos you added in the previous execution should be displayed. They should have been saved to disk when you exited the project before and then reloaded when you ran it again.

13. Save your project as before.

ADDITIONAL TOPICS ON GENERAL PROCEDURES

General procedures are a very useful programming tool, because they provide reusable code as well as reducing the complexity of a project. In this section, we will consider an advanced use of subs and functions termed *passing by value* that combines some of the features of functions with those of subs. We will also consider some of the common errors that occur when you use functions and subs.

Passing by Value in Subs

As we mentioned earlier, parameters in functions and subs share the same memory location with the corresponding arguments in the statement that invokes the sub. When a parameter variable is modified within the sub, the corresponding argument variable is also modified. The argument–parameter pair creates a *two-way* communication link between the sub or function and the statement that invokes it. This is termed **passing by reference**. In the previous examples, the lists passed to the Sort subs were passed by reference and modified by the subs. Another way to pass values into subs and functions is called **passing by value**; in it there is a *one-way* street for passing values into, but not out of, the sub or function.

There are advantages to both approaches; in some cases it is useful to modify the arguments, and in others it is not. For example, while we want to rearrange the lists that are sorted, we probably do not want to change the number of elements in the array that is also passed to the sub. It turns out that it is possible to have it both ways—to pass some parameters by reference and to pass other parameters by value. The default condition is to pass parameters by reference. However, we can change any parameter to passing by value by adding the **ByVal** keyword before it. The *ByVal* keyword is a way to protect an argument from being changed in a sub or function.

When a parameter is defined as being passed by value in a sub or function, it becomes a local variable in the sub that is initialized to the value of the corresponding argument. In essence, it is a *local copy* of the argument that cannot leave the sub.

If we wanted to make sure that the number of array elements would not be modified within the sub that is used to sort the membership and video arrays in the Vintage Videos scenario, the Sub definition statement would be:

```
Public Sub Sort(strList1() As String, strList2() As _
    String, curList3() As Currency, ByVal intNum As Integer)
```
With the use of **ByVal**, if the intNum parameter is changed within the sub, it will *not* be changed outside the sub.

> **TIP:** An alternative way to specify by value passing is to use parentheses around the variable name in the reference statement instead of putting the keyword ByVal in the procedure declaration.

As an example of the effect of the *ByVal* keyword, assume that we will modify the Reverse and ReverseStr subs used in the PartList.vbp project to pass the first parameter by value. The revised Sub definition statement is:

```
Sub Reverse(ByVal curFirst As Currency, curSecond _
    As Currency)
```
If the PartList.vbp project is opened and the Reverse and ReverseStr subs are modified to pass the first parameter by value, the result of running it, sorting the parts list, and displaying the parts would be as shown in Figure 7-22.

FIGURE 7-22. Effect of passing parameters by value

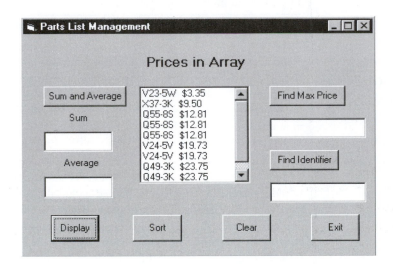

Note in Figure 7-22 that some values are repeated while others are missing. This occurs because the first parameter in the two Reverse subs is not changing while the second parameter is changing.

Common Errors

General procedures have their own special set of errors of which you should be aware, including the number of arguments and parameters not matching, the data types of the arguments and parameters not matching, and arguments being out of order.

In the first case, unless you have defined one or more parameters as optional, then the number of arguments must match the number of parameters. If this error is encountered, one of several error messages referring to a type mismatch will be displayed. Figure 7-23 shows a possible error message.

Figure 7-23 Type mismatch error message

In the second case, unless you have defined parameters as the Variant data type, then the data type of the arguments *must* match the data type of the parameters. If this error occurs, the error message will likely be the same as that for an incorrect number of arguments, since both errors can result in the same situation—a mismatch in the data types. The same type of error can occur when arguments are out of order and data types do not match. However, a worse case is when arguments are out of order but the data types still match. This will *not* result in an error message, but it will result in incorrect results. Using Breakpoints and Watches along with the Local window and Watch window is often the only way to find this error in programmer logic.

It's Your Turn!

1. What is the difference between passing a variable by reference and passing a variable by value? When should you pass a variable by value?

2. Describe how you may use the Watch and Immediate windows to aid in debugging your general procedures.

SUMMARY

In this chapter, we have introduced you to a powerful new programming form—the general procedure. Unlike event procedures, general procedures are not associated with a specific event and can be used anywhere on a form or in the project as needed. They increase the capability of dividing up the work in creating a Visual Basic project. General procedures also offer the potential to reuse code in multiple locations and to reduce the complexity of event procedures.

Two types of general procedures—function procedures and sub procedures—are written by the programmer rather than being built into Visual Basic. Function procedures return a value through their name, while sub procedures (commonly referred to as *subs*) do not return a value. However, subs are very useful for modifying arguments passed to them. Both functions and subs must be invoked by an event procedure or general procedure, and they must be defined in the General object of the form or Code module. When a function or sub is defined, there must be a one-to-one correspondence between the arguments in the calling event or general procedure and the parameters in the function or sub.

A common use of a function is to create a single value that is assigned to a variable or output. The name of the function must be assigned a value in the function. Functions and subs discussed in this chapter included a function to find the income tax due, a sub to sort an array using another sub to reverse two array values, and a sub to search an array.

A sub is often used for manipulating the arguments passed to it. A sub can invoke another sub; for example, a sub to sort an array can invoke a sub to reverse two array elements. Sorting an array requires that nested loops be used to repeat the comparison–reversal process until the array is sorted.

The use of global variables and general procedures was also discussed in this chapter. Global variables are declared in the Code module of the project and are known to all forms and procedures in the project. However, if a global variable is changed anywhere in the project, this change is reflected everywhere. Global general procedures are also defined in the Code module and are known to all forms and procedures.

String functions were used to search for parts of a string or to extract a substring from within a longer string. They were used here to search for partial names. Useful string functions include UCase, InStr, Len, Right, Left, and Mid.

Adding to, deleting from, and printing arrays were also discussed in this chapter. Adding to an array is simply a matter of increasing the number of elements in the array and copying the new value into the last position in the array. Deleting from an array requires that all elements *below* the element to be deleted be copied up one position and the number of elements decreased by one. The same Sort sub can be used to sort different sets of arrays as long as they are the same data types. The semicolon and Tab characters can be used to print arrays in exact positions either on the printer or to the Debug object.

Arguments can be passed to a sub or function by reference or by value. When an argument is passed by reference, if the corresponding parameter is changed in the sub or function, this change is reflected in the argument. If the argument is passed by value, any changes in the corresponding parameter are not reflected in the argument. The ByVal keyword is used in the Procedure definition statement to define an argument to be passed by value.

Errors in using general procedures most often involve the number or type of the arguments not matching the number or type of the corresponding parameters. Having the arguments out of order can also result in an error.

NEW PROGRAMMING STATEMENTS

Statement to reference a programmer-defined function variable = functionName(arg1, arg2, ..., argn)
Statement to reference a programmer-defined sub procedure subName arg1, arg2, ..., argn
Statement to create programmer-defined function **Function** *type*FuncName(parameter1 as type, parameter2 as type, ...) as type
Statement to create programmer-defined sub procedure **Sub** SubName(parameter1 as type, parameter2 as type)
Statement to publicly declare a variable in Code module **Public** varName1 as type, varName2 as type, ...
Statement to declare a parameter to by passed by value **Sub** SubName(**ByVal** parameter1 by type)

KEY TERMS

bubble sort
code module
event procedure
function procedure (function)
general procedure

global declaration
parameter
passing by reference
passing by value

programmer-defined general
procedures
reusable code
sub procedure (sub)

EXERCISES

1. For each of the following, write the scope (local, module, or global) of the variables described.

   a. Variable sngY declared inside sub procedure called CalcInterest.

b. Array variable intAge declared using the keyword Dim in the general declaration section of the form frmEmployee.frm.

c. Variable intSize declared using the keyword Public in the general declaration section of the code module modSearch.mod.

d. Variable blnStatus declared as a parameter of the function blnCheck.

e. Variable intNumber declared using the keyword Dim in the general declaration section of the code module modSort.mod.

2. Write function procedures for each of the following:

a. Write a function that, when passed an array of letter grades and the number of grades, will calculate a grade point average (GPA). Use the scale: A = 4.0, B = 3.0, C = 2.0, D = 1.0, and F = 0.0.

b. Write a function that will have as parameters a single variable representing degrees of temperature and a string variable representing a code that can be either "F" for Fahrenheit or "C" for Celsius. If the code is F, then the original temperature is in degrees Celsius and should be converted to degrees Fahrenheit. If the code is C, then the original temperature is in degrees Fahrenheit and should be converted to degrees Celcius. The formula to convert from Celsius to Fahrenheit is: $F = (9/5)*C + 32$.

c. Write a function that will receive two integer values and return a random number between these values. A formula for doing this using the Rnd function may be written as: Int((intUBnd - intLBnd + 1) * Rnd + intLBnd), where intUBnd is the higher of the two values passed to the function and intLBnd is the lower of the two values passed to the function.

3. Write sub procedures for each of the following:

a. Write a sub procedure that will accept an array of names and the number of names, and return a second array with initials. The original array has names in last name first format separated by a comma and a space, for example "Smith, John." The new array should contain the initials in order with periods, for example "J. S."

b. Write a sub procedure for a computerized testing program that will receive three variables: a boolean variable blnAnswer; an integer variable intNumCorrect; and an integer variable intNumTried. When blnAnswer is True, then intNumCorrect should be incremented and a message should appear saying: "That's Correct." When blnAnswer is False, a message should appear saying: "That's Incorrect." In either case, the variable intNumTried should be incremented and a message should appear showing how many answers are correct out of the number attempted.

c. A short term parking lot charges based on the time a car has been in the lot. Less than 15 minutes is no charge, first half hour is $0.50, second half hour is $0.75, and every portion of an hour after that is $1. In addition, employees who work in a building adjacent to the lot receive a 20% discount of the total parking charge. Write a sub procedure that will receive a boolean variable indicating whether or not a patron works in the adjacent building and two date variables, one representing the time in the parking lot and the other representing the time out. Your sub should calculate the amount owed, display the amount owed in a message to the patron, and pass the amount owed back to the calling routine.

4. For each of the following, explain what is wrong with the code. What error messages would you see, if any? What can you do to fix it?

```
a. Public Sub (sngX As Single) As Boolean
     If sngX >= 0 And sngX < 100 Then
        blnCheck = True
     Else
        blnCheck = False
     End If
   End Sub
b. Public Function lngCube(intX As Integer) As Long
     Dim intX As Integer
     lngCube = intX ^ 3
   End Function
c. Public Function intSum() As Sum
     Public intX As Integer
     Public intY As Integer
     Public intZ As Integer
     intSum = intX + intY + intZ
   End Function
```

5. Use the Visual Basic Help facility or the MSDN on-line library to answer the following questions.

   a. What is a bookmark? How do you use it?

   b. Can public variables in different modules share the same name? If so, how can you differentiate between them in code?

   c. In addition to form and standard modules, what third type of module is available in Visual Basic and what is it used for?

   d. What method can be used to simulate errors when testing your code?

PROJECTS

1. Retrieve Ex6-1.vbp from your data disk and add a button that will invoke a sub to sort and display the student records in *descending order* of the quiz average. Write the corresponding sub(s). Also, write a String data type function to replace the code that assigns a letter grade to each student and a Single data type function to find and display the average of the quiz scores. Finally, write a sub to replace the code to find and display the information on the students with the highest *and* lowest quiz scores. Why could you not write a function for this purpose? Run and test your project with the Student.txt data file. Save your project as **Ex7-1.frm** and **Ex7-1.vbp** in the Chapter7 folder on your data disk.

2. Retrieve Ex6-2.vbp from your data disk and add a button that will invoke a sub to sort the customer names in *descending order* of the sales. Write the corresponding sub(s). Add a button that will invoke a function to find the average sales. Display this value in a text box with an appropriate label. Add a new array that will contain the customer sales status. This status is determined as HIGH if the customer sales are more than 20 percent above average, LOW if the sales are more than 20 percent below average, and AVERAGE otherwise. You will need to add a sub to make this calculation and assignment. Finally, replace the code to find and display the customers with the highest and lowest sales with a sub. Run and test your project with the CustSales.txt data file. Save your project as **Ex7-2.frm** and **Ex7-2.vbp** in the Chapter7 folder on your data disk.

3. Retrieve Ex6-3.vbp from your data disk and add a button that will invoke a sub to sort and display the golfer records in *ascending* order of the golf scores. Write the corresponding sub(s). Replace the code that assigns a designation to each golfer with a String

data type function. Replace the code that finds and displays the name and score of the golfers with highest and lowest scores with a sub. Run and test your project with the Golfers.txt data file. Save your project as **Ex7-3.frm** and **Ex7-3.vbp** in the Chapter7 folder on your data disk.

4. Retrieve Ex6-4.vbp and replace the code used to search for the Zip code for a city name with a function. Also, add a button to invoke a sub to sort the list of cities in alphabetical order and display them and their Zip code in a list box. Add a Click event procedure for the list box that will invoke the same search function you wrote earlier. Add another function that provides the capability of reversing the search—that is, the capability of inputting a Zip code and displaying the corresponding post office. Test your project with the ZipCodes.txt data file and save it as **Ex7-4.frm** and **Ex7-4.vbp** in the Chapter7 folder on your data disk.

5. Retrieve Ex6-5.vbp and replace the code used to find an insurance premium with a function. Test your project with the data shown in Chapter 6 and save it as **Ex7-5.frm** and **Ex7-5.vbp** in the Chapter7 folder on your data disk.

6. Retrieve Ex7-1.vbp and add the Ex6-6Two.frm file to it. Modify this project so that the student names and quiz score arrays are loaded only *once* and all subs and functions are known to both forms. Make the following changes and additions:

    a. Replace the code on the second form with a global sub that will display a given student's average and letter grade.

    b. Replace the code on the second form with a global sub that will respond to the option button by displaying all student names with quiz scores above the corresponding quiz scores (90-80-70-60).

    c. Add a third form which should be named **frmStudentAdd**. The user should be able to switch to this form by clicking a button on the main form. The new form should allow the user to add new students and quiz scores to the student list, determine letter grades for the new students as they are added, and print a list of all students, their quiz scores, and their letter grades in alphabetical order (use existing subs wherever possible).

    d. Modify the Exit button on the main form so that the revised student name and quiz score arrays are saved to the data file upon exit. Test your project with the Student.txt data file.

    e. Save the files as **Ex7-6One.frm, Ex7-6Two.frm, Ex7-6Three.frm, Ex7-6.bas** and **Ex7-6.vbp**.

7. Retrieve Ex7-2.vbp and add the Ex6-7Two.frm file to it. Modify this project so that the customer names and sales arrays are loaded only *once* and all subs and functions are known to both forms. Make the following changes and additions:

    a. Replace the code on the second form with a global function that will display a given customer's sales.

    b. Replace the code on the second form with a global sub that will respond to the option button by displaying all customer names with sales less than a designated value in a list box (use the same values as in Chapter 6).

c. Add a third form, which should be named **frmCustomerAdd**. The user should be able to switch to this form by clicking a button on the main form. The new form should allow the user to add new customers and sales to the customer list and print a list of all customers and their sales in alphabetical order (use existing subs wherever possible).

d. Modify the Exit button on the main form so that the revised customer name and sales arrays are saved to the data file upon exiting the project.

e. Run your project with the CustSales.txt data file. Save the files as **Ex7-7One.frm, Ex7-7Two.frm, Ex7-7Three.frm, Ex7-7.bas** and **Ex7-7.vbp**.

8. Retrieve Ex7-3.vbp and add the Ex6-8Two.frm file to it. Modify this project so that the golfer names and scores arrays are loaded only *once* and all subs and functions are known to both forms. Make the following changes and additions:

a. Replace the code on the second form with a global function that will display a given golfer's score.

b. Replace the code on the second form with a global sub that will respond to the option button by displaying all golfer names with scores above a certain score (use the same values as in Chapter 6).

c. Add a third form, which should be named **frmGolferAdd**. The user should be able to switch to this form by clicking a button on the main form. The new form should allow the user to add new golfers and scores to the golfer list, determine the status for the new golfers as they are added, and print a list of all golfers, their scores, and their status in alphabetical order (use existing subs wherever possible).

d. Modify the Exit button on the main form so that the revised golfer name and score arrays are saved to the data file upon exiting the project.

e. Run your project with the Golfer.txt data file and save it as **Ex7-8One.frm, Ex7-8Two.frm, Ex7-8Three.frm, Ex7-8.bas,** and **Ex7-8.vbp**.

9. Validation of user input is an important part of many programs. In addition, much of the necessary validation is similar from program to program—so much so, that you may find yourself writing similar code over and over to perform the same validation tasks. To save time writing future programs, create a Visual Basic module file of validation functions. This module can then be added to any project that requires input validation. Each function should receive relevant parameters to perform the validation and then return a boolean value. The boolean return value may be true when the input value is correct and false when it is not correct. You will probably need to write different functions for each data type. As a start to your validation library, write functions to validate for the following items:

a. Validate that a string value has been entered into a textbox.
b. Validate that an item entered into a text box is a number.
c. Validate that an integer value falls between an upper and a lower bound.
d. Validate that a string value contains a specific character.
e. Validate that an item has been selected from a list box.

Save your module as **Ex7-9.bas**.

10. Currency exchange rates are important for both the world traveler and the investor alike. But since they fluctuate on a daily basis, it is often difficult to keep up with answers to questions such as: How many pesos are equivalent to a 1 US dollar? How many French francs make a Japanese yen? If a pound of tea costs 10 Russian rubles,

what does it cost in China? Write a Visual Basic project to create a table of equivalent currency values. Include a subroutine that will read a file containing a list of currencies and the equivalent amount in US dollars. Each record in this file will contain a String representing the currency name, and a value representing the amount of the currency equal to 1 US dollar, for example "FR francs", 6.75 would mean that 6.75 French francs are equal to one US dollar. Create a second sub procedure that will generate a table like that shown in Table 7-7. By reading across the table, we can read the amount of foreign currency indicated by the column heading that equals one unit of the curency indicated by the row heading. Create two functions to perform your calculations. One function may be used to calculate the exchange values between one US dollar and any given foreign currency. The second function may be used to calculate exchange values between two foreign currencies. Note that to find values between two foreign currencies you may need two conversions, the first currency to US dollars followed by converting US dollars to the second currency. Save your project as **Ex7-10.-frm**, and **Ex7-10.vbp**.

TABLE 7-7: Currency Exchange Table

	US Dollar	**Fr. Franc**	**Jap. Yen**	**Mex. Peso**
US dollar	1	7.29	124.03	9.405
Fr franc	0.137	1	17.01	1.29
Jap. yen	0.0081	0.059	1	13.19
Mex. new peso	0.106	.775	0.076	1

11. Chef Lutz has been keeping a recipe collection for years on notecards. He has recently decided to save these recipes in two files. One file will contain a list of ingredients and amounts while the other will be a text file containing the step-by-step instructions. He would like to have a Visual Basic program to help him manage his recipe collection. An interesting twist to his collection is that some of his recipes were obtained in his homeland of Germany, while others were obtained in the United States. The main difficulty this brings is in converting the various measures from German to US measures and vice versa. He has decided to input each file using its original values and measurements and then incorporate into the program the capability of converting between the measurement scales. An example recipe file is shown in Table 7-8.

TABLE 7-8: Recipe File Format

"American Apple Pie"
"Serves:", 8 **"Scale:", "American"** **"Items:", 6** **"White Flour", 2.4, "cups"** **"Sugar", 2, "tbsp"** **"Salt", .25, "tsp"** **"Cold Butter", 0.5, "cups"** **"Vegetable Shortening", 5, "tbsp"** **"water", 8, "tbsp"**

Build a recipe management project for Chef Lutz. Include as many general sub procedures and functions in your code as possible. Your project should allow Chef Lutz to enter a new recipe, retrieve a recipe by selecting it from a list box (you may need another file with a list of recipe names), convert a recipe from American measures to European measures and vice versa, calculate measures when the required number of people to serve is different from the amount served by a particular recipe, and print a recipe with calculated measures. Conversion factors for some common measurements are found in Table 7-9 as are some internal American conversion factors. Save your project as **Ex7-11.-frm,** and **Ex7-11.vbp.**

TABLE 7-9: Recipe Conversion Factors

	American	European
Flour	1 cup	125 grams
Sugar or Butter	1 cup	250 grams
Liquids	1/4 cup 1 cup 1 quart	5 cL 2.5 dL 1 L
	2 tablespoons = 1 ounce	
	1 cup = 8 ounces	
	3 teaspoons = 1 tablespoon	

12. One way to compute a person's fitness level is based on the time that it takes for the person to walk 3 miles without running. Table 7-10 shows the standards for five general fitness levels for a woman from 20 to 29 years of age. These standards can be extended to men by subtracting 2 minutes from each of the times listed in the table. They can be extended to younger people, aged 13 to 19 years, by subtracting 1 minute from each time.

TABLE 7-10: Fitness Level Standards (Women, 20–29)

Fitness Level	Time to Walk 3 Miles
1	Over 48 minutes
2	Over 44 but less than or equal to 48 minutes
3	Over 40 but less than or equal to 44 minutes
4	Over 36 but less than or equal to 40 minutes
5	36 minutes or less

Write a program that can determine a person's fitness level based on these standards. Your program should allow the user to enter the person's first and last name, age, gender, and time to walk 3 miles in minutes. Be sure to validate all input using an appropriate function. The program should store the input information in a fitness profile structure along with the person's fitness level. Create a function that will determine the fitness level based on the input. The fitness profile should also be displayed as a report on the screen. If the person's age is outside of the 13 to 29 age, display a message indicating that the fitness level cannot be determined. Use as many general sub and function procedures as needed. Save your project as **Ex7-12.frm,** and **Ex7-12.vbp.**

PROJECT: JOE'S TAX ASSISTANCE (CONT.)

That Sunday afternoon, Angela and Joe took Zooey home to her parents and joined them for dinner. Joe was having a conversation with Tony, Zooey's father, as they grilled a few steaks on the barbecue.

"Thanks for having Zooey over for the weekend. Did you have a nice time?" Tony asked.

"Oh, yes! Zooey is always a delight to have around. We did some swimming and worked on the tax program that she's helping me with," replied Joe. "How was your weekend?"

"Not so great up to now. I had to work most of the time. My crew is working on the new building downtown."

"Why are you having to work on the weekends? Aren't you the boss?"

Tony responded, "That's why I had to go in. We've been having some problems with a couple of our subcontractors and I had to go in to straighten them out. That's what the boss does."

"What are the problems?" Joe inquired.

"Are you familiar with how subcontracting works? Basically, each subcontractor, such as a plumber or an electrician, has a specific job to do. We supply the subcontractor with information in the form of blueprints and materials, the subcontractor does the job, and then supplies us with a finished product. In one case, the right materials for installing the bathroom fixtures weren't getting to the plumber. In another, the electricians—who, by the way, had the right material—just weren't doing the job right."

A light went on in Joe's mind. He smiled and said, "That sounds like functions and subroutines."

Perplexed, Tony demanded, "What are you talking about?"

"Today Zooey was explaining some programming techniques called functions and subroutines. They sound a lot like your subcontractors. They are basically smaller programs with specific duties to perform. The main program, or the general contractor in your case, sends material in the form of variables to the subprogram, the subprogram does its job, and sends back values to the main program. The main program is like you: It supervises. It decides when the subprogram should be called and what it should get."

"Zooey said you were excited about this program you're writing," Tony remarked. "It sounds like you're learning a lot."

"Yes, I'm quite excited. The neat thing is that many of the programming techniques end up like something in real life. The trick to understanding them sometimes boils down to just finding the right analogy."

"An old dog like you ought to have plenty of life's analogies in that head of yours. Let's go have a steak."

Questions

1. Write a function for your tax program that calculates the value to be entered on line 36 of the 1040 form. The program will pass the number of exemptions and the adjusted gross income to the function, and the function will return the value for line 36. The instructions for the 1040 line 36 should give you ideas on how to write the function.

2. Write a subroutine procedure for calculating the tax for line 38 of the 1040 form. The calculated tax will depend on the value of line 37 (Taxable Income) and the tax category of the person (Single, Married filing jointly, etc.). Use the Tax Rate Schedules in the 1040 booklet to guide you in writing the subroutine.

3. Run and test your program.

8   Security, Menus, and Files

Learning Objectives

After reading this chapter, you will be able to:

❖ Require a password to protect the information system from unauthorized access.

❖ Create a menu for a project using the Menu Editor.

❖ Add code to the menu items to execute actions when an item is selected.

❖ Create a memo editor using a multiline text box.

❖ Add and use the common dialog box control to open, save, and close files.

❖ Work with the Windows clipboard to cut, copy, and paste information in the memo editor.

❖ Use a menu control array to control many menu items with one event procedure.

Scenario: Adding More Functionality to the Vintage Videos Project

"Hi, Ed. What are you doing?" Clark asked as he doffed his coat and backpack. "By the way you're whistling, you must be having fun."

Ed looked up from his video catalog as he finished off the chorus to *Singing in the Rain.* "Hi, Clark. I've been thinking of placing some orders to increase our selection of musicals. You know, Fred Astaire, Gene Kelly. Many of our more romantic customers just love that kind of film."

"It sounds like you might enjoy them yourself," Clark prodded.

"I have to admit, the tunes are catchy," Ed replied.

It had been several weeks since the grand opening of Vintage Videos, and business was booming. Because of their initial success, the owners had decided to hire some part-time help to mind the counters. This would allow them time to take care of the management aspects of their small business and, they hoped, give them time to enjoy the fruits of their labors. In addition, they found it necessary to purchase additional computer equipment to increase their checkout capacity.

"What brings you down today?" Ed asked. "You've been so busy with your studies lately that you only seem to appear around supper time."

"Now that you mention it, I am getting hungry," Clark replied with a grin. "Actually, Yvonne called to let me know that the new computers had arrived, and since midterms are over I have some time to help you get them set up. I also have a few things to do to our Visual Basic program."

"The computers are still in their boxes. They are in the back room awaiting your inspection," Ed explained. "The program is working great so far. The member search routine you added seemed to really speed it up. But I also have a couple of things I'd like to see if you can include. What were you planning to do?"

"For one thing, I think it would look more professional if I changed some of the interface to a menu system instead of all buttons. Most programs for Microsoft Windows have menus and use buttons for shortcuts."

"That sounds okay, but will it make it harder to use?" Ed inquired thoughtfully.

"Not really. Menus are still very easy to use, and they also provide a way to better organize the commands. For instance, I can group all file-related commands on one menu and have other menus for working with video or member data," Clark continued.

"Great! It sounds like you have been giving the program some thought," said Ed. "The new clerks we've hired have given me a couple of ideas. For one, would it be possible to put a password on the system so that not just anybody can start it up each day?"

"Hmmm, I think so. It would be a matter of checking a password the user enters against the system password that we designate. I'll give it some thought."

"Second, the clerks occasionally leave us notes and memos to let us know about video requests. Can we add a capability for recording comments or memos?"

A smile started to appear on Clark's face. "That sounds like you need a sort of an in-house e-mail system. That would be neat. I'll have to think about how to do it though, but it would be good practice. I'll get started after I set up the computers."

Excited, Clark headed to the back room, seemingly unaware of the spring in his step and the tune he was now whistling. Ed smiled to himself and thought: "I told him those tunes are catchy."

Discussion of Scenario

In this chapter, we have several major points to address for the Vintage Videos information system: including a password system to ensure that only authorized persons are starting the system each day; changing from a button-oriented interface to one that uses menus; and developing a system in which memos can be created, edited, saved, and printed.

Ed and Yvonne have asked Clark to add password protection to the information system he has been creating to protect it from unauthorized access. They also feel that it would be very useful to add a memo creation and editing element to the information system. This would enable them to enter requests from customers for particular movies, to write memos to Clark about problems and suggestions for the information system, and to write memos to themselves, to each other, and to staff regarding issues or problems as they arise.

Replacing the button-oriented interface with a menu-driven one is Clark's idea as a way to respond to the need for a memo creation system with an interface that is more professional-looking and easier to use. For this reason, we will deal with creating a menu interface before we create the memo creation and editing system.

USING PASSWORDS FOR SECURITY

Security is an important concept in information systems that is aimed at protecting them from unauthorized entry. Virtually every day you hear about a hacker breaking into a computer system for "fun" or with criminal intent. One of the most widely used (and abused) systems for providing protection for an information system is to require a **password** that is known only to an authorized user. The user is typically given some number of chances to enter his or her password, which is compared to the password associated with the user's account ID number. If the user does not enter the correct password within the allotted number of tries—say, three—then the user is "kicked off" the system.

> **TIP:** Passwords should be at least six characters long and should not be anything that can be easily guessed, like Test, Password, or first names of family members.

Password Security System

To create a password validation system for Vintage Videos, we need to add a form that will request the user to enter a password when the project is started. Associated with the Form_Load event for the new form should be a procedure that will request the user to enter a password. The sequence of characters entered by the user should be checked against the correct password and, if the sequence is correct, the frmVintage form should be displayed. The user should be given three chances to enter a correct password before the project is automatically terminated.

To add a password form, you should either click the New Form icon or select the **Project | New Form** menu option. In either case, a new form is added to the project. Table 8-1 shows the properties for this form that should be set at design time.

TABLE 8-1: Password Form Properties

Property	Value
Name	frmPassword
Caption	Password
BorderStyle	Fixed Single
Control Box	False

You should be familiar with the first two properties (Name and Caption), but the BorderStyle and Control Box properties are new to you. The **BorderStyle** property determines the style for the border of the form. Since we do not want the user moving or resizing the password form, we set it to *Fixed Single* to prevent movement or resizing. Also, since we do not want the user closing the box without entering a valid password, we set the **Control Box** property to False. This presents an immovable form that cannot be resized or closed without the user entering a valid password.

> **TIP:** To create a secure password that is easy for you to remember, make-up your own rule for creating your password based on something you can remember and using a variety of keyboard characters.

We also need to include a single text box, *txtPassword*, and two command buttons—one to accept the password that has been entered in the text box (*cmdAccept*) and one to cancel the password process and exit the project (*cmdCancel*). The resulting password form is shown in Figure 8-1. Note that since there is no control box in the upper left-hand corner of the form, a user cannot bypass the form without entering a password.

FIGURE 8-1.
Password form

When the password form shown in Figure 8-1 is displayed, the user must enter the correct password in the text box and click the Accept button (or press ENTER). If they want to terminate the password entry process and exit the project, they would click the Cancel button (or press ESC).

Making frmPassword the Startup Object

Note that just adding the frmPassword form does not make it the first form that is displayed. Unless the project properties are changed, the first form added to the project is the first form displayed—the **Startup object**. To make a different form or module the Startup object, the **Project|Properties** menu option should be selected. If this is done, the Project Properties dialog box shown in Figure 8-2 will be displayed, with the current Startup object (frmVintage) being displayed in the Startup object window. Using the drop-down list box, we can change the Startup object—in this case, to frm-Password. If this is done, the Password form will be displayed when the project is started. The combination of making frmPassword the Startup object and giving it a fixed border with no control box means that the user must go through it to reach any other forms in the project.

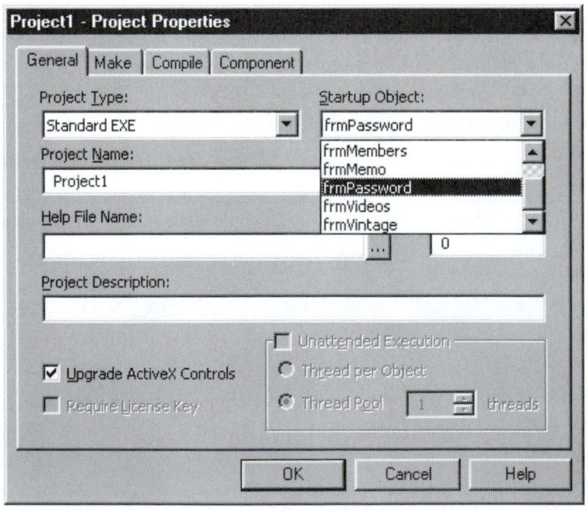

FIGURE 8-2.
Startup object
dialog box

Setting Other Properties for the Password Form

The txtPassword text box has two very useful properties for checking whether the user has entered a valid password: the Tag and PasswordChar properties. The **Tag** property is a string that can be associated with a text box (and other controls) at design time and is not available to the application's user. This property is useful for storing extra data needed for the project. By setting the Tag property of the text box at design time, we have an easy way to check whether the user has entered the correct password.

The **PasswordChar** property for a text box sets the character that will be displayed when the user types characters into the text box. For example, if we set the PasswordChar property to the asterisk (*), this character will be displayed in place of every character, while the Text property for the text box is still whatever the user typed. This provides protection from someone reading the password off the screen as it is being input.

For the two command buttons, there are two new properties of interest: the Default and Cancel properties. If the **Default** property is set to True for a command button, then its Click event will be executed when the **ENTER** key is pressed. On the other hand, if the **Cancel** property is set to True for a command button, then its Click event is activated by the **ESC** key. In both cases, to avoid conflicts, only *one* command button on the form can have the Default property set to True and only *one* command button can have the Cancel property set to True. For the Password form, the cmdAccept button's Default property should be set to True and the cmdCancel button's Cancel property should be set to True. This enables the user to enter a password and press ENTER to accept it, or to press ESC to cancel the password entry process. The properties for the controls on the Password form are summarized in Table 8-2.

TABLE 8-2: Controls and Properties for Password Form

Control	Property	Value
txtPassword	Tag	MorrisTheCat
txtPassword	PasswordChar	* (asterisk)
cmdAccept	Default	True
cmdCancel	Cancel	True

Adding Code to the Password Form

The code for the Accept button compares the contents of the text box to the Tag property of the text box using the UCase function to convert both the user's input (txtPassword.text) and the txtPassword Tag property into uppercase characters. If the user has entered the correct password and there is a match, this form is closed with the Unload Me command (the *Me* keyword is a shortcut way of referring to the current form) and the focus is shifted to the customer name text box on the main form. The **Unload** command is used here instead of the Hide method, since the form will not be used again and should be removed from memory.

> **Tip:** While you are testing your password system, set the Text property of the password text box to the password to avoid repeatedly entering the password. Clear the text box before using the project.

On the other hand, if the user has entered an incorrect password, there is no match and the user is requested to try again. After three attempts to enter the correct password, the user is not allowed any more attempts and the project is terminated. The number of attempts at entering a correct password is saved in the Static variable *int-NumTries,* so it is not reset between Click events of the Accept button. The code for the Accept button is shown in VB Code Box 8-1, and the dialog when an incorrect password (*morris*) is entered is shown in Figure 8-3 (the correct password is *MorrisThe-Cat*).

Mini-Summary 8-1: Password Security

1. Passwords are a common method of providing security for information systems.

2. Password protection can be added to a Visual Basic project with the Tag property of a text box and a startup form to which the user must respond.

3. The user's input to the text box can be compared to the Tag property; if the user fails to match the Tag property in three tries, the project is terminated.

VB Code Box 8-1. Code for Accept button	

```
Private Sub cmdAccept_Click()
   Static intNumTries as Integer
   If UCase(txtPassword.text) = UCase(txtPassword.Tag) Then
     frmVintage.Show   'Go to main form
     Unload Me
   Else 'No match found
     intNumTries = intNumTries + 1 'Increase number of attempts
     If intNumTries >= 3 Then 'Too many attempts
       MsgBox "Too many attempts", vbCritical, "Access Denied"
       End
     Else 'Try again
       MsgBox "Press Ok and try again", vbExclamation, _
       "Incorrect Password"
       txtPassword.Text = ""
       txtPassword.SetFocus
     End If
   End If
End Sub
```

Figure 8-3. Entry of incorrect password

It's Your Turn!

1. Why is the system exited after three attempts at entering the password?

2. Why do we use an asterisk as the password character?

3. How can you avoid having to enter the password during the development and testing process?

4. What property is set to **True** for a command button to cause its Click event to be executed when the **Enter** key is pressed?

5. What is the **Static** keyword used for?

6. Would the tag property be appropriate for storing passwords for multiple users? Why or why not? What could you do differently?

To revise the Vintage Videos project to use a password to check for unauthorized users, do the following:

7. Start Visual Basic and open the **Vintage7.vbp** project from the Chapter7 folder on your data disk.

8. Use the Add Form icon or the **Project|Add Form** menu selection to add a new form to the project which should be named **frmPassword**. Create a new folder on your data disk named **Chapter8** and save the password form as **Password.frm** in this folder. Change the properties for the form to those shown in Table 8-1.

9. Use the **Project|Properties** menu selection to make frmPassword the Startup object.

10. Add the text box, label, and command buttons as shown in Figure 8-1 to the Password form, and give them the names and captions discussed in the text. Change their properties to those shown in Table 8-2.

11. Add the code shown in VB Code Box 8-1 to the Click event for the cmdAccept command button. Add the End command to the cmdCancel command button.

12. Run the project and test the password form by entering the correct password (*MorrisTheCat*). Exit the project and run it again and enter an incorrect password three times. What happens? Use the **File|Save as...** option to create a new folder with a name of Chapter8. Save the project as **Vintage8.vbp** in the Chapter8 folder on your data disk.

CREATING A MENU SYSTEM FOR VINTAGE VIDEOS

The owners of Vintage Videos have asked Clark to add a memo creation and editing feature to the information system he has been developing. This will add a capability to the system beyond that of processing transactions. In thinking about this new feature, Clark has realized that another button on the main form—in addition to the six that are already there (Check Name, Find Video, Calculate, Print, Clear, and Exit) plus the three video type option buttons—would make the screen entirely too cluttered. To make the memo capability available to the user, while at the same time not adding buttons, Clark has decided to revise the screen to use menus.

Menus from which users select an option have been a part of computer programs for many years, going back to the days when the text-oriented DOS operating system controlled the majority of personal computers. Menus are easy to use, while providing the user with a wide variety of options. You have been using a menuing system since we first introduced you to Visual Basic back in Chapter 2. While command buttons are useful for many operations and are widely used on Windows toolbars, menus are able to provide many more choices in a more compact manner.

Using the Menu Editor

Menu Editor

To make creating menus in Visual Basic easy, a **Menu Editor** has been included in the development system. To access the Menu Editor, click the Menu Editor icon from the standard toolbar or select the **Tools | Menu Editor** menu option. This will cause the Menu Editor dialog box to be displayed, as shown in Figure 8-4.

With the Menu Editor, it is possible to create custom menus for your application and to assign properties to them with the dialog box options. These options include creating a caption for a menu item, naming it, assigning a shortcut key to a menu item, initially enabling a menu item, and adding or deleting menu items. At the bottom of the dialog box is a list box that displays a hierarchical list of menu items. Submenu items are indented to indicate their hierarchical position or level. Table 8-3 shows some of the more commonly used Menu Editor dialog box options and their results.

FIGURE 8-4. Menu Editor dialog box

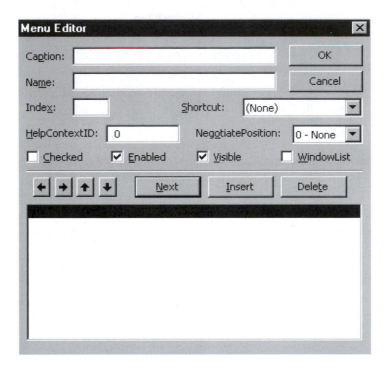

Application to Vintage Videos

To see how the Menu Editor works, we will use it to convert some of the existing buttons into menu items and to add new functionality through menus. We will demonstrate additional uses of the Menu Editor when we use it in the menu creation and editing system.

To start with, we need to decide the menu structure for the main Vintage Videos form. One criterion for deciding when operations should remain as buttons and which should be converted to menu items is frequency of use. A rule of thumb is that frequently used operations should remain as buttons, since they are easier to find and click than menu items. In our case, there are six command buttons and three option

TABLE 8-3: Commonly Used Menu Editor Dialog Box Options

Dialog Box Option	Action	Result
Caption	Enter a caption for menu item	Caption appears in menu list
Name	Enter a name for menu item	Use this name for menu item in code
Index	Assign a numeric value	Determines menu item's position in a control array
ShortCut	Select a shortcut key	Menu item can be selected directly with a shortcut key
Checked	Check or uncheck this check box	Determines if menu item initially has a check mark beside the menu caption
Enabled	Check or uncheck this check box	Determines if menu item can respond to events
Visible	Check or uncheck this check box	Determines if menu item is initially visible
Left/Right Arrows	Click an arrow	Creates a menu item as a main menu item or submenu item
Up/Down Arrows	Click an arrow	Moves menu item up/down
Next	Click button	Moves to next line in menu list
Insert	Click button	Inserts a blank menu item above current line
Delete	Click button	Deletes current menu item

buttons on this form, and only the Calculate command button and the three option buttons are used for every video. Three others—Check Name, Print, and Clear—*may* be used for each customer (if the clerk forgets to use the Check Name button, the validation routine added in Chapter 7 requests that they do so before continuing). The Find Video button is used only when a customer asks if the store carries a particular video, and the Exit button is used only at the end of the day. Based on this frequency of use, we should leave the Calculate, Print, and Clear operations as command buttons and the Video Type selections as option buttons. On the other hand, it would seem appropriate to convert the Check Name, Find Video, and Exit buttons to menu items along with the new Create Memo operation. Table 8-4 shows the various operations and whether they will be command buttons or menu items.

Once the type of control for each operation is decided, the next step is to decide on the number of main menu items under which the menu items will fall. While we could put all five operations on the menu bar, this would quickly clutter it. Instead, we need to include the operations in submenus that are displayed whenever a menu bar item is selected. Of the five operations, it would seem that the Check Member and Find Video operations fall under a menu bar item of *Members/Videos*, and the Create Memo operation should fall under a *Memo* menu bar item. Finally, it is traditional for the Exit operation to fall under a *File* menu bar item. For completeness, we should also

TABLE 8-4: Operations and Type of Control

Operation	Type of Control
Video Type selection	option buttons
Calculate	command button
Print	command button
Clear	command button
Exit	menu item
Check Name	menu item
Find Video	menu item
Create Memo	menu item

include a *Help* menu bar item under which we will include an About operation that will display information about the project. Table 8-5 shows the menu bar headings and the submenu items that will fall under each one.

TABLE 8-5: Main Menu Headings with Submenu Items

Menu Bar Item	Submenu items
File	Exit
Members/Videos	Check Member Find Videos
Memos	Create Memo
Help	About

Using the Menu Editor

To use the Menu Editor to create a menu bar for the Vintage Videos application, we need to first click on the Menu Editor icon or select the Tools|Menu Editor menu option, as discussed earlier. This will display the Menu Editor dialog box shown in Figure 8-4.

The next step is to enter the caption for the first menu bar item—**File**—in the caption text box of the Menu Editor dialog box and then give it a name. Names for menu controls begin with the prefix *mnu*, so an appropriate name for this menu bar item would be *mnuFile*, which should be entered in the Name text box. Since the File menu bar item is not part of a menu control array, and we do not want it checked but do want it enabled and visible, no other Menu Editor dialog box options should be changed. The File menu bar item now appears as the first item in the menu list box at the bottom of the dialog box.

To include the exit operation under the File menu bar item, the next step is to click the **Next** button and then the **right arrow** button. This will advance the pointer to the next menu item and make it a submenu item to the File menu bar item. If you then enter a caption of **Exit** with a name of *mnuFileExit*, the Menu Editor dialog box will appear as shown in Figure 8-5. Submenu items usually include the name of the submenu and the menu item to which they belong. While this can generate long names, it enables someone reading your code to understand the relationship of the submenu item to the overall menu structure.

In Figure 8-5, note that the File menu bar item is flush with the left margin, but the Exit submenu item is indented and preceded by four dots (....) to indicate that it is a submenu item to the menu bar item above it.

FIGURE 8-5. Menu Editor dialog box

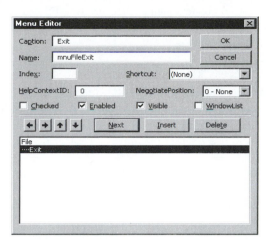

To create the second menu bar item—*Members/Videos*—first you need to press **Next** and the **left arrow** button to *outdent* back to the menu bar level. Note: Performing these actions in the reverse order results in the Exit submenu item being made a menu bar item! Second, you then enter the caption for this item—**Members/Videos**—and the name—*mnuMemVid*. The two submenu items are entered in the same way as the Exit submenu item, except that you do not need to press the right arrow button for the second submenu item. Pressing the Next button enables you to enter the caption and a name for it at the same level as the first submenu item.

> **TIP:** The following common menu creation errors will result in syntax errors: failure to provide values for the Name and Caption properties, attempting to add a check to a top-level menu, and attempting to assign a shortcut key to a top-level menu.

Access and Shortcut Keys

In addition to clicking on a menu option to select it, we can create access and shortcut keys for the menu and submenu options. An **access key** is a key on the keyboard that by itself or combined with the Alt key can be used to access a menu or submenu option. For example, if the access key for the File menu bar option is F, then pressing Alt and F together (press Alt and while holding it down, press F) will display the File submenu. Access keys for submenus do not require the Alt key to activate the submenu option. For example, if X is the access key for the File|Exit option, then once the submenu is displayed, you can press X by itself to exit the project. Access keys are denoted on the menu and submenu by being underlined—for example, File and Exit.

To create an access key, you simply place an ampersand (&) immediately before the letter in the menu caption in the Menu Editor that you wish to be the access key. For example, to make F the access key for the File menu option, the caption for mnuFile in the Menu Editor should be changed to &*File*. Similarly, to make X an access key for the File|Exit option, the caption should be changed to *E&xit*.

Shortcut keys are a special set of keys with which you can directly access a submenu option (main menu items or menu or submenu items with submenu items cannot have a shortcut key). Shortcut keys are typically the function keys (F1, F2, and so on) or the Ctrl or Shift key combined with a letter and/or a function key. For example, if F5 is the shortcut key to create a memo, then pressing F5 will take you directly to the Memo form without going through the menu system. Shortcut keys are displayed on the menu or submenu list to the right of the item.

> **TIP:** Access keys that appear on the same menu must be different. However, the same access key may be used on different menus. All shortcut keys must be different, but you should try to use industry standard shortcut keys to establish a consistent look and feel. For example, use Ctrl+C for copy or Ctrl+S for save.

To create a shortcut key, you simply choose one from the list of available key combinations in the Shortcut key drop-down list on the Menu Editor. For example, if you want to use the F2 function key as a shortcut to the File|Exit option, you select this key from the Shortcut key list.

If all of the menu bar and submenu items shown in Table 8-5 are entered using the Menu Editor, the resulting dialog box is shown in Figure 8-6. Figure 8-7 shows the resulting menu system for the Vintage Videos project with the Members/Videos menu bar item selected. Note the underlined access keys and shortcut keys listed to the right of the submenu options.

FIGURE 8-6. Menu Editor after menu items are entered

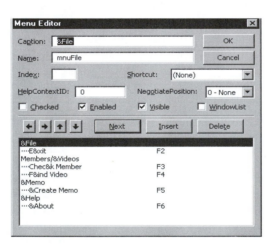

FIGURE 8-7. Members/Videos submenu

Mini-Summary 8-2: Using the Menu Editor

1. The Menu Editor makes it easy to create menu system for any Visual Basic application by entering a caption, name, and selecting any other options for the menu item.

2. Menu item names include a prefix of *mnu*, while submenu items also include any menu and submenus names to which the submenu belongs.

3. Hierarchical levels in the menu system are controlled by the indention of submenu items and outdention of menu items.

4. Access keys can be assigned by including an ampersand (&) in the caption, and shortcut keys can be assigned by selecting from a drop-down list box.

It's Your Turn!

1. Why would we replace command buttons with a menu system?

2. What are the menu options that almost always appear in a Windows-based system menu system?

3. What is the difference between access and shortcut keys?

4. What shortcut keys are standard for Windows applications?

Completing the remaining questions will enable you to create the Visual Basic project discussed in the text.

5. Make **frmVintage** the current form and use the Menu Editor icon on the tool bar or the **Tools | Menu Editor** menu option to open the Menu Editor dialog box. Identify each of the elements of the dialog box shown in Table 8-3.

6. Use the Menu Editor to enter the items shown in Table 8-5 with the captions, names, access keys, and shortcut keys (where applicable) shown in Table 8-6.

TABLE 8-6: Menu Captions, Names, Access Keys, Shortcut Keys, and Types

Menu Element Caption	Name	Access Key	Shortcut Key	Type
&File	mnuFile	F		Menu bar
E&xit	mnuFileExit	x	F2	Submenu
Members/&Videos	mnuMemVid	V		Menu bar
Chec&k Member	mnuMemVidCheck	k	F3	Submenu
F&ind Video	mnuMemVidFind	i	F4	Submenu
&Memo	mnuMemo	M		Menu bar
&Create Memo	mnuMemoCreate	C	F5	Submenu
&Help	mnuHelp	H		Menu bar
&About	mnuHelpAbout	A	F6	Submenu

This table also indicates if an item is a menu bar item (flush left in the menu list) or a submenu item (indented). Use the access keys and shortcut keys. Your resulting menu list should appear as shown in Figure 8-6, and the menu bar on the Vintage form should appear as shown in Figure 8-7.

7. Save the revised form and project under their existing names.

ADDING CODE TO MENU ITEMS

Creating a menu system for a Visual Basic application is just the first step in using menu items to execute procedures in response to events. The second step is to write the code for the menu item Click event procedure. The Click event is the only event for *all* menu items. This step is similar to that used to add code to the event procedures we discussed earlier, with two exceptions. First, there will be no code for menu bar items that have submenus; all of the code will be associated with the submenu items. For example, there will be no code for the mnuFile menu bar item, since it has a submenu. There will be code for mnuFileExit item, since it is a submenu with no additional submenu. Second, instead of double-clicking a control to display the corresponding default event procedure, you click the menu item *once* to display the Code window.

If the code being added to menu or submenu items contains totally new code, then the code is entered the same as for any other event. On the other hand, when an application like Vintage Videos is being converted from using command buttons or other controls to using a menu system, many of the code procedures for the command buttons can be transferred to the menu items without having to be retyped. We will consider this case first.

Converting Event Procedures

In the Vintage Videos application, three command buttons (Check Name, Find Video, and Exit) are being converted to submenu items. While we could retype the code for these event procedures, it is much more efficient to use the Editor capabilities of Visual Basic to *cut and paste* the code from the command button event procedure to the corresponding submenu item event procedure. This entails a six-step process (all at design time):

1. Open the Code window by double-clicking the command button for which the code is to be transferred.
2. Use the mouse to highlight the code for that event procedure [do not include the first (Sub) and last (End Sub) statements].
3. Cut the code using the **Edit | Cut** menu option (use **Ctrl-x** as a shortcut for this operation) and delete the first and last statements of the empty event procedure.
4. Open the Code window for the corresponding submenu item Click event by clicking it *once* or by just changing to the menu item in the Code window.
5. Paste the code into the submenu item Click event procedure using the **Edit | Paste** menu option (use **Ctrl-v** as a shortcut for this operation).
6. Delete the command button control from the form.

For example, to transfer code from the Exit command button Click event procedure to the Exit submenu item Click event procedure at design time, here are the six steps:

1. Open the cmdExit_Click Code window by double-clicking the Exit command button.
2. Highlight the code for this event procedure with the mouse, as shown in Figure 8-8.
3. Use **Edit|Cut** to remove the highlighted code and delete the first and last statements of the now empty event procedure.
4. Open the Code window for the mnuExit procedure by clicking the File menu bar option and then clicking the Exit submenu option.
5. Use **Edit|Paste** to paste the code into the event procedure.
6. Click the View Object button on the Project Explorer to display the frmVintage form; highlight the Exit command button and delete it.

These same operations should be carried out for the Check Member and Find Video command buttons.

In addition to transferring code from command button event procedures to menu item event procedures, we must revise any references to the command button event procedures. To make sure that we find and revise all references to a control event procedure, we can use the **Edit|Replace** menu option to search for the command button references and replace them with menu item references.

FIGURE 8-8.
Highlighted code in cmdExit_Click() event procedure

```
Project1 - Form1 (Code)

cmdExit                          Click

Private Sub cmdExit_Click()
    Dim intCounter As Integer
    Open "a:members7.dat" For Output As #10
    For intCounter = 0 To intNumMembers - 1
        Write #10, strMembers(intCounter), strPhoneNumbers
    Next
    Open "a:videos.dat" For Output As #3
    For intCounter = 0 To intnumvideos - 1
        Write #3, strVideos(intCounter), curVideoPrice(int
    Next
    Close #3
    Close #10
```

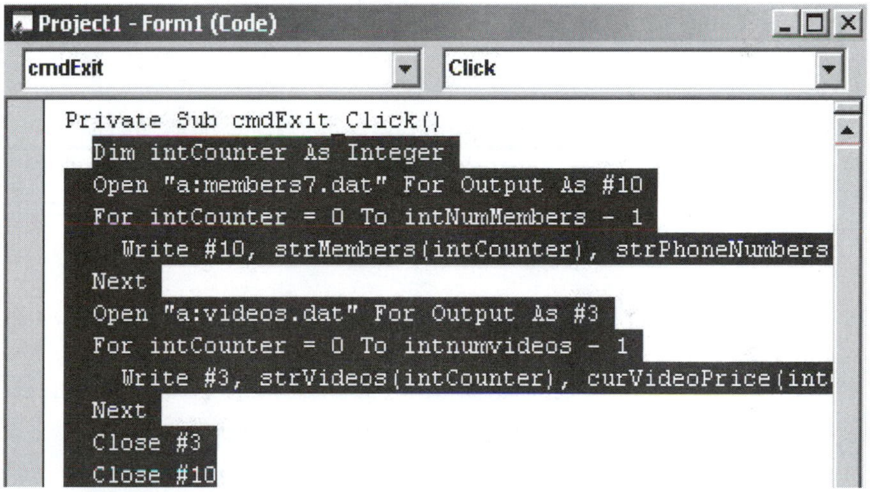

Adding the Help/About Option

The Memo and Help menu bar items are both new to the Vintage Videos application. Since the Memo item requires a new form and will be discussed extensively in the remainder of this chapter, we will confine ourselves right now to the Help item. Recall that this item has one submenu item—About—which provides information on the application. While Help options on most Windows systems also provide helpful information on using the application, this is beyond the scope of this textbook and we will restrict ourselves to providing information about the application.

To provide information about the application, we need to add a new form that will be displayed when the About submenu item is clicked with the instructions in the mnuAbout_Click event procedure:

```
frmAbout.Show
```

This new form should have a label that displays the required information and a button that returns control to the main form, as shown in Figure 8-9. Note that the information about the application is stored in the label caption in 12-point font. The Ok button returns control to the main form with the instruction:

```
Unload Me
```

where the *Me* keyword refers to the current form.

FIGURE 8-9. About form

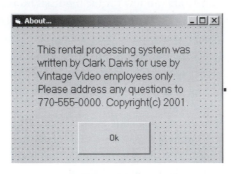

Mini-Summary 8-3: Adding Code to Menu Items

1. For menu items to work, you must add code to them in the same way you added code to command buttons or other controls.

2. It is easy with Visual Basic's editing options to move code from other controls to menu items.

3. Help/About forms are commonly found in most commercial software.

It's Your Turn!

1. How do we move the code from command buttons and other controls to the menu system?

2. What shortcut way do we have of referring to the current form?

3. Why would we unload a form rather than simply hiding it?

Completing the remaining questions will enable you to create the Visual Basic project discussed in the text.

4. Use the instructions in the text to cut the code from the cmdExit command button event procedure and paste it into the corresponding submenu item (mnuFileExit). Delete the Exit command button from the form and delete the corresponding beginning and ending statements from the Code window.

5. Repeat the operations to move the code from the cmdCheck and cmdFindVideo command button event procedures to the mnuMemVidCheck and mnuMemVidFind submenu items. Remember to delete the command buttons from the form and the corresponding beginning and ending statements from the Code window.

6. Use the **Edit | Replace** menu option to find and replace any references to cmdExit, cmdCheck, and cmdFindVideo with the corresponding menu controls (there should be none).

7. Use **Project|Add Form** or the new form icon to add a new form to the project. Give it a name of **frmAbout** and a caption of **About...**, and save it as **About.frm**. Add the code necessary to display it from the mnuHelpAbout submenu item, that is:

```
frmAbout.Show
```

8. Add a label to the frmAbout form. Give the label a name of **lblAbout** and add the caption shown in Figure 8-9 in a 12-point font.

9. Add a command button to frmAbout with a name of **cmdOk** and a caption of **Ok**. Add the code necessary to unload frmAbout when the Ok button is clicked, that is:

```
Unload Me
```

10. Run your project and test the menu options to which you have transferred code from command buttons. Now test the About submenu option and the Ok button on the About form.

11. Save your project under the same name as before.

CREATING A MEMO EDITOR

The next feature requested by the owners of Vintage Videos is a system to create, save, and print new memos and retrieve and edit existing memos. This will allow the employees to easily make notes of customer requests for favorite videos or to write memos to one another about problems with the operation of the store or with the information system Clark is creating. To create this feature, Clark has already added a menu bar item, *Memos,* with the submenu item *Create Memo.* The Create Memo submenu item should allow the user to create and save a completely new memo or to edit an existing memo. For example, the first time a customer requests a particular video, the employee would use the Create Memo option to create a new memo with the video listed and save it as, say, *Requested Videos.txt* (recall that Windows 95 allows long file names with embedded blanks). The next time a customer requests a video, an employee could retrieve this file and add the new video name to it. When Ed and Yvonne order videos, they could then edit the file to show that the video was ordered on such-and-such date. Finally, when the video arrives, the file could be edited again to show the date it was added to the store's inventory, or if it cannot be obtained, that information could also be added to the listing. Periodically, the list would need to be purged of old customer requests to keep it from becoming too long.

To create the Memo Editor function, Clark needs to add another form, called *frm-Memo,* that will contain the actual memo creation and editing area plus a menu system. The memo creation and editing area will be in a text box called *txtMemo.* The menu system is needed to carry out file operations (open, save, print, and so on), editing operations (cut, copy, paste, and so on), and formatting operations (selecting a font or style for the memo). This form will be displayed by selecting the Create Memo submenu item.

The mnuMemoCreate event procedure will have two instructions:

```
frmMemo.Show
frmMemo.txtMemo = ""
```

where the second instruction clears the text box on the frmMemo form.

The frmMemo Form

The frmMemo form is added to the project like any other new form—with the New Form icon or the **Project|Add Form** menu option. This form should be named *frmMemo* with a caption of **Memos**. Adding this form increases the number of forms in this project to five. To help you see the relationship of all the forms to the overall project, Figure 8-10 provides a *roadmap* to the current project.

FIGURE 8-10.
Roadmap to current project

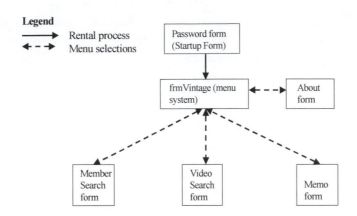

Only one control other than the menu system needs to be added to the form: a text box in which the memo text is entered and edited. As with any other text boxes, the default Text1 value for the text property should be deleted. The text box should be given a name of *txtMemo* and its **Multiline** property should be set to **True**. The Multiline property allows any text entered in the text box to *wrap* to the next line when it reaches the boundary of the text box. If the Multiline property were left as False, only one line of text would appear in the text box no matter how large the box is made. Finally, the **ScrollBars** property should be set to **Vertical** to create the capability to scroll down the text box if the text goes beyond the available space.

> **TIP:** When the Multiline property is set to True, you can also set the Alignment property to align text as centered, left or right justified. It is left justified by default. When Multiline is False, setting the Alignment property has no effect.

While we could make the text box as large as the form at design time, what happens when the user resizes the form while the project is running? The text box size does not change to match the new size of the form. What we need is a way to automatically resize the text box to fit the size of the form. To make this happen, a new event is needed: the form's **Resize** event. This event is executed any time the user displays or resizes the form. Using the Resize event, we can force the text box to fill the form by setting its Height and Width properties equal to the form's *interior* height and width. At any time, the form's interior height and width are equal to its ScaleHeight and Scale-Width properties. So, to set the interior height of the txtMemo text box equal to the form's height, the instruction in the form's Resize event procedure is:

```
txtMemo.Height = ScaleHeight
```

VB Code Box 8-2 shows the frmMemo Resize event procedure, and Figure 8-11 shows the resulting form at design time and at run time, with the text box changing size to fill the form.

VB CODE BOX 8-2. Form_Resize event procedure to resize text box	```Private Sub Form_Resize() txtMemo.Height = ScaleHeight txtMemo.Width = ScaleWidth End Sub```

FIGURE 8-11. Memo form at design time (left) and run time (right)

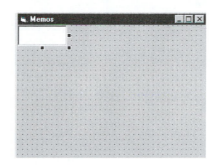 

The Memo Menu System

With the multiline property of the txtMemo text box set to True, you can now enter text into the text box. This text will wrap to the next line when you reach the boundary of the text box. However, to do anything other than enter text, we need to add a menu system to the Memo form with file, editing, and formatting operations. This menu system should have three menu bar items—File, Edit, and Format—each of which will have at least two submenu items. Table 8-7 shows these three menu bar options with the corresponding submenu items and the purpose of each. It should be noted that the Font and Style submenu items have submenus that list the fonts or styles from which the user can select. We will discuss them in more detail when we take up these two submenus.

With the exception of two submenu items, you should understand all of these items. The new items are the two dashes (-) that are displayed on the menu as a separator line; hence the names mnuFileSep and mnuEditSep. These separator lines are useful for separating groups of menu items. If the Menu Editor dialog box is opened for the Memo form and these items are entered, the form will appear as shown in Figure 8-12, where the File menu bar item has been selected. Note that seven submenu items are displayed, with the first six separated from the Exit item by a horizontal line. We will discuss each of the three menu bar items—File, Edit, and Format—in different sections, with the File option divided up among two sections.

Mini-Summary 8-4: Creating a Memo Editor

1. Text editors are among the most widely available types of software.

2. To create a text editor in Visual Basic, we use a text box with the multiline property set to true plus vertical scrollbars.

3. The Resize event can be used to force the text box to fill the form whenever the form is displayed.

FIGURE 8-12. Menu system for frmMemo

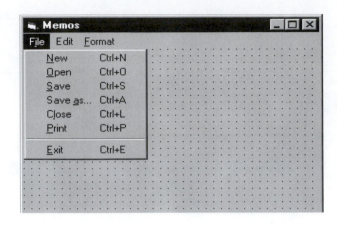

TABLE 8-7: Memo Form Menu System

Menu Bar Caption	Submenu Caption	Name	Shortcut Key	Purpose
F&ile		mnuFile		Displays submenu of File-related items
	&New	mnuFileNew	Ctrl+N	Begin new memo
	&Open	mnuFileOpen	Ctrl+O	Retrieve existing memo file
	&Save	mnuFileSave	Ctrl+S	Save memo under current name
	Save &as...	mnuFileSaveAs	Ctrl+A	Save memo under new name
	C&lose	mnuFileClose	Ctrl+L	Close this memo but do not exit memo system
	&Print	mnuFilePrint	Ctrl+P	Print contents of text box
	-	mnuFileSep		Separator line
	&Exit	mnuFileExit	Ctrl+E	Exit memo system
&Edit		mnuEdit		Displays submenu of Editing items
	C&ut	mnuEditCut	Ctrl+X	Remove selected portion of text
	Cop&y	mnuEditCopy	Ctrl+C	Copy selected portion of text
	Pas&te	mnuEditPaste	Ctrl+V	Insert most recently cut or copied text
	-	mnuEditSep		Separator line
	Clea&r all	mnuEditClear	Ctrl+R	Clear text box
&Format		mnuFormat		Displays submenu of Format-related items
	Fo&nt	mnuFormatFont		Select a font for the text
	&Style	mnuFormatStyle		Select a style (bold, italics, and so on) for the text.

It's Your Turn!

1. What control do we use in a text editor to input and edit text? How do we make it handle multiple lines of text?

2. How do we make this control fill the form in which it is located?

3. How do we add separators to a menu?

Completing the remaining questions will enable you to create the Visual Basic project discussed in the text.

4. Add a new form to the Vintage Videos project, and give it a name of **frmMemo** with a caption of **Memos**.

5. Add the following instruction to the Create Memo submenu item on the frmVintage form to display the new memo creation form:

```
frmMemo.Show
frmMemo.txtMemo = ""
```

6. Add a text box named **txtMemo** to frmMemo. Change its **Multiline** property to **True**, its **Scrollbars** property to **Vertical**, and its **Left** and **Top** properties to **zero**.

7. Open the Code window for the frmMemo object and switch to the Resize event. Enter the code shown in VB Code Box 8-2 to force the text box to fill the form.

8. Use the Menu Editor system to add the menu bar and submenu items shown in Table 8-7. Clicking on the File menu bar item should display a submenu like that shown in Figure 8-12.

9. Run your project and click the **Memo** menu bar on the main form option to display a submenu. Click on the **Create memo** option to display frmMemo. It should look like the right side of Figure 8-11. Click the **Close** icon in the upper right-hand corner to return to the main form. Click the **File | Exit** menu option.

10. Save the new form as **Memo.frm** and save the project under the current name.

WORKING WITH THE FILE SUBMENU

In the File submenu on the frmMemo form, the first item, New, clears the text box of any existing text in preparation for starting a new memo. While this is automatically done when the Create memo submenu item is selected from the main form, it may also be necessary to clear the screen from within the menu system. The next four items—Open, Save, Save As..., and Close involve file operations. We will discuss creating and saving a memo in this section and then take up the other operations in the next section.

Creating a Memo

If you run the Vintage Videos project and select the *Memo | Create Memo* option from the menu bar item from the main Vintage Videos screen, the frmMemo form is displayed with the cursor in the upper left corner. At this point you may type any text you wish in the text box. Note that if you enter text that extends beyond the right side of the form, it *wraps* to the next line. Figure 8-13 shows the memo form with this paragraph entered in it. Note that you can move the cursor around in the text and insert new text or delete existing text as with any word processing package.

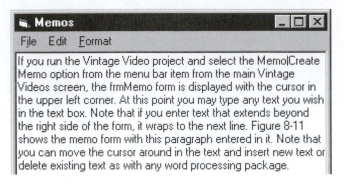

To create a new memo without saving this one, we need to use the *File | New* menu option to clear the screen. There is only one instruction for this submenu item:

```
txtMemo = ""
```

Using the common dialog control

file list box

directory list box

drive list box

Once a memo has been created, the next step is to save it. This should be possible with either the *File | Save* or *File | Save as...* menu option, with the difference being that the first option will save the text under an existing file name if one exists or display a Save File dialog box if no file name exists. In the second case, the Save File dialog box is displayed automatically, so the user can enter a file name or change the file name.

The Standard Visual Basic Toolbox has three controls that are meant for working with files: the file list box, directory list box, and drive list box. However, using these controls to work with (save and open) files can be somewhat complicated, and it is easier to use a control that is not initially on the Toolbox—the **common dialog control**. This control combines all of the operations of the other three controls into one central dialog box that is very easy to use.

To use the common dialog control, you must first add it to the Toolbox if it is not already there. To do this, select **Project | Components** to display the Components dialog box as shown in the left side of Figure 8-14. Note that there is a list of controls with check boxes beside them. Clicking in a check box and then clicking Ok will add the corresponding control to your Toolbox. Checking the Microsoft Common Dialog Control 6.0 check box adds this control to the bottom of your toolbox as shown in the right side of Figure 8-14 (where the new control is pointed out).

Once you have added the common dialog control to the Toolbox, you can then add it to the form in the usual manner and give it a name beginning with a *dlg* prefix. In this case, we will call it **dlgMemo**. While you can locate the common dialog control anywhere you wish on the form during design time, you have *no* control over where it will appear at run time. At this time, it is also useful to change another property, **CancelError**, from False to True. The reason for doing this will become evident later. The common dialog control has many uses. It can be used to work with files, colors, and fonts as well as to control the manner in which output should be printed. It can also be used to display a Help file selected by the user. In our case, we will restrict out discussion to working with files.

FIGURE 8-14.
Components dialog
box

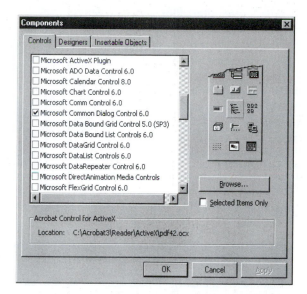

> **TIP:** In addition to opening and saving files, the common dialog box
> can be used to show standard forms for adjusting colors or fonts, con-
> trolling the printer, and showing help.

To use the common dialog control to work with files, you need to add code to the
appropriate submenu item Click event to *connect* the event to the common dialog control. For the common dialog control, this is accomplished with either the **ShowSave**
method or the **ShowOpen** method. For example, to display the common dialog control to save a file, the instruction is:

```
dlgMemo.ShowSave
```

To display the common dialog control to open a file, the instruction is:

```
dlgMemo.ShowOpen
```

Saving a New Memo We should be able to save a new memo—that is, one that does not already have a file
name—with either the File|Save option or File|Save as... option. The best way to do
this is to write the code for the Save as... event procedure and then call it from the Save
event procedure when no file name exists.

Before using the ShowSave instruction to connect the common dialog control to
a form, we need to display a list of file types from which the user can select a type to
save the file as. This is done with the **Filter** property of the common dialog box with
the following syntax:

dlgName.Filter = "description1| filter1| description2| filter2| etc."

where *descriptionN* is a description of the file type [All Files (*.*), Text files (*.txt), and
so on] and *filterN* is the actual filter (*.*, *.txt, and so on) for the *Nth* description and
filter. Also, the pipe symbol (|) is required to separate descriptions and filter strings.
For example, the filter instruction to display all types of files and text files for the dlg-
Memo common dialog control is:

```
dlgMemo.Filter = "All files(*.*)|*.*|Text files(*.txt)|*.txt"
```

To indicate the default type of file—that is, the type that the file will automatically
be saved as—we use the **FilterIndex** property (this is also the type of file that is displayed in the dialog box). This property has the following form:

dlgName.**FilterIndex = N**

where N equals the number of the type of file in the Filter property statement. For example, to make text files the default file type for the dlgMemo common dialog control, the statement is:

```
dlgMemo.FilterIndex = 2
```

where text files are the second file type in the filter statement.

If the three statements shown in VB Code Box 8-3 are included in the mnuFileSaveAs_Click event procedure, a file Save As dialog box similar to the one shown in Figure 8-15 will be displayed.

VB CODE BOX 8-3. Code to set up Filter property	```dlgMemo.Filter = "All Files (*.*)|*.*|Text Files(*.txt)|*.txt"```
	```dlgMemo.FilterIndex = 2```
	```dlgMemo.ShowSave```

FIGURE 8-15. Save As dialog box

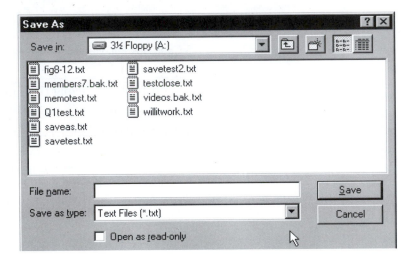

Note in Figure 8-15 that only files with a .txt extension are shown in the list box. Users can select one of these files as the file name for the memo, thereby writing over the previous contents, or they can enter a new file name in the File Name text box at the bottom of the dialog box. Note that the *Save as Type* drop-down list box shows that the file will be saved as a txt file.

Once we have entered a file name in the File Name text box either by typing or by selecting an existing file, this becomes the **FileName** property for the common dialog control. If we assign this property to a string variable, *TheFileName*, it can be used in the Open statement. The string variable should be declared at the form level so that the name of the file can be shared by the Save, SaveAs, and Open event procedures.

Once the file is opened, the contents of the txtMemo text box can be written to the file with the Print # statement and the file can then be closed. For example, if the file number is 1, the statement would be:

```
Print #1, txtMemo.Text
```

Once the file is saved, a form-level Boolean variable *Saved* is set equal to True. This variable will be used in the Close procedure to determine if the memo has been saved before closing it. VB Code Box 8-4 shows the complete mnuFileSaveAs_Click event procedure.

| VB CODE BOX 8-4. Code for Save As event procedure | ```
Private Sub mnuFileSaveAs_Click()
  Dim intFileNum As Integer
  On Error GoTo ErrHandler 'User clicked Cancel
  intFileNum = FreeFile 'Use next available file number
  dlgMemo.Filter = "All Files(*.*)|*.*|Text Files(*.txt)|*.txt"
  'Set up filter and set default to text files
  dlgMemo.FilterIndex = 2
  dlgMemo.ShowSave 'Display dialog box
  strTheFileName = dlgMemo.filename 'Select file name
  Open strTheFileName For Output As #intFileNum
  Print #intFileNum, txtMemo.Text
  Close #intFileNum
  blnSaved = True
  Exit Sub
ErrHandler:
  Exit Sub
End Sub
``` |

In looking at VB Code Box 8-4, you will note two other new coding features: the use of the **FreeFile** function and the **On Error GoTo** statement. In the first case, once you start working with multiple files at the same time, you may not always be able to recall which file numbers have already been used. To help you with this, the FreeFile function returns the next available file number. By setting an Integer variable, intFile-Num, equal to the FreeFile function and using it everywhere we would have had to use a value for the file number, we no longer have to worry about what actual file number is being used.

The On Error GoTo statement instructs the code to jump to a *label* somewhere else in the code when an error is encountered. In this case, the label is *ErrHandler:* (where the colon is an essential part of the label), and it comes after the code to open the file. If the *CancelError* property of the dlgMemo common dialog control has been set to True as we did earlier, then clicking the Cancel button will generate an error that is detected by the On Error GoTo statement and execution of the procedure is termi-nated. We will use this same mechanism with the other file operations to check if the user has clicked the Cancel button on the dialog box. Note: It is important to include the Exit Sub statement *before* the ErrHandler: label to avoid executing error handling code as a normal step in the code.

Mini-Summary 8-5: Using the Common Dialog Control

1. The common dialog control is useful when working with files as well as with other features.

2. The common dialog control ShowSave and ShowOpen methods are used to display Save As and Open File dialog boxes. The Filter and FilterIndex properties control which types of files are displayed and which one is the default type.

3. The common dialog Filename property is used to transfer the name of the file being saved or opened. Text is written to a file with the Print #*n* instruction.

4. The FreeFile function returns the next available file number, and the On Error GoTo instruction is used to check for the user clicking the Cancel button.
```

It's Your Turn!

1. What statement is used to clear the memo in preparation for creating a new one?

2. Where is the control that is used to work with files found? How do we add it to the Toolbar?

3. What two command dialog control methods are used to save files or open existing files?

4. What property of the common dialog control is used to determine what types of files are displayed? How do we make one of these file types the default type?

5. What does the FreeFile function do? What happens if the On Error Goto statement encounters an error?

6. What property of the common dialog control must be set to True in order for the Cancel button to work correctly?

Completing the remaining questions will enable you to create the Visual Basic project discussed in the text.

7. Run your project and select the **Memo | Create memo** menu option. The frm-Memo form should be displayed with the txtMemo text box completely filling the form.

8. Test your memo creation application by entering the first two sentences of the paragraph with the *Creating a memo* heading. It should look similar to Figure 8-13. Close this form by clicking the **Close** icon and then close the project.

9. Go to the frmMemo form and to the **File | New** menu item and add this lines of code:

```
txtMemo.Text = ""
strTheFileName = ""
```

10. If the common dialog control is not there already, add it to your tool bar by using the **Project | Components** menu option and clicking the **Microsoft Common Dialog Control 6.0** check box.

11. Add the common dialog control to the frmMemo form and give it a name of **dlg-Memo**. Change the **CancelError** property to **True**.

12. Click the **File | SaveAs...** menu item to add code to it and add the code shown in VB Code Box 8-4. Also, declare a String variable **strTheFileName** and a Boolean variable **Saved** as form-level variables.

13. Run your project and select the **Memo | Create memo** menu option. Once again, enter the first two sentences of the paragraph with the *Creating a memo* heading, only this time use the **File | SaveAs...** menu item to display the Save As dialog box.

14. Use the Save As dialog box to save the text as **a:\Exer6.txt**. Clear the screen with the **File | New** option, close this form by clicking the **Close** icon, and then close the project.

15. Open the WordPad text editor application (do not close Visual Basic), retrieve the file **Exer6.txt** from the a:\ drive, and compare it to the file you just saved. They should be the same. Close WordPad and return to Visual Basic.

16. Save frmMemo and the project under their current names.

OTHER FILE OPERATIONS

Once a file has been created and saved, we need a way to retrieve the file and save it again. We also need a way to close a memo. These three operations will be discussed in this section along with the Print and Exit options. The Open submenu item opens an existing file, and the Save item saves a file under the same name as originally opened or, if the file is new, saves it under a new file name. The Close item checks whether the text has been saved. If it has, it clears the screen. If the file has not been saved, the user is queried as to whether to save the text to a file and then the screen is cleared. The next item, Print, prints the contents of the memo. Finally, the Exit item closes the current text and exits the memo creation and editing screen.

Opening a File

Opening an existing file involves displaying the Open File common dialog box, highlighting an existing file or entering the name of one to open, and clicking the Open button to assign this file name to the Filename property of common dialog control. If the user tries to open a blank file name in the Open File dialog box, nothing happens. The user must either select or enter a file name to open the dialog box or click the Cancel button to close it.

Much of the code to display the Open File dialog box is the same as that for the Save As operation, with the same Filter and FilterIndex property statements being used. The key difference is that the ShowOpen method is used with the common dialog control instead of the ShowSave method and the contents of the file are input to the text box. The resulting Open File dialog box is shown in Figure 8-16. Note that the file saved in the last *It's Your Turn!* exercises (Exer6.txt) is now in this list and is highlighted for opening.

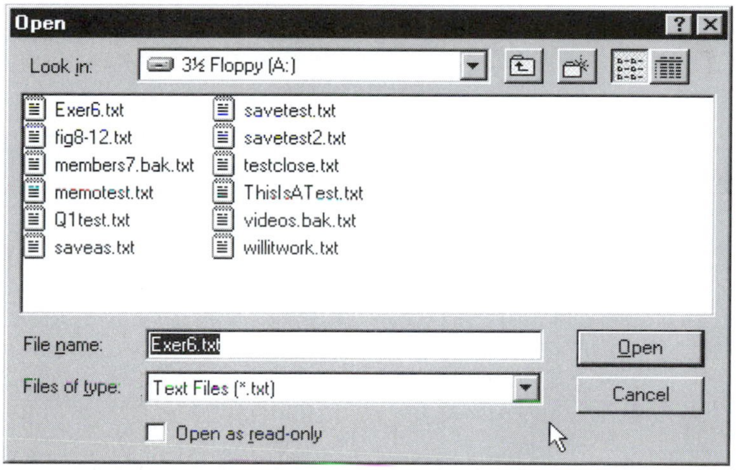

FIGURE 8-16. Open File dialog box

Note in the Open File dialog box in Figure 8-16 that only files with a .txt extension are displayed. This is due to our setting the default file type for the Open File dialog box to the txt extension with the FilterIndex property of the common dialog control (FilterIndex = 2). If we had set it to All Files with FilterIndex = 1, then all of the files on the disk would have been displayed. You can also display other available file types with the Files of Type drop-down list box.

As with the Save As operation, the Filename property of the common dialog control must be assigned to a string variable, *strTheFileName*. This variable will be used in the Open *filename* for Input statement to open the file. As mentioned earlier, this variable has been declared at the form level, so the Save procedure will be able to save the contents of the text box using the name under which it was opened or previously saved. Also, as with the Save As procedure, we will use the *FreeFile* function to determine the file number to use in the Open statement and the On Error GoTo statement to check if the user has clicked the Cancel button.

Once the file is opened, its contents must be transferred to the text box. The easiest way to do this is to use the ***Input$*** function. The form of this function is:

Input$(*number, #FileNumber*)

where *number* = the number of characters in the file that is identified by *#FileNumber*.

In looking at this function, you will probably note that it requires the number of characters in the file—a value we do not know. Fortunately, there is another function that we can use to find this value, the **LOF(FileNumber)** function. This function can be inserted in the Input$ function in place of the *number* argument. For example, if the file number is the Integer variable *intFileNum*, then the statement to input all characters in the file into the txtMemo text box is:

```
txtMemo.Text = Input$(LOF(intFileNum), #intFileNum)
```

Once the text has been input into the text box, the input file is closed as usual. For the mnuFileOpen_Click( ) event procedure, the code is shown in VB Code Box 8-5.

VB CODE BOX 8-5. Code to open a file	```Private Sub mnuFileOpen_Click()```

```
Private Sub mnuFileOpen_Click()
  Dim intFileNum As Integer
  On Error GoTo ErrHandler 'If cancel clicked, do this
  intFileNum = FreeFile 'Find next available free file
  dlgMemo.Filter = "All Files (*.*)|*.*|Text Files (*.txt)|*.txt"
  'Set up filter and set default to text files
  dlgMemo.FilterIndex = 2
  dlgMemo.ShowOpen 'Display dialog box
  strTheFileName = dlgMemo.FileName 'Select file name
  Open strTheFileName For Input As #intFileNum
  txtMemo.Text = Input$(LOF(intFileNum), #intFileNum)
'Read all text in file
  Close #intFileNum
  blnSaved = True
  Exit Sub
ErrHandler: 'User clicked Cancel on dialog box
  Exit Sub
End Sub
```

Saving a File

The purpose of the File|Save menu option is to save the current memo text using the name under which it was previously opened or saved as. The code to handle this operation is much like that for the Save As operation, except that there is no need to display the Save As dialog box because the file name is already known. Recall that the file name was saved earlier as the form-level String variable *strTheFileName*. When we use this variable, the statements to save the text in txtMemo to the same file name are shown in VB Code Box 8-6, where *intFileNum* is an Integer variable generated by the FreeFile function. Also, as in the Save As procedure, the form-level Boolean variable *blnSaved* is set to True.

| **VB CODE BOX 8-6.** Code to write text to a file | ```
Open strTheFileName for Output as #intFileNum
Print #intFileNum, txtMemo.Text
Close #intFileNum
blnSaved = True
``` |
|---|---|

However, there is one problem with this code: What happens if a user tries to use the Save procedure when the file has not been previously given a name in the Save As operation? Since the variable strTheFileName has nothing in it, this will generate an error. One way to avoid this error is to check if the variable, strTheFileName, has anything stored in it; if it does, then the code shown in VB Code Box 8-6 should be implemented. If strTheFileName is empty, the mnuFileSaveAs_Click( ) event procedure is called, so the user can enter a file name using the Save As dialog box. The complete mnuFileSave_Click( ) is shown in VB Code Box 8-7.

| **VB CODE BOX 8-7.** Revised Code for Save option | ```
Private Sub mnuFileSave_Click()
    Dim intFileNum As Integer
    On Error GoTo ErrHandler 'Do if user clicked cancel
    intFileNum = FreeFile 'Use next available file number
    If strTheFileName <> "" Then
      Open strTheFileName For Output As #intFileNum
      Print #intFileNum, txtMemo.Text 'Print contents to file
      Close #intFileNum
      blnSaved = True 'This file has been saved
    Else 'No file name; call Save As operation
      Call mnuFileSaveAs_Click
    End If
    Exit Sub
    ErrHandler: 'User clicked Cancel on dialog box
    Exit Sub
End Sub
``` |
|---|---|

The Print, Close, and Exit Options

The last three file operations are Print, Close, and Exit. The Print operation simply involves printing the contents of the txtMemo text box to a printer or to the Debug object. In the latter case, the single instruction to do this is:

```
Debug.Print txtMemo.Text
```

We would replace Debug with Printer to direct the output to a printer.

The Close option

The Close operation involves clearing the txtMemo text box *after* determining whether or not the text has been saved. This is where the Boolean variable *blnSaved* is used; if it is True, then the text has been saved and the text box can be cleared. If it is False, the text has not been saved, and the user should be queried as to whether to save the file. If the answer is Yes, the file should be saved using the mnuFileSave_Click event procedure and then the text box and *strTheFileName* variable are cleared. The code to accomplish this is shown in VB Code Box 8-8.

The Close operation works fine *unless* the user has changed the text and has forgotten to save the revised text. To ensure that the user is given the opportunity to save the revised text, we need to use the text box Change event to set the Saved variable to

| **VB CODE BOX 8-8.** Code for Close submenu option | ```
Private Sub mnuFileClose_Click()
    Dim intYesNo As Integer
    If Not blnSaved Then 'File not previously saved
        intYesNo = MsgBox("File not saved! Save it?", _
        vbYesNo, "Save File?") 'Query user about saving file
        If intYesNo = VBYes Then 'User wants to save file
            Call mnuFileSave_Click
        End If
    End If
    txtMemo = "" 'Clear text box
    strTheFileName = "" 'Clear file name
End Sub
``` |
|---|---|

False whenever there is a change to the text box. You can add this instruction by double-clicking the txtMemo text box to display the txtMemo_Change event procedure and adding the following instruction:

```
blnSaved = False
```

The Exit option   Exiting the memo creation and editing option involves executing the Close operation, unloading frmMemo, and displaying the main form. We call the mnuFileClose option to check for unsaved text before exiting the procedure. We use the Unload instruction instead of the Hide instruction for frmMemo to reduce the number of forms saved in memory at one time. The code for this procedure is shown in VB Code Box 8-9

| **VB CODE BOX 8-9.** Code for Exit option | ```
Private Sub mnuFileExit_Click()
    Call mnuFileClose_Click
    Unload frmMemo
    frmVintage.Show
End Sub
``` |
|---|---|

Mini-Summary 8-6: Opening and Saving Files

1. The common dialog box can be used to open files with the ShowOpen method. The same Filter and FilterIndex methods and FileName property as before are also used.

2. To retrieve the contents of the file, the Input$(LOF(FileNumber), FileNumber) function is used, where LOF returns the length of the file.

3. A previously opened or saved file can be saved using the Print #FileNumber instruction. If a file has not been opened or saved, the mnuFileSaveAs event procedure should be called.

4. A form-level variable can be used to determine whether a file has been saved or not.

It's Your Turn!

1. What property of the common dialog control must be set equal to the name of the file being saved?

2. To open a file, what statement is used to read the contents? How do we determine the number of characters being input?

3. To save a file, what statement is used to write the contents of the memo box into a file?

4. How do we keep track of whether or not there have been any changes to a memo?

Completing the remaining questions will enable you to create the Visual Basic project discussed in the text.

5. Display frmMemo and click on the **File | Open** menu option to display the Code window for this event procedure. Enter the code shown in VB Code Box 8-5 to create the mnuFileOpen _Click event procedure.

6. Run your project and test the **File | Open** option by opening the file you created in the previous exercises (**Exer6.txt**). Terminate the project.

7. Open the Code window for the mnuFileSave_Click event procedure and enter the code shown in VB Code Box 8-7.

8. Use the Object list to open the Code window for the txtMemo_Change event procedure and add the instruction:

```
blnSaved = False
```

9. Run your project, open **Exer6.txt** again, and modify it in some way. Test the Save option by saving this modified text.

10. Click the **File | New** option and enter your name, address, and phone number in the text box. Click the **File | Save** option and save this text as **MyInfo.txt**. Terminate your project.

11. Create the mnuFilePrint_Click event procedure by entering this instruction:

```
Debug.Print txtMemo.Text
```

12. Enter the code shown in VB Code Box 8-8 to create the mnuFileClose_ Click event procedure.

13. Enter the code shown in VB Code Box 8-9 to create the mnuFileExit_ Click event procedure.

14. Run your project and test the remaining Print, Close, and Exit options. Use the Exit option to terminate the Memo system and then exit the project. Save your project under the current file names.

THE EDITING SUBMENU

Once text has been entered in the text box, the next step is to edit it. Some editing can be done by inserting and deleting text. However, three key operations need to be added: the capability to *copy* or *cut* text from one location in the text box and to *paste* it into another location. Recall that copying text and cutting text are similar in that both are used to transfer highlighted text to some other location. They are different in that text that is *cut* is removed from the text box while text that is *copied* remains in the text box. We also want to add the capability to clear the text box (Clear All).

All three of the Copy, Cut, and Paste operations use the Clipboard object. The **Clipboard object** is a Windows object on which text or graphics from any Windows application can be stored and later retrieved. In using the Clipboard, it is important to remember that only one piece of text can be on the Clipboard at one time. (While data in different formats can be on the Clipboard simultaneously, we will not consider that case.)

The Clipboard object has no properties, but it has two important methods: the **SetText** method and the **GetText** method. The SetText method is used to transfer selected text to the Clipboard, and the GetText method is used to retrieve the current contents of the Clipboard to some destination. Figure 8-17 shows this process.

> **TIP:** The Clipboard object is shared by all applications in Windows. This means that the contents are subject to change whenever you switch to another application.

With the Clipboard object, it is quite easy to write the code for the Copy, Cut, and Paste Edit submenu options. For the Copy and Cut options, all that is needed is to clear the Clipboard with the **Clear** method and then use the SetText method to copy highlighted text on the txtMemo text box to the Clipboard object. Any highlighted text in a text box is stored in the **SelText** property of the text box, so this is what the SetText method stores on the Clipboard. The code to clear the Clipboard and store the highlighted text in the text box on it is:

```
Clipboard.Clear
Clipboard.SetText txtMemo.SelText
```

FIGURE 8-17.
SetText and GetText
methods with
Clipboard object

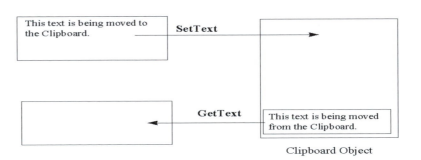

Clipboard Object

This code is used for both the Cut and Copy operations, but we need one more statement for the Cut operation to remove the selected text from the text box by setting the SelText property to an empty string:

```
txtMemo.SelText = ""
```

Finally, the code for the Paste operation reverses the procedure used in the Cut and Copy operations by using the GetText method as shown below:

```
txtMemo.SelText = Clipboard.GetText()
```

where the SelText property is the location where the text will be pasted. Figure 8-18 shows the Code window for the Cut, Copy, Paste, and Clear All sub menu options.

*Enabling Menu
Options*

In working with the Cut, Copy, and Paste editing options, note that one or more of these options should not be active at various times during the editing process. For example, when the editing text box is empty, all three options should be disabled. Similarly, if no text has been cut or copied to the Clipboard object, then the Paste option should not be active, since there is nothing to paste. In both cases, we can use the **Enabled** property of the menu control to control whether or not a menu item is

FIGURE 8-18.
Code for editing
operations

```
mnuEditClearAll                        ▼    Click

     Private Sub mnuEditClearAll_Click()
        txtMemo = ""
     End Sub

     Private Sub mnuEditCopy_Click()
        Clipboard.Clear
        Clipboard.SetText txtMemo.SelText
     End Sub

     Private Sub mnuEditCut_Click()
        Clipboard.Clear
        Clipboard.SetText txtMemo.SelText
        txtMemo.SelText = ""
     End Sub

     Private Sub mnuEditPaste_Click()
        txtMemo.SelText = Clipboard.GetText()
     End Sub
```

active. If this property is set to True, then the menu item is active and is displayed in black print. If the property is set to False, the menu item is inactive and is grayed out. For example, to disable the Edit|Paste menu option, the instruction is:

```
mnuEditPaste.Enabled = False
```

with False being replaced by True to enable the option.

In the first case, all editing menu options should be inactive when the Memo form is loaded, since nothing is in the editing text box. Similarly, all editing options should be disabled whenever the text box is cleared—after the File|New and File|Close options and after the Edit|Clear All option. On the other hand, when there is a change in the text box, the Cut, Copy, and Clear All options should be enabled. In the second case, the Paste option should be disabled until the Cut option or Copy option has been used.

To disable all editing options, a sub procedure like the one shown in VB Code Box 8-10 should be used. Note that it has instructions to disable the Edit Cut, Copy, Paste, and Clear All options. This sub procedure should be called from the frmMemo Form_Load, mnuFileNew, mnuFileClose, and mnuEditClear event procedures.

| **VB CODE BOX 8-10.** Code to disable the Edit Menu | ```
Sub EditDisable()
    mnuEditCopy.Enabled = False
    mnuEditCut.Enabled = False
    mnuEditClear.Enabled = False
    mnuEditPaste.Enabled = False
End Sub
``` |
| --- | --- |

To activate the Edit Cut, Copy, and Clear All menu options whenever there is a change to the text box, the enabling instructions should be entered in the txtMemo_Change event procedure. Finally, an instruction to enable the Edit|Paste option should be included in the mnuEditCopy and mnuEditCut event procedures. The revised code for the Form Load and mnuEdit event procedures is shown in Figure 8-19 along with the Edit submenu after text has been entered in the editing text
```

box but before any text has been cut or copied. Note that the Paste option is grayed out since it is not enabled.

Mini-Summary 8-7: Using the Windows Clipboard

1. The Windows Clipboard object is used for the Cut, Copy, and Paste editing operations.

2. The Clipboard SetText and GetText methods make this possible by working with the SelText property of the text box.

3. Menu options can be enabled or disabled through the Enabled property.

FIGURE 8-19.
Code to enable/disable menu options

```
Private Sub Form_Load()
     EditDisable
End Sub
Private Sub Form_Resize()
   txtMemo.Height = ScaleHeight
   txtMemo.Width = ScaleWidth
End Sub
Private Sub mnuEditClearAll_Click()
     txtMemo = ""
     EditDisable
End Sub
Private Sub mnuEditCopy_Click()
   Clipboard.Clear
   Clipboard.SetText txtMemo.SelText
   mnuEditPaste.Enabled = True
End Sub
Private Sub mnuEditCut_Click()
   Clipboard.Clear
   Clipboard.SetText txtMemo.SelText
   txtMemo.SelText = ""
   mnuEditPaste.Enabled = True
End Sub
Private Sub mnuEditPaste_Click()
   txtMemo.SelText = Clipboard.GetText()
End Sub
```

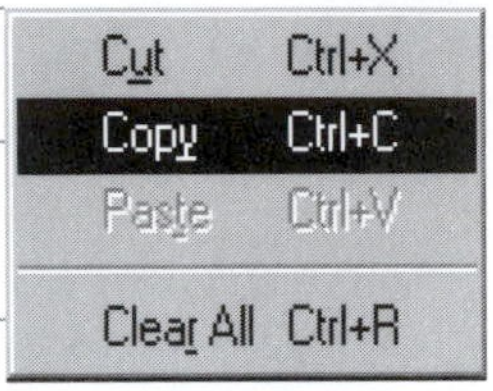

Cut	Ctrl+X
Copy	Ctrl+C
Paste	Ctrl+V
Clear All	Ctrl+R

It's Your Turn!

1. What object is used for the copy, cut, and paste editing operations? What two methods are used to carry out these operations?

2. What method is used to clear the Clipboard of any existing material? What property of the text box is used to store highlighted text?

3. What property is used to control whether or not a menu item is active?

Completing the remaining questions will enable you to create the Visual Basic project discussed in the text.

4. Add the code shown in Figure 8-19 to the Click event procedures for the mnuEdit-Copy, mnuEditCut, mnuEditPaste, and mnuEditClear menu controls.

5. Add the code shown in Figure 8-19 to the Form Load event procedure to disable the Edit submenu options. Also add the sub procedure **EditDisable** to the code module.

6. Add the following code to the txtMemo_Change event procedure to enable the Cut, Copy, and Clear All menu options:

> **mnuEditCopy.Enabled = True**
>
> **mnuEditCut.Enabled = True**
>
> **mnuEditClear.Enabled = True**

7. Run your project and test the editing capabilities of the memo creation system.

 a. First note the characteristics of the Edit submenu when the form is loaded and then again after you enter several lines of text or retrieve a file you previously saved.

 b. Next, cut a line of text from your memo and paste it at the end of the text. Now, copy the same line and paste it at the beginning to the text.

 c. Finally, clear all of the text and exit the memo system.

8. Save the project and frmMemo under the same names as before.

THE FORMAT SUBMENU

The last memo menu bar option submenu we need to consider is Format. This menu bar option has only two options: Font and Style, both of which also have submenus. The Font submenu is a list of font types from which the user can choose, and the Style submenu has a list of styles from which the user can choose. While it would also be possible to include a list of font sizes under the Format menu option, for the purposes of this text we will consider only font types and style types.

For both fonts and styles, we will use **menu control arrays**. Like the control arrays for individual controls, menu controls arrays allow us to use a single name for all fonts and a single name for all styles, with the individual fonts or styles being distinguished by an index value. When the user selects a particular font or style by clicking it in the Font or Style submenu, the associated index value will be passed to the menu control array Click event procedure and a Select Case decision structure can be used to determine which font or style was selected. Unlike control arrays for which the index values are automatically set as you enter them, menu control arrays require that you set the index values manually. A good way to do this is to set them in the Menu Editor as they are added. We will discuss the Font submenu first and then the Style submenu.

The Font Submenu

Fonts determine the shape of the characters that are displayed on the screen and printed. While there are a large number of fonts to choose in Visual Basic, we will use only seven fonts for demonstration purposes: Arial, Courier New, Modern, MS Sans Serif, MS Serif, Times New Roman, and WingDings. The WingDings font is more "just for fun" than for actual use.

To create the Fonts submenu, open the Menu Editor and click on the Style submenu item. Next, click on the Insert button to open a space between the Font submenu item and the Style submenu item (the Insert button always inserts *above* the current item). By clicking the right arrow, you can indent the next item as a submenu to the Font submenu. The name of this new item should be **mnuFormatFontName**, the caption should be **Arial**, and the index value should be set to zero. Repeating this operation opens a new space for the next Font submenu item with the same name, a caption of **Courier New**, and an index value of 1.

Note that there are eight dots in front of this submenu item, indicating that it is a submenu item to the Font submenu. Note also that it has an index value of 1. Repeating this process of adding Font submenu items for each of the four remaining fonts, all with the same name (mnuFormatFontName) and with index values from 2 to 6, generates a menu control array. Figure 8-20 shows the submenu list box after all Font submenu options have been added.

Figure 8-20. Font submenu list box

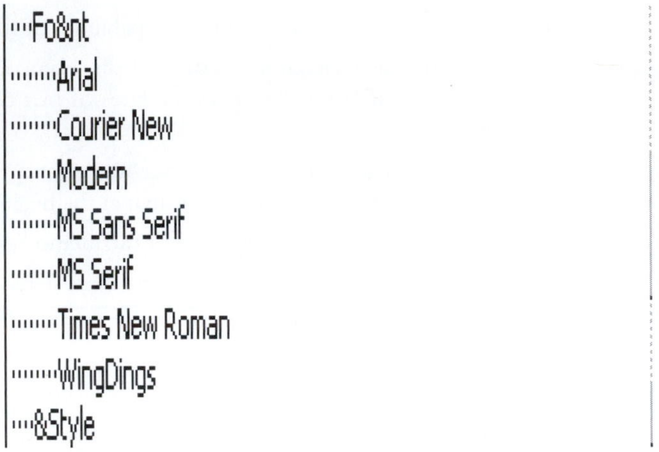

```
····Fo&nt
········Arial
········Courier New
········Modern
········MS Sans Serif
········MS Serif
········Times New Roman
········WingDings
····&Style
```

To add the code needed to select a font when the user clicks a Font submenu item, click Ok to close the Menu Editor if it is still open and then click any of the Font submenu fonts to open the mnuFormatFontName_Click event procedure. As mentioned earlier, clicking a font name passes the corresponding index value to the Click event procedure, so we need to determine which value has been passed. The best way to do this is to use a Select Case decision structure to determine the value of Index and to set the **FontName** property of the txtMemo text box to the appropriate font type. The code to do this is shown in VB Code Box 8-11.

VB Code Box 8-11. Code to select font for the text box

```
Select Case Index
    Case 0
       txtMemo.FontName = "Arial"
    Case 1
       txtMemo.FontName = "Courier New"
    Case 2
       txtMemo.FontName = "Modern"
    Case 3
       txtMemo.FontName = "MS Sans Serif"
    Case 4
       txtMemo.FontName = "MS Serif"
    Case 5
       txtMemo.FontName = "Times New Roman"
    Case 6
       txtMemo.FontName = "WingDings"
End Select
mnuFormatFontName(Index).Checked = True
```

While the Select Case structure shown in VB Code Box 8-11 is sufficient to select a font for the text box, we have added another statement immediately after the End Select statement that adds a check mark beside the font on the submenu. This enables the user to easily determine the current font. The check mark is added by setting the **Checked** property of the selected menu item to True.

To make sure that no other fonts are checked, add the code shown in VB Code Box 8-12 immediately *prior* to the Select Case statement to "uncheck" any previously checked fonts. If the Modern font is selected, the text box and submenu will appear as shown in Figure 8-21.

VB CODE BOX 8-12. Code to uncheck all fonts	```Dim intCounter As Integer For intCounter = 0 To 6 mnuFormatFontName(intCounter).Checked = False Next```

FIGURE 8-21. Font submenu with checked font

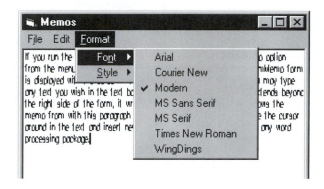

The Style Submenu

The Style submenu is very similar to the Font submenu in that it controls how the text will look. However, instead of selecting a particular type of font, the style submenu selects an appearance feature: none of the styles, bold style, italics style, underline style, or a combination of bold and italics styles. Creating the Style submenu is very similar to creating the Fonts submenu in that a menu control array is used and the Select Case structure is used to select a style to be implemented. In this case, the name of the Styles submenu control is **mnuFormatStyleType**, and it will have the five entries with index values running from zero to four.

FIGURE 8-22 Styles submenu

One key difference between the Font submenu and the Style submenu is that for the Style submenu instead of assigning a font name to the FontName property of txtMemo text box, we assign the **FontBold**, **FontItalics**, or **FontUnderline** properties of the text box to be True or False. If, for instance, the FontBold property of the text box is True, then all of the text in the text box will be bold. (With both fonts and styles, *all* of the text in the text box must take on the selected font or style; it is not possible to have the property apply to only a selected portion of the text.)

The Style submenu is shown in Figure 8-22, and the mnuFormatStyleType_Click event procedure to implement this menu is shown in VB Code Box 8-13. Note, for example, that the *Regular* submenu option is implemented by setting all style properties to False and that text in both bold and italics is created by setting both properties to

True. Note in Figure 8-22 that we have added shortcut keys to the styles to make changing the style more efficient .

Mini-Summary 8-8: Working with Fonts and Styles

1. A menu control array includes multiple menu items, all of which have the same name but each of which is distinguished by its index.

2. The menu Editor does not automatically add index values to menu control array items. These must be added using the Menu Editor at the time the menu item is created.

3. Once you have created the menu control array, clicking an option passes its index value to the event procedure, where a Select Case statement is used to detect the clicked option.

4. The FontName text box property can be used to determine the font for the text box, and FontBold, FontItalics, and FontUnderline can be used to determine the style.

| **VB CODE BOX 8-13.** Code to select a style for the text | ```
Private Sub mnuFormatStyleType_Click(Index As Integer)
    Select Case Index
        Case 0
            txtMemo.FontBold = False
            txtMemo.FontItalic = False
            txtMemo.FontUnderline = False
        Case 1
            txtMemo.FontBold = True
            txtMemo.FontItalic = False
            txtMemo.FontUnderline = False
        Case 2
            txtMemo.FontBold = False
            txtMemo.FontItalic = True
            txtMemo.FontUnderline = False
        Case 3
            txtMemo.FontBold = False
            txtMemo.FontItalic = False
            txtMemo.FontUnderline = True
        Case 4
            txtMemo.FontBold = True
            txtMemo.FontItalic = True
            txtMemo.FontUnderline = False
    End Select
End Sub
``` |
|---|---|

It's Your Turn!

1. What property of the text box is used to determine the style of the text?

2. What type of array is used to store the fonts and styles used to format the text? How is the font array then used to actually change the font?
```

3. How do you make the text bold, italicized, or underlined? How is this different from setting the font?

4. How is it possible to show which font or style has been selected?

Completing the remaining questions will enable you to create the Visual Basic project discussed in the text.

5. With frmMemo on the screen, use the Menu Editor to add the seven fonts discussed in the text and shown in Figure 8-20 for the Format|Font submenu. Give all seven the same name—**mnuFormatFontName**—and give each a caption that matches the corresponding font type. Starting with the first one, add index values running from zero to six.

6. After closing the Menu Editor, click on *any* of the options in the Font submenu to display the Click event procedure. Begin this event procedure with the code shown in VB Code Box 8-12 to remove any existing check marks. Then add the code shown in VB Code Box 8-11 to select the font and place a check mark beside it.

7. Run your project and select the **Memo|Create memo** option. Enter several lines of text or retrieve a text file. Use the **Format|Font** submenu to format the text as Modern. Then format it as Courier New and then as WingDings (where the latter will not be readable!). Finally, format the text as Arial and then exit the memo creation system without saving the file. Also exit the project.

8. With frmMemo on the screen, use the Menu Editor to add the five styles discussed in the text and shown in Figure 8-21 to create the Format|Style submenu. Give all five the same name—**mnuFormatStyleType**—and give each a caption that matches the corresponding style type. Starting with the first one, add index values zero to four.

9. After closing the Menu Editor, click on any of the options in the Style submenu to display the Click event procedure. Add the code shown in VB Code Box 8-13 to select the style.

10. Run your project and select the **Memo|Create memo** option. Enter several lines of text or retrieve a text file. Use the **Format|Style** submenu to format the text as boldface. Then format it as italics and then as underline. Finally, format the text as bold and italics and then exit the memo creation system without saving the file.

11. Save the form and project under the same names.

SUMMARY

In this chapter, we discussed providing security for the Vintage Videos information system, creating a menu system to replace some of the command buttons, and added a new option: creating a memo system for creating, editing, saving, and printing memos.

Passwords are a common method of enforcing security for information systems. Password protection can be added to a Visual Basic project by using the Tag property of a text box and a startup form to which the user must respond. The user's input to the text box can be compared to the Tag property, and if the user fails to match the Tag property in three tries, the project is terminated.

The Menu Editor makes it easy to create a menu system for any Visual Basic application by entering a caption and name and selecting any other options for the menu item. Menu item names include a prefix of *mnu*, while submenu items also include any menu and submenus names to which it belongs. Hierarchical levels in the menu system are controlled by the indention of submenu items and outdention of menu items. Access keys can be assigned by including an ampersand (&) in the caption, and shortcut keys can be assigned by selecting from a drop-down list box.

For menu items to work, you must add code to them in the same way you added code to command buttons or other controls. It is easy with Visual Basic's editing options to move code from other controls to menu items. Help/About forms are commonly found in most commercial software.

Text editors are among the most widely available types of software. To create a text editor in Visual Basic, we use a text box with the multiline property set to true plus vertical scrollbars. The Resize event can be used to force the text box to fill the form whenever the form is displayed.

The common dialog control is useful for working with files as well as with other features. The common dialog control ShowSave and ShowOpen methods are used to display Save As and Open File dialog boxes. The Filter and FilterIndex properties control which types of files are displayed and which one is the default type. The common dialog FileName property is used to transfer the name of the file being saved or opened. Text is written to a file with the Print #*n* instruction. The FreeFile function returns the next available file, and the On Error GoTo instruction is used to check for the user clicking the Cancel button.

The common dialog box can be used to open files with the ShowOpen method. The same Filter and FilterIndex methods and FileName property as before are also used. To retrieve the contents of the file, the Input$(LOF(FileNumber), FileNumber) function is used, where LOF returns the length of the file. Saving a previously opened or saved file is accomplished with the Print #FileNumber instruction. If a file has not been opened or saved, the Save As event procedure should be called. A form-level variable can be used to determine whether a file has been saved or not.

The Windows Clipboard object is used for the Cut, Copy, and Paste editing operations. The SetText and GetText methods make this possible by working with the SelText property of the text box. Menu options can be enabled or disabled through the Enabled property.

A menu control array includes multiple menu items; all of them have the same name, but each is distinguished by its index. Creating a menu control array requires that you manually add the index values using the Menu Editor. Once you have the menu control array created, clicking an option passes its index to the event procedure, where a Select Case statement is used to detect the clicked option. The FontName text box property can be used to determine the font for the text box, and the FontBold, FontItalics, and FontUnderline properties can be used to determine the style.

You can create the new elements for the Vintage Videos project by adding the code shown in VB Code Boxes 8-1 to the Password form and copying the code from the cmdExit, cmdCheck, and cmdFindVideo command buttons to the corresponding menu items on the Vintage form. Also, add the code in VB Code Boxes 8-2, 8-4, 8-5, 8-7, 8-8, and 8-9 to the Memo form. For the Edit menu option on the Memo form, add the code shown in VB Code Box 8-10 and Figure 8-19. To the code window for the Format menu option on the Memo form, add the code shown in VB Code Boxes 8-11 through 8-13.

EXERCISES

1. In some applications, Personal Identification Numbers (PIN) are used instead of passwords. Create a form that accepts a PIN as a password. Instead of using the tag to hold the password, create a sub procedure that checks if a PIN is valid. For this prob-

NEW VISUAL BASIC ELEMENTS

Control/Object	Properties	Method	Event
form object	BorderStyle ControlBox ScaleHeight ScaleWidth		Resize
text box control	Alignment Multiline PasswordChar Height/Width SelText Scrollbars Tag		
command button control	Default Cancel		
menu control	Name Caption Enabled Checked		Click
common dialog control	Name CancelError FileName Filter FilterIndex	ShowOpen ShowSave	
Clipboard object		Clear GetText SetText	

NEW PROGRAMMING STATEMENTS

Statement to check for an error **On Error GoTo** ErrorLabel: ErrorLabel:
Statement to Input text from file **Input$(LOF(**FileNum), #FileNum)
Statement to save text to a file **Print** #FileNum, txtName.text

KEY TERMS

clipboard object   Menu Editor   shortcut keys

common dialog control   menus   startup form

menu control array   password

lem, use the rule that a valid PIN is composed of a two digit month value and a two digit day value. For example, on January 21 the valid PIN would be 0121 and on November 3 the valid PIN would be 1103. The Visual Basic Date, Month, and Day functions should be useful in comparing the entered PIN with the current date values.

2. Write a program that contains one upper-level menu with the name **Appearance**. Include in this menu two submenus, **Color** and **Size**. For the color submenu, write a series of menu items such as **Black**, **White**, **Green**, etc. When each Color menu item is selected, the BackColor of the form should change to the corresponding color. In addition, the selected menu item is checked. For the Size submenu, create three menu items, **Big**, **Medium**, and **Small**. When each of these is selected, the size of the form should adjust to match the selected menu item and the menu item is checked. Select appropriate access and short-cut keys for each menu item.

3. One way to save time when developing Visual Basic projects is to begin by using an existing form or template that already contains standard features that you may use for most of your projects. Create a template form with standard, functioning menu items. At a minimum include a **File** and **Help** menu. On your file menu include the submenus **Open**, **Close**, **Save**, **Save as** ..., and **Exit**. Write code for each of these and set appropriate access and shortcut keys. On the Help menu, include a submenu with the caption **About**. For this submenu, have it generate a message box for which the message may be easily edited to describe the current project.

4. For each of the following, explain what is wrong with the code. What error messages would you see, if any? What can you do to fix it?

a. The code shown below corresponds to menu items for cutting, copying, and pasting items in a textbox.

```
Private Sub mnuCopy_Click()
    Clipboard.SelText Text1.GetText
End Sub

Private Sub mnuCut_Click()
    Clipboard.SelText Text1.GetText
    Text1.SelText = ""
End Sub

Private Sub mnuPaste_Click()
    Text1.SetText = Clipboard.SelText
End Sub
```

b. The following code should open a file for a program. The file will then be available for use by other code until it is closed when a different button is clicked.

```
Private Sub Command1_Click()
  Dim intFileNum As Integer
  On Error GoTo ErrHandler
  intFileNum = FreeFile
  dlgDialog1.Filter = "Text (*.txt)|*.txt| _
    All files (*.*)|*.*"
  dlgDialog1.FilterIndex = 2
```

```
        dlgDialog1.ShowOpen
        strFileName = dlgDialog1.FileName
        Open strFileName For Input As #intFileNum
    ErrHandler:
        Close All
        Exit Sub
    End Sub
```

5. Use the Visual Basic Help facility or the MSDN on-line library to answer the following questions.

    a. For each upper level menu, how many levels of submenus can you have?

    b. What is the Path property? Can it be used with the App object?

    c. What is the difference between a modal and a modeless form? How do you make a form modal?

    d. What is the Resume statement? When and where is it used?

PROJECTS

If you have not already added the common dialog control to your toolbar, you should do this before attempting any of these exercises. All files should be saved in the Chapter8 folder on your data disk.

1. Retrieve Ex7-1.vbp (or Ex7-6.vbp if you completed it) from your data disk and modify it to display a password form when the initial form is loaded. Use a password of your choosing, but make sure that it is not displayed when entered. Also, revise the main form to replace all buttons with a menu system with two menu bar options: File and Students. Include the Exit operation in the File submenu and all other operations in the Students submenu. In addition, add an About menu bar option that displays a third form with information about you and this project. Finally, add an Open option to the File submenu that will allow you to select the data file you wish to use with this project. If you are modifying the project for Exercise 7-6, then also replace the command button operations on the second and third forms with appropriate menu selections. Save the files for this project in the Vintage8 folder with a project file name of **Ex8-1.vbp**. Use appropriate names for the other files.

2. Retrieve Ex7-2.vbp (or Ex7-7.vbp if you completed it) from your data disk and modify it to display a password form when the initial form is loaded. Use a password of your choosing, but make sure that it is not displayed when entered. Also, revise the main form to replace all buttons with a menu system with two menu bar options: File and Customers. Include the Exit operation in the File submenu and all other operations in the Customers submenu. In addition, add an About menu bar option that displays a third form with information about you and this project. Finally, add an Open option to the File submenu that will allow you to select the data file you wish to use with this project. If you are modifying the project for Exercise 7-7, then also replace the command button operations on the second and third forms with appropriate menu selections. Save the files for this project in the Vintage8 folder with a project file name of **Ex8-2.vbp**. Use appropriate names for the other files and save everything in the Chapter8 folder, but make sure they do not conflict with file names used with projects saved in this folder.

3. Retrieve Ex7-3.vbp (or Ex7-8.vbp if you completed it) from your data disk and modify it to display a password form when the initial form is loaded. Use a password of your

choosing, but make sure that it is not displayed when entered. Also, revise the main form to replace all buttons with a menu system with two menu bar options: File and Golfers. Include the Exit operation in the File submenu and all other operations in the Golfers submenu. In addition, add an About menu bar option that displays a third form with information about you and this project. Finally, add an Open option to the File submenu that will allow you to select the data file you wish to use with this project. If you are modifying the project for Exercise 7-8, then also replace the command button operations on the second and third forms with appropriate menu selections. Save the files for this project in the Vintage8 folder with a project file name of **Ex8-3.vbp**. Use appropriate names for the other files and save everything in the Chapter8 folder, but make sure they do not conflict with file names used with projects saved in this folder.

4. A local pet shop, Pets R Us, would like you to build their new system for creating coupons to be mailed to existing customers who have made recent special-order purchases. The user can choose to send customers a 10%-off coupon on their next purchase or a coupon for a large bag of pet food with a $15 purchase. Your application should input the names and addresses of existing customers from a sequential file that is selected from a common dialog box. This file has an EOF marker and is in the following form:

name
street address
city, state, Zip code

Save these data in three String arrays (maximum 100 strings per array), and add the names to a list box that is displayed on the opening form. When you select a name from the list box, a second form should be displayed that creates a form letter based on the information you input from the file. The form with the list box on it should be the opening form and should have a File menu that will have options enabling a user to input a data file from a dialog box, print the contents of the three arrays, switch to the second form, and exit the program. The menu option to switch to the second form should check to ensure that all the necessary fields are complete for the customer selected and then display the coupon form. If any information is missing, this menu option should display an error message alerting the user to the problem. Be sure to use appropriate shortcut and access keys on the menu.

Because this project gives valuable coupons to customers, the user should have to enter a password before being able to use the project. There should also be an About form that can be reached from a menu option and that displays information about you and this project.

Once the second form is displayed, it should have a text box for the name and address of the customer and a multiline text box into which one of two messages can be displayed depending on a menu selection. If the customer is to be given a 10%-off coupon, then the following message should be displayed:

Dear Customer:

This coupon entitles you to a 10% discount on your next purchase. Thank you for shopping at Pets R Us.

On the other hand, if the customer is to be given large bag of pet food with a $15 purchase, the following message should be displayed:

Dear Customer:

This coupon entitles you to a free large bag of pet food with the purchase of $15 or more of merchandise. Thank you for shopping at Pets R Us.

In addition to a menu option that will enable the user to select the type of coupon, there should be a File submenu on the second form that will enable the user to print the coupon form or exit the coupon form back to the Startup form. You should also add a third form named frmCustomerAdd. The user should be able to switch to this form by selecting a menu bar option on the main form. The new form should allow the user to add new customers and their addresses to the customer list and print a list of all customers and their addresses in alphabetical order.

You should also modify the Exit button on the main form so that the revised customer name and address arrays are saved to the data file when the user exits the project. Save your project as **Ex8-4.vbp** giving the form files appropriate names. Save everything in the Chapter8 folder, but make sure the file names do not conflict with file names used with projects saved in this folder.

5. Professor Hardnose's policy is that the number of times a student is absent is subtracted from the student's exam average to compute a modified quiz average. Thus, for a student with an exam average of 81.50 and 3 absences, the modified exam average would be 78.50. Professor Hardnose determines the final letter grade based on the modified exam average using a 60-70-80-90 scale. Your mission, should you decide to accept it, is to input the name, ID number, number of absences, and exam average for his students from a file, with the ID number being displayed in a list box. When an ID number if selected from the list box, a modified exam average is calculated and a letter grade is assigned. All of the information on the student is added to a second list box.

You will also need to create File and Summary menu bar options. The File submenu should include Open, Print, and Exit options with a separator bar above the Exit option. The Open submenu option should allow the professor to choose a file from which to input data (he teaches several different classes.) The Print submenu option should print the contents of the list box containing the modified average and letter grade for all students, and the Exit submenu option should exit the project. The Summary menu bar option should display a second form with a list box and option buttons for each letter grade. Clicking an option button should display a list of student names assigned that letter grade. There should be a Return command button on this form to return control to the main form.

Because this project involves sensitive information on student grades, there should be a password security form that must be satisfied before the main form can be accessed. Name this project **Ex8-5.vbp** and give the forms appropriate file names. Save everything to the Chapter8 folder, but make sure the file names do not conflict with file names used with projects saved in this folder.

6. Since the manager of Pets R Us often wants to write letters to very special customers offering them a unique discount, a memo creation option is required for this application. Add a menu bar option on the main form that enables the user to switch to a memo creation form similar to that discussed in the text. You should also create the memo creation form discussed in the text and add it to this project. Name this project **Ex8-6.vbp**, and give the forms appropriate file names. Save everything to the Chapter8 folder, but make sure the file names do not conflict with file names used with projects saved in this folder.

7. Professor Hardnose's tough grading policy brings many queries from students regarding their grades. To avoid with having to deal with these queries, the professor would like to have a memo editor added to his grading information system. With it, he

could retrieve and modify standard memos that explain why a student received a particular grade. He could also create new memos when a student was particularly interested in his grade. Please retrieve the Ex8-5.vbp project from your data disk and modify it to add the capability to create, edit, and save memos. Save the revised project as **Ex8-7.vbp** with the new editing form saved as **Ex8-7Memo.frm.** Do not change the names of any other forms you may have created for the previous exercise.

8. Many systems are set up for more than one authorized user. Generally, the user of such a system will provide both a user ID and a password. For a system such as this to work, a mechanism is needed to store a list of users and passwords securely. One method is to store the list in a file with the IDs and the passwords encrypted. When the program begins the file may be read into two arrays and then the values may be decoded. Once they are decoded the arrays may be searched for matching user IDs and passwords. Encryption rules may range from the fairly simple to the complex. For example, a simple rule might be to convert each character in the password to its ASCII value (using the Asc( ) function) and then add a constant. This is easily reversed by first subtracting the constant from each ASCII value and then converting back to a character (using the Chr( ) function). The more complex the encryption rule the more secure the password file.

Create a password system for a Visual Basic program that utilizes both a user ID and a password. Include on a main program form a menu item that allows a user once they have entered the system to change their password. This feature should require that the user re-enter their current password and then enter the new password. Once a button is clicked, the old password should be verified and then the user should be requested to verify the new password by retyping it into an input box. If the old password is correct and the new password has been entered correctly twice, the new password should be encrypted and saved to the password file. If items are entered in error, provide an appropriate message and exit the sub. For added security, make up your own encryption/decryption rule. Name this project **Ex8-8.vbp**, and give the forms appropriate file names. Save everything to the Chapter8 folder, but make sure the file names do not conflict with file names used with projects saved in this folder.

9. The most popular feature of The Ila Weekly World Journal is the classified advertisement section. The cost of each advertisement is calculated using an initial cost of $1 plus $0.01 per character (including spaces). Bubba Hearst, the managing editor of the classifed section, wishes to create a simple program for entering, editing, and pricing classified ads. Ads will be typed into a Multiline text box. Menu items will be provided for editing the advertisement. These should include cut, copy, and paste features. In addition, the user may choose various font styles and sizes from a format menu. The default font style and size is provided at no extra cost; an additional cost of $.25 is added if a different format is selected. On a file menu, provide options to Clear and Submit the ad. The Clear option will clear the text box and initialize the cost. The Submit option will generate a common dialog box for saving the ad. Once the ad has been saved, a form will appear with a listbox showing a receipt for the ad. The receipt will show the number of characters (Hint: the LOF( ) or Len( ) functions may be useful here), a breakdown of the costs for the ad, and a total cost. Include a button for printing the receipt and one for canceling this form. When cancel is clicked, the program should return to the main form and be ready for creating the next classified advertisement. Name this project **Ex8-9.vbp**, and give the forms appropriate file names. Save everything to the Chapter8 folder, but make sure the file names do not conflict with file names used with

projects saved in this folder.

PROJECT: JOE'S TAX ASSISTANCE (CONT.)

As he started to shut down his laptop, Joe muttered to himself, "It just doesn't look or feel like these other Windows programs yet."

He had just spent a couple of hours exploring some of the software that was on his laptop. He had noticed that many of the programs written for the Windows operating system had the same look and feel. Most seemed to have a main area where work is performed, they all seemed to have a row or two of buttons for performing some operations, and Joe noticed that just about all of the programs that he saw had a row of pull-down menus along the top of the window.

He began to realize how important this was for people learning the software. "You know," he thought, "after getting used to one of these Windows software programs, it's not too difficult to get started with another, because they have a lot in common."

"That's what I need to do with our program," he said half out loud. "All of these big buttons on the screen just don't look right anymore."

It took him only a second to pick up the phone and dial Zooey's number.

"Hi, Tony, it's Joe," he said to Zooey's father on the other end of the line. "I'm fine. And you? Great! I was wondering if Zooey's available. Yes, I want to talk about our program again." When he got excited about something, Joe would often forget to slow down and observe the niceties of small talk, but his family had come to expect and accept such little eccentricities.

When Zooey came on the line, Joe said just one word. "Menus!" he exclaimed.

"What are you talking about, Grandpa?" Zooey asked. Laughing, she added, "This is Zooey, you know. Not Chinese take-out. Did you dial the wrong number again?"

"Not this time. What I mean is, I want to change our program so that it has menus," he explained. "You know. Like the other Windows software."

"I think we can do that, Grandpa. I can come over tomorrow after school." Zooey replied. "But why do you want to do that? Don't you like the way we have it now?"

"Yes, I'm happy with the program so far. I just think it would be improved if we make it more like other Windows programs. Especially if I'm going to make it available for other VITA volunteers."

Zooey replied, "You're probably right. Also, we could eventually make it so that the screen is not so cluttered. This would move most of the main form into the menu, where it is always available, instead of behind the other forms."

"I didn't think of that." Joe beamed. "You sure are a bright girl. You probably get that from my side of the family."

"Ha! Ha! I wouldn't let Dad hear you say that." Zooey laughed. "Well, I have to finish some homework before bed. See you tomorrow, Grandpa."

"Good night, Zooey" Joe said as they hung up.

"Hmm, I think I'll look at some more menus for ideas," Joe thought as he opened the laptop again.

Questions

1. Look at various Windows software. List the menus and menu items that they have in common.

2. Set up a menu structure for the VITA program that includes some of these common

menus. For now, just develop the structure. Functionality can be added later as your skills progress. Include, at a minimum, the following menus: File, Edit, Window, and Help.

3. Add an additional menu called Forms. In this menu include an item corresponding to each of the forms that might go along with the 1040 tax form. These include the 1040 itself and the schedules that support various calculations. For the 1040 menu item, create a submenu that includes items corresponding to the buttons of the original program. Set up each of these items so that when an item is selected the proper commands are executed.

4. Run and test your program.

9 INTRODUCTION TO WORKING WITH DATABASES IN VISUAL BASIC

LEARNING OBJECTIVES	After reading this chapter, you will be able to:

- ❖ Understand how databases are used to store business data and how they differ from arrays.
- ❖ Describe the parts of a database and understand database concepts.
- ❖ Discuss database operations, including querying, editing, adding, and deleting.
- ❖ Add the data control to a form and connect it to a database table through the Recordset property.
- ❖ Use bound controls to display the contents of selected database fields.
- ❖ Add controls to browse the database records, add new records, and delete existing records.
- ❖ Find database records with field contents that match a specified value or string.

SCENARIO: USING A DATABASE AT VINTAGE VIDEOS

Clark leaned on the piano and stared across the crowded, smoke-filled bar at the girl of his dreams. As the music played, her eyes met his and he shyly averted his gaze. As the piano man came to the end of the song, Clark sighed and muttered, "Play it again, Sam."

A giggle and a sharp poke in the ribs awoke Clark from his daydream. Reddening and wondering if he had spoken out loud, he turned to see that his sister Yvonne had somehow snuck up on him. Little wonder, he realized, since he had been far away in thought.

"So I see that you like the new clerk, Monique." Yvonne goaded. As they watched, Monique began helping a customer rent some videos. Using the new menu system, she entered the names of the videos and selected a video type to display the price information. After accepting the money and printing the receipt, she smiled and asked the customer if there would be anything else.

Noticing her brother's smitten look, Yvonne decided to bring him back to reality. "What's next for the store program, Clark?" she inquired. "It seems to be working pretty well for Monique."

Once again Clark was cruelly drawn out of his reverie. He took a deep breath and began answering his sister's question. "I've come to realize that the current system of using sequential files and arrays for storing and manipulating the store's data is becoming inadequate," he said in his most businesslike voice. "Since both the number of customers and the number of videos keep growing, we need a more efficient way to store the data. Fortunately, I've already had a class in databases, and there are database controls available with Visual Basic."

"What's a database?" Yvonne asked. "Isn't that just the word for information that is stored on the computer? I thought we were already doing that!"

"Well, yes and no. A database is basically information that is stored on a computer system, but it's more than that," Clark explained. "There are several standard ways of creating databases, such as a relational database. These standard formats allow for the data to be structured in an organized fashion so that it is more easily managed. You know—adding or deleting data, modifying data, or even querying the database for certain information. All of these things are easier and more efficient with a well-organized database."

"I see. But why do *we* need one?" she inquired. Clark could tell that she really was interested, and he almost forgot about Monique as he continued to explain.

"Databases help solve several problems related to storing lots of data, and believe me, our data requirements are getting bigger every day. Databases also help reduce the storage of redundant information and maintain the accuracy, integrity, and security of the data as well. Before long our data may be one of the most important assets that we have! In addition, we can use a database to replace the paper and pencil system we've been using to track who rented what video and compute late fees on overdue videos. This will also give me the reason I need to reorganize the entire project to take advantage of using a database."

"You should explain some of this to Monique. Girls often like a man who is passionate about his work. It's a fundamental insight," Yvonne teased.

Clark blanched. Somehow, he had known that his daydream was neither unnoticed nor forgotten. His fears were confirmed when Yvonne said: "Besides, as Sam's song says, 'The fundamental things apply as time goes by.'"

Discussion of Scenario

While the current transaction processing system for Vintage Videos is working well as far as it goes, there definitely is room for improvement. The current system of sequential files and arrays has been adequate for a small number of members and videos, but as the store has grown, this system does not allow for the type of processing that is needed. For example, there is no computerized method for keeping track of when a video was rented, when it was returned, and what the late fee is, if there is one. While the paper and pencil method is currently sufficing, it will not work much longer. In addition, since the array of member names is stored in memory, data can be lost if a computer "hangs" and has to be rebooted or if the system "crashes."

For these and a variety of other reasons, Clark has suggested using a database to store data about the members and about the videos in such a way that it will be possible to carry out all of the searches that currently are being done only for members and videos. More important, using a database will make it possible to keep up with videos as they are rented and returned and, as a result, to be able to determine the status of any video in the store—if it has been rented, and, if so, when it is due back in. Using a database will also make it possible to automatically add late fees to a customer's record for movies returned late. Finally, the database will make it possible to automatically add the price of a video to the transaction, thereby speeding up the transaction process.

Clark has also indicated that he wants to reorganize the project to take advantage of using a database to store information on videos and customers. We will delay discussing his proposed reorganization until after we have covered important database concepts and the use of Visual Basic to work with databases.

DATABASE CONCEPTS

Given all of the improvements that are possible in just the Vintage Videos transaction system, it is no wonder that databases have become an essential part of all information systems. In fact, developing a database for an information system is usually the first step in designing and creating the system. For this reason, we dedicate this entire chapter to rewriting the Vintage Videos transaction project to use databases rather than sequential files and arrays.

To start this discussion, we need to formally define a database: a **database** is *the storage of different types of data in a such a way that the data can be easily manipulated and retrieved by an end user.* Every database is composed of a series of elements, beginning with fields. A **field** is *a single fact or data item. It is the smallest unit of named data that has meaning in a database.* Examples of fields include a name, address, or phone number on a membership list; a product number in an inventory list; or a price in a price list. Fields are given **field names** that are used to identify them. *A collection of related data that is treated as a unit* is referred to as a **record**. Basically, records are collections of fields that pertain to a single person, place, or thing. For example, we might have a membership list record that contains numerous fields, including name, phone number, street address, city, state, Zip code, and other information of interest.

A related collection of records, all having the same fields, is referred to as a **table**. For example, a table for the Vintage Videos membership list would have a record for each person on the list, with each record referring to a different person and having the same fields. In a table, the records are commonly referred to as the **rows** of the table and the fields are the **columns** of the table. Figure 9-1 shows the first few records of the Membership table. Note the rows and columns of this table.

FIGURE 9-1.
Membership table

		Name	Phone_Number	Street_Address	City	State	Zip	Late_Fees
▶	+	Smith, Joe	706-555-0012	120 Hilltop Rd	Watkinsville	GA	30677	$0.00
	+	Mullins, Janice	706-555-0777	25 Greenwood Way	Watkinsville	GA	30677	$1.07
	+	Smith, Joe	706-555-1234	489 Prince Ave.	Watkinsville	GA	30677	$0.00
	+	Randall, Ray	706-555-3214	225 Ryan Ave.	Athens	GA	30606	$3.20
	+	Arons, Suzy	706-555-3587	293 Milledge Ave.	Watkinsville	GA	30677	$16.00
	+	Crider, Alice	706-555-3660	121 Andrews Ct.	Athens	GA	30605	$10.65
	+	Carroll, Ann	706-555-3700	105 Washington St.	Athens	GA	30605	$4.26
	+	Goodly, Alice	706-555-4244	400 Holman Rd.	Watkinsville	GA	30677	$3.18
	+	Roberts, Judy	706-555-4783	707 Westbury Ct.	Athens	GA	30604	$0.00
	+	Hyatt, Ashley	706-555-5355	1249 Atlanta Highway	Watkinsville	GA	30677	$0.00

Relational Databases

Finally, if we have multiple tables that are related, we then have a special type of database known as a **relational database**. This is the most common type of database used today, and it is the type we will use in this text. As an example of a relational database, consider the Vintage Videos database composed of the Membership table shown in Figure 9-1 along with a second Video table with fields for the video ID and name, the rental price, the location in the store, and to determine whether or not the video is rented. Finally, there will be a third table that contains information on each rental, including fields for the video ID number, the phone number of the person renting the video, and the date the video is to be returned. In this case, the Membership table is related to the Rental table through the customer phone number that is common to both tables, and the Video table is related to the Rental table through the video ID number that is common to both tables. Since both the Membership table and the Video table are related to the Rental table, they are also related to each other. These relationships are shown in Figure 9-2.

FIGURE 9-2.
Relationships in Vintage Videos database

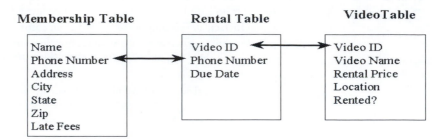

You may ask: Why are these particular fields related, rather than some others? It has to do with ensuring that there is no ambiguity about the records being referenced. If we assume that every Vintage Videos member has a phone and that there is only one membership per household, then the phone number is a unique identifier for each member with no two members having the same phone number; in database terminology, the phone number is the **primary key** for the Membership table. Similarly, the video ID is the primary key for the Video table. In the Rental table, these two keys become what is known as **foreign keys**, because they identify records from another table in this table. However, note that each transaction is now uniquely identified by the phone number of the person renting it and the video ID of the video being rented. Through this relationship, for example, we will be able to find out information about the rental status of a video or the number of videos that a person has rented at any one time. In many database packages, the table is automatically sorted on the primary key. For example, Figure 9-1 is arranged in ascending order of telephone number, since this is its primary key. Note: While the Rented field in the Videos table is redundant (this information is available from the Rental table), we will include it to avoid having to perform multiple operations early in the chapter.

> **Tip:** When entering a new record into a database, you must provide a value for the primary key field and the value must not duplicate the primary key value of any other record in the table.

Since this is not a textbook on database design, we will not go any further into the manner in which the tables and keys are designed and selected. For further information on this topic, you may wish to refer to a book on relational databases.[1]

Database Operations   The primary use of a database is to enable the user to obtain information from it in a usable form by constructing **queries** to the database. For a relational database, these queries are written in a special language known as **SQL** (for *Structured Query Language*), and they enable database users to find records from a table that meet some stated criterion or to create composite records from multiple tables that meet the criterion. While knowing SQL is a must for working with multiple tables, Visual Basic has pro-

---

1. An excellent discussion of relational databases can be found in *Data Management* 3rd. by Richard T. Watson (New York: John Wiley and Sons, 2002).

vided tools that allow us to query a single table without writing any SQL. We will spend this chapter discussing the use of Visual Basic to query a single table, and then discuss the use of SQL to query multiple tables in Chapter 10.

Once a query has been used to find a database record, it is then possible to **edit** the record—that is, make changes to the contents of one or more fields—or to **delete** a record if it is no longer needed in the database. It is also possible to **add** new records to the database. For example, if a member paid his or her late fees, we would want to query the Membership table for this member's record and edit the late fees amount to make it zero. We will also want to edit the record to add late fees when the renter returns a video after the due date. Similarly, if a new person joins Vintage Videos, we would want to add a record for that person to the Membership table. Finally, if a video is removed from stock, we would need to find the record in the Videos table and delete it.

Databases vs. Arrays

A question that may come to you in reading this discussion is this: Why are databases so superior to the file and array system we have been using? While arrays are very useful for working with moderate-sized lists and tables in computer memory, databases are superior for the type of processing faced by Vintage Videos and countless other organizations for several reasons:

1. A database table can store multiple types of data in the same table, while arrays are restricted to a single data type.
2. Any changes to the database are immediately saved to disk as they occur.
3. We can use a sophisticated database engine to handle the processing.
4. It is very easy to connect multiple computers to the same database, so that any changes are immediately known to all computers.

In the first case, instead of having to work with multiple arrays, each holding a different type of data, we can work with a single table that stores different types of data. For example, the Membership table shown in Figure 9-1 has Text, Numeric, and Currency data types in it. In the second case, by storing changes in the database as they occur rather than waiting until the end of the processing period, we avoid potential losses in data due to power outages or other problems. In the third case, instead of the programmer having to develop the logic and write the code to search for a specific record, we can depend on the database engine to handle this operation. The programmer has to be concerned only with ensuring that the correct request is passed to the engine. Finally, an array can reside on only one computer, and any changes to it are not known to other computers, even if those computers have a similar array on them. This means that changes such as new members or rented videos would have to be reconciled between computers at the end of the day—an onerous job at best! For all of these reasons, in this chapter we will discuss converting the Vintage Videos transaction processing application to a database system.

Databases in Visual Basic

To work with a database in Visual Basic, we will assume that it has already been created either by someone else or by you using Microsoft Access 2000 or some other database software package. Visual Basic is equipped to work with databases created by virtually any personal computer software as well as databases that are stored on another computer. For the purposes of this text, we will assume that a Microsoft Access 2000 relational database already exists and that we will be working with it. As you may know, Microsoft Access files have an *.mdb* (Microsoft database) extension. In Visual Basic we will be using the Microsoft Jet database engine to work with databases just as if we were using Microsoft Access. It should be noted that the individual tables in a Microsoft Access database are *not* saved separately—they are all saved in a single .mdb file.[2]

One of our goals in using Visual Basic to work with a database is to provide users with a friendly front end to the database that will allow them to carry out operations on the database without having to know the appropriate Visual Basic or SQL instructions. For example, if we want to find all members with late fees greater than a certain amount, the Visual Basic front end should make it possible to enter the amount and click a button to have this list generated. Or, if we want to check in a returned video, we should be able to display information on the video simply by entering its ID number.

> **Tip:** The Learning Edition of VB6 shipped with this book does not have Access 2000 compatibility. You can add this feature by downloading the VS Service Pack 4 from the Microsoft Web site (http://msdn.microsoft.com/vstudio/sp/vs6sp4/default.asp) and installing it.

In this chapter, you will work with a database named **Vintage.mdb**, which can be downloaded from the Web site associated with this text. Both Access 97 and Access 2000 versions are available and can be viewed with the appropriate version of Access.

Mini-Summary 9-1: Database Concepts

1. A database is a way of storing different types of data so that the data can be easily manipulated and retrieved by an end user.

2. Databases are composed of fields, records, and tables, where fields are single facts or data items that have field names. A collection of related data that is treated as a unit is referred to as a record, and a related collection of records all having the same fields is referred to as a table.

3. Tables in a relational database are related through fields that contain the same information. The primary key is a field that is unique to each record. A primary key which is used as a field in another table is a foreign key.

4. Database operations include querying to find specific records as well as adding, editing, and deleting records.

5. Databases have some advantages over arrays, including permanence as well as the ability to store multiple types of data, to use database engines, and to use the same information on multiple computers.

It's Your Turn!

1. List the key elements of any database. Why is a relational database so named?

2. What is the difference between a primary key and a foreign key in a relational database table?

---

2. The material in this chapter works for either Access 97 or 2000. For more information on upgrading to Access 2000, visit the Web site associated with this text.

3. What are databases typically used for? What is SQL?

4. How is using a database for processing superior to using files and arrays?

5. Why would you want to use a Visual Basic front end instead of just allowing users to access the database using a DBMS such as Microsoft Access?

6. Go to **Student** section of the text Web page and download the Vintage.mdb database from the Chapter 9 area and save it to the *root folder* of your data disk.

7. If you have access to Microsoft Office, use the Access database program to view the Members table in the database; it should look like that shown in Figure 9-1

THE DATA CONTROL

data control

The control that allows us to work with a database in Visual Basic is the **data control**. This control acts as a link between the Visual Basic project and the database stored on disk. The data control is linked to a table of the database or to a virtual table. It accesses database records in the table or from the query one at a time with an internal pointer denoting the **current record** in the database. We will restrict ourselves to working with database tables until we take up using SQL in the latter portion of the chapter. The data control has CD player-like controls on it at run time that allow you to move backward and forward through the database either one record at a time or from the first or last record in the database.

The data control is added to a form in the same way as any other control. Once it is added to a form, three properties need to be set at design time: Name, Caption, and DatabaseName.[3] While you are already familiar with the Name and Caption properties, the other one is new. The **DatabaseName** property refers to the file name (including the drive and path name) of the database. A fourth property, the **Record-Source** property, is also often set at design time and defines the database table that the data control accesses.

> **Tip:** In addition to an individual table, the RecordSource property may be set to a Query defined in the database or the results of an SQL statement written within the Visual Basic code.

To help you understand the data control and how it is used to display database records, we will begin creating the new Vintage Videos transaction processing system project with a single form that will display the database records in the Members table of the Vintage.mdb database you downloaded earlier. Later, we will add other new forms to this project as well as adding existing forms from the old Vintage Videos project that are not affected by the switch to a database system.

This new form, named *frmMemberInfo,* will have a data control named *datMembers* with a caption of **Members** (the name prefix for the data control is **dat**). To set the DatabaseName property, click on it to display a dialog box button (with three dots on it). If you click on this button, you can then select a database from a dialog box by searching for it and then clicking on it. In our case, the DatabaseName property is set to *a:\vintage.mdb* (assuming the Vintage.mdb database was downloaded to your data disk). Once you have set the DatabaseName property, you can set the RecordSource

3. If the *Connect* property is not set to the version of MS Access you are using, you will have to set it as well.

FIGURE 9-3 Record-
Source property

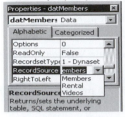

property by clicking on it and then clicking on the down arrow to select a database table from the resulting list. Figure 9-3 shows the RecordSource property with a list of tables displayed. In our case, we will select the *Members* table.

The form will also have text boxes in which the customer name, street address, city, state, Zip code, phone number, and late fees, if any, are displayed. These textboxes will be named, respectively, *txtCustName, txtAddress, txtCity, txtState, txtZip, txtPhone-Num,* and *txtLateFees.* It will also have the Vintage Videos slogan and logo, since we will eventually integrate them into the Vintage Videos transaction processing system. The resulting form is shown in Figure 9-4, with the data control pointed out.

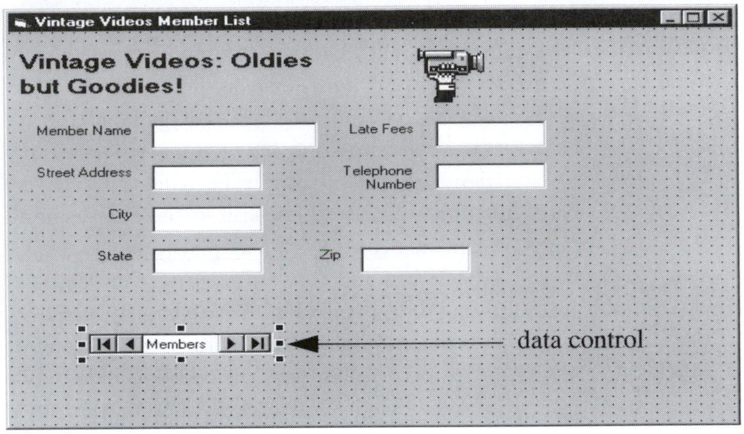

FIGURE 9-4.
frmMemberInfo
form with data
control

The data control links the Visual Basic project to the database; bound controls link other controls to the data control so they can be used to display the contents of fields in the current record. A **bound control** (also known as a **data-aware control**) accesses and displays data corresponding to a field in the table associated with the data control. This is accomplished through the bound control's **DataField** property. Bound controls with which you are familiar include the text box, label, check box, image, list box, and combo box controls. In addition, there are DBList, DBCombo, and DBGrid controls that are meant specifically to work with databases. All of these controls are editable; that is, in addition to viewing the contents of the database, you can change the database through the controls.

> **Tip:** It's important that you set data properties in the proper order. For instance, for the data control, you should set the DatabaseName property before selecting the RecordSource. For a bound control such as a text box, set the DataSource property before setting the DataField property.

For example, in the form shown in Figure 9-4, all of the text boxes will be bound to the corresponding fields in the Members table of the a:\Vintage.mdb database. At design time, they are bound to the fields through the **DataSource** and the DataField text box properties. The DataSource property is linked to the name of the data control, which is, in turn, linked to a database table. The DataField property is linked to a field of the table that is defined in the RecordSource property of the data control. In both cases—DataSource and DataField—a drop-down list box displays the appropri-

Bound Controls

ate choices. If datMembers is selected as the DataSource property, then all of the fields in the Members table of the Vintage.mdb database are displayed in the DataField drop-down list box. For the txtCustName, the associated data field name would be the Name field in the Members table. Table 9-1 shows the text boxes in the frmMember form and the data fields to which each text box should be bound.

TABLE 9-1: Bound Text Boxes on Form

Text Box	Data Field
txtCustName	Name
txtAddress	Street_Address
txtCity	City
txtState	State
txtZip	Zip
txtLateFees	Late_Fees
txtPhoneNum	Phone_Number

Once the data control is linked to a database table and these text boxes are bound to the corresponding database fields, running the project will automatically display the contents of the first record in the database table. You can browse the records by clicking on the first, previous, next, and last controls on the datMembers data control. Figure 9-5 shows the Members form with the first database record displayed.

Mini-Summary 9-2: The Data Control

1. In Visual Basic, the data control is the link to the database through its DatabaseName and RecordSource properties.

2. Bound or data-aware controls are those controls that are automatically linked to a field in the database through the data control's DataSource and DataField properties.

FIGURE 9-5.
Database record
displayed

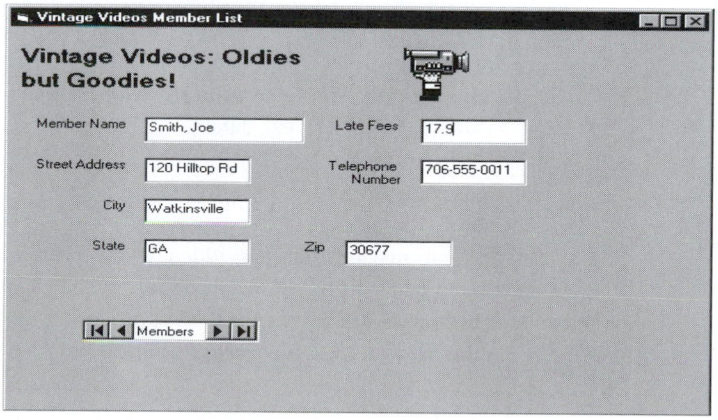

It's Your Turn!

1. What is the function of the data control? Which of its properties must be set for it to be useful?

2. What is a *bound* control? To bind a textbox to a data control, which properties must be set?

3. What is another name for a bound control?

4. What other Visual Basic controls can be bound to a database?

Completing the remaining questions will enable you to create the Visual Basic project discussed in the text.

5. Start a new project with a single form called **frmMemberInfo**. Add the controls shown in Figure 9-4, including the data control to the form. (Recall that the graphic of the video camera is found in the Graphics\Icons\Misc folder as Camera.ico and that it goes in an image control.) Give the text box controls the names shown in Table 9-1; name the data control as **datMembers** and give it a caption of **Members**.

6. For the data control, the DatabaseName property should be **a:\vintage.mdb** and the RecordSource property should be the **Members** table from this database.

7. Set the **DataSource** property for each of the text boxes to the DatMembers data control and set the **DataField** property for each text box to the appropriate data field shown in Table 9-1. Run your project and verify that the first record of the database is displayed as shown in Figure 9-5. Try out each of the VCR buttons on the data control to browse the database records.

8. Create a new **Chapter9** folder on your data disk and save the form as **Member-Info.frm** and the project as **Vintage9.vbp** in this folder.

ADDING NAVIGATIONAL BUTTONS

To improve the use of this form, we can add a number of features in the form of navigational buttons and menu options to add records and to delete the current record. The navigational buttons will replicate those shown on the data control, thereby allowing us to make the data control invisible to the user through its **Visible** property. We can also display the current record number and add a button that will exit the project (later, this will be used to move to another form). Two of these navigational buttons will use the image control for more than just looking pretty: It will be clickable to move to the previous or next database record. The names of the five controls to be added are shown in Table 9-2 in the order they will appear across the bottom of the form, along with the types of controls, the purpose of each, and any other pertinent properties.

If navigational buttons are added to the bottom of the frmMemberInfo form along with an exit button, the resulting form will be as shown in Figure 9-6. While you may not be able to see it because it has no caption, the record number label is located between the previous and next image controls.

Coding the Navigational Buttons

Because of the powerful database methods that are included in Visual Basic, coding these new navigational buttons is not really difficult. However, one important concept you should understand is that of the Recordset. The **Recordset object** represents the

TABLE 9-2: Navigational Buttons

Control	Name	Purpose	Other Properties
command button	cmdFirst	Move to first record	Caption property = "First"
image	ImgPrevious	Move to previous record	Picture property =...\icons\arrows\Arw01lt.ico
label	lblRecordNumber	Display the current record number	Caption property is blank
image	ImgNext	Move to next record	Picture property =...\icons\arrows\Arw01rt.ico
command button	cmdLast	Move to last record	Caption property = "Last"

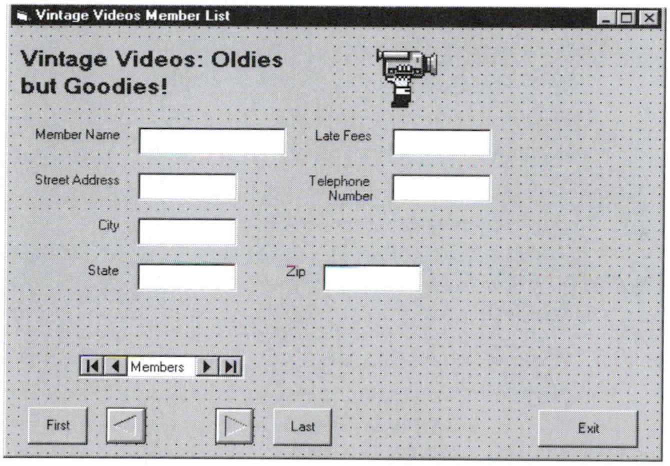

FIGURE 9-6.
Database form with navigational buttons

records in a database table or the records that can result from running a query on the database. In essence, it is the current set of records. For the time being, we will concern ourselves only with the case involving a single database table—the one set as the RecordSource property at design time.

With the Recordset object, numerous methods can be used to move the database around or modify it. Some of the navigational methods are shown in Table 9-3, along with their purpose.

TABLE 9-3: Recordset Methods

Method	Purpose
MoveFirst	Move to the first record in the Recordset
MoveLast	Move to the last record in the Recordset
MoveNext	Move to the next record in the Recordset
MovePrevious	Move to the previous record in the Recordset

Other Recordset object methods for adding or deleting records, querying a database, or editing a record will be discussed later. In each case, the Recordset method is used in a statement of the following form:

datName*.Recordset.*method

For example, to move to the next record in the Vintage database that is linked to the datMembers data control, the statement would be:

```
datMembers.Recordset.MoveNext
```

Using the Recordset methods, you can add the necessary code to the various navigational buttons on the Members form.

Initializing the record number counter

To keep track of the current record, we have added a record number counter in the form of a label (lblRecordNum). As we move through the database, this counter will be updated. However, it needs to be initialized to the current record in the database each time the form is displayed. This requires the use of a new form event—the Activate event. This event occurs whenever the form is made visible by the Show method. This event is used instead of the Load event because the form will be loaded into memory only once.

To find the current database record, we can use the AbsolutePosition property of the Recordset object to set the record counter label to the appropriate number. Since this property starts counting at zero, we need to add one to its value to determine the appropriate record number. The code for the Form_Activate event procedure is shown in VB Code Box 9-1.

VB CODE BOX 9-1. Code for Form_Activate event procedure	```Private Sub Form_Activate() lblRecordNumber.Caption = Str(datMembers. _ Recordset.AbsolutePosition + 1)End Sub```

Moving to the first record

To move to the first record when the cmdFirst button is clicked, we use the Recordset MoveFirst method. The record counter should also be reset using the AbsolutePosition property in this event procedure, as shown in VB Code Box 9-2.

VB CODE BOX 9-2. Code for cmdFirst_Click() event procedure	```Private Sub cmdFirst_Click() datMembers.Recordset.MoveFirst lblRecordNumber.Caption = Str(datMembers. _ Recordset.AbsolutePosition + 1)End Sub```

Moving to the last record

Moving to the last record is very much like moving to the first record, replacing MoveFirst with MoveLast. However, instead of setting the record number counter to a specific value for the last record, we will use as an alternative the RecordCount property of the Recordset object, which is equal to the number of records in the Recordset. The appropriate code is shown in VB Code Box 9-3.

VB CODE BOX 9-3. Code for CmdLast_Click() event procedure	```Private Sub cmdLast_Click() datMembers.Recordset.MoveLast lblRecordNumber.Caption = Str(datMembers. _ Recordset.RecordCount)End Sub```

Moving to the next record	The code to move to the next record would seem to be very similar to the code to move to the first or last record, and it is. However, we need to add code to ensure that the pointer has not been moved past the end of the Recordset. To do this, we need to check the EOF (end of file) property of the Recordset object. The EOF property is True if the record pointer has been moved beyond the last record in the database, otherwise, it is False. If the EOF property is True, then we need to set the pointer back to the end of the database. The code to do this is shown in VB Code Box 9-4. Note in this code that if the record pointer is not past the end of the database after the MoveNext method is applied, the record counter is simply set using the AbsolutePosition property as before. We do this instead of incrementing the counter to avoid any conflicts between the counter value and the location of the record pointer that might be caused by additions and deletions of records. If the record pointer is past the end of the database, a message is displayed and the pointer is moved to the end of the table. It is not necessary to change the record number counter in this case, because the pointer was already at the end of the database.

VB CODE BOX 9-4. Code for moving to the next record	
| | ```
Private Sub imgNext_Click()
  datMembers.Recordset.MoveNext
  If Not (datMembers.Recordset.EOF) Then
    lblRecordNumber.Caption = Str(datMembers.Recordset. _
    AbsolutePosition + 1)
  Else
    MsgBox "Already at end of table", vbInformation
    datMembers.Recordset.MoveLast
  End If
End Sub
``` |

Moving to the previous record	Moving to the previous record is very similar to moving to the next record, with one exception: Instead of checking the EOF property, we check the BOF (beginning of file) property. If the record pointer has been moved before the first record, the BOF property is True, and this can be checked in the same way that the EOF property was checked. The resulting code is shown in VB Code Box 9-5.

VB CODE BOX 9-5. Code for moving to the previous record	
| | ```
Private Sub imgPrevious_Click()
  datMembers.Recordset.MovePrevious
  If Not (datMembers.Recordset.BOF) Then
    lblRecordNumber.Caption = Str(datMembers.Recordset. _
    AbsolutePosition +1)
  Else
    MsgBox "Already at beginning of table", vbInformation
    datMembers.Recordset.MoveFirst
  End If
End Sub
``` |

Mini-Summary 9-3: Adding Navigational Buttons

1. The Recordset object is the current set of records linked to the data control, and the AbsolutePosition property provides the record number for the current record.

Mini-Summary 9-3: Adding Navigational Buttons (Continued)

2. Browsing methods of the data control include MoveFirst, MoveNext, MovePrevious, and MoveLast.

3. The EOF (end-of-file) and BOF (beginning-of-file) properties indicate that the record pointer is beyond the end of the recordset or before the beginning of the recordset, respectively.

It's Your Turn!

1. What does the Data Control Visible property do?

2. What is the Recordset object composed of?

3. Indicate whether each of the following is a property or a method of the Recordset object and give its purpose:

> a. MoveNext
>
> b. RecordCount
>
> c. BOF
>
> d. AbsolutePosition
>
> e. MoveLast

4. Why do we use the Form_Activate event instead of the Form_Load event to set the record number?

Completing the remaining questions will enable you to create the Visual Basic project discussed in the text.

5. Add the navigational controls shown in Figure 9-6 along with an Exit button. Use the names and other properties for the navigational buttons shown in Table 9-2 and **cmdExit** for the Exit button.

6. Add the code shown in VB Code Boxes 9-1, 9-2, and 9-3 for the Form_Activate event procedure and for the cmdFirst and cmdLast navigational buttons. Use the code shown in VB Code Box 9-4 for the imgNext button and the code shown in VB Code Box 9-5 for the imgPrevious button. Finally, add the **End** statement of the cmdExit button.

7. Run your project and try out each of the navigational buttons on the form to browse the database records. Note that the record number changes to match the current record. If you are sure the navigational buttons are working properly, set the Visible property for the datMembers data control to **False** to make it invisible.

8. Save the form and project under their current names.

ADDING, EDITING, AND DELETING RECORDS

Once you have browsed the records in the database, you may wish to add a new record to the database, edit the current record by changing one or more fields, or delete the current record. To accomplish these operations on the database, we need additional Recordset object methods, including the AddNew, Update, and Delete methods. While you may think that we also need an Edit method to modify the contents of the database fields, this is not necessary. Because the text boxes are data-aware, any change to a text box is automatically incorporated into the corresponding database field when the record pointer is moved or the Update-Record method is executed.

To make these operations easier, we will add a menu system to this form with a menu bar item of **Member Operations**. There will be four submenu items: **Add Member**, **Delete Member**, **Save Member**, and **Cancel Operation**, where the last two operations are related to the Add Member operation. The Save Member menu item will provide a method of ensuring that a new member's information is saved to the database. The Cancel Operation menu item enables the user to cancel the process of adding a new member. The menu items are named *mnuMemberAdd*, *mnuMemberDelete*, *mnuMemberSave*, and *mnuMemberCancel*.

Adding a New Record   While a database must exist before Visual Basic can be used to access it, you can easily add records to an existing database using the **AddNew** method. Adding records to the database is a three-step process:

1. Use the Recordset AddNew method to create a blank record in the database.

2. Input a value or string for each field of the new record.

3. Save the record with the Save Member operation.

When the blank record is created in the database in Step 1, the text boxes on the form are all cleared (or set to zero if they correspond to numeric fields). The data for the new record can then be entered directly into the text boxes. If a text box corresponds to a numeric field (late fees or Zip code), then the zero must be replaced with the a new value.

After the data for all the fields have been entered, the database is updated with the UpdateRecord method in the Save Member menu operation with the instruction:

```
datMembers.UpdateRecord
```

Notice that in this case, the entire database represented by the data control (datMember), not just the Recordset, is updated. This makes the change permanent. The code for the Add Member menu option is shown in VB Code Box 9-6, and the code for the Save Member menu option is shown in VB Code Box 9-7.

VB CODE BOX 9-6. Code to add record for new members	```Private Sub mnuMemberAdd_Click() varCurrentRecord = datMembers.Recordset.Bookmark datMembers.Recordset.AddNew blnAddingRecord = True End Sub```

VB CODE BOX 9-7. Code to save record for new member	```Private Sub mnuMemberSave_Click() datMembers.UpdateRecord If blnAddingRecord Then cmdLast_Click blnAddingRecord = False End If End Sub```

In looking at these two code tables, you will notice that two form-level variables are used: *blnAddingRecord* and *varCurrentRecord*. The blnAddingRecord variable is a Boolean data type variable that indicates if a new record is being added. The varCurrentRecord is a Variant data type variable that stores the position of the current record before adding a new record. This information is provided by the **Bookmark** property of the Recordset, which uniquely identifies each record in the database. By saving this information, we can return to a record if we need to. Both the blnAddingRecord variable and the varCurrentRecord variable will be used in the Cancel operation—the former to indicate if a record is being added and the latter to set the record pointer back to the record that was current before the Add operation was implemented.

> **Tip:** A record's AbsolutePosition can change as other records are added or deleted. A BookMark is more stable because it always points to the same physical location for the record.

The mnuMemberSave_Click event procedure uses the UpdateRecord method to update the database. If the blnAddingRecord variable has been set to True, the cmdLast_Click event is called to move the pointer to the end of the database to display the new record. Also, the blnAddingRecord variable is set to False after the record is added. We need this If-Then block so that we can use the Save Member operation to save any changes to existing database records without needing to move to the end of the database.

The mnuMemberCancel_Click event procedure is shown in VB Code Box 9-8, where we have used the **UpdateControls** method to make the contents of the current bound controls match those in the corresponding database record. Once again, this is useful if we want to cancel an editing operation. If a record is being added as indicated by the blnAddingRecord variable, then the Cancel operation sets the Recordset Bookmark to the varCurrentRecord variable. Recall that this variable stores the location of the current record before the Add operation is initiated. Once again, the blnAddingRecord variable is set to False after the operation is canceled.

VB CODE BOX 9-8.
Code to cancel
current operation
	```Private Sub mnuMemberCancel_Click()```
	``` datMembers.UpdateControls```
	``` If blnAddingRecord Then```
	``` datMembers.Recordset.Bookmark = varCurrentRecord```
	``` blnAddingRecord = False```
	``` End If```
	```End Sub```

For example, if we want to add a new record for John Lister, with phone number of 770-555-2579 and address of 292 Ashford Way in Bogart, GA 30622, we would click on the Member Operations menu bar option and then click on Add Member. This will clear all text boxes except the ones for late fees and Zip code which are set to zero. The user can then enter the pertinent information. When all information has been entered, the user saves the record to the database by clicking on the Save Member submenu option. It should be noted that the new record is saved as the *last* record in the database, but when the database is reopened later, it will be resorted to put the new record in its appropriate location.

If we wanted to cancel the process of adding a new member, we could simply click the Cancel Operation submenu option.

Editing Records

As mentioned earlier, because all of our text boxes are data-aware, any changes to a text box are automatically incorporated into the database when the record pointer is moved to a new record or the UpdateRecord method is executed. This means that all you need to do to edit a record is to use the navigational buttons to find it and make it the current record, and then edit the field(s) by making any changes in the corresponding text boxes. For example, in the record for Janice Mullins (the second record in the database), to correct the phone number to be 706-555-0778 instead of 706-555-0777, you would move the record pointer to the record containing her information and correct the phone number by typing over it or editing it. Moving to another record or clicking the Save Member submenu option will update the database and make this change permanent. Later we will handle the situation where a user makes changes and then exits *without* saving them.

Deleting Records

In addition to adding new records and editing existing records, we need to provide the capability to delete an existing record. As with the other features, Visual Basic has provided the Recordset **Delete** method to remove a record from the database. Once the pointer is positioned on the record to be removed, the Delete method automatically handles the delete operation. However, it is useful to ask the user as to whether they are sure they want to delete this record, because once a record is deleted, it cannot be undeleted.

The code to handle the query uses the capability of the MsgBox function to return a value depending on which button the user clicks. The statement to check whether the user really wants to delete the record would be:

```
intResponse = MsgBox(strDelete, vbYesNoCancel + _
    vbCritical + vbDefaultButton2, "Delete Record")
```

where

intResponse = an Integer variable that will be checked to determine which button was clicked

strDelete = a user-defined constant with the message "Are you sure you want to delete this record?"

vbYesNoCancel = a Visual Basic constant resulting in the Yes, No, and Cancel buttons being displayed

vbCritical = a Visual Basic constant resulting in an "X" in a red circle being displayed

vbDefaultButton2 = a Visual Basic constant that makes the second (No) button the default button (the one with the focus)

"Delete Record" = the title for the message box

This Msgbox will cause a window to be displayed like the one shown in Figure 9-6.

FIGURE 9-7. Delete Record message box

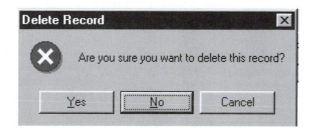

As discussed in Chapter 6, if the user clicks on "Yes" to delete the record, then the value of Response is equal to 6; if the user clicks on "No," the value of intResponse is 7; and if the user clicks on "Cancel," the value is 2. However, it is not necessary to remember these values, because there are vbYes, vbNo, and vbCancel constants that are equal to them. If intResponse is equal to the vbYes constant, then the record is deleted; otherwise, the event procedure is terminated. The code for the Delete menu option is shown in VB Code Box 9-9.

| **VB CODE BOX 9-9.** Code to delete a record | ```
Private Sub mnuMemberDelete_Click()
    Const strDelete as String = "Are you sure you want to " _
    & "delete this record?"
    Dim intResponse As Integer
    intResponse = MsgBox(strDelete, vbYesNoCancel + _
    vbCritical + vbDefaultButton2, "Delete Record")
    If intResponse = vbYes Then
      datMembers.Recordset.Delete
      datMembers.Recordset.Movenext
      If datMembers.Recordset.EOF then
        cmdLast_Click
      End if
    End If
End Sub
``` |
|---|---|

Note that if the user selects "Yes" to delete the record, the Recordset Delete method is executed and the record pointer is moved to the next record. This could move the pointer beyond the last record in the database, so it is necessary to check the Recordset EOF property. If the property is True, then the cmdLast_Click event procedure is called to move the pointer back to the last record *and* to revise the record number label.

Mini-Summary 9-4: Adding, Editing, and Deleting Records

1. The Recordset AddNew method can be used to add a new record to the database. When this method is used, bound textboxes are cleared or set to zero for numeric fields at which point data can be entered into the fields.

2. Once a new record is entered, it can be saved by moving to a new record or by using the UpdateRecord method.

3. A Boolean variable can be used to keep track of whether a new record has been added or not. This information can be useful when the user cancels an operation.

3. The Bookmark property provides a unique identifier for each record in the database as a Variant data type. When the value of the Bookmark property is saved to a variable, it is always possible to return to a record using the value of that variable. This is a more stable method of saving the position than the AbsolutePosition property which can change as other records are added.

4. The contents of data-aware controls can be edited by changing the contents of the control. The changes are saved by moving to another record.

5. Records can be deleted with the Delete method. It is useful to query the user before making the deletion permanent by moving to another record.

```

It's Your Turn!

1. What Recordset method is used to add new records to the database?

2. What is the purpose of the blnAddingRecord and varCurrentRecord variables in the project discussed in the text? What data types are they and why?

3. What Recordset property do we use to find the value of the varCurrent Record variable?

4. How do we make the contents of bound controls match those of the corresponding database record?

5. Why do you not need to remember the integer values of the "Yes" and "No" responses to the Message Box query?

Completing the remaining questions will enable you to create the Visual Basic project discussed in the text.

6. Add a menu bar option to the frmMemberInfo form with a caption of **Member Operations** and a name of **mnuMember**. Add submenu options with the captions and names shown in Table 9-4.

TABLE 9-4: Properties for Member Operations Submenu

Caption	Name
Add Member	mnuMemberadd
Delete Member	mnuMemberDelete
Save Member	mnuMemberSave
Cancel Operation	mnuMemberCancel

7. At the form level, declare **blnAddingRecord** as a Boolean variable and **varCurrentRecord** as a String variable.

8. Add the code shown in VB Code Box 9-6 to the mnuMemberAdd event procedure to enable the user to add records to the database.

9. Add the code shown in VB Code Box 9-7 to the mnuMemberSave event procedure to enable the user to save changes to the database.

10. Add the code shown in VB Code Box 9-8 to the mnuMemberCancel event procedure to enable the user to cancel changes to the database.

11. Add the code shown in VB Code Box 9-9 to the mnuMemberDelete event procedure to enable the user to delete a record from the database.

12. Run your project and add the new member discussed in the text (**John Lister**, with phone number of **770-555-2579**, residing at **292 Ashford Way** in **Bogart, GA 30622**). Use the Save Member option to save this new record.

13. Edit the record for Janice Mullins to change her phone number to be **706-555-0778** instead of 706-555-0777. Move to another record and then move back to see that the change has been saved.

14. Save your form and project under the same name.

FINDING RECORDS

While a browser screen like the one created in the previous sections can be useful for navigating records, the real power of a database comes from being able to find records by *querying* the database for records that meet some criteria. These criteria must be written in Visual Basic the same way they would be written in SQL, which can be a little confusing. However, we will try to make clear what is going on in each query, so you can learn to write your own queries.

Visual Basic provides us with several Recordset methods for finding records. These include **FindFirst, FindNext, FindLast,** and **FindPrevious**, where each method is used the same way, that is, as a combination of the Find method and a query string. For the FindFirst method, the form is as shown below. The other Find methods work in exactly the same manner.

*dat*Name**.Recordset.FindFirst** *query string*

Query Strings

The key to finding a record in the Recordset object is the query string. There are several things to remember about the query string. First, it is always a string. Second, it is usually a combination of a database field name, a comparison operator, and a value or string to which the field name is being compared. For example, if you wanted to find the first record in the Members table of the Vintage database (the current Recordset) with late fees greater than zero, the query string would look like:

```
datMembers.Recordset.FindFirst "Late_Fees > 0"
```

where the query string is "Late_Fees > 0". In this case, the field name is Late_Fees, the comparison operator is the greater-than symbol, and the contents of the Late_Fees field are being compared to zero.

While we could simply display this value in a text box, it would be more useful to display all the names and amounts of the late fees from all records that match this criterion in a list box. To do this, we need to add a command button named **cmdFindLateFees** with a caption of *Find Late Fees* and a list box named **lstLateFees** to the current frmMemberInfo in the bottom right-hand corner of the form. We also need to use the FindNext method to find the second and subsequent records, and we need to continue searching the database until there are no more matching records. This implies the use of a Do Until loop with the Recordset **NoMatch** property as a condition for continuing the loop. The NoMatch property returns a value of False each time a record is found that matches the query string. If no more records are found that match the query string, it returns a value of True.

The contents of the matching Name and Late_Fee fields are found through the Recordset **Field** property which has the form **Field(*"fieldname"*)**. For example, the contents of the matching Name field is found in

```
datMembers.Recordset.Field("Name")
```

It is not actually necessary to include the keyword *Field*, that is, the expression can be shortened to:

```
datMembers.Recordset("Name")
```

To list the matching records, the Name and Late_Fees Field properties for matching records are concatenated and added to the list box with the AddItem method. The code for the cmdFindLateFees event procedure is shown in VB Code Box 9-10.

Three things are notable about this code: First, instead of including the query string in both the FindFirst method and the FindNext method, we set a string variable equal to the query string and include it instead. While doing this is not terribly important here, it will become very useful when we start working with more complex query

> **Tip:** Some database management systems allow field names with spaces, for example Company Name. When used in code, you must place square brackets [] around field names containing spaces as in datCustomers.Recordset.("[Company Name]").

VB CODE BOX 9-10. Code to find members with late fees	
| | ```
Private Sub cmdFindLateFees_Click()
Dim strQueryString As String, varBookMark As Variant
varBookMark = datMembers.Recordset.Bookmark
strQueryString = "Late_Fees > 0"
lstLateFees.Clear 'Clear late fee list
datMembers.Recordset.FindFirst strQueryString 'Find 1st one
Do Until datMembers.Recordset.NoMatch
  lstLateFees.AddItem datMembers.Recordset("Name") & _
  " " & Format(datMembers.Recordset("Late_Fees"), _
  "currency") 'Add record to list box
  datMembers.Recordset.FindNext strQueryString 'Find next 1
Loop
datMembers.Recordset.Bookmark = varBookMark
End Sub
``` |

strings. Second, we use a Variant type variable, *varBookMark*, to save the location of the record before the search by setting it equal to the Bookmark property. After the search is completed, we set the Bookmark property of the Recordset to the variable to return to the original record. There is no need to change the Record Number label, since we go back to the record corresponding to the current value. Third, and last, we use the Clear method to automatically clear the Late Fees list box before adding names to it. We will do this with all of our searches. The form resulting from clicking the Late Fees button is shown in Figure 9-8.

FIGURE 9-8. List of members with late fees

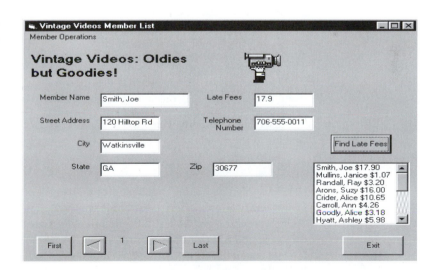

More on Query Strings

The query string used in the previous example included all of the criteria in a single string, that is, "Late_Fees > 0". However, the real power of Visual Basic comes from allowing the user to input the criteria. For example, instead of restricting the query to
```

all late fees greater than zero, we might want to allow the user to input a late fees value, say, $10, and use this value in the query rather than a cutoff of zero. Or, we might want to find the late fees for a specific member by entering the member's telephone number. We will look at creating query strings for both of these situations; the key difference between them is that the first query involves a numeric value while the second involves a string. Addressing this difference requires two different approaches to creating the query string. However, it is important to remember that the query must *always* be a string, just as the query string "Late_Fees > 0" was a string even though it involved a numeric comparison.

In the first case, the query string involves a numeric comparison like that used to find all members with late fees. Now, however, the user can input a value to be used in the comparison. This requires concatenating the first part of the comparison with this value. For example, if an InputBox is used to input the value that is stored in the string variable, strMaxLateFee, then the statement to input the cutoff values and to create the query string would be written as:

```
strMaxLateFees = InputBox("What is the cutoff value?")
strQueryString = "Late_Fees > " & strMaxLateFees
```

Note that even though the cutoff value is a numeric value, it must be written as a string in the query string.

In the second case—finding the late fee for a given telephone number—the comparison involves a string variable: the telephone number. This requires that the string variable be enclosed in apostrophes within the quotation marks of the query string. For example, if the telephone number being searched for is 770-555-1294, the query string should look like **"Phone_Number = '770-555-1294'"**. This requires concatenating the telephone number string with apostrophes before and after it and then concatenating this combination with the first part of the comparision. If an InputBox is used to input the telephone number as a string variable, strPhoneNum, then the statement to input the telephone number and to create the query string would be written as:

```
strPhoneNum = InputBox("What is the telephone number?")
strQueryString = "Phone_Number = " & "'" & strPhoneNum &
   "'"
```

which will result in a query string like the one in boldface shown above.

The easiest way to ensure that the apostrophe is added correctly to the query string is declare it as a constant at the beginning of any event or sub procedure in which it is used, that is,

```
Const strApos as String = "'"
```

and then to concatenate this constant with the rest of the query string as shown below:

```
strQueryString = "Phone Number = " & strApos & strPhoneNum & _
strApos
```

To apply this to the Members project, we will create another menu bar option named *mnuFind* with a caption of **Find**. This menu bar option will have two submenu options: *mnuFindLateFees* with a caption of **Find Late Fees** and *mnuFindPhoneNumber* with a caption of **Find Phone Number.** We will also delete the existing cmdFind button and cut and paste its code into each of the new submenu option event procedures. In the case of the late fees, the new code will be almost exactly the same as the cmdFind code shown earlier in VB Code Box 9-10, with the addition of declaring the appropriate string variables and modifying the query string as shown above. The code for the mnuFindLateFees is shown in VB Code Box 9-11.

> **Tip:** To work with date data types, you must surround them with the pound sign (#) instead of the apostrophe.

| **VB CODE BOX 9-11.** Code to find members with late fees above a cutoff value | ```vb
Private Sub mnuFindLateFees_Click()
  Dim strQueryString As String, strLateFees As String
  Dim varBookMark as Variant
  strLateFees = InputBox("What is the late fees cutoff?")
  varBookMark = datMembers.Recordset.Bookmark
  strQueryString = "Late_Fees > " & strLateFees
  lstLateFees.Clear
  datMembers.Recordset.FindFirst strQueryString 'Find first one
  Do Until datMembers.Recordset.NoMatch
    lstLateFees.AddItem datMembers.Recordset("Name") & _
    " " & Format(datMembers.Recordset("Late_Fees"), _
    "currency") 'Add record to list box
    datMembers.Recordset.FindNext strQueryString 'Find next one
  Loop
  datMembers.Recordset.Bookmark = varBookMark
End Sub
``` |

In the case of the telephone number query, we need to add the statement to create the strApos string constant containing the apostrophe in addition to declaring a new string variable. Since there is only one membership for a given phone number, there is no need to repeat the search after the first instance is found and there is no need to remember where the pointer was before the search. If the varBookMark references are deleted, all of the fields for the record found by the search will be displayed and there is no need to copy the information to the list box. However, it is necessary to update the lblRecordNumber caption by setting it equal to the AbsolutePosition + 1. In addition, a message needs to be displayed if no phone number matches the one input by the user, and the name needs to be added to the list box if a match is found. The code for the mnuFindPhoneNumber is shown in VB Code Box 9-12.

| **VB CODE BOX 9-12.** Code to find a member with a given telephone number | ```vb
Private Sub mnuFindPhoneNumber_Click()
  Const strApos as String = "'"
' Create this constant to avoid typing apostrophes
  Dim strQueryString As String, strPhoneNum As String
  strPhoneNum = InputBox("What is the phone number?")
  strQueryString = "Phone_Number = " & strApos & _
    strPhoneNum & strApos
  lstLateFees.Clear
  datMembers.Recordset.FindFirst strQueryString 'Find match
  If datMembers.Recordset.NoMatch Then
    MsgBox "No match for this phone number", vbExclamation
  End If
  lblRecordNumber.Caption = Str(datMembers.Recordset. _
  AbsolutePosition + 1)
End Sub
``` |

FIGURE 9-9. Members with late fees > $10.00

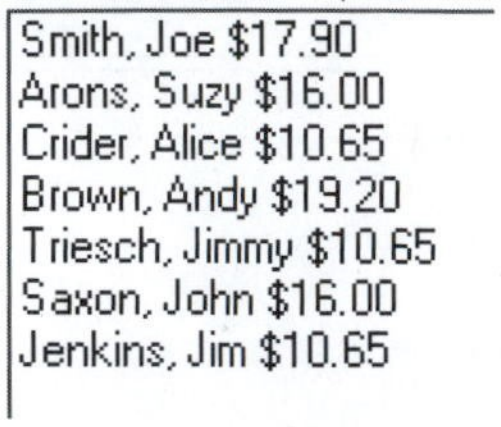

Smith, Joe $17.90
Arons, Suzy $16.00
Crider, Alice $10.65
Brown, Andy $19.20
Triesch, Jimmy $10.65
Saxon, John $16.00
Jenkins, Jim $10.65

If we run the project, select the *Find Late Fees* submenu option, and input a value of $10.00, the resulting list of names is shown in Figure 9-9.

If we then clear the list box, select the *Find Phone Number* submenu option, and enter the phone number mentioned above (770-555-1294), all of the information boxes about Stams, Lonnie will be displayed in the text (Do **not** enclose the phone number in quotation marks!). If a non-existent telephone number is entered (say, 706-555-1294), a message will be displayed stating that this telephone number was not found in the database.

Mini-Summary 9-5: Finding Records

1. Records are found by querying the database. The query string must include the field name, a comparison operator, and the subject of the comparison.

2. Query strings are created by concatenating the various parts together. If the subject of the comparison is a string, it must be enclosed in apostrophes. In Visual Basic, the user can input the subject of the query string.

3. The FindFirst, FindNext, FindPrevious, and FindLast methods can be used with the query string to actually move the pointer to a matching record.

4. The NoMatch property returns a value of True if there are no matching records. A Do Until NoMatch loop can be used with the FindNext method to find multiple matching records.

5. The Field property of the data control can be used to transfer the contents of the various fields to list or text boxes.

It's Your Turn!

1. Why is it not necessary to know SQL to query a database from Visual Basic?

2. What does the Recordset NoMatch property tell us? The Field property?

3. What Recordset methods are typically used with a query?

4. How do we construct a query string that can be used to find matching records? Is there anything different about searching for a character string?

5. How do we return the current record after we have found a matching record?

Completing the remaining questions will enable you to create the Visual Basic project discussed in the text.

6. Add a list box and command button to the frmMemberInfo form in the lower right-hand area of the form as shown in Figure 9-8. Name the list box **lstLateFees** and the command button **cmdFind**. Add a caption of **Find Late Fees** to the command button.

7. Add the code shown in VB Code Box 9-10 to the cmdFind event procedure. Run your project and click the cmdFind command button. You should see the same output as shown in Figure 9-8.

8. Add a **mnuFind** menu bar option with a caption of **Find** to the form. Add three submenu options with the properties shown in Table 9-5.

TABLE 9-5: mnuFind Submenu Options

Name	Caption
mnuFindLateFees	Find Late Fees
mnuFindPhoneNumber	Find Phone Number
mnuFindClear	Clear

9. Copy and paste the code from the cmdFind event procedure into the mnuFindLate-Fees and mnuFindPhoneNumber event procedures you just created. Modify the code for the mnuFindLateFees event procedure to match that shown in VB Code Box 9-11. Finally, add the instruction:

```
lstLateFees.Clear
```

to the mnuFindClear event procedure.

10. Run your procedure and test this submenu option by entering a value of **10.00**. The result should match that shown in Figure 9-9. Clear the list box and try some other higher and lower values. If everything works, delete the cmdFind command button and the corresponding event procedure from the code window.

11. Modify the code for the mnuFindPhoneNumber event procedure to match that shown in VB Code Box 9-12. Run your procedure and test this submenu option by entering a telephone number of **770-555-1294**. Lonnie Stam's name, late fees ($2.12), and other information will be displayed in the text boxes. Now enter a telephone number of **706-555-1294**. A message that there is no match for this phone number should be displayed. Finally, enter another phone number for a member who is in the database, and verify that the correct name and late fees are displayed.

12. Save your project and form under the current names.

SUMMARY

A database stores different types of data in a such way that an end user can easily manipulate and retrieve the data. Databases are composed of fields, records, and tables, where fields are single facts or data items that have field names. A collection of related data that is treated as a unit is referred to as a record, and a related collection of records all having the same fields is referred to as a table. Tables in a relational database are related through fields that contain the same information. The primary key is a field that is unique to each record. When a primary key appears in another table, it is a foreign key. Database operations include querying to find specific records as well as adding, editing, and deleting records. Databases have some advantages over arrays, including permanence and the ability to store multiple types of data, to use database engines, and to be used on multiple computers.

In Visual Basic, the data control is the link to the database through its Database-Name and RecordSource properties. Bound or data-aware controls are those that are automatically linked to a field in the database through the data control's DataSource and DataField properties. The Recordset object is the current set of records linked to the data control. Browsing methods of the data control include MoveFirst, MoveNext, MovePrevious, and MoveLast. The EOF (end-of-file) and BOF (beginning-of-file) properties indicate that the record pointer is beyond the end of the Recordset or before the beginning of the Recordset, respectively.

To add a record to the database, we use the AddNew method with the Field property of the Recordset. We can edit the contents of data-aware controls by changing the contents of the control. We can save the changes by moving to the another record or using the Update method. We can delete records with the Delete method.

We find records by querying the database. The query string must include the field name, a comparison operator, and the subject of the comparison. Query strings are created by concatenating the various parts together. If the subject of the comparison is a string, it must be enclosed in apostrophes. In Visual Basic, the user can input the subject of the query string. The FindFirst, FindNext, FindPrevious, and FindLast methods can be used with the query string to actually move the pointer to a matching record. The NoMatch property returns a value of True if there are no matching records. A Do Until NoMatch loop can be used with the FindNext method to find multiple matches. The Field property of the data control can be used to transfer the contents of the various fields to list or text boxes.

The complete code for the frmMemberInfo form in Vintage9.vbp is shown in VB Code Box 9-13.

| **VB CODE BOX 9-13.** Complete code for frmMemberInfo form | <pre>Dim varCurrentRecord as Variant, blnAddingRecord as Boolean
Private Sub cmdFirst_Click()
    datMembers.Recordset.MoveFirst
    lblRecordNumber.Caption = Str(datMembers. _
    Recordset.AbsolutePosition + 1)
End Sub
Private Sub cmdLast_Click()
  datMembers.Recordset.MoveLast
  lblRecordNumber.Caption = Str(datMembers. _
  Recordset.RecordCount)
End Sub
Private Sub imgNext_Click()
  datMembers.Recordset.MoveNext
  If Not (datMembers.Recordset.EOF) Then
    lblRecordNumber.Caption = Str(datMembers.Recordset. _
    AbsolutePosition + 1)
  Else
    MsgBox "Already at end of table", vbInformation
    datMembers.Recordset.MoveLast
  End If
End Sub
Private Sub imgPrevious_Click()
  datMembers.Recordset.MovePrevious
  If Not (datMembers.Recordset.BOF) Then
    lblRecordNumber.Caption = str(datMembers.Recordset. _
    AbsolutePosition +1)
  Else
    MsgBox "Already at beginning of table", vbInformation
    datMembers.Recordset.MoveFirst
  End If
End Sub</pre> |

VB CODE BOX 9-14. Complete code for frmMemberInfo form (Cont.)	```vb
	Private Sub Form_Activate()
	    lblRecordNumber.Caption = Str(datMembers. _
	    Recordset.AbsolutePosition + 1)
	End Sub
	Private Sub mnuMemberAdd_Click()
	  varCurrentRecord = datMembers.Recordset.Bookmark
	  datMembers.Recordset.AddNew
	  blnAddingRecord = True
	End Sub
	Private Sub mnuMemberSave_Click()
	  datMembers.UpdateRecord
	  If blnAddingRecord Then
	      cmdLast_Click
	      blnAddingRecord = False
	  End If
	End Sub
	Private Sub mnuMemberCancel_Click()
	    datMembers.UpdateControls
	    If blnAddingRecord Then
	        datMembers.Recordset.Bookmark = varCurrentRecord
	        blnAddingRecord = False
	    End If
	End Sub
	Private Sub mnuMemberDelete_Click()
	    Const strDelete as String = "Delete this record?"
	    Dim intResponse As Integer
	    intResponse = MsgBox(DeleteYesNo, vbYesNoCancel + _
	    vbCritical + vbDefaultButton2, "Delete Record")
	    If intResponse = vbYes Then
	      datMembers.Recordset.Delete
	      datMembers.Recordset.Movenext
	      If datMembers.Recordset.EOF then
	        cmdLast_Click
	      End if
	    End If
	End Sub
	Private Sub mnuFindLateFees_Click()
	  Dim strQueryString As String, varBookMark As String
	  varBookMark = datMembers.Recordset.Bookmark
	  strQueryString = "Late_Fees > 0"
	  lstLateFees.Clear 'Clear late fee list
	  datMembers.Recordset.FindFirst strQueryString 'Find 1st one
	  Do Until datMembers.Recordset.NoMatch
	    lstLateFees.AddItem datMembers.Recordset("Name") & _
	    " " & Format(datMembers.Recordset("Late_Fees"), _
	    "currency") 'Add record to list box
	    datMembers.Recordset.FindNext strQueryString
	  Loop
	  datMembers.Recordset.Bookmark = varBookMark
	End Sub
	``

| VB Code Box 9-14. Complete code for frmMemberInfo form (Cont.) | ```Private Sub mnuFindPhoneNumber_Click()
  Const strApos as String = "'"
  Dim strQueryString As String, strPhoneNum As String
  strPhoneNum = InputBox("What is the phone number?")
  strQueryString = "Phone_Number = " & strApos _
  & strPhoneNum & strApos
  lstLateFees.Clear
  datMembers.Recordset.FindFirst strQueryString 'Find match
  If datMembers.Recordset.NoMatch Then
      MsgBox "No match for this phone number", vbExclamation
  End If
  lblRecordNumber.Caption = Str(datMembers.Recordset. _
  AbsolutePosition + 1)
End Sub``` |

New Visual Basic Elements

Control/Object	Properties	Methods	Events
data control	Name Caption DatabaseName RecordSource	Refresh UpdateRecord UpdateControls	
text box control	DataField DataSource		
image control	Picture		Click
RecordSet object	AbsolutePosition BOF BookMark EOF Field NoMatch	AddNew Delete FindFirst FindLast FindNext FindPrevious MoveFirst MoveLast MoveNext MovePrevious	

Key Terms

bookmark
bound control
column
current record
data control
data-aware control

database
field
fieldname
foreign key
primary key
query

record
recordset object
relational database
row
table

Exercises

1. Suppose that the database table, Food.mdb, is as shown in Table 9-6. Describe what each procedure does in the code shown after the table:.

TABLE 9-6: The Food.mdb Database

ItemID	Item	Item Price
1	Hamburger	1.50
2	Hot Dog	0.95
3	French Fries	0.85
4	Soda	0.90
5	Milk Shake	2.10
6	Pizza	2.75
7	Wings	3.55
8	Gyro	4.25

```
Private Sub cmdCompleteOrder_Click()
  Dim sngTax As Single
  Dim curTotal As Currency
  sngTax = 0.05 * CCur(txtTotal.Text)
  curTotal = CCur(txtTotal.Text) + sngTax
  txtTotal.Text = Format(curTotal, "Currency")
End Sub
Private Sub cmdFood_Click(Index As Integer)
  Dim strQuery As String
  Dim curTotal As Currency
  strQuery = "ItemID = " & CStr(Index + 1)
  datFood.Recordset.FindFirst strQuery
  curTotal = CCur(txtTotal.Text) + _
    datFood.Recordset("[Item Price]")
  txtTotal.Text = Format(curTotal, "Currency")
End Sub
Private Sub cmdNewOrder_Click()
  txtTotal.Text = Format(0, "Currency")
End Sub
Private Sub Form_Load()
  txtTotal.Text = Format(0, "Currency")
End Sub
```

2. Write query strings for each of the following:

a. For the Vintage Video Membership table (shown in Figure 9-1), write a query string to find all customers who live in the city of Bogart.

b. For the Food database in Table 9-6, write a query string to find all items that cost less than $1.

c. For the Mystery Book database of Table 9-10, write the necessary code to create a query string that will find books by an author name provided by the user. The user enters the author name in a textbox called txtAuthor.

d. For the Stocks database described in Table 9-12, create a query string to find stocks with a purchase price between $20 and $50.

3. Given the table from a database shown in Table 9-10 and the following code, determine the value displayed in:

   a. Text1.Text _____

   b. Text2.Text _____

   c. Text3.Text _____

   d. Text4.Text _____

   e. Text5.Text _____ .

```
Private Sub cmdGo_Click()
  Dim intI As Integer
  Dim strQuery1 As String
  Dim strQuery2 As String
  Dim strQuery3 As String
  datMystery.Recordset.MoveLast
  Text1.Text = datMystery.Recordset("BookTitle")
  datMystery.Recordset.MoveFirst
  For intI = 1 To 5
      datMystery.Recordset.MoveNext
  Next intI
  Text2.Text = datMystery.Recordset("BookAuthor")
  datMystery.Recordset.MoveLast
  strQuery1 = "BookAuthor = 'Hillerman'"
  datMystery.Recordset.FindPrevious strQuery1
  Text3.Text = datMystery.Recordset("BookTitle")
  strQuery2 = "Pages <= 250"
  datMystery.Recordset.FindFirst strQuery2
  Text4.Text = datMystery.Recordset("BookTitle")
  strQuery3 = "BookAuthor = 'Christie'"
  datMystery.Recordset.FindFirst strQuery3
  Text5.Text = datMystery.Recordset("BookTitle")
End Sub
```

4. For each of the following, explain what is wrong with the code. What error messages would you see, if any? What can you do to correct the code?

   a. The code shown on the following page should find the first item with a price
   that satisfies the query string using the Food database of Table 9-6.

```
Private Sub cmdGo_Click()
  Dim strQuery As String
  strQuery = "Item Price > 1"
  datFood.Recordset.FindFirst strQuery
  txtDisplay.Text = datFood.Recordset("Item Price")
End Sub
```

   b. The following code should find all items that satisfy the query string using the
   Food database of Table 9-6.

```
Private Sub cmdGo_Click()
  Dim strQuery As String
  strQuery = "Price > 1"
  Do Until datFood.Recordset.NoMatch
    lstDisplay.AddItem datFood.Recordset("Item")
    datFood.Recordset.FindNext strQuery
  Loop
End Sub
```

c. The following code should find all items that satisfy the query string using the Mystery Book database of Table 9-10.

```
Private Sub cmdGo_Click()
  Dim strQuery As String
  Dim strAuthor As String
  strAuthor = txtAuthor.Text
  strQuery = "BookAuthor = " & strAuthor
  Do Until datMystery.Recordset.NoMatch
    lstDisplay.AddItem datMystery.Recordset("BookTitle")
    datMystery.Recordset.FindNext strQuery
  Loop
End Sub
```

5. Use the Visual Basic Help facility or the MSDN on-line library to answer the following questions.

a. What are the EOFAction and BOFAction properties of the Data Control? What are their possible settings and what happens for each?

b. What is the CancelUpdate method and when can it be used?

c. What is new about data access in Visual Basic 6.0 over previous versions?

d. What tools are provided with Visual Basic 6.0 that let you to help create and manage data-driven applications? In what editions of Visual Basic 6.0 are they available?

PROJECTS

1. Assume that a list of student names, ID numbers, and quiz averages is stored in a database called *Students.mdb*. You may download the Students.mdb file from the text Web site and save it to the root folder of your data disk. The fields and field names are shown in Table 9-7, where the Letter_Grade field is initially blank.

TABLE 9-7: Fields and Field Names for Students.mdb Database

Field	Field Name
Student Name	Name
Student ID Number	ID_Number
Quiz Average	Quiz_Average
Letter Grade	Letter_Grade

Create a project to access this database and to process the data. Your project should use a single form to carry out the following operations:

a. Display information on each student in text boxes with appropriate labels on the main form. You should add browser buttons and a record number counter to the main form.

b. Enable the user to use a 90-80-70-60 scale to determine the letter grade for a single student or for all students and add the grade to the database in the Letter_Grade field for that student.

c. Enter a quiz average value and display the names of all students with a quiz average *higher* than the value you entered.

d. Enter an ID number and display the name and information for the corresponding student in the text boxes.

e. Add, delete, or edit student records as necessary, and save the result of this action.

f. Save this project as **Ex9-1.vbp** and **Ex9-1.frm** to the Chapter9 folder on your data disk.

2. Assume that customer information in the form of names, telephone numbers, and sales amounts is stored in a database file called *CustSales.mdb*. You may download the CustSales.mdb file from the text Web site and save it to the root folder of your data disk. The fields and field names are shown in Table 9-8, where the Category field is initially blank.

TABLE 9-8: Fields and Field Names for CustSales.mdb Database

Field	Field Name
Customer Name	CustName
Telephone Number	PhoneNum
Sales Amount	Sales
Sales Category	Category

Create a project to access this database and to process the data. Your project should use a single form to carry out the following operations:

a. Display information on each customer in text boxes with appropriate labels on the main form. You should add browser buttons and a record number counter to the main form.

b. Enable the user to use the scale shown in Table 9-9 to determine the Sales Category for a single customer or for all customers and add it to the database in the Category field for that customer.

TABLE 9-9: Sales Amounts and Categories

Sales Amount	Category
$1,000 or less	Light
$1,001 to $5,000	Average
Greater than $5,000	Heavy

c. Enter a sales value and display the names of all customers with sales values *lower* than the value you entered.

d. Enter an telephone number and display the name and information for the corresponding customer in the text boxes.

e. Add, delete, or edit customer records as necessary, and save the result of this action.

f. Save this project as **Ex9-2.vbp** and **Ex9-2.frm** to the Chapter9 folder on your data disk.

3. Assume that Jane has created a database of her favorite mystery novels using the data shown in Table 9-10. Create the same database and create a Visual Basic application that will answer the following questions:

    a. List all books with more than some number of pages.

    b. List all books by a specific author. .

TABLE 9-10: Mystery Database

BookID	BookTitle	BookAuthor	Detective	Pages
1	Free Fall	Crais	Elvis Cole	265
2	Hush Money	Parker	Spenser	239
3	Murder on the Orient Express	Christie	Hercule Poirot	188
4	Purple Cane Road	Burke	Dave Robicheaux	320
5	Lullaby Town	Crais	Elvis Cole	287
6	Family Honor	Parker	Sunny Childs	225
7	A Is for Alibi	Grafton	Kinsey Milhone	185
8	Hunting Badger	Hillerman	Joe Leaphorn and Jim Chee	238
9	Sacred Clowns	Hillerman	Joe Leaphorn and Jim Chee	255
10	The Murder of Roger Ackroyd	Christie	Miss Marple	190
11	I the Jury	Spillane	Mike Hammer	215
12	Stalking the Angel	Crais	Elvis Cole	320
13	Pastime	Parker	Spenser	250
14	The Secrete of Annex Three	Dexter	Inspector Morse	210
15	Murder After Hours	Christie	Miss Marple	256

4. Create a project that will allow the user to input a city name and find that city's Zip code. Assume that the name and Zip code for each city are stored in a database named *ZipCode.mdb*. You may download the ZipCode.mdb file from the text Web site and save it to the root folder of your data disk. The two field names for this database are City and Zip_Code.

Assume that the user can input either a city or a Zip code from the main form of the project. Depending on the user's selection, a secondary form is displayed asking the user to enter the appropriate information (there are two different forms). Once the user has entered the appropriate information, the city and Zip code are displayed in text boxes on the main form. The user should also be able to browse through the city–Zip code pairs using browsing buttons that you have added to the main form. The user should also be able to add, delete, or edit city–Zip code records and save the results. Save this project as **Ex9-3.vbp** and **Ex9-3.frm** to the Chapter9 folder on your data disk.

5. Assume that the FlyByNite Insurance company wishes to use a database to store information on its customers. This information should include the customer's name, Social Security number, age, and insurance premium. Assume that this information is stored in the *Insured* table in a database named *a:\Insurance.mdb*. In addition, this database has a *Life* table that has two fields: Age and Premium. You may download the Insurance.mdb file from the text Web site and save it to the root folder of your data disk. The fields and field names for the Insured table are shown in Table 9-11, where the Amount field is initially blank.

TABLE 9-11: Fields and Field Names for CustSales.mdb Database

Field	Field Name
Name of Insured	Name
SS Number	SSNum
Age	Age
Does insured smoke?	Smoker
Premium Amount	Amount

Your project should display information about the company's customers in the Startup form in text boxes with browser buttons to navigate among the customer records. There should be another form that computes the premium amount using the Insured and Life tables. A customer is assigned the premium in the Life table that has the first Age field higher than his age; that is, age 31 and below have a premium of $65, but age 32 jumps to $95 (see Exercise 5 in Chapter 6). If the insured smokes, there is a surcharge equal to 30% of the premium amount. The second form should show the insured's name, age, and smoker status (yes or no) from the main form, and it should calculate the premium from the Life table, the surcharge if any, and the amount due using the Smoker status and the Life table. There should be a way to print this information and to return to the main form. When the command is given to return to the main form, the second form should be cleared and the amount due should be saved in the Amount field of the Insured table.

Save this project as **Ex9-4.vbp**. Save the main (Startup) form as **Ex9-4One.frm** and the second form as **Ex9-4Two.frm** to the Chapter9 folder on your data disk.

6. Annie Warbucks is attempting to increase her personal wealth by investing in stocks. To aid her in her struggle, she has created a database to store information about the stocks in her portfolio. The fields in her database are shown in Table 9-12.

TABLE 9-12: Fields and Field Names for Stocks.mdb Database

Field	Field Name
Sticker Symbol	Symbol
Company Name	CompName
Purchase Date	PDate
Purchase Price	PPrice

TABLE 9-12: Fields and Field Names for Stocks.mdb Database

Field	Field Name
Current Price	CPrice
Number of Shares Owned	Shares

Create a Visual Basic program that Annie can use to manage her database. The program should include all functions needed to manage the database, that is: browse, add, delete and update records. In addition, provide controls for calculating and displaying the following statistics for the stocks:

Change in Price = Current Price–Purchase Price

Current Position = Shares * Current Price

Total Value = Sum of All Current Positions

Also, provide features that allow Annie to query the database. This should include: a search for stocks that have been purchased before or after a particular date, a search for stocks that have a negative or positive current position, and a search for stocks that have increased in value by a given percentage.

Notice that this database is set up under the assumption that all shares of a particular stock are purchased at a single time. How would you change the database to allow for multiple purchases of the shares from the same company?

7. Scott Aficionado spends a lot of time managing his fantasy baseball team. In order to use his time more efficiently and hopefully improve his standing in the league, he has decided to create a database with a Visual Basic front end. He hopes to use the program to help him search through and analyze baseball statistics. He can then use the results of his analysis to build a formidable team. He begins by creating a database table with fields shown in Table 9-13. This table contains information that can be used to analyze a player's success at batting. Scott will be able to populate this table using information available at many sites on the Web. Create a Visual Basic program to manage Scott's database. The program should include all functions needed to manage the database, that is: browse, add, delete and update records. In addition, provide controls for calculating and displaying the following statistics for the players:

a. Batting Average = Divide the number of hits by at-bats

b. Slugging Percentage = Divide the total bases of all hits by the total times at bat where single = 1 base, double = 2 bases, triple = 3 bases, home run = 4 bases.

c. On-Base Percentage = Divide the sum of hits plus walks plus number of hit-by-pitch by the total number of plate appearances.

For an additional challenge, provide features for Scott to search for players who have a minimum value for one of the three calculated statistics..

TABLE 9-13: Fields and Field Names for Baseball.mdb Database

Field	Field Name
Player ID	PLID
Player Name	Name
Team Name	Team
Player Position	Pos

TABLE 9-13: Fields and Field Names for Baseball.mdb Database (Continued)

Field	Field Name
At Bats	AB
Runs Scored	Runs
Total Hits	Hits
Doubles	Doubles
Triples	Triples
Home Runs	HR
Runs Batted In	RBI
Walks	BB
Hit-By-Pitch	HBP
Sacrifice	SF

8. Chance Ivory conducts simulation studies for a leading manufacturer of video gaming machines. Since simulation studies often require multiple runs, Chance would like to develop a method that would allow him to store the results of many simulations in a database.

As a prototype he decides to conduct simple simulations of rolling a single, standard die. Each simulation run will consist of multiple throws of the die. Each time a simulation is conducted, Chance wants to save a simulation ID, the number of throws of the die for the simulation, and counts of how many times each possible die value appears. The fields and field names for the Simulation table are shown in Table 9-14.

Initially, all records are blank. New records are added when each simulation is conductedYour form should contain: a data control for linking to the database; seven text boxes, one for each field in the database table. (This does not include the SimID field. This field is automatically generated by the database); one command button for running the information and storing the results in the database; and one command button to end the program.

When the button is pressed, a record should then be added to the database and the user should be prompted to enter the number of rolls to be conducted during the current simulation. As the simulated rolls are executed, counts for each possible die roll are stored in an array. When the total number of rolls has been executed, the die counts are assigned to the text boxes and the new record in the database is updated. Finally, the values for the current simulation are displayed in the textboxes.

TABLE 9-14: Fields and Field Names for Simulation.mdb Database

Field	Field Name
Simulation ID	SimID
Number of Ones occurred in each simulation.	Ones
Number of Twos occurred in each simulation.	Twos
Number of Threes occurred in each simulation.	Threes
Number of Fours occurred in each simulation.	Fours

TABLE 9-14: Fields and Field Names for Simulation.mdb Database (Continued)

Field	Field Name
Number of Fives occurred in each simulation.	Fives
Number of Sixes occurred in each simulation.	Sixes

PROJECT: JOE'S TAX ASSISTANCE (CONT.)

That much dreaded time of year, tax time, was approaching again, but for Joe the prospect was exciting. He would soon be able to test his new program in action at his VITA site. He could hardly wait to start using the program, and it was with a sense of happy anticipation that he began to get organized.

There were the usual materials that one uses when rendering tax assistance: pencils and other office supplies, newly purchased; tax forms and manuals of Tax Code; and, of course, Joe's laptop and program. These were the tools of the VITA volunteer's trade, so to speak.

Joe reached up and pulled a dusty binder off the shelf. On its cover the binder had the label "Client Ledger." Being very systematic, as auditors tend to be, Joe had been keeping records of all of the clients he had served while volunteering at the VITA site. The ledger included each client's name and Social Security number, the date of the meeting, the total amount of time that Joe had spent with that person, and the amount of refund received or tax paid. There was a separate page for each day that Joe had worked at the VITA site. Of course, Joe had boxes full of tax return copies tucked away in the attic.

Joe blew the dust off the cover, opened the binder, and began looking over the lists of former clients, wondering which ones would be back this year.

From the doorway, Angela said, "It looks like you're getting ready early this year. Wouldn't have anything to do with your new interest in computers, would it?"

"Yes. I'm anxious to see if our new Visual Basic program will help me do the work better and be more productive," Joe responded. "So, I thought I'd get a few things ready. I was just starting to look through the old client list and prepare a few new pages."

"Are you still using that old binder? It looks like it's seen its best days, if you ask me," Angela observed. "I thought that you were doing everything by computer now."

Joe looked at his binder and then back at Angela. "You know," he said, as his face lit up with a smile, "I hadn't even thought of putting this stuff on the computer. And Zooey mentioned something about being able to handle all sorts of data on the computer with Visual Basic."

"Oh, no! It sounds like I've got you started again," Angela moaned. "I suppose that the garage cleaning you promised is going to be put off for a few more weeks now."

"Just remember, it was your idea," Joe said as he gave her a peck on the cheek. "Zooey and I will take you out to dinner to celebrate when we get it finished. And then maybe I'll work on the garage."

Questions

1. Assume that Joe has created a database file named Clients.mdb which may be downloaded from the text Web site. This file has one table with five fields: Date, Name, SSNum (for Social Security number), Time (in minutes), and Amount (refunded or owed—a negative value).

2. Create a form for the VITA program that will be used when Joe wants to work with the database. Include the database functions that you have learned in this chapter. Add a menu to the VITA program with items for working with the database.

3. Run, test, and debug your program.

10 ADVANCED DATABASE OPERATIONS

LEARNING OBJECTIVES

After reading this chapter, you will be able to:

❖ Revise an existing Visual Basic project by combining new and old forms.

❖ Use the GotFocus event to execute code when a control receives the focus.

❖ Set the RecordSource property of a data control at run time to a table or query and use the Edit and Update methods to change existing field values.

❖ Use database-oriented controls such as DBList box, DBCombo, and DBGrid to display specific fields of a database or entire records.

❖ Use SQL statements that involve more than one table as the RecordSource for a data control.

SCENARIO: REVISING VINTAGE VIDEOS

Ed continued to read the list from the card. "1938 by MGM, cast included Reginald Owen, Gene Lockhart, and Terry Kilburn, directed by Edwin L. Marin. . ."

"*A Christmas Carol!*" Monique burst in excitedly.

Three jaws dropped as the others stared at her in disbelief. Ed, Yvonne, Clark, and Monique had been spending some rare free time playing a new movie trivia game that they had begun to sell at the store. Monique had been doing well the entire game, but the obscure reference of this latest question proved too much for the other players.

"How did you ever know that one?" inquired Yvonne.

Monique looked a little guilty as she replied. "Well, I have been populating Clark's database. And, it's difficult to type in all that information about our videos without learning something."

Clark looked thoughtful. He said, "Great job, Monique. You know, that movie reminds me of my Vintage Video program."

Now it was Clark's turn to be on the receiving end of disbelieving stares. "No, I'm serious, guys. Think about it: Scrooge got a look at his future, didn't like it, then did something about it by making some major changes."

"Are you trying to tell us something?" Ed asked.

"Well . . ." Clark hesitated. "As I told you before, using a database for our information will be much better than using sequential files. But, in order to use our program with a database, I'll need to make a few more changes."

"But I thought that the program was finished!" Yvonne protested.

Ed, coming to Clark's defense, responded, "Hold on. Clark told us that we've been working with a prototype, and he warned us that improvements might mean big changes." To Clark he added, "What changes do you need to make?"

Regaining his confidence, Clark explained, "I'm adding a few of the tools that are provided in VB for working with the database. To do this, I'm going to have to rework some of the forms from the current program. Also, we need to be able to work with the other tables in the database. These new tools along with some more complex querying will let us do that."

He added, "It's not as much as it sounds. I can reuse some parts of the current version. Also, we'll keep the current prototype working while I make the changes. I don't think it will come to this, but if the modifications don't work out I can continue with what we have now."

"Alright, sounds like you know what you're doing. Go for it," said Ed.

Satisfied, Yvonne added, "And if we do have to stay with what we've got, it'll be like another old Christmas classic, *It's a Wonderful Life*. You know, feeling depressed about his life, man gets to see how it would be different if he had made different choices and decides his life isn't so bad after all."

"1946 by MGM, cast included Jimmy Stewart, Donna Reed, and Lionel Barrymore, directed by Frank Capra," Monique added, smugly.

Discussion of Scenario

As mentioned in the Vintage Videos scenario for this chapter, Clark wants to take advantage of switching to a database system to revise the entire project. You may be surprised at this willingness to revise the project, but you should remember two important concepts. First, since the project is written as self-contained objects, it will *not* be necessary to rewrite those elements of the project that are not affected by the switch to a database system. For example, the password form will not change, and neither will the memo creation editing portion of the project. Even those forms that will be affected by the change to a database system will retain much of their existing code. This is an important feature of object-oriented programming: Because objects are reusable, they can be reused in a revised version of the same project.

The second concept to remember was discussed by one of the pioneers of developing information systems—**Frederick Brooks**. Dr. Brooks was an early innovator of many concepts still used in computing. He wrote a classic book in the field of systems development, *The Mythical Man Month,* in which he noted that system's developers should "plan to throw one [system] away; you will anyhow."[1] In the Vintage Videos case, Clark is doing nothing but following the long-understood concept that, no matter how much thought goes into the first version of an information system, that first version usually must be replaced by a second, improved version.

Objectives for Vintage Videos Project

In rewriting parts of the Vintage Videos transaction processing application, we will have the following objectives:

1. To be able to enter a member's phone number and have that member's name, address, telephone number, and late fees, if any, be displayed in the appropriate text boxes on a member information form.

---

1. Brooks, Frederick P., *The Mythical Man-Month: Essays on Software Engineering* (Reading, MA: Addison-Wesley, 1975), p. 116.

2. To be able to browse the member information form and add new members or delete existing members; also, to be able to display the names and late fees for members who owe more than a certain amount.

3. To be able to enter the ID number for a video on a Rental form, have the name and price for this video be displayed automatically in the appropriate text boxes, and process the rental of multiple videos in this manner.

4. For each video that is rented, to have the ID number added to a database table along with the phone number of the person renting it and the date it is due to be returned.

5. To be able to search for videos with a particular name or partial name to determine if they are in stock, and if they are, to display their price, location, and availability; this form will also be used to add videos to the store's inventory and to delete worn-out videos.

6. For videos that are overdue, to be able to call the customers who have rented them and request they be returned.

7. To be able to check videos back in when they are returned, and to automatically update the availability status of the video and, if it is late, the late fee amount owed by the person returning it.

While this sounds like a lot to do, using a database will ease the effort a great deal. The first four operations can be handled without resorting to any SQL commands, but we will need to use SQL to carry out the last three operations. In all cases, we will be using the Vintage.mdb database file, which you should have already downloaded from the Web site for this book and modified in previous exercises.

Plan for Revising Vintage Videos Project

The plan for the revised Vintage Videos project is shown in Figure 10-1, where the solid black lines indicate the order in which the typical video rental process will proceed and the dashed lines represent supplemental operations accessed from the menu.

FIGURE 10-1. Plan for revised Vintage Videos project

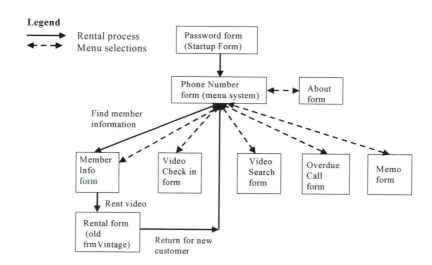

Once the correct password has been entered, control is switched to the Phone Number form, on which the store clerk determines if the customer is a member by entering the customer's telephone number. If the customer is a member, then control is shifted to the Member Information form, where the name, address, and late fees, if any, corresponding to the phone number are displayed. This form can also be used to browse the membership list and add or delete members.

Once the membership information has been validated, the clerk switches to the Rental form and enters a video ID number, thereby displaying the video's name and price. As this is done for each video rented by the customer, the prices and taxes are summed and combined with the late fees, if any, to determine the amount due. When the transaction is completed, control is switched back to the Phone Number form for a new customer.

It will also be possible to switch to the Member Information form from the Phone Number form through a menu system that will be moved from the old Vintage Videos main form (frmVintage). As shown by the dashed lines, the menu system can also be used to search for a video, carry out such video operations as adding new or deleting old videos, check in returned videos, call customers about overdue videos, create and edit memos, and view the About form. As denoted by the return arrows on the dashed lines, there should be a way to return from each of these forms to the Phone Number form.

Creating this revised transaction processing system for Vintage Videos requires that many of the forms from the previous Vintage Videos project be added to this new project and that three new forms be created. In the first case, the frmMemo, frmPassword, frmAbout, frmVintage8, and frmVideos7 forms should be added to the new project from the project created in Chapter 8 and in previous chapters. Also, the frmMemberInfo form from Chapter 9 should be added. The frmPassword form should be designated as the Startup form using the Project|Project1 Properties menu option. In addition, the frmVintage8 form should be renamed *frmRental*. Note that we do not add the frmMembers form, because we are replacing it with the frmMemberInfo form.

In the second case, the three new forms that must be added are the frmPhone form, the frmCheckin form, and the frmOverdue form. The first (*frmPhoneNum*) is required to input the telephone number. Control should be transferred to this form when an acceptable password is entered in the startup Password form. The second form (*frmCheckin*) will be used to check in returned videos and to add new videos or delete worn-out videos. The third new form (*frmOverdue)* will be used to call customers about overdue videos.

In addition to adding the old and new forms to the revised Vintage Videos project, we will need to make a variety of additions and changes to some of the forms. These additions and changes will be discussed as we develop the project.

Adding Old and New Forms to the Project

As mentioned earlier, many of the forms that were a part of the old Vintage Videos project need to be added to the new project. Adding forms from one project to another is very easy: While in design mode for the new project, you simply use the **Project|Add File** menu option, display the drive and folder in which the forms are located, and select a form to add. For example, to add frmPassword from the Vintage8.vbp project, you select the Project|Add File menu option, locate the Vintage8 folder using the File Open dialog box, open it, and then add the Password.frm file to the current project by double-clicking it. This should be done for all other forms that need to be added to the new project. This form should also be made the startup form for the new project.

As each existing form is added to the project, you should immediately use the **Save frm*name*.frm as...** command to save the form to a new folder named *Chapter10*. Once all forms have been added, the project must be saved in order for the forms to be made a permanent part of the project.

A new form should be added to the project with the **Project|Add Form** menu option or the **Add Form** icon. This new form should contain a single text box in which the telephone number of a member can be entered. There should be a command button to use to find the member with this telephone number. The store slogan and logo as well as all of the menu and submenu items that are currently on the frm-Rental (the old frmVintage8) form should be transferred to this form and deleted from that form. It should be named *frmPhoneNum* and saved as **PhoneNum.frm**. The resulting form is shown in Figure 10-2.

FIGURE 10-2. New form to input member telephone number

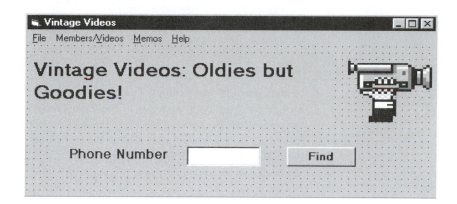

The code for all of the submenu options except Exit is the same as that on the old frmVintage8. For the Exit submenu option, the code is much simpler since we no longer have to worry about writing revised information back to disk—it consists of the **End** command. In addition to the existing Members/Videos submenu items, we need to add submenu items to call about overdue videos and to check in returned videos. The first submenu option should have a caption of **Overdue Videos** and a name of *mnuMemVidLate*. The second submenu option should have a caption of **Check in videos** and a name of *mnuMemVidChkVid*. The code necessary to display the frmOverdue and frmCheckin forms should also be added. The code for the submenu options is shown in VB Code Box 10-1.

Verifying Member Status

In addition to having the menu system that provides access to other forms, the primary purpose of the frmPhoneNum form is to check the phone numbers of customers to verify that they are members before allowing them to rent videos. When the clerk enters a phone number in the text box and clicks on Find, the Member Information form (frmMemberInfo) should appear with the customer's name, address, telephone number, and late fees displayed. To accomplish this, we need to add the appropriate code to the Find button.

The code for this button will be similar to that used in the Member Information form to search for a member with a matching telephone number. One difference will

| **VB CODE BOX 10-1.** Menu options for frm-PhoneNum | ```
Private Sub mnuFileExit_Click()
    End
End Sub
Private Sub mnuHelpAbout_Click()
    frmAbout.Show
End Sub
Private Sub mnuMemoCreate_Click()
    frmMemo.Show
End Sub
Private Sub mnuMemVidCheck_Click()
    frmMemberInfo.Show
End Sub
Private Sub mnuMemVidChkVid_Click()
    frmCheckin.Show
End Sub
Private Sub mnuMemVidFind_Click()
  frmVideos.Show
  frmVideos.txtSearch.SetFocus
End Sub
Private Sub mnuMemVidLate_Click()
  frmOverDue.Show
End Sub
``` |

be that, since the datMembers data control is on the frmMemberInfo form, we must include the form name as a part of the data control name. Also, before trying to find the phone number with the FindFirst method, we need to check its length to be sure it has 12 characters. Finally, after finding the record, we need to hide the frmPhoneNum form and display the frmMemberInfo form. VB Code Box 10-2 shows the code for the cmdFind button.

| **VB CODE BOX 10-2.** frmPhoneNum Code for cmdFind button | ```
Private Sub cmdFind_Click()
  Const strApos as String = "'"
  Dim strTarget As String
  If Len(txtPhoneNum.Text) <> 12 Then
    MsgBox "Input 12 character telephone number!", _
      vbExclamation, "Membership verification"
  Else
    strTarget = "Phone_Number = " & strApos & txtPhoneNum _
    & strApos
    frmMemberInfo.datMembers.Recordset.FindFirst strTarget
    If frmMemberInfo.datMembers.Recordset.NoMatch Then
      MsgBox "No member with that telephone number!", _
        vbExclamation, "Membership Verification"
      txtPhoneNum = ""
    Else
      frmPhoneNum.Hide
      frmMemberInfo.Show
    End If
  End If
End Sub
``` |

Figure 10-3 shows the effect that entering a valid telephone number in frmPhone-Num has on frmMemberInfo. Note that we have added a **Back** button to the frm-

MemberInfo form to transfer control back to frmPhoneNum and we have changed the caption on the cmdExit button to *Rental.*

FIGURE 10-3.
Result of finding
member information

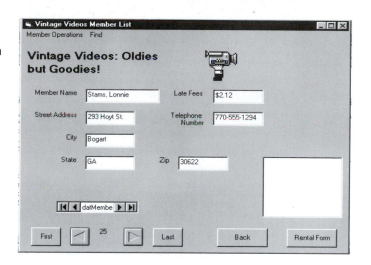

*Transferring
Information to the
Rental Form*

Once the membership information has been verified in the Member Info form, control should be transferred to the video rental transaction form—frmRental. To do this, we need to revise the *Exit* button on frmMemberInfo to transfer control to frmRental along with the user's name and late fees, if any. This means the caption of this button should be changed to reflect its new purpose (which is to display the Rental form instead of exiting the project) as shown in Figure 10-3, and the statements shown in VB Code Box 10-3 should replace the *End* statement in the cmdExit event procedure in order to transfer information and control to the frmRental form. .

VB CODE BOX 10-3. frmMemberInfo Code to switch to frmRental form	```Private Sub cmdExit_Click() frmMemberInfo.Hide frmRental.Show frmRental.txtCustName.Text = txtCustName.Text frmRental.txtLateFees.Text = txtLateFees.Text End Sub```

Mini-Summary 10-1: Revising the Project

1. Projects almost always end up being changed from their original forms. However, with VB this is easy to do since existing forms can be reused.

2. Developers should create a plan for projects that include both old and new forms and their relationship.

3. It is possible to reference a data control on another form by giving the "full name" of the data control, that is, include the form name in front of the data control name.

It's Your Turn!

1. Why is it not unusual to need to scrap the first version of a systems development project and create a new one?

2. Is it easier to create a new version of a systems development project with Visual Basic than to use earlier languages that do not share its object-oriented properties? Why or why not?

3. If you need to refer to an object on another form, what must you include as a part of its name?

Completing the remaining questions will enable you to create the Visual Basic project discussed in the text.

4. Open the **Vintage9.vbp** project from the **Chapter9** folder in design mode. Use the **File | Save MemberInfo.frm as...** menu option to save the form to a new folder named **Chapter10** on your data disk. Then use the **File | Save Project as...** option to save the **Vintage9** project to the new **Chapter10** folder as **Vintage10.vbp**.

5. Use the **Project | Add File** to add the following form files to the **Vintage10** project from the **Chapter8** folder: **Vintage8.frm**, **Memo.frm**, **About.frm**, **Video7.frm**, and **Password.frm**. As you add each file, use the **Save** *frmName* **As...** command to save it to the **Chapter10** folder. In the save process, change the file name of **Vintage8.frm** to **Rentals.frm** and the name of **Videos7.frm** to **Videos.frm**. Use the **Project | Project1 Properties** submenu option to make the **frmPassword** form the Startup object. (This is very important!) Also, change the name of the **frmVintage** form to **frmRental**. After all form files have been added and saved, resave the project under the same name.

6. While still in design mode for the Vintage10 project, use the **Project | Add Form** or the **Add Form** icon to add a new form. Cut and paste the store slogan ("Vintage Videos: Oldies but Goodies!") from the frmRental form to the new form. Also, cut and paste the logo to the new form. Add to this form a text box named **txtPhoneNum**, a label to describe it (**lblPhoneNum**), and a command button named **cmdFind** with a caption of **Find**. Set the Default property for this command button to **True** so the user can enter a telephone number and press **Enter** to search for it. The resulting form should look like Figure 10-2. Name the form **frmPhoneNum**, give it a caption of **Vintage Videos**, and save it as **PhoneNum.frm** to the **Chapter10** folder.

7. Modify the **File | Exit** submenu option of the frmMemo form to display the frmPhoneNum form rather than the old frmVintage form.

8. Use the Menu Editor to create the same menu and submenu options on the frmPhoneNum form as are currently being used on the frmRentals form (these are shown in Table 8-6 in Chapter 8). When you have completed this operation, add two other submenu items with captions of **Overdue Videos** and **Check in videos** and names of **mnuMemVidLate** and **mnuMemVidChkVid** to the **Members/Videos** menu option. Add the code shown in VB Code Box 10-1 to the submenu options on this form. Lastly, use the Menu Editor to remove the menus from frmRentals and the code editor to remove the corresponding code.

9. Add the code shown in VB Code Box 10-2 to the Find command button. Run your project and test the Find button by entering a telephone number with fewer than 12 characters. Now enter **770-555-1294**. This should result in the database record for Lonnie Stams being displayed. Exit the project and run it again entering **770-555-1095**. You should get a message that there is no member with this telephone number.

10. Change the caption for the cmdExit button on the frmMemberInfo form to **Rental Form** and add the code statements shown in VB Code Box 10-3 to replace the **End** statement in the cmdExit event procedure to transfer information and control to the frmRental form. Also, add a button named **cmdBack** with a caption of **Back**. Add code to this button to hide frmMemberInfo and display frmPhoneNum.

11. Save the forms and project under their current names in the Chapter10 folder.

RENTING VIDEOS

The next step in revising the Vintage Videos transaction processing system is to modify the frmRental form (the old frmVintage form) to use the Vintage.mdb database. This involves determining the name and price of a video for a given ID number to use in the calculation of taxes and amount due, designating the video as being rented, and removing any late fees from the record of the person renting it (customers must pay all late fees before renting any new videos).

To do all this, we need to modify the frmRental form to include a data control (*datVideos*) that will be linked to the Vintage.mdb database, but, for reasons to be discussed shortly, not to any specific table. We also need to include a text box in which the video ID number will be entered (*txtVideoID*). The option buttons that have been used to determine the price for the video are no longer needed, so they should be removed. The menu bar options and Vintage Videos slogan and logo should already have been removed and a new heading label added. In addition, the cmdCalc_Click event procedure needs to be modified to clear the txtVideoID text box and to set the focus back to it rather than to the txtVideoName text box. The resulting frmRental form is shown in Figure 10-4.

Determining Name and Price of Video

When videos are presented to the clerk to be rented, the clerk enters the ID number for the video on the frmRental form to automatically display the video name and price. This process involves four actions:

1. Validate that the txtVideoID text box is not blank.
2. Validate that the video ID number matches a video on the database.
3. Validate that the video is not already rented.
4. Display the name and price of the video.

Actions 2 and 3 might seem unnecessary, since the clerk is entering the ID number of a video presented by the customer; however, since the clerk could easily input an incorrect number, these checks are necessary to avoid Visual Basic errors. The potential for input errors is one of the reasons bar codes are so widely used today for input. Once the first three validations have been made, then the last action can be carried out.

All of these actions need to be executed *before* the Calculate button is clicked to compute the taxes and amount due, and we can use the **GotFocus** event for the cmdCalc command button for this purpose. The corresponding event procedure is executed whenever a control receives the focus. To force the cmdCalc command button

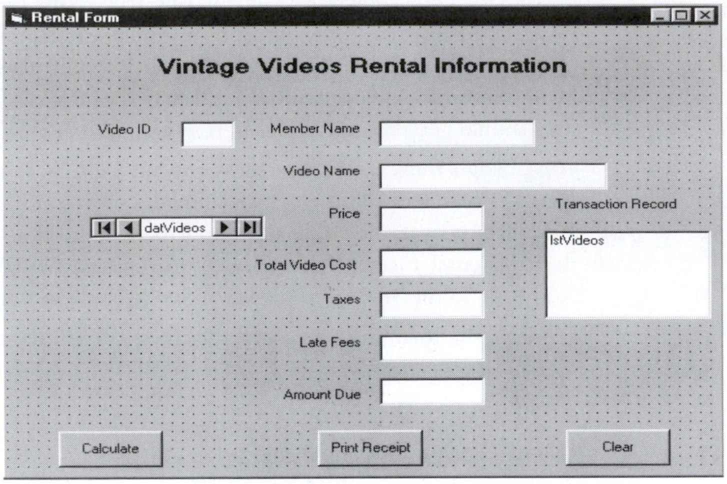

FIGURE 10-4.
Revised frmRental
form

to receive the focus when the video ID number is entered and the Tab key is pressed, we need to set the TabIndex property of the txtVideoID text box to zero and the Tab-Index property of the cmdCalc command button to 1. When the GotFocus event procedure is executed, the first action is to validate that an ID number has been entered. As with previous data entry validation, this simply involves checking the contents of the appropriate text box.

> **Tip:** An alternative to the GotFocus event for performing data validation is the Validate event. The Validate event occurs before the focus shifts to a (second) control that has its CausesValidation property set to True.

The next two actions both involve checking if a video ID exists in a database table. However, this validation must be carried out on two different database tables: the Videos table and the Rental table. Because we are working with two different tables, the RecordSource property for the data control will not be set at design time, so the database fields are *not* bound to specific text boxes and the data control Record-Source property is set to the appropriate table in the code. This requires two statements—one to assign the RecordSource property to the name of a database table and one to refresh the database with the data control **Refresh** method, as shown below:

dat*Name*.RecordSource = "*TableName*"

dat*Name*.Refresh

For example, to define the Videos table as the RecordSource for the datVideos data control, the statements would be:

```
datVideos.RecordSource = "Videos"
datVideos.Refresh
```

In addition to being set equal to a database table, the RecordSource property can be set equal to an SQL query or even to a query created in Microsoft Access. We will use the SQL approach later in the chapter to work with both single and multiple tables.

Once the RecordSource property has been set with these two statements, we can use the FindFirst method to determine if there is a video with this ID number. This is accomplished with code similar to that used to check for the member name corresponding to a telephone number, except that since the ID number is numeric, the apostrophes are not needed. If there is no video with this number, the txtVideoID text box is cleared and the focus is set to it. The complete code to check if a video exists is shown in VB Code Box 10-5 which includes code shown in VB Code Box 10-4.

| **VB CODE BOX 10-4.** frmRental Code to search for video by number | ```
datVideos.RecordSource = "Videos"
datVideos.Refresh
strTarget = "ID_Num = " & txtVideoID.Text
datVideos.Recordset.FindFirst strTarget
If datVideos.Recordset.NoMatch Then
    MsgBox "Video does not exist", vbCritical, "Video Status"
    txtVideoID = ""
    txtVideoID.SetFocus
End If
``` |
| --- | --- |

To check if the video corresponding to the ID number exists but is rented, the Recordset Field property discussed earlier is used. The comparison condition is:

```
If datVideos.Recordset("Rented") Then
```

since the Rented field of the Videos tables is a Yes/No (Boolean) field and no comparison is necessary.

It is not necessary to create another If-Then statement for this condition; we can simply combine it with the previous If-Then using the Or operator to create a single If-Then statement; that is:

```
If datVideos.Recordset.NoMatch Or _
datVideos.Recordset("Rented") Then
```

We can also use the Field property to transfer the contents of the Video_Name and Price fields to the corresponding text boxes. The complete cmdCalc_GotFocus event procedure is shown in VB Code Box 10-5.

| **VB CODE BOX 10-5.** frmRental cmdCalc_- GotFocus code to display the video name and price | ```
Private Sub cmdCalc_GotFocus()
  Dim strTarget As String
  If txtVideoID.Text = "" Then
    MsgBox "You must enter a valid ID number."
    txtVideoID.SetFocus
    Exit Sub
  Else
    datVideos.RecordSource = "Videos" 'Define RecordSource
    datVideos.Refresh
    strTarget = "ID_Num = " & txtVideoID.Text 'Set up query
    datVideos.Recordset.FindFirst strTarget 'Search for ID Num
    If datVideos.Recordset.NoMatch Or _
      datVideos.Recordset("Rented") Then 'ID not found
      MsgBox "Video does not exist or is rented", _
        vbCritical, "Video Status"
      txtVideoID.Text = ""
      txtVideoID.SetFocus
    Else 'ID Found
      txtVideoName.Text = datVideos.Recordset("Video_Name")
      txtVideoPrice.Text = Format(datVideos.Recordset_
        ("Price"),"currency") 'Copy name and price to boxes
    End If
  End If
End Sub
``` |
| --- | --- |

Designating the Video as Being Rented

Once the name and price of the video are displayed in text boxes, the next step is to use the cmdCalc_Click event procedure to calculate the taxes and amount due and to designate this video as being rented. The former step is already handled by the cmd-Calc button, but the latter step involves both editing the *Rented* field for this video in the Videos table and adding a row to the Rental table. The fact that two different tables are modified to designate a video as being rented is indicative of the redundancy in this database design, as mentioned earlier. To reduce the complexity of the cmdCalc event procedure, both of these operations will be written as procedures (UpdateVideos and UpdateRental). These procedures are referenced in the cmdCalc_Click event procedure immediately before the txtVideoID, txtVideoName, and txtVideoPrice text boxes are cleared. The focus is set back to the txtVideoID text box instead of to the txtVideoName text box as was done previously. The complete code for the cmdCalc_Click event procedure including the references to UpdateVideos and Up-dateRental is shown in VB Code Box 10-6, with the new or revised statements in boldface.

| VB CODE BOX 10-6. frmRental cmdCalc_-Click code to update Videos and Rental tables | ```
Private Sub cmdCalc_Click()
    Const sngTaxRate As Single = 0.07 'Use local tax rate
    Dim curPrice As Currency, curAmountDue As Currency
    Dim curTaxes As Currency, curLateFees As Currency
    If txtCustName.Text = "" Then 'Check for customer name
     txtCustName.Text = InputBox("Enter customer name and try again.")
        Exit Sub 'No customer name entered
    End If
    If txtVideoName.Text = "" Then 'Check for video name
        txtVideoName.Text = InputBox("Enter video name and try again.")
        Exit Sub 'No video name entered
    End If
    curPrice = CCur(txtVideoPrice.Text)
    curTotalCost = curTotalCost + curPrice 'Add price to total cost
    curTaxes = curTotalCost * sngTaxRate 'Compute taxes
    curLateFees = CCur(txtLateFees.Text)
    curAmountDue = curTotalCost + curTaxes + curLateFees
      'Compute amount due
    txtLateFees.Text = Format(curLateFees, "currency")
    txtTotalCost.Text = Format(curTotalCost, "currency")
    txtTaxes.Text = Format(curTaxes, "currency")
    txtAmountDue.Text = Format(curAmountDue, "currency")
    txtVideoPrice.Text = Format(curPrice, "currency")
    lstVideos.AddItem txtVideoName.Text & " " & txtVideoPrice.Text
    UpdateVideos
    UpdateRental
    txtVideoName.Text = ""
    txtVideoPrice.Text = ""
    txtVideoID.Text = ""
    txtVideoID.SetFocus
End Sub
``` |
|---|---|

To edit the Rented field in the Videos table for this video, we use the Recordset Edit and Update methods. The Edit method makes it possible to change one or more fields in the current record using the Field property, and the Update method makes these changes permanent in the database. The Rented field needs to be set to True, since it is a Yes/No field in the database. These operations will be accomplished in the Update Videos sub procedure, as shown in VB Code Box 10-7.
```

VB CODE BOX 10-7. frmRental UpDate-Videos Sub procedure	```
	Sub UpdateVideos()
	  datVideos.Recordset.Edit
	  datVideos.Recordset("Rented") = True
	  datVideos.Recordset.Update
	End Sub
	``

> **Tip:** You cannot use the Edit method to change the contents of a data-aware field.

It is also necessary to add a row to the Rental table to link the phone number of the person renting the video to the ID number of the video being rented. The due date for the video is also included in this row. To accomplish this, we need to set the datVideos.RecordSource property equal to this table name (Rental), add a new row (record) with the AddNew method, and assign the various fields of the table values with the Field property. These operations will be accomplished in the UpdateRental sub procedure as shown VB Code Box 10-8.

VB CODE BOX 10-8. frmRental Update-Rental Sub procedure	```
	Sub UpdateRental()
	  datVideos.RecordSource = "Rental"
	  datVideos.Refresh
	  datVideos.Recordset.AddNew
	  datVideos.Recordset("Video ID") = CInt(txtVideoID.Text)
	  datVideos.Recordset("Phone Number") = frmMemberInfo. _
	  txtPhoneNum.Text
	  datVideos.Recordset("Date Due") = Date + 2
	  datVideos.Recordset.Update
	End Sub
	``

Note in VB Code Box 10-8 that the Video ID database field is set equal to the contents of the txtVideoID text box and the Phone Number field is set equal to the txtPhoneNum text box on the frmMemberInfo form. Since all videos rented from Vintage Video are two-day rentals, the Date Due field is set equal to the system date plus two. To do this, we use the **Date** function to find the system date and then add two days to it

> **Tip:** Visual Basic built-in functions for working with dates and times include the Date, Time, Timer, and DateDiff functions as well as many more.

Removing Late Fees from Member Record

When the member rents a video, he or she must pay any late fees in addition to the rental costs for the current videos. This payment of the late fees must be recognized in the database by modifying the Late_Fees field in the Members table to set it to zero when the receipt is being printed and the transaction is completed. The easiest way to do this is to use the datMembers data control on the frmMemberInfo form, since the RecordSource is already equal to the Members table and the record for the member renting the video is the current record. The code to accomplish this should be added to the end of the cmdPrint_Click event procedure as shown in VB Code Box 10-9.

VB CODE BOX 10-9. Code to set late fees to zero	`frmMemberInfo.datMembers.Recordset.Edit`
	`frmMemberInfo.datMembers.Recordset("Late_Fees") = 0`
	`frmMemberInfo.datMembers.Recordset.Update`

Returning to the Phone Number Form

To return to the Phone Number form, we need to add three statements to the cmdClear_Click event procedure: one to unload the Rental form and two to display the frmPhoneNum form and clear the txtPhoneNum text box. These are shown in VB Code Box 10-10. In addition, the statement to set the focus back to the txtCust-Name text box should be deleted. The revised cmdPrint_Click and cmdClear_Click event procedures are shown in VB Code Box 10-11 with the new code statements in boldface.

VB CODE BOX 10-10. Code to return to frm-PhoneNum	`Unload Me`
	`frmPhoneNum.Show`
	`frmPhoneNum.txtPhoneNum.Text = ""`

| **VB CODE BOX 10-11.** frmRental complete code for cmdClear and cmdPrint | ```
Private Sub cmdPrint_Click()
  Dim intNumber As Integer, intCounter As Integer
  lstVideos.AddItem "Total video price " + txtTotalCost.Text
  lstVideos.AddItem "Taxes " + txtTaxes.Text
  lstVideos.AddItem "Late Fees " + txtLateFees.Text
  lstVideos.AddItem "Total price = " + txtAmountDue.Text
  lstVideos.AddItem "Thanks for your business!"
  intNumber = lstVideos.ListCount - 1
  For intCounter = 0 To intNumber
    Debug.Print lstVideos.List(intCounter)
  Next
  frmMemberInfo.datMembers.Recordset.Edit
  frmMemberInfo.datMembers.Recordset("Late_Fees") = 0
  frmMemberInfo.datMembers.Recordset.Update
End Sub
Private Sub cmdClear_Click()
  txtCustName.Text = ""
  txtVideoName.Text = ""
  txtVideoPrice.Text = ""
  txtTaxes.Text = ""
  txtAmountDue.Text = ""
  txtTotalCost.Text = ""
  txtLateFees.Text = ""
  curTotalCost = 0
  lstVideos.Clear
  Unload Me
  frmPhoneNum.Show
  frmPhoneNum.txtPhoneNum.Text = ""
End Sub
``` |
|---|---|

Running the project

We are now ready to run the project to use the Vintage database in the rental process. For example, if we run the project and enter the same telephone number as before (770-555-1294), the form shown in Figure 10-3 is displayed. Clicking the **Rental** com-
```

mand button displays the frmRental form. Entering a video ID of **23** and pressing Tab automatically displays the corresponding video name and price, as shown in Figure 10-5.

Clicking the Calculate button will calculate the amount owed; clear the txtVideoID, txtVideoName, and txtVideoPrice text boxes; and return control to the txtVideoID text box. If you now attempt to enter the same video ID as before, an error message will be displayed. Instead, clicking the Print button prints a receipt to the Debug window and sets the member's late fees to zero.

Now, if you clear the Rental form, return to the Phone Number form, and enter the same phone number as before, you should see that the member's late fees, which were $2.12, are now equal to zero.

FIGURE 10-5.
Result of entering a video ID number

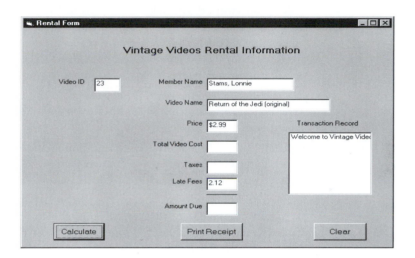

Mini-Summary 10-2: GotFocus Events, Designating the RecordSource, and Editing Fields

1. The GotFocus event, which occurs when a control receives the focus, is a good way to automatically display information.

2. You can designate the RecordSource for the data control at run time. The Refresh method must be used to make this change.

3. The Edit and Update methods can be used with the Field property to edit fields that are *not* bound.

It's Your Turn!

1. What event is automatically executed any time an object is given the focus?

2. If you choose to define the RecordSource property of a data control in the code, what data control method must follow this statement?

3. Assume you have a data control named **datStudents** and you wish to set the RecordSource property equal to a query created in Access named **sqlTopStudents.** Write the statements to carry out this operation.

4. What other method *must* be used with the **Edit** method of the data control Record-Set object?

5. Assume for the **datStudents** data control defined above, you wish to modify the Name field for the current record to set it to a null value (""). Write the statements necessary to do this (assuming the field is *not* bound to a control.)

Completing the remaining questions will enable you to create the Visual Basic project discussed in the text.

6. Modify the frmRental form to have a caption of **Rental Form** and to include a heading label with a caption of **Vintage Videos Rental Form**. You should also add data control named **datVideos** that has a database name property of **a:\Vintage.mdb** with a Visible property of **False**. Also, add a text box named **txtVideoID**. Set the Tab-Index property for the txtVideoID text box to **0** and to **1** for the cmdCalc button. Add appropriate labels and delete the Frame and Option Buttons used to select the type of video being rented. Delete the event procedure for the Option Buttons. Finally, change the caption for the cmdPrint button to be **Print Receipt**. The resulting form should appear as shown in Figure 10-4.

7. Delete all code in the Form Load event procedure for the frmRental form with the exception of the instruction that adds the message "Welcome to Vintage Videos" to the list box.

8. Double-click the Calculate command button and use the Procedures list box to switch to the GotFocus event. Enter the code shown in VB Code Box 10-5 to validate the video ID number entered in txtVideoID and to display the video name and price in the appropriate text boxes.

9. Modify the cmdCalc_Click event procedure to refer to the UpdateVideos and UpdateRental sub procedures before clearing the txtVideoName and txtVideoPrice text boxes as shown in VB Code Box 10-6. Also, add statements to clear the VideoID text box and to set the focus back to it. Finally, delete the instruction setting the focus to the txtVideoName textbox at the end of the procedure.

10. Create the **UpdateVideos** sub procedure using the code shown in VB Code Box 10-7. Also create the **UpdateRental** sub procedure using the code shown in VB Code Box 10-8.

11. Add the code shown in VB Code Box 10-9 to the cmdPrint_Click event procedure to set the member's late fees to zero.

12. Add the code shown in VB Code Box 10-10 to the cmdClear_Click event procedure to return to the frmPhoneNum form.

13. Run your project with the member phone number and video ID discussed in the text (770-555-1294 and 23). You should see the same form as shown in Figure 10-5. Click the Calculate command button to total the price plus taxes and set the focus back to the txtVideoID. Try entering the same video ID again and see what happens. Try entering a video ID number of **999** and see the results.

14. Click the Print button and then the Clear button to return to the frmPhoneNumber form; enter the same phone number as before. The late fees should now be zero.

15. Enter the data shown in Table 10-1 for three persons renting videos.

16. Exit the project and save all forms and the project under the same file names.

TABLE 10-1: Three Rental Transactions

Phone Number	Video IDs
706-555-1234	1, 11, 31
770-555-1010	3, 26, 50
706-555-9475	15, 37

WORKING WITH VIDEOS

In addition to converting the transaction forms to use the Vintage.mdb database, we want to convert the form used to search for videos matching a search string and to add new videos or delete existing videos to work with the database. Recall that this form is named **frmVideos** and was originally added in Chapter 6 to search through arrays. To revise this form to work with databases, we need to add a data control and replace the list box control with a new type of control especially designed to work with databases—the DBList control.

First, let's add a data control named **datFind** to the frmVideos form and link it to the same database as the other data controls by setting its DatabaseName property to the name of the database (**a:\vintage.mdb**). Also, set the RecordSource property for datFind to **Videos**. Since this data control does not need to be seen, its Visible property is set to **False**.

Now, we need to delete the lstVideos listbox and replace it with one of the DB controls that are very useful for displaying information in databases. The three controls are the **DBList, DBCombo,** and **DBGrid** controls. We can display an entire database table or a combination of selected rows and a selected column depending on which control is used. Since these controls are not originally available in the toolbox, we need to add them the same way we added the common dialog box control in Chapter 8. (If these controls are not shown, see the supporting Web site for information on adding them.) Use the Visual Basic **Project|Components** menu option to display a list of controls that can be added to the toolbox and select the *Microsoft Databound Grid* and *List* controls by clicking the checkbox beside each one. This will add the appropriate icons for the three controls to the toolbox for future use. Once we have added these three controls to the toolbox, we can use them in forms to display data in the database. The three letter prefixes for these controls are dgd, dbl, and dbc for the DBGrid, DBList, and DBCombo controls, respectively.

DBList Control

DBCombo Control

DBGrid Control

The DBGrid control can be used to display an entire table or selected rows and columns. It is also very powerful (as well as somewhat dangerous) in that it can be used to dynamically edit the database by saving changes that are entered in the various cells of the control. The DBGrid control is linked to the database by setting its **Data-Source** property equal to a data control on the same form. The DBList and DBCombo controls are useful for displaying just one column of the database table for all or selected rows. They are *read-only* controls in that you *cannot* edit the database through them. In our case, we will use the DBList control to display names of videos that match the search string entered in that textbox.

> **Tip:** To prevent the user from changing the contents of DBGrid cells, set the AllowUpdate property to False.

To do this, we start by going to frmVideos form and deleting the existing listbox (lstVideos) and adding a DBList control named *dblVideos*. The DBList has two key properties for displaying records: the RowSource and ListField properties. The **Row-Source** property points to the data control that will provide the database records to be listed. The **ListField** property designates the database field that will be displayed. In our case, the RowSource property is set equal to the datFind data control and the List-Field property is set equal to the Video_Name field. Note that drop down list boxes are available for these properties so that you don't need to remember data control and field names.

Since we are looking for videos *like* the search string in the txtSearch text box, we need to set the RecordSource for the datFind data control equal to an **SQL query** that searches for matching records in the Videos table of the database. As we mentioned earlier, in addition to database tables being the RecordSource for a data control, an SQL query—whether created in the code at run time, entered in the RecordSource property at design time, or created in Microsoft Access and referenced at either run time or design time—can be used as the RecordSource property. In this case, the SQL query will be created in the code and referenced at run time.

Before we go into using an SQL query as the RecordSource property, let's review the form of an SQL query:

SELECT *fieldnames* FROM *tables* WHERE *query*

where the *query* part of the SQL statement looks exactly like the queries we have been using with the FindFirst and FindNext methods in Visual Basic. For example, we might write an SQL statement to find all of the fields for all records in the Members table that live in Athens as:

```
SELECT * FROM Members WHERE City = 'Athens'
```

where the asterisk is used to find all fields.

To find video names like the search string, we will use a new type of comparison operator: the "LIKE" operator. This operator type allows us to look for Video names that partially match a search string input by the user. The query combines the LIKE operator with the asterisk wild-card character (*) to search for records containing the search string regardless of what precedes or follows the search string. The result is exactly the same as when we used the InStr() function with arrays in Chapter 6.

The general form of the query using the LIKE Operator is:

SELECT * FROM Table WHERE *FieldName* LIKE '*SearchString*'

with both the asterisks and the search string being enclosed in apostrophes in the query string. For example, if the search string is "And", then the query would find "Dogs And Cats", "And she loves you", or "The great And".

As with the apostrophe by itself, the best way to work with the string constant combining an apostrophe with the wildcard character is to create constants with the Const keyword—that is,

```
Const strAposAst as String = "'*", strAstApos as String = "*'"
```

—and to use them before and after the search string in the query.

We will define a string data type variable, strSQLQuery, to hold the query; the RecordSource property will be set equal to this string variable and the data control refreshed with the Refresh method to actually run the query. Combining the LIKE query and these two constants with the rest of the SQL statement yields:

```
strSQLQuery = "SELECT * FROM Videos WHERE Video_Name LIKE " _
& strAposAst & strSearch & strAstApos
```

where strSQLQuery is the string that stores the SQL statement and strSearch is the search string from txtSearch.

To search for and display all video names matching some query, we simply set the RecordSource property for datFind equal to strSQL and then refresh datFind. The

> **Tip:** If you use a database system other than MS Access, remember that not all are created equal. SQL is case sensitive on some systems, some do not support the Like operator, and wildcard characters may vary from system to system.

matching video names will automatically be displayed in the dblVideos DBList box. The code for the cmdSearch_Click event procedure is shown in VB Code Box 10-12.

VB CODE BOX 10-12. frmVideos Code to search database for matching videos

```
Private Sub cmdSearch_Click()
  Const strAposAst As String = "'*", _
  strAstApos As String = "*'"
  Dim strSQL as String, strSearch as String
  strSearch = txtSearch.Text
    If strSearch = "" Then
      MsgBox "You must enter a video name!"
      txtSearch.SetFocus
  Else
    strSQL = "SELECT * FROM Videos WHERE Video_Name LIKE " _
    & strAposAst & strSearch & strAstApos
    datFind.RecordSource = strSQL
    datFind.Refresh
    If datFind.Recordset.EOF Then
        MsgBox "No matching videos"
    End If
  End If
  txtVideoInfo.Text = ""
End Sub
```

Two points in this code are worth noting. First, the txtSearch text box is validated and then used as the search string. Second, the complete SQL string uses the LIKE comparison operator to search for any video whose name contains the search string.

Selecting a Specific Video

If we want information on a specific video after displaying the names of matching videos, we need to add code to the dblVideo_Click event procedure to display the video's name, price, store location, and rental status when a video name is clicked in the list box. Clicking a video in the dblVideo DBList control should display information about it in a text box beneath the list box. For any matching video, the value of the Rented field is determined; if the value is True, then the video is rented; otherwise the video is available. In either case, the result is assigned to a string variable, strStatus, that is displayed in the text box along with the name, price, and location. This is more meaningful than just displaying True or False.

To do this, we use the **SelectedItem** property of the dblVideos DBList control. This property returns a variant value that is equal to the Bookmark for this record and, as such, can be used to find the matching record in the datFind Recordset. The code is shown in VB Code Box 10-13.

If the project is run, the Find Videos option is selected from the Members/Videos menu bar option on the frmPhoneNumber form, and the search string "and" is entered in the text box. The result of clicking the Search command button is shown in Figure 10-6. Note in Figure 10-6 that five videos were found with "and" somewhere in their name, and that *Willy Wonka and the Chocolate Factory* has been selected, but that it is rented at this time.

VB Code Box 10-13. frmVideos code to select a video	```
	Private Sub dblVideos_Click()
	  Dim varSelIndex as Variant, strStatus As String
	  varSelIndex = dblVideos.SelectedItem
	  datFind.Recordset.Bookmark = varSelIndex
	  If datFind.Recordset("Rented") Then
	    strStatus = "Rented"
	  Else
	    strStatus = "Available"
	  End If
	  txtVideoInfo.Text = datFind.Recordset("Video_Name") & " " _
	  & Format(datFind.Recordset("Price"), "currency") & " " & _
	    datFind.Recordset("Location") & " " & strStatus
	End Sub
	``

Figure 10-6.
Result of searching for "and"

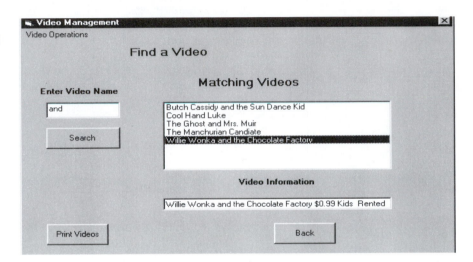

Adding, Deleting, and Printing Videos

Just as with arrays, we will need to add videos to the database. Also, as videos become worn out, they will either be sold or discarded and their records will need to be deleted from the database. As was done for the frmMemberInfo form, we can do this with a menu bar option of **Video Operations** and two submenu options: **Add Video** and **Delete Video**. The code for these two options will be very similar to that used for the corresponding operations on the frmMemberInfo form. Because of this similarity, we will present the code with no further discussion other than to say that a video *must* be selected in the list box before it can be deleted; otherwise there will be no current video and the last video on the list will be deleted. This is validated by checking if the SelectedItem property is empty with the **IsNull()** function; if it is, there is nothing to be deleted. The code to add and delete videos is shown in VB Code Box 10-14.

The last modification we need to make to this form is to revise the cmdPrint_Click event procedure to print the contents of the Videos table, instead of several arrays as was done in Chapter 7. To do this, we need to use the EOF property and MoveNext method of the Recordset as shown in VB Code Box 10-15, where only the video name and availability are printed. Note in this code that a loop is used to print records *until* the database EOF property is encountered. The MoveNext method is used to move the record pointer to the next record.

VB CODE BOX 10-14. frmVideos Add and Delete event procedures	`Private Sub mnuVidOpsAdd_Click()`

```
Private Sub mnuVidOpsAdd_Click()
    datFind.Recordset.AddNew
    datFind.Recordset("Video_Name") = InputBox("Input Name")
    datFind.Recordset("Price") = CCur(InputBox("Input Price"))
    datFind.Recordset("Location") = InputBox("Input Location")
    datFind.Recordset.Update
End Sub
Private Sub mnuVidOpsDel_Click()
  Const strWarning as String = "Delete this video?"
  Dim intResponse as Integer
  If IsNull(dblVideos.SelectedItem) Then
    MsgBox "Please select a video to delete"
  Else
    intResponse = MsgBox(strWarning, vbYesNoCancel + _
    vbCritical + vbDefaultButton2, "Delete Video")
    If intResponse = vbYes Then
        datFind.Recordset.Bookmark = dblVideos.SelectedItem
        datFind.Recordset.Delete
        datFind.Refresh
    End If
    txtVideoInfo.Text = ""
  End If
End Sub
```

VB CODE BOX 10-15. frmVideos code to print Videos table	

```
Private Sub cmdPrint_Click()
    Dim strStatus As String
    datFind.Recordset.MoveFirst
    Do Until datFind.Recordset.EOF
      If datFind.Recordset("Rented") Then
          strStatus = "Rented"
      Else
          strStatus = "Available"
      End If
      Debug.Print datFind.Recordset("Video_Name") & "   " _
      & strStatus
      datFind.Recordset.MoveNext
    Loop
End Sub
```

Mini-Summary 10-3: Working with Videos

1. The DBList, DBCombo, and DBGrid are controls that can be bound to the data control to show lists one field, multiple fields, or entire records from a database.

2. The DBList can be used to show a field from a table or SQL query with the RowSource property being set equal to a data control and the ListField property being equal to the field to be displayed. The SelectedIndex property can be used to determine which item in the DBList has been selected.

3. SQL (Structured Query Language) can be used as the RecordSource property for data controls. The Refresh method must be used after assigning the RecordSource property in the code. Keywords commonly used in an SQL statement are SELECT, FROM, and WHERE.

Mini-Summary 10-3: Working with Videos (Continued)

4. The LIKE comparison operator can be used to find strings that partially match the contents of a database field. The subject of the search should have wildcard asterisks on either side of it, with everything enclosed in apostrophes.

5. The SelectedItem property of the DBList control can be used to find the bookmark in the database of the selected item or to ensure an item has been selected using the IsNull function.

6. To print a database, you need to use an Until loop and the MoveNext method.

It's Your Turn!

1. In addition to a database table, to what other entities can the data control Record-Source property be set equal?

2. Write the SQL statement to select all fields from the Videos table that have a price of $2.99.

3. How does the DBList box differ from the list box you have been using in previous chapters?

4. What information does the **SelectedItem** property of the DBList box control provide? What data type is it?

5. Write the statements necessary to display all videos with price of $2.99 in a DBList box named dblClassics. Assume the same data control is used in this case as was used in the example.

6. Why do we use the **IsNull** function to check if an item in a DBList box has been chosen?

Completing the remaining questions will enable you to create the Visual Basic project discussed in the text.

7. Modify the existing frmVideos form by adding a menu bar item named **mnuVidOps** with a caption of **Video Operations**. To this menu bar item, add two submenu items named **mnuVidOpsAdd** and **mnuVidOpsDel** with captions, respectively, of **Add Video** and **Delete Video**.

8. Add a data control to the frmVideos form with a name of **datFind**. Set the DatabaseName property to **a:\Vintage.mdb**, the RecordSource property to **Videos**, and the Visible property to **False**. Also, add a text box beneath the list box. Make it the same width as the list box and give it a name of **txtVideoInfo**.

9. Replace the existing code for the cmdSearch_Click event procedure with that shown in VB Code Box 10-12 to search for videos. Also, replace the existing code for the lstVideos_Click event procedure with that shown in VB Code Box 10-13.

10. Run your project and test it by entering a search string of "and". You should see a list like that shown in Figure 10-6. Click on *Willie Wonka and the Chocolate Factory* to see the price, location, and availability of this video. It should be rented.

11. Add the code for the mnuVidOpsAdd_Click( ) and mnuVidOpsDel_ Click( ) event procedures shown in VB Code Box 10-14 to the two menu items.

12. Run your project and test it by adding a new video, ***True Grit***, with a price of **$1.99** and with a location of **Western**. Also, delete the existing video, ***The Manchurian Candidate***.

13. Replace the code in the cmdPrint_Click event procedure with the code shown in VB Code Box 10-15. Test this code to ensure that a complete list of all videos in the database will be printed to the Immediate window.

14. Save your forms and project under the same names.

MORE ON THE DB CONTROLS

As we noted in the last section, the DBList, DBCombo, and DBGrid controls are useful for displaying all or part of a record from a database table or query. In this section, we will combine the DBList and DBGrid controls to enable the employees of Vintage Videos to call customers about overdue videos. Recall that all videos rented from Vintage Videos are due back in two days and that there is only one copy of each video. To find overdue videos, we will need to query the Rental table to find videos whose due date is before the current date; e.g., a video with a due date of November 1 is overdue if the current date is November 2. For each matching record, we need to find the corresponding customer name and video name so the employee can call a customer, say, Alice Harris, and ask about a specific video, say, *The Robe*.

Unfortunately, the information necessary to make these calls is not in the Rentals table alone; instead, it is distributed among the three tables of the database: Members, Videos, and Rentals. The Rentals table contains a record for each rental of a video including the customer telephone number, the video ID number, and the date the video is due back. The Members table contains the name and telephone number of all customers, and the Videos table contains the ID number and name of each video.

However, the DBList box (and DBCombo) control has the capability to be linked to another DB control in such a way that the field name in the DBList control is updated by clicking a record in the other DB control. In our case, if the records for overdue videos are displayed in a DBGrid control, we can link a DBList control containing customer names to the DBGrid so that the customer name corresponding to the current or highlighted record in DBGrid is also highlighted in the DBList control. Similarly, we can add a DBList control with video names that is also linked to the DBGrid so the overdue video name is highlighted. An example of this is shown in Figure 10-7. Note that the video is due on January 25, 2001, but the date this was run was January 26, 2001 as shown in the *Today's Date* textbox.

Adding the frmOverdue Form

As a start to linking the controls on this form, let's start by using **Project|Add Form|New Form** menu command to add a new form to the project. The new form should have as its name *frmOverdue* with a Caption property of *Overdue Videos*. To this form add a data control named *datOverdue* with its DatabaseName property the same as before (a:\vintage.mdb). Make this data control invisible but don't define the RecordSource property at design time; instead, we will use an SQL statement as the RecordSource as we did in the last section. In this case, the required SQL statement should find all records that are overdue and is shown below:

SELECT * FROM Rental WHERE [Date Due] < #Date#

FIGURE 10-7.
Example of linking
DB controls

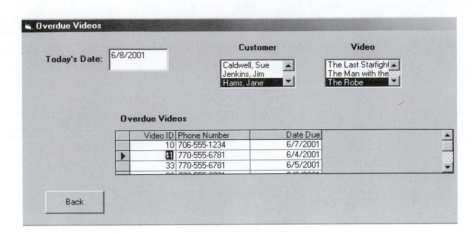

where the Date Due field is enclosed in brackets because of the space in the field name. The **Date** function returns the current date and is enclosed in pound signs to force the Access database engine used by Visual Basic to treat it as a date. This statement can be used as the RecordSource for the datOverdue data control by including it in the Form_Load event procedure as shown in VB Code Box 10-16.

VB CODE BOX 10-16. frmOverdue Form_Load event procedure	```Private Sub Form_Load() Dim strSQL as string txtToday.Text = Date strSQL = "SELECT * FROM Rental WHERE [Date Due] < #" & Date & "#" datOverDue.Recordsource = strSQL datOverDue.Refresh End Sub```

The next step is to add a DBGrid control named *dgdOverDue* and set its **Data-Source** property equal to the datOverdue data control. If this is done, the project run, and the Overdue Videos option selected from the Members/Videos main menu item, any overdue videos will be listed in the DBGrid control in a manner similar to that shown in Figure 10-7.

Linking the Controls

To link a DBList to the dgdOverdue DBGrid control, we need to consider three other properties of the DBList that make the linking possible: the DataSource, DataField, and BoundColumn properties. The **DataSource** property is the name of the data control with the recordset to be updated, typically the same data control as the DBGrid control. The **DataField** property is the field to be updated in the changing recordset. Finally, the **BoundColumn** is the name of the field with the value to be inserted in the table being updated. Note that the BoundColumn and DataField properties point to the same field in different database tables.

For our example, we need to add a data control named **datCustomer** that points to the Members table of the Vintage.mdb database and set the properties of dblCustomer as shown in Table 10-2. If this is done and the Overdue Videos form accessed as before, then the name displayed in dblCustomer will correspond to the current record in dgdOverdue in a manner similar to that shown in Figure 10-7.

Note that the first two properties of dblCustomer, that is, RowSource and List-Field, display the names of customers in the DBList. The BoundColumn property

TABLE 10-2: Linking and Display Properties for dblCustomer

Property	Value
RowSource	datCustomer
ListField	Name
BoundColumn	Phone_Num
DataSource	datOverdue
DataField	Phone Number

points to the Phone_Num field in the same database table as the customer names. The DataSource property points to the same data control as does dgdOverdue, and the DataField property points to the same field in the Rental table (Phone Number) as does the BoundColumn property in the Members table. This equivalence provides the linking between the dblCustomer and dgdOverdue. This relationship is shown in Figure 10-8.

FIGURE 10-8.
Linking
relationships

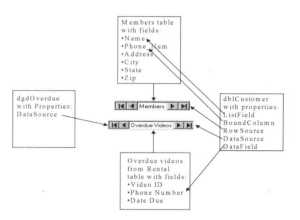

To display the name of the video that is overdue as well as the customer name and the rental record, an approach should be taken with a second DBList control (**dblVideoName**) that is similar to that done with the first. To do this, add another data control (**datVideoName***) pointing to the Videos table and set the properties of dblVideoName as shown in Table 10-3. Note that the datOverdue data control is the common element for both DBList boxes as it is the linking element.

TABLE 10-3: Properties for dblVideoName

Property	Value
RowSource	datVideoName
ListField	Video_Name
BoundColumn	ID_Num

TABLE 10-3: Properties for dblVideoName (Continued)

Property	Value
DataSource	datOverdue
DataField	Video ID

Mini-Summary 10-4: More on the DB Controls

1. In addition to using the DBList control to list the records in a Recordset, it is possible to link it to other DB controls.

2. The DBGrid only has a DataSource property, but it shows all fields and records in the corresponding Recordset.

3. The DataSource, DataField, and BoundColumn properties of the DBList control can be used to link it to other DB controls by setting the DataSource property to the same data control as the other DB control. The DataField and BoundColumn must be set equal to the same field but in different Recordsets to create the link.

It's Your Turn

1. How does the DBGrid control differ from the DBList box or DBCombo box controls?

2. Why would you want to link the DBList box control to another DB control?

3. What properties of the DBList box control are used to link it to another DB control? Explain how this linking is carried out.

4. What is different about a SQL query involving dates?

Completing the remaining questions will enable you to create the Visual Basic project discussed in the text.

5. Use the **Project|Add Form|New Form** menu command to add a new form to the current project. The new form should have as its name **frmOverdue** with a Caption property of **Overdue Videos**. To this form add a data control named **DatOverdue** with its DatabaseName property the same as before (**a:\vintage.mdb**). Make this data control invisible but don't define the RecordSource property at design time. Also add a textbox named **txtDate** and clear the **Text** property.

6. Add a DBGrid control named **dgdOverDue** and set its **DataSource** property equal to the datOverdue data control. In the Form_Load event for this form, add the code shown in VB Code Box 10-16. Save the new form as **Overdue.frm** and save the project.

7. Before running your project, use the Windows 95/98/2000 Start Menu to display the Date/Time icon on the Control Panel. Double-click this icon to display the Date/Time window (or simply double-click the time in the bottom right-hand corner). Advance the date six days from the current date. (Remember to return it to today's date when you are finished.)

8. Run your project and switch immediately to the new form using the **Members/ Videos|Overdue Call** menu option. When this is done, you should see a DBGrid control similar to that shown in Figure 10-7 with all overdue videos. (This will depend on which ones you rented in earlier exercises.)

9. Add DBList and data controls to display the customer name as shown in Figure 10-7. Set the properties for these controls as shown in Table 10-4. Run your project as

TABLE 10-4: Control Properties

Properties for dblCustomer	Value	Properties for datCustomer	Value
Name	dblCustomer	Name	datCustomer
RowSource	datCustomer	DatabaseName	a:\vintage.mdb
ListField	Name	RecordSource	Members
BoundColumn	Phone_Num		
DataSource	datOverdue		
DataField	Phone Number		

before. You should now be able to click on a row in the DBGrid control and see the name of the person who rented the overdue video.

10. Add a second DBList control and a second data control with properties shown in Table 10-5. Run your project as before. You should now be able to click on a row in the DBGrid control and see the name of the overdue video as well as the person who rented it.

TABLE 10-5: Control Properties

Properties for dblVideoName	Value	Properties for datVideoName	Value
Name	dblVideoName	Name	datVideoName
RowSource	datVideoName	DatabaseName	a:\vintage.mdb
ListField	Video_Name	RecordSource	Videos
BoundColumn	ID_Num		
DataSource	datOverdue		
DataField	Video ID		

11. Save the form and project.

USING SQL TO CHECK IN VIDEOS

The last feature that we want to add to the Vintage Videos transaction processing system is the capability to check in videos when they are returned. This process involves using SQL (Structured Query Language) to work with all three tables in the database simultaneously. Up to this point in the chapter, we have not assumed that you have any previous experience with relational databases. However, to completely understand this discussion, you should have some knowledge and experience in this area.

Checking in videos requires that we accomplish four objectives:

1. When the form is loaded, the system date should be displayed in a text box. When the ID number for the returned video is entered in a text box, the video name and price from the Videos table and the date due from the Rental table should be automatically displayed via an SQL query.

2. When a command button is clicked, the system date on the computer should be compared to the due date in the Rental table. If the system date is later than (greater than) the due date, then the late fees for the video are computed by multiplying the number of days overdue by the video price found on the Videos table.

3. The late fees must then be added to any existing late fees to update the late fees amount on the Members table. The late fees should be zero when the first video is returned, but will change if multiple late videos are returned before any more are rented.

4. The Rented field on the Videos table should then be updated to show that this video is no longer rented, and the row of the Rental table corresponding to this video should be deleted.

The form for carrying out these operations is shown in Figure 10-9. Recall that we reach this form from the frmPhoneNum menu system by selecting the Check In submenu option of the Members/Videos menu. Note that a data control named **datCheckIn** has been added to the form. This data control will be used to display the information about the returned video as well as to update the three tables. The controls that have been added are summarized in Table 10-6.

The GotFocus event for cmdCheckIn will also be used to display the video and member information corresponding to the video ID number by running a query and using this query as the recordsource for the data control..

TABLE 10-6: Controls for frmCheckin

Control	Purpose
txtVideoID	Video ID number for video being checked in
txtVideoName	Name of video being checked in
txtVideoPrice	Price of video being checked in
txtDateDue	Date the video was due
txtLateFees	Late fees (both old and new)
txtDate	Date the video is being checked in
txtPhoneNum	Phone number of member returning video
cmdCheckIn	Calculates late fees (if any) and updates database tables
cmdClear	Clears text boxes before next video is checked in
cmdReturn	Returns control to frmPhoneNum

FIGURE 10-9. Form to check in returned videos

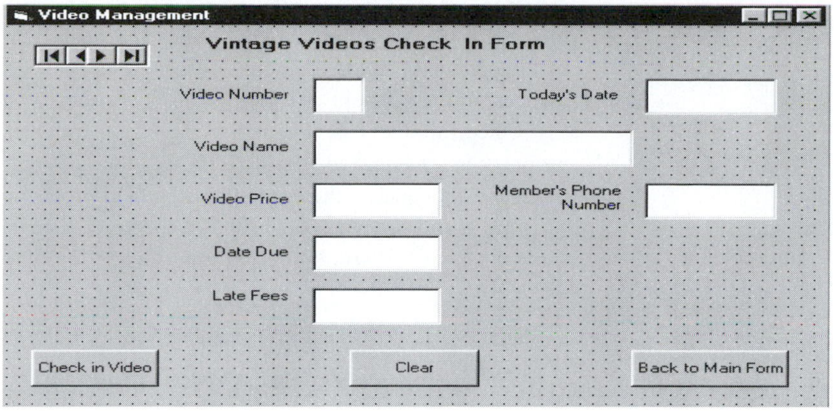

Finding Information on Returned Video

The query to check in a video is quite complex involving three tables and is shown in VB Code Box 10-17. To determine if a match has been found, we use an If-Then statement to check the EOF property of the Recordset. If the EOF property is found to be True, the record pointer is beyond the end of the database and no match was found. If the EOF property is False, a match was found. Once it has been determined that a match has been found, the next step is to assign the contents of the various fields to the corresponding text boxes using the Field property. The complete code for the cmdCheckIn_GotFocus event is shown in VB Code Box 10-17.

VB CODE BOX 10-17. frmCheckin code to display information on video using SQL

```
Private Sub cmdCheckIn_GotFocus()
    Dim strSQLQuery As String
    strSQLQuery = "SELECT Rental.[Date Due] as DateDue," _
    & " Rental.[Video ID] as VID, Members.Late_fees as" _
    & " LateFees, Videos.Video_Name as VideoName," _
    & " Videos.Price as Price, Members.Phone_Number" _
    & " as PhoneNum FROM Videos, Rental, Members" _
    & " WHERE Videos.ID_Num = Rental.[Video ID]" _
    & " and Members.Phone_Number = Rental.[Phone Number]" _
    & " and Videos.Id_Num = " & CLng(txtVideoID.Text)
    datCheckIn.RecordSource = strSQLQuery
    datCheckIn.Refresh
    If datCheckIn.Recordset.EOF Then
      MsgBox "Video not rented", vbExclamation, "Video Status"
      txtVideoID.Text = ""
      txtVideoID.SetFocus
      Exit Sub
    Else
      txtDateDue.Text = datCheckIn.Recordset("DateDue")
      txtVideoPrice.Text = datCheckIn.Recordset("Price")
      txtVideoName.Text = datCheckIn.Recordset("VideoName")
      txtLateFees.Text = datCheckIn.Recordset("Latefees")
      txtPhoneNum.Text = datCheckIn.Recordset("PhoneNum")
    End If
End Sub
```

In looking at this code, you should first note that the query uses standard SQL commands—SELECT, FROM, and WHERE—to select the fields and rows that match the query. Note that the *dot method* is used to combine tables and fields to qualify the field name, as in Rental.[Date Due]. The query also contains unique aliases for the various database fields to avoid confusion later on. For example, DateDue is an alias for Rental.[Date Due].

Once the query is assigned to the string variable, the datCheckIn RecordSource property is set equal to it and refreshed, the EOF property is checked, and the text boxes are set equal to the corresponding field properties. When a video ID number of 41 is input and the focus is shifted to the cmdCheckIn command button, the result is shown in Figure 10-10. Note that this video is four days overdue.

FIGURE 10-10.
Checking in a late video

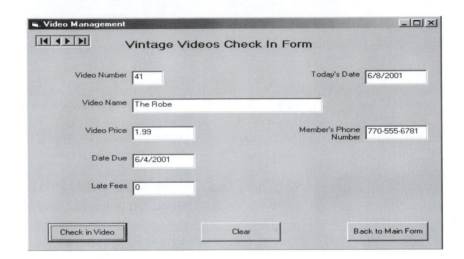

Updating Tables

With the information in the text boxes, we can now write the code to update the various tables. Even though the record pointer is currently pointing to the matching record in each table, we cannot simply edit the record defined by the SQL query. Instead, we must define each table as the RecordSource and then use the FindFirst method to find the record in that table. Once the record has been found, then it can be modified. In the Members table, we must use the telephone number to find the Late Fees field and then modify it by adding the new late fees associated with overdue rentals. In the Videos table, we must use the video ID number to find and change the Rented field to False since the video has now been returned. Finally, in the Rental table, we must find and delete the record associated with this rental. This must all be accomplished in the cmdCheckIn_Click event procedure as shown in VB Code Box 10-18, where all of the updating is accomplished in three sub procedures: UpdateMembers, UpdateVideos, and UpdateRental. Note that there is no confusion with these sub names since they are local to this form.

Note in this code that the due date and video price we found earlier and stored in the txtDateDue and txtLateFees text boxes are used to compute the additional late fees. The date in the txtDateDue text box is compared to the system date returned by the Date function. If the rental is overdue (Date > dtmDate_Due), then the late fee is equal to price times days overdue plus any existing late fees. The Late Fees field is then edited in the UpdateMembers sub procedure to make it equal to this value. Next, the Rented field is modified in the UpdateVideos sub procedure and the record is deleted in the UpdateRental sub procedure. When all changes have been made, cmdClear_Click event procedure is invoked to clear the text boxes in preparation for

| VB CODE BOX 10-18. frmCheckin code to check in returned videos | ```
Private Sub cmdCheckIn_Click()
    Dim dtmDate_Due As Date, curPrice As Currency
    Dim curLateFees as Currency
    curPrice = txtVideoPrice.Text
    dtmDate_Due = txtDateDue.Text
    curLateFees = CCur(txtLateFees.Text)
    If Date > dtmDate_Due Then
        curLateFees = (Date - dtmDate_Due) * curPrice + curLateFees
    End If
    txtLateFees.Text = Format(curLateFees, "Currency")
    UpdateMembers
    UpdateRental
    UpdateVideos
    cmdClear_Click
End Sub
``` |

checking another video. This same event procedure can be invoked to cancel the check-in process and clear the text boxes. When all returned videos have been processed, the cmdReturn button should unload the current form and return control to the frmPhoneNum form.

Obviously, the key to the check-in process is the three sub procedures that update the various tables. All three sub procedures work in a similar manner: find the record corresponding to the values in the appropriate text box, modify it, and update the record. These three sub procedures are shown in VB Code Box 10-19.

Mini-Summary 10-5: Using SQL to check in videos

1. SQL is required whenever you wish to draw data from multiple tables at the same time.

2. To link a data control to multiple database tables, it must be linked to an SQL statement.

3. A multiple table query cannot be edited; each table must be edited separately. However, after the query is executed, the record pointers for the various tables will be pointing to the records that are to be edited.

It's Your Turn!

1. Why was a multi-table SQL statement used to handle the return of videos to Vintage Videos? Can you explain another way to handle this problem?

2. Why were aliases used in the SQL statement?

3. Why was it necessary to run queries to update the tables involved in returned videos?

Completing the remaining questions will enable you to create the Visual Basic project discussed in the text.

4. Create the frmCheckIn form as shown in Figure 10-9 with the text boxes and command buttons listed in Table 10-6. Also add a data control (**datCheckIn**) with a DatabaseName property of a:\vintage.mdb. Add code to the Form_Load event procedure to set the txtDate text box equal to the Date function.

5. After defining appropriate TabIndex properties to make the txtVideoID text box the first text box in the tab sequence and the cmdCalc command button the second control, add the code shown in VB Code Box 10-17 to the cmdCheckIn_GotFocus
```

| **VB CODE BOX 10-19.** frmCheckin sub procedures to update database tables | ```
Sub UpdateMembers()
    Const strApos As String = "'"
    datCheckIn.RecordSource = "Members"
    datCheckIn.Refresh
    datCheckIn.Recordset.FindFirst "Phone_Number = " _
    & strApos & txtPhoneNum.Text & strApos
    datCheckIn.Recordset.Edit
    datCheckIn.Recordset("Late_Fees") = CCur(txtLateFees.Text)
    datCheckIn.Recordset.Update
End Sub
Sub UpdateVideos()
    datCheckIn.RecordSource = "Videos"
    datCheckIn.Refresh
    datCheckIn.Recordset.FindFirst "ID_num = " & _
    txtVideoID.Text
    datCheckIn.Recordset.Edit
    datCheckIn.Recordset("Rented") = False
    datCheckIn.Recordset.Update
End Sub
Sub UpdateRental()
    datCheckIn.RecordSource = "Rental"
    datCheckIn.Refresh
    datCheckIn.Recordset.FindFirst "[Video ID] = " _
    & txtVideoID.Text
    datCheckIn.Recordset.Delete
End Sub
``` |

event procedure. Run your project, switch to this form, enter a VideoID of **23**, and press **Tab** to move the focus to the cmdCheckIn button. A form similar to that shown in Figure 10-10 should be displayed.

6. Exit the project and add the code shown in VB Code Box 10-18 to the cmdCheckIn_Click event procedure. Next, create the three sub procedures shown in VB Code Box 10-19 at the form level.

7. Add the code necessary to clear the text boxes and set the focus to the txtVideoID text box in the cmdClear_Click event procedure. Also, add the code necessary to return control to the frmPhoneNum form by unloading the current form and displaying that form. Save the form as **CheckIn.frm** and the project under the same name.

8. Before running your project, use the Windows Start Menu to display the Date/Time icon on the Control Panel. Double-click this icon to display the Date/Time window. Advance the date six days from the current date. (Remember to return it to today's date when you are finished.)

9. Run your project, switch to the frmCheckIn form, once again, enter a video ID number of **23**, and press **Tab**. This time, note that the date due is before the current date (by how much depends on when you carried out the earlier exercise to simulate renting videos). Click the cmdCheckIn button and switch to the frmMembers form to note the change in the late fees due to the video being returned late.

10. Click the cmdClear button and try entering a video ID number of **23** again. Note the result. Now enter a video ID number of **50** and carry out the check-in process. Clear the text boxes, return to the frmPhoneNum form, click the Find Video submenu
```

option, and perform the same search as before. Note that *Willie Wonka and the Chocolate Factory* is now listed as available, since it has been checked in. (Return the system date to today's date.)

USING THE DATA VIEW WINDOW

Data View icon

The **Data View window** is a new feature of Visual Basic 6 that allows you to view and modify a database from within Visual Basic. Previously, to view a database, you had to switch out of Visual Basic and into the appropriate database management system. Now, with the Data View window, you simply connect to the database and then view it and make any needed changes, saving much time and effort. The Data View window is a design time tool that cannot be used during run time.

Creating the Data Link

Data Link icon

To connect to your database, you must click on the Data View icon in the toolbar or select Data View window from the View menu bar option. When this is done, the Data View window appears as shown in Figure 10-11. Note that there is a Data Links folder and a Data Environment Connections folder. If you have created data links or environment connections, they would be displayed here. At the top of the window are icons for refreshing the data view, adding a new data environment connection, and adding a new data link. We will use the last of the three to create a data link to a Microsoft Jet database (for example, an Access 2000 database).

FIGURE 10-11. Data View window

If the icon on the top of the Data View window to create a new data link is clicked, a wizard will walk you through the process of linking to a database. The first thing you will see in this process is the Data Link Properties window in which you will need to set the database properties. In our case, we want to select the Microsoft Jet Engine 4.0 (assuming the Service Pack 4.0 has been installed on version of Visual Basic) as the *provider* as shown in Figure 10-12 and then click the Next button.

Clicking Next will display the Connection tab from the Data Link Properties window in which you must enter the name of the database to which you wish to connect. In our case, we will assume we are connecting to the Vintage.mdb database on a floppy diskette in the A: drive. You can enter this information directly or use the dialog box button to the left of the database name text box to select it. In either case, the resulting window is shown in Figure 10-13. You do not need to worry about changing anything else in this window. You can check if your connection worked by clicking the *Test Connection* button at the bottom of the screen and then Click *Ok* to return to the Data View window.

If your connection is set up properly, you should now see a new icon named *DataLink1* beneath the Data Links folder in the Data View window. Clicking on the plus sign beside it will display Tables, Views, and Stored Procedures folders. Clicking

FIGURE 10-12. Data Link Properties window

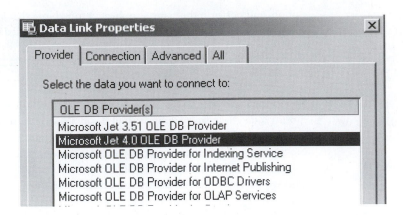

FIGURE 10-13. Data base name added

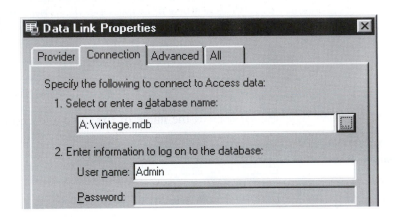

the Tables folder will display the tables in your database. For the Vintage.mdb database, this is shown in Figure 10-14

FIGURE 10-14. Data View window with new connection

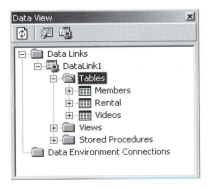

To actually view the contents of a table of the database, double-click the corresponding table icon in the Data View window. For our example, double-clicking the Members table icon will result in the contents of that table being displayed as shown in Figure 10-15 after the Data View window has been closed to show the table. You can also click the plus sign beside any table to view the fields of the table and the detail of the fields.

FIGURE 10-15.
Members Table of
Vintage.mdb
database

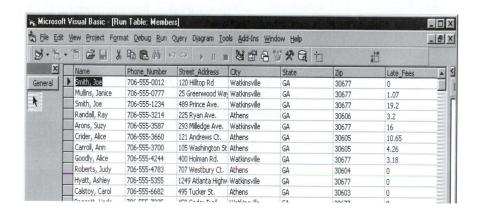

It should be noted that once created, a link in the Data View window does not have to be redone if the database changes; simply clicking the Refresh Data View icon will take care of connecting to the revised database. Once the table is displayed, you can edit the contents of a field by placing the cursor in the field contents and making any desired changes. You can also view and change the field definitions by clicking the plus beside a table name and then double-clicking a field name.

> **Tip:** Right-click the name of the table and choose **Design** to view or modify the table definition. This allows you to change the structure of the table, the columns it contains and the column properties.

Mini-Summary 10-6: Using the Data View Window

1. The Data View window is an addition to Visual Basic that enables you to look at a database without exiting Visual Basic.

2. Accessing a database using the Data View window involves setting up the Data Link by providing information on the database provider.

3. Once the Data Link is set up, the tables, queries, and stored procedures in the database can be viewed.

4. The field definitions as well as the contents of the tables can be changed and saved using the Data View window.

It's Your Turn!

1. What is the Data View window and what capabilities does it provide us?

2. What is the Data Link?

Completing the remaining questions will enable you to create the Visual Basic project discussed in the text.

3. In Visual Basic, click the Data Window icon in the Toolbar to display the Data View window. In the Data View window, create a data link by clicking the Data Link icon and following the wizard. Select the **Microsoft OLE DB 4.0 Provider** if you are using Access 2000. Select the Vintage.mdb database on the a:\ drive.

4. You should now see a new data link (**DataLink1**). Click the plus sign to display the tables, views, and stored procedures for the database. Click the plus sign beside the **Members** table to view the associated fields.

5. Double-click the **Members** table to view its contents as shown in Figure 10-15.

6. Close the Members table and then close the Data View window to return to Visual Basic.

SUMMARY

Projects almost always end up being changed from their original form. However, with VB this is easy to do since existing forms can be reused. Developers should create a plan for projects that include both old and new forms and their relationship. It is possible to reference a data control on another form by giving the "full name" of the data control, that is, include the form name in front of the data control name.

A good way to automatically display information is with the GotFocus event, which occurs when a control receives the focus. We can designate the RecordSource for the data control at run time; the Refresh method must be used to make this change. The Edit and Update methods can be used with the Field property to edit fields that are not data-aware.

The DBList, DBCombo, and DBGrid are controls that can be bound to the data control to show lists of one field, multiple fields, or entire records from a database. The DBList can be used to show a field from a table or SQL query with the Row-Source property being set equal to a data control and the listfield property being equal to the field to be displayed. The SelectedIndex property can be used to determine which item in the DBList has been selected.

SQL (Structured Query Language) can be used as the RecordSource property for data controls. The Refresh method must be used after assigning the RecordSource property in the code. Keywords commonly used in an SQL statement are SELECT, FROM, and WHERE. The LIKE comparison operator can be used to find strings that partially match the contents of a database field. The subject of the search should have wildcard asterisks on either side of it, with everything enclosed in apostrophes. The SelectedItem property of the DBList control can be used to find the bookmark in the database of the selected item or to ensure an item has been selected using the IsNull function. To print a database, you need to use an Until loop and the MoveNext method.

In addition to using the DBList control to list the records in a recordset, it is possible to link it to other DB controls. The DBGrid only has a DataSource property, but it shows all fields and records in the corresponding Recordset. The DataSource, DataField, and BoundColumn properties of the DBList control can be used to link it to other DB controls by setting the DataSource property to the same data control as the other DB control. The DataField and BoundColumn must be set equal to the same field but in different recordsets to create the link.

SQL is required whenever you wish to draw data from multiple tables at the same time. To link a data control to multiple database tables, it must be linked to an SQL statement. The multiple-table query cannot be edited; each table must be edited separately. However, after the query is executed, the record pointers for the various tables will be pointing to the records that are to be edited.

The Data View window is an addition to Visual Basic that enables you to look at a database without exiting Visual Basic. Accessing a database using the Data View window involves setting up the Data Link by providing information on the database provider. Once the Data Link is set up, the tables, queries, and stored procedures in the database can be viewed. The field definitions as well as the contents of the tables can be changed and saved using the Data View window.

Since this is a revised project, summary information on the new procedures may be helpful to you. Instead of displaying all of the code for this project, which would take at least six pages, we will use two tables to show you where the code in the various VB Code Boxes should appear, that is, in the phone number form (frmPhoneNum), the membership information form (frmMemberInfo), the video information form (frmVideos), the rental form (frmRentals), the late videos form (frmOverdue), or the video check in form (frmCheckin). Note that we don't include code for the other forms in this project since they have not changed. Table 10-7 lists each VB Code Box in order and indicates the new lines of the procedure, its location, and its status, that is, whether it is new to this chapter or a modification of previous code. On the other hand, Table 10-8 shows the six forms of the revised Vintage.vbp project listed above the VB Code Boxes containing code that is new or modified in this chapter for that form. If an event procedure is not shown in either table, it is not changed from previous chapters and remains in the Vintage Videos (Vintage.vbp) unchanged. You should consider these two tables to be a *roadmap* to the changes and modifications that have taken place in this chapter.

TABLE 10-7: Location of Code in VB Code Boxes in Revised Vintage Videos Project

VB Code Box	General or event procedure	Location	Status
10-1	Multiple menu options	frmPhoneNum	New
10-2	cmdFind_Click event procedure	frmPhoneNum	New
10-3	cmdExit_Click event procedure	frmMemberInfo	New
10-5	cmdCalc_GotFocus event procedure	frmRental (old frmVintage)	New
10-6	cmdCalc_Click event procedure	frmRental (old frmVintage)	Modified
10-7	UpdateVideos sub procedure	frmRental (old frmVintage)	New
10-8	UpdateRental sub procedure	frmRental (old frmVintage)	New
10-11	cmdClear_Click and cmdPrint_Click event procedures	frmRental (old frmVintage)	Modified
10-12	cmdSearch event procedure	frmVideos	New
10-13	dblVideos_Click event procedure	frmVideos	New
10-14	mnuVidOpsAdd_Click and mnuVidOpsDel_Click event procedures	frmVideos	New
10-15	cmdPrint_Click event procedure	frmVideos	Modified
10-16	Form_Load event procedure	frmOverdue	New
10-17	cmdCheckin_GotFocus event procedure	frmCheckin	New
10-18	cmdCheckin_Click event procedure	frmCheckin	New
10-19	UpdateMembers, UpdateVideos, and UpdateRental sub procedures	frmCheckin	New

Table 10-8: Location of New or Modified code in Revised Vintage Videos Project

frmPhoneNum	frmMemberInfo	frmRental	frmVideos	frmOverdue	frmCheckin
VB Code Box 10-1	VB Code Box 10-3	VB Code Box 10-5	VB Code Box 10-12	VB Code Box 10-16	VB Code Box 10-17
VB Code Box 10-2		VB Code Box 10-6	VB Code Box 10-13		VB Code Box 10-18
		VB Code Box 10-7	VB Code Box 10-14		
		VB Code Box 10-8	VB Code Box 10-15		
		VB Code Box 10-11			

New Visual Basic Elements

Control/Object	Properties	Methods	Events
command button control			GotFocus
data control	RecordSource	Refresh	
DBCombo	DataField ListField		
DBGrid	DataSource		
DBList	BoundColumn DataField DataSource ListField		
Recordset object		Edit Update	

Key Terms

Brooks, Frederick

Date function

IsNull function

Structured Query Language (SQL)

New Programming Statements

Creating SQL Query String
strSQLQuery = "SELECT * FROM *tablename* WHERE *query*"

Using LIKE condition
strSQLQuery = "SELECT * FROM *tablename* WHERE *fieldname* LIKE '*searchstring*'"

Exercises

1. Find *The Mythical Man-Month: Essays on Software Engineering* by Frederick Brooks in your library and read the article about having to throw away the first version of a project. Write a two page paper on how this applies to projects created with Visual Basic.

For the following exercises, assume that you have a database named CUSTOMERS with three tables—Calls, Contacts, and ContactTypes. The Calls table has the fields—CallID, ContactID, CallTime, Subject, and Notes. The Contacts table has the fields—

ContactID, FirstName, LastName, CompanyName, Address, City, State, Email, Phone, LastMeetingDate, and ContactTypeID. The ContactTypes table has the fields—ContactTypeID, and ContactType. Use this database for exercises 2 and 3.

2. Describe the results that will be shown if the following SQL queries are executed.

a. strSQLQuery = "SELECT FirstName, LastName, WorkPhone, City FROM Contacts WHERE City='New York'"

b. strSQLQuery = "SELECT * FROM Contacts WHERE LastMeeting-Date>#1/1/2000#"

c. strSQLQuery = "SELECT * FROM Contacts WHERE LastMeeting-Date>#1/1/2000# AND State ='TN'"

d. strSQLQuery = "SELECT Contacts.FirstName, Contacts.LastName, Contacts.Email, ContactTypes.ContactType FROM Contacts, ContactTypes WHERE Contacts.ContactTypeID = ContactTypes.ContactTypeID AND Contact-Types.ContactType = 'Email'"

3. Write a Visual Basic SQL statement to obtain results for each of the following.

a. Get a list of all contacts at Microsoft.

b. List the first and last names of all people who were called since December of last year.

c. List the first and last names of all people who were called since December of last year about the subject "Merger."

d. List the first and last names of all people who were contacted via email about the subject "Merger." Note: This one may require a JOIN which is discussed in any database text.

Assume you have a database named SALES with three tables—Customers, Products, and Transactions. Assume the Customer table has two fields—Name and IDNum, and the Products table has three fields—ProdNum, Description, and Price. Finally, the Transactions table has three fields—ID, ProdID, and DateSold where the ID is a foreign key for the Customers table and the ProdID is the foreign key for the Products table. Use this information for Exercises 4, 5 and 6.

4. Assume that a data control exists on the current form named **datSold**. Write the statements to set this data control equal to the Transactions table and to add a new record to this table that contains the IDNum of a customer in the ID field, the Prod-Num of a product in the ProdID field, and the date of the sale in the DateSold field.

5. Write the statements to find and print to the Debug window all records in the Product table that have a price higher than $10.00. Use a data control named **datGeneral.**

6. Write the statements to find and print to the Debug window all records in the Customer table with a name containing the letters "ar". Use the same data control as above.

PROJECTS

1. Yeehaw Technical University wishes to analyze its students in terms of majors, GPA, and courses taken. To do this, the school has prepared a database called *newstud.mdb*. You may download the newstud.mdb file from the Chapter 10 data files section of the textbook Web site and save it to the root folder of your data disk. This file has three

tables: Info, Course IDNum, and Course. The tables and fields in each table are shown in Table 10-9. (You may assume that each course has only one section and that the course name is unique.)

TABLE 10-9: Fields in Each Table in NewStud.mdb

Table	Field1	Field2	Field3	Field4
Info	Name	IDNum	Major	GPA
Course IDNum	Course	StudNum		
Course	Course	Professor	Building	

Write a Visual Basic project using this database to carry out the following operations. In many cases, you must use your judgment to design the forms.

a. Create a Startup form from which you may switch to other forms or exit the project. It should be possible to return to this opening screen from any primary form by clicking an Ok button on that form.

b. Create a primary form that will display student names, ID numbers, majors, and GPAs in text boxes. This form should have navigational aids to display next, previous, first, and last student records and to return to the opening screen.

c. Create a form in which the user can display in a list box the names of all students for a major that the user inputs, along with the number of students in this major and the major itself.

d. Create a form in which the user can display in a list box the names of all students with a GPA above a value that the user inputs, along with the number of students achieving this value and the GPA value. This form should have an option to show this information just for students in a given major.

e. Create a form that, for a student ID number input by the user, will display in a list box the student's name, the courses taken by the student, and the professors and buildings for those courses.

f. Save this project as **Ex10-1.vbp**. Save the various forms as **Ex10-1One.frm**, **Ex10-1Two.frm**, and so on, in the Chapter10 folder on your data disk.

2. In an effort to improve sales, the sales manager at the local Toyosun dealership has created a database file named Cars.mdb which may be downloaded from the Chapter 10 data files section of the textbook Web site. This database file has three tables: SALESPERSON, VEHICLE, and SALES. The SALESPERSON table contains the SS Number, first name, and last name of the salespersons at the dealership, and their sales to date for this period. The VEHICLE table contains the ID Number, dealer's cost, MSRP, and vehicle type (car, SUV, or truck.) When a vehicle is sold, the vehicle ID number, salesperson's SS Number, and the date of the sale are entered in the SALES table. In addition, the sales to date field in the SALESPERSON table is updated with the amount of this sale.

Write a Visual Basic project to use this database to carry out the following operations. In many cases, you must use your own judgement to design the forms. Your complete project should carry out the following operations:

a. Create a start up form to handle the sale of a vehicle. You should be able to enter the vehicle ID number and display the MSRP and vehicle type when a **Vehicle** button is clicked. Similarly, you should be able to enter the salesperson's SS Number and display their first and last names when a **Salesperson** button is clicked. When a Calculate button is clicked, the sale goes through and the SALES and SALESPERSON tables are updated. You should be able to switch to the secondary forms or exit the project from this form using a menu system.

b. Create a *secondary* form that will automatically display the ID number, dealer cost, MSRP, and model of vehicle for records in the VEHICLE table in textboxes. This form should have navigation aids to display next, previous, first, and last automobile records and to return to the opening screen. Add a list box to this form in which clicking a **Vehicle Type** button should display the ID numbers of all vehicles for a vehicle type selected from a list box by the user. The form should also display the number of this type vehicle in the database.

c. Create a *secondary* form in which you should also be able to display in a list box the ID numbers and model of all vehicles with an MSRP *above* a value that the user inputs in a text box along with the number of vehicles with MSRP above this value. You should be able to return to the opening form.

d. This dealership has a five-day return policy. Add a *secondary* form to your project that will handle these returns. Note that this form should check the current date against the sales date to insure that no more than 5 days have elapsed. This transaction should remove the associated record from the SALES table and reduce the sales-to-date field in the SALESPERSON table by the amount of the MSRP for this vehicle. You should be able to return to the opening form.

e. Save this project as **Ex10-2.vbp**. Save the various forms as **Ex10-2One.frm**, **Ex10-2Two.frm**, and so on, in the Chapter10 folder on your data disk.

3. Have you ever dreamed of winning the lottery? It may not be as great as you may think. Very large amounts of money would require multiple accounts in order to manage your money. Cheer up! With your lottery winnings you should be able to afford a laptop with Visual Basic and database software. Then you can easily manage your many accounts using a ledger database while sipping frosty beverages beside your new pool. In preparation for your lucky day, create the ledger database described here or download it from the textbook Web site. This database will store transaction information, accounts, and classifications of account numbers. The tables and fields for the Ledger.mdb database, which can be downloaded from the Chapter 10 data files section of the textbook Web site, are shown in Table 10-10.

TABLE 10-10: Fields in Each Table in Ledger.mdb

Table	Field1	Field2	Field3	Field4	Field5	Field6
Transactions	TransactionID	TransDate	TransType	AccountID	Withdrawal Amt	DepostAmt
Accounts	AccountID	AccNumber	AccName	AccTypeID		
AccountTypes	AccTypeID	AccountType				

Write a Visual Basic project to use this database to carry out the following operations. In many cases, you must use your own judgement to design the forms. Save the project and all forms in an appropriately titled folder on your disk. Your complete project should carry out the following operations:

a. Create a start form that will request a userID and a password. If the values are entered correctly, a message should appear welcoming the user and enabling the buttons on the form. If they are entered incorrectly, a message should notify the user and a second and third attempt should be allowed. If after the third try the user has still not entered the correct information, the program should end. The buttons on the form should provide access to the secondary forms listed below.

b. Create a *secondary* form for adding new transaction entries to the database. Use textboxes and labels to allow the user to enter the appropriate values for each field. Each value entered should be validated before the database is updated with the new entry.

c. Create a *secondary* form that will allow you to choose a specific account from a listbox and enter two dates. After clicking a button you should see a listing of all transactions that occurred between the dates entered for that account. Your listing should include for each transaction the transaction date, type, and amount.

d. Create a *secondary* form that, when a button is clicked, will display a listing of all accounts and the current balance for each account. For each listing, include the account number, name, type, total amount withdrawn, total amount deposited, and balance. Below the listing, display the grand total withdrawn, deposited, and balance for all accounts.

e. Save this project as **Ex10-3.vbp**. Save the various forms as **Ex10-3One.frm**, **Ex10-3Two.frm**, and so on, in the Chapter10 folder on your data disk.

4. For many information system consultants, traveling and filling out expense reports is a part of life. Stephanie Taylor has been trying to keep up with the expense reports she receives in her job as Support Manager for The E-Consultant Group, an IS consulting group specializing in on-line systems. In order to more quickly reimburse the consultants and in the full spirit of the "paper work reduction movement," she has decided to create a database to help her manage consulting expenses. The tables and fields for the Expenses.mdb database, which may be downloaded from the Chapter 10 data files section of the textbook Web site, are shown in Table 10-11.

TABLE 10-11: Fields in Each Table in Expenses.mdb

Table	Field1	Field2	Field3	Field4	Field5	Field6
Employees	EmployeeID	SSNumber	Name	Title	Extension	Phone
ExpReports	ExpReportID	EmployeeID	ExpenseType	AdvanceAmt	DeptCharged	Paid
ExpDetails	ExpDetailsID	ExpReportID	ExpCatID	ExpItemAmt	ExpItemDesc	ExpDate
ExpCategories	ExpCatID	ExpCategory	ExpCatAcct			

Write a Visual Basic project to use this database to carry out the following operations. In many cases, you must use your own judgement to design the forms. Save the project and all forms in an appropriately titled folder on your disk. Your complete project should carry out the following operations:

a. Create a start up form that would allow Stephanie to browse the ExpReports table. Your form should contain buttons that allow her to go to the first, next, previous, and last record in the table. The fields for a current record should be displayed using textboxes that are bound to the fields. This form should also contain buttons that allow her to load each of the remaining forms listed below.

b. Create a *secondary* form that will allow Stephanie to select a specific expense report and then view the details of that report. The items displayed for the report should include the employee ID, the expense type, the date submitted, the advance, amount and whether or not the employee has been reimbursed. In a listbox list each item for which an expense was reported. For each item, list the item amount, description, date, and category. Your form should also calculate and show the total amount of expenses on the report and the amount owed to the employee (total expenses - advance amount).

c. Create a *secondary* form that will allow Stephanie to select an employee name from a listbox and enter a date. Add a command button with code to display a listing of the employee's expense reports that have been submitted after the inputted date. For each expense report, display the expense type, the date submitted, the amount of the advance, and the total amount of expenses on the report.

d. Create a *secondary* form to display a listing of all employees who still need to be reimbursed for some expenses. For each employee owed, list their name and the total amount owed.

e. Save this project as **Ex10-4.vbp**. Save the various forms as **Ex10-4One.frm**, **Ex10-4Two.frm**, and so on, in the Chapter10 folder on your data disk.

PROJECT: JOE'S TAX ASSISTANCE (CONT.)

Joe, a little rumpled in his pajamas and house slippers, grumbled to himself as he stared at the screen. He was still staring and sipping from his mug of coffee when he barely noticed movement at the door to the room.

"What's wrong, Grandpa? You're sounding a little gumpy today," he heard Zooey ask as she entered.

Not bothering to look up, Joe wiped absently at the coffee dribbling down his chin and said, "Just trying to figure out what's up with this client database. It worked fine when we started using it, but now it seems to be acting up, dang it!"

"Well . . ." Zooey began. "Here's Mr. Wells, my high school programming teacher. He came to give us some help."

A surprised and embarrassed Joe, looked up to see Zooey's instructor smiling at him. After re-wiping his chin, Joe stood to shake hands with him.

"Nice to meet you. I'll be grateful for the help," Joe said in greeting. "Although, you could've given me a little notice," he added with a side-long glance at Zooey.

"It's a pleasure, sir," said Mr. Wells. "Call me Scott. Zooey told me about your programming project and your work with taxes. I was intrigued and thought maybe I could lend a hand."

After the introductions had been made, Mr. Wells sat down to have a look at the pair's program and database. Zooey and Joe watched and explained various aspects and their current problem over his shoulder.

"I'm impressed. It seems that Zooey has learned something in my class after all," he said with a wink. "I think I see what's causing your problem."

He continued. "Your current database was okay as long as you only met with a client once. Because it's composed of a single table though, you start to get something called 'data redundancy' when you see a client a second or third time."

"I think I see what you mean," Joe replied. "What should we do next?"

"First, we need to redesign the database. Then, we can start to work on some new VB forms to work with it. Also, I can show you how to use a couple more controls that make working with databases easier."

The trio put their heads together and in a short time they came up with a new database design. The tables and fields of their new database are shown in Table 10-12.

TABLE 10-12: Fields in Each Table in Revised Clients.mdb

Table	Field1	Field2	Field3	Field4	Field5
Clients	ClientID	SSNum	Name	Phone	
Contacts	ContactID	ClientID	Date	Time	Met?
FormUsed	FormUsedID	ContactID	FormID	Qty	
Forms	FormID	FormType	FormDesc		

His initial embarrassment long since dissipated by his excitement, Joe said, "Scott, I think that this will do it."

"Don't be so sure," replied Mr. Wells. "It will probably work fine, but eventually you'll think of additions or modifications that you want to make. Useful systems like this are almost always evolving."

"Okay, but now we have someone to turn to when we get stuck," Joe replied. "Zooey, go ask your Grandma for some money to pay the man."

"No, please don't," Wells protested. "But, there is something you can do for me. Zooey, where did I leave my box?"

As Zooey retreived the box from it's hiding place in the hallway, Joe began to realize what was coming next.

"I took the liberty of bringing along some receipts from last year...," Mr. Wells began.

Questions

1. Assume that Joe has revised the database file named Clients.mdb which may be downloaded from the textbook Web site. This file contains the tables and fields shown in Table 10-12.

2. Create forms for the VITA program that Joe can use to manage (add and delete entries, browse the database.) Add a menu to the VITA program with items for working with the database.

3. Add forms which will allow Joe to get answers to the following questions:

   a. When was the last visit by a specific client and which tax forms were used?

   b. List the dates and times of client meetings that have not met yet? (Note: the Met? field in the Contacts table is Boolean with True when the meeting has already occurred and False when it has not yet occurred.)

   c. How many of each tax form were used within a particular time period?

4. Run, test, and debug your program.

11 USING VISUAL BASIC TO CREATE GRAPHICS

LEARNING OBJECTIVES

After reading this chapter, you will be able to:

❖ Understand the use of graphics to visually display data and information.

❖ Describe the types of business graphics and the ways they are used to aid business decision makers.

❖ Discuss the use of the picture box control as an area to display graphics.

❖ Create a graph of a mathematical function on the picture box using the PSet method.

❖ Create line charts using the Line method.

❖ Use the DrawStyle property to distinguish between multiple lines.

❖ Add titles and legends to charts.

❖ Create bar charts using the box option for the Line method.

❖ Use the FillStyle property to distinguish between multiple bars.

❖ Use the Circle method to create pie charts and scatter diagrams.

SCENARIO: USING GRAPHICS TO ANALYZE SALES AT VINTAGE VIDEOS

Clark stepped up onto the sidewalk and shook the snow off of his boots. He took a last look at the falling snow before heading into the store and smiled as he thought of last night's date with Monique. "It really is a wonderful life."

On the bus, he had begun to count off the important things that had happened to him recently. In addition to his starting to date Monique, Ed's and Yvonne's Vintage Videos store had been pretty successful. Clark felt that he had a hand in that success, not only with management duties, but with developing the Visual Basic program that was an integral part of the store's information system. Finally, Clark thought about graduating at the end of the semester and that he might have to move on to another job and leave Vintage Videos. These thoughts were still running through his mind as he entered Vintage Videos and saw Ed and Yvonne poring over some papers at the counter.

Yvonne looked up from the papers and smiled. "Hi, 'Bro," she said.

Clark took off his coat as Ed waved him over to the counter. "Just who we need to talk to. Come over here a minute and join us," Ed called out excitedly.

Ed continued, "You know, Clark, we've been doing pretty well and the store has been more successful than we imagined. Yvonne and I have been discussing it and I think that we've decided to open up another store across town."

Clark was speechless, and his mind began to race through all the possibilities that this entailed for his information system. Networking, the need for a server to handle a larger database, and equipment needs for the new store were among the many thoughts that began to flood his consciousness.

Yvonne giggled when she saw the look on his face. "I think Monique has him a little starry-eyed these days," she teased. "Anyway, we still have to get the loan first."

"That's right," said Ed. "That's where we need your computer expertise once again, Clark. We need to come up with a nice, professional business loan application to present to the bank."

"We have lots of good data showing how our sales have increased. Look here. Our rental sales revenue has increased in almost every month. We had around $9,000 in video rental revenue in December alone, plus about another $4,000 in miscellaneous revenue," Ed continued.

"That's great," Clark agreed after returning to reality. "But why do you need my computer expertise?" he asked.

"It's for the loan application," Yvonne responded. "We would like to show this information in the form of nice, professional-looking graphs and charts. We don't currently have the software that could do it, and besides, Ed hasn't kept up with the latest versions."

"You know, it's possible to write programs using Visual Basic that can generate various charts and graphs," Clark replied. "All of the data is already stored in the computer, and you wouldn't need to buy or learn new software."

"What types of charts could you make?" Ed inquired. "I was thinking of maybe a line or bar chart showing the revenue increases."

Clark responded confidently, "I'm sure we can do that. We could also do a pie chart showing the various categories of videos and the percentages rented of each. And maybe even tie that into revenues. I have a few days until school starts again. Let me see if I can work something up."

Ed put his arm around Yvonne and smiled. "You know, honey, after the loan goes through, we'll need someone to be in charge of the other store," he said, with a nod and a wink in Clark's direction.

All of a sudden Clark's impending career decision seemed a little clearer. As the bell on the door signaled the arrival of the first customer of the day, Clark thought, "I must have my own guardian angel!"

Discussion of Scenario

In this scenario, Ed and Yvonne need to create graphics to provide a dramatic display of Vintage Videos' growth for a loan application. Instead of purchasing and learning a full-blown spreadsheet package like Microsoft Excel or Lotus 1-2-3, Clark is going to use the capabilities of Visual Basic to create the specific charts they need. Graphs and charts are another way to display the results of processing. In many cases, they can portray data in a far more useful way than tables of numbers.

While spreadsheet or other charting packages would most likely be used for general charting needs, Visual Basic can be useful in creating custom charts that will be same from period to period except for the data used to generate them. That way, the user can simply click on a menu option to immediately see the new chart. Charts created by Visual Basic can also be useful to the novice user since they do not require a knowledge of spreadsheets or other software.

COMPUTER GRAPHICS

As you have seen in the first ten chapters of this book, lists and tables are very useful in displaying numeric and textual information. However, they do not always do a good job of helping a business decision maker find trends or make comparisons between groups of numbers, especially when there are a large number of values to consider. On the other hand, **graphics** are very useful for handling data or information visually. Mathematicians and scientists have been using graphics for years to display equations. Similarly, engineers have used graphics to design a wide variety of machines and structures using **CAD** (computer-aided design) **graphics**, and artists use graphics to create images for both business and artistic purposes. We have already used **clipart graphics** created by others in some of our projects.

Since the advent of the personal computer, graphics have commonly been used to display information about business and industry. For example, if the owners of Vintage Videos wanted to learn more about video rentals, they might very well want to look at a graphic representation rather than poring over tables of numbers. Such graphics are commonly referred to as **analysis** or **business graphics**. Business graphics can help a decision maker better understand or analyze the data. Common uses for charts in business include pictorial representations of sales, budgets, or expenses, and comparisons either over time or between different groups at the same time.

Most business graphics are created with spreadsheet packages. These graphics include such types as line, bar, and pie charts. **Line charts** are often used to show trends over time. The incline or decline of each line segment demonstrates the change in values on the vertical axis for each unit change on the horizontal axis. **Bar charts** can be used to compare quantities using vertical or horizontal bars, where the length or height of the bar represents each quantity. **Pie charts** can be used to compare parts of some quantity (budget, income, and so on) using a circular diagram. Finally, **scatter diagrams** can be used to look for patterns in data. Figure 11-1 shows a line chart for the number of rentals by month and a pie chart indicating the distribution of types of rental for the entire year. These charts were created in Microsoft Excel.

FIGURE 11-1. Line and pie charts from Excel

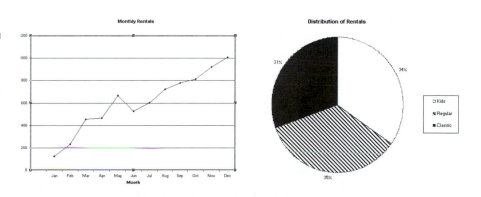

Graphics in Visual Basic

Visual Basic offers the capability to create a wide variety of graphics. In addition to the business graphics discussed earlier, you have already seen the use of the image control to display a logo for Vintage Videos. It is also possible to include a variety of shapes in a project using the **shape** control or to draw *freehand* pictures in a Visual Basic project. Animated graphics are also possible with Visual Basic. It is also possible with the Professional Version of VB to add the MSChart control to use in creating graphics.

In this chapter, we will begin our discussion of graphics by plotting a mathematical equation. We will then turn our attention to creating business graphics—that is, line, bar, and pie charts—for the Vintage Videos scenario. This will include displaying multiple line and bar graphs on the same chart using various types of lines or types of fill (solid, crosshatch, and so on). Finally, we will include a brief demonstration of creating a scatter diagram. While all of these charts could be created with the MSChart control, it is also useful for you to understand how to write programs to create your own charts.

Mini-Summary 11-1: Computer Graphics

1. Computer graphics including CAD, clipart, and business graphics are an important computer application.

2. Business or analysis graphics can help a decision maker understand large amounts of data. They include line charts, bar charts, pie charts, and scatter diagrams.

3. While commonly created using a spreadsheet package, business graphics can also be created using Visual Basic.

It's Your Turn!

1. List three types of commonly used graphics and give an example of the use of each.

2. List the various types of business graphics in common use and give an example of the use of each.

3. How are business graphics commonly created?

CREATING GRAPHICS USING VISUAL BASIC

To plot mathematical equations or create business graphics, we will follow a six-step approach:

1. Decide on a type of control to use in creating the graphic.
2. Set up the coordinate system for the control.
3. Add horizontal and vertical axes to the control.
4. Add division marks and labels to the axes.
5. Draw the graphic on the control.
6. Add titles and legends to the graphic.

To demonstrate these steps, we will begin with a mathematical example with which you should be familiar from your algebra courses: graphing a quadratic equation. As you know, this will result in a parabola being displayed. In our case, the quadratic equation to be graphed is:

$$f(x) = 2x^2 - 5x - 25$$

We will divide our discussion of the six steps into two sections. The first section will cover the first three steps: choosing a control, setting up the coordinate system for the control, and adding horizontal and vertical axes to the control. The next section will cover the latter three steps: adding division marks and labels to the axes, drawing the graphic on the control, and adding titles and a legend.

Choosing a Control

In Visual Basic, there are several standard controls, including the form, image, command button, option button, and picture box controls, that can be used to display graphics. However, the only ones that can be used to *draw* graphics are the form and picture box controls. We will start out using the picture box control on which to draw graphics and then add a situation in which a form is used. In both cases, we will set the **BackColor** property to White to facilitate easier viewing of the graphs.

Setting Up the Coordinate System

Once a control has been selected on which to create a graphic image, the next step is to set up a coordinate system for the control. Since graphics are drawn in Visual Basic by plotting points on a coordinate system, we must have control over that system. The default coordinate system for the form or for any other graphic control is measured in twips, with the upper left-hand corner having the coordinates (0, 0) and the coordinates increasing as you move down and to the right. For example, if you placed a picture box on a form, the coordinates of the upper left-hand corner might be (240, 240) and the coordinates of the lower right-hand corner might be (2775, 2055). You may have noticed coordinates like these at the right end of the toolbar when a control is selected. Figure 11-2 shows a picture box on a form along with its coordinates as shown on the toolbar.

FIGURE 11-2.
Picture box on form
with coordinates

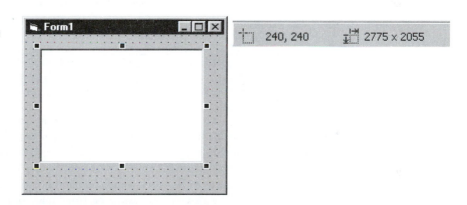

A coordinate system measured in twips with the origin (0, 0) at the upper left-hand corner is often awkward to work with. For this reason, it is usually best to change both the units of measure and the location of the origin point. Both of these changes can be made using the **Scale** method. The general form of the Scale method is:

object.**Scale** *(HUL, VUL) - (HLR, VLR)*

where

> *HUL* = horizontal measure of the upper left-hand corner
>
> *VUL* = vertical measure of the upper left-hand corner
>
> *HLR* = horizontal measure of the lower right-hand corner
>
> *VLR* = vertical measure of the lower right-hand corner

For example, for a picture box named picQuad that will display the quadratic graph, if we want the horizontal measurement to run from –10 to 10 and the vertical measurement to run from –100 to 100, the appropriate Scale method would be:

```
picQuad.Scale (-10, 100) - (10, -100)
```

resulting in the upper left-hand corner having the coordinates (–10, 100) and the lower right-hand corner having the coordinates (10, –100). Note that this results in the origin point being in the middle of the control.

Once the Scale method has been used to create a coordinate system for a picture box or any other control, all references to points in that control must work with this coordinate system. Attempting to reference a point outside the coordinate system will result in an error.

It is also possible to set up the coordinate system using the **ScaleTop, Scale-Height, ScaleLeft**, and **ScaleWidth** picture box properties. The ScaleTop property sets the coordinate for the top of the picture box, and the ScaleHeight property determines the number of units between the top and bottom of the picture box. Similarly, the ScaleLeft property sets the coordinate for the left side of the picture box and the ScaleWidth property determines the number of units between the left and right sides of the picture box. For our example, the statements to set up the same coordinate system as before using these properties are:

```
picQuad.ScaleTop = 100
picQuad.ScaleLeft = -10
picQuad.ScaleWidth = 20
picQuad.ScaleHeight = -200
```

Note that the ScaleHeight property is set to a *negative* value. This forces the top coordinate to be larger than the bottom coordinate. If the ScaleHeight value is positive, the bottom coordinate will be larger.

Like any property, the various Scale properties can be used to determine information about the picture box; that is, the ScaleWidth property will return the width of the picture regardless of how the ScaleWidth property was initially determined.

> **TIP:** Recall that the ScaleHeight and ScaleWidth properties were used in Chapter 8 to expand a text box to fill the form.

Add Axes to Control   Once the coordinate system has been added to the control, the next step is to add **axes**. These are the horizontal and vertical lines that provide a reference system for the chart. You should be familiar with the concept of graph axes from your mathematics courses in which you used X and Y axes to plot points on a coordinate axis. The only difference between the axes used for mathematical plots and the axes used for charts is that for charts the axes are not always measured numerically. For example, in the Vintage Videos case, while the vertical axes will be measured in number of rentals, the horizontal axis will be measured in months. Not all chart types require axes; for example, pie charts do not need axes to measure the distribution of values. On the other hand, line and bar charts require axes to provide a frame of reference for the data being charted. Graphs like the one we will create for the quadratic equation also need axes to provide a reference for the parabola.

Creating axes involves the use of the **Line** method. The general form of this method is:

object.**Line** *(HUL, VUL) – (HLR, VLR)*

where *HUL, VUL, HLR*, and *VLR* have the same meanings as with the Scale method, except that now they refer to the left and right ends of the line being drawn.

For example, with the coordinate system defined earlier for the picQuad picture box, the following Line method will draw a line from a point 5 units to the left of the origin and 50 units above it (−5, 50) to a point 3 units to the right of the origin and 30 units below it (3, −30):

```
picQuad.Line (-5, 50) - (3, -30)
```

The resulting line is shown in the left side of Figure 11-3. In looking at this figure, it is easy to see the need for some form of axes for reference. If we had not added the coordinates to the end of the line, it would not have been very meaningful. Just as we used the Line method to draw this downward-sloping line, we can also use it to draw horizontal and vertical axes that cross at the origin. For this, the appropriate commands are:

```
picQuad.Line (-10, 0) - (10, 0)
picQuad.Line (0, 100) - (0, -100)
```

If these commands are given along with the previous Line method, the coordinate axes in the picQuad picture box with the line running through them will be displayed as seen in the right side of Figure 11-3.

FIGURE 11-3. Use of Line method (left) and addition of axes (right)

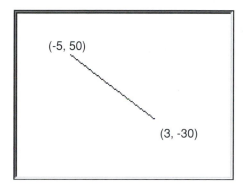
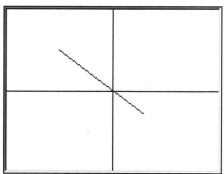

Scale and Line commands should be placed in the Form_Load event procedure so that they will be implemented before the quadratic equation (or any other equation or chart) is graphed. In addition to the Scale and Line method commands, we need to use the **AutoRedraw** property of the picture box. Setting the AutoRedraw property to True automatically draws the output from the Line and other graphics methods in the picture box. Setting it to False makes the graphics *persistent*; that is, they will remain when other graphics are cleared from the screen with the **Cls** method. While we could have also used the Me.Show method to display the coordinate system, they would have been cleared along with other graphics by the Cls method. The code to determine the coordinate system and to draw the axes is shown in VB Code Box 11-1.

VB CODE BOX 11-1. Code to determine coordinate system and add axes	``` Private Sub Form_Load() picQuad.Scale (-10, 100)-(10, -100) picQuad.AutoRedraw = True ' Turn on AutoRedraw. picQuad.Line (-10, 0)-(10, 0) picQuad.Line (0, 100)-(0, -100) picQuad.AutoRedraw = False ' Turn off AutoRedraw. End Sub ```

Mini-Summary 11-2: Creating a Graphic

1. The first three steps in creating a graphic are to select a control, set the coordinate system, and draw the horizontal and vertical axes. The picture box is one of a variety of controls that can be used for drawing graphics. Others include the form and command button controls.

2. The coordinate system is set using the **Scale** method or the **ScaleTop**, **ScaleLeft**, **ScaleHeight**, and **ScaleWidth** properties.

3. Straight lines can be drawn using the **Line** method, in which the beginning and ending values of the line are specified. The Line method is often used to draw axes for a graph.

4. The **AutoRedraw** property must be used in the Form_Load event procedure to display the axes.

It's Your Turn

1. List the steps to create a business graphic in Visual Basic.

2. Which Visual Basic control is commonly used for creating graphics?

3. How do we go about setting the coordinate system for a business graphic or equation (two ways)?

4. What method is used to create axes for a graphic? What parameters must be set to do this?

5. What does the AutoRedraw property do to a graph?

6. For each of the following, write the Visual Basic code that will set up the coordinate system described.

> a. Create a coordinate system 100 units wide and 100 units high with the origin in the center of the picture box.

> b. Create a coordinate system 50 units wide and 50 units high with the origin in the bottom left corner of the picture box.

> c. Create a coordinate system 1000 units wide and 1000 units high. Set the origin at 100 units to the right and 100 units above the lower left corner of the picture box.

> d. Create a coordinate system 100 units wide and 100 units high. Set the origin above and to the right of the lower left corner so that if a line were drawn from the lower left corner to the origin it would be exactly 5 units long.

7. For each of the following, draw the line described. Assume that the scale has been set using: `picDisplay.Scale (-50, 50) - (50, -50)`.

> a. Draw a line starting at the lower left corner, through the origin, to the upper right corner.

> b. Draw a horizontal line that bisects the picture box through the origin.

> c. Draw a vertical line that bisects the picture box through the origin.

> d. Draw a line from the center of the top edge of the picture box to the center of the right edge of the picture box.

Completing the remaining questions will enable you to create the Visual Basic project discussed in the text.

8. Start a new project with a Standard EXE form that is approximately 5220 x 6150 twips in size. Add a picture box control to the form, and make it 4455 x 4455 twips that is centered in the form (the reason it does not look square is that twips are a printer measurement, not a screen measurement). Set its BackColor property to White.

9. Give the form a name of **frmQuadPlot** and a caption of **Quadratic Plot**. Name the picture box **picQuad**.

10. Add the code shown in VB Code Box 11-1 to the Form_Load event procedure. When you run the project, your result should have horizontal and vertical lines that cross in the middle of the picture box, as shown in the right side of Figure 11-3 (without the downward sloping line.)

11. Add a command button named **cmdPlot** with a caption of **Plot Graphic**. Add a single line of code to this command button:

```
picQuad.Line (-5, 50) - (3, -30)
```

When you click this command button, the downward-sloping line will be added to the picture box, as shown on the right side of Figure 11-3.

12. Add another command button named **cmdClear** with a caption of **Clear**. Add a single line of code to this command button:

```
picQuad.Cls
```

When you click the cmdClear command button, the Cls method will cause the downward-sloping line to disappear, but the coordinate axes should remain. Try clicking the Plot and Clear buttons to ensure that your project works.

13. Add a third command button to exit the project.

14. Create a new folder on your data disk named **Chapter11** and save the form as **QuadPlot.frm** and the project as **QuadPlot.vbp** in this folder.

CREATING GRAPHICS (CONTINUED)

In this section, we will continue our discussion of creating graphics in Visual Basic. At this point, you should have added a picture box named picQuad to a blank form, set up a coordinate system for picQuad, and added vertical and horizontal axes to the picture box. Now we will add division marks and labels to the axes, graph the quadratic equation in the picture box, and add a title to the graph.

Adding Division Marks to Axes

To make the horizontal and vertical axes meaningful, we need to provide some type of dividing marks along each of the axes, along with a description of each dividing mark. For example, the horizontal axis for the quadratic plot runs from −10 to 10 and the vertical axis runs from −100 to 100. As we did with the coordinate axes, we can draw these division marks with the Line method. However, in this case they must be much shorter—around 3–5 percent of the total length of the axes.

For example, the vertical division marks we want to draw on the horizontal axis would run from 5 units above the horizontal axis to 5 units below it. Since the division marks on the horizontal axis should be placed at each unit between −9 and 9 (no mark is needed at either edge of the picture box), we would use a For-Next loop to place them:

```
For intCounter = -9 to 9
  picQuad.Line (intCounter, 5) - (intCounter, -5)
Next
```

Note that the horizontal line coordinate is equal to the counter value in the For-Next loop, with the vertical coordinate running from 5 to –5.

The horizontal division marks on the vertical coordinate axis are placed in a similar manner with two differences: The For-Next loop runs from –90 to 90 in steps of 10 and the horizontal coordinates of the division marks run from –0.5 to 0.5, as shown below:

```
For intCounter = -90 to 90 Step 10
   picQuad.Line (-0.5, intCounter) - (0.5, intCounter)
Next
```

If these two For-Next loops are added to the previous code for Form_Load event procedure for the picQuad picture box control, it would appear as shown in Figure 11-4 (where the line graphic has been cleared).

FIGURE 11-4.
Addition of division marks to axes

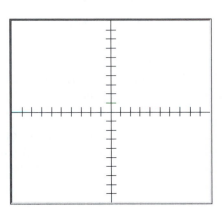

Adding Labels to the Axes

While the division marks are a great help in adding a reference system to the picture box, we also need to add labels to define the meaning of the division marks. In the case of the quadratic plotting example, the labels along the horizontal axis should be the integers –9 to 9 and the labels along the vertical axis should be the integers –90 to 90 in increments of 10. To place these labels, we need to use the **CurrentX** and **CurrentY** properties of the picture box. These properties can be used either to determine the current location on the graph or to move to some other location. In our case, we want to use the CurrentX and CurrentY properties to center the labels beneath or to the side of the division marks.

To center the labels beneath the division marks on the horizontal axis, we need to go through four steps as a part of the For-Next loop that draws the division marks:

1. Determine the width of the label with the **TextWidth** property.
2. Divide the label width by two and subtract the result from the current location to determine the value of CurrentX where the label should be added.
3. Set the CurrentY for the label to the value at the bottom of the division marks.
4. Add the label to the graph or chart with the picture box **Print** method.

For example, if the counter is equal to –5, then this is the label to be displayed beneath the horizontal axis. If the TextWidth property is set equal to the counter value (after we convert it to a string), the result is 0.4358 (remember that the scale is now between –10 and 10). If this is divided by two and subtracted from the current location (the value of the counter), the value of CurrentX is –5 –0.4358/2 = –5.2179. This is the horizontal value at which the label should begin. The vertical value should be immediately below the end of the division mark. Recall that the division mark ran vertically from 5 to –5, so an appropriate CurrentY value for the label would be –5. The *HorizontalAxis* sub procedure to draw the division marks and add the labels to the horizontal axis is shown in VB Code Box 11-2. Note that the labels for counter values of 0 and 1 are not displayed. This is done to avoid congestion of labels around the intersection of the axes.

| **VB CODE BOX 11-2.** Code to add division marks and labels to horizontal axis | ```
Sub HorizontalAxis()
    Dim intCounter As Integer, sngLabelwidth As Single
    For intCounter = -9 To 9 'Add division marks
       picQuad.Line (intCounter, 5)-(intCounter, -5)
       Labelwidth = picQuad.TextWidth(Str(intCounter))
       picQuad.CurrentX = CSng(intCounter) - sngLabelwidth/2
       picQuad.CurrentY = -5
       If intCounter < 0 Or intCounter > 1 Then
         picQuad.Print intCounter 'Add labels
       End If
    Next
End Sub
``` |
|---|---|

> **TIP:** You can also avoid label congestion by moving some labels to the other side of the axis.

Adding labels to the vertical axis follows the same four-step process as adding labels to the horizontal axis, with one exception: Instead of centering the labels horizontally, we must center them vertically. This is handled with the **TextHeight** property to determine the correct CurrentY property. The CurrentX property is set equal to the right-hand coordinate of the division mark plus some value—0.1 in this case. The *VerticalAxis* sub procedure to draw the division marks and add the labels to the vertical axis is shown in VB Code Box 11-3.

| **VB CODE BOX 11-3.** Code to add division marks and labels to the vertical axis | ```
Sub VerticalAxis()
    Dim intCounter As Integer, sngLabelHeight As Single
    For intCounter = -90 To 90 Step 10
       picQuad.Line (0.5, intCounter)-(-0.5, intCounter)
       sngLabelHeight = picQuad.TextHeight(Str(intCounter))
       picQuad.CurrentY = CSng(intCounter) - sngLabelHeight / 2
       picQuad.CurrentX = 0.6
       If intCounter > 0 Or intCounter < -10 Then
           picQuad.Print intCounter
       End If
    Next
End Sub
``` |
|---|---|

If the two For-Next loops in the Form_Load event procedure are replaced with references to the HorizontalAxis( ) and VerticalAxis( ) sub procedures and the project is run, the resulting project will appear as shown in Figure 11-5. Note that the axes, division marks, and labels now appear in the picture box as we want them.

FIGURE 11-5.
Addition of labels to
axes

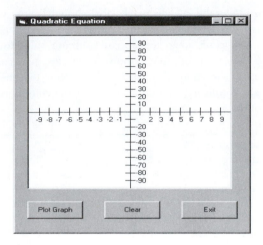

Graphing the Equation   Now that we have the coordinate axes, division marks, and labels, we are ready to graph the quadratic equation given earlier. Graphs such as this one are drawn with the **PSet method**. The PSet method plots X and Y values on the coordinate system defined earlier and has the form *PSet(X,Y)*. For example, in the current coordinate system, picQuad.PSet(5, 30) would place a point in the picQuad picture box at the point (5, 30).

In the PSet method, the Y argument is often an expression or a function—either one that is already available in Visual Basic or one that the programmer creates. In our case, we will create a function called Quadratic and call it from the PSet method. The code to create this function is shown in VB Code Box 11-4.

| **VB CODE BOX 11-4.** Function to compute quadratic equation | ```
Function sngQuadratic(sngXValue As Single) As Single
    sngQuadratic = 2 * sngXValue ^ 2 - 5 * sngXValue - 25
End Function
``` |
| --- | --- |

To plot all possible points in the quadratic equation, we need to use a For-Next loop that runs from –10 to 10 in small increments—say, 0.01. If we used much larger increments, the plot would have "holes" in it. In this case, the For-Next loop counter variable will take the place of the X argument in PSet and the code to plot the quadratic equation will replace the code in the cmdPlot button previously used to plot the line. This code is shown in VB Code Box 11-5.

| **VB CODE BOX 11-5.** Code to plot quadratic equation | ```
Private Sub cmdPlot_Click()
    Dim sngXValue As Single
    For sngXValue = -10 To 10 Step 0.01
        picQuad.PSet (sngXValue,sngQuadratic(sngXValue))
    Next
End Sub
``` |
| --- | --- |

> **TIP:** For complicated functions, you will need to experiment with the proper step value in the For-Next loop to find the best value.

Adding a Title to Graph

Adding a title to the graph is much like adding labels to the axes: We use the CurrentX and CurrentY properties to define the position of the title and we use the Print method to display the title. In the case of the quadratic graph, we would like to place a title in the lower left-hand corner. To do this, we should set the CurrentX value to –9 and the CurrentY value to –90. We can also use the Fontsize and FontBold properties to control the font size and to highlight the title. The resulting code to add a title to the quadratic graph is shown in VB Code Box 11-6. This code should be added to the cmdPlot_Click event procedure.

VB CODE BOX 11-6. Code to add title to graph	``` picQuad.CurrentX = -9 picQuad.CurrentY = -80 picQuad.Fontsize = 6 picQuad.FontBold = True picQuad.Print "Y = 2*X^2 - 5*X - 25" ```

The entire code for this project is shown in VB Code Box 11-7. If the project is then run, the quadratic function will be graphed along with a title as shown in Figure 11-6.

FIGURE 11-6. Graph of quadratic equation

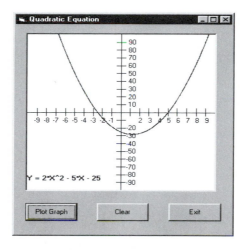

It's Your Turn!

1. How do we go about adding division marks to the axes of a graph?

2. What two methods are key to creating labels in the correct locations on the graph?

3. What are the four steps that should be included to center labels beneath the division marks on the horizontal axis?

4. What method is used to graph an equation?

Completing the remaining questions will enable you to create the Visual Basic project discussed in the text.

| **VB CODE BOX 11-7.** Complete code for graphing equation | ```vb
Private Sub Form_Load()
    picQuad.Scale (-10, 100)-(10, -100)
    picQuad.AutoRedraw = True   ' Turn on AutoRedraw.
    picQuad.Line (-10, 0)-(10, 0)
    picQuad.Line (0, 100)-(0, -100)
    picQuad.AutoRedraw = False ' Turn off AutoRedraw.
End Sub
Sub HorizontalAxis()
    Dim intCounter As Integer, sngLabelwidth As Single
    For intCounter = -9 To 9 'Add division marks
        picQuad.Line (intCounter, 5)-(intCounter, -5)
        sngLabelwidth = picQuad.TextWidth(Str(intCounter))
        picQuad.CurrentX = CSng(intCounter) - sngLabelwidth/2
        picQuad.CurrentY = -5
        If sngCounter < 0 Or sngCounter > 1 Then
            picQuad.Print sngCounter 'Add labels
        End If
    Next
End Sub
Sub VerticalAxis()
    Dim intCounter As Integer, sngLabelHeight As Single
    For intCounter = -90 To 90 Step 10
        picQuad.Line (0.5, intCounter)-(-0.5, intCounter)
        sngLabelHeight = picQuad.TextHeight(Str(intCounter))
        picQuad.CurrentY = intCounter - sngLabelHeight / 2
        picQuad.CurrentX = 0.6
        If intCounter > 0 Or intCounter < -10 Then
            picQuad.Print intCounter
        End If
    Next
End Sub
Function sngQuadratic(sngXValue As Single) As Single
    sngQuadratic = 2 * sngXValue ^ 2 - 5 * sngXValue - 25
End Function
Private Sub cmdPlot_Click()
  Dim sngXValue As Single
  For sngXValue = -10 To 10 Step 0.01
    picQuad.PSet (sngXValue,sngQuadratic(sngXValue))
  Next
  picQuad.CurrentX = -9
  picQuad.CurrentY = -80
  picQuad.Fontsize = 6
  picQuad.FontBold = True
  picQuad.Print "Y = 2*X^2 - 5*X - 25"
End Sub
``` |

5. Create the **HorizontalAxis** and **VerticalAxis** sub procedures shown in VB Code Box 11-2 and VB Code Box 11-3. Add references to these sub procedures to the Form_Load event procedure *prior* to turning the AutoRedraw method off. Run your project. The picture box should appear as shown in Figure 11-5.
```

6. Add the code shown in VB Code Box 11-4 to the project to create the **Quadratic** function. Replace the existing code for the cmdPlot_Click event procedure with the code shown in VB Code Box 11-5 to plot the graph of the quadratic equation.

7. Add the code shown in VB Code Box 11-6 to the cmdPlot_Click event procedure to display a title on your graph. Your complete code for this project should appear as shown in VB Code Box 11-7.

8. Run your project and click the Plot command button; a graph of the quadratic function along with a title should appear in the bottom left-hand corner of the picture box, as shown in Figure 11-6.

9. Save your form and project under the same name.

10. Modify the code for the Plot command button by changing the step value for the For-Next loop from 0.01 to 0.1. Run your project again. What happens? Now change the step value to 0.5 and run the project again. What was the result? Do NOT save the revised project.

CREATING BUSINESS GRAPHICS

As we mentioned earlier, business graphics use various types of charts to display information on business operations. For Vintage Videos, we need to create line, bar, and pie charts. For the line charts and bar charts, we need to create two charts of each type: one to display the total rentals for each month and one to display the rentals for each type of video—Kids, Regular, and Classic. The pie chart will be used to display the distribution of total videos rented for the year. This means that five different charts are going to be created for Vintage Videos:

1. a line chart for total rentals
2. line charts for the three types of rentals
3. a bar chart for total rentals
4. bar charts for the three types of rentals
5. a pie chart for distribution of total rentals

Since displaying the various charts for Vintage Videos is not a part of the rental transaction information system, we will begin a new project for this purpose with a menu system that will allow the user to select the type of chart to display. This new project will be named *Charts.vbp* and will have a single form named *frmCharts*.

Adding the Picture Box Control

As we did in plotting a graph for the quadratic equation, we will use the picture box control to display the various charts used to analyze the number of rentals. This picture box control will be named *picRentals* and will cover most of the frmCharts form. In addition, we will use a menu system with two menu bar options: File and Charts. The File menu bar option will enable the user to clear the existing chart or exit the project. The Charts menu bar option will enable the user to select the type of chart to be displayed. The resulting form is shown in Figure 11-7, with a portion of the menu system displayed.

Entering Data to Be Analyzed

The graph for the quadratic equation did not have any data associated with it. Most business graphics, however, are used to display data about sales, operations, cost, and so on. Typically, these data are available in a database like those discussed in Chapters 9 and 10. The Vintage Videos case would involve a database table that tracks the number

FIGURE 11-7. Form used to display charts

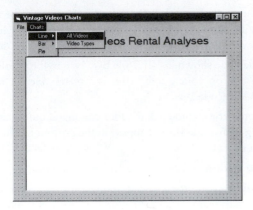

of rentals of each type of video for each month. However, since we did not design our database in Chapter 9 to include this table, we will assume the data have been transferred to a sequential access file from which they can be accessed to use in displaying the various types of charts—line, bar, and pie. These data are shown in Figure 11-8.

FIGURE 11-8. Rental data for Vintage Videos

```
"Jan",140,140,151
"Feb",175,350,294
"Mar",350,700,546
"Apr",700,700,235
"May",525,1050,760
"Jun",711,738,400
"Jul",704,825,575
"Aug",1050,900,574
"Sep",970,1050,700
"Oct",1050,1081,739
"Nov",1227,1450,1050
"Dec",1418,1485,1133
```

The frmCharts Form_Load event is used to input these monthly data into a String data type array (*strMonths*) and three Integer data type arrays (one for each of the three types of video). These data are also summed to create a fifth array of total rental data (*intAllRentals*). These five arrays will be used to create all of the charts, and they are declared at the form level to hold 25 months of data. The code necessary to declare these arrays at the form level and to input the data from a sequential file named *a:\VideoRentals.txt* is shown in VB Code Box 11-8.

It's Your Turn!

1. What five charts are going to be created for Vintage Videos? What will be the business reason for each chart?

2. Why do we declare the various arrays at the form level?

Completing the remaining questions will enable you to create the Visual Basic project discussed in the text.

| VB CODE BOX 11-8. Code to input chart data | ```
Option Explicit
Dim strMonths(24) as String, intKids(24) as Integer
Dim intRegular(24) as Integer, intClassic(24) as Integer
Dim intAllRentals(24) as Integer, intNumMonths as Integer

Private Sub Form_Load()
  Dim intCounter As Integer
  Open "a:\VideoRentals.txt" For Input As #1
  intCounter = 0
  Do Until EOF(1)
    Input #1, strMonths(intCounter), intKids(intCounter), _
    intRegular(intCounter), intClassic(intCounter)
    intAllRentals(intCounter) = intKids(intCounter) + _
    intRegular(intCounter) + intClassic(intCounter)
    intCounter = intCounter + 1
  Loop
  Close #1
  intNumMonths = intCounter
End Sub
``` |
|---|---|

3. Start a new project by adding a standard form. Expand this form so that it is approximately 7400 by 6200 twips. To this form, add a label with a caption of **Vintage Videos Rental Analysis.**

4. Add a picture box control to this form with a name of **picRentals** and expand it to almost fill the form. Make its BackColor property White.

5. Use the Menu Editor to add two menu bar items with captions of **File** and **Charts**. Give them names of **mnuFile** and **mnuCharts**. To these two menu bar items, add the submenu items shown in Table 11-1. The result should appear like that shown in Figure 11-7.

TABLE 11-1: Menu Items for frmCharts

Menu Bar Item	Submenu Item Caption	Submenu Item Name	Sub Submenu Caption	Sub Submenu Name
File	Clear	mnuFileClear		
	- (Separator Bar)	mnuFileSep		
	Exit	mnuFileExit		
Charts	Line	mnuChartsLine	All Videos	mnuChartsLineAll
			Video Types	mnuChartsLineTypes
	Bar	mnuChartsBar	All Videos	mnuChartsBarAll
			Video Types	mnuChartsBarTypes
	Pie	mnuChartsPie		

6. Open the Declarations section of the form and add the array declaration shown at the top of VB Code Box 11-8. Next, open the Form_Load event and add the code shown in the lower section of Code Table 11-8.

7. Add the following single line of code to the mnuFileClear_Click event procedure:
```

`picRentals.Cls`

8. Add the **End** instruction to the mnuFileExit_Click event procedure.

9. Save the form as **Charts.frm** and the project as **Charts.vbp** in the Chapter11 folder on your data disk.

10. Use NotePad to create a sequential access file named **VideoRentals.txt** with the data shown in Figure 11-8, and save it to your data disk. You may also download it from Web site for the text.

PREPARING TO CREATE LINE AND BAR CHARTS

Line charts are often used to show the change in values over time. Bar charts, on the other hand, can be used to show information over time or over other criteria. In the case of Vintage Videos, the owners have expressed an interest in seeing how the number of rentals has changed over time, and they would like to see this information shown as both line charts and bar charts. Since the same rental values will be plotted over the same time period, the same coordinate system, axes, division marks, and labels will be appropriate for both types of chart. In this section, we will discuss getting ready to create line and bar charts by setting up the picture box and axes on which they will be plotted.

Creating line and bar charts involves the same steps shown on page 452 for plotting the quadratic equation, plus one preliminary step: sketching a design for the chart. In this section, we will discuss the design step plus steps 1 through 4 for both line charts and bar charts. In later sections, we will discuss creating the charts using the work done here and then show how to create a pie chart.

Design the Chart

We need to sketch a design for the line and bar charts in order to determine the maximum and minimum values that will be plotted on the chart. This information becomes very important when we set up the coordinate system for the chart. For example, to design the coordinate system for the total number of rentals for the first twelve months of operation for Vintage Videos, we need to determine the *maximum* number of rentals that will occur in any one month. Looking at the data in Figure 11-8, we can see that this occurs in December with a value of 4,036 *total* rentals. Given that we will want to have division marks at some even number—say, every 500 rentals—we should increase this to 4,500. (Note that since the number of horizontal units is already known to be twelve months, this determination is not necessary for the horizontal axis.) The resulting design is shown in Figure 11-9, where we have sketched in the vertical and horizontal axes, showing the maximum values on each. Since at this point we are still simply designing the chart, the actual line chart is not shown.

Setting Up the Coordinate System

Since we have already decided to use the picture box as the control on which to display the charts for Vintage Videos, we will skip the step of choosing a control and go right into setting up the coordinate system.

Based on the chart design completed in the preliminary step, the next step is to set the coordinate system for the picture box using the Scale method, as we did with the quadratic equation. For the Vintage Videos case, the horizontal measure is the number of months (12) that the chart will cover *plus* some extra space to include the vertical axis and labels. Similarly, the vertical measure is the *maximum* number of rentals for any

FIGURE 11-9.
Design for line and
bar charts

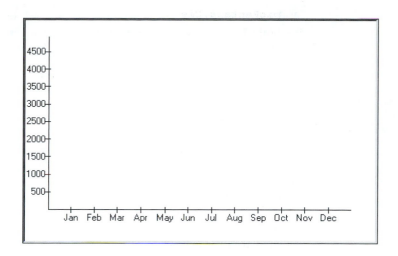

one month. For the total rentals case shown in Figure 11-9, the maximum is 4,500, plus some extra space around the edges for titles and labels.

Once the coordinate system has been set, adding the vertical and horizontal axes is similar to plotting the quadratic equation, except that the vertical axis should be placed to the left of the origin (0, 0) point (assuming that January is the 0th month.) The axes should extend almost to the edge of the picture box. We say *almost* to the edge, because we need to leave space for titles and labels. Also, charts just *look* better when there is empty space around the edges of the picture.

While the coordinate system and axes shown in Figure 11-9 are adequate for the single case of charting the sum of the monthly rental values shown in Figure 11-8, this approach will not be appropriate for charting the various types of rentals—that is, Kids, Regular, and Classic. For this reason, we need to use a more general approach to setting up the coordinate system and adding the axes that will work regardless of the type of chart being plotted. Also, since line and bar charts will use the same coordinate axes, taking a more general approach will allow the sub procedures we create to work in all four cases—that is, in the line and bar charts for total rentals and for types of rentals.

To do this, we first need to note that the coordinate system and axes depend on the number of months and the maximum number of rentals to be charted. For example, for the total rentals case the maximum number of rentals to be plotted is around 4,000, but for the Kids type rentals case the maximum is less than 1,500. While the number of months probably will not change, there is no reason not to allow for more than twelve months.

In either case, we need to make the coordinate system and the position of the axes dependent on the maximum number of rentals and number of months being charted, rather than fixing it at some value as was done for the quadratic equation. That way, the procedures and functions necessary to create the coordinate system and position the axes can be referenced from the appropriate menu option Click event procedure. Note that the same coordinate system and axes will work for either the bar charts or the line charts, so the functions and procedure created here can be used in either case.

Since we are already counting the number of months when we input the data, we do not need to doing anything special to compute this value. To handle the operation of determining the maximum number of rentals, however, we need to create a function called *intMostRentals.* The intMostRentals function will be very much like those discussed in Chapter 6 on arrays, and it will use the number of months computed when the data are input to determine the number of repetitions of the For-Next loop. This function is shown in VB Code Box 11-9.

| **VB CODE BOX 11-9.** Function to find maximum number of rentals | ```
Function intMaxRentals(intRentals() As Integer) As Integer
  Dim intCounter As Integer
  intMaxRentals = 0
  For intCounter = 0 To intNumMonths - 1 'Find Maximum Rentals
    If intRentals(intCounter) > intMostRentals Then
      intMaxRentals = intRentals(intCounter)
    End If
  Next
End Function
``` |
|---|---|

Using the intMaxRentals function, we can write a sub procedure to determine the value of the global variable, *intMostRentals,* for the case where the total number of rentals is being plotted. This sub procedure, which we will call *MaxAll,* will also compute another global variable, *intIncrement,* that will be used in adding the division marks to the axes and rounding off the value of intMostRentals. If the total number of rentals is less than 1,500, intIncrement is set at 100; otherwise, it is set at 500. The intIncrement variable is then used to round the maximum number of rentals up to the next highest multiple of intIncrement. This results in labels on the vertical axis being in increments of 100 or 500, with the highest label being larger than the maximum number of rentals. VB Code Box 11-10 shows the MaxAll sub procedure.

| **VB CODE BOX 11-10.** Sub procedure to find intMostRentals value for the All Rentals case | ```
Sub MaxAll()
  intMostRentals = intMaxRentals(intAllRentals())
  If intMostRentals <= 1500 Then
    intIncrement = 100
  Else
    intIncrement = 500
  End If
  intMostRentals = intIncrement * (IntMostRentals _
  / intIncrement + 1)
End Sub
``` |
|---|---|

For example, if the maximum number of rentals is 4,036 (for all videos), then the increment will be 500 and the maximum number will be rounded up to 4,500. On the other hand, if the maximum number of rentals is, say, 1,133 (for a type of video), the increment will be 100 and the maximum number will be rounded up to 1,200.

> **TIP:** You may need to select increment values other than 100 and 500 for the problems you work on.

For the three types of videos (Kids, Regular, and Classic) to be displayed on the same chart, we need to go one step further to determine the highest of these three values in a sub procedure called *MaxTypes,* shown in VB Code Box 11-11. The maximum of the three video types is stored in intMostRentals, and once again, intIncrement is computed and the value of intMostRentals is rounded off.

Once the value of maximum number of rentals has been found as the global variable intMostRentals, setting up the coordinate system and adding the axes is straight-

| VB CODE BOX 11-11. Sub procedure to find intMostRentals value for Maximum Rentals cases | ```
Sub MaxTypes()
  intMostRentals = 0
  If intMaxRentals(intKids()) > intMostRentals Then
      intMostRentals = intMaxRentals(intKids())
  ElseIf intMaxRentals(intRegular()) > intMostRentals Then
      intMostRentals = intMaxRentals(intRegular())
  ElseIf intMaxRentals(intClassic()) > intMostRentals Then
      intMostRentals = intMaxRentals(intClassic())
  End If
  If intMostRentals <= 1500 Then
    intIncrement = 100
  Else
    intIncrement = 500
  End If
  intMostRentals = intIncrement * (intMostRentals / _
  intIncrement) + 1)
End Sub
``` |
|---|---|

forward. We will use some percentage of the maximum number of rentals—say, 20 percent—to determine the spacing around the coordinate axes. The *DrawAxes* sub procedure to set the coordinate system is shown in VB Code Box 11-12.

| VB CODE BOX 11-12. Sub procedure to set up coordinate system and draw axes | ```
Private Sub DrawAxes()
  Dim sngSpacing As Single
  sngSpacing = 0.2 * intMostRentals
  picRentals.Scale (-2, intMostRentals + sngSpacing) - _
  (intNumMonths + 1, -sngSpacing)
  picRentals.Line (-1, 0) - (intNumMonths, 0)
  picRentals.Line (-1, 0) - (-1, intMostRentals + 0.5 * _
  sngSpacing)
End Sub
``` |
|---|---|

Note in this sub procedure that the upper left-hand coordinate is (–2, intMost-Rentals + intSpacing) and that the lower right-hand coordinate is (13, –intSpacing). If the intMostRentals value is 4,500 as discussed above, these translate into (–2, 5400) and (13, –900)—fairly close to the design shown in Figure 11-9. On the other hand, if intMostRentals is 1,500, then the coordinates are (–2, 1800) and (13, –300). The vertical axis runs through the –1 horizontal coordinate, placing it one unit to the left of the first month. It also runs from 0 up to the intMostRentals value plus 50 percent of the spacing, thus leaving the desired empty space at the top and bottom. If we use the mnuChartLineAll_Click event procedure as an example, the code to set up the coordinate system is shown in VB Code Box 11-13, where the global variables intMostRentals and intIncrement are computed in the MaxAll sub procedure and are used in the DrawAxes procedure to set up the coordinate system and draw the axes. Note that the picRentals picture box is cleared at the beginning of the event procedure in case another chart had been previously plotted.

| VB CODE BOX 11-13. Code for line chart total rentals menu options | ```
Private Sub mnuChartsLineAll_Click()
  picRentals.Cls
  MaxAll
  DrawAxes
End Sub
``` |
|---|---|
```

The code for the mnuChartsBarAll is exactly the same as that shown in VB Code Box 11-13, while the code for the mnuChartsLineTypes_Click and mnuCharts-BarTypes_Click event procedures would call the MaxTypes sub procedure instead of the MaxAll sub procedure to compute the intMostRentals and intIncrement variables. If the project is run with these additional functions and procedures and any one of the line or bar chart menu options is selected, the picture box will have vertical and horizontal axes.

Adding Division Marks and Labels

As shown in the design sketch in Figure 11-9, the horizontal axis of the Vintage Videos line chart should have twelve vertical division marks to represent each of the twelve months, and each division mark should have a label denoting the month. Similarly, the vertical axis should have a number of equally spaced division marks representing the number of rentals. While the horizontal axis division marks will remain the same for all of the line and bar charts, the vertical axis division marks will change depending on whether the total rentals or the types of rentals are being charted. The global variable, intIncrement, becomes important here, because there will be a division mark on the vertical axis for each value of this variable.

For the division marks on the horizontal axis to be an appropriate size, their length should depend on the units used on the vertical axis. For example, if intMostRentals is 4,500, then the vertical division marks should be about 200 units long. (There is no set value for this, so trial and error is often the best way to determine it.) This implies that the marks should run from about 100 units above the horizontal axis to 100 units below it. On the other hand, if intMostRentals is 1,500, this mark length would be inappropriate. So, rather than use an absolute value for the division mark length, we can use a percentage of intMostRentals—say, 2 percent—as the length above and below the axis.

We add labels to the division marks on the horizontal axis in a manner similar to that used to add labels for the quadratic graph. The primary difference here is that the labels on the horizontal axis are the three-letter abbreviations for the months of the year stored in the strMonths( ) array. The *HorizontalLabels* sub procedure to add division marks and labels to the horizontal axis is shown in VB Code Box 11-14, and the resulting horizontal axis is shown in Figure 11-10.

VB CODE BOX 11-14. Code to add horizontal labels to chart	

```
Sub HorizontalLabels()
  Dim intCounter As Integer, sngDivMark As Single
  Dim sngMonthWidth As Single
  For intCounter = 0 To intNumMonths - 1
    sngMonthWidth = picRentals.TextWidth(strMonths(intCounter))
    sngDivMark = 0.02 * intMostRentals
    picRentals.Line (intCounter, -sngDivMark) - _
     (intCounter, sngDivMark)
    picRentals.CurrentX = intCounter - sngMonthWidth / 2
    picRentals.CurrentY = -sngDivMark
    picRentals.Print strMonths(intCounter)
  Next intCounter
End Sub
```

The approach for adding division marks and labels to the vertical axis is almost identical to that used in the quadratic graph example, with one exception: The length of the division marks is computed as being 1 percent of the number of months. This is

FIGURE 11-10.
Horizontal axis

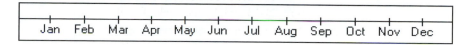

> **TIP:** For labels involving multiple words, you can add a second row.

done to make the code more flexible in case the number of months does change. The *VerticalLabels* sub procedure to add division marks and labels to the horizontal axis is shown in VB Code Box 11-15.

VB CODE BOX 11-15.
Code to add vertical labels to chart

```
Sub VerticalLabels()
    Dim intCounter As Integer, sngDivMark As Single
    Dim sngRentalWidth As Single, sngRentalHeight As Single
    For intCounter = intIncrement To intMostRentals _
    Step intIncrement
        sngRentalWidth = picRentals.TextWidth(Str(intCounter))
        sngRentalHeight = picRentals.TextHeight(Str(intCounter))
        sngDivMark = 0.01 * intNumMonths
        picRentals.Line (-1 - sngDivMark, intCounter)- _
        (-1 + sngDivMark, intCounter)
        picRentals.CurrentX = -1 - sngDivMark - sngRentalWidth
        picRentals.CurrentY = intCounter - sngRentalHeight / 2
        picRentals.Print Str(intCounter)
    Next intCounter
End Sub
```

If these two sub procedures (HorizontalLabels and VerticalLabels) are added to the Charts project and referenced in the various menu item event procedures, the appropriate division marks and labels will be drawn. For example, the mnuChartsLineAll_Click event procedure should look like the code shown in VB Code Box 11-16.

VB CODE BOX 11-16.
Event procedure to draw axes for total rentals

```
Private Sub mnuChartsLineAll_Click()
    picRentals.Cls
    MaxAll
    DrawAxes
    HorizontalLabels
    VerticalLabels
End sub
```

The Click event procedures for the other three types of line and bar charts will look virtually the same, except that the reference to MaxAll should be replaced with a reference to MaxTypes in those cases where the three types of videos are being charted. Figure 11-11 compares the axes, division marks, and labels that will appear for the total rental and rental types cases if the project is run. Notice that because the increment value is small for the rental types, there are more division marks to show finer detail.

FIGURE 11-11.
Comparison of chart setup for total rentals (left) and rentals by type (right).

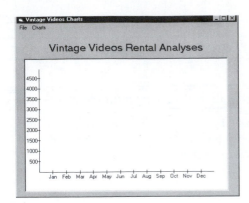

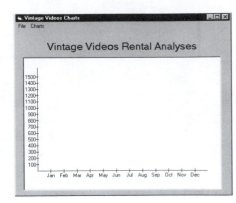

Mini-Summary 11-3: Preparing to Create Line and Bar Charts

1. The first step in creating a chart is to design the chart showing the axes and labels.

2. The second step is to set the coordinate axes. This often involves using different scales for the vertical and horizontal axes and placing the origin off-center.

3. The third step is to add the division marks and labels on the vertical and horizontal axes.

It's Your Turn!

1. What preliminary step is required before the four step procedure described earlier can be implemented to create business graphics? Why is this step needed?

2. In the Vintage Videos project, why is it necessary to determine the most rentals that occurs in any month? What is this value used for in the project?

3. For each of the following, write Visual Basic code to create the axes described.

    a. An x-axis from 0 to 100 with tick marks at 10 unit intervals and a y-axis from 0 to 100 with tick marks at 10-unit intervals.

    a. An x-axis from 0 to 100 with tick marks at 10 unit intervals and a y-axis from 0 to 100 with tick marks at 20 unit intervals.

    b. An x-axis from -100 to 100 with tick marks at 10 unit intervals and a y-axis from -100 to 100 with tick marks at 20 unit intervals.

    c. An x-axis from -50 to 100 with tick marks at 10 unit intervals and a y-axis from -20 to 100 with tick marks at 20 unit intervals.

Completing the remaining questions will enable you to create the Visual Basic project discussed in the text.

4. Declare **intMostRentals** and **intIncrement** to be Integer variables at the form level. Create the **intMostRentals** function shown in VB Code Box 11-9 to find the maximum number of rentals.

5. Create the **MaxAll** sub procedure shown in VB Code Box 11-10 to find values for the intMostRentals and intIncrement form level variables for the total rentals case.

6. Create the **MaxTypes** sub procedure shown in VB Code Box 11-11 to find values for the intMostRentals and intIncrement global variables for the rental types case.

7. Create the **DrawAxes** sub procedure shown in VB Code Box 11-12 to set up the coordinate system and draw the axes.

8. Create the Menu Option event procedures for the two line chart cases and the two bar chart cases. Recall that for the line and bar charts for the total rentals cases, the code shown in VB Code Box 11-13 is appropriate. For the rental types cases, the reference to the MaxAll sub procedure should be replaced with a reference to the MaxTypes sub procedure. Run your project and click on any chart Menu Option.

9. Create the **HorizontalLabels** and **VerticalLabels** sub procedures shown in VB Code Box 11-14 and VB Code Box 11-15 at the form level. Add references to these sub procedures in your Menu Option event procedures. For the line and bar charts for the total rentals cases, the code shown in VB Code Box 11-16 is appropriate. Run your project and select Line Chart for All Rentals. The result should look like the left side of Figure 11-11. Now select the Video Types option from the Line Charts submenu. The result should look like the right side of Figure 11-11.

10. Save your form and project under the same names.

DRAWING LINE CHARTS

Once the coordinate system, axes, division marks, and labels have been created, the next step is to actually draw the line and bar charts. Unlike the quadratic equation, in which we used the PSet method, both types of charts will be drawn using the Line method. We will discuss drawing line charts in this section and bar charts in the next section.

Drawing a line chart is simply an extension of using the Line method to create the axes for the line and bar charts. The idea is to connect the coordinates with lines. For example, if the number of rentals for January is 431, then coordinates for this point are (0, 431). Similarly, if the number of rentals for February is 819, the coordinates are (1, 819). The line connecting these points is then defined as:

```
picRentals.Line (0, 431) - (1, 819)
```

To generalize this approach, we can use a For-Next loop to connect each point to the next point in the data set. The statement in the For-Next loop is:

```
picRentals.Line(intCounter,intAllRentals(intCounter)- _
(intCounter + 1,intAllRentals(intCounter + 1))
```

where the For-Next Loop counter variable runs from 0 to intNumMonths – 2.

The *DrawLineAll* sub procedure to draw the line chart for the total rentals case is shown in VB Code Box 11-17. A reference to this sub procedure should be added to the mnuChartsLineAll_Click event procedure that was shown earlier as VB Code Box 11-16. If this code is created and a reference to it is added to the mnuChartsLineAll_Click event procedure, running the project and selecting this option will result in a line chart like that shown in Figure 11-12.

VB CODE BOX 11-17. Sub procedure to draw line chart for all videos	<pre>Sub DrawLineAll()
	  Dim intCounter as Integer
	  For intCounter = 0 To intNumMonths - 2
	      picRentals.Line (intCounter, intAllRentals(intCounter))- _
	      (intCounter + 1, intAllRentals(intCounter + 1))
	  Next
	End Sub</pre>

FIGURE 11-12. Line chart for all videos

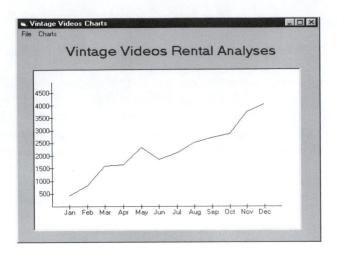

Adding Titles and Legends

Now that we have a line chart for total rentals for the first year of operation, we need to finalize the chart by adding titles and legends. We need a title at the top left of the picture box and a title beneath the horizontal axis. A legend is not needed for this chart, but will be for the line chart showing multiple video types.

We create titles for this chart in the upper left-hand corner of the picture box in a manner similar to the one we used to add a title to the graph of the quadratic equation: We use the CurrentX and CurrentY properties to position the title, the Fontsize and FontBold properties to define the appearance of the title, and the Print method to actually display it.

In the case of the title in the upper left-hand corner, we know that the top of the picture box is defined as intMostRentals value plus some spacing value—in this case, 20 percent of intMostRentals. We also know that the left-hand side of the picture box is defined as –2 and that the vertical axis is set at –1. Using this information, we should print the title in the area below the top and to the right of the vertical axis, beginning at, say, (–0.5, 1.2 * Most-Rentals).

Similarly, to print a title beneath the horizontal axis, we first need to recall that the division marks extend down by an amount equal to 2 percent of intMostRentals and that the month abbreviations are below them. To print the title below the month abbreviations, make the CurrentY value of the title equal to the length of the division marks plus the height of the month abbreviations. (Due to the orientation of the coordinate system, the TextHeight method returns a negative value.) This title also needs to be centered beneath the horizontal axis, just as the month abbreviations are centered beneath the division marks. Since these labels will be used for both the line charts and the bar charts, in all four cases we need to create a *PrintTitles* sub procedure to use to print the titles. This sub procedure is shown in VB Code Box 11-18.

You should note in this code that the last two lines return the font size and style to their default settings, so that future uses of this sub procedure will not be affected by this use. Also note that we have replaced the pairs of CurrentX and CurrentY assignment statements with a reference to a sub procedure, *FindXandY,* that accomplishes the same purpose. This sub procedure is shown in VB Code Box 11-19, where we have the ByVal keyword to ensure that the arguments are not changed by the sub procedure.

VB CODE BOX 11-18. Sub procedure to print chart titles	```Private Sub PrintTitles()```

```
Private Sub PrintTitles()
  Dim sngMonthWidth As Single, sngMonthHeight As Single
  Dim sngDefaultSize as Single
  FindXandY -0.5, 1.2*intMostRentals 'Find position for title
  sngDefaultSize = picRentals.FontSize
  picRentals.FontSize = 10 'Set size and style
  picRentals.FontBold = True
  picRentals.Print "Video Rentals by Month" 'Print title
  sngMonthWidth = picRentals.TextWidth("Month")
  sngMonthHeight = picRentals.TextHeight("Jan") '(Labels(0))
  FindXandY intNumMonths / 2 - sngMonthWidth / 2, _
    -0.02 * intMostRentals + sngMonthHeight
' Center title beneath horizontal axis
  picRentals.Print "Month" 'Print title
  picRentals.FontSize = sngDefaultSize
  picRentals.FontBold = False
End Sub
```

VB CODE BOX 11-19. Code for sub to set X and Y values	

```
Private Sub FindXandY(ByVal sngX As Single, _
  ByVal sngY As Single)
  picRentals.CurrentX = sngX
  picRentals.CurrentY = sngY
End Sub
```

If a reference to the PrintTitles sub procedure is added to the mnuChartsLineAll_Click event procedure *after* the code to plot the line, the resulting code is as shown in VB Code Box 11-20. If the project is run with this menu option being selected, the result is as shown in Figure 11-13.

VB CODE BOX 11-20. Final event procedure to draw line chart for all videos	

```
Private Sub mnuChartsLineAll_Click()
  picRentals.Cls
  MaxAll
  DrawAxes
  HorizontalLabels
  VerticalLabels
  DrawLineAll
  PrintTitles
End sub
```

Drawing Multiple Lines

The next step is to draw multiple lines on the chart: one for each of the three video types—Kids, Regular, and Classic. Drawing the three individual lines is handled in exactly the same way as drawing the single line, with one exception: To distinguish between the lines, we need to use the **DrawStyle** property. This property determines the appearance of the lines drawn in the picture box. The various options are shown in Table 11-2, where you can set the property to either the VB constant or the value.

For example, to draw a line that is composed of a dash followed by two dots, the command would be:

```
picRentals.DrawStyle = vbDashDotDot
```

To draw lines representing rental values for the three types of videos, we simply change the DrawStyle property between drawing each type of line. Other than that, the

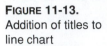

FIGURE 11-13.
Addition of titles to
line chart

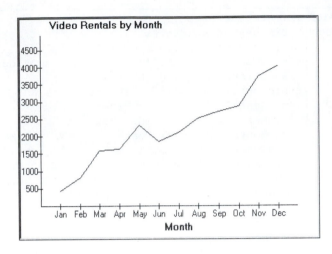

TABLE 11-2: DrawStyle Property Constants and Values

Line Style	VB Constant	Value
Solid	vbSolid	0
Dash	vbDash	1
Dot	vbDot	2
Dash Dot	vbDashDot	3
Dash Dot Dot	vbDashDotDot	4
Transparent	vbTransparent	5
Inside Solid	vbInsideSolid	6

> **TIP:** You can also draw the lines in color by adding a VB color constant (VB + the color) at the end of the Line method statement.

DrawLineTypes sub procedure is very much like the sub procedure used to draw the line for all rentals. The code for this new sub procedure is shown in VB Code Box 11-21.

VB CODE BOX 11-21.
Sub procedure to
draw multiple lines

```
Private Sub DrawLineTypes()
    Dim intCounter As Integer
    For intCounter = 0 To intNumMonths - 2
      picRentals.DrawStyle = vbSolid
      picRentals.Line (intCounter, intKids(intCounter))- _
      (intCounter + 1, intKids(intCounter + 1))
      picRentals.DrawStyle = vbDash
      picRentals.Line (intCounter, intRegular(intCounter))- _
      (intCounter + 1, intRegular(intCounter + 1))
      picRentals.DrawStyle = vbDot
      picRentals.Line (intCounter, intClassic(intCounter))- _
      (intCounter + 1, intClassic(intCounter + 1))
    Next
    picRentals.DrawStyle = vbSolid 'Makes line style solid
End sub
```

If a reference to this sub procedure is added to the mnuCharts-LineType_Click event procedure and the project is run, the result of selecting this option is as shown in Figure 11-14.

> **TIP:** The DrawWidth property can be used to adjust the width of lines on an object between 1 and 32,767 in pixels..

FIGURE 11-14.
Result of drawing multiple line charts

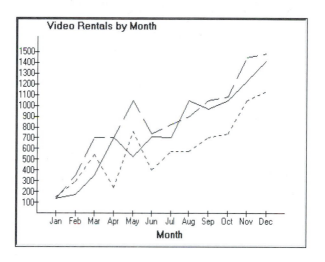

Adding a Legend to the Chart

Note in Figure 11-14 that the three types of lines have different line styles. To make this understandable to the viewer, we need to add a legend beneath the chart title that explains the meaning of each of the various line styles. Adding this legend is similar to adding a title, except that we need to use the Line method to include an example of each of the various types of lines.

The primary concern here is to line up the sample lines with the corresponding descriptive text. Once a line has been drawn, the CurrentX and CurrentY values are equal to the end of the line. To make the labels match the lines, after drawing a line, we need to move up one-half the height of the text as measured by the TextHeight property before printing the label. Once the label is printed, we then need to move down by one character height before drawing the next line. For example, assume we set the variable, *sngLegendHeight*, equal to the TextHeight property and start the first line at a CurrentY value equal to intMostRentals. The line will be drawn at this CurrentY value. To print the label, we need to move *up* by one-half of sngLegendHeight and over a small amount. Once the label is printed, we need to move back to the original CurrentX value and down to a new value of CurrentY that is equal to the CurrentY value after the label *plus* sngLegendHeight is printed. (Due to the orientation of the coordinate axes, the TextHeight property is negative, so we have to add rather than subtract it to move down.)

If we also create in the Form_Load event an array called *strTitles( )* that contains the names of the three types of videos, then we can use a For-Next loop to create the legends for the various types of lines. Since we used the DrawStyle Visual Basic constants equal to values of 0, 1, and 2 to create the lines, we can simply set the DrawStyle property to the For-Next loop counter value. The *LegendLine* sub procedure to carry out this process is shown in VB Code Box 11-22.

VB CODE BOX 11-22. Sub procedure to add legend to line chart	``` Sub LegendLines() Dim sngLegendHeight As Single, intCounter As Integer Dim sngX as Single, sngY as Single 'Set sngLegendHeight to the TextHeight of any character sngLegendHeight = picRentals.TextHeight("A") FindXandY -0.5, intMostRentals 'Start at -0.5 and intMostRentals For intCounter = 0 To 2 picRentals.DrawStyle = intCounter ' sngX = picRentals.CurrentX sngY = picRentals.CurrentY picRentals.Line(sngX,sngY) - (sngX + 2, sngY) 'Draw legend line and move up 0.5 character to line up label sngX = picRentals.CurrentX FindXandY sngX + 0.1, sngY - 0.5 * sngLegendHeight picRentals.Print strTitles(intCounter) 'Now move down before drawing next line FindXandY -0.5, picRentals.CurrentY + sngLegendHeight Next picRentals.DrawStyle = vbSolid 'Set Drawstyle to default End Sub ```

If this sub procedure is added to the Code window for the project, a reference to it is added to the mnuChartsLineTypes event procedure, and the project is run, the result will be as shown in Figure 11-15.

FIGURE 11-15. Multiple-line chart with legend added

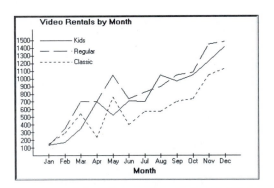

┌───┐
│ **TIP:** If you use color to distinguish the lines on the chart itself, then │
│ you will need to use color for them in the legend as well. │
└───┘

┌───┐
│ **Mini-Summary 11-4: Drawing Line Charts and Adding Titles and Legends** │
│ │
│ 1. Line charts are drawn using the Line method to connect the points on the chart. │
│ │
│ 2. Titles are added to a line chart in a manner similar to that used to add labels. │
│ │
│ 3. We can draw multiple lines on a chart by using the **DrawStyle** property to distinguish between the various lines. │
│ │
│ 4. For multiple-line charts, a legend is also needed to show the purpose of each line. │
└───┘

It's Your Turn!

1. What method is used to draw a line chart? How do we connect each point to the next point in the data set?

2. What is the value of the VB constant for each of the following line types:

    a. Solid

    b. Dot

    c. Dash

    d. Inside solid

3. What would you do to draw the lines in color?

4. How do we go about creating legends for multiple lines on a line chart?

5. For each of the following, draw the line or lines described. Assume that the scale has been set using: `picDisplay.Scale (-50,50) - (50, -50)`.

    a. A dashed line from the origin to the top right corner of the picture box.

    b. A red, dash-dash-dot line from the origin to the bottom left corner of the picture box.

    c. A green, dotted line from the origin to the top left corner of the picture box that is 5 pixels wide.

    d. A series of 5 vertical lines stretching from the bottom edge to the top edge of the picture box. The first line should cross the horizontal axis ten units to the left of the origin and each successive line should be drawn 5 units to the right of its predecessor. Use a different DrawStyle, size and color for each line.

Completing the remaining questions will enable you to create the Visual Basic project discussed in the text.

6. Add the code shown in VB Code Box 11-17 to create the DrawLineAll sub procedure to draw the line chart for total rentals. This sub procedure should be referenced in the mnuChartsLineAll_Click event procedure.

7. Add the code shown in VB Code Box 11-19 to create the FindXandY sub procedure to set the values of the CurrentX and CurrentY properties.

8. Add the code shown in VB Code Box 11-18 to create the PrintTitles sub procedure to print titles at the top left of the chart and beneath the horizontal axis. NOTE: This sub procedure should be referenced in **all** of the line and bar chart event procedures. The final version of the event procedure to display a line chart for total videos is shown in VB Code Box 11-20. Run the project again and select the line chart for all videos. The result should look like Figure 11-13.

9. Add the code shown in VB Code Box 11-21 to create the DrawLineTypes sub procedure to draw three types of lines, one for each type of video. This sub procedure should be referenced in the mnuChartsLineTypes_Click event procedure. Run the project again and select the line chart for video types. The result should look like Figure 11-14.

10. Add the code shown in VB Code Box 11-22 to create the LegendLines sub procedure to print a legend at the upper left of the chart. This sub procedure should also be referenced in the mnuChartsLineTypes_Click event procedure. Also, at the form level,

declare the Titles( ) string array to have a maximum subscript value of 2 and assign the names of the video types to it in the Form_Load event procedure with "Kids" being assigned to Titles(0), "Regular" being assigned to Titles(1), and "Classics" being assigned to Titles(2). Run the project again and select the line chart for all videos. If the line chart for video types is selected, the result should look like Figure 11-15.

11. Save your form and project under the same name.

DRAWING BAR CHARTS

Drawing bar charts also uses the Line method but in a way that creates a two-dimensional box rather than a one-dimensional line. As we shall see, these boxes can be transparent, filled completely, or crosshatched with a variety of designs. The general form of the line method necessary to draw a box instead of a line is:

> *object*.**Line (***HC1, VC1***) – (***HC2, VC2***), *Color*, BF**

where

HC1 = the horizontal coordinate of the starting corner of the box

VC1 = the vertical coordinate of the starting corner of the box

HC2 = the horizontal coordinate of the corner of the box *diagonally* opposite the starting corner

VC2 = the vertical coordinate of the corner of the box *diagonally* opposite the starting corner

Color = the color in which the box is drawn

B = statement that this is a box rather than a line

F = statement that the box is filled

Note: While the Color, B, and F parameters are optional, to draw a box we must include the B parameter.

TIP: You cannot use the F parameter without the B parameter.

For example, for a box using the coordinate system for total rentals that is centered over the second division mark on the horizontal axis (Feb), is 1 unit wide, and has a height of 1,000, the appropriate command would be:

```
picRentals.Line (.5, 0) - (1.5, 1000), , B
```

and the resulting box would appear as shown in Figure 11-16 (where we have zoomed in on the pertinent section of the chart).

FIGURE 11-16. Box drawn on horizontal axis

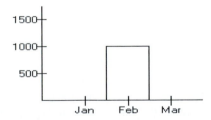

Since we can use the same coordinate system and axes for the bar charts as we did for the line charts, our only task here is to draw bars like the one shown in Figure 11-16. However, instead of the bar chart taking up all of the space around a month, we need to leave some space between the bars— say, the same amount of space as was allocated to the bars. This implies that instead of the bar width going from 50 percent before the division mark to 50 percent after the mark for the total rentals case, the bar should go from, say, 25 percent before to 25 percent after. In each case, the height of the bar should be equal to the total rentals for that month as stored in the intAllRentals( ) array. A For-Next loop is used to draw the bars for each month in the *DrawBarAll* sub procedure, as shown in VB Code Box 11-23.

VB CODE BOX 11-23. DrawBarAll sub procedure	```
	Private Sub DrawBarAll()
	   Dim intCounter as Integer
	   For intCounter = 0 To intNumMonths - 1
	      picRentals.Line (intCounter - 0.25, 0)- _
	      (intCounter + 0.25, intAllRentals(intCounter)), , B
	   Next intCounter
	End Sub
	``

The mnuChartsBarAll_Click event procedure should look *exactly* like the mnuChartsLineAll_Click event procedure shown in VB Code Box 11-20, except that the reference to the DrawLineAll sub procedure should be replaced with a reference to the DrawBarAll sub procedure. If the project is run and the All rentals option is selected from the Bar Charts submenu, the result will be as shown in Figure 11-17.

FIGURE 11-17. Bar charts for all rentals

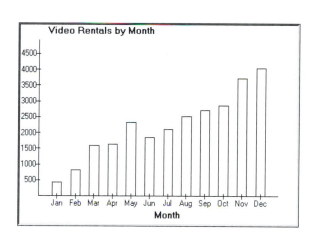

Drawing Bar Charts for Rental Types

Drawing the bar charts for the three types of rentals is similar to drawing the bar chart for total rentals. The primary difference is that, for each month, three bars must be drawn rather than just one. We also need to find a way to distinguish among the bars for the three rental types. In the first case, instead of having a single bar covering 50 percent of the space around a division mark, we will have three bars, each taking up 20 percent of the space. The three bars will take up 60 percent of the space, leaving 40 percent between the sets of bars. This means that the first line will run from intCounter – 0.3 to intCounter – 0.1, the second from intCounter – 0.1 to intCounter + 0.1, and the third from intCounter + 0.1 to intCounter + 0.3.

To handle the second problem—that is, distinguishing among the three types of rentals—we can use two approaches. First, to fill the box in the same color as it is drawn, we can add the F option to the Line method. Alternatively, to fill the box with a design, we would omit the F option and *precede* the Line method command with the **FillStyle** property. The FillStyle options are shown in Table 11-3.

TABLE 11-3: FillStyle Property Options

Fill Style	VB Constant	Value
Solid	vbFSSolid	0
Transparent	vbFSTransparent	1
Horizontal Lines	vbHorizontalLine	2
Vertical Lines	vbVerticalLine	3
Upward Diagonal Lines	vbUpwardDiagonal	4
Downward Diagonal Lines	vbDownwardDiagonal	5
Crosshatching	vbCross	6
Diagonal Crosshatching	vbDiagonalCross	7

> **TIP:** If you add the F parameter to the Line method, the box is always filled solid and you can use the Color parameter of the Line method with the VB color constants to distinguish the various lines.

To draw three bars with the first one solid (FillStyle = 0), the second one transparent (FillStyle = 1), and the third one having a horizontal line pattern (FillStyle = 2), the single Line command for the total rentals bar chart should be replaced with three combinations of FillStyle and Box Line commands in a For-Next loop. If this is done, the *DrawBarTypes* sub procedure will look like that shown in VB Code Box 11-24.

| **VB CODE BOX 11-24.** Sub procedure to draw multiple bars | ```
Sub DrawBarTypes()
Dim intCounter As Integer
 For intCounter = 0 To intNumMonths - 1
     picRentals.FillStyle = 0
     picRentals.Line (intCounter - 0.3, intKids(intCounter))- _
     (intCounter - 0.1, 0), , B
     picRentals.FillStyle = 1
     picRentals.Line (intCounter - 0.1, _
     intRegular(intCounter))- (intCounter + 0.1, 0), , B
     picRentals.FillStyle = 2
     picRentals.Line (intCounter + 0.1, _
     intClassic(intCounter))- (intCounter + 0.3, 0), , B
   Next intCounter
End Sub
``` |

To create a legend for the types of bars, we can modify the code in the LegendLines sub procedure (VB Code Box 11-22). The modifications involve drawing bars rather than lines and lining up the labels at the tops of the bars instead of on the lines. The resulting *LegendBars* sub procedure should look like that shown in VB Code Box 11-25.

If both the DrawBarTypes sub procedure and the LegendBars sub procedure are referenced in the mnuChartsBarTypes event procedure, as was done in the mnuChartsLineTypes event procedure, and the project is run, the resulting bar charts will look like those shown in Figure 11-18.
```

| VB CODE BOX 11-25. Sub procedure to add legends to bar charts | ```
Sub LegendBars()
  Dim sngLegendHeight As Single, intCounter As Integer
  sngLegendHeight = picRentals.TextHeight("A")
  picRentals.CurrentY = intMostRentals - sngLegendHeight
  For intCounter = 0 To 2
    picRentals.FillStyle = intCounter
    picRentals.Line(-0.5,picRentals.CurrentY + _
    sngLegendHeight) - (0.5,picRentals.CurrentY + 2 * _
    sngLegendHeight), , B
    FindXandY picRentals.CurrentX + 0.1, _
    picRentals.CurrentY - sngLegendHeight
    picRentals.Print strTitles(intCounter)
  Next
  picRentals.FillStyle = 0
End Sub
``` |

FIGURE 11-18. Multiple bars on a single chart

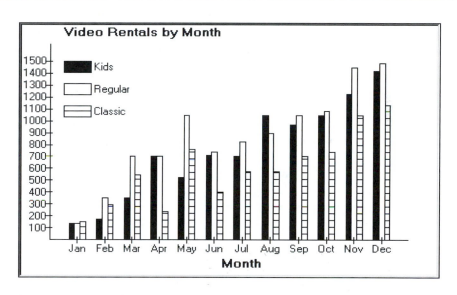

Mini-Summary 11-5: Drawing Bar Charts

1. Bar charts are drawn using the B (box) option with the Line method. The parameters for the Line method give the coordinates of the corners of the box.

2. Multiple bars can be distinguished using the **FillStyle** property.

3. A legend is added for multiple bars in much the same way as for multiple lines.

It's Your Turn!

1. What method is used to create a bar chart? How is its use different for a bar chart than from previous uses?

2. What parameter must be added to the method to make it a box? To fill it?

3. What property is used to determine the style of fill to be used in the box?
```

4. How are legends added to distinguish between bars in a bar chart?

5. For each of the following, use the Line method to draw the bars or boxes described. Assume that the scale has been set using: `picDisplay.Scale (-50,50) - (50, -50)`.

 a. Draw a solid black box, 50 units wide in the exact center of the picture box.

 b. Draw a green, cross-hatched box 50 units wide in the exact center of the picture box.

 c. Draw five boxes of varying sizes and colors. Each box should be centered at the origin. The first box should fill the picture box with it's color. Each succeeding box should have a width that is 20 units smaller than it's predecessor and a different color. The result should look something like a square bulls-eye. For a greater challenge use a loop instead of five Line method statements.

 d. Draw five red bars spaced evenly across the picture box. Each should be 4 units wide and they should grow from height of 10 units for the first bar to a height of 50 units for the last. The bottom of each bar should rest at the y = 0 level. The first bar should be centered at x = -40 the last should be centered at x = 40. For a greater challenge use a loop instead of five Line method statements.

Completing the remaining questions will enable you to create the Visual Basic project discussed in the text.

6. Add the code shown in VB Code Box 11-23 to create the DrawBarAll sub procedure to draw the bar chart for total rentals. This sub procedure should be referenced in the mnuChartsBarAll_Click event procedure. The final version of this event procedure should be similar to the mnuChartsLineAll_Click event procedure, *except* that the DrawBarAll sub procedure is referenced instead of the DrawLineAll sub procedure.

7. Run the project again and select the bar chart for all videos. The result should look like Figure 11-17.

8. Add the code shown in VB Code Box 11-24 to create the DrawBarTypes sub procedure to draw three types of bars, one for each type video. This sub procedure should be referenced in the mnuChartsBarTypes_Click event procedure.

9. Add the code shown in VB Code Box 11-25 to create the LegendBars sub procedure to create a legend for the multiple bars. This sub procedure should also be referenced in the mnuChartsBarType_Click event procedure. Run the project again and select the bar chart for all videos. If the bar chart for video types is selected, the result should look like Figure 11-18.

10. Save the form and project under the same names.

DRAWING PIE CHARTS

As shown back in Figure 11-1, pie charts use a circle divided into sectors to show the distribution of some parts of the whole. In the Vintage Videos case, we want to show how the total rentals for the year are distributed among the three types of videos.

Using the Circle Method

To draw a pie chart, we need to be able to draw a circle and then divide this circle into sections known as **sectors**. We also need to be able to fill the sectors and provide a legend to explain what each sector represents.

To create a circle or a portion of a circle, we use the **Circle** method. The form of this method is shown below:

*object.***Circle (*x, y*),** *radius, color, start, end*

where

x, y = the center of the circle

radius = the radius of the circle

color = the color for the circle

start = the starting point in radians for any sector of the circle

end = the ending point in radians for any sector of the circle

Most of these parameters should be self-explanatory, but you may not be familiar with the use of radians to determine the starting and ending points for a sector. However, if you remember that there are 2 pi radians (where pi = 3.14159) in an entire circle, then creating a sector just involves multiplying the fraction of the circle in the sector times 2 pi to determine the starting and ending points. For the lines connecting the sector to the center point to be displayed, the values of the starting and ending points must be negative. If the starting and ending points are not included, then an entire circle is drawn.

> **TIP:** To draw a line from the center point to a sector at angle 0, use a small negative value instead of zero as the starting point.

For example, to create an entire circle with center at (0, 0) and radius of 10, the command would be:

```
Circle (0, 0), 10
```

To create a sector with the same center point and a radius that starts at a point 10 percent of the way around the circle and continues to a point 40 percent of the way around, with the sector being connected to the center point, the command would be:

```
Circle (0, 0), 10, , -0.10 * TwoPI, -0.40 * TwoPI
```

where sngTwoPI is a constant that has been set equal to 2 * 3.14159. If the command to draw the sector is given on a blank form for which the scale has been set so that the origin is in the center of the form, the result is shown in Figure 11-19.

FIGURE 11-19.
Sector of a circle

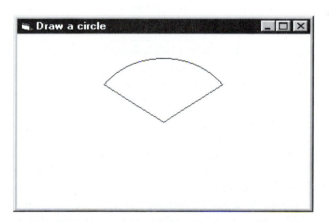

> **TIP:** The *color* parameter affects only the lines describing the circle, not the interior of the circle.

Drawing a pie chart is simply a matter of connecting a series of sectors, one for each item to be charted. That is, the ending point for one sector will be the beginning point for the next sector. For example, assume there are three items, with the first item accounting for 20 percent of the total, the second item accounting for 35 percent of the total, and the third item accounting for 45 percent of the total. In this case, we would use three Circle method commands to draw three connecting sectors:

```
Circle (0, 0), 10, , 0, -.2 * sngTwoPI
Circle (0, 0), 10, , -0.2 * sngTwoPI, -.55 * sngTwoPI
Circle (0, 0), 10, , -.55 * sngTwoPI, -sngTwoPI
```

Note that we used the *cumulative* fractions to start and end each sector. For example, the cumulative fraction for the second sector is equal to the sum of the fractions for the first and second sectors. If these three statements are entered in the Form_Load event for the same form as before, along with the AutoRedraw property, and the project is run, the result will appear as shown in Figure 11-20.

FIGURE 11-20.
Circle divided into sectors

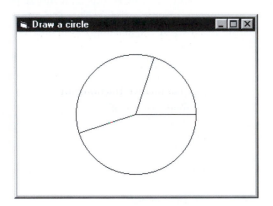

Adding a solid fill or crosshatching to the sectors is handled in the same way as for a bar chart: We simply place a FillStyle property statement before each Circle method statement. This does require one change: Instead of starting the first sector at zero, which cannot be negative, the first sector should start at −2 Pi, thus creating a line to begin the sector. You must have a line at the beginning and end of each sector that you wish to fill.

> **TIP:** You can omit an argument in the middle of the syntax for methods like Circle, but you must include the argument's comma before including the next argument.

Application to Vintage Videos Scenario

Rather than use the same picture box for the pie chart as we used for the line and bar charts, we will use a separate form—frmPie. When the pie chart is selected from the Charts menu, the frmPie form will be displayed with the pie chart on it.

To draw a pie chart for the distribution of rentals for Vintage Videos, we first need to sum the rentals for each type of video and for all videos and then find the fraction of the whole for each type of rental. To carry out this operation, we need to add a sub procedure called *ComputeTotals* that is referenced in the mnuChartPie_Click event procedure. This sub procedure is shown in VB Code Box 11-26. Note that it computes the fraction of rentals associated with each type of video and stores this information in an array called *sngFraction( )*. This array is then passed back to the mnuChartPie_Click event procedure.

| **VB CODE BOX 11-26.** ComputeTotals sub procedure | ```Private Sub ComputeTotals(sngFraction() As Single)
  Dim intCounter As Integer, intSumFirst As Integer,
  Dim intSumSecond As Integer, intSumThird As Integer
  Dim intSumtotal As Integer
  For intCounter = 0 To intNumMonths - 1
    intSumFirst = intSumFirst + intKids(intCounter)
    intSumSecond = intSumSecond + intRegular(intCounter)
    intSumThird = intSumThird + intClassic(intCounter)
    intSumtotal = intSumtotal + intAllRentals(intCounter)
  Next
  sngFraction(0) = CSng(intSumFirst) / CSng(intSumtotal)
  sngFraction(1) = CSng(intSumSecond) / CSng(intSumtotal)
  sngFraction(2) = CSng(intSumThird) / CSng(intSumtotal)
End Sub``` |

Once the fraction of total rentals for each type has been computed, we can proceed to draw the pie chart on the new form. The sub procedure to do this, *DrawPie*, involves three key steps:

1. Compute the cumulative fractions for each of the three types of videos.
2. Set the coordinate system for the form.
3. Draw the pie chart using the Circle method.

The first step simply involves summing the individual fractions that are passed to the sub procedure and storing them in a new array called *sngCumFraction( )*. The second step is similar to what was done earlier, but is stated in terms of the radius of the circle. That way, no matter what value is selected for the radius, everything will be relative to it. In our case, we want to leave room in the upper left-hand corner for a title and a legend, so the scale is set so that the origin is about three-fifths from the left and top of the form. Finally, the pie chart is drawn with the first sector filled, the second sector empty, and the third sector filled with crosshatching. The DrawPie sub procedure is shown in VB Code Box 11-27.

> **TIP:** To color the sectors of a circle, you must set the FillStyle property to 0 (solid) and then use the **FillColor** property to fill each sector.

Adding Title and Legend

Adding a title and a legend to the pie chart are virtually the same as for the bar chart, except that the scale is different. However, we still use the TextHeight property to line up the legend and descriptive labels. The Title-Pie sub procedure to add a title to the pie chart is shown in Code Table 11-28. Note that the radius is passed to this procedure as the local variable sngR and is used to position the title relative to the top and left side of the form.

The *LegendPie* sub procedure is shown in VB Code Box 11-29, where the radius is used to position the legend relative to the left side of the form. The final mnuChartsPie_Click event procedure is shown in VB Code Box 11-30.

If the project is run and the pie chart option is selected, the result will be as shown in Figure 11-21. Notice that we have added a Clear button to the form that unloads the form and returns control to the main form.

| **VB CODE BOX 11-27.** DrawPie sub procedure | ```
Private Sub DrawPie(sngFraction() As Single,_
  sngRadius As Single)
  Const sngTwoPI As Single = 2 * 3.14159
  Dim sngCumFraction(2) As Single, intCounter As Integer
  sngCumFrac(0) = sngFraction(0)
  For intCounter = 1 To 2
    sngCumFraction(intCounter) = _
    sngCumFraction(intCounter - 1) + sngFraction(intCounter)
  Next
  sngRadius = 1 'Value of Radius does not matter
  frmPie.Scale (-3 * sngRadius, 3 * sngRadius)- _
  (2 * sngRadius, -2 * sngRadius)
  frmPie.FillStyle = 0
  frmPie.Circle (0, 0), sngRadius, , -sngCumFraction(2) * _
  sngTwoPI, -sngCumFraction(0) * sngTwoPI
  frmPie.FillStyle = 1
  frmPie.Circle (0, 0), sngRadius, , -sngCumFraction(0) * _
  sngTwoPI, -sngCumFraction(1) * sngTwoPI
  frmPie.FillStyle = 2
  frmPie.Circle (0, 0), sngRadius, , -sngCumFraction(1) * _
  sngTwoPI, -sngCumFraction(2) * sngTwoPI
End Sub
``` |
|---|---|

| **VB CODE BOX 11-28.** TitlePie sub procedure | ```
Private Sub TitlePie(sngR As Single)
Dim sngDefaultSize As Single
  sngDefaultSize = picRentals.FontSize
  frmPie.FontSize = 10 'Set size and style
  frmPie.FontBold = True
  frmPie.CurrentY = frmPie.ScaleTop - 0.01 * sngR
  frmPie.CurrentX = frmPie.ScaleLeft + 0.01 * sngR
  frmPie.Print "Vintage Videos Rental Distribution"
  frmPie.FontSize = sngDefaultSize
  frmPie.FontBold = False
End Sub
``` |
|---|---|

| **VB CODE BOX 11-29.** LegendPie sub procedure | ```
Private Sub LegendPie (sngR As Single)
    Dim sngLegendHght As Single, sngX As Single,
    Dim sngY As Single, intCounter As Integer
    sngLegendHght = frmPie.TextHeight("A")
    sngY = frmPie.CurrentY + sngLegendHght
    sngX = frmPie.ScaleLeft + 0.1 * sngR
    For intCounter = 0 To 2
      frmPie.FillStyle = intCounter
      frmPie.Line (sngX, sngY)- _
      (sngX + 0.5 * sngR, sngY + LegendHght), , B
      frmPie.CurrentY = Y
      frmPie.CurrentX = frmPie.CurrentX + 0.1 * sngR
      frmPie.Print strTitles(intCounter)
      sngX = frmPie.ScaleLeft + 0.1 * sngR
      sngY = frmPie.CurrentY + sngLegendHght
    Next
End Sub
``` |
|---|---|
```

| **VB CODE BOX 11-30.** mnuChartsPie_Click event procedure | ```
Private Sub mnuChartsPie_Click()
    Dim sngFracRentals(2) As Single, sngRadius As Single
    picRentals.Cls
    frmPie.Show
    ComputeTotals sngFracRentals()
    DrawPie sngFracRentals(), sngRadius
    TitlePie sngRadius
    LegendPie sngRadius
End Sub
``` |
|---|---|

FIGURE 11-21.
Final pie chart for Vintage Videos

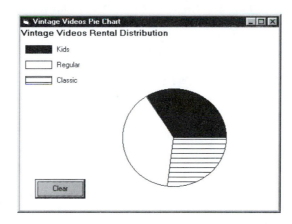

Mini-Summary 11-6: Drawing Pie Charts

1. Pie charts are drawn using the **Circle** method, where the center of the circle and the radius determine the location and size of the circle.

2. To draw the segments of the pie chart, we add parameters to the Circle method that will draw sectors rather than complete circles. These sectors are measured in radians.

3. For the center of the circle to be connected to the sectors, the sector parameters must be negative.

4. In a manner similar to that used for bar charts, the sectors can be filled using the FillStyle property and a legend can be added.

It's Your Turn!

1. When is a pie chart preferable to a bar chart? Are there times when either will do?

2. For each of the following, use the Circle method to draw the circles or slices described. Assume that the scale has been set using: `picDisplay.Scale (-50,50) - (50, -50)`.

    a. Draw a green circle with a radius of 10 units centered at the origin.

    b. Draw a green circle with a radius of 10 units centered 10 units to the right of the origin. Fill the circle with black vertical bars.
```

c. Draw a circle with a radius of 30 units centered at the origin. Divide the circle into 4 equal size slices each filled with a different color. For an extra challenge, try to do this using a loop.

d. Draw a bulls-eye consisting of five concentric circles each of different colors. The outer ring should have a radius of 50 units and the inner circle should have a radius of 10 units. For an extra challenge, try to do this using a loop.

Completing the remaining questions will enable you to create the Visual Basic project discussed in the text.

3. Add a new form to the current project with a name of **frmPie** and a caption of **Vintage Videos Pie Chart**. Make the BackColor property of this form White. Add a command button in the lower left-hand corner with a name of **cmdClear** and a caption of **Clear**.

4. Add the code shown in Code Boxes 10-6, 10-7, 10-8, and 10-9 to frmCharts form in the project to draw the pie chart, add the titles to it, and add a legend.

5. Add the code shown in VB Code Box 11-30 to the event procedure for the **mnuChartsPie_Click** menu option.

6. Code the Clear button on frmPie to unload the frmPie form and return control to frmChart.

7. Run the project and select the Pie Chart option. The result should look like Figure 11-21.

8. Save frmPie as **Pie.frm** and save the project under the same name as before.

9. Modify the LegendPie sub procedure to include in the legend the percent of the total for each video type. (Hint: You will need to pass the sngFraction( ) array to this sub procedure and use it for this exercise.) Save the form and project under their current names.

DRAWING SCATTER DIAGRAMS

The owners of Vintage Videos did not request a scatter diagram, because the line charts provide most of the information they need. However, they may see a need for such charts in the future, since scatter diagrams are often used to look for patterns in data. For example, the owners of Vintage Videos might want to look at the number of rentals for periods of the day in order to determine staffing requirements. They might also want to look at the distribution of video types for each day of the week with an eye toward allowing longer or shorter rentals for certain types of videos on specific days.

In our case, since we have already done all of the work to create a coordinate system and have added division marks, labels, titles, and a legend, we will demonstrate the use of scatter diagrams for the same rental data as before—that is, the distribution of types of rentals for the past twelve months. This will allow us to use the same setup procedures as for the bar and line charts. To do this, the first step is to add to the Charts menus a Scatter submenu option that will display the scatter diagram.

The key to creating the scatter diagram for the rental data is the *ScatterDraw* sub procedure, which uses the FillStyle property and the Circle method to plot points for each type of video for each month. The center of each circle is at the array index for the month and the number of rentals for that month. The radius of the circle is arbitrarily set at 1 percent of the number of months. The ScatterDraw procedure is shown in VB Code Box 11-31.

| VB CODE BOX 11-31. Code to create scatter diagram | ```
Private Sub ScatterDraw()
  Dim intCounter As Integer
  For intCounter = 0 To intNumMonths - 1
    picRentals.FillStyle = 0
    picRentals.Circle (intCounter, intKids(intCounter)), _
    0.01 * intNumMonths
    picRentals.FillStyle = 1
    picRentals.Circle (intCounter, intRegular(intCounter)), _
    0.01 * intNumMonths
    picRentals.FillStyle = 6
    picRentals.Circle (intCounter, intClassic(intCounter)), _
    0.01 * intNumMonths
  Next intCounter
End Sub
``` |
|---|---|

The LegendScatter sub procedure for adding a legend for the scatter diagram is similar to the LegendBar sub procedure that adds legends to the bar chart, except that circles are used in the legend rather than bars. Similarly, the mnuChartsScatter_Click event procedure is virtually the same as for the mnuChartsBarTypes_Click event procedure, except that the reference to the DrawBarType sub procedure is replaced with a reference to ScatterDraw and the reference to the LegendBar sub procedure is replaced with a reference to the LegendScatter sub procedure. If the project is run and the **Charts|Scatter** option is selected, the resulting chart will be as shown in Figure 11-22.

FIGURE 11-22.
Scatter diagram for rental data

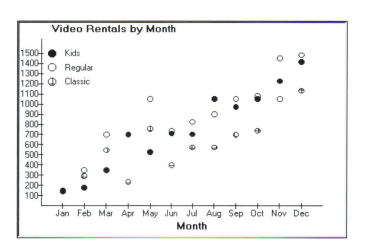

TIP: You can use colors instead of patterns to distinguish the circle used in a scatter diagram. To do this, set the FillStyle to solid (0) and then use a different FillColor property for each circle.
```

Mini-Summary 11-7: Scatter Diagrams

1. Scatter diagrams help the user look for patterns in data.

2. A scatter diagram can be drawn in Visual Basic by using the FillStyle property and the Circle method to draw circles.

3. The circles are plotted for pairs of values, with the radius of each circle being set to a small fraction of the horizontal axis scale.

It's Your Turn!

1. Use the Menu Editor to add a **Scatter** option to the Chart submenu with a name of **mnuChartsScatter**.

2. Copy the code for the mnuChartsBarTypes_Click event procedure to the mnuChartsScatter_Click event procedure. Change the reference to **DrawBarTypes** to be **ScatterDraw** and the reference to **LegendBar** to be **LegendScatter**.

3. Create the ScatterDraw sub procedure by adding the code in VB Code Box 11-31 to the project.

4. Create the LegendScatter sub procedure by modifying the LegendBar sub procedure to replace the Line method with the Circle method.

5. Run your project and select the Scatter option from the Chart submenu. The results should look like those shown in Figure 11-22.

6. Save your forms and project under the same names as before.

SUMMARY

Graphics are very useful for viewing data or information visually. Mathematicians and scientists have been using graphs for years to display equations. Graphics are also commonly used to display information about business and industry. Known as business graphics, these primarily include line, bar, and pie charts.

The first three steps in creating a graphic image in Visual Basic are to select a control, set the coordinate axis, and draw the horizontal and vertical axes. The picture box is one of a variety of controls that can be used for drawing graphics. Other controls include the Form object and the image control. The coordinate axis is set using the Scale method or the ScaleTop, ScaleLeft, ScaleHeight, and ScaleWidth properties. Straight lines can be drawn using the Line method, in which the beginning and ending values of the line are specified. The AutoRedraw property must be used in the Form_Load event procedure to make the axes persistent.

The next three steps in creating a graphic are to add division marks and labels to the axes, draw the graphic on the control, and add titles and legends to the graph. The CurrentX and CurrentY properties are used to determine the location of division marks and labels on the graph. The division marks are added to the axes with the Line method. The labels are added to the division marks with the Print method. The TextHeight and TextWidth properties are used to help position the labels. The actual graph for a mathematical function is plotted using the PSet method within a For-Next Loop. The increments in the loop must be kept small to avoid gaps in the graph.

The first step in creating a line chart or a bar chart is to sketch a design of the chart showing the axes and labels. The second step is to set the coordinate axes. This often involves using different scales for the vertical and horizontal axes and placing the origin off-center or using different scales for multiple types of charts. The third step is to add the division marks and labels on the vertical and horizontal axes.

Line charts are drawn using the Line method to connect the points on the chart. Titles are added to a line chart in a manner similar to that used to add labels. Bar charts are drawn using the B (box) option with the Line method. The parameters for the Line method give the coordinates of the corners of the box. Multiple bars can be distinguished using the FillStyle property. A legend for multiple bars is added in a manner similar to that used for multiple lines.

Pie charts are drawn using the Circle method, where the center of the circle and the radius determine the location and size of the circle. To draw the segments of the pie chart, parameters are added to the Circle method to draw sectors rather than complete circles. These sectors are measured in radians. For the center of the circle to be connected to the sectors, the sector parameters must be negative. The sectors can be filled using the FillStyle property, and a legend can be added in a manner similar to that used for bar charts.

Scatter diagrams are used to look for patterns in data. In Visual Basic, a scatter diagram can be drawn by using the FillStyle property and Circle method to draw circles. The circles are then plotted for pairs of values, with the radius of each circle being set to a small fraction of the horizontal axis scale.

The code for the business graphics project for Vintage Videos is found in VB Code Boxes 11-8 through 11-31.

NEW VISUAL BASIC ELEMENTS

Control/Object	Properties	Methods	Events
picture box control	AutoRedraw CurrentX CurrentY DrawStyle FillStyle ScaleHeight ScaleLeft ScaleTop ScaleWidth TextHeight TextWidth	Circle Cls Line Print PSet Scale	
Form object	FillColor FillStyle	Circle	

KEY TERMS

analysis graphics

axis

bar chart

business graphics

clipart graphics

computer-aided design (CAD)

graphics

line chart

pie chart

scale

scatter diagram

EXERCISES

1. Which type of chart would you use to illustrate each of the following? Why?

a. A meteorologist wants to show a comparison of the daily high temperatures for the last five days.

b. A marketing manager wants to report on the market share for a product for his company and four of their competitors.

c. An analyst would like to plot the daily price of a stock for the last month.

d. A scientist wants to plot data collected from an experiment. The data consists of tomato plant growth measurements in inches for plants that were grown under different constant temperatures ranging from 40 to 100 degrees fahrenheit.

e. A pollster wants to report the percentage of voters who are in favor of each of four candidates.

2. Write code to create each of the following objects in a picture box. Assume that the scale has been set using: `picDisplay.Scale (-50, 50) - (50, -50)`.

a. Draw a circle centered at the origin with a radius of 10 units. Around the circle, draw a square with sides that are tangential to the circle.

b. Repeat exercise 2a, but with a radius that is provided in a textbox by the user.

c. Repeat exercise 2a, but this time draw a series of circles in squares. Start with a circle centered at the origin with a radius of five units, and continue until you have a circle with a radius of 50 units inside a corresponding square.

3. For each of the following code segments, describe what appears in the picture box after the code has been executed.

```
a. Private Sub cmdGo_Click()
     Dim intI As Integer
     Dim intJ As Integer
     Dim blnK As Boolean
     blnK = True
     picDisplay.Scale (-50, 50)-(50, -50)
     For intI = 50 To -45 Step -5
       For intJ = -50 To 45 Step 5
         If blnK Then
           picDisplay.Line (intJ, intI)- _
             (intJ + 5, intI - 5), vbGreen, BF
           blnK = False
         Else
           picDisplay.Line (intJ, intI)- _
             (intJ + 5, intI - 5), vbRed, BF
           blnK = True
         End If
       Next intJ
       blnK = Not blnK
     Next intI
   End Sub
```

```
b. Private Sub cmdGo_Click()
     Dim sngTwopi As Single
     sngTwopi = 2 * 3.1415
     picDisplay.Scale (-50, 50)-(50, -50)
     picDisplay.Circle (0, 0), 5
     picDisplay.Circle (15, 15), 5
     picDisplay.Circle (-15, 15), 5
```

```
        picDisplay.Circle (0, 0), 25, , _
          0.55 * sngTwopi, 0.95 * sngTwopi
        picDisplay.Circle (0, 0), 35
      End Sub

c.  Private Sub cmdGo_Click()
      Dim intX As Integer
      Dim sngY As Single
      picDisplay.Scale (-50, 50)-(50, -50)
      For intX = -30 To 30 Step 4
        sngY = 25 - 0.4 * intX
        picDisplay.Circle (intX, sngY), 1
      Next intX
    End Sub

d.  Private Sub cmdGo_Click()
      Dim sngY(5) As Single, intJ As Integer
      Dim intI As Integer, intK As Integer
      picDisplay.Scale (-10, 70)-(110, -10)
      picDisplay.Line (0, 0)-(0, 60)
      For intI = 1 To 5
        sngY(intI) = Rnd() * 100 + 1
        intJ = intI * 10 - 2
        intK = intI * 10 + 2
        picDisplay.Line (0, intJ)-(sngY(intI), intK), , BF
      Next intI
    End Sub
```

4. For each of the following, explain what is wrong with the code. What error messages would you see, if any? What can you do to correct the code?

a. The following code should generate a vertical bar chart for the values (13, 10, 8, 15, 11) that are stored in the form level array intNum( ). The bars should be 4 units wide, drawn with solid fill and evenly spaced along the entire length of the horizontal axis.

```
Private Sub cmdGo_Click()
  Dim intI As Integer
  picDisplay.Scale (-10, 20)-(50, -10)
  picDisplay.Line (-5, 0)-(45, 0)
  For intI = 0 To 4
    picDisplay.Line (intI - 2, 0)- _
      (intI + 2, intNum(intI)), , F
  Next intI
End Sub
```

b. The following code should generate a pie chart for the values (0.35, 0.23, 0.09, 0.33), which are stored in the form level array sngNum( ).

```
Private Sub cmdGo_Click()
  Dim intI As Integer, sngStart As Single
  Dim sngRad As Single, sngStop As Single
  sngRad = 2 * 3.1415
  picDisplay.Scale (-50, 50)-(50, -50)
  sngStart = -0.001
  For intI = 0 To 3
    sngend = -(Abs(sngStart) + sngNum(intI))
    picDisplay.Circle (0, 0), 30, , sngStart, sngend
```

```
        sngStart = sngend
      Next intI
    End Sub
```

5. Use the Visual Basic Help facility or the MSDN on-line library to answer the following questions.

    a. What values are the CurrentX and CurrentY properties set to immediately after the Line method is executed?

    b. How can the optional keyword Step be used with the Circle method?

    c. What property can you change to plot larger dots when using the PSet method?

    d. What happens if you use the Scale method without specifying any coordinates?

PROJECTS

In each of the following projects, you should include titles and legends where appropriate. You should also make the code to set the coordinate system and axes as general as possible. Wherever possible, consider using color instead of crosshatching to distinguish parts of the charts.

1. Revise the QuadPlot.vbp project to plot the equation $y = x^3$ using the same axes as before. Save the project as **Cubic.vbp** and the form as **Cubic.frm**.

2. Assume that the weekly box office receipts (in $100,000s) for a first-run movie can be described by the equation $R = at - bt^2$ where $t =$ the time in weeks that the movie has been out and a and b are parameters that are different for each movie. For example, if $a = 4$ and $b = 0.4$, the movie will bring in $360,000 in the first week, $640,000 in the second week, and so on. In this model, however, by the tenth week the box office sales fall to zero. Create a Visual Basic project that will allow the user to input values for the a and b parameters (where a > b and b < 1.0) and then plot the graph of box office receipts. Save the form as **Ex11-2.frm** and the project as **Ex11-2.vbp** in the Chapter11 folder on your data disk.

3. Revise the graphics project discussed in this chapter (Charts.frm, Pie.frm, and Charts.vbp) so that instead of showing the number of rentals for each month, the various charts display the revenue. Hint: Revenue will be equal to the number of videos of each type rented times the rental price for that type of video. Save the revised forms as **ChartRev.frm** and **PieRev.frm** and the project as **ChartsRev.vbp** in the Chapter11 folder on your data disk.

4. Table 11-4 shows the data that the Allatoona Regional Medical Center has reported about its growth over the past ten years (in millions of dollars).

TABLE 11-4: Financial Data for Allatoona Regional Medical Center

Year	Total Assets	Additions	Operating Income
1988	15	2.8	1.8
1989	26	2.7	1.0
1990	28	3.0	0.3
1991	20	2.5	0.6
1992	21	2.6	1.0
1993	25	2.5	1.8

TABLE 11-4: Financial Data for Allatoona Regional Medical Center

Year	Total Assets	Additions	Operating Income
1994	29	3.0	2.4
1995	49	5.6	2.0
1996	50	9.0	3.0
1997	67	15.0	4.5

Create a Visual Basic project that will input these data from a sequential access file and display the following items:

  a. A line chart showing the change in assets over the 10-year period

  b. Line charts showing the change in additions and operating income over the 10-year period

  c. A bar chart to show the change in assets over the 10-year period

  d. Bar charts to show the change in additions and operating income over the 10-year period

Why is it inappropriate to show all three financial values on the same chart?

Save the form as **Ex11-4.frm** and the project as **Ex11-4.vbp** in the Chapter11 folder on your data disk.

5. Table 11-5 shows data on hourly wages for different types of workers for 1988 and 1998.

TABLE 11-5: Hourly Wages for Selected Professions

Profession	1988 Hourly Wage	1998 Hourly Wage
Plumber	20.75	24.75
Mechanic	18.25	21.55
Teacher	15	17.50
Nurse	16	20.35
Programmer	19.50	31.25
Accountant	25.50	28.75
College Professor	24.00	26.25

Create a Visual Basic project that will:

  a. Input this data from a sequential access file.

  b. Create a bar chart that compares hourly wages for 1988 to those for 1998. Use abbreviations for the various professions as labels on the horizontal axis.

  c. Create a scatter diagram that plots the 1988 and 1998 values. Be sure to include a legend that distinguishes among the data points.

Save the form as **Ex11-5.frm** and the project as **Ex11-5.vbp** in the Chapter11 folder on your data disk.

6. A survey showed the data in Table 11-6 regarding the purpose of corporate Web sites. Use this data to create a Visual Basic project that will display a pie chart that represents these data. Save the form as **Ex11-6.frm** and the project as **Ex11-6.vbp** in the Chapter11 folder on your data disk.

TABLE 11-6: Corporate Web Site Purposes

Web Site Purpose	Percent of Total
Advertising or Public Relations	66
Electronic Commerce	7
Customer Support	9
Other	18

7. Data on the growth of the four most popular Internet Domain names from recent surveys are shown in Table 11-7. Create a Visual Basic project to carry out the following operations:

    a. Input the data from a sequential access file and store it in a two-dimensional array.

    b. Create line and bar charts to display the total of all Domain names for each survey period. Do the same for each Domain name.

    c. Create a pie chart for the Jan. 1998 data.

TABLE 11-7: Growth in Internet Domains (100,000s) (Source: Network Wizards)

Domain	Jan. 1998	July 1997	Jan. 1997	July 1996
.com	8201	4501	3965	3224
.edu	3944	2943	3654	2114
.net	5283	2165	1549	1232
.org	520	435	313	N/A

Save the forms as **Ex11-7.frm** and **Ex11-7Pie.frm** and the project as **Ex11-7.vbp** in the Chapter11 folder on your data disk.

8. Assume that the owners of Vintage Videos have collected data on the number of videos rented on each day of the week for the past four weeks. These data are shown in Table 11-8. Write a Visual Basic project to input the data from a sequential access file, store them in a two-dimensional array, and use them to create a scatter diagram that displays the number of videos rented in relation to the days of the week. Save the form as **Ex11-8.frm** and the project as **Ex11-8.vbp** in the Chapter11 folder on your data disk.

9. A time series represents a collection of measurements that are obtained over time. Time series are useful in analyzing how a particular phenomenon behaves over time. For example, a marketing manager might be interested in analyzing sales data to see if there are any seasonal effects, or a stock analyst may want to use the price history of a stock to predict its future value.

TABLE 11-8: Number of Rentals for Days of Week

Day of Week	Week 1	Week 2	Week 3	Week 4
Monday	129	136	128	134
Tuesday	133	128	131	129
Wednesday	166	157	171	169
Thursday	141	138	142	147
Friday	191	197	202	203
Saturday	203	211	206	212
Sunday	166	171	166	164

Analysts often attempt to develop a mathematical model that can be used to describe a time series that has been observed. The model can then be used to obtain plots of the series and make estimations of future or missing values. These models often incorporate past periods' data in order to predict future periods. Suppose an analyst developed the following model after analyzing the price of a particular stock over time:

$$\text{Price}(i) = -2 + 0.988 * \text{Price}(i-1) - 0.02 * \text{Price}(i-2) + 0.001 * \text{Price}(i-3)$$
$$+ 5 * \text{Rnd}(\,)$$

where $\text{Price}(i)$ is the stock price in period i, $\text{Price}(i-1)$ is the stock price one period earlier, $\text{Price}(i-2)$ is the stock price two periods earlier, and $\text{Price}(i-3)$ is the stock price 3 periods earlier. $\text{Rnd}(\,)$ is a random element that represents that portion of the stock's price behavior that cannot be explained by the previous three periods' prices. For example, if the prices for periods 1, 2, and 3 are $10, $15, $13, then the price of the stock in period 4 would be $10.64 plus a random value determined by $5 * \text{Rnd}(\,)$.

Write a Visual Basic program that will plot this time series for 100 periods. Use a dot to plot each point and connect them with a line. You will need to provide values for the first three periods to begin the series. Save the form as **Ex11-9.frm** and the project as **Ex11-9.vbp** in the Chapter11 folder on your data disk.

PROJECT: JOE'S TAX ASSISTANCE (CONT.)

Joe clicked on the button, and the information about his latest VITA clients—the Millers—was saved in his laptop. He leaned back in his chair and smiled. The Visual Basic program that he and Zooey had written was turning into a definite time-saver. He would have to sit down with Zooey and talk about what to work on next. As he sat thinking, he heard a knock at the door.

"Come in," he called. His smile grew bigger as Zooey and Janet walked in.

"Hi, Dad!" "Hi, Grandpa!" they said almost simultaneously.

"Well, what brings two of my favorite ladies down here?" Joe asked and rose to give them a hug.

Janet replied, "We stopped by to take you to lunch, and Zooey wants to find out how the program is working."

"Yeah, Grandpa, I want you to tell me all about it at lunch," Zooey added excitedly.

Joe beamed. "Okay! Let me grab a couple of things and lock up. How about Chinese?"

After arriving at the restaurant and passing through the buffet line, they settled into a booth to enjoy their conversation over lunch.

"You know, Zooey, the program is great. Thank you again for all your help," Joe began. "It's helped me to keep all of the clients' information better organized, I can access it easier than before, and it's even helped me cut down on the time I spend with each client."

Zooey's smile grew wider. "That's awesome. I told one of my teachers about it. She wants me to demonstrate it in class if you'll let me."

"That's fine by me, Zooey," Joe replied. "I can come to your school to help you show it if you want. I've been thinking of sharing it with the world anyway," he added.

"What do you mean, Dad?" inquired Janet.

"Well, I've been thinking of making the program available to other VITA volunteers through the IRS. But I think I'll have to sell them on the benefits first."

Janet responded: "Sounds like you need to make a good business sales presentation."

"You're right. That's exactly what I need. I've got lots of numbers showing how the program has improved my work: time to see clients, both before and after, amounts of refunds/payments, etc. All of it's stored in the computer and on disks, thanks to Zooey's database."

"Grandpa, you know we can use Visual Basic to turn all of those numbers into good-looking charts and graphs," Zooey interjected.

"That's just what you need for a good business presentation, Dad," said Janet. "It looks like my daughter here has a good head for business."

"And, Grandpa, you can practice your presentation at my school before presenting it to the VITA people," said Zooey.

"Well, now," replied Joe, looking prouder than ever. "It sounds like we have a plan. Zooey might need to spend another weekend with her grandparents. How about it, girls?"

"You'll just have to take her to softball practice and it's fine with me," said Janet.

"Me, too," said Zooey, "and maybe I can bring some friends over to swim afterwards."

"You've got it," said Joe. "It's the least I can do for my chief programmer."

1. Prepare a data file with the information shown in Table 11-9. Joe began using the Visual Basic program on February 24, 2001.

TABLE 11-9: Client Information

Date	Number of Clients
2/11/01	7
2/12/01	8
2/13/01	4
2/16/01	5
2/17/01	7
2/18/01	6
2/19/01	4
2/20/01	6
2/23/01	5

TABLE 11-9: Client Information (Continued)

Date	Number of Clients
2/24/01	7
2/25/01	6
2/26/01	8
2/27/01	11

2. Create Visual Basic code that uses the date file to create a line chart showing the number of clients per day.

3. In Table 11-10 is a frequency distribution showing the number of clients who fall within certain categories of refunds due or taxes owed. Here the value is positive if the client gets a tax refund and negative if the client owes taxes. Create Visual Basic code that displays these data as a bar chart showing the number of clients per category. This type of chart is commonly called a frequency histogram.

TABLE 11-10: Frequency Distribution

Refund/Owed	Number
-150 to -100	3
-99 to -50	5
-49 to 0	8
1 to 50	14
51 to 100	12
101 to 150	7
151 to 200	2
201 to 250	3

4. Much of the information above could be derived from the database created for the VITA case of Chapter 9. For a slightly more challenging exercise, add code to your program so that a line chart that exhibits the number of clients per day can be generated from the database entries. You can calculate the number of clients per day simply by adding up all the records that occur on a particular date.

5. Run, test, and debug your program

12

USER-DEFINED DATA TYPES, DIRECT ACCESS FILES, AND OBJECT CLASSES

After reading this chapter, you will be able to:

❖ Understand how to create user-defined data types to facilitate processing data into information.

❖ Work with record types to store multiple types of data in a single array.

❖ Use direct access files to store information.

❖ Understand some of the principles of object-oriented programming, including the concepts of classes and encapsulation.

❖ Discuss the steps in designing a class on which to base objects.

❖ Create new Class modules using the Class Builder wizard.

❖ Declare and use objects based on these classes.

❖ Add methods and properties to these objects.

**SCENARIO:
CREATING A
PAYROLL
SYSTEM AT
VINTAGE
VIDEOS**

Clark sat at the desk in the back room of the new Vintage Videos store, staring at nothing. The stacks of papers and open ledgers piled haphazardly in front of him attested to the cause of his stupor. Clark had been the manager of the new store for about two weeks now, and he was beginning to feel that he might be in over his head. Even the sound of Monique's voice as she called from the store barely registered to him.

"Clark? What are you doing? Didn't you hear?" Monique asked. Clark was startled to see that she was standing right next to him.

"I'm sorry. I must have been lost in thought," he replied. "I've been trying to figure out all of these accounts and I feel like a character in one of those classic 'fish out of water' stories. I'm not sure that I'm prepared to be a manager," he continued. "I'm having an especially hard time figuring out a way to manage this payroll. Some of us are salaried and some are hourly. Everything is different for each—pay rate, overtime, taxes, insurance, Social Security . . . it's so complicated."

"Why don't you approach it like a problem from one of your information systems classes?" Monique asked. "I believe you worked on several business applications in them, from what you told me."

Clark straightened up and said, "Hey, that's not a bad idea. I could approach the payroll from an IS viewpoint and even write a program or two. I'm sure that Ed wouldn't mind having payroll automated for the whole company, either."

"Wow, the whole company sounds like a big job," replied Monique. "Aren't we getting a little too excited?"

"You're right as usual, but I can do this in small steps. I'll use some programming techniques that will make the initial prototype small and fast so we can try it out. Then I can make adjustments as I go," Clark replied.

Clark looked at Monique and smiled. "You always know what to say to encourage me. I think that I'll have to keep you around. Come on! I'll treat you to dinner and a movie from the collection."

As they walked toward the front hand in hand, Monique glanced sideways at Clark and suggested: "How about one of those Japanese monster movies? *Godzilla in Tokyo* has to be one of the best examples of a 'fish out of water'."

"Oh, no," Clark groaned. "I think that maybe I have created a monster."

Discussion of Scenario

In the current situation facing Vintage Videos, Clark has taken over as manager of the new store and is facing a problem common to management: computation of payroll. At Vintage Videos some employees, such as Clark, are salaried, while most are part-time hourly employees. The salaried employees are paid the same salary regardless of the number of hours they work, while the hourly employees are paid an hourly wage rate and must be paid overtime if they work more than 40 hours in a week. Both categories of employees are subject to withholding taxes equal to 15 percent for federal taxes plus 7.45 percent for Social Security and Medicare taxes. In addition, salaried employees have $25 per week deducted for health insurance. (We are assuming this is a state with no state income tax.)

The task facing Clark is to create a prototype employee payroll information system in Visual Basic that will allow a user to add new employees or to delete individuals who are no longer employed at Vintage Videos. He also wants to be able to select an employee from a list and display a screen that will allow the user to compute the gross and net pay for that employee based on payroll status (hourly or salaried), pay rate, and hours worked. While this project could be handled as a database project such as that discussed in Chapter 9, Clark wants to store much of the information in internal memory to speed processing. He also does not want to spend much time designing a database until he is sure that this project is going to be useful.

In the first case, we will discuss the use of user-defined data types, which will enable us to avoid problems with arrays discussed earlier—that is, the requirement that all data in an array must be of the same type. In the second case, we will use a type of data file known as direct access files, which can be programmed to support the addition and deletion of records just as with a database but without the need for database design. Finally, we will take a look at object-oriented programming (OOP) in Visual Basic within this same payroll framework.

USER-DEFINED DATA TYPES

As discussed in Chapters 6 and 9, one of the shortcomings of arrays is that only one type of data can be stored in them. For example, an array might be defined as a String array, an Integer array, or a Single array, but not as all three at the same time. Fortunately, if we are willing to create our *own* data types in Visual Basic, we can circumvent this problem. These new data types are commonly referred to as *user-defined data types,* although that is something of a misnomer since it is not the person using the program but the programmer creating the project who does this. For this reason, we will refer to them as **user-defined data types.**

User-defined data types in Visual Basic are made up of elements, where each element is declared to be a standard data type (String, Integer, and so on) or a previously declared user-defined data type. User-defined data types in Visual Basic are much like database records. (In fact, in some programming languages, a user-defined data type is referred to as a *record type*.) For example, a user-defined data type for a college student might include the student's ID number, last name, first name, middle initial, and grade point average (GPA). By creating an array of college student data types, we become able to store all this different type of information under one name in memory.

Using user-defined data types is a two-step process. First, the data type must be declared in a Code module, and second, a variable or array must be declared to be of that data type in the procedure in which it is going to be used. You *cannot* use the user-defined data type as the variable; you must declare a variable (or array) to be of that type and then use it in your code.

Declaring a Data Type   The first step in using a user-defined data type is to declare the data type globally in a Code module using the **Type** statement with the Public keyword. The various elements that will make up that data type are then listed along with their data types. The type declaration process is terminated with an **End Type** statement. The form of the Type statement is:

> **Public Type** *typename*
>   *elementname1 as type*
>   *elementname2 as type*
>   *etc.*
> **End Type**

where *typename* and the various *elementname* values must follow the standard variable-naming rules. Also, the *type* values must be standard data types or previously declared user-defined data types. The elements in a Type statement can be individual variables or arrays.

> **TIP:** You may also declare the data type as Private, in which case it can be used only in the module in which it is declared. However, this does not affect the scope of a variable declared to be of that type.

For example, the Type statement to declare the college student data type discussed earlier in a Code module is shown in VB Code Box 12-1, where we have used **fixed-length strings** instead of the variable-length strings we have been using throughout this text. Using fixed-length arrays in a Type statement forces all variables of this type to be the same length, which will be useful for formatting information in a list box and for saving the variables to a file.

Using a User-defined Data Type   Once a programmer defined data type has been declared globally in a Code module, it can then be used in declaring variables or arrays anywhere in the project, just as any other data type would be used to declare variables. For our example, to declare a variable udtOneStudent to be of the type CollegeStudent, the statement would be:

```
Dim udtOneStudent as CollegeStudent
```

Note that the variable prefix for a user-defined data type is *udt*.

VB CODE BOX 12-1. Code to define a data type	`Public Type CollegeStudent`
	`    lngIDNumber as Long`
	`    strLastName as String * 20`
	`    strFirstName as String * 10`
	`    strMidInit as String * 2`
	`    sngGPA as Single`
	`End Type`

Now, the variable udtOneStudent is composed of the same five elements that were declared for the type CollegeStudent with the structure shown in Figure 12-1. From this, it is easy to see why this data type is referred to as a record data type in other languages.

FIGURE 12-1.
Structure of variable
udtOneStudent

udtOneStudent

lngIDNum
strLastName
strFirstName
strMidInit
sngGPA

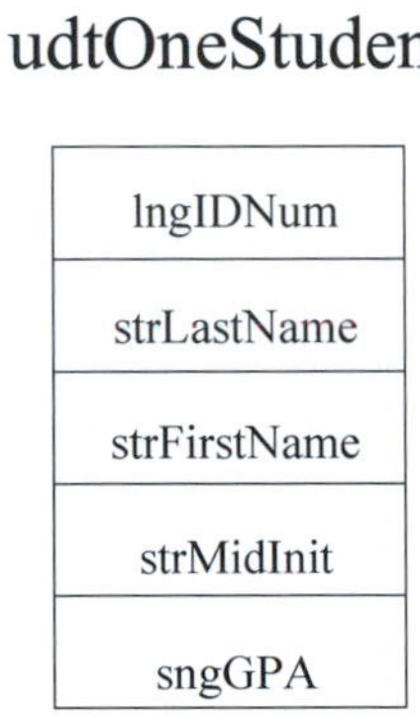

To refer to the individual elements of the udtOneStudent variable, we use the **dot notation**—that is, *VariableName.ElementName*. For example, to assign a student name to the strLastName element of the variable udtOneStudent, the statement would be:

```
udtOneStudent.strLastName = "Burdell"
```

Similarly, to assign a grade point value to the GPA element, the statement would be:

```
udtOneStudent.sngGPA = 3.12
```

If the data on a student are being input from text boxes on a form like that shown in Figure 12-2, the complete set of statements to input the data and clear the text boxes would be as shown in VB Code Box 12-2 (where the sub procedure ClearTextBoxes clears the text boxes and sets the focus back to the txtIDNumber text box).

> **TIP:** If two variables are declared as the same user-defined type, you can assign one to the other. This will assign all of the elements in one variable to all of the elements in the other.

Using the With Statement

To reduce the redundancy in working with data type variables like udtOneStudent, we can use the **With** statement, which allows us to work with multiple elements of a single object. The form of the With statement is:

With *object*
  statements
End With

FIGURE 12-2.
Student information
form

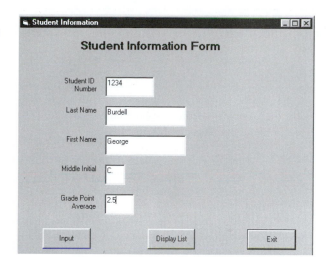

VB CODE BOX 12-2. Code to input student data	```Private Sub cmdInput_Click()```
	``` Dim udtOneStudent As CollegeStudent```
	``` udtOneStudent.lngIDNumber = CLng(txtIDNumber.Text)```
	``` udtOneStudent.strLastName = txtLastName.Text```
	``` udtOneStudent.strFirstName = txtFirstName.Text```
	``` udtOneStudent.strMidInit = txtMiddleInitial.Text```
	``` udtOneStudent.sngGPA = CSng(txtGPA.Text)```
	``` ClearTextBoxes```
	```End Sub```

where all of the statements would normally begin with the object name followed by a period and then the rest of the statement. The With statement allows you to mention the object name once and then begin each statement with a period.

> **TIP:** If you create a variable of a user defined type and then declare a Watch on that variable, the Watch window will display the name of the variable and a plus sign. You then need to click on the plus to unfold and see the elements of the variable.

For example, the five statements to input data to the udtOneStudent variable from text boxes as shown in VB Code Box 12-2 can be replaced using the With statement as shown VB Code Box 12-3:

VB CODE BOX 12-3. Use of With statement	```With udtOneStudent```
	``` .lngIdNumber = CLng(txtIDNumber.text)```
	``` .strLastName = txtLastName.Text```
	``` .strFirstName = txtFirstName.Text```
	``` .strMidInit = txtMiddleInitial.Text```
	``` .sngGPA = CSng(txtGPA.text)```
	```End With```

The With statement can also be used to assign properties to a control. For example, to assign the properties to the txtIDNumber text box, the statements might be: as shown in VB Code Box 12-4.

VB CODE BOX 12-4.
Use of With statement
for setting property
values
	```With txtIDNumber```
	``` .TabIndex = 0```
	``` .Height = 1500```
	``` .Width = 2500```
	```End With```

If we have a second form (*frmList*) with a list box (*lstStudents*) to which we want to add the elements of the udtOneStudent variable, we can use the With statement to reduce the redundancy in the AddItem method as shown below:

```
With udtOneStudent
    frmList.lstStudents.AddItem .lngIDNumber & "   " & _
    .strLastName & "   " & .strFirstName & "   " & _
    .strMidInit & "   " & Format(.sngGPA, "fixed")
End With
```

Adding this code to the revised cmdInput_Click event procedure results in the final code to input student information and add it to the list box on the frmList form shown in VB Code Box 12-5. If several names are input and added to the list box and the list is displayed with the Click button, the result is shown in Figure 12-3.

VB CODE BOX 12-5.
Revised Code to input
student information
and add to list box
	```Private Sub cmdInput_Click()```
	``` Dim udtOneStudent As CollegeStudent```
	``` With udtOneStudent```
	``` .lngIDNumber = CLng(txtIDNumber.Text)```
	``` .strLastName = txtLastName.Text```
	``` .strFirstName = txtFirstName.Text```
	``` .strMidInit = txtMiddleInitial.Text```
	``` .sngGPA = CSng(txtGPA.Text)```
	``` End With```
	``` With udtOneStudent```
	``` frmList.lstStudents.AddItem .lngIDNumber & " " & _```
	``` .strLastName & " " & .strFirstName & " " _```
	``` & .strMidInit & " " & Format(.sngGPA, "fixed")```
	``` End With```
	``` ClearTextBoxes```
	```End Sub```

FIGURE 12-3.
Result of adding
student names

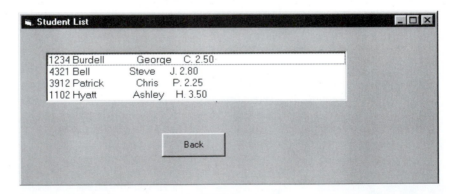

You might note that the names in Figure 12-3 do not line up very well, even though we used fixed-length strings for all of the variables except the GPA value. This problem is caused by the use of a **proportional font** (in this case MS Sans Serif) in which different characters take up different amounts of space. To resolve this problem, simply change the list box font to a **monospace font** like Courier; the items now line up one beneath the other as shown in Figure 12-4. Note that we have also added a label above the list box to provide headings for the columns in it. (While monospace fonts are somewhat less attractive than proportional fonts, they do give you more control over the placement of strings and values in a list box.)

FIGURE 12-4.
Result of changing list box font to Courier

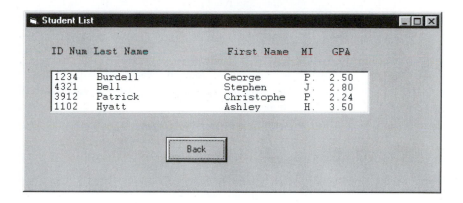

ID Num	Last Name	First Name	MI	GPA
1234	Burdell	George	P.	2.50
4321	Bell	Stephen	J.	2.80
3912	Patrick	Christophe	P.	2.24
1102	Hyatt	Ashley	H.	3.50

TIP: A monospace font uses more space than a proportional font to display the same number of characters.

Mini-Summary 12-1: User-defined Data Types

1. The Type statement is used to create a user-defined data type that is composed of standard data types or previously defined data types. User-defined data types are usually defined in a Code module, so they are known to all modules of the project.

2. Before variables can be used, they must be declared to be of the user-defined data type; the type itself **cannot** be used as a variable.

3. By using a user-defined data type, we can create an array that will store multiple data types.

4. The With statement enables the programmer to work with multiple elements of a single object.

5. A monospace font can be used to line up items in a list box.

It's Your Turn!

1. Denote each of the following statements as True or False:

   a. User-defined data types are usually defined in a code module.

   b. You can use the user-defined data type name as a variable.

   c. It is possible using user-defined data types to create arrays that store multiple data types.

   d. The With statement enables you to refer to object properties without repeating the object name.

2. Write the statements necessary to create a new user-defined data type with name equal to **NewType** that has three elements: an Integer type called **Element1**, a String type called **Element2**, and a Currency type named **Element3.**

3. Write a user-defined data type for the elements of each of the following scenarios:

    a. A university bookstore wishes to work with the following information about the textbooks that are sold: title, author, publisher, year of publication, wholesale price, and retail price.

    b. A trucking company wishes to store the following information about each truck in its fleet: truck ID, manufacturer, model, year of purchase, and current mileage.

    c. A shipping company wishes to work with the following information when tracking packages: invoice number, sender, receiver, send date, and current location.

4. Write a With statement to set in run time the name property of a new form equal to **frmQ2,** the caption property to **Set at run time**, and the control box property to **False.**

Completing the remaining questions will enable you to create the Visual Basic project discussed in the text.

5. Create the form shown in Figure 12-2 with the controls shown in Table 12-1 along with appropriate labels or captions. Name this form **frmStudentInfo**.

TABLE 12-1: Controls for Student Information System

Control	Control
txtIDNumber	txtGPA
txtLastName	cmdInput
txtFirstName	cmdDisplay
txtMiddleInitial	cmdExit

6. Open a Code module and, as shown in VB Code Box 12-1, define the **CollegeStudent** data type. Save this module as **StudentInfo.bas**.

7. Add a second form named **frmList** with a list box named **lstStudents** and make its font **Courier** with a font size of **10** points. Add a label as shown in Figure 12-4 above the list box, with its font changed to 10-point Courier to match the contents of the list box. Add a command button (**cmdBack**) and the corresponding code to return control to the main form.

8. Add the code shown in VB Code Box 12-5 to the cmdInput_Click event procedure to input student information and add it to lstStudents. Write a sub procedure called **ClearTextBoxes** to clear all text boxes and set the focus back to the txtIDNumber text box.

9. Add the necessary code to the cmdDisplay_Click event procedure to display the second form (frmList). Also, add the necessary code to the cmdExit_Click event procedure.

10. Run your project and add the four students shown in Table 12-2 to your project. Switch to the second form to ensure that the names are being added to the list as shown in the same figure. Your result should look like Figure 12-4 (you may have to adjust the label above the list box.).

TABLE 12-2: Student Data

ID Number	Last Name	First Name	MI	GPA
1234	Burdell	George	C.	2.50
4321	Bell	Stephen	J.	2.80
3912	Patrick	Christopher	P.	2.24
1102	Hyatt	Ashley	H.	3.50

11. Create a new folder on your data disk named **Chapter12.** Save the first form as **StudentInfo.frm** in this. Save the second form as **StudentList.frm** and save the project as **StudentInfo.vbp.**

MORE ON PROGRAMMER-DEFINED DATA TYPES

As we said earlier, one reason to use user-defined data types is to be able to include different types of data within an array. For example, using standard data types, we would need five different arrays to store the five elements of the student record with which we have been working. These arrays would include a Long Integer data type array for the student ID; String arrays for the last name, first name, and middle initial; and a Single array for the grade point average. While it is not difficult to declare these arrays and input data into them, manipulating them would require that we use the same index value for each array—a much more complicated process than if we simply declared an array of type CollegeStudent. If this latter process is done, all of the data are stored in a single array.

An array that uses a user-defined data type is declared in the same way as an array for a standard data type:

Dim *arrayName(max index)* as *data type*

The only difference is that now the *data type* is a user-defined type. The same is true with regard to passing a user-defined data type variable or array to a sub procedure or function: You replace the standard types with the user-defined data type.

For example, to declare an array to be of type CollegeStudent, the statement is:

```
Dim udtManyStudents(100) as CollegeStudent
```

Once an array is declared to be of a user-defined data type, we refer to the elements of the array by giving the array name plus the data type element name, separated by a period. For example, to assign a value to the LastName element of the tenth student record in the udtManyStudents array, the statement would be:

```
udtManyStudents(9).strLastName = "McGahee"
```

Similarly, to display the GPA value for the twentieth student in a text box, the statement would be:

```
txtGPA.Text = Str(udtManyStudents(19).sngGPA)
```

Including Arrays in User-defined Data Types

Just as user-defined data types can be included in an array, it is also possible to include arrays within a user-defined data type. For example, assume that, in addition to including the student's ID number, name, and GPA data, we wanted to include a list of all courses which the student has taken while in college. This list could include up to 60 courses, so clearly we would need an array to handle it. The array declaration for the array should be included within the Type statement, immediately before the End Type statement, as:

```
strCourses(60) as String * 10
```

If this element definition is added to the CollegeStudent Type statement and the same udtManyStudents array declaration as above is used, we can now add up to 61 courses to each record in this array. To add the third course to the record for the twentieth student, the statement could be:

```
udtManyStudents(19).strCourses(2) = "Math 116"
```

It would be fairly easy to extend the small project in which we input information about a student and displayed it in a list box to also include information about the courses the student has completed. Doing this would require adding to the CollegeStudents data type an array that stores the courses for which the student has credit and an Integer type data element that would hold the number of courses completed. This would enable us to display the list of courses in another list box.

Building upon Existing User-defined Data Types

Once the programmer has defined a data type, it enjoys the same status as a standard data type in that it can be passed to sub procedures and functions and can be used in the creation of other user-defined data types. For example, if we wanted to create a user-defined data type that consists of the personal student information currently stored in variables of type CollegeStudent *plus* financial information on the student, including residency status, fees paid status, and amount of fines outstanding, the Type statement might look like:

```
Public Type StudentInfo
    udtPersonal As CollegeStudent
    strResidency As String
    blnFeesPaid As Boolean
    curFinesOutstanding As Currency
End Type
```

Note that the element udtPersonal has been declared to be of the type CollegeStudent, which means that any variable declared to be of type StudentInfo can store *all* of the data that can be stored in a variable of type CollegeStudent *plus* the residency, fees paid, and outstanding fines data—a great deal of information under one variable name!

Application to Vintage Videos Scenario

Recall that the Vintage Videos scenario involved creating a prototype payroll information system for a project that will use payroll data in the form of employee name, Social Security number, pay status (salaried or hourly), pay rate, and hours worked to compute the gross and net pay for each employee. The gross pay will depend on pay status and hours worked, while the net pay will involve subtracting federal payroll taxes, Social Security taxes, and, for salaried employees, health insurance premiums from the gross pay.

To handle these processing needs, we can create a user-defined data type with elements for the first name, last name, Social Security number, telephone number, pay type, and pay rate. If this data type is called *EmpRecord*, then the type declaration in a Code module is shown in VB Code Box 12-6, along with a declaration of the variable *udtEmployees( )* as an array of this type and two Integer type variables, *intEmpCntr* and *intCurrEmp*, that represent the number of items in the array and the index of the current item in the array, respectively.

| **VB CODE BOX 12-6.** Type and variable declarations in Code module | ```
Public Type EmpRecord
    strFName As String * 15
    strLName As String * 25
    strSSNum As String * 11
    strPhone As String * 14
    strPaytype As String * 8
    curPayRate As Currency
End Type
Public udtEmployees() As EmpRecord
Public intEmpCntr As Integer
Public intCurrEmp As Integer
``` |
|---|---|

It should be noted that the array udtEmployees( ) is declared without an upper limit on the subscript. This means that the array is being declared as a dynamic array. **Dynamic arrays** are just that: arrays whose size can grow or shrink as needed. Dynamic arrays conserve memory, since no space is set aside for them until they are actually needed within an event or a sub procedure or a function and then only the minimum size is allocated. Compare this with fixed-size arrays, which are declared for the maximum *possible* number of elements, leading to unneeded memory being set aside for them.

When a dynamic array is needed, its size is declared using the **ReDim** statement to the actual maximum subscript that will be used within the procedure or function. Dynamic arrays become important when we are working with lists of user-defined variables where each variable can represent a great deal of data. In our case, the dynamic array Employees( ) will grow as the number of employees grows or shrink as employees leave the company.

> **TIP:** You **cannot** use the ReDim statement to redeclare the size of an array for which the size was explicitly declared earlier.

Mini-Summary 12-2: User-defined Data Types and Dynamic Arrays

1. It is possible to create an array composed of user-defined data types.

2. Arrays can be defined as an element of a user-defined data type.

3. A user-defined data type can be included in other user-defined data types.

4. The size of a dynamic array is not defined until it is needed. The ReDim statement is used to define the size of the array when the size becomes known.
```

It's Your Turn!

1. Declare a variable as an array of type **Newtype** declared in the last exercise with a maximum of 100 elements.

2. Declare the same array as above as a dynamic array. Also, write the statement necessary to redimension this array.

3. Write a user-defined data type for the elements of each of the following scenarios:

a. An online news company wishes to store the following information about each news report on its site: article ID, author, date written, subject category, and an array of 10 keywords.

b. A manufacturing company gathers a set of five measurements at set periods and plots the average on a control chart as part of a quality control program. As part of a Visual Basic program the production manager wishes to store the following information: machine number, product ID, date, time, and an array of five measurements (single data type).

Completing the remaining exercises will enable you to create the Visual Basic project discussed in the text.

4. Begin a new project and add a Code module to it named **EmpInfoSys**.

5. Add the code shown in VB Code Box 12-6 to the Code module to define the **EmpRecord** data type, declare **udtEmployees()** as a dynamic array of the EmpRecord type, and declare the other global variables.

6. Give the default form a name of **frmEmpInfoSys** and a caption of **Employee Information System.** Do not change anything else about it at this time.

7. Save the Code module as **EmployeeInfo.bas**, the form as **EmpInfoSys.frm**, and your project as **VintageEIS.vbp** (for Employee Information System) in the Chapter12 folder.

VINTAGE VIDEOS PAYROLL PROJECT

To create the Vintage Videos payroll project, we need three forms:

1. a startup form to display a list of employee names, phone numbers, and pay types;
2. a form to add data on a new employee;
3. a form to calculate gross and net pay based on the information stored about a given employee.

Startup Form to Display Information on Employees

The Startup form has two primary purposes: displaying a list of employees and providing a menu system from which the user can choose to save the list of employees to a file, print the list, exit the project, go to the Add Employee form, or delete an employee. This employee information form, named **frmEmpInfoSys**, is shown in Figure 12-5 with the Employee submenu being selected.

The code to print the list of employees involves using a For-Next loop, as we have done in previous examples. Similarly, the code to exit the project uses the End command. The code to save the list of employees to file will involve the use of a new type of file that we will discuss in a later section. The Add Employee menu option will

FIGURE 12-5.
Employee
information form

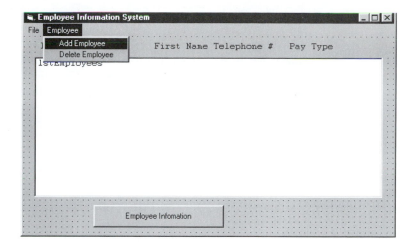

transfer control to the second form, on which new employees are added to the list box on this form and to the udtEmployees( ) array declared globally in the Code module.

To access the form used to add employees (*frmAddEmp*), we need to write code for the *Add Employee* submenu option. This code consists of two statements, one to display the frmAddEmp form and one to hide the current form:

```
frmAddEmp.show
Me.Hide
```

Adding Employees   Since initially there are no employees in the system, the next step in creating this payroll prototype project is to create the form and write the code to add employees to the list box and the udtEmployees( ) array. We have already started this process by declaring a user-defined type (EmpRecord) to store employee information and declaring a dynamic array of that type [udtEmployees( )] in the EmpInfoSys Code module. The frmAddEmp form is shown in Figure 12-6. Note that the user enters the new employee's first and last names, Social Security number, phone number, and pay rate in the text boxes and selects a pay type from the pay type combo box. Clicking the *Add Employee* command button adds this information to the array of employee records.

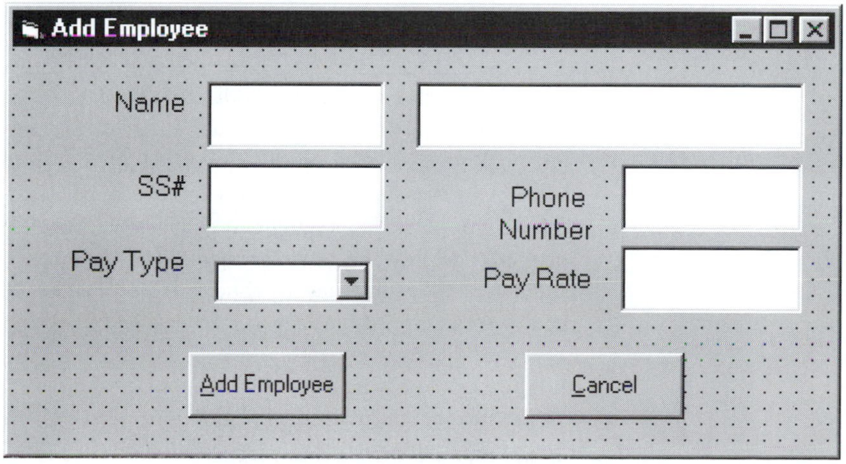

FIGURE 12-6. Form
to use in adding
employees

The next step is to open the Code window for the Add Employee command button and add the code necessary to transfer the contents of the various text boxes to the udtEmployees( ) array and to the lstEmployees list box on the Startup form. The code to handle this operation is written as a sub procedure called *AddEmpRecord* that is called when the command button is clicked. Once this sub procedure is completed, the Startup form is displayed and frmAddEmp is unloaded. (It will not be used frequently, so we do not need to keep it in memory.) The code for the AddEmpRecord sub procedure is shown in VB Code Box 12-7, and the cmdAddEmp_Click event procedure is shown in VB Code Box 12-8.

| **VB CODE BOX 12-7.** Sub procedure to add record to list box | ```
Sub AddEmpRecord()
    Dim udtEmp As EmpRecord
    With udtEmp
     .strFName = txtFname.Text
     .strLName = txtLname.Text
     .strSSNum = txtSSnum.Text
     .strPhone = txtPhoneNum.Text
     .strPaytype = cboPayType.Text
     .curPayRate = CCur(txtPayRate.Text)
    End With
    intEmpCntr = intEmpCntr + 1
    ReDim Preserve udtEmployees(intEmpCntr) As EmpRecord
    udtEmployees(intEmpCntr) = udtEmp
    With udtEmployees(intEmpCntr)
     frmEmpInfoSys.lstEmployees AddItem .strLName & " " _
      & .strFName & " " & .strPhone & " " & .strPaytype
    End With
End Sub
``` |
|---|---|

| **VB CODE BOX 12-8.** cmdAddEmp_Click event procedure | ```
Private Sub cmdAddEmp_Click()
    AddEmpRecord
    frmEmpInfoSys.Show
    Unload Me
End Sub
``` |
|---|---|

TIP: To see the code for a sub procedure or function, double-click the reference to it to highlight it and then press **Shift-F2**.

Note in the code for the AddEmpRecord sub procedure that the contents of the text boxes are added to a local variable, *udtEmp,* and the employee counter (intEmpCntr) is incremented. This value of the employee counter is then used to increase the size of the array udtEmployees using the **ReDim Preserve** statement. The ReDim part of this statement changes the size of the dynamic array, and the Preserve part retains the existing contents of the array. Failure to include the *Preserve* parameter will result in the array being cleared by the ReDim statement. This way, only the minimum size of the array is ever needed but previous data is retained.

After the array is redimensioned, the employee information is added to the array and the last name, first name, phone number, and pay type are added to the lstEmployees list box on the frmEmpInfoSys form. As with the student application, we will change the Font property for the list box to select the Courier monospace font so the items will line up. Figure 12-7 shows the process of adding a name to the employee list and the result of pressing the Add Employee command button.

> **TIP:** You can also use the **Chr(9)** character function to insert the Tab operation between items in a list box.

FIGURE 12-7.
Adding employee (top) and employee list (bottom)

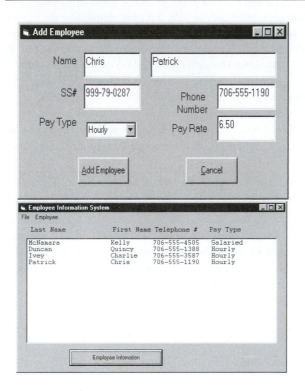

The code for the Cancel button on the frmAddEmp form is the same as for the Add Employee button shown in VB Code Box 12-8, *except* that the AddEmpRecord sub procedure is *not* referenced.

Using the List Box ItemData Property

A shortcoming of the current lstEmployees list box is that it is not shown in alphabetical order of last name. While it is very easy to set this up using the list box Sorted property, if we do not link the items in the list box to the corresponding items in the array of employee records, they will no longer match. For example, the names in the list box in Figure 12-7 are in the same order as the names in the udtEmployees( ) array (the order in which they were input). However, once the Sorted property is applied to these records, they will not be in the same order, because the list box will no longer be linked to the array.

To link the list box and the array, we need to use the **ItemData** property of the list box. This property allows us to add information about each record that stays with the record no matter where it is in the list box. In our case, setting the ItemData property of the list box item equal to the subscript of the corresponding array element will provide the needed link. In computer science terminology, the ItemData property will be a **pointer** to the corresponding array element. If this is done, no matter what the order of the items in the list box, we will always be able to find the corresponding array element.

The form of the ItemData property is shown below:

list.**ItemData(***index***) = *array subscript***

where the ***index*** value is the number of the item in the list box.

To use the ItemData property, we need to assign the array subscript value to it at the same time that we add the array element to the list box with the AddItem method. Visual Basic even has a property that will provide the *index* value for the next item in the list—the **NewIndex** property of the list box. The complete form then becomes:

list.**ItemData(***list*.**NewIndex) = *array subscript***

For our project, we need to declare a new variable, ***intIndex***, and add the statements shown in VB Code Box 12-9 to the AddEmpRecord sub procedure in the frmAddEmp form (shown earlier as VB Code Box 12-7) immediately before the End Sub statement. Once we do this, we will be able to sort the list box while still knowing the corresponding array subscript through the ItemData property.

VB Code Box 12-9. Using the ItemData property	`intIndex = frmEmpInfoSys.lstEmployees.NewIndex` `frmEmpInfoSys.lstEmployees.ItemData(intIndex) = intEmpCntr`

To see how this works, consider Table 12-3, which shows the names for the records shown earlier in Figure 12-7, but in alphabetical order. We have also shown in the ItemData property for each record which matches the order in which they were input and are stored in the udtEmployees( ) array.

Table 12-3: Use of ItemData Property

Last Name	**First Name**	**ItemData Property**
Duncan	Quincy	2
Ivey	Charlie	3
McNamara	Kelly	1
Patrick	Chris	4

Deleting Employees   The use of the ItemData property will also make deleting employees much easier. Instead of having to worry about how to delete a record from the array and the list box, we simply use the RemoveItem property to remove the record from the list box. Then, since no list box item has an ItemData property corresponding to the subscript of the deleted record, it will never be referenced. So, while it is still in the array, it will not be referenced and when we save the array later, we will not write that array element to disk, effectively deleting it. The code to delete an item in the list box is shown in VB Code Box 12-10, where we make sure that an item has been selected in the list box and that the user really wants to delete it before carrying out the Delete operation.

For example, if the name Charlie Ivey is deleted from Table 12-3, there will no longer be a list box item with its ItemData property equal to 3—so the corresponding array element will not be referenced.

Mini-Summary 12-3: The ReDim Preserve Statement and ItemData Property

1. The ReDim Preserve statement redimensions a dynamic array while preserving the existing contents of the array.

2. The ItemData property of a list box can be used to store information about the item in the list box, including a pointer to an array subscript.

3. The ItemData property can be set using the NewIndex property of the list box.

4. The array elements corresponding to items deleted from a list box are not physically deleted, but their array subscript does not appear as an ItemData property.

| **VB CODE BOX 12-10.** Code to delete an employee | ```
Private Sub mnuEmpDel_Click()
    Dim intYesNo as Integer
    If lstEmployees.ListIndex > -1 Then
        intYesNo = MsgBox("Delete the selected employee?", _
        vbCritical + vbYesNo, "Confirm Deletion")
        If intYesNo = vbYes Then
            lstEmployees.RemoveItem lstEmployees.ListIndex
        End If
    Else
        MsgBox "You must select an employee first", _
        VBCritical
    End If
End Sub
``` |
|---|---|

It's Your Turn!

1. Why do we need to use the Redim Preserve statement? What happens if you use the Redim statement without the Preserve parameter?

2. What is the ItemData property of a listbox used for? Why do we need it?

3. What is the NewIndex property of the listbox used for?

Completing the remaining exercises will enable you to create the Visual Basic project discussed in the text.

4. Modify the existing Startup form the employee payroll system (frmEmpInfoSys) to look like that shown in Figure 12-5 with the control and menu item names shown in Table 12-4. Add the labels to match the controls listed there.

5. Create the lblHeadings label with headings shown in Table 12-5. Change the Font property for the lstEmployees list box and the lblHeadings label to be 10-point Courier. Adjust the contents of lblHeadings to match the positioning of the items in the list box. (You can do this using the string lengths for each element defined earlier plus one extra space.) Save the form as **EmpInfoSys.frm** to the Chapter12 folder on your data disk.
```

TABLE 12-4: Control and Menu Item Names for frmEmpInfoSys Form

Control or Menu Item Name	Control or Menu Item Name
lstEmployees	mnuFileExit
cmdEmpInfo	mnuEmp
mnuFile	mnuEmpAdd
mnuFileSave	mnuEmpDel
mnuFilePrint	lblHeadings

TABLE 12-5: Headings for lblHeading label

Headings
Last Name
First Name
Telephone #
Pay Type

6. Create the form shown in Figure 12-6 to add employees to the project (frmAddEmp) with the control names shown in Table 12-6. Add the necessary labels for the text boxes and combo box. Finally, add two items to the combo box: **Salaried** and **Hourly**.

TABLE 12-6: Controls for frmAddEmp

Control Names	Control Names
txtFName	txtPhone
txtLName	cboPayType
txtSSNum	cmdAddEmp
txtPayRate	cmdCancel

7. Add the code to the mnuEmpAdd_Click event procedure necessary to switch to the frmAddEmp form.

8. Create the AddEmpRecord sub procedure shown in VB Code Box 12-7 as a part of the frmAddEmp Code module. Add the code shown in VB Code Box 12-8 to the cmdAddEmp_Click event procedure. Also, add the appropriate code to the cmdCancel_Click event procedure. Save this form as **AddEmp.frm** in the Chapter12 folder on your data disk.

9. Add the code shown in VB Code Box 12-9 to the AddEmpRecord sub procedure and declare **Index** to be an Integer variable. This code will create the ItemData property for the list box. Set the Sorted property for the lstEmployees list box to **True**.

10. Add the code shown in VB Code Box 12-10 to the mnuEmpDel_Click event procedure.

11. Add the code necessary for the **File | Print** menu option to print the contents of the list box. Also add the code for the **File | Exit** menu option to exit the project.

12. Run your project and add the employee names shown in Table 12-7 to your project. The results should look like the bottom part of Figure 12-7, *except* that the names are now in alphabetical order.

TABLE 12-7: Employee Data

First Name	Last Name	Social Security Number	Phone Number	Pay Type	Pay Rate
Kelly	McNamara	999-29-0861	706-555-4505	Salaried	$25,000
Quincy	Duncan	999-65-9538	770-555-1388	Hourly	$6.00
Charlie	Ivey	999-69-4198	706-555-3587	Hourly	$6.00
Chris	Patrick	999-79-0287	706-555-1190	Hourly	$6.50

13. Delete the record for Charlie Ivey and then add it back again.

14. Save your project in the Chapter12 folder under the same names as before.

CALCULATING GROSS AND NET PAY

Once the employee data have been entered, we need to compute the gross and net pay for an employee record, by switching from the frmEmpInfoSys form to a third form named *frmShowEmp* when the employee's record in the lstEmployees list box is *double-clicked*. (It should also be possible to do this by highlighting a record and clicking the *Employee Information* command button.) At the same time, the ItemData property of the item in the list box (which corresponds to the array subscript of this record) is saved in the global variable *intCurrEmp*. Since the operations should be possible from two different events, we will write them in the *ShowEmployee* sub procedure as seen in VB Code Box 12-11.

| **VB CODE BOX 12-11.** Sub ShowEmployee | ```
Sub ShowEmployee()
    intCurrEmp = lstEmployees.ItemData(lstEmployees.ListIndex)
    frmShowEmp.Show
    Me.Hide
End Sub
``` |
|---|---|

The frmShowEmp form for calculating payroll is shown in Figure 12-8. Note that it has text boxes for all of the employee information, and all of the information *except* the hours worked will come from the udtEmployees( ) array. The user will enter the hours worked for hourly employees and then click the *Calculate Pay* command button to display the gross and net pay. For a salaried employee, it is only necessary to click the command button since it won't matter how many hours were worked. The user can also print the form or cancel the operation and return to the first form by clicking *Print* or *Cancel* command buttons at the bottom of the form.

As we said earlier, the ShowEmployee sub should be used to display the payroll calculation form when the name is double-clicked in the list box or when it is highlighted and the command button at the bottom of the form is clicked. We use the dou-
```

FIGURE 12-8.
Payroll calculation
form

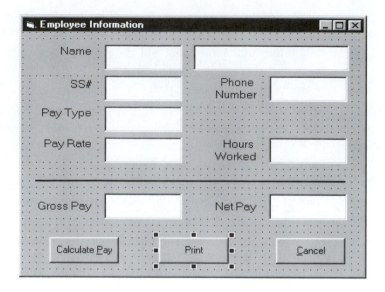

ble-click event for the list box so that it is possible to highlight a name without immediately switching to the pay calculation form. To ensure that a name is indeed highlighted before the click event for the Show Information command button attempts to display the employee information, we need to check the ListIndex of the list box to validate, that is, it is greater than -1. This click event procedure is shown in VB Code Box 12-12. It is not necessary to check that a name is highlighted for the list box double-click event since this is automatically accomplished by the event itself.

VB CODE BOX 12-12. Code to check for valid ListIndex value	```Private Sub cmdEmpInfo_Click() If lstEmployees.ListIndex > -1 Then ShowEmployee End IfEnd Sub```

When the frmShowEmp form is displayed, the employee's data should be transferred from the udtEmployee( ) array element corresponding to the intCurrEmp variable saved earlier to the text boxes. This should occur in the Form_Activate event procedure. The Activate event is used here instead of the Load event, because this form will be hidden between uses rather than being unloaded. The frmShowEmp Form_Activate event procedure is shown in VB Code Box 12-13.

VB CODE BOX 12-13. frmShowEmp Form_Activate event procedure	```Private Sub Form_Activate() With udtEmployees(intCurrEmp) txtFName.Text = .strFName txtLName.Text = .strLName txtSSnum.Text = .strSSNum txtPhone.Text = .strPhone txtPayType.Text = .strPaytype txtPayRate.Text = Str(.curPayRate) End WithEnd Sub```

Once the employee data are displayed in list boxes on the form, the next step is to calculate the gross and net pay based on the pay type, pay rate, and, for hourly employees, number of hours worked. To do this, we need to add code to the cmdCalcPay command button. If the employee is hourly, we need to make an overtime calculation similar to that discussed in Chapter 4 to compute the gross pay. If the employee is salaried, we simply divide the annual pay rate by 52 to compute the weekly gross pay. In either case, we compute the net pay by subtracting 22.45 percent of the gross pay (15 percent for federal taxes and 7.45 percent for Social Security taxes.) Finally, if the employee is salaried, we subtract an additional $25 per week for health insurance premiums. The cmdCalc_Click event procedure is shown in VB Code Box 12-14. If the third person in the list box (Charlie Ivey) is selected and 45 is entered as the number of hours worked, the result of clicking the Calculate Pay command button is as shown in Figure 12-9.

VB CODE BOX 12-14. Code for Calculate Pay button	

```
Private Sub cmdCalcPay_Click()
  Dim sngHrsWrked As Single, curPayRate As Currency
  Dim curGrossPay As Currency, curNetPay As Currency
  Dim strPayType As String
  strPayType = Trim(txtPayType.Text) 'Remove extra spaces
  curPayRate = CCur(txtPayRate.Text)
  If strPayType = "Hourly" Then 'Check pay type
    If txtHrsWrked.Text = "" Then 'Check for missing data
      txtHrsWrked.Text = InputBox("Please input hours worked")
      Exit Sub
    Else
      sngHrsWrked = CSng(txtHrsWrked.Text)
    End If
    If sngHrsWrked > 40 Then 'If hourly, check for overtime
      curGrossPay = 40 * curPayRate + 1.5 * (sngHrsWrked - 40) _
      * curPayRate
    Else
      curGrossPay = sngHrsWrked * curPayRate
    End If
  Else
    curGrossPay = curPayRate / 52
  End If
  txtGrossPay.Text = Format(curGrossPay, "Currency")
  curNetPay = curGrossPay - curGrossPay * (0.15 + 0.0745)
  If PayType = "Salaried" Then
    curNetPay = curNetPay - 25
  End If
  txtNetPay.Text = Format(curNetPay, "Currency")
End Sub
```

The cmdPrint button should print the contents of the text boxes to the Debug object with appropriate labels, and the cmdCancel button should clear the text boxes and return control to the Startup form.

FIGURE 12-9.
Calculation of gross
and net pay

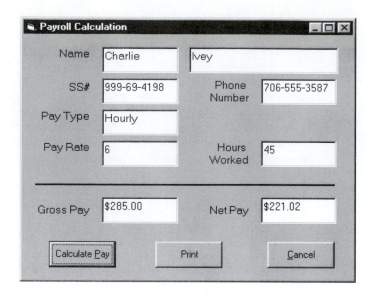

It's Your Turn!

Completing the remaining exercises will enable you to complete the Visual Basic project discussed in the text.

1. Add the code for the ShowEmployee sub procedure shown in VB Code Box 12-11 to the frmEmpInfoSys form. Add the code shown in VB Code Box 12-12 to the cmdInfoEmp_Click event procedure. Add a reference to the ShowEmployee sub procedure to the lstEmployees_DblClick event procedure.

2. Create the form to calculate gross and net pay shown in Figure 12-8, using the control names shown in Table 12-8. Add appropriate labels to the form and give it a caption of **Employee Information** and a name of **frmShowEmp**. Save this form as **ShowEmp.frm** to the Chapter12 folder on your data disk..

TABLE 12-8: Controls for frmShowEmp

Control Name	Control Names
txtFName	txtHrsWrked
txtLName	txtGrossPay
txtPayType	txtNetPay
txtPayRate	cmdCalcPay
txtSSNum	cmdPrint
txtPhone	cmdCancel

3. Add the code shown in VB Code Box 12-13 to the Form_Activate event procedure for the frmShowEmp form.

4. Add the code shown in VB Code Box 12-14 to the cmdCalcPay_Click event procedure.

5. Add appropriate code to the Cancel button to return control to the Startup form. In addition, add necessary code to the Print button to print the contents of the text boxes with appropriate labels.

6. Run your project and enter the names of the employees shown in Table 12-7 on page 521. Select the record for **Charlie Ivey** and enter a value of **45** for the number of hours worked. Calculate the gross and net pay for this employee. The result should look like that shown in Figure 12-9.

7. Change the number of hours worked for this employee to **30** and recalculate the gross and net pay.

8. Click Cancel to clear the text boxes and return to the frmEmpInfoSys form. Select the record for **Kelly McNamara** and calculate her gross and net pay *without* entering a value for the number of hours.

9. Save your project under the same file names.

USING DIRECT ACCESS FILES

While the application we have created does a good job of enabling the user to enter employee data and display them in a list box, it does not save these data between executions of the project. Previously, we have used sequential access files (Chapter 5) and database files (Chapter 9) for this purpose. While we might use a database to save the employee data entered as a part of this project, sequential access files would not be appropriate, for several reasons. Recall that in sequential files, records are stored on the file in the same order that they were written, and they are read back in that same order. This can be cumbersome when the order of processing records on a file differs from the order in which those records are physically stored or when records are being added or deleted during the processing.

Clark has already decided that since his payroll system for Vintage Videos is going to be a prototype, he does not want to go to the trouble of designing a database for it. Fortunately, there is another type of file that combines the flexibility of a database to access records in any order with the ease of access of a sequential access file from Visual Basic: the **direct access file**. These files are record-oriented like a database, but they can be accessed from Visual Basic just like sequential access files without the need to add another control.

Pictorially, a direct access file would appear as shown in Figure 12-10. Note that all records in a direct access file are assumed to have the same fields and to be of the same size. This is why we used fixed-length strings in the declaration of the EmpRecord data type. Direct access files (also known as **random access files**) are so named because the user can access any record on this type of file directly without going through any other records.

The key parameter for a direct access file is the **record number**. This is a positive Integer value that is assigned to the record when it is written onto the file. Once a record is written onto a file with a given record number, it can always be identified for processing. The record number of a direct access file is analogous to the subscript on a one-dimensional array in which each record corresponds to an element in the array. While the order of the records on a direct access file is the same as the order of their

Record Number

	Field 1	Field 2	Field 3	Field 4
1				
2				
3				
4				
5				
6				

record numbers, any record, regardless of its physical position, can be written, read, or rewritten by having the user simply specify its record number.

Given the flexibility and ease of use of the direct access file, we will use it to save the records created in the employee information system to secondary storage. Later, if Clark and the owners of Vintage Videos decide to implement the system across both stores, Clark will probably want to convert to a database system like that used for the video rental transaction system discussed in Chapter 9.

Creating a Direct Access File

Creating a direct access file in Visual Basic is very similar to creating a sequential access file, with one major exception: Instead of using the Print command or the Write command to save data or information to the file, we use the **Put** command. Also, when data or information is being retrieved from a direct access file, we use the **Get** command instead of the Read command.

In either case—adding data to or retrieving data from a direct access file—the file must first be opened, just as was done with sequential access files. The Open statement for a direct access file has the following form:

Open *filename* For Random As *file number* Len = *record length*

where the *Random* parameter denotes the file as a direct access file regardless of whether it is being used for input or for output. The ***Len = record length*** parameter defines the number of bytes required to write a record to disk. The record length must be the same for every record on the file. The Close statement for direct access files is exactly the same as for sequential access files.

> **TIP:** Since the record length should be the same for all records in a random access file, all values in a record should use data types that are of a fixed size. Avoid using the Variant data type, do not use dynamic arrays, and use fixed length strings for character data.

Rather than having to determine the record length manually, we can rely on a Visual Basic function called the **Len( )** function, which returns the number of bytes required to store a variable or record. For example, to open a direct access file to store the employee records created by the employee payroll system discussed earlier, the statement could be:

```
Open "a:\VideoEmp.dat" for Random as #2 Len = Len(udtEmp)
```

where *Len(udtEmp)* is the length of the variable udtEmp, which was declared to be an EmpRecord data type.

Once a direct access file is opened, the next step is to write data on the file. As mentioned earlier, this is accomplished with the Put command, which has the following form:

Put #*file number, record number, variable name*

where the *record number* parameter is optional. If the record number is deleted, the new record is written after the record that was referenced by the last Put or Get statement.

In the employee payroll system, we need to write code for the **File | Save** procedure. This involves writing the udtEmployees( ) array element corresponding to each item in the list box to a file, as shown in VB Code Box 12-15.

VB CODE BOX 12-15. Code to save a direct access file	```Private Sub mnuFileSave_Click() Dim intCounter As Integer, intIndex As Integer Dim udtEmp As EmpRecord, intFileNum As Integer On Error Resume Next intFileNum = FreeFile Kill App.Path & "\VideoEmp.dat" Open App.Path & "\VideoEmp.dat" For Random As _ #intFileNum Len = Len(udtEmp) For intCounter = 0 To lstEmployees.ListCount - 1 intIndex = lstEmployees.ItemData(intCounter) udtEmp = udtEmployees(intIndex) Put #intFileNum, , udtEmp Next Close #intFileNum End Sub```

In the code to save the file, we use the FreeFile function to return an unused file number. We also use a new object and property: **App.Path**. The App object specifies information about the current application—in this case, its path. If a file of any type—sequential, database, or direct access—is in the *same* file folder as the application, we can always reference it using App.Path as the path for the file. This is true whether the file is being referenced within the Visual Basic environment or as an executable file.

Finally, we use the **Kill** statement to delete the existing data file to avoid problems when the number of records being saved to it is less than the number currently in the file. In this situation, if we did not delete the file some of the old records would still be in the file. To avoid having an error message displayed the very first time the file is created, we also add the *On Error Resume Next* statement. This will allow processing to continue even though there is no file to delete with the Kill statement.

Note also that the record number is not referenced in the Put statement, because we are adding the udtEmp variable to the end of the current direct access file immediately after the last record written to the file. If we wanted to specify the record number into which the variable is to be written, we could have done so in the Put statement.

Retrieving Data from a Direct Access File

Once employee records at Vintage Videos have been saved on a direct access file, the next step is to retrieve them in the Form_Load event procedure of the Startup form when the project is restarted at a later date. The records are retrieved with the Get command, the form of which is shown below:

Get #*file number, record number, variable name*

where the parameters are the same as with the Put command and, also as with the Put command, the record number is optional. If we are retrieving records in sequence and the record number parameter is omitted, the next record in order is retrieved.

In our case, the objective is to input the employee records, add them to the udtEmployee( ) array, and display them in the lstEmployees list box. If the number of records on the file is known, a For-Next loop can be used to retrieve them. Fortunately, just as the record length can be determined with the Len function, the total length of the file (in bytes) can be found with the **LOF** (length of file) function. Once this value is known, we can find the number of records on the file by using Integer division to divide the LOF value by the Len value. For example, if the LOF value is 1,000 and the Len value is 100, then there are $1,000\backslash100 = 10$ records on the file. The number of employees, intEmpCntr, is also set equal to this value at the end of the procedure.

Using the number of records on the file, which we found by using the LOF and Len functions, we can input each one, add it to the udtEmployee( ) array, display it in the lstEmployees list box, and set the ItemData property in a For-Next loop. The GetEmployeeList sub procedure to handle this operation is called from the Form_Load event procedure for frmEmpInfoSys. It is shown in VB Code Box 12-16.

To create the complete employee payroll computation project, you will need to refer to the code shown in VB Code Boxes 12-6 through 12-16.

| **VB Code Box 12-16.** Sub procedure GetEmployeeList | <pre>Sub GetEmployeeList()
    Dim udtEmp As EmpRecord, intFileNum As Integer
    Dim strEmpString As String, intMaxFile As Integer
    Dim intCounter as Integer, intIndex as Integer
    intFileNum = FreeFile
    Open App.Path & "\VideoEmp.dat" For Random As _
    #intFileNum Len = Len(udtEmp)
    frmEmpInfoSys.lstEmployees.Clear
    intMaxFile = LOF(intFileNum) \ Len(udtEmp)
    ReDim udtEmployees(intMaxFile) As EmpRecord
    For intCounter = 0 To intMaxFile - 1
        Get #intFileNum, , udtEmployees(Counter)
        frmEmpInfoSys.lstEmployees.AddItem _
            udtEmployees(intCounter).strLName & " " & _
            udtEmployees(intCounter).strFName & " " & _
            udtEmployees(intCounter).strPhone & " " & _
            udtEmployees(intCounter).strPayType
            intIndex = frmEmpInfoSys.lstEmployees.NewIndex
            frmEmpInfoSys.lstEmployees.ItemData(intIndex) _
            = intCounter
    Next
    Close #intFileNum
    intEmpCntr = intMaxFile
End Sub</pre> |

Mini-Summary 12-4: Direct Access Files

1. A direct (or random) access file is a record-oriented file in which records can be accessed and manipulated in any order through their record number.

2. Direct access files are opened with the Open statement, with the record length being defined by the Len() function.

3. The Put statement is used to write records to a direct access file, and the Get statement is used to read records from the file.

4. We can find the number of records in a direct access file by dividing the number of bytes in the files found through the LOF( ) function by the length of one record.

5. The Path property of the App object can be used to define the folder in which the application is located.

It's Your Turn!

1. How does a direct access file differ from a sequential access file? Why is it often also referred to as a random access file?

2. Why do we need the record number and record length parameters when working with a direct access file?

3. What statement is used to write information to a direct access file? Read information from it?

4. Why do we use fixed length strings in the user-defined data type that is being stored in a direct access file?

5. Assume that each of the following statements applies to the same program. Also, assume that the following data type has been declared with a record length of 78 bytes.

```
Public Type Speaker
    strFName as String*15
    strLName as String*25
    strTopic as String*30
    dtmLectureDate as Date
End Type
```

a. Write a statement that opens the file Schedule.rnd for random access. Each record uses the Speaker user defined data type.

b. Write a statement that retrieves the 34th record from the file Schedule.rnd. The values retrieved should be assigned to the variable udtGuest that has been declared as data type Speaker.

c. Write a statement that writes the values stored in the variable udtGuest that has been declared as data type Speaker to the next available location in the file Schedule.rnd.

Completing the remaining exercises will enable you to complete the Visual Basic project discussed in the text.

6. Add the code shown in VB Code Box 12-15 to the mnuFileSave event procedure to save the contents of the udtEmployees( ) array to the direct access file.

7. Add the code shown in VB Code Box 12-16 to the Code window for the frmEmp-InfoSys form to create the GetEmployeeList sub procedure. This sub procedure should be referenced in the Form_Load event procedure.

8. Run your project and add the same names you added earlier (shown in Table 12-7). Click the **File | Save** menu option to save the names to a direct access file named "VideoEmp.dat" in the same folder as the program file. Exit the project and then restart it. These same names should automatically appear in the lstEmployees list box.

9. Save your forms and project under the same name as before.

CREATING OBJECTS IN VISUAL BASIC

As we mentioned in Chapter 1, Visual Basic is an object-oriented, event-driven computer language because it uses objects that respond to events. In that chapter we defined *objects* as identifiable shapes, each of which has certain properties and can respond to a variety of events. In that definition, we were referring to **visual objects**, that is, objects that can be seen on the screen. However, Visual Basic is not restricted to visual objects only; objects that are not displayed on the screen can also be used. Commonly referred to as **application objects**, these are objects that the programmer constructs to improve the efficiency of the project. Like visual objects, application objects have properties and methods that are defined by the programmer. While Visual Basic is not a completely **object oriented language (OOP)**, it can be used to create and work with application objects.

A more general definition of **objects** is that they are *self-contained modules that combine data and program code and that cooperate in the program by passing strictly defined messages to one another.* This methodology is easier to work with, because it is more intuitive than traditional programming methods, which divide programs into hierarchies and separate data from programming code. To understand why objects are extremely valuable programming tools, it is necessary to understand that all programs consist of data that require processing and procedures for processing that data. As long as the data and procedures remain the same, the program will work; however, if either the data or the procedures change, the program may not work. Object-oriented programming transforms programming by binding data and procedures in objects. Users can combine the objects with relative ease to create new systems and extend existing ones. Around us is a world made of objects, so the use of objects to create information systems provides a natural approach to programming.

Object-Oriented Programming Concepts

To work with objects in Visual Basic (or any other computer language), it is necessary to understand some basic concepts. First, in order to create an object, you must first create a **class**, that is, a *template with data and procedures from which objects are created.* One way of looking at a class is to think of it as the *cookie cutter* and the actual object as the resulting *cookie.*[1]

All of the actual work in creating an object is accomplished in creating the class; an object is created by defining it to be an **instance** of a class, with the elements of the object being known as **instance variables**. An example of a visual class is a form that you create; you can use it to create new forms with the same characteristics as the class

---

1. Cornell, Gary, *Visual Basic 5 from the Ground Up* (Berkeley: Osborne/McGraw-Hill, 1997), p. 376.

form. Similarly, the controls in the toolbox are classes from which you can create instances on a form. However, you cannot use these instances to create similar objects.

Two other object-oriented programming concepts with which you should be familiar are encapsulation and inheritance. **Encapsulation** refers to a key concept: It should never be possible to work with instance variables directly; they must be addressed through the object's properties and methods. This implies a *black-box* view of an object, in which the programmer does not need to know what is going on inside the object, but only needs to know how to work with the object's methods and properties. For example, for the last eight chapters you have been using text boxes without knowing exactly how the SetFocus method moves the cursor to a text box; you just know that it does.

The second key concept in object-oriented programming, **inheritance**, refers to the capability to create classes that descend from other classes—so-called *subclasses*. This capability makes it easier to build a new class by having it inherit properties and methods from another class. However, since Visual Basic does not support inheritance, we will not consider this concept any further.

Creating a Class

As an example of creating application objects, we will use the same payroll prototype project discussed earlier in the chapter. Recall that the form used to compute the gross and net pay involved a command button that checked the pay type and then computed the gross and net pay based on the pay rate and hours worked. Since this is a fairly common situation, it seems like a good one for which to create objects to handle these operations—say, a ComputePay object with properties equal to the data on the employee and methods equal to the gross and net pay computation. That way, this object can be used in many other situations, just as text boxes are used in many different projects.

To create a class from which the ComputePay object can be generated, we must use a new type of module: the **Class module**. Class modules are similar to Code modules in that they are both pure code with no visual objects. However, the code in a Class module can only be used to create the properties and methods for a class; it cannot be used to write general-purpose sub procedures and functions. Like Code modules, Class modules must be saved—but with a **.cls** extension.

Creating a Class module involves a six-step process to develop the procedures and functions that carry out the operations for an object derived from this class. These six steps are:

1. Add the Class module to the project.
2. Declare local variables to be used in the module.
3. Initialize the Class properties of the object.
4. Write the statements necessary to enable the class to have values assigned to its properties or to assign its properties to variables outside of the object.
5. Write the functions that will create methods that will carry out processing within the class.
6. Save the module as a .cls file.

Notice how steps 2 through 5 provide encapsulation for application objects within Visual Basic. Step 2 sets up *local* variables that will not be accessible from outside the class. Step 3 provides initial values for Object properties, while step 4 provides a way for the object's properties to be changed or used without the properties directly interacting with the project. Finally, step 5 creates the functions that will carry out processing within the object without being exposed to the outside world of the project. Once the class has been created, you can declare any number of objects to be of that class. All of these objects will share the same properties and methods created in the class.

We will provide a brief discussion of the first four steps and then spend more time on using the Class Builder wizard to set up a Class module that will handle the gross and net pay calculations for the employee.

Adding the Class module

You add Class modules to the project using the **Project|Add Class Module** main menu option, just like you add Code modules or new forms. Doing so will display a screen like that shown in Figure 12-11, from which you can click on the Class Module icon to add a new Class module manually or click on the VB Class Builder icon to use this wizard to help you with the process. We will discuss using the Class Builder approach later. Like any form or module, the class should be given a name. In our case, we are adding a class named **EmployeeClass**.

FIGURE 12-11. Add Class Module window

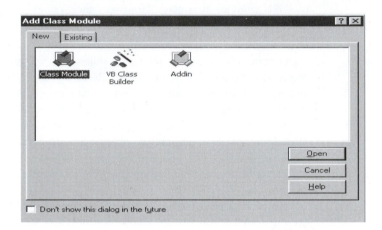

Declaring local variables

Since we want to encapsulate objects derived from the EmployeeClass module, all variables used in the class should be declared as local variables with the *Private* keyword. We need a local variable for each and every property of the class, because these variables will store the values assigned to the properties. In our case, since the properties of the class represent the same values as the elements of the EmpRecord data types—that is, first name, last name, Social Security number, pay type, phone number, and pay rate—we need to declare local variables for each of these. For example, for the First-Name property of this class, we will assign a variable **mvarFirstName**. (We show an *mvar* prefix with each variable because the Class Builder wizard does this.) These variables are declared in the Declarations section of the General object of the Class module that we are creating. The declarations for this example are shown in VB Code Box 12-17. We have also declared a local variable, *curTemp*, which we will use in the NetPay method for this class.

VB CODE BOX 12-17. Declaring local variables for the Class module	```Private mvarFirstName As String Private mvarLastName As String Private mvarSSNumber As String Private mvarPayType As String Private mvarPhone As String Private mvarPayRate As Currency Private curTemp As Currency```

Initializing properties

Just as visual objects like the text box have default properties, such as Text1 for the Text property, so also do application objects have default properties. The only difference is that because we are creating the class from which the object is derived, we must set the default properties in the Class_Initialize sub procedure by assigning values to the corresponding local variable. In our case, we want to initialize the Social Security number to "000-00-0000," which must be replaced. Similarly, the default employee type should be Hourly and the default pay rate should be $6.00. No other default values should be set. The code to set up the Class_Initialize sub procedure is shown in VB Code Box 12-18.

VB CODE BOX 12-18. Class_Initialize event procedure	```Private Sub Class_Initialize()```
	 ``` mvarSSNumber = "000-00-0000"```
	 ``` mvarPayType = "Hourly"```
	 ``` mvarPayRate = 6.00```
	 ```End Sub```

Creating Properties for the Class

Once the Class module has been added and named and the local variables have been declared and, if necessary, initialized, the next step is to set up the properties for the class. Setting up the properties is a two-way street; it must be possible to assign values to these properties from the outside and to determine from the outside what the current values of a property are. Just as we can change the Text property of a text box or use the current Text property in our code, we should be able to do the same thing with an application object. Working with properties is accomplished with two types of statements: Property Let and Property Get.

> **TIP:** Creating a property by using a Property procedure pair (for example Get/Let) allows for error checking, and ensures that the value passed is valid.

We can change the properties of application objects by setting up Property Let statements in the Class module. A **Property Let** statement assigns a value to a property in a special type of sub procedure. The form of this special type of sub procedure is shown below:

> **Public Property Let** *propertyName***(ByVal** *OutsideVar* **as** *type*)
>   *mvarLocalVariable = OutsideVar*
> **End Property**

In this special sub procedure, the value being assigned to the property is passed in through the OutsideVar in the Property Let statement and then assigned to the local variable associated with this property. Notice that the ByVal keyword is used to insure that the direction of flow is strictly *into* the sub procedure. The OutsideVar variable is usually a dummy variable through which the value flows to the local variable; its name has no significance.

For example, to assign a value to the FirstName property of the EmployeeClass module, the Property Let statement would be:

```
Public Property Let FirstName(ByVal vData as string)
   mvarFirstName = vData
End Property
```

where *vData* is the outside variable through which the first name will pass.

If the object ComputePay is declared to be of the class EmployeeClass, then this Property Let statement will allow us to assign a value to the FirstName property with a statement like that shown below:

```
ComputePay.FirstName = "Chris"
```

To allow the "outside world" to work with the properties of an object, we need to use the Property Get statement in the definition of the Class module. The **Property Get** statement assigns the value of the local variable to the property through a special type of function that has the following form:

>**Public Property Get** *propertyName()*
>   *propertyName = mvarLocalVariable*
>**End Property**

Note that this is indeed a function, since a value is assigned to the property name within the function.

TIP: The default scope for a property is Public.

For example, to determine the value of the FirstName property of the Employee-Class module, the Property Get statement would be:

```
Public Property Get FirstName()
    FirstName = mvarFirstName
End Property
```

If the object ComputePay is declared to be of the class EmployeeClass, then this Property Get statement will allow us to assign the FirstName property to a variable anywhere in the project using a statement like that shown below (where strEmployeeFirstName has been declared as a string):

```
strEmployeeFirstName = ComputePay.FirstName
```

Mini-Summary 12-5: Object-Oriented Programming

1. Object-oriented programming is an efficient way to write computer programs that are easily combined and reused.

2. Objects are self-contained modules that combine data and program code that cooperate in the program by passing strictly defined messages to one another. Application objects are like visual objects in that they have properties and methods.

3. Key concepts in object-oriented programming are classes, encapsulation, and inheritance. A class is a template with data and procedures from which objects are created. Classes are created first, and then objects are created from the classes. Class modules are saved as .cls files.

4. Properties are created in Visual Basic via the Property Let and Property Get statements. Methods are created by writing functions that carry out needed processing.

It's Your Turn!

1. Why is object-orient programming becoming a popular way to build applications?

2. What is the difference between an object and a class?

3. Which of the capabilities of object-oriented programming does Visual Basic not support?

4. What are the six steps to creating a Class module?

5. Define the following terms: object, class, instance, encapsulation, inheritance.

6. What do the Property Let and Property Get statements have to do with encapsulation?

USING THE CLASS BUILDER WIZARD

To work with the properties of an object, we must create Property Let and Property Get statements for each and every property. We must also, create the functions for the methods. Since this can become quite tedious, we will use the Class Builder wizard to take much of the work out of the process of creating a Class module operation. To start the Class Builder wizard, you simply click on the VB Class Builder icon instead of the Class Module icon when you select the Project | Add Class Module. When you click on the VB Class Builder icon, the **Class Builder** window is displayed. The top portion of this window is shown in Figure 12-12.

FIGURE 12-12.
Class Builder window

Note that this window has two panes. The left-hand pane shows all of the existing Class modules in the project; clicking on an existing Class module enables it to be edited. The right-hand pane shows the properties and methods in the selected Class module.

You may also create a new Class module from within the Class Builder window. Selecting the **File | New | Class** menu option or clicking on the far left-hand icon will create a new class, which is given a name in the **Class Module Builder** window. This top portion of this window, with the name **EmployeeClass** entered, is shown in Figure 12-13. Once you have named the new class, it will appear in the left-hand pane of the Class Builder window and you can start adding properties to it.

FIGURE 12-13.
Class Module Builder window

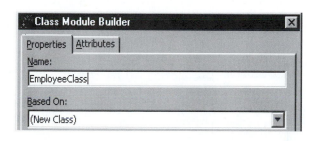

Adding Class Properties

New Property Icon

Regardless of how a Class module is added, the next step is to add properties to it. To add a property to a class, you click on the new class in the Class Builder window and then either select **File | New | Property** or click on the Add New Property icon in the Class Builder toolbar. Doing this displays the **Property Builder** window, as shown in Figure 12-14.

FIGURE 12-14.
Property Builder
window

Entering a name for the property, setting the data type, and clicking Ok will declare the appropriate local variables and generate the Let and Get statements for this property. For the example shown in the figure, the resulting code is shown in VB Code Box 12-19.

VB CODE BOX 12-19. Result of using Property Builder window to create one property	```Private mvarFirstName As String 'local copy```

	```Public Property Let FirstName(ByVal vData As String)```
	``` mvarFirstName = vData```
	```End Property```

	```Public Property Get FirstName() As String```
	``` FirstName = mvarFirstName```
	```End Property```

If this same operation is carried out for all six of the properties (FirstName, LastName, SSNumber, PhoneNum, and EmpType as String and PayRate as Currency), all of the associated local variables will be declared and the necessary Let and Get statements will be created. In addition, the property names and types will be added to the Class Builder window in alphabetical order, as seen in Figure 12-15. The Class Builder creates the shell for the Class_Initialize sub procedure, but actual initialization code must be added by the programmer.

FIGURE 12-15.
Properties in Class
Builder window

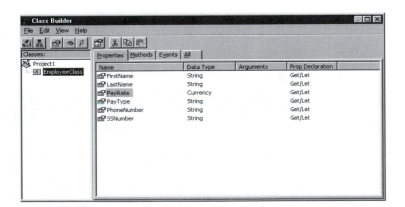

Creating Class Methods

After creating all of the properties for the Class module, our next step is to create the methods for the class. In our scenario, we need to create two methods for this class: the GrossPay method and the NetPay method. The GrossPay method will compute the gross pay for the employee based on the Class properties and the hours worked, and the NetPay method will compute the net pay for the employee based on the Pay-Type property and the result of the GrossPay method.

The VB Class Builder wizard can also help in creating Class methods by creating the *first* and *last* lines of the functions corresponding to the methods. Unlike the properties, the functions require that you add the logic in order to implement them. To create a Class method, you should first select the Class module in the Class Builder window that you created earlier and then, instead of clicking the Add New Property icon, click the Add New Method icon. Doing this displays the **Method Builder window**.

New Method Icon

Since Class methods are functions, we need to define the type of the function and any arguments that are passed to it. The type of the function can be selected from the drop-down list box at the bottom of the Method Builder window. We can add arguments to the function by clicking on the plus (+) sign at the right of the window and filling out the necessary information in the **Add Argument** window that is displayed. Figure 12-16 shows the Method Builder window and the Add Argument window after the method name (**GrossPay**) has been entered and the plus sign has been clicked to add the **HoursWorked** argument.

FIGURE 12-16.
Method Builder window

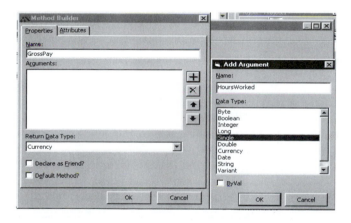

Clicking Ok in the Add Argument window will add this argument to the function in the Method Builder window, and clicking Ok in the Method Builder window will add the method to the right-hand pane of the Class Builder. This same procedure should be carried out for the NetPay method. If the All tab in this pane is clicked, the properties and methods are displayed simultaneously.

As mentioned earlier, when a method is added to the Class module, only the first and last statements of the corresponding function are added to the Code window and you must add the logic necessary to implement the method. The logic for the Gross-Pay and NetPay methods is the same as the logic used earlier in the cmdCalcPay button on the frmShowEmp window (VB Code Box 12-14). The GrossPay function is shown in VB Code Box 12-20.

Note that the mvarPayType and mvarPayRate local variables defined by the Class Builder wizard are used here, along with the sngHoursWorked variable that is passed

VBCODEBOX12-20. GrossPay function in Class module	```Public Function GrossPay(sngHoursWorked As Single) As Currency If mvarPayType = "Hourly" Then If sngHoursWorked <= 40 Then GrossPay = mvarPayRate * sngHoursWorked Else GrossPay = (mvarPayRate * 40) + _ (mvarPayRate * 1.5 * (sngHoursWorked - 40)) End If Else GrossPay = CCur(mvarPayRate) / 52 End If curTemp = GrossPay End Function```

to the function to compute the gross pay. The resulting gross pay value is saved to the *curTemp* local variable for use in the NetPay function shown in VB Code Box 12-21.

VB CODE BOX 12-21. NetPay function in Class module	```Public Function NetPay() As Currency NetPay = curTemp - (0.15 + 0.0745) * Temp If mvarPayType = "Salaried" Then NetPay = NetPay - 25 End If End Function```

Mini-Summary 12-6: Using the Class Builder Wizard

1. The Class Builder wizard enables the programmer to build classes quickly and easily by adding properties and methods.

2. The Property Builder is used to add properties to the class. It declares the necessary local variables and adds the Let and Get statements to create the properties.

3. The Method Builder creates the first and last statements of the functions needed to create methods, including any arguments passed to the functions.

4. The Class Builder creates the first and last statements for the Class_Initialize procedure.

It's Your Turn!

1. Why do we use functions to create the methods of a class?

2. How does the Class Builder wizard help us create classes? Could we do this without the wizard?

Completing the remaining exercises will enable you to complete the Visual Basic project discussed in the text.

3. Select **Project|Add Class Module** and then click on the VB Class Builder icon to start the wizard.

4. Click on the **New Class** icon (or select **File|New|Class** from the menu) and change the name to **EmployeeClass**.

5. Click on **EmployeeClass** in the left-hand pane of the Class Builder window and then click on the **Add New Property** icon to create a new property in this class. Give it a name of **FirstName** with a data type of **String**. Select **File | Update Project** and the Code window for the EmployeeClass Class module should look like VB Code Box 12-19 (where we have not shown comments added by the Class Builder wizard.)

6. Use the same approach to add the properties shown in Table 12-9. The appropriate variable declaration and Let and Get statements should be added to the Code window by the Class Builder wizard. Once you exit the Class Builder wizard, you will see them in the code window.

Table 12-9: Properties Added to EmployeeClass

Property	Data Type
LastName	String
SSNumber	String
PhoneNum	String
PayType	String
PayRate	Currency

7. Click on **EmployeeClass** and then click on the **Add New Method** icon to create a new method. Give it a name of **GrossPay** with a data type of **Currency**. Click on the plus sign to add an argument named **HoursWorked**, which is a **Single** data type. The first and last statements of the corresponding function are added to the Code window.

8. Repeat Exercise 5, but give the method a name of **NetPay** and a data type of **Currency**. There are no arguments for this function. The first and last statements of the corresponding function are added to the Code window.

9. Close the Class Builder wizard and open the Code window for the EmployeeClass Class module. Declare the **curTemp** variable as **Currency** in the general declarations. Add the code shown in VB Code Box 12-20 to the GrossPay function and add the code shown in VB Code Box 12-21 to the NetPay function.

10. Add the code shown in VB Code Box 12-18 to the **Class_Initialize** event procedure.

11. Save the Class module under the same name, but rename the project **ObjEmpInfosys.vbp**.

DECLARING AND USING OBJECTS

Once a class is created, the next steps are to declare an application object to be of this class and to then to use that object. Objects are declared at the module or form level, just like variables, with one major difference: The **New** keyword is used to denote this as a new object from a class rather than as a variable declaration. The general form of this Declaration statement is:

Dim *objectname* As New *classname*

For example, to declare an object called **objShowingEmp** to be of the class EmployeeClass, the statement would be:

```
Dim objShowingEmp As New EmployeeClass
```

where the variable name of *obj* is used to define an object. In our case, this Declaration statement should be included at the form level of the frmShowEmp form, where the gross pay and net pay are calculated.

Once an application object has been declared, its properties are used in much the same way as those of visual objects. That is, properties are assigned values and variables are assigned Object properties. Also, an application's object methods are used to process data and return values, in a similar manner to that used by visual objects. In our case, the Object properties will hold the information about the current employee, and the methods will be used to calculate gross and net pay in the frmShowEmp form, replacing the existing calculations with much simpler code.

Using ShowingEmp Object Properties

To demonstrate the use of objects in the frmShowEmp form, we will add another command button to the existing Calculate, Print, and Cancel buttons. This button will display the objShowingEmp Object properties. While this change is not necessary, it will allow you to see the use of the default Object properties created in the Class_ Initialize event procedure by making the Text properties of the form's text boxes equal to the Object properties in a sub procedure named *ShowProperties*. This sub procedure is called in the Form_Activate event procedure to display the default objShowingEmp object properties when the form is loaded. The declaration of the object, the Show-Properties sub procedure, and the Form_Activate event procedure are shown in VB Code Box 12-22.

| **VB CODE BOX 12-22.** Code to use object properties | ```
Option Explicit
Dim objShowingEmp As New EmployeeClass
Private Sub Form_Activate()
    ShowProperties
End Sub
Sub ShowProperties()
    With objShowingEmp
      txtFname.Text = .strFirstName
      txtLname.Text = .strLastName
      txtSSnum.Text = .strSSNumber
      txtPhone.Text = .strPhoneNum
      txtPayType.Text = .strPayType
      txtPayRate.Text = Str(.curPayRate)
    End With
End Sub
``` |
|---|---|

The first time the frmShowEmp form is loaded, several things happen: The objShowingEmp object is defined, the Class_Initialize event procedure is executed, and the form is displayed with the default properties as shown in Figure 12-17.

To modify the objShowingEmp object properties to match those of the employee selected from the lstEmployees list box and to display them on the frmShowEmp form, we use the Display button. The code for this button is shown in VB Code Box 12-23, where we have used the ShowProperties sub procedure to display the current Object properties.

Using Object Methods

Once the Object properties have been set, the next step is to use the Object methods to compute the gross and net pay when the Calculate button is clicked. Since all of the hard work has been done in defining the Class module, this computation involves only
```

FIGURE 12-17.
Default Object
properties

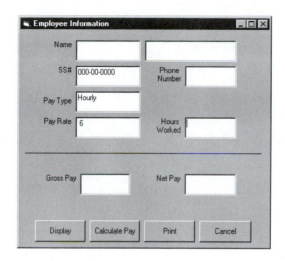

| **VB CODE BOX 12-23.** Code to display object properties | ```
Private Sub cmdDisplay_Click()
    With objShowingEmp
        .strFirstName = udtEmployees(intCurrEmp).strFName
        .strLastName = udtEmployees(intCurrEmp).strLName
        .strSSNumber = udtEmployees(intCurrEmp).strSSNum
        .strPhoneNum = udtEmployees(intCurrEmp).strPhone
        .strPayType = Trim(udtEmployees(intCurrEmp).strPayType)
        .curPayRate = udtEmployees(intCurrEmp).curPayRate
    End With
        ShowProperties
        txtHrsWrked.Text = "0"
End Sub
``` |
|---|---|

two lines of code that compute the gross pay and net pay and assign them to the appropriate text boxes. The code for the Calculate button is shown in VB Code Box 12-24.

| **VB CODE BOX 12-24.** Code for cmdCalcPay command button | ```
Private Sub cmdCalcPay_Click()
    Dim sngHoursWorked as Single
    sngHoursWorked = CSng(txtHrsWrked.Text)
    txtGrossPay.Text =Format(objShowingEmp.curGrossPay( _
    sngHoursWorked),"currency")
    txtNetPay.Text = Format(objShowingEmp.curNetPay,"Currency")
End Sub
``` |
|---|---|

Note that the contents of the txtHrsWrked text box are passed to the GrossPay method, but that nothing is passed to the NetPay method. If the project is run and the same employee is selected as before, the result of clicking the Display button, entering 45 as the number of hours worked, and clicking the Calculate button is shown in Figure 12-18. Note the results are exactly the same as shown before in Figure 12-9 for this same employee.

The only item left is the Cancel button, in which we set the contents of the objShowingEmp object back to their default values in preparation for displaying the next employee, show the frmEmpInfoSys form, and unload the current form. The code for this purpose is shown in VB Code Box 12-25.

FIGURE 12-18.
Result of
calculating pay

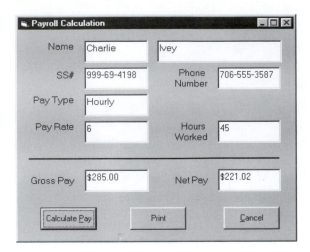

| VB CODE BOX 12-25. Code for cmdCancel button | ```
Private Sub cmdCancel_Click()
   With objShowingEmp
      .strFirstName = ""
      .strLastName = ""
      .strSSNumber = "000-00-0000"
      .strPhoneNum = ""
      .strPayType = "Hourly"
      .curPayRate = 6
   End With
   frmEmpInfoSys.Show
   Unload Me
End Sub
``` |
|---|---|

Final Remarks on Objects

While we have given only a brief introduction to objects, we hope it has shown the power of this approach to programming, especially in the area of reusability. For example, the Class module EmployeeClass can be used to create multiple versions of the same type of object in other parts of this current project. On a more global scale, the EmployeeClass.cls file can be transferred to other projects and can be used to create payroll objects there the same as it does here.

Mini-Summary 12-7: Declaring and Using Objects

1. Objects are declared at the form level or project level with the Dim...As New... statement.

2. Once declared, an application object's properties and methods can be used just like those of a visual object

---

It's Your Turn!

1. What statement is used to declare an object? What must always be the last element in this statement?

2. What is the difference between a visual object and an application object? Do they have any similarities?
```

3. How are an application object's properties and methods used?

Completing the remaining exercises will enable you to complete the Visual Basic project discussed in the text.

4. Add a new button named **cmdDisplay** to the frmShowEmp form and give it a caption of **Display**.

5. Open the Code window for the frmShowEmp form and delete all existing code.

6. Insert the first section of code from VB Code Box 12-22 in the Declarations section of the general procedure to declare ShowingEmp as a new form-level object of the EmployeeClass class.

7. Insert the bottom two sections of code from VB Code Box 12-22 to create the ShowProperties sub procedure and the Form_Activate( ) event procedure.

8. Add the code shown in VB Code Box 12-23 to the cmdDisplay_Click( ) event procedure.

9. Add the code shown in VB Code Box 12-24 to the cmdCalcPay_Click( ) event procedure.

10. Add the code shown in VB Code Box 12-25 to the cmdCancel_Click( ) event procedure.

11. Run your project and select **Charlie Ivey** as the employee for whom to calculate gross and net pay. The frmShowEmp form should initially appear like that shown in Figure 12-17. Click the Display button to view the properties for this employee. Enter **45** as the number of hours worked and click the Calculate Pay button to see the gross and net pay for the employee. It should be the same as shown in Figure 12-18. Finally, click the Cancel button to return to the frmEmpInfoSys form.

12. Save the frmShowEmp form as **objShowEmp.frm**. Save all other forms and modules under their current names. Save the project under its current name.

SUMMARY

By using a user-defined data type, it is possible for an array to store multiple data types. The Type statement is used to create a user-defined data type, which is composed of standard data types or previously defined data types. User-defined data types are usually defined in a Code module so that they will be known to all modules of the project. The With statement enables the programmer to work with multiple elements of a single object. It is possible to create an array composed of a user-defined data type, and arrays can be defined as an element of a user-defined data type.

Dynamic arrays are arrays for which a maximum subscript does not need to be defined until it is needed. The ReDim statement is used to define the size of the array when it is known. The ReDim Preserve statement is used to redimension a dynamic array while preserving the existing contents of the array.

The ItemData property of a list box can be used to store information about the item in the list box, including a pointer to an array subscript. This property can be used to link a list box and an array while still allowing the list box to be sorted. The Item-Data property can be defined using the NewIndex property of the list box. The array elements corresponding to items deleted from a list box are not physically deleted, but their array subscript does not appear as an ItemData property.

A direct (or random) access file is a record-oriented file in which records can be accessed and manipulated in any order through their record number. Direct access files are opened with the Open statement, with the Random parameter and the record length parameter being set equal to the Len( ) function. The Put statement is used to write records to a direct access file, and the Get statement is used to read records from the file.

Object-oriented programming is an efficient way to write computer programs that are easily combined and reused. *Objects* are self-contained modules that combine data and program code that cooperate in the program by passing strictly defined messages to one another. Application objects are like visual objects in that they have properties and methods. Key concepts in object-oriented programming are classes, encapsulation, and inheritance. A class is a template with data and procedures from which objects are created. Classes are created first, and then objects are created from the classes. Properties are created in Visual Basic via the Let and Get statements. Methods are created by the programmer writing functions that carry out needed processing.

The six steps to create a class are as follows:

1. Add the Class module to the project.
2. Declare local variables to be used in the module.
3. Initialize the Class properties of the object.
4. Write the statements necessary to enable the class to have values assigned to its properties or to assign its properties to variables out side of the object.
5. Write the functions that will create methods that will carry out processing within the class.
6. Save the Class module with a .cls extension.

The Class Builder wizard enables the programmer to build classes quickly and easily by adding properties and methods. The Property Builder, which is used to add properties to the class, declares the necessary local variables and adds the Let and Get statements to create the properties. The Method Builder creates the first and last statements of the functions needed to create methods, including any arguments that are to be passed to the functions. The Class Builder does not add the Class_Initialize procedure or the logic for the method functions.

Objects are declared at the form level or project level with the Dim ... As New ... statement. Once declared, an application object's properties and methods can be used just like those of a visual object.

New Visual Basic Elements

Control/Object	Properties	Methods	Events
list box control	ItemData(index) NewIndex		
App object	Path		

New Programming Statements

Statements to define a user-defined data type
Public Type typename
  elementName1 as type
  elementName2 as type
End Type

With statement **With**   statements **End With**
Statement to declare an array of a user-defined data type **Dim** arrayName(Max Index) as data type
Statement to declare a dynamic array **Dim** arrayName( ) as data type
Statement to declare size of a dynamic array **ReDim** arrayName(max index) as type
Statement to declare size of dynamic array while preserving existing elements **Redim Preserve** arrayName(max index) as type
Statement to open a direct access file **Open** filename **for Random As** file number **Len =** record length
Statement to write data on a random access file **Put #**file number, record number, variable name
Statement to input data from a random access file **Get #**file number, record number, variable name
Statements to create a property of an object class **Public Property Let** propertyName (**ByVal** Outside variable as type)   mvarLocalVariable = Outside Variable **End Property**
Statements to assign property of an object class to outside variable **Public Property Get** propertyName ( )   propertyName = mvarLocalVariable **End Property**
Statement to declare an object of a certain class **Dim** objectName **As New** classname

Key Terms

application object	encapsulation	pointer
class	fixed length string	proportional font
class module	inheritance	random access file
direct access file	monospace font	record number
dot notation	object	user-defined data type
dynamic array	object-oriented programming (OOP)	visual object

EXERCISES

1. Assume that each of the following are for the same Visual Basic program:

a. Write the statements to create a data type called Player with five attributes: name (a string with 30 characters), weight (an integer), height (a single), points per game (a single), and rebounds per game (a single).

b. Write the statements to declare a variable, TheBest, to be an instance of the type Player and use a With statement to assign the following values to TheBest: Name: M. Jordan; Weight: 200; Height: 76; Points per game: 30.5; Rebounds per game: 2.5.

c. Write the statements to define a dynamic array called NCAA82 to be of type Player and assign the first element of this array to be equal to TheBest.

d. Write the statements to input other values to the NCAA82 array from a dynamic access file.

2. Describe the object class Word.cls that is created with the following code. What are its properties and methods?

```
Option Explicit
Private mvarText As String
Private mvarSize As Integer
Private mvarNumVowels As Integer
Private mvarNumConsonants As Integer
Private Sub Class_Initialize()
    mvarText = ""
    mvarSize = 0
    mvarNumVowels = 0
    mvarNumConsonants = 0
End Sub
Public Property Let Text(ByVal vWord As String)
    mvarText = vWord
End Property
Public Property Get Text() As String
    Text = mvarText
End Property
Public Property Get Size() As Integer
    mvarSize = Len(mvarText)
    Size = mvarSize
End Property
Public Property Get NumVowels() As Integer
    Dim intI As Integer
    Dim strW As String
    mvarNumVowels = 0
    If mvarSize > 0 Then
        strW = mvarText
        For intI = 1 To mvarSize
            Select Case UCase(Left(strW, 1))
            Case "A", "E", "I", "O", "U"
                mvarNumVowels = mvarNumVowels + 1
            End Select
            strW = Right(strW, Len(strW) - 1)
        Next intI
    End If
    NumVowels = mvarNumVowels
```

```
End Property
Public Property Get NumConsonants() As Integer
    mvarNumConsonants = mvarSize - mvarNumVowels
    NumConsonants = mvarNumConsonants
End Property
Public Function Upper() As String
    Upper = UCase(mvarText)
End Function
```

3. For each of the following, explain what is wrong with the code. What error messages would you see, if any? What can you do to correct the code?

   a. The following should declare a user defined data type:
```
Public DataType as Type
   strCompanyName as String
   intCompanyEmp as Integer
   CurCompanyRev() as Currency
End With
```

   b. The following code should allow the outside world to work with a Boolean property called ProperNoun for object class Word.cls of exercise 2.
```
Public Property Get ProperNoun()
    If Left(mvarText, 1) = UCase(Left(mvarText, 1)) Then
        mvarProperNoun = True
    Else
        mvarProperNoun = False
    End If
End Property
```

4. Use the Visual Basic Help facility or the MSDN on-line library to answer the following questions.

   a. When is it possible to open a file using a different file number without first closing the file?

   b. What is the maximum size allowed for a fixed length string?

   c. Can you define properties for a class without using the Property Get and Let statements?

   d. What is polymorphism and what does it allow you to do?

PROJECTS

1. Assume that a list of student names, ID numbers, and quiz averages is stored in a direct access file called *Students.dat*. You may download the Students.dat file from the Chapter 12 section of the text web site and save it to the root folder of your data disk. The fields are shown in Table 12-10, where the LetterGrade field is initially blank.

TABLE 12-10: Fields for Students.dat

Field
StudentName (last name first form)
StudentID

TABLE 12-10: Fields for Students.dat (Continued)

Field
QuizAverage
LetterGrade

Create a project to access this direct access file and to process the data. Your project should use a multiple forms and programmer defined types to carry out the following operations:

a. Display the list of students in a list box sorted on the name field. Double-clicking a student name or highlighting it and clicking a command button should display information on each student in text boxes with appropriate labels on a second form.

b. On the second form, the professor should be able to implement a 90-80-70-60 scale to determine the letter grade for the current student and add the grade to the Letter Grade field for that student.

c. The professor should be able add, delete, or edit student records as necessary, and save the result of this action. It should also be possible to print the list of students.

d. Save this project as **Ex12-1.vbp, Ex12-1.bas, Ex12-1List.frm, Ex12-1Add.frm** and **Ex12-1Details.frm** to the Chapter12 folder on your disk.

2. Assume that customer information in the form of names, telephone numbers, and sales amounts is stored in a direct access file called *CustSales.dat*. You may download the CustSales.dat file from the Chapter 12 section of the text web site and save it to the root folder of your data disk. The fields are shown in Table 12-11, where the Sale Category field is initially blank.

TABLE 12-11: Fields and Field Names for CustSales.dat

Field
CustomerName (in last name first form)
PhoneNumber
SalesAmount
SalesCategory

Create a project to access this direct access file and to process the data. Your project should use multiple forms and programmer defined data types to carry out the following operations:

a. Display the list of customers in a list box sorted on the name field. Double-clicking a student name or highlighting it and clicking a command button should display information on each student in text boxes with appropriate labels on a second form.

b. Display on the second form information on each customer in text boxes with appropriate labels.

c. Enable the user to use the scale shown in Table 12-12 to determine the Sales Category for a single customer and add it in the Category field for that customer.

TABLE 12-12: Sales Amounts and Categories

Sales Amount	Category
$1,000 or less	Light
$1,001 to $5,000	Average
Greater than $5,000	Heavy

d. Add, delete, or edit customer records as necessary, and save the result of this action. It should also be possible to print the list of customers or the results of the computation.

e. Save this project as **Ex12-2.vbp, Ex12-2.bas, Ex12-2List.frm, Ex12-2Add.frm,** and **Ex12-2Details.frm** to the Chapter12 folder on your disk.

3. Assume that a direct access file *RealEstate.dat* exists with the name, Social Security number, a withholding percentage, year-to-date sales, and year-to-date withholding for real estate agents at the Champions Real Estate agency. You may download this file from the Chapter 12 section of the text web site. The withholding percentage is the percentage of each transaction that the salesperson wants withheld for income tax purposes. When a transaction occurs, the salesperson is paid on the type of transaction—that is listing, sale, or both, and the percent to be withheld. If the transaction involved a listing by the agent, he or she receives 1.5 percent of the sales amount; if the transaction was a sale by the agent, they receive 2 percent of the sales amount. Finally, if the agent both listed and sold the property, they receive 4 percent of the sales amount (1.5 percent for listing, 2 percent for selling, and 0.5 percent as a bonus for doing both.)

For example, assume that Howard Ellis has specified that 20 percent of any amount coming to him is to be withheld. If Howard both lists and sells a property for $100,000, then his gross amount due is $100,000 x 0.04 = $4,000. His net amount due is then $4,000 x (1 - 0.20) = $3,200.

a. Your program should allow the managing partner for the firm to click on a name whenever a sale occurs and display the name, Social Security number, and withholding percentage on a second form. He or she should then be able to determine the gross and net amounts due the agent and print this information with appropriate labels.

b. At the same time, the year-to-date sales and withholding fields should be updated based on the latest sale and the file saved to disk.

c. The manager should be able add data on new agents, delete agents that have left the firm, print a list of agents, and edit information on agents whenever they change their withholding percentage.

d. Save your project as **EX12-3.vbp, EX12-3.bas, EX12-3List.frm, Ex12-3Add.frm** and **EX12-3Compute.frm** in the Chapter12 folder.

4. Universal Widgets sells to a variety of specialized products to a small group of rather large customers each of which has negotiated its own discount arrangement with Universal. For example, Sears receives a 12 percent discount while WalMart receives a 13

percent discount. Assume that the names of the customers, corresponding discount rates, and year-to-date gross and net sales values are stored on a direct access file named *Universal.dat*. You may download this file from the Chapter 12 section of the text web site.

a. Your program should display the customer names in sorted order. The sales manager for Universal should be able to click on the name of a customer to transfer it and the discount rate to a second form where he or she can enter the number of units to be sold and their price. They should then be able to compute the gross amount due, the discount due the retailer, and the net amount due to Universal. He or she should be able to print this information with appropriate labels.

b. At the same time that the information is being printed, the year-to-date gross and net sales values for this customer should be updated base do this transaction and the file saved to disk.

c. The sales manager should be able add data on new customers, delete customers when necessary, print a list of customers, and edit information on customers whenever the negotiated discount rate changes.

d. Save your project as **EX12-4.vbp, EX12-4.bas, EX12-4List.frm**, and **EX12-4Compute.frm** in the Chapter12 folder on your data disk.

5. Assume that Bulldog Computers has a variety of computer combinations which they sell to both businesses and individuals. A combination typically includes everything the user will need to start work—CPU, hard, floppy, and CD-ROM drives, monitor, modem, printer, associated cables, and personal productivity software. The price of each combination depends on the speed of the CPU, the size of the hard drive, the quality of the printer, the size of the monitor, and the speed of the modem. Assume that the information of these computer combinations is stored on a direct access file named *BulldogCombos.dat*. Also, assume that the total number of each combination sold to date are stored on this file. You may download this file from the Chapter 12 section of the text web site. This information includes the SKU number, the name given it by Bulldog, the price of the combination, and the number sold.

a. Your program should allow a Bulldog salesperson to click on the name of a combination and display the name, SKU number, and price on a second form. They should then be able to input the number of units sold and applicable tax rate to determine the gross price and price including taxes on the purchase. They should be able to print this information with appropriate labels.

b. At the same time as this information is being printed, the number of units of this combination should be updated on the file and the file saved to disk.

c. A sales manager should be able add data on new combinations, delete combinations no longer being sold by Bulldog, print a list of combinations, and edit information on combinations whenever prices change (a frequent occurrence).

d. Save your project as **EX12-5.vbp, EX12-5.bas, EX12-5List.frm**, and **EX12-5Compute.frm** in the Chapter12 folder on your data disk.

6. Redo Exercise 1 using object-oriented programming techniques. Save the revised project as **EX12-6.vbp, EX12-6.bas, EX12-6List.frm, EX12-6Details.frm** and **EX12-6.cls** in the Chapter12 folder on your data disk.

7. Redo Exercise 2 using object-oriented programming techniques. Save the revised

project as **EX12-7.vbp, EX12-7.bas, EX12-7List.frm, EX12-7Details.frm** and **EX12-7.cls** in the Chapter12 folder on your data disk.

8. Redo Exercise 3 using object-oriented programming techniques. Save the revised project as **EX12-8.vbp, EX12-8.bas, EX12-8List.frm, EX12-8Compute.frm** and **EX12-8.cls** in the Chapter12 folder on your data disk.

9. Redo Exercise 4 using object-oriented programming techniques. Save the revised project as **EX12-9.vbp, EX12-9.bas, EX12-9List.frm, EX12-9DCompute.frm** and **EX12-9.cls** in the Chapter12 folder on your data disk.

10. Redo Exercise 5 using object-oriented programming techniques. Save the revised project as **EX12-10.vbp, EX12-10.bas, EX12-10List.frm, EX12-10Compute.frm** and **EX12-10.cls** in the Chapter12 folder on your data disk.

11. Use object-oriented programming techniques to a create a class called **Dataset.cls**. Each instance of the Dataset object represents a list of numerical data with related properties and methods. The dataset object should allow the user to maintain a set of values with no limit to the number of items in the list. Begin by placing at the module level of the class the declaration:

```
Private sngData() as Single
```

Your object should include the following properties. A Count property that represents the total number of values in the data set. A Minimum property that represents the smallest value in the data set. A Maximum property that represents the largest value in the data set. An Average property that represents the average of all values in the list. A Range property that represents the difference between the minimum and maximum values in the list. Use appropriate data types for each property that you define.

Also include the following methods for working with the dataset class. An Initialize method that sets the original Count to zero. An Add method that provides a mechanism for adding an item to the data set. An Update method that is used to recalculate property values. A GetItem method that allows for retrieval of a specific item from the data set. A DeleteItem method that allows for the deletion of a specific item from the data set. Finally, include a Clear method that will erase the entire data set when invoked. Save your class so that it may be used as part of future projects.

What additional properties and methods could you add to the Dataset class?

PROJECT: JOE'S TAX ASSISTANCE (CONT.)

Joe and Angela walked in the door. Joe had just returned from a VITA conference in Washington, DC. It was the height of the tax season, and the IRS was interested in finding out how things were going at the various VITA sites around the country. Joe had been excited to attend the conference and had taken the opportunity to show off his Visual Basic program. He had just set his suitcase and laptop down, and was taking off his jacket, when the phone rang.

Joe picked up the receiver and said, "Hello?"

"Hi, Grandpa! How was your trip?" came the reply from Zooey.

"Hi, pun'kin. I had a nice time," Joe replied. "The cherry trees on the south end of the Mall are beautiful this time of year."

"I'm glad you had a good time, Grandpa," Zooey said quickly. "But, how did they like your program?"

"Well, now," Joe laughed. "Getting right down to business, aren't you?" he teased, giving Angela a wink.

Angela smiled. "She must be asking about the program. That's all she could think about while you were gone."

"Okay, Zooey, I won't keep you waiting," Joe said. "The general response was positive."

"What does that mean, Grandpa?" Zooey pressed. "Did they like it?"

"It means that they liked the idea and thought that it showed promise, but they offered some suggestions for improvement," he replied. "They did say that they would like to look at it in more detail after tax season is over. And they also seemed impressed by the charts."

"I guess that's okay, Grandpa, but I'd hoped that they would love it," said Zooey. "What kind of changes did they have in mind?"

"There were two or three, but the main one had to do with more instructions and help built into the program. You know, like they have in most of the word processors and spreadsheets. I was thinking of adding a Help menu," Joe explained.

"I've got another idea," exclaimed Zooey. "My teacher showed us about context-sensitive help. That's when the Help system shows you just what you need depending on what you're working on at that moment. For instance, if you are using a particular button or text box, when you click on Help, it would automatically give help related to that object. We could also use some other things that I've learned, like user-defined variable types and random access files."

"Wow, you have been busy!" praised Joe. "But hold your horses. I need to get cleaned up and rested from my trip. How about I call you later and we can discuss the details?"

"Okay, Grandpa. You have a good rest and I'll start thinking of how we can work out the Help system. See ya!" Zooey said as she rang off.

"Ah, the energy of youth," sighed Joe, and he and Angela headed off to unpack.

Questions

1. Using a user-defined data type, create a form and a short Visual Basic program that would allow Joe to create and save Help comments for each line of the IRS 1040 form. The data types should include the form, the form section, the line number, and a Help comment. Your program should save Help comments in a random access file. Debug and test the program. Using an IRS 1040 form for reference, enter several records into the files.

2. Joe would like to be able to press a button and have a Help comment appear for whichever entry he is currently working on. This is a form of context- sensitive help. Create an object class that can be used for showing Help comments. The class should be able to take as input the current location of the cursor (a specific text box) and read from the Help file. An object from the class would then display the appropriate comment.

3. Test and debug your program.

13   INTRODUCTION TO VBSCRIPT

LEARNING OBJECTIVES

After reading this chapter, you will be able to:

❖ Understand the use of scripting languages like VBScript in electronic commerce Web sites.

❖ Discuss the use of client/server technology on the World Wide Web.

❖ Describe the difference between client-side and server-side scripting.

❖ Discuss the differences between Visual Basic and VBScript.

❖ Understand how VBScript works with HTML to produce dynamic Web pages.

❖ Discuss the use of VBScript to validate input from various types of input objects.

❖ Describe how VBScript can be used to make calculations on a Web page.

SCENARIO: VINTAGE VIDEO GOES ONLINE

The phone rang at the store just as Clark was heading out to make a delivery.

Monique, standing on a ladder with her arms full of videos said, "Clark, can you get that before you go?"

Clark picked up the phone thinking that it might be another delivery order. He was surprised when he heard his brother-in-law's voice.

"Hi Ed," Clark said. "How's the convention going? Everything's fine here on the home front."

"It's a little hectic but we're learning some things. Yvonne's attending a session right now entitled *Why Don't Customers Rewind? Strategies and Tips*." Ed replied.

Rolling his eyes, Clark laughed and responded, "I think I'm glad that I'm back here. What's up? I'm in a hurry. I've got a couple of deliveries to make."

"That's kind of what I wanted to talk to you about," said Ed. "There are a lot of sessions here about using the Web and e-commerce in the video business."

His interest piqued, Clark set the videos down on the counter and made himself comfortable on a stool. "What's on your mind?" He asked.

"I've been thinking. What if, in addition to taking phone orders for deliveries, we set up something on our Web site that will allow our customers to request videos for delivery?" Ed inquired. "Have you learned anything like that in your computer classes?"

"Sure," said Clark. "In fact, I've recently been studying a form of Visual Basic for the Web. It's called VBScript, and it works along with HTML."

"Great!" said Ed. "I've got a few minutes before the next session. Let's talk."

The two hashed out a strategy. They decided that Clark should prepare a page for Vintage Vidoes.com that would allow users to select a video from a predefined list for delivery. Once a video has been selected, the cost of the video, delivery charge, and total charge will be displayed. Then, if the customer wishes to complete the request, she may click a button to submit it as E-mail to Vintage Videos. In addition, a button will be included that will allow the customer to reset the form to start over.

Clark said, "It's been a little slow today. Maybe I can get started after I get back from these deliveries."

"Good," said Ed. "I have to get going, too. I'm off to hear about *Blockage Reduction in the 24 Hour Drop-Box.*"

"Well, at least you may be able to catch a few winks." Clark teased. "Have a good trip and see you soon."

Discussion of Scenario

In this scenario, we are encountering a common situation in today's networked economy where a retailer wishes to use the power of the Internet to make their goods and services available to consumers or other businesses. Commonly known as **electronic commerce**, the use of Web sites to sell goods and services over the Internet is a fast growing part of our economy. The vast majority of electronic commerce applications occur on the World Wide Web or as it is more commonly known, simply the Web. The **World Wide Web (Web)** is *a body of software and a set of protocols and conventions based on hypertext and multimedia that make the Internet easy to use and browse.* The Web along with e-mail are the primary reasons for the tremendous growth of the Internet during the 1990s. It uses a capability to *jump* between and within documents virtually at will known as **hypertext.** On the Web, hypertext links in a document are underlined, and by clicking on them, a user can navigate throughout the system limited only by his or her mental connections. The World Wide Web is based on this concept of hypertext where documents are located on Web servers around the world.

The Web is a special type of **client/server network**. With client/server computing, processing is shared between multiple small computers known as **clients** that are connected via a network to a host computer known as a **server.** It is important to note that while the terms *client* and *server* are often used to refer to the machines being used, it is actually the *client software* and *server software* that carry out the processing. For example, a Web browser like Netscape or Internet Explorer is a Web client that runs on your computer with Web server software running on servers all over the world. Your browser can communicate with these servers by sending the **uniform resource locator (URL)** to produce the Web page you see. Figure 13-1 shows the relationship between the browser on your PC and a Web server.

FIGURE 13-1. Browser and Web server

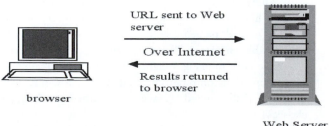

When displaying information sent to it from the server, the browser processes formatting instructions included in the text file retrieved from the server. For example, assume that the creator of a document stored on a Web server has decided a certain phrase should appear in bold when displayed. Instead of saving the file with a bold font, the server stores the data with **tags** to indicate which text will be in bold when displayed. The tags in the World Wide Web are part of a special publishing language called **hypertext markup language (HTML)** and the documents on the Web all have an html (or htm) extension. Documents on the Web are referred to as **Web pages** and their location is a **Web site.** Since HTML is standard for all computers, any Web browser can request an HTML document from any Web server. For instance, a browser running on a PC using Windows 98 can access files on a Macintosh or Unix-based server with no problems.

Review of HTML

While this is *not* a text on creating Web pages, it is impossible to discuss client-side script without some knowledge of HTML. There are books and Web sites[1] dedicated to this topic. In addition, you can now create Web pages with such word-processing like software as Microsoft FrontPage and Netscape Composer without knowing HTML. In this section, we will provide a brief introduction/review of HTML.

To start with, HTML tags are enclosed in angle brackets (< >)to set them off. For example, the tag for bolding is <B>[2]. Also, most HTML tags work in pairs. One tag is used to start formatting or an action, and one is used to turn off the formatting or action. The tags that make up the pair are similar with the second tag beginning with a slash (/) character. For instance, the following character string stored on a server as:

The <B>World Wide Web</B> is the <I>key</I> to electronic commerce.

will be displayed by the client as:

The **World Wide Web** is the *key* to electronic commerce.

because the browser interprets the tag <B> as turn *on* bolding and the tag </B> as turn *off* bolding and <I> and </I> as turning italics on and off. While most tags require both a beginning and an end tag, there are exceptions. Exceptions to this rule include the line break tag (<BR>) and various input elements such as text boxes (<INPUT TYPE=text>.) Table 13-1 shows some of the most commonly used HTML tags along with example results of using them .

TABLE 13-1: Commonly Used HTML Tags

Tag	Operation	Example	Result
<B>	Boldface text	<B>Hello</B>	**Hello**
<I>	Italicize text	<I>Hello</I>	*Hello*
<CENTER>	Center text	<CENTER>Hello</CEN-TER>	Hello
 	Break line and begin new line	End this line. Start another line	End this line. Start another line
<HTML>	Begin/End HTML	<HTML>... </HTML>	Begins and ends Web page

---

1. For example see http://hotwired.lycos.com/webmonkey/authoring/ for a variety of tutorials on HTML.

2. HTML tags are *not* case sensitive, but we will capitalize them to ensure that they are evident.

TABLE 13-1: Commonly Used HTML Tags (Continued)

Tag	Operation	Example	Result
<TITLE>	Begin/End title of Web page	<TITLE>Web page for Chapter 13</TITLE>	"Web page for Chapter 13" appears in header bar of browser
<BODY>	Begin/End body of Web page	<BODY> ... </BODY>	Begins and ends the body of the Web page
<P>	Start/End paragraph	<P>Begin text</P> <P>Begin more text</P>	Begin text Begin more text
<H1>	Create type 1 (largest) heading (also type 2, 3, 4)	<H1>Biggest</H1> <H2>Big </H2> <H4>Small</H4>	# Biggest ## Big Small
<IMG SRC = ... >	Include image in Web page	<IMG SRC = family.jpg>	jpg image file named "Family" is displayed
<FORM>	Create an input form on Web page	<FORM NAME = Order>... </FORM>	Creates an input form named "Order"
<INPUT TYPE = text>	Create text box for input	<INPUT TYPE = text NAME = txtOrder>	Create a text box for input (goes inside form tags)

FIGURE 13-2.
General form of Web page

```
<HTML>
<HEAD>
<TITLE>
Title of Web page goes here
</TITLE>
Other heading material goes here
</HEAD>
<BODY>
Body of Web page goes here
</BODY>
</HTML>
```

The general form of an HTML page is shown in Figure 13-2. In relation to scripting in the Web page, it is important to note that script placed within the <HEAD>..</HEAD> tags is *not* executed unless referred to in the body of the HTML page. On the other hand, script placed in the body is automatically executed as the Web page is loaded into the browser. This means that the head section is a good place to locate event handlers that are executed when an event occurs in the body.

Figure 13-3 shows a fairly simple web page and the HTML source language necessary to display it. Tags used in this code include **H1, H2, H3,** and **H4** for four sizes of headings, **I** to italicize text, **CENTER** to center text, **IMG** for an image, **HR** for a horizontal line, and **Align** to put text on the left or right side of the page.

FIGURE 13-3. Web page and HTML source code

Welcome to Vintage Videos Online!

Oldies but Goodies!

Last updated: May 3, 2001

Ed and Yvonne Monk: Owners

Clark Davis: Webmaster

```
<HTML>
<HEAD>
<TITLE>Vintage Videos Online Web Page</TITLE></HEAD>
<BODY>
<H1><center>Welcome to Vintage Videos Online!</H1>
<IMG src="Camera.jpg" border=1>
<h2><I>Oldies but Goodies!</I></h2></center>
<h4><P align=right>Last updated: May 3, 2001</h4></P><HR>
<H3 align=left>Ed and Yvonne Monk: Owners</H3>
<h4><P align=left>Clark Davis: Webmaster</P></h4>
</BODY>
</HTML>
```

Scripting in the browser

A very important use of Web browsers in electronic commerce is to enter information such as name, address, items ordered, and credit card numbers into Web pages that are sent back over the Internet to the server for processing and eventual shipment of the order. Before returning the completed form over the Internet, it is often useful to validate the input to ensure that all input has been included and that it is appropriate. For example, did the user complete all of the necessary information in the name and address boxes, and did they include the appropriate number of digits in the credit card number? It is also sometimes useful to make simple calculations on the browser to give the user some idea how much the total bill will be. Both validation of input and calculations on the browser can be carried out via a type of computer programming known as scripting. **Scripting** is similar to other types of computer programming in that it uses variables and statements to carry out a desired set of logical operations, but it is also different. Instead of being executed by the computer's processor as is a compiled program such as an exe file, it is executed by another program, in our case the Web browser. In general, scripting languages are easier to work with than compiled languages such as C++ and Java and are ideal for carrying out the limited needs of validating input and making simple calculations on a Web browser. However, a script takes longer to run than a compiled program since each instruction is being interpreted rather than being executed directly by the processor.

The two most widely used scripting languages for working with Web pages are Javascript and VBScript. **Javascript** tends to use a C-like syntax and can run on either Netscape or Internet Explorer browsers. On the other hand, **VBScript** is based on Visual Basic, but runs only on Internet Explorer. Both Javascript and VBScript, when used on the browser, are termed **client-side scripting** since they are running on the Web client. VBScript is also widely used in the Active Server Page (ASP) approach to directing Microsoft Web server software that runs on Windows NT or 2000 operating systems. So-called **server-side scripting** using VBScript is beyond the scope of this chapter, but is quite easy to learn once you have a good understanding of Visual Basic and VBScript. Figure 13-4 shows an example of VBScript used in ASP. In looking at this figure, everything inside the server-side VBScript code tags <% and %> is VBScript and everything else is HTML. You will recognize many of the VBScript statements as being the same as their Visual Basic counterparts.

> **Tip:** VBScript will execute with Internet Explorer versions 3.0 or later.

FIGURE 13-4.
VBScript used in ASP

```
<%Option Explicit%>
<!-- #include file="DBConnect.asp"-->
<HTML>
<BODY>
<%dim DBConn, RSMembers, DatabaseLocation, VideoName, SQLStmt, RS
Dim Location, Price, Rented, ID, Status
if Request("txtExact")="" then%>
<H1>Input the name of the video and click the Search Button</H1><BR>
<FORM ACTION="exact.asp" METHOD=POST NAME=form1>
Video Name:<INPUT TYPE=text NAME=txtExact><BR>
<INPUT TYPE=submit VALUE=Search NAME=submit1>
</FORM>
<%else
    VideoName = Request("txtExact")
DatabaseLocation = Server.mappath("Vintage.mdb")
ConnecttoDB DBConn, Databaselocation
SQLStmt = "Select * from Videos where Video_Name = " & _
"" & VideoName & ""
Set RS = DBConn.execute(SQLStmt)
If RS.EOF then
Response.Write("No Matching Videos by that name")
else
Response.Write("<H2>Click on the video you wish to rent." & _
"If none are listed, all are rented.</H2>")%>
<!--#Include file="ListVideos.asp"-->
<%end if
end if%>
</BODY>
</HTML>
```

Mini-Summary 13-1: Client and Server Side Scripting

1. Electronic commerce is based on use of the World Wide Web which is a client/server network with clients running Web browsers that can interpret information sent from Web servers.

2. The information sent from servers is in the form of hypertext markup language (HTML) which is composed of tags that the browser uses to format the information.

3. Scripting is a form of computer programming that can run on either the Web browser or Web server. Commonly used scripting languages are VBScript and JavaScript.

4. Scripting on the client is referred to as *client-side scripting* while scripting on the server is *server-side scripting*.

It's Your Turn!

1. What does the World Wide Web have to do with electronic commerce?
2. How does the browser communicate with a Web server to display Web pages?
3. What does *HTML* stand for?
4. What is the HTML tag for boldface? Centering? New line?
5. What is the difference between scripting and compiled computer languages?
6. What types of browser does VBScript run on?

USING VBSCRIPT

As mentioned above, VBScript is a scripting language based on Visual Basic that is used for both client- and server-side scripting on the World Wide Web. In this chapter, we will discuss the use of VBScript as a client-side scripting tool for validating e-commerce Web page input and for carrying out simple calculations on Web pages *before* sending them back to the server for order fulfillment. Since VBScript is based on Visual Basic, you should find this material very easy. However, you should review the use of HTML since VBScript and HTML must work together to carry out these operations.

VBScript is based on Visual Basic in that they both use a version of the Basic computer language for the code that carries out the desired logic. For example, all of the code you've been writing to execute event procedures, general subs, and functions uses a form of Basic. VBScript uses exactly the same coding rules as does Visual Basic with a few exceptions that will be discussed in the next sections. For example, the form of assignment statements, decisions, and loops are very much the same as are the creation of arrays, subs, and functions and the use of files.

Differences between VBScript and Visual Basic

While VBScript is based on Visual Basic, there are some significant differences between the two languages. These differences are listed in Table 13-2 and will be discussed in detail in this section.

TABLE 13-2: Differences between VBScript and Visual Basic

Visual Basic	VBScript
Uses different types of variables and constants	Uses only one type of variable--the Variant
Can be compiled into an exe file	Is interpreted by the Internet Explorer browser software
Uses event procedures to react to events	Uses event handlers to react to events
Has an easy-to-use integrated development environment (IDE)	Does not have an easy-to-use IDE specifically for VBScript
Runs as stand-alone language	Must be integrated with HTML

Variable types. In the first case, Visual Basic has many different types of variables that you can you use in your coding including string, single, double, integer, date, currency, and so on. On the other hand, VBScript has only one type of variable—the

Variant. The Variant variable type, which is also available in Visual Basic, is a chameleon variable type that takes on whatever data type is necessary for a given situation. For example, if you assign a string of characters to a variant variable, it will become a string data type. On the other hand, if you assign the number 3.141523 to a variant variable, it will become a single variable type.

Usually, the VBScript interpreter handles this correctly but there can be problems, especially if it's not clear what data type the variable should be. For example, VBScript will automatically assume that everything in a text box is text and this can lead to problems when the contents of a text box are assigned to a variable that should be numeric. To avoid this problem, we encourage you to use the conversion functions for VBScript to create a Variant of a specific subtype which acts like the Visual Basic data type. For example, if you set a VBScript variable equal to CSng(txtPrice), it will be a Variant subtype of single and act like a Visual Basic single data type variable. As it turns out, the conversion functions are the same as those for Visual Basic. Initially shown as Table 3-7, we have shown them again here as Table 13-3.

TABLE 13-3: VBScript Conversion Functions

VBScript Function	Purpose
CBool	Converts argument to a Variant of subtype Boolean
CCur	Converts argument to a Variant of subtype Currency
CDate	Converts argument to a Variant of subtype Date
CInt	Converts argument to a Variant of subtype Integer
CSng	Converts argument to a Variant of subtype Single
CDbl	Converts argument to a Variant of subtype Double
CStr	Converts argument to a Variant of subtype String

Interpreted language. In the second case, while it is possible to create a binary version of most computer languages like Visual Basic, C++, or Java by compiling them, VBScript programs must be interpreted by other software, usually the Internet Explorer browser on the client side and Web server software on the server side. This makes VBScript and other scripting languages run more slowly than compiled software. However, except in the most processing intensive cases, you won't notice this difference.

Event handlers. In Visual Basic, we wrote code to respond to events like button-clicks or change or form load. This code was written in sub programs called **event procedures** where each procedure determined what would happen if a specific event occurred for a specific object. For example, we used the command button Click event to respond to the user clicking a command button. In VBScript, we can write code to respond to the same events, only now the subprograms are referred to as **event handlers.** While the names are different and, as we shall discuss in the next section, the manner in which they are created is different, event procedures and event handlers are essentially the same. We will be discussing the use of event handlers to handle events in this chapter.

No Easy-to-Use IDE. In working with Visual Basic, you have used the Visual Basic **Integrated Development Environment (IDE)** to create forms, add code to event procedures, and write necessary functions and sub programs. This IDE made working with Visual Basic very easy since it did much of the work for you. You have a form automatically displayed to use in creating your projects and there are a wide variety of controls from which to choose. For example, if you want a command button, you simply double-click one in the toolbox and it appears on your form. Beyond the interface, Visual Basic provides a large number of tools including automatic event procedures for the controls, syntax checking as you write the code, a variety of types of help, and powerful debugging tools.

Unfortunately, there is no IDE specifically for VBScript. The closest thing to an IDE for VBScript is Microsoft's Visual InterDev (VID). VID is a part of the same Visual Studio package as Visual Basic, but is a multipurpose development tool that is used for both JavaScript and VBScript on both the client and server. These multiple capabilities make it a very powerful tool that at the same time can be very confusing to use for client-side scripting with VBScript. It may also be true that you do not have Visual InterDev installed on your machine.

Since there is no easy-to-use IDE for VBScript that is always readily available, we will show you how to use a text editor like NotePad or an HTML editor to carry out all of the activities you are used to having with Visual Basic. This will include using HTML to create the controls necessary to generate a form on the browser, writing the VBScript code to create event handlers and other logic, and then testing your code by saving it and switching to Internet Explorer. You will probably find the lack of an IDE and the integration with HTML discussed next to be the biggest differences between Visual Basic and VBScript.

Integration with HTML. Because VBScript is running on a Web page, it must be tightly integrated with the HTML that is used to display text, graphics, and images on the page. Where Visual Basic is a "stand alone" language, VBScript must work with HTML for both input and output. That is, input must come from HTML forms such as text and list boxes and output must also be in the form of HTML. This is necessary since browsers can accept only HTML.

In addition, any client-side VBScript commands **must** be enclosed in special script tags of the form <SCRIPT> ... </SCRIPT> (in server-side scripting these are the <% ... %> tags). These tags cause the browser to interpret anything inside them as code that should be executed. Anything outside of the script tags is interpreted as HTML code. This is often a confusing issue with first-time users of VBScript since they are not used to integrating a computer language with a formatting language like HTML.

Other Differences. In addition to these major differences between Visual Basic and VBScript, there are other, less significant differences associated with the language itself. For example, with the Select Case statement in VBScript, you can use only one or multiple values or strings separated by commas as the condition format. A range of values or comparison conditions like those discussed in Chapter 4 for Visual Basic will not work for VBScript. As these differences come up, we will point them out.

The <Script> Tag   As mentioned above, all VBScript code must be enclosed in HTML script tags. These tags for VBScript are of the form:

<SCRIPT language="VBScript"> ... </SCRIPT>

The same type tags are used for Javascript with a change in the language parameter.

VBScript code is typically located in two places in the Web page—in the HEAD section and in the BODY section. When VBScript is placed in the HEAD section, it is in the form of functions and sub programs that act as event handlers; that is, they are referenced in the BODY section of the HTML or are executed in the BODY section when an event occurs. For example, if a button is clicked, an OnClick event handler may be called to execute the VBScript code.

If the VBScript code appears in the BODY section of the HTML code, it is executed when the page loads. For example, a message box should automatically be displayed when a Web page is loaded into the browser. The VBScript code to accomplish this should be located in the BODY section of the page. In this discussion, we will restrict ourselves to writing event handlers in the HEAD section, but writing VBScript code in the BODY section is very similar. It is important to remember, though, that wherever the VBScript code appears, it must be enclosed in the <SCRIPT> </SCRIPT> tags or it will be interpreted as HTML.

Mini-Summary 13-2: Using VBScript

1. VBScript is a reduced version of Visual Basic that can be used for client- or server-side scripting. On the client, VBScript only runs on Microsoft's Internet Explorer.

2. Important differences between Visual Basic and VBScript involve variable types used, capability to be compiled, using event procedures instead of event handlers, having a built-in IDE, and capability to run as a stand-alone language instead of being integrated with HTML.

3. VBScript must appear within the <Script>...</Script> tags.

4. VBScript appears two places in the Web page—in the HEAD section for event handlers and in the BODY section to be executed when the page loads.

It's Your Turn!

1. What type(s) of variables are supported by VBScript?

2. Why is it important to use conversion functions with VBScript?

3. Does the Variant data type have any subtypes? How do they relate to the variable types in Visual Basic?

4. What is an event handler? How do they relate to event procedures in Visual Basic?

5. What is the Script tag, and what is its purpose in a Web page?

6. Why does VBScript run more slowly than compiled languages?

7. In what two locations in a Web page is VBScript found? What are the purposes of VBScript in the two locations?

WEB PAGE CREATION

As we mentioned above, the three primary uses of VBScript for client-side scripting are to validate Web page input, carry out simple calculations and lookups, and to create dynamic Web pages based on user input. In this section, we will discuss creating a Web page that will be used for input. Later sections will discuss validating the input to this Web page as well as the other uses of VBScript.

> **Tip:** It's a good idea to inform users who load your pages with an alternative browser that some portions of your web page will only work with Internet Explorer.

Vintage Video Online Rental Web Form

Before validating input from a Web page or processing it, we need to create the form that will be used to capture the input. While this is strictly an HTML operation, we need to complete it before we can discuss validation. In the case of our scenario, Vintage Videos requires a Web page that will enable a member to input their name, telephone number, and e-mail address and then select one of the ten videos that are available for home delivery. The cost of the video is then computed and a delivery charge added to determine the total cost *before* the data are sent to the Web server at Vintage Videos where the database is checked to ensure the videos are still available. While the Web page displayed *should* only show videos that are available to rent, it is possible that a video could have been rented by another person between the time the page was generated at the server and the member decided which video to rent. The dynamic generation of the page at the server is an example of server-side scripting since it uses the database that is on the server. As noted earlier, client-side scripting cannot do anything in the way of querying or modifying a database on the server so this must be handled by server-side scripting. The Web page we want to create is shown in Figure 13-5 with some of the objects pointed out.

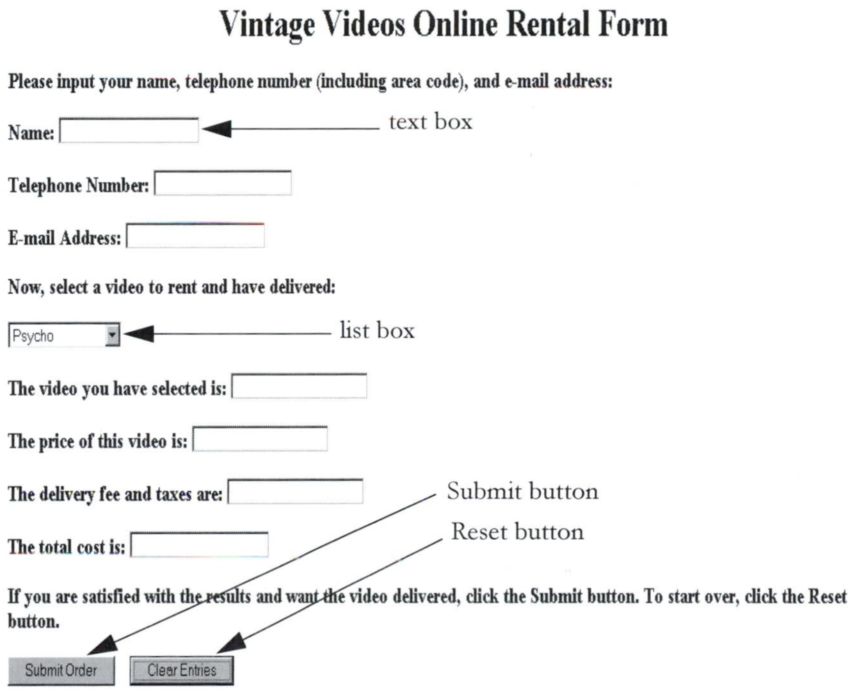

FIGURE 13-5.
Vintage Videos
Online Rental Form

Vintage Videos Online Rental Form

Please input your name, telephone number (including area code), and e-mail address:

Name: [ ] ◄——— text box

Telephone Number: [ ]

E-mail Address: [ ]

Now, select a video to rent and have delivered:

[Psycho ▼] ◄——— list box

The video you have selected is: [ ]

The price of this video is: [ ]

The delivery fee and taxes are: [ ] ——— Submit button

The total cost is: [ ] ——— Reset button

If you are satisfied with the results and want the video delivered, click the Submit button. To start over, click the Reset button.

[Submit Order] [Clear Entries]

Note that the Web page in Figure 13-5 has three text boxes and a list box for input and four text boxes to display to the user the name and price of the video which they have selected as well as the taxes and delivery fee and total cost of the item. In this case, we will want to both validate the input of a name, telephone number, and e-mail address as well as the selection of a video to rent. We will also want to display the name and price of the video in addition to computing and displaying the taxes and delivery fee and total cost of the video. The user clicks on the Submit button to send this information to the server for processing or the Reset button to clear his or her entries to start over again.

Using Form Tags

To create this page, we will use some of the standard formatting HTML tags such as <CENTER>, <H1>, and <H3> to create the headings and labels for the various text and list boxes. We will also want to use form tags to create the text and list box objects as well as the Submit and Reset buttons. Table 13-4 shows the form tags that are used to create these four types of objects plus some other form tags that are commonly used on Web pages.

TABLE 13-4: Form Tags in Web Pages

Form Tag/ Object Created	Example
Form	<FORM ACTION=Mailto:videosv@negia.net NAME=frmInput METHOD=post ENCTYPE = text/ plain>...</FORM>
Text box	<INPUT TYPE=text NAME=txtPhoneNum>
List Box	<SELECT NAME=lstVideos> ... </SELECT>
Item in list box	<OPTION VALUE=1>Bambi</OPTION>
Radio Button	<INPUT TYPE=radio NAME=optChooseOne>
Check Box	<INPUT TYPE=checkbox NAME=chkFirstOption>
Submit Button	<INPUT TYPE=Submit VALUE="Submit Order" NAME=cmdSubmit>
Reset Button	<INPUT TYPE=Reset VALUE="Start Over" NAME=cmdReset>
Button	<INPUT TYPE=Button VALUE=Calculate NAME= cmdCalc>

In looking at the examples in Table 13-4, it should be noted that the attribute values must only be included in quotation marks when they include a space. For example, while it is not necessary to include any of the NAME properties in quotation marks, it is necessary to include the value attribute for the submit button (Submit Order) in quotation marks because it has imbedded spaces. We will briefly discuss each of these tags and how they are used.

<FORM> Tag. To use any of the form tags to create objects, you must enclose all of them in the <FORM> ... </FORM> tags. These indicate to the browser that any tags between the pair of FORM tags refer to objects like text and list boxes that are used for input and output on the Web page. Like all of the primary form tags, the <FORM> tag should have a NAME attribute with a three letter prefix. This name will be used later to identify the various input and output items so it is essential that it be included.

The <FORM> tag also has several other important properties, some of which are shown in this example. These include the ACTION, METHOD, and ENCTYPE properties. The *ACTION* and *ENCTYPE* parameters determine what will happen to the data in the input controls like text boxes when the Submit button is clicked and the form of the data. In this case, the data will be e-mailed to a special address at Vintage Videos in plain or text form. Another typical action is to send the data to a page on the server where it is processed. The *METHOD* attribute is used to determine the manner in which data are sent to the server—behind the scenes as in the *post* value shown here or through the URL with the *Querystring* attribute. An example of the <FORM> tag would be:

```
<FORM NAME=frmInput ACTION="mailto:videosv@negia.net"
METHOD=post ENCTYPE=plain/text>
```

Note: videosv@negia.net is *not* an actual e-mail address. If you use this address and attempt to submit the form, it will bounce back to you as an undeliverable message.

Text box Tag . The <INPUT TYPE=text> tag creates a text box object for either input or output. The name of this object should begin with the txt prefix, and its size can be modified with the *TYPE* attribute. The contents of this and other form objects is determined by the *value* attribute. This parameter replaces a variety of properties used in Visual Basic including the text box and list box text attribute and the label caption attribute. In some cases like the list box object and the various buttons, the value attribute is set at design time; with other objects like the text box, it is typically set at run time. An example of the text box tag is:

```
<INPUT TYPE=text NAME=txtName>
```

List box Tags. The <SELECT> tag creates a list box which is populated at design-time through a series of <OPTION> tags. The value of the <SELECT> tag is equal to the value of the selected option in the list box. For example, to create a list box with three video options, the <SELECT> tag and three <OPTION> tags would appear as follows:

```
<SELECT NAME=lstVideos>
<OPTION VALUE=2>Psycho</OPTION>
<OPTION VALUE=1>Bambi</OPTION>
<OPTION VALUE=2>Ghost</OPTION>
</SELECT>
```

In looking at this example, the text between the <OPTION> and </OPTION> tags is what is actually displayed in the list box. However, the value attribute is what is important because it is what can be processed by the client-side VBScript and sent to the server. In this case, the value attribute is used to determine the price of each video that will be displayed on the Web page when a video is selected: 1 for $.99, 2 for $1.99, and 3 for $2.99. If there is not an explicit value attribute, it defaults to the text or content attribute. It is *not* necessary to have the </OPTION> tag but we have shown it for completeness.

> **Tip:** An HTML SELECT element can be used like either a VB combo box or a list box, depending on its SIZE property. If you set the SIZE property to 1 then it acts like a drop-down combo box, but if its SIZE is set to more than one then it becomes a list box.

Button, Submit, and Reset Buttons. These three Input tags all create clickable buttons on the Web page but have decidedly different results. The <INPUT TYPE=Button> tag is a general purpose button for which an event handler must be written to respond to it being clicked. For example, if the button is named *cmdCalc*, then we might want to write an event handler sub program called *cmdCalc_OnClick* that will be executed when this particular button is clicked. We can also write a general sub called *Calc* that can be called from the tag itself with the addition of the statement: *Onclick=Calc* to the end of the tag. For example, the button tag statement might be:

```
<INPUT TYPE=button NAME=cmdCalc VALUE=Calculate ONCLICK=Calc>
```

where the value attribute determines the caption for the button. A tag like the one shown here allows the same event handler to be used for multiple events. If an event handler for the onclick event has been specifically created for this button like cmdCalc_OnClick discussed previously, the last attribute should not be included.

The <INPUT TYPE=Submit> tag creates a button, which when clicked will submit the contents of the Web page to the location specified in the <FORM ACTION> attribute. For our example, we specified the action as mailto:videosv@negia.net, so clicking the submit button will cause this to happen. If no value attribute is included, Submit buttons will have a caption of "Submit". An example of the tag for a submit button is:

```
<INPUT TYPE=Submit NAME=cmdSubmit VALUE="Submit Order">
```

There is no need for an event handler for a submit button since the result of clicking this button is automatic.

The <INPUT TYPE=Reset> tag creates a button, which when clicked, will clear or "reset" the contents of the Web page input form. If no value attribute is included, Reset buttons will have a caption of "Reset". An example of the tag for a reset button is:

```
<INPUT TYPE=Reset NAME=cmdReset VALUE="Start Over">
```

There is no need for an event handler for a reset button since the result of clicking this button is automatic.

> **Tip:** You can make an HTML object invisible by setting the height and width properties to 0.

Putting it all together

We are now ready to put all of these tags together to create the desired Web page using Notepad or other text editor. To recall, our order page for an online video rental order includes headings, three text boxes with associated labels, a list box with a label, four more text boxes with associated labels, a submit button, and a reset button. The complete HTML code for the input form on the Web page is shown in VB Code Box 13-1. To discuss this page, we will break it into three pieces—the first will contain the headings, FORM statement, and first three text boxes; the second piece will contain the list box and associated labels; and the last piece will contain the last four text boxes plus the submit and reset buttons. In the first piece, we include a title for the Web page and use a centered size one heading for the top of the page. The FORM statement defines the input area and indicates where and how the input is to be submitted. We use size three headings for the other headings and labels associated with the text boxes. The last items in the first part of the HTML page are the text boxes named txtName, txtPhoneNum, and txtEmail.

> **Tip:** You should try out each portion of your Web page as it is created by retrieving it into Internet Explorer. This helps avoid encountering a large number of HTML errors at the same time.

The second section of HTML code creates the list box and associated labels. Even though there are only 10 videos, there are 11 items listed in separate option tags. In all cases except the first, the value attribute is used to determine the price of each video—1 for $.99, 2 for $1.99, and 3 for $2.99. The first item with a value of zero and no video name is a dummy selection which is used to ensure that user selects a video. Finally, the HTML code for the second set of four text boxes, the submit button, and the reset button, is shown in VB Code Box 13-1. Note that there are four output text boxes named txtVideo, txtPrice, txtDeliveryFee, and txtTotalCost in which the name, price, delivery fee ($2.00), and the computed total cost will be displayed. There are also two buttons—a submit button named cmdSubmit and a reset button named cmdReset. Note the value attributes for these buttons are enclosed in quotation marks because they contain imbedded space. Finally, there are ending FORM, BODY, and HTML tags.

| **VB CODE BOX 13-1.** HTML code for input form | ```html
<HTML>
<HEAD>
<TITLE>Vintage Videos Online Rental System</TITLE>
</HEAD>
<BODY>
<H1 ALIGN=center>Vintage Videos Online Rental Form</H1>
<FORM NAME=frmInput METHOD=post ACTION=mailto:videosv@negia.net
ENCTYPE=text/plain>
<H3>Please input your name, telephone number including area code, and
e-mail address:</H3>
<H3>Name: <INPUT TYPE=text NAME=txtName></H3>
<H3>Telephone Number: <INPUT TYPE=text NAME=txtPhoneNum></H3>
<H3 align=left>E-mail Address: <INPUT TYPE=text NAME=txtEmail></H3>
<H3>Now, select a video to rent and have delivered:</H3>
<SELECT NAME=lstVideos>
<OPTION value=0> </OPTION>
<OPTION value=2>Psycho</OPTION>
<OPTION value=1>Bambi</OPTION>
<OPTION value=2>Ghost</OPTION>
<OPTION value=3>Star Wars</OPTION>
<OPTION value=1>Dumbo</OPTION>
<OPTION value=2>Rain Man</OPTION>
<OPTION value=2>Blazing Saddles</OPTION>
<OPTION value=2>Ben Hur</OPTION>
<OPTION value=3>Spartacus</OPTION>
<OPTION value=2>Tootsie</OPTION>
<OPTION value=3>The Sting</OPTION>
</SELECT>
<H3>The video you have selected is: <INPUT TYPE=text NAME=txtVideo>
The price of this video is: <INPUT TYPE=text NAME=txtprice>
The delivery fee and taxes are: <INPUT TYPE=text NAME=txtDeliveryFee>
<H3>The total cost is: <INPUT TYPE=text NAME=txtTotalCost>
<H3>If you are satisfied with the results and want the video
delivered, click the Submit button. To start over, click the Reset
button.</H3>
<INPUT TYPE=submit NAME=cmdSubmit VALUE="Submit Order">

<INPUT NAME=cmdReset TYPE=reset VALUE="Clear Entries">
</FORM>
</BODY>
</HTML>
``` |

Mini-Summary 13-3: Web Page Creation

1. In addition to the standard formatting HTML tags, form tags are used to create input objects such as text and list boxes.

2. Form tags include those for creating text and list boxes, radio buttons, and checkboxes as well as submit, reset, and command buttons. In all cases, the object tags must be enclosed within the <FORM>...</FORM> tags.

3. The Submit button will send the input to an e-mail site or to the Web server and the Reset button will clear the user input.

It's Your Turn!

1. How are form tags used? List three form tags and give their purpose as well as their format.

2. What are the purposes of the METHOD and ACTION parameters in the form tag?

3. What is the purpose of the Submit button? What other buttons can you use?

4. Write the HTML code to create an input box named **txtInputName** and a list of age categories (less than 21, 21-30, 31-40, 41-50, 51-60, and greater than 61) called lstAges from which to choose the age corresponding to the same person. Also add a Submit button. Assume that the form will be submitted via e-mail to videosv@negia.net.

5. Describe what will be displayed when each of the following lines of HTML code are interpreted by your browser.

    a. <INPUT TYPE = text NAME = txtAverage VALUE = Average>

    b. <INPUT TYPE = radio NAME = optOption1>Under 18
       <INPUT TYPE = radio NAME = optOption2>Between 18 and 50
       <INPUT TYPE = radio NAME = optOption3>Over 50

    c. <INPUT TYPE = checkbox NAME = chkCheck1>Sports
      <INPUT TYPE = checkbox NAME = chkCheck2>Travel
      <INPUT TYPE = checkbox NAME = chkCheck3>Entertainment

    d. <INPUT TYPE = Button VALUE = Go NAME = cmdGo>

6. Write HTML code that will display each of the following in your Web browser.

    a. A text box for entering in a person's first name.

    b. A list box that allows a user to select a day of the week.

    c. A command button that will allow the user to perform a calculation.

    d. A command button that allows the user to reset the form.

Completing the remaining questions will enable you to create the Visual Basic project discussed in the text.

7. Open Notepad or another text editor and begin creating the Vintage Videos Online Rental Form by entering the HTML code shown in VB Code Box 13-1. Create a folder named Chapter13 on your data disk. Save this page in it by selecting **File | Save**, chang-

ing to the a:\ drive and to this folder, changing the file type to **All Files**, and entering a name of **VideosOnline.htm.** (We will assume you are using Notepad; if you are using some other text editor, carry out the appropriate operations to save the file.)

8. Open Microsoft Internet Explorer and use the **File | Open** menu option to open the file **a:\Chapter13\VideosOnline.htm**. You can do this by entering the file name directly or by using the Browse option of the dialog box. When you do this, you should see the part of the Web page shown earlier as Figure 13-5 but with no video selected. If you do not, check your HTML code to make sure it is correct.

VALIDATING WEB PAGE INPUT

Whenever a Web page is used for input to a Web server, it is necessary to validate that the input is complete and in the correct form, if possible. In the first case, validation involves checking input to ensure that all required fields are filled out. For example, a registration form might involve a number of fields such as name, address, e-mail address, telephone number, and so on, but only some of these fields may be required for the registration to be accepted. Rather than sending incomplete data to the server, client-side scripting can be used to check the contents of required fields and alert the user to add necessary missing information before the data are sent to the server.

In addition to using client-side scripting with VBScript to validate that the input is correct, it is often useful to carry out some processing before sending the data to the server for processing. We will cover the validation step here and the computation step in the next section.

The Validation Process

The validation process on a Web page is similar in many ways to the validation process for Visual Basic forms discussed in Chapters 4 and 5 in that it is necessary to check for empty text boxes and for list boxes where no option has been selected. In addition, with Web pages that are involved with e-commerce, it is often necessary to check that the contents of a text box are appropriate. For example, typical validation questions are:

❖ Is there an appropriate number of digits in a name or telephone number?

❖ Is there an @ sign in an e-mail address with a sufficient number of characters?

❖ Are there exactly nine digits in a Social Security number with dashes in the correct location?

❖ Are there an appropriate number of characters in a credit card number?

While there are definitely other validation checks, we will restrict ourselves to checking for text boxes with an appropriate number of characters or the presence of a required character and for the selection of a list box option.

To check for an appropriate number of digits or characters, the Len function is used and the InStr function is used to check for the presence of a required character in a specific location. Checking for a selected list box option requires determining the value of the SelectedIndex property of the list box; if it is greater than -1, then an option has been selected.

The validation process is typically carried out when some event occurs through an event handler sub or function. For the example Web page shown earlier as Figure 13-5, clicking the "Submit Order" button (cmdSubmit) should activate an event handler function that will check to ensure that all of the text boxes are completed before submitting the data via e-mail to videosv@negia.net. In other situations, events other than a button click can be used to fire an event handler. For example, changing the selection of a list box option or the contents of a text box, scrolling a list box, and moving the focus to a form object are all possible events that can cause an event handler to execute.

Validation Event Handler

As mentioned earlier, to handle events you must write event handler subs and functions. These procedures should be placed in the HEAD section of the HTML page, but are activated by events involving FORM input controls that are located within the BODY section of the page. In our case, when the cmdSubmit submit button is clicked, we want to make a number of checks including checking that:

1. a name that is at least five characters long has been entered in the txtName text box;
2. a telephone number that has *exactly* 12 digits in it has been entered in the txtPhoneNum text box;
3. an e-mail address with an "@" sign in it and that is at least five characters long has been entered in the txtEmail text box;
4. an option from the lstVideo list box has been selected.

Since all of these checks are made when the cmdSubmit button is clicked, they should all be a part of the same event handler procedure that is executed when the user tries to submit the form. For that reason, the event handler procedure will be named frmInput_OnSubmit. The next question is: should it be a sub or function? In this case, we can use a function that returns a value of true or false depending on whether the form should be submitted or not.

The general form of a function in VBScript is exactly the same as in Visual Basic; that is, it begins with the Function name statement and ends with the End Function statement. The difference lies in the fact that any event handler function or sub must be within the <Script Language = "VBScript"> and </Script> tags and must be contained in the HEAD section of the HTML code. In our case, the statements to set up the frmInput_OnSubmit function are shown in VB Code Box 13-2 along with the surrounding HTML statements. Note that we have used a comment statement to point where the VBScript code will go.

> **Tip:** Unlike the Visual Basic Function statement, the Function statement in VBScript does not include a data type declaration.

VB Code Box 13-2. Setting up event handler function	``` <HTML> <HEAD> <TITLE>Vintage Videos Online Rental System</TITLE> <Script Language="VBScript"> Function frmInput_OnSubmit 'VBScript Code goes here End Function </Script> </HEAD> ```

Validating Text Box Input

Since the text box is a primary form of input for Web pages, we will consider validating text box input first and then consider validating list box selections. For the text boxes of the Vintage Videos online rental system, we need to consider the first three validation checks, which are listed above as follows

❖ Does the name text box contain a minimum number of characters, in this case 5?

❖ Does the text box in which the telephone number is entered have exactly 12 characters?

❖ Does the text box for the e-mail address contain an @-sign and at least five characters?

Just as with Visual Basic, it is best to use a variable to validate the contents of a text box. When setting a variable equal to the contents of any form object, you *must always* use the complete name of the object including the form name. The general form to do this for a text box is:

strVariable = frmFormName.txttext box.Value

where *strVariable* is the name of the variable and *frmFormName.txttext box.Value* is the complete name of the contents of the text box. For example, for the txtName text box, this becomes:

```
strName = frmInput.txtName.Value
```

Once a string variable has been set equal to the contents of the text box, we could use it to check for an empty text box just like we did in Visual Basic, that is, compare it to the null string as shown below:

If *strVariable* = "" Then

However, since we are requiring the name be at least five characters long, we don't need to do this particular check. Instead, we can use the following general form to check if there are an adequate number of characters in the text box:

If Len(*strVariable*) < *MinNumber* Then

where *strVariable* is the same as above and *MinNumber* is the minimum allowable characters in the text box. The check for an exact number of characters is similar with the replacement of the less than operator with the equal to or not equal to operators. For our example with the string variable set equal to the contents of the txtName text box, this becomes:

```
If Len(strName) < 5 Then
```

> **Tip:** If you are viewing a Web page in Internet Explorer, using **View|Source** menu option will display the HTML code in Notepad which you can then add to or edit it and then save with the **File|Save As...** option.

For the telephone number, since we want it to be exactly equal to 12 characters, the validation check would be (where strPhone has been set equal to the contents of the txtPhoneNum text box):

```
If Len(strPhone) <> 12 Then
```

To check for the @-sign or any other required character in a text box, we use the same InStr function that was discussed in Chapter 6 to determine if a character appears in a string. The general form of this function is:

InStr(*start*, *string to be searched*, *search string*, *end*)

where *start* and *end* are numeric values representing the position in the string to be searched where the search begins and ends. If these parameters are omitted, they are assumed to be equal to the beginning position (1) and the ending position in the string. As with Visual Basic, the InStr function returns the position in the string to be searched where the search string occurs. If it returns a value of zero, then the search string does not occur. In the case of the e-mail text box, the statement to check for the presence of the @-sign would be (where strEmail has been set equal to the contents of the txtEmail text box):

```
If InStr(strName,"@") = 0 Then
```

If any of these three text box validation checks evaluates to true, that is, the text box does not have an acceptable entry, a number of actions are taken, including:

1. a message box is used to display a request that the user enter a name that is at least five characters long

2. the function name (frmInput_OnSubmit) is set to false to cancel the submission of the form

3. the text box is cleared by setting its value property to the null string ("")

4. the focus is set back to the text box that was found to be empty.

5. the function is exited since no other checks need be made once one has failed.

If, on the other hand, the length check evaluates to false, that is, there are a sufficient number of characters, the function continues on to the next validation check.

The message box in VBScript is the same as in Visual Basic. Also, setting the function name equal to false and setting the contents of the text box to the null string are the same. Just remember that with VBScript you must use the *full name* of the text box including the form name. On the other hand, setting the focus back to the now empty text box in VBScript uses the **Focus** method instead of the SetFocus method. The general form of this statement is:

> ***frmFormName.txttext box*.Focus**

The statements to carry out all of the text box validation checks are shown in VB Code Box 13-3. These statements should come *immediately* after the HTML <HEAD> tag in the code shown in VB Code Box 13-1.

VB CODE BOX 13-3. VBScript statements to check for empty or short text box	
| | ```
<SCRIPT LANGUAGE ="VBScript">
Function frmInput_OnSubmit
Dim strName, strEmail, strPhone, strVideo, intSelIndex
strName = frmInput.txtName.Value
strPhone = frmInput.txtPhoneNum.Value
strEmail = frmInput.txtEmail.Value
If Len(strName) < 5 Then
    Msgbox "Please input a name at least 5 characters long!"
    frmInput.txtName.Value = ""
    frmInput.txtName.Focus
    frmInput_OnSubmit = False
    Exit Function
ElseIf Len(strPhone) <> 12 Then
    Msgbox "Please input a phone number with exactly 12 dig-
its!"
    frmInput.txtPhoneNum.Value = ""
    frmInput.txtPhoneNum.Focus
    frmInput_OnSubmit = False
    Exit Function
ElseIf InStr(strEmail,"@") = 0 Or Len(strEmail) < 5 Then
    Msgbox "Please input an e-mail address with an @ sign" _
        & "and at least 5 characters!"
    frmInput.txtEmail.Value = ""
    frmInput.txtEmail.Focus
    frmInput_OnSubmit = False
    Exit Function
End If
End Function
</SCRIPT>
</HEAD>
``` |
```

Note that we start with the <SCRIPT> tag followed by the variable declarations to be used in the function and then set three string variables equal to the contents of the three text boxes. These three string variables are used in an If-Then-ElseIf structure to make the validation checks. First the txtName text box is checked to determine if it has fewer than 5 characters. If it does, the five actions discussed above are taken; otherwise, the txtPhoneNum text box is checked to determine if there are exactly 12 characters. If it does not have exactly 12 characters, the five actions are taken; if it has 12 characters, the txtEmail text box is checked both for the presence of an @-sign and for at least five characters.

Failure to make a correct input into any of the three text boxes should now result in a message box being displayed, the text box cleared, and the focus set back to the text box. Figure 13-6 shows the message box that results from clicking the Submit Order button when the telephone number has only 11 digits.

Tip: To cancel an event, return a Function value of false.

FIGURE 13-6.
Message box
indicating incorrect
text box input

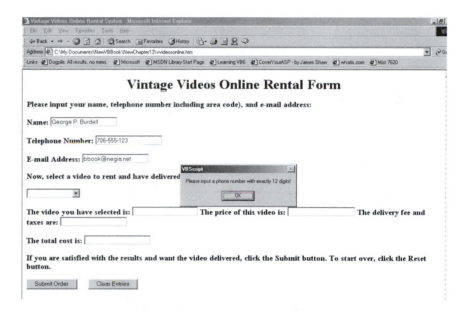

*Checking for
Unselected List Box
Option*

In addition to checking for incorrect input in text boxes, we need to check for an unselected list box option. To do this, we use the *SelectedIndex* attribute of the list box. This attribute is equal to the index of the selected option and is equal to minus one (-1) if no option is selected. The SelectedIndex attribute for a form list box is very similar to the ListIndex attribute for list and combo boxes in Visual Basic discussed in Chapter 5. So, to ensure that an option in a list box is selected, we simply need to set an Integer variable equal to the SelectedIndex property and then check if it is less than 1 as in the general form shown below:

intVariable = *frmName.lstName.*SelectedIndex
If *intVariable* < **1 Then**

Since the first, blank option has a SelectedIndex of zero, if intVariable is less than 1, no option has been selected and the validation check fails. In this case, we need to carry out all but one of the actions carried out for invalid text boxes; we don't need to set the list box contents to the null string. VB Code Box 13-4 shows the statements necessary to validate the selection of an option for the lstVideos list box on the online rental form. These statements need to be inserted into the frmInput_OnSubmit function *immediately* prior to the End Function statement.

| VB CODE BOX 13-4. List boxes validation | ```
intSelIndex = frmInput.lstVideos.SelectedIndex
If intSelIndex < 1 Then
    Msgbox "You must select a video!"
    frmInput.lstVideos.Focus
    frmInput_OnSubmit = False
    Exit Function
End If
``` |
|---|---|

Mini-Summary 13-4: Validating Web Page Input

1. Validation is necessary whenever input comes from a Web page to ensure that it is complete and in the correct form before sending it to the Web server for processing.

2. Types of Web page validation include checking for the appropriate number of characters or digits in a text box, checking for the presence of a required character, checking for characters appearing in the correct location, and ensuring that an option has been selected from a list or combo box or that a radio button or checkbox has been selected.

3. Event handlers are used to validate Web page input by checking input when a button is clicked or when some other event occurs.

4. The Len function is used to check for an appropriate number of characters and the InStr function is used to check for the presence of a required character.

5. Checking for a selected option in a list box uses the SelectedIndex property.

It's Your Turn!

1. Where in the HTML page do functions and subs go? Where are they referenced in the page?

2. Write a function to test the contents of a text box called **txtSSNumber** to:

    a. check if it has exactly 11 characters in it

    b. check if it has dashes in it

    c. check if the first dash comes at the fourth position in the string

    d. and check if the second dash comes at the seventh position in the string.

3. Write a function to test the contents of a text box called **txtPhoneNumber** to:

    a. check if it has exactly 13 characters in it

    b. check that the 1st and 5th characters are right and left parenthesis

    c. check if the 9th character is a dash

    d. check that all other characters are integers

4. Write a function to validate that at least one of a set of checkboxes has been checked.
```

5. How can we use the SelectedIndex property of the list box?

Completing the remaining questions will enable you to create the Visual Basic project discussed in the text.

6. If your VideosOnline.htm file is not already open in Notepad, open it now. Go to the HEAD section of the HTML code and enter the code shown in VB Code Box 13-3. Save your revised file and switch to Internet Explorer. Use the **File | Open | Browse** option to retrieve your modified VideosOnline.htm file into Internet Explorer.

7. Without entering anything into the text boxes, click the Submit Order button. You should see the message box shown in Figure 13-6 and the input cursor should now appear in the Name text box. Enter a name less then five characters long, say, Joe, and click the Submit order button again. What happens?

8. Try out the other two input text boxes, entering both incorrect and correct data. If you enter all correct data, a message box should appear telling you that the data is about to be e-mailed to the e-mail address you entered in your <Form> statement. You should press Cancel unless you are sure your computer is set up to send e-mail. (You should be aware that many university and college computer laboratory machines are not set up to send e-mail and an error message will result from attempting to do so.)

9. Switch to Notepad and enter the code shown in VB Code Box 13-4 to validate the selection of an option from the lstVideos list box in the VideosOnline.htm file immediately prior to the End Function statement. Save the revised file and switch back to Internet Explorer. Click the Refresh button to load the revised VideosOnline.htm file. Enter appropriate data in all of text boxes but do not select an option from the list of videos. You should receive an error message when you click the Submit Order button. Now select a video and click the Submit Order button again. As before, click Cancel on the e-mail message box. Note: if you are sure that there is a default e-mail client on your computer and you want to see how the input would appear were it sent via e-mail, change the e-mail address in the FORM statement to your own address and click Ok on the e-mail message box.

10. While still in Internet Explorer with appropriate data entered and a selection made from the list of videos, click the Clear Entries button. All of your input should be cleared by doing this.

USING VB-SCRIPT FOR CALCULATIONS

In addition to validating input for Web pages, we can use VBScript to make calculations on Web pages. While we cannot access a database with client-side scripting, we can work with lists of items to select one and determine a value for it. We can also use assignment statements, decisions, loops, and arrays just like in Visual Basic to carry out calculations on the Web page. This can be very useful for the user to determine the cost of an order prior to submitting it to the server for processing.

In our case, we want to use VBScript to enable the user to select a video to rent from the Web page by clicking on it from the list box to display its name and price and then calculate the total rental costs. In the online case, these costs include the price of the video plus a delivery fee of $2.00 and the usual taxes. Recall that the video price depends on the type of video, that is, $.99 for kids videos, $1.99 for regular videos, and $2.99 for classic videos. If the user is satisfied with the information displayed, he or she can then click on the Submit Order button which validates the entry of a user name, telephone number, and e-mail address and then sends *all* of the information (including that input by the user and that calculated by the client-side processing) via e-mail to the address specified in the HTML FORM statement. If the user is unhappy with any of the information, they can click the Clear Entries button to clear the Web page and start over or not rent a video at all. The latter event may occur when the user sees the additional $2.00 delivery fee that they must pay!

Carrying out these operations is accomplished with VBScript in a three-step process:

1. Determine and display name of selected video.
2. Determine and display price of selected video.
3. Calculate and display total cost of online rental.

These three steps need to be executed through an event handler function or sub when some event occurs. What event should this be? You might automatically say clicking the Submit Order button, but that would submit the order before the user has a chance to look at it and decide whether or not to proceed with ordering the video. A better event to consider is clicking on a video in the list box since this does not carry out the submit operation. The final question is do we use function or sub as the event handler? Since this event does not require a return value, a sub named lstVideos_OnClick is appropriate. As with the frmInput_OnSubmit function event handler, the lstVideos_Onclick sub must appear in the HEAD section of the HTML code. Since we have already included the <SCRIPT LANGUAGE = "VBScript"> tag, we don't need to add it in again; all we need to do is to write the sub to carry out the three operations before or after the frmInput_OnSubmit function in the HEAD section.

> **Tip:** The Option Explicit statement can be used in VBScript much like it is in Visual Basic. However, it behaves differently when encountering undeclared variables by causing a Run Time error.

Displaying Name of Selected Video

If you recall the Vintage Videos Web page that we created earlier, the list box displays the name of the video and each video has a value property set to 1, 2, or 3 depending on the price of the video. To display the name of the selected video, we need to find the SelectedIndex property of the lstVideos list box to determine which one was selected. This value is then used to display the text property of the corresponding list box item in the txtVideo text box. The beginning of the lstVideos_OnClick sub and the statements necessary to display the video name are shown in VB Code Box 13-5.

| **VB CODE BOX 13-5.** Displaying video name in text box | ```
Sub lstVideos_OnClick
    Dim strVideoName, curVideoPrice, curTaxes
    Dim intIndex, intPrice, curTaxesFees, curTotal
    Const curDeliveryFee = 2.00
    intIndex = frmInput.lstVideos.SelectedIndex
    strVideoName = frmInput.lstVideos.Options(intIndex).Text
    frmInput.txtVideo.Value = strVideoName
End sub
``` |
|---|---|

Note in this code that we begin by naming the sub and declaring variables. We also declare curDeliveryFee to be a constant with value of 2.00. This is the delivery fee that is added to the rental cost of all videos rented online. The last three statements determine the index value of the selected option, find the corresponding video name, and transfer it to the txtVideo text box. The statement:

```
strVideoName = frmInput.lstVideos.Options(intIndex).Text
```

is critical since it uses the index of the selected video (intIndex) to find the corresponding video name as the text property of the selected item in lstVideos and assigns it to a string variable.
```

Displaying Price of Video

Displaying the price of the video requires that we first determine the value property of the selected item in lstVideos since this value (1, 2, or 3) indicates the price of the video. Finding the value property of the selected item in lstVideos is easier than finding the name of the video since it is equal to the value property of lstVideos itself; that is, if intPrice is a variable to which we assign this value property, then the statement to assign the value follows:

```
intPrice = frmInput.lstVideos.Value
```

Once we know the value of intPrice, we can use this to determine the price of the selected video and assign it to the curVideoPrice variable with a Select Case statement. Once the price has been determined, it is displayed in the txtPrice text box by assigning its Value property to the curVideoPrice variable formatted as currency. Note the different form of the format function used in VBScript. This code is shown in VB Code Box 13-6 and comes right after the previous code in the lstVideos_OnClick sub program.

VB CODE BOX 13-6. Code to determine and display price of video	`intPrice = frmInput.lstVideos.Value`
	`Select Case intPrice`
	`Case 1`
	`   curVideoprice = .99`
	`Case 2`
	`   curVideoPrice = 1.99`
	`Case 3`
	`   curVideoPrice = 2.99`
	`End Select`
	`frmInput.txtPrice.Value = FormatCurrency(curVideoPrice)`

Figure 13-7 shows the result of selecting the video *Star Wars* from the list box and displaying the name and price.

FIGURE 13-7. Displaying Name and Price of Video

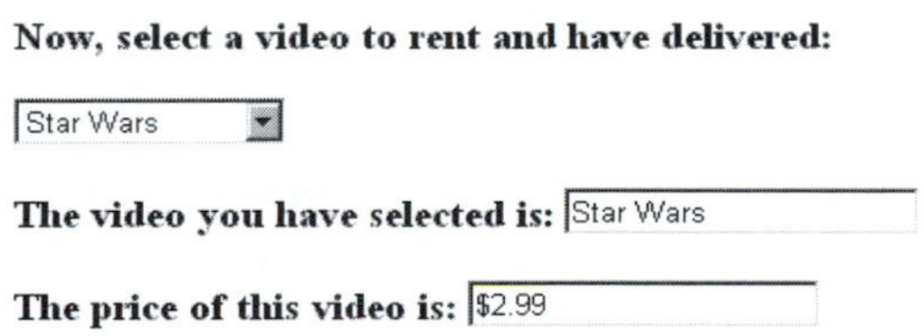

Now, select a video to rent and have delivered:

Star Wars ▼

The video you have selected is: Star Wars

The price of this video is: $2.99

Calculating Total Rental Cost

Once we know the price of the video, we can compute the taxes as 7 percent of the video price and add them to the delivery fee of $2.00 to determine the additional costs of renting the video. This value is displayed in the txtDeliveryFee text box using the FormatCurrency function. Finally, the VBScript code to compute and display the total rental cost in the txtTotalCost text box shown in VB Code Box 13-7 is added to the lstVideos_OnClick event handler. The complete sub procedure is shown in VB Code Box 13-8.

If the resulting Web page is retrieved into Internet explorer, it will appear as shown in Figure 13-8. Note that the user has entered all personal information and has selected *Star Wars* which has a rental price of $2.99, taxes and delivery fees of $2.21, and a total rental cost of $5.20.

| VB CODE BOX 13-7. Code to compute rental costs | ```
    frmInput.txtPrice.Value = FormatCurrency(curVideoPrice)
    curTaxes = 0.07 * curVideoPrice
    curTaxesFees = curTaxes + curDeliveryFee
    frmInput.txtDeliveryFee.Value = FormatCurrency(curTaxesFees)
    curTotal = curVideoPrice + curTaxesFees
    frmInput.txtTotalCost.Value = FormatCurrency(curTotal)
End sub
``` |
|---|---|

| VB CODE BOX 13-8. Complete code of the OnClick event handler | ```
Sub lstVideos_OnClick
    Dim strVideoNamePrice, strVideoName, curVideoPrice, curTaxes
    Dim intIndex, intPrice, curTaxsFees, curTotal
    Const curDeliveryFee = 2.00
    intIndex = frmInput.lstVideos.SelectedIndex
    strVideoName = frmInput.lstVideos.Options(intIndex).Text
    frmInput.txtVideo.Value = strVideoName
    intPrice = frmInput.lstVideos.Value
    Select Case intPrice
    Case 1
        curVideoprice = .99
    Case 2
        curVideoPrice = 1.99
    Case 3
        curVideoPrice = 2.99
    End select
    frmInput.txtPrice.Value = FormatCurrency(curVideoPrice)
    curVideoTaxes = 0.07 * curVideoPrice
    curTaxesFees = curVideoTaxes + curDeliveryFee
    frmInput.txtDeliveryFee.Value = FormatCurrency(curTaxesFees)
    curTotal = curVideoPrice + curTaxesFees
    frmInput.txtTotalCost.Value = FormatCurrency(curTotal)
End sub
``` |
|---|---|

FIGURE 13-8. Final video rental Web page

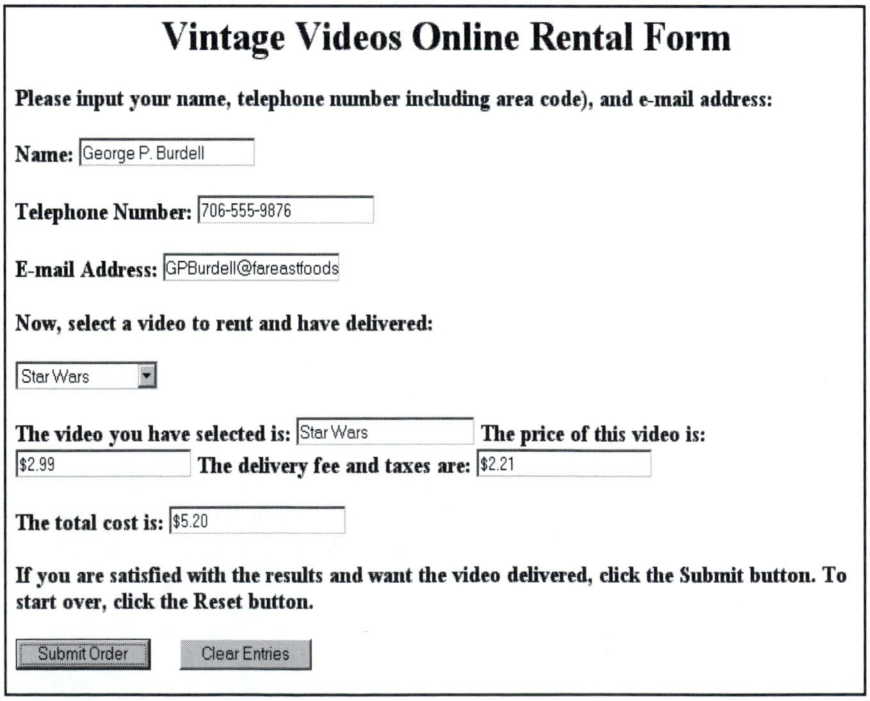

Vintage Videos Online Rental Form

Please input your name, telephone number including area code), and e-mail address:

Name: George P. Burdell

Telephone Number: 706-555-9876

E-mail Address: GPBurdell@fareastfoods

Now, select a video to rent and have delivered:

Star Wars

The video you have selected is: Star Wars   **The price of this video is:** $2.99   **The delivery fee and taxes are:** $2.21

The total cost is: $5.20

If you are satisfied with the results and want the video delivered, click the Submit button. To start over, click the Reset button.

Submit Order   Clear Entries

If the Submit button were clicked for this page, the resulting e-mail message would appear as shown in Figure 13-9. Note that the control (for example, txtName) is shown with its corresponding value. It would be very easy to write a program using string functions to **parse** this type of E-mail to determine the name of the video to be delivered (*Star Wars*) and the amount to be charged to the customer ($5.20) just by looking for the corresponding text box name (txtVideo and txtTotalCost).

FIGURE 13-9. Result of submitting the form

```
txtName=George P. Burdell
txtPhoneNum=706-555-9876
txtEmail=GPBurdell@fareastfoods.com
lstVideos=3
txtVideo=Star Wars
txtprice=$2.99
txtDeliveryFee=$2.21
txtTotalCost=$5.20
```

Mini-Summary 13-5: Using VBScript for Calculations

1. VBScript can be used on the client browser to carry out simple calculations but not to access a database. The calculations are usually very much like those in Visual Basic.

2. Finding the text that is displayed in a list box uses the text property of the selected list box option.

3. The value property of the list box can be used to determine a corresponding value through the Select Case statement.

It's Your Turn!

1. Why can VBScript not be used to access a database through the browser?

2. Why do we have to use the SelectedItem property of the list box to determine the text of the highlighted element?

3. Rewrite the code in VB Code Box 13-6 to use an If-Then-ElseIf decision form to determine the price of the video being selected.

4. Assume that a web page contains a list box named lstDays listing the days of the week. Write a function that when a day is selected, a messagebox will appear confirming which day was selected. Note: the syntax for a messagebox for VBScript is just like that of Visual Basic.

5. Assume that, instead of a flat $2.00 for delivery, the fee is equal to ten percent of the rental price. Rewrite the code in VB Code Box 13-8 to compute the total cost under these assumptions.

Completing the remaining questions will enable you to create the Visual Basic project discussed in the text.

6. If your VideosOnline.htm file is not already open in Notepad, open it now. Go to the HEAD section of the HTML code and enter the code shown in VB Code Box 13-5 to create the lstVideos_OnClick event handler sub program. Save your revised file

and switch to Internet Explorer. Use the **File | Open | Browse** option to retrieve your modified VideosOnline.htm file into Internet Explorer and select *Star Wars* as the video to be rented. Its name should now appear in the txtVideo text box.

7. Return to Notepad and add the code shown in VB Code Box 13-6 to the lstVideos_OnClick sub immediately after the existing code. Save the code and return to Internet Explorer. Click the Refresh button and select the same video as before. Your Web page should now look like that shown in Figure 13-7 with the video name and price being displayed.

8. Once again, switch to Notepad and add the rest of the code shown in VB Code Box 13-7 to the lstVideos_OnClick sub immediately prior to the End sub statement. Save the code and return to Internet Explorer. Click the Refresh button and select the same video as before. Your Web page should now look like that shown in Figure 13-8 with the additional costs and total cost being displayed along with the video name and price.

9. Use Notepad to change the destination e-mail from videosv@negia.net to your own e-mail address. Retrieve the file into Internet Explorer, enter the same data, and click the Submit button. You should receive an e-mail similar to that shown in Figure 13-9. (If you don't change the e-mail address and submit the form, you will still receive the e-mail, but it will be because the message has been bounced back to you.)

10. Try some other videos, especially those that are not in the "Classic" category. Now go back into the code of the VideosOnline.htm file and change the name of the lstVideos_OnClick event handler sub to lstVideos_OnChange. Save the file and switch to Internet Explorer. Click the Refresh button and select any video you wish. It should work the same as before since the OnChange event is activated when any change occurs to the list box. Before exiting Notepad, change the name back to the lstVideos_OnClick for this event handler and resave the file.

SUMMARY

Electronic commerce is based on use of the World Wide Web which is a client/server network with clients running Web browsers that can interpret information sent from Web servers. The information sent from servers is in the form of hypertext markup language (HTML) which is composed of tags that the browser uses to format the information. Scripting is a form of computer programming that can run on either the Web browser or Web server. Commonly used scripting languages are VBScript and JavaScript. Scripting on the client is referred to as *client-side scripting* while scripting on the server is *server-side scripting*.

VBScript is a reduced version of Visual Basic that can be used for client- or server-side scripting. On the client, VBScript only runs on Microsoft's Internet Explorer. Important differences between Visual Basic and VBScript involve variable types used, capability to be compiled, using event procedures instead of event handlers, having a built-in IDE, and capability to run as a stand-alone language instead of being integrated with HTML. VBScript must appear within the <Script>...</Script> tags. VBScript appears two places in the Web page—in the HEAD section for event handlers and in the BODY section to be executed when the page loads.

In addition to the standard formatting HTML tags, form tags are used to create input objects such as text and list boxes. Form tags include those for creating text and list boxes, radio buttons, and checkboxes as well as submit, reset, and command buttons. In all cases, the object tags must be enclosed within the <FORM>...</FORM>

tags. The Submit button will send the input to an e-mail site or to the Web server and the Reset button will clear the user input.

Validation is necessary whenever input comes from a Web page to make sure that it is complete and in the correct form before sending it to the Web server for processing. Types of Web page validation include checking for an appropriate number of characters or digits in a text box, checking for the presence of a required character, checking for characters appearing in the correct location, and ensuring that an option has been selected from a list or combo box or that a radio button or checkbox has been selected. Event handlers are used to validate Web page input by checking input when a button is clicked or some other event occurs. The Len function is used to check for an appropriate number of characters, and the Instr function is used to check for the presence of a required character. Checking for a selected option in a list box uses the SelectedIndex property.

VBScript can be used on the client browser to carry out simple calculations but not to access a database. The calculations are usually very much like those in Visual Basic. Finding the text that is displayed in a list box uses the text property of the selected list box option. The value property of the list box can be used to determine a corresponding value through the Select Case statement. The complete code for the VideosOnline.htm Web page is found in VBScript Boxes 13-1, 13-3, 13-4, and 13-8.

VBSCRIPT FORM ELEMENTS

Element	Properties	Methods	Events
text box	Name Value	Focus	
list box	Name SelectedIndex Text		OnClick OnChange
submit button	Name Value		OnClick
reset button	Name Value		OnClick

VBSCRIPT PROGRAMMING STATEMENTS DIFFERENT FROM VISUAL BASIC

HTML Tag for VBScript <SCRIPT LANGUAGE ="VBScript">...</SCRIPT>
Format function variable or property = ***Formattype(variable)***
Setting the Focus to a text box *formname.txtname.***Focus**
Checking for a selected item in a list box **If** *frmname.lstname.***SelectedIndex = -1 Then**

KEY TERMS

client/server network

clients

client-side scripting

electronic commerce

event handler

event procedures

hypertext

hypertext markup language (HTML)

Integrated Development Environment (IDE)

Javascript

scripting

server

server-side scripting

uniform resource locator (URL)

VBScript

Web pages

Web site

World Wide Web (Web)

EXERCISES

1. Discuss briefly the concept of client/server networks and their relationship to the World Wide Web.

2. Discuss the importance of the Form HTML tag in electronic commerce.

3. List the differences between Visual Basic and VBScript other than their purpose.

4. For each of the following form elements, give the HTML code to create it:
   a. text box
   b. check box
   c. radio button
   d. list box
   e. list box element
   f. button
   g. submit button
   h. clear button

5. In each of the following cases, give the property that is requested:
   a. stores the contents of a text box
   b. displays text for an element of a list box
   c. stores the actual contents of an element of a list box
   d. indicates the index of a selected item in a list box
   e. the name of the submit button
   f. the caption of a submit button

PROJECTS

1. Create a Web page with five text boxes and corresponding labels. The first text box should allow the user to input a student's name, and the next three text boxes are for input of three quiz scores. The last text box is to display the average of the three quiz scores. Use a command button to sum the three test scores and compute and display the average of the three scores (use the Fixed Numeric format for the average.) Add validation statements to the code for this command button. These validation statements should check that the user has entered a student name and three quiz scores. Also, add a command button to clear the text boxes. Save the resulting project as **Ex13-1.htm** in the Chapter13 folder on your data disk. Test it on Internet Explorer with a student name of **Chris Patrick** and test scores of **71, 79,** and **85.**

2. Create a Web page that will provide an estimate of the cost to treat a lawn with pre-emergent. Add four text boxes and corresponding labels. The first text box should allow the user to input the customer's name. The next two text boxes should allow the user to input the square footage for a lawn and the cost per square foot for a given type of treatment. The fourth text box should display the cost of the treatment, which is equal to the square footage times the cost per square foot. Add validation statements to the code for the command button that computes the treatment cost. These statements should check that the user has entered a customer name and the number of square feet.

Use a command button to compute and display the treatment cost. Format the cost per square foot and treatment cost as dollars and cents. Add a command button to clear the text box. Save the resulting project as **Ex13-2.htm** in the Chapter13 folder on your data disk. Test it on Internet Explorer with a customer name of **Caroline Myers** with square footage of **3250** square feet and a treatment cost of **$.002** per square foot.

3. Create a Web page that allows the user to input a make of automobile and data about fuel use. There should be four text boxes and corresponding labels. The first text box should allow the user to input the make of the car being tested. The second and third text boxes should allow the user to input the miles driven and the gallons of gas used. The fourth text box should display the miles per gallon, which is equal to the miles driven divided by the gallons used. Use a command button to compute and display the miles per gallon (use the Fixed Numeric format). Add a command button to clear the text boxes. Save the resulting project as **Ex13-3.htm** in the Chapter13 folder on your data disk. Test it on Internet Explorer with a **Toyonda** make of car that was driven **225** miles on **7.3** gallons of gas.

4. Create a Web page to compute the income tax for a single person using the 2000 federal tax rates shown in Table 13-5, assuming the standard deduction is taken. Taxable income is found by subtracting $2,800 for each exemption plus the Standard Deduction ($4,400). For example, if your gross income is $60,000 with one exemption, your taxable income will be $60,000 – $2,800 – $4,400 = $52,800 and your taxes will be $3,937.50 + 0.28 * ($52,800 – $26,250) = $11,371.50. Use text boxes to input the taxpayer's name and income and a list box to allow the user to select a number of exemptions from 0 to 4. Use a command button to compute and display the taxes due. (Use the Currency format.) Add a command button to clear the text boxes. Save the resulting project as **Ex313-4.htm** in the Chapter13 folder on your data disk. Test it on Internet Explorer for **Elmer Fudd** with an income of $95,000 and 3 exemptions.

TABLE 13-5: Tax Brackets

Taxable Income	Taxes Due
$0–$26,250	15% of taxable income
$26,250–$63,550	$3937.50 plus 28% of taxable income over $26,250
$63,550–$132,600	$14,385.50 plus 31% of taxable income over $63,550

TABLE 13-5: Tax Brackets (Continued)

Taxable Income	Taxes Due
$132,600–$288,350	$41,170.50 plus 36% of taxable income over $132,600
$288,350 and over	$86,854.50 plus 39.6% of taxable income over $288,350

5. Assume your company is selling software over the Internet for listening to audio(MP3) files and viewing video files. You market three types of software: the basic audio software for $29.95, the basic video software package for $34.95, and a combination audio and super video package for $59.95. Please create a Web page to handle this transaction where the user name and e-mail are input in text boxes and the type of software package is selected from a list box. When a Submit button is clicked, the page should be checked to ensure that the name and e-mail address fields are "appropriately" completed and that some software package has been selected before allowing a submission of the order form. You should also calculate the amount due so that it changes whenever a software package is selected. Save your page as **Ex13-5.htm** and save it in the Chapter13 folder on your data disk. Test it on Internet Explorer with a name of **Buster Browne**, an e-mail address of **bbrowne@nosuchaddress.org,** and a selection of the super video package.

6. Info2You.com is a free Internet service that allows you to subscribe to e-mail discussion lists. The lists include topics ranging from Entertainment News to VBtips. A user may visit the Info2You site and select the e-mail lists for which they have an interest. Once selected, information and news about the topic will be sent to the user's e-mail on a periodic basis. Create a Web page that will allow a user to subscribe to various lists. Your page should include 10 checkboxes and corresponding labels which allow a user to select one or more topics of interest. The page should also include a text box where the user may type their e-mail address. Include two radio buttons that will allow the user to select their preferred format for the E-mail, either HTML or Text. Include two buttons - one for resetting the page and one for submitting the information. Your code should validate that at least one topic has been selected and that the e-mail is in a proper format. Save your page as **Ex13-6.htm** and save it in the Chapter13 folder on your data disk. Test it on Internet Explorer with a name of **Curious George**, an e-mail address of **cgeorge@nosuchaddress.org,** and with three of the topics selected.

PROJECT: JOE'S TAX ASSISTANCE (CONT.)

"So, who are these guys in the picture?" Joe inquired.

Zooey blushed. "That's The Corner Boyz," she admitted. "I like their songs...and besides, I think Dylan is dreamy." In an attempt to change the subject she added, "But Grandpa, that's not what I wanted to show you."

Zooey and Joe were looking at Zooey's web page. She had called him up earlier sounding excited and asking to come over right away.

Zooey clicked a link saying Guessing Game and a new page appeared. Joe saw a page displaying 3 text boxes and 3 buttons. Text on the page directed him to click on the Start button to begin and then to guess a number between 1 and 1000 and enter it in an appropriate text box. Joe entered a guess and then clicked on a button labeled Guess. In one text box the words "Guess lower" appeared and in another the number 1 appeared showing him how many guesses he had made. He guessed lower, then continued to make guesses until eventually the message read "Good job!" It had taken him 11 guesses to get the correct number.

"Nice game," he said to Zooey. "But what made you so excited?"

"Mr. Wells showed us how to program some simple VBScript," She replied. "Afterwards, I went home and played around with it a little and came up with this. We can use it for your VITA Web site."

"Whoa, there," said Joe. "I don't think that a guessing game would be appropriate for my VITA Web site..."

Zooey interrupted, "No silly, I didn't mean the game. I meant we could use VBScript."

A little puzzled, Joe asked, "What do you mean?"

"Don't you see, VBScript lets a person work interactively with the web page. They can enter information and then click buttons to do something with it—even send it as e-mail."

"I still don't see how we can use it for the VITA Web site."

"Remember the other day when Grandma was complaining about taking messages from your VITA clients who wanted to set up appointments?" Getting more excited now, Zooey continued. "What if you had a page on your web site that could let the client request an appointment which can be sent to you by e-mail? Then, you can confirm positively or negatively back to them by phone or e-mail."

Beginning to see the light, Joe said, "You may be on to something. That might reduce the phone calls and Grandma won't have to take as many of my messages. Shall we get started?"

Beaming, Zooey said, "Yes! Let's do it!"

"I'm proud of you Zooey. Not only are you learning programming but you've certainly had good ideas for my VITA work," Joe remarked. "For all your help, I promise that if any of The Corner Boyz request an appointment, especially Dylan, you'll be the first to know."

Questions

1. Create a Web page for Joe's VITA Web site that will allow clients to request appointments. The page should request the client's name, phone number, and E-mail address (if any). Set up a list box that contains dates for the next two weeks excluding Saturday and Sunday. Set up a second list box that will contain times in 30 minute intervals between 9:00am and 4:00pm. Additional text on the page should let the client know that the appointment date and time are subject to confirmation by Joe. Include buttons for submitting the information to Joe via e-mail and resetting the form. Your VBScript code should validate that all information has been entered or selected correctly before submitting.

2. Run, test, and debug your program.

Index

Microsoft®
Visual Basic 6.0 Working Model Edition
to accompany
Learning to Program with Visual Basic 6.0, Second Edition
by Patrick G. McKeown and Craig A. Piercy
©2002 John Wiley & Sons, Inc.

Installation Instructions

Inserting the Visual Basic 6.0 Working Model Edition CD-ROM into your computer should automatically lead you through the process of installing the applications and components you'll need to accomplish your programming tasks. However, if the installation screen does not automatically appear, please follow the procedure below:

1. Insert the CD in the CD-ROM drive.
2. From the Program Manager, select File/Run. (If using Windows 95, select Start/Run.)
3. In the space provided, type **d:/setup.exe** (where "d" is your CD-ROM drive), and press OK.
4. Follow the on-screen instructions for the set up.

Wiley Technical Support
(212) 850-6753
http://www.wiley.com/techsupport
MSDN Online help found at www.msdn.microsoft.com

_____

This program was reproduced by John Wiley & Sons, Inc. under a special arrangement with Microsoft Corporation. For this reason, John Wiley & Sons, Inc. is responsible for the product warranty and for support. If your CD-ROM is defective, please return it to John Wiley & Sons, Inc., which will arrange for its replacement. PLEASE DO NOT RETURN IT TO MICROSOFT CORPORATION. Any product support will be provided, if at all, by John Wiley & Sons. PLEASE DO NOT CONTACT MICROSOFT CORPORATION FOR PRODUCT SUPPORT. End users of this Microsoft program shall not be considered "registered owners" of a Microsoft product and therefore, shall not be eligible for updgrades, promotions, or other benefits available to "registered owners" of Microsoft products.

System Requirements

–Personal computer with 486DX/66 (Pentium 90 or higher microprocessor recommended)
–Microsoft Windows 95 or later, Windows NT 4.0, with Service Pack 3 or later (Service Pack 3 included)
–Minimum memory: 24 MB for Windows 95 or later, 24 MB for Windows NT 4.0 (32 MB recommended for all)
–Hard disk space required:
       –Typical installation: 52 MB
       –Maximum installation: 65 MB
–Microsoft Internet Explorer Service Pack 1 (included); additional hard disk space required for Microsoft Internet
 Explorer: 43 MB typical, 59 MB maximum
–CD-ROM drive
–VGA or higher-resolution monitor (Super VGA recommended)
–Microsoft Mouse or compatible pointing device